THE COLONIZED APOSTLE

PAUL IN CRITICAL CONTEXTS

The Paul in Critical Contexts series offers cutting-edge reexaminations of Paul through the lenses of power, gender, and ideology.

Apostle to the Conquered: Reimagining Paul's Mission
Davina C. Lopez

The Arrogance of Nations: Reading Romans in the Shadow of Empire
Neil Elliott

The Politics of Heaven: Women, Gender, and Empire in the Study of Paul
Joseph A. Marchal

Christ's Body in Corinth: The Politics of a Metaphor
Yung Suk Kim

Galatians Re-Imagined: Reading with the Eyes of the Vanquished
Brigitte Kahl

THE COLONIZED APOSTLE

PAUL
THROUGH
POSTCOLONIAL
EYES

Edited by

CHRISTOPHER D. STANLEY

Fortress Press
Minneapolis

THE COLONIZED APOSTLE
Paul through Postcolonial Eyes

Copyright © 2011 Fortress Press. All rights reserved. Except for brief quotations in critical articles or reviews, no part of this book may be reproduced in any manner without prior written permission from the publisher. Visit http://www.augsburgfortress.org/copyrights/contact.asp or write to Permissions, Augsburg Fortress, Box 1209, Minneapolis, MN 55440.

Some scripture quotations are based on the New Revised Standard Version Bible, copyright © 1989 by the Division of Christian Education of the National Council of the Churches of Christ in the USA. Used by permission. All rights reserved.

Some scripture quotations are based on the Revised Standard Version of the Bible, copyright © 1946, 1952, 1971 National Council of the Churches of Christ in the USA. Used by permission. All rights reserved.

Chapter 5 first appeared in *The Conrad Grebel Review* 21 (2003): 82–103.
Chapter 7 first appeared in *Theoforum* 35 (2004): 173–93.
Chapter 9 was published in *What Is Asian American Biblical Hermeneutics?* (Honolulu: University of Hawai'i Press, 2008), 75–97, and is reprinted by kind permission of University of Hawai'i Press.
Chapter 10 first appeared in *Journal of Feminist Studies in Religion* 22 (2006): 5–32.
Chapter 16 first appeared in *Asia Journal of Theology* 19/1 (April 2005): 188–220.

Cover design: Laurie Ingram
Cover image: The apostle Paul being led toward martyrdom; detail of a stone relief from the lower panel of the sarcophagus of Junius Bassus (fourth century C.E.), Museum of the Treasury, St. Peter's Basilica, Rome. Photograph © Erich Lessing/Art Resource, N.Y.
Book design: The HK Scriptorium

Library of Congress Cataloging-in-Publication Data

The colonized Apostle : Paul through postcolonial eyes / edited by Christopher D. Stanley.
    p. cm.
Includes bibliographical references and index.
ISBN 978-0-8006-6458-9 (alk. paper)
1. Bible. N.T. Epistles of Paul—Postcolonial criticism. I. Stanley, Christopher D.
BS2650.52.C65   2011
227'.06—dc22
                                                                2011016178

15 14 13 12 11   1 2 3 4 5 6 7 8 9 10

Contents

Contributors	xi
Foreword by Efraín Agosto	xiii

Part One: What Is Postcolonial Studies? 1

Introduction 3
Christopher D. Stanley

1. Paul after Empire 9
Stephen D. Moore
    The Beginnings of Postcolonial Studies 9
    The Beginnings of Postcolonial Biblical Criticism 12
    Interrogating the "Postcolonial" in Postcolonial Biblical Criticism 21

2. Critical Perspectives on Postcolonial Theory 24
Susan B. Abraham
    The Feminist Frame 26
    The Pedagogical Frame 29

3. Marxism and the Postcolonial Study of Paul 34
Neil Elliott
    Elements of Marxist Interpretation 35
    Marxist Interpretation of Early Christianity 37
    Marxism and Postcolonial Criticism 39
    Marxist Challenges for
        the Postcolonial Interpretation of Paul 42
    A Future for Marxist Criticism?
        A Christian-Marxist Coda 49

PART TWO: PAUL AND ANCIENT FORMS OF COLONIALISM — 51

A. PAUL AND ROMAN COLONIAL RULE

4. Pauline Agency in Postcolonial Perspective — 53
Subverter of or Agent for Empire?
JEREMY PUNT

- Introduction: The Problematic Paul — 53
- Paul and Empire: Accounting for an Ambivalent Situation — 54
- A Postcolonial Optic on Paul and Empire: Power and Agency — 55
- Paul, Power, and Agency: The Corinthian Community — 56
- Challenging Empire? Weakness and Foolishness as Subversion — 57
- Paul, Agent for Empire? Asserting Power and Strength — 59
- Conclusion — 61

5. The Politics of Paul — 62
His Supposed Social Conservatism and the Impact of Postcolonial Readings
GORDON ZERBE

- The Underlying Millenarian Script — 65
- The Use of Politically Loaded Terms — 68
- Paul's Experience at the Hands of Roman and Civic Authorities — 70
- Romans 13 and the Monumental Contradiction — 70
- Conclusions — 72

6. Visualizing Significant Otherness — 74
Reimagining Paul(ine Studies) through Hybrid Lenses
DAVINA C. LOPEZ

- A State of Postcolonial Affairs — 74
- Whither Postcolonial Paul(ine Studies)? — 76
- Hybridity as a Complex, Contestable Signifier in Postcolonial Paul(ine Studies) — 78
- Resourcing Visual Representation for Potentially Hybrid Postcolonial Reimaginations of Paul(ine Studies) — 79
- Trajan's Column: Visualizing Romans and Paul as Unstable, Hybrid Figures — 81
- Visualizing Hybridity and Honesty: Reimagining Relationships, Then and Now — 92

Contents

B. PAUL, COLONIALISM, AND ETHNICITY

7. **Reading Romans 7 in Conversation**
   with Postcolonial Theory 95
   Paul's Struggle toward a Christian Identity of Hybridity
   L. ANN JERVIS
       Identity in Postcolonial Theory 96
       Hybridity 96
       Analogical Relationships between Romans 7 and Postcolonial Theory 97
       The Identity of the Speaker in Romans 7 99
       Conclusion: The Hybrid Identity Described in Romans 7 108

8. **Paul the Ethnic Hybrid?** 110
   Postcolonial Perspectives on Paul's Ethnic Categorizations
   CHRISTOPHER D. STANLEY
       Introduction 110
       Setting the Stage 112
       The "Hybridity" Debates 113
       Paul and Postcolonial Studies 116
       Paul's Ethnic Worldview 117
       Postcolonial Musings 122
       Conclusion 126

9. **Redressing Bodies at Corinth** 127
   Racial/Ethnic Politics and Religious Difference
   in the Context of Empire
   TAT-SIONG BENNY LIEW
       Embodying Corinthian Rhetoric and Politics 128
       Paul's Rejected Body 131
       Body Building over Jesus' Dead (Jewish) Body 133
       (Other) Bodies Feminized and Sexualized 139
       Conclusion 143

C. PAUL, COLONIALISM, AND GENDER

10. **Imperial Intersections and Initial Inquiries** 146
    Toward a Feminist, Postcolonial Analysis of Philippians
    JOSEPH A. MARCHAL
        Prompting Need: Gaps, Erasures, and Conflicts 147
        Procedure and Precedent 151

Interpreting Philippians: A Postcolonial Paul?	152
Connections and Conclusions	158

11. Beyond the Heroic Paul   161
Toward a Feminist and Decolonizing Approach to the Letters of Paul
MELANIE JOHNSON-DEBAUFRE AND LAURA S. NASRALLAH

The Heroic Political Paul	162
Disrupting the Heroic Traveling Missionary:	
1 Thessalonians and Acts as Test Cases	168
Conclusions	173

12. To What End?   175
Revisiting the Gendered Space of 1 Corinthians 11:2-16 from a Feminist Postcolonial Perspective
JENNIFER G. BIRD

Mapping the Method	177
To What End?	178
Conclusion	185

PART THREE: PAUL AND MODERN WESTERN COLONIALISM   187

13. Wrestling with the "Macedonian Call"   189
Paul, Pauline Scholarship, and Nineteenth-Century Colonial Missions
ROBERT PAUL SEESENGOOD

Introduction: Another Look at Hybridity and the Pauline Writings	189
The Bible and Nineteenth-Century Missions	191
Historicity and Paul: Two Competing Views	196
Paul and Arguments for (Colonial) Enslavement	200
Conclusion: Hybridity in the Reading of Paul	204

14. Galatians and the "Orientalism" of Justification by Faith   206
Paul among Jews and Muslims
BRIGITTE KAHL

Edward Said: Decolonizing Orientals and Occidentals,	
Muslims and Jews	208
Galatians Colonizing Phrygians, Turks, Jews, and Muslims:	
William M. Ramsay	209
The Dying Galatian and the Justification of the Occidental Self:	
Critical Reimagination I	213

Christ Crucified and the Justification of the Other:
   Critical Reimagination II 217
Galatian Foreskin as Sign of Noncompliance and Nonconformity:
   Critical Reimagination III 219
Conclusion 222

15. Paul, Nation, and Nationalism 223
A Korean Postcolonial Perspective
JAE WON LEE
Paul and Nation 224
Postcolonialism and National Relationships 226
Empire Criticism 228
Paul and Nationalism 230
Conclusion 235

16. Constructions of Paul in Filipino Theology of Struggle .. 236
GORDON ZERBE
The Vision of a New World Coming (Emerito Nacpil,
   Julio Labayen, and Carlos Abesamis) 238
Kenōsis and the Unmasking of and Victory over the Powers
   (Levi Oracion) 244
Dismantling Oppressive Structures, Freedom from Bondage,
   and Transcendence as a Critique of All Human Projects
   (Benito Dominguez) 246
Tortured Conscience, Justification by Faith, and the Dialectical
   Separation of Gospel and Law (Everett Mendoza) 248
Paul as a Model of Contextual Theologizing, Conversion
   as Illumination (José de Mesa and
   Lode L. Wostyn, C.I.C.M.) 251
Summary and Conclusions 253

Notes 256

Indexes 351

Contributors

SUSAN B. ABRAHAM is Assistant Professor of Ministry Studies at Harvard Divinity School in Cambridge, Massachusetts.

EFRAÍN AGOSTO is Professor of New Testament and Dean at Hartford Seminary in Hartford, Connecticut.

JENNIFER G. BIRD is Assistant Professor of Religion and Director of the Women's and Gender Studies Program at Greensboro College in Greensboro, North Carolina.

NEIL ELLIOTT is Acquiring Editor in Biblical Studies at Fortress Press and teaches courses in biblical studies at Metropolitan State University and United Theological Seminary in New Brighton, Minnesota.

L. ANN JERVIS is Professor of New Testament at Wycliffe College, University of Toronto, Canada.

MELANIE JOHNSON-DEBAUFRE is Associate Professor of New Testament at Drew University Theological School in Madison, New Jersey.

BRIGITTE KAHL is Professor of New Testament at Union Theological Seminary in New York, New York.

JAE WON LEE is Assistant Professor of New Testament at McCormick Theological Seminary in Chicago, Illinois.

TAT-SIONG BENNY LIEW is Professor of New Testament at the Pacific School of Religion in Berkeley, California.

DAVINA C. LOPEZ is Assistant Professor of Religious Studies at Eckerd College in St. Petersburg, Florida.

JOSEPH A. MARCHAL is Assistant Professor of Religious Studies at Ball State University in Muncie, Indiana.

STEPHEN D. MOORE is Professor of New Testament at Drew University Theological School in Madison, New Jersey.

LAURA S. NASRALLAH is Associate Professor of New Testament and Early Christianity at Harvard Divinity School in Cambridge, Massachusetts.

JEREMY PUNT is Associate Professor of New Testament at the University of Stellenbosch, South Africa.

ROBERT PAUL SEESENGOOD is Assistant Professor of Religious Studies at Albright College in Reading, Pennsylvania.

CHRISTOPHER D. STANLEY is Professor of Theology at St. Bonaventure University in St. Bonaventure, New York.

GORDON M. ZERBE is Professor of New Testament at Canadian Mennonite University in Winnipeg, Canada, and served as Visiting Professor at Silliman University Divinity School, Dumaguete City, Philippines, in 1996–98 and 2002–4.

Foreword

Efraín Agosto

I am pleased to offer a foreword for a volume devoted to readings of the apostle Paul from different perspectives of postcolonial criticism. In recent years, as I have furthered my own study of postcolonial theory and its application to biblical studies, I have yearned for such resources. There is much to be learned and put into practice in postcolonial approaches, and the present volume is an important step in the right direction.

Several years ago, Professor Fernando F. Segovia of Vanderbilt University, a pioneer of postcolonial biblical criticism, asked me to contribute an essay on Philippians to *A Postcolonial Commentary on the New Testament Writings* (2009), which he co-edited with R. S. Sugirtharajah. I was glad for that first opportunity to analyze a Pauline letter from a postcolonial perspective.[1] From Professor Segovia I learned the necessity of engaging a "postcolonial optic," an approach that resonated very much with my own interpretive approach to Paul up to that point. I was already looking for signs in Paul's mission and ministry of a commitment to liberation and a concern to provide access and opportunity for "the least of these" in his communities, even as I recognized that Paul's approach was marked with serious inconsistencies, as we see, for example, when we examine the role of women in the Pauline mission.[2]

In order to employ a postcolonial optic in biblical criticism,[3] Segovia posits that we should ask about those signs of imperial domination over colonized peoples that are present in the world of the biblical texts. The New Testament documents, of course, emerged from communities dominated by the Roman imperial order of the first century. The apostle Paul, in particular, founded his communities in the imperial colonies of the Greek East. When we read Paul's letters, a postcolonial optic requires us to ask how the overwhelming power and reality of the Roman Empire impacted the recipients of the correspondence. More specifically, we must examine the extent to which Paul's letters, and indeed all New Testament documents, show accommodation or resistance to the imperial dominance and concomitant colonialism of their context.

Second, Segovia insists that a postcolonial reading of the New Testament must revisit historic interpretations of biblical texts and the methodologies used to study them, especially traditional historical-critical methods. These methods emerged in the eighteenth and nineteenth centuries in the context of imperial activity by Spain, France, Germany, and England. Imperialism, as defined by postcolonial theorists, involves a dominant country's imposition of its culture upon another, distant nation, usually for economic purposes. Generally speaking, the imperialism of Spain, Portugal, France, Germany, and England from the fifteenth to the nineteenth centuries carried with it a missionary agenda as well, along with appropriate biblical interpretations to support both imperialism and the evangelization of conquered peoples in the so-called new world (the lands renamed "North America" and "South America"), as well as the continents of Africa and Asia. In addition, in the nineteenth and twentieth centuries, U.S. imperialism, under such euphemistic labels as "manifest destiny," also exercised increasing political and economic hegemony, in particular over Latin America and the Caribbean, with the support of religious bodies and their techniques of scriptural interpretation. Segovia argues, vehemently and rightly, that the biblical interpretations and historical-critical methodologies that accompanied imperialism should not be left to dominate our own readings but should be subject to close, critical analysis.

Thus we see that postcolonial criticism questions imperial domination, wherever it might be found, in both the ancient and modern worlds. But this is not all: Segovia also posits a third set of questions connected to the modern context. What is the role of "the children of the colonized," to use Segovia's term, in the whole enterprise of biblical interpretation? As people who have experienced the effects of colonial domination for generations, they are in a unique position to read imperial and colonial reality as integral aspects of the biblical text. For this reason Segovia insists that it is imperative for the profession of biblical criticism to include the children and grandchildren of the colonized in the task of biblical interpretation. This focus on the children of the colonized as legitimate interpreters of biblical texts allows for a shift of biblical interpretation from text to reader. Such a shift is necessary in our postcolonial era because the effects of the long colonial history of the West over non-Western cultures, including non-Western minorities in the United States, still dominate the global landscape. Because many readers from non-Western cultures know what imperialism and colonialism look and feel like, their participation in the interpretive process produces new and insightful readings of the biblical texts.

My own research on Paul and postcolonial theory provides an example of the point. My Puerto Rican heritage has led me recently to investigate the intertextual echoes between Paul, the "Apostle to the Gentiles," and the "Apostle of Puerto Rican Independence," Pedro Albizu Campos. Born in 1893, Pedro Albizu Campos was a Harvard-educated Puerto Rican lawyer who, in the 1920s, began to lead the independence party in Puerto Rico, a territory acquired by the United States as spoils of the Spanish-American War. By 1937, after a peaceful protest by Puerto Rican nationalists in Ponce against U.S. occupation turned violent when U.S.-backed police forces began to fire on the unarmed protesters, Albizu Campos was targeted by the U.S. government as a dangerous revolutionary. Albizu Campos was imprisoned in the 1940s, spending

Foreword xv

time in an Atlanta federal prison, and then again for a much longer period in the 1950s. The second imprisonment came shortly after two separate shooting incidents by groups of *independentistas*, one outside the presidential residence at Blair House in 1950 and another outside Congress in 1954. Puerto Rican independence party leaders, including Albizu Campos, were rounded up and jailed, regardless of whether they had anything to do with the shootings. Albizu Campos spent most of the next fifteen years in U.S. and Puerto Rican prisons and was released only shortly before his death in April 1965.

Because of his leadership, intelligence, concern for the independence of Puerto Rico, and eloquent representation of the Puerto Rican cause, Albizu Campos came to be known as the Puerto Rican "Apostle of Independence."[4] Albizu Campos was a fiery and eloquent speaker, and many of his speeches from his years as leader of the independence party in Puerto Rican are readily available. Less available, and rarely studied, are his letters, including his letters from prison.

My exploration of the resonances between Albizu Campos and the apostle Paul shows how postcolonial theory can allow the biblical critic to explore both the imperial and the anti-imperial implications of ancient texts. Many scholars have noted that the apostle Paul was both a subject of the Roman imperial order and an anti-imperial agent creating assemblies that were dedicated to a "lord" other than the emperor, Jesus the Christ. The postcolonial critic, however, does not limit scholarly investigation to the first century; two additional hermeneutical moves are required. In the first place, the postcolonial critic labors to ensure that the interpretive methods that were developed under the shadow of Western imperialism do not continue to dominate the way we read religious texts today but remain subject to critique and reversal. In the second place, the postcolonial critic insists that the voices of those who have been colonized (together with their contemporary descendants) must be taken seriously in the analysis of these texts and the creation of appropriate, empowering reading strategies.

This last point explains why I, as a child of Puerto Rican immigrants to New York City in the 1950s who were born only a few decades after the U.S. appropriated Puerto Rico, read the first-century letters of Paul not only as relics of an ancient imperial world but also as exemplars of the nefarious persistence of imperialism and colonization through the centuries. I insist also on putting those ancient texts, which reveal the influence of a Roman imperial worldview even as they champion anti-imperial resistance, into conversation with similar efforts today, when our ostensibly *post*colonial world continues to suffer the ill effects of the imperialism of past centuries. By examining the connections between the anti-imperial resistance of the apostle Paul and that of another, later "colonized apostle," who also wrote letters to his constituents and followers (including some from an imperial prison), I hope to show that studying Pedro Albizu Campos in the context of twentieth-century imperialism resonates with the study of Paul twenty centuries ago. In both men we see some of the universal signposts of imperial domination and anti-imperial resistance. Studying Albizu Campos helps us to understand not only our postcolonial world but also Paul's imperial world, including the role of religious belief in both settings. It is instructive to note, even before we dig into the reasons why this is the case, that Albizu Campos's followers used New

Testament imagery to describe his impact. Like Paul, he was an "apostle" and, like Paul, he proclaimed a "gospel."

In short, postcolonial theory impels me to ask what it is about religion and its adherents that both promotes and resists imperialism and colonization. I contend that a better understanding of how religious belief both motivates and curtails resistance to empire, whether in the ancient world or in our own day, can help us to make faith and religion more positive forces in our world.

The essays in this volume explore Paul's status as a subject of the Roman Empire and take the measure of his apostolic work. Some contributors argue that Paul was attempting to create alternative, anti-imperial societies in the major urban centers of the empire, while others contest that conclusion. All of these readings may nevertheless serve as valuable signposts for our theorizing and practice of postcolonial hermeneutics.

PART ONE

WHAT IS POSTCOLONIAL STUDIES?

Introduction

Christopher D. Stanley

The last few decades have witnessed the gradual erosion of the long-standing hegemony of the historical-critical method in the field of biblical studies. The myth of scholarly objectivity that lay at the heart of historical-critical scholarship has been undermined by the rise of feminist studies, reader-response criticism, and postmodern philosophy, among other developments. In the process, the way has been cleared for the application of new methods and perspectives to the study of the Jewish and Christian Scriptures, including some that eschew any effort at remaining "objective" in favor of self-consciously political concerns.

While there have been many positive results from these new approaches, one of the less sanguine results has been the further fragmentation of an already fragmented field. No one can possibly keep up with even the most significant developments in the various subfields and submethods that are now being used in the field of biblical studies. The fact that different methods often begin with different presuppositions and have different goals makes it even more difficult for scholars to build bridges between subdisciplines and communicate about their work.

One of the more recent methodological entrants to the field of biblical studies is postcolonial criticism. As Stephen Moore explains in the opening essay of this volume, tracing the origins and history of postcolonial criticism (or "postcolonial studies")[1] is a fool's errand, since the banner of "postcolonial" has been applied to so many different authors and materials, including some figures (e.g., Edward Said and Gayatri Chakravorty Spivak) who actively eschew the label. Its distant roots lie in the work of authors such as Frantz Fanon, Aimé Césaire, Chinua Achebe, C. L. R. James, Albert Memmi, and Ngugi wa Thiong'o, each of whom lived through the transition from colonialism to postcolonialism in a specific cultural context and engaged in sustained reflection on the insidious effects of colonialism and/or the daunting challenges of decolonization.[2] Yet none of these authors would have used the term "postcolonial criticism" to describe their work. The framing of "postcolonial studies" as a mode of academic discourse is a product of the Western academy, particularly in the field of literary studies, where it grew out of the "canon wars" of the 1980s and the related "discovery" of non-Western literatures by Western scholars. The writings of these scholars in turn influenced other disciplines, including history, anthropology, area studies, and cultural studies. The two streams (i.e., "Western" and "non-Western") came together in the work of scholars such as Gayatri Chakravorty Spivak and Homi Bhabha, whose writings combine a thorough familiarity with Western modes of academic discourse with a deeply personal awareness of the effects of colonialism on formerly colonized peoples.

At the heart of postcolonial criticism lies a concern to identify and combat the negative social, economic, political, and psychological effects of colonialism in all of its forms, including the various types of "neo-colonialism" that have replaced formal political domination as contemporary systems of social control. More specifically, postcolonial analysis seeks to expose the various social and ideological mechanisms that colonial powers use to maintain hegemony over the minds and bodies of colonized peoples and to explain how both colonizers and colonized are molded by their participation in such a system.

Viewed in this way, postcolonial criticism can be practiced by anyone, regardless of scholarly pedigree or place of origin. In practice, however, much of the seminal work in this area has been performed by scholars who grew up (and in many cases still reside) in formerly colonized territories while receiving their education in Western academic institutions. This is understandable, since the experience-based knowledge of such individuals gives them insight into social realities that are less obvious to "outsiders," while their familiarity with Western academic discourse provides a means of expressing those insights in terms that "outsiders" can understand. As a result of their labors, scholars who have never lived under direct colonial rule have learned to see the world at least vicariously through "postcolonial eyes" (hence the subtitle of this volume) and to practice "postcolonial criticism" in conscious solidarity with those who have been (and continue to be) more immediately affected by colonial domination.

While it might seem obvious that postcolonial critics should have paid substantial attention to the use of religion (specifically, Christianity and the Bible) as a means of social control by Western colonial authorities, the reality is that the role of religion has been under-theorized by those who have worked in this area. In part this can be traced to the limited attention given to religion by the early critics of Western colonial rule, whose interests were driven more by the struggle for social and political liberation than by an abstract concern to describe the function of societal institutions. In part it reflects the historical development of "postcolonial studies" within academic disciplines such as literary studies, where questions of religion are less central. In part it simply mirrors the secular outlook of much of Western academic scholarship. Whatever the reason, religion has played at best a very minor role in the work of most postcolonial scholars.

Even in the field of biblical studies, postcolonial analysis has operated largely on the margins since it was first propounded by scholars such as R. S. Sugirtharajah and Fernando Segovia in the 1990s.[3] Two broad (and mostly distinct) currents can be discerned in the studies that have been performed in this area. One approach seeks to illuminate the many and varied ways in which the Bible (and the Christian religion in general, particularly in its missionary mode) has been used both to support and to challenge the ideology, activities, and institutions of Western colonialism. Studies of this type represent a natural and mostly noncontroversial extension of "mainstream" postcolonial analysis to fill the lacunae that exist in postcolonial models concerning the role of religion in the colonial enterprise. The second approach seeks to mine the works of postcolonial authors for insights and methods that might illuminate the operation and influence of colonial rule in the world(s) in which the Hebrew and Christian Scriptures were composed, edited, and transmitted. Scholars who follow this approach believe that there are substantial parallels in the operations and effects of colonial domination in different times and places and that an awareness of these cross-cultural patterns can enhance our understanding of the Bible and its world. The assumptions embedded in this approach would be challenged on theoretical grounds by many postcolonial scholars who would insist that the value of their insights is limited to the specific circumstances of modern Western colonialism and its capitalistic framework.[4] But this has not stopped biblical scholars (together with scholars in other historical fields) from drawing on the insights of various postcolonial critics to help them analyze the colonial circumstances under which the literature of the Bible originated and the relation of the biblical texts to those circumstances. Scholars from formerly colonized nations have played an important and growing role in both of these areas.

Until recently, most of the work that had been done on postcolonial interpretation of the New Testament focused on the Gospels and the book of Revelation.[5] The letters of Paul had received little attention apart from a handful of studies by "Western" scholars that were scattered among the four volumes of essays edited by Richard Horsley from 1997 through 2004 under the aegis of the "Paul and Politics" section of the Society of Biblical Literature.[6] As recently as 2008, it was difficult to find more than a dozen articles that drew explicitly on secular postcolonial theorists and publications, and nearly all of these were published in out-of-the-way venues.[7] The present volume was designed to fill that lacuna by demonstrating some of the ways in which postcolonial criticism might enhance our understanding of the life and letters of Paul. Since it was approved for publication, a number of important books and articles have appeared that analyze Paul's letters through a postcolonial lens.[8] As a result, this book can now serve as a critical introduction to what is quickly becoming a "new wave" in Pauline studies.

The book is divided into three sections.

1. The first section, entitled "What Is Postcolonial Studies?" includes (in addition to the present essay) articles by Stephen Moore and Susan Abraham that offer a historical and critical overview of postcolonial studies for the sake of readers who are new to the area, though even the most seasoned postcolonial critics will find points in both pieces that will challenge their ideas. The section also includes an essay by Neil Elliott on the uneasy relationship between postcolonial studies and Marxism, including the potential benefits of applying both approaches to the study of Paul and his letters.

2. The second and largest section, entitled "Paul and Ancient Forms of Colonialism," consists of nine articles that examine various ways in which postcolonial studies might enhance our understanding of the historical Paul and his letters. The length of

this section reflects both the diversity of interests of the individual contributors and the judgment that insufficient work had been done in this area until fairly recently.

This part of the book is divided into three subsections. The first subsection, which includes essays by Jeremy Punt, Gordon Zerbe, and Davina Lopez, focuses on the political dimension of Paul's writings, with special attention to the ways in which his thought patterns and rhetoric might have been affected by his social location as a colonized citizen (?) of the Roman Empire. All three articles grapple in different ways with the question of whether Paul should be viewed as resisting, rejecting, or reinscribing the ideology, values, and practices of Roman imperial/colonial rule. Their sophisticated and nuanced treatment of these issues and the conclusions that they draw pose challenges for much of the work that has been done in recent years under the "Paul and Politics" rubric.

The second subsection contains essays by Ann Jervis, Christopher Stanley, and Tat-siong Benny Liew that use a postcolonial lens to analyze Paul's statements about personal and ethnic identity. Ann Jervis points out a number of analogies between Paul's description of the human plight in Romans 7 and Homi Bhabha's understanding of "hybridity," while Christopher Stanley questions the value of "hybridity" as a category for interpreting the ethnic categorizations that permeate Paul's letters. Finally, Tat-siong Benny Liew explores the tensions that would have existed between Paul and his Gentile audiences (specifically, the Corinthians) as a result of the Jewish physical identity of both the apostle and the Messiah whom he preached.

The third subsection turns a postcolonial eye toward Paul's statements about gender, with individual essays by Joseph Marchal and Jennifer Bird and a joint essay by Melanie Johnson-DeBaufre and Laura Nasrallah. Joseph Marchal draws on the insights of postcolonial feminist scholars to analyze Paul's relation to Roman imperial ideology in his letter to the Philippians, while Melanie Johnson-DeBaufre and Laura Nasrallah offer a feminist critique of the tendency to valorize the views and activities of Paul in contemporary scholarship. Finally, Jennifer Bird looks again at the gendered language of 1 Corinthians 11 from a postcolonial perspective to see if it yields any new insights beyond those that have been uncovered already by feminist scholars.

3. The third major section of the book brings Paul into the modern (and postmodern) world, tracing some of the ways in which his letters have been or could be used either to support or to challenge the ideologies and practices of Western colonialism. The materials in this section are fairly diverse. Robert Seesengood examines how academic scholarship on the letters of Paul in the nineteenth century was influenced by popular Christian beliefs about missionary activity and slavery, both of which were implicated in Western colonial activities. Brigitte Kahl analyzes how a number of important Pauline scholars appropriated ancient stereotypes of "the Galatians" and turned Paul into a protagonist of Roman/Christian/Occidental civilization doing combat with inferior barbarians/Orientals/Muslims/Turks. Jae Won Lee draws on postcolonial critiques of nationalism and the attitudes of contemporary Korean-Americans toward their homeland to make sense of the tension between nationalism and transnationalism that she identifies in Paul's letters. Finally, Gordon Zerbe investigates how Paul's letters have

Introduction 7

been read and used by contemporary Filipino scholars and church leaders as part of their effort to promote popular resistance to authoritarian neo-colonial rulers.

The essays included in this volume do not begin to exhaust the possible relevance of postcolonial criticism to the letters of Paul, but they do demonstrate some of the ways in which a serious postcolonial engagement with Paul might proceed. In some cases the authors are quite explicit about the role of postcolonial theory in their analysis, while in others the sources and theories upon which they are drawing are relegated to the footnotes. Readers who wish to learn more about postcolonial criticism will find a treasure trove of helpful material in these notes, including works by both "secular" and biblical scholars. If the articles in this volume serve to encourage more Pauline scholars to read and interact with the insights of postcolonial studies, then it will have achieved its purpose. Postcolonial criticism is no passing fad, and scholars of Paul would do well to become familiar with it.

CHAPTER ONE

Paul after Empire

STEPHEN D. MOORE

The Beginnings of Postcolonial Studies

Beginning his book *Beginnings*, Edward Said ponders the difference between an origin and a beginning. The former he pronounces "divine, mythical and privileged," while the latter he styles "secular, humanly produced, and ceaselessly reexamined."[1] According to the tale most often told about the beginnings of postcolonial studies—the academic analysis of colonialism, imperialism, and other related phenomena—the field had its inception in Said's own book, *Orientalism*.[2] This tale is and is not true, in the way of such tales, and so this putative inception begs careful reexamination. Such reconsideration will not take us deeply into postcolonial studies, but it will at least take us around its perimeter, after which we will be better positioned to consider Paul's relations to the imperial, the colonial, and the postcolonial.

First beginning. The term "postcolonial(ism)" appears to have been coined in the geopolitical aftermath of World War II and first employed in such expressions as "the post-colonial nation-state." Whether or to what extent the term ever expressed an unequivocal conviction that colonialism was now securely relegated to the past (such pastness being the import of the "post-") is debatable. What is certain is that any such conception of the postcolonial has long seemed naïve or utopian, old-style colonialism having mutated inexorably into neocolonialism, the latest and most insidious manifestation of which, many would argue, is globalization.[3]

Second beginning. It was only in the 1990s that postcolonial studies coalesced fully and finally as an academic field. The field is frequently condensed to the emblematic names of Edward Said, Gayatri Chakravorty Spivak, and Homi Bhabha. None of the three, however, played any significant role in the naming or institutionalization of the field. The primary catalysts in that regard were a less glamorous trio, Bill Ashcroft, Gareth Griffiths, and Helen Tiffin, who produced two of the textbooks that were key in constituting the field, namely, *The Empire Writes Back* and *The Post-Colonial Studies Reader*.[4] But they were not alone. As the 1990s unfolded, field-constituting "postcolonial" titles began to proliferate at a remarkable rate. The disciplinary expansion took place primarily in the United States—and, not coincidentally, in a context in which the United States had recently become the sole superpower, further consolidating its position as the most far-reaching and efficient empire the world had ever seen. And whereas postcolonial studies would ultimately make relatively deep inroads in a number of academic fields (including biblical studies), its heaviest concentration from the outset has been in the field of literary studies.

Third beginning. This nascent field of postcolonial studies, like any other such field, needed its myth of origins, however modest, and its intellectual heroes. Thus we return to the late Edward Said and his 1978 book *Orientalism*. Poststructuralist theory was the lingua franca of the literary studies field in which postcolonial studies began to proliferate in the 1990s.[5] Poststructuralist analysis of the literatures and other cultural artifacts of colonial and postcolonial societies thus became the hallmark of that burgeoning field. Said was the first to engage in this style of analysis; thus his *Orientalism* came to be seen retrospectively as the charter document of postcolonial studies, notwithstanding the fact that the book itself employed neither "postcolonial" nor "postcolonialism" in its terminological armature. *Orientalism* did, however, make strategic use of the analytic categories of Michel Foucault to excavate the West's multi-discursive construction of the "Orient." The book analyzes the emergent academic disciplines, political discourses, literary representations, and cultural stereotypes by which the East, especially the Middle East, became the West's constitutive Other, particularly during the incremental expansion and consolidation of the modern European empires.

The second putative originator of "colonial discourse analysis" (later termed "postcolonial theory") was Gayatri Chakravorty Spivak. As a deconstructive feminist preoccupied with the systemic omissions and blind spots that enable texts and entire societies to function, Spivak modeled a postcolonial reading strategy attuned to hyper-exploited individuals and populations, particularly women of the global South. Her 1985 essay "Can the Subaltern Speak?" was an immensely subtle and controversial meditation on the impossibility of "speaking for" those who subsist below the radar of official histories or political systems of representation. The essay helped to set the agenda for the emerging field of postcolonial studies, as did her 1987 collection, *In Other Worlds*. By contrast, her 1999 magnum opus, *A Critique of Postcolonial Reason*, finds her deeply critical of the field with which her name had become nearly synonymous, and that critical stance has, if anything, subsequently sharpened.[6]

The third putative originator of postcolonial theory was Homi Bhabha, who also began in the mid-1980s to engage in poststructuralist analysis of modern colonialism and its multifarious aftermath. Bhabha's major essays were collected in *The Location of Culture*, a book that may be said to epitomize postcolonial theory more than any other.[7] Unlike the field of biblical studies, postcolonial studies does not pivot on the concept of method. It has yielded little in the way of readily identifiable methodologies or easily repeatable strategies of reading. A partial exception to this rule can be seen in the analytic categories of colonial ambivalence, mimicry, and hybridity as set forth (in thoroughly unsystematic fashion) in *The Location of Culture*.[8] These three interrelated concepts provide a suggestive reading grid that can readily, if not unproblematically, be superimposed on texts emerging from empire, including biblical texts. For Bhabha, the relationship between colonizer and colonized is characterized by simultaneous attraction and repulsion, which is to say *ambivalence*. In consequence, resistance and complicity coexist in different measures in each and every colonial subject. Colonial *mimicry*, meanwhile, results when the colonized is seduced or coerced into internalizing and replicating the colonizer's culture—a process replete with opportunity for the colonized, according to Bhabha, as mimicry readily teeters over into mockery. *Hybridity*, finally, in Bhabha's deconstructive version of it, is never a simple synthesis or syncretic fusion of two originally discrete cultures, since a culture can never be pure, prior, original, unified, or self-contained but is always already infected by impurity, secondariness, mimicry, self-splitting, and alterity—in a word, by hybridity.[9]

Fourth beginning. While postcolonial theory has been the most visible and influential variant of postcolonial studies, it is by no means the whole of it. An older, more diffuse tradition of postcolonial criticism has deep roots in Marxist theory and tends to frame (modern) colonialism squarely as an übercapitalist enterprise and to analyze it accordingly, with due attention to economic, military, political, and administrative matters, whereas postcolonial theory tends to focus on the subtler operations of colonial discourse and counter-discourse, as we have seen, such as Orientalizing, representing the subaltern, and colonial mimicry.[10]

Yet even if postcolonial studies did not begin with postcolonial theory, the question nonetheless arises: Is postcolonial studies, whatever its variants, to be viewed as a Western academic product, purely and simply? (One cannot help noting, for instance, that even Benita Parry's materialist critique of postcolonial studies was published by Routledge, the press that, more than any other, was responsible for the creation of postcolonial studies as a lucrative academic enterprise.) In answer, it is important to emphasize that the more remote beginnings of postcolonial studies do not lie in academia per se, whether Western or otherwise. Contemporary histories of the field customarily trace its roots to a disparate group of post–World War II intellectuals, artists, and revolutionaries, notably Frantz Fanon, Aimé Césaire, Chinua Achebe, C. L. R. James, Albert Memmi, and Ngugi wa Thiong'o, each of whom lived through the transition from colonialism to postcolonialism in a specific cultural context and engaged in sustained reflection on the insidious effects of colonialism and/or the daunting challenges of decolonization.[11]

Likewise, Said, Spivak, and Bhabha were born and raised in the global South. They elected, however, to work and reside in the West. Although they have written from positions external to the West, they have also written from the pinnacle of the Western academic profession—specifically, from prestigious chairs at U.S. Ivy League institutions. In consequence, their work is viewed by some as compromised, a criticism that, however, relies on certain oversimplifications, as I have argued elsewhere.[12]

Postcolonial biblical criticism, meanwhile, is less haunted by the specter of institutional success. Endowed chairs in Bible and Postcolonialism at Harvard or Yale, Oxford or Cambridge, Heidelberg or Tübingen do not seem to be an immediate threat to this fledgling subfield. This is not to say, however, that postcolonial biblical criticism is not itself a curiously convoluted phenomenon. To these complex twists we now turn.

The Beginnings of Postcolonial Biblical Criticism

According to the tale now routinely told about the inception of postcolonial biblical criticism, it began with Laura Donaldson's *Postcolonialism and Scriptural Reading*, a special issue of the journal *Semeia*, which appeared in 1996.[13] Richard Horsley's *Paul and Empire* followed soon thereafter, appearing in 1997.[14] To style this story a myth of origins would be excessive. All the more reason, then, to reexamine it.

This tale, too, is and is not true. Because of the notorious *Semeia* backlog, which eventually led to the discontinuation of the journal, it is unlikely that any reader, however eager, clutched *Postcolonialism and Scriptural Reading* in his or her hands prior to 1997. More importantly, it is clear from Horsley's introduction to *Paul and Empire* that he had not seen the *Semeia* issue.[15] In real terms, then, postcolonial biblical criticism does not have a single beginning, much less a single origin.[16] In the beginning—or *a beginning*, at any rate—was a full-length work on Paul (or three; for all intents and purposes, *Paul and Empire*, *Paul and Politics*, and *Paul and the Roman Imperial Order* may be regarded as a trilogy).[17] How does that programmatic work begin? How does its editor frame it?

Whatever reservations some biblical scholars might have about some of Horsley's scholarship, there is no question that he is capable at times of reframing the field in electrifyingly original ways. Nowhere is this more evident than in his introduction to *Paul and Empire*. Central to the rhetorical strategy of the introduction is Horsley's thoroughly counterintuitive argument that the "New Perspective" on Paul does not constitute a major paradigm shift in Pauline studies.[18] Why not? Because "[t]he issues of the law, sin, righteousness, and faith in their 'Christian' versus their 'Jewish' configuration remain at the center of discussion," eliciting a "corresponding focus" on Galatians and Romans "where those issues are prominent."[19] While the New Perspective has added considerable nuance to the traditional Augustinian-Lutheran construal of Paul as standing over against Judaism, it has not succeeded in displacing this construal. For that a still newer perspective is required. "Recent recognition that ... prominent Pauline terms such as 'gospel,' 'the cross/crucified,' 'salvation,' and perhaps even 'faith' were borrowed from and stand over against Roman imperial ideology suggests a reexamination of what it is that Paul is against primarily."[20] Horsley then proceeds to argue (with a particular nod to the work of Dieter Georgi, to be discussed further below) that it is the Roman imperial order that Paul's gospel is primarily designed to counter. This is especially evident in 1 Thessalonians, 1 Corinthians, and Philippians, but it can be seen also in Romans and Galatians.[21] In 1 Thessalonians, for instance, destruction is promised to those "who trust in the Roman imperial 'peace and security'"; in 1 Corinthians, "Christ crucified on a Roman cross" stands over against "the rulers of this age, who are doomed to perish"; while in Philippians, "real citizenship" is said to be in heaven, from which one should "expect the true 'Savior.'"[22]

In his critique of the New Perspective, Horsley twice characterizes it as a "deconstruction" of the Augustinian-Lutheran construction of Paul.[23] Yet Horsley is arguing in effect that the New Perspective is *insufficiently* deconstructive, that it is still enclosed within a constricting dualism (Judaism/Christianity) or a "closed field of oppositions," as Jacques Derrida himself might have phrased it.[24] A second phase is therefore necessary in the deconstructive operation, a shift of attention to a third object of analysis, one that intersects with both terms of the binary opposition so as to propel us onto fresh terrain not delimited or determined in advance by the opposition,[25] that terrain being the Roman imperial order. Consciously or not, Horsley is dancing the classic deconstructive two-step in his critique of the New Perspective, employing a strategy that enables him to stake out a "beyond the New Perspective" position that cannot be reduced to finely calibrated cautions about throwing out the Pauline baby with the Lutheran bathwater.

Of course, it is a strategy not without risks. Amy-Jill Levine has argued passionately and compellingly that postcolonial criticism of the New Testament cannot afford to set aside as of secondary importance the task of attending thoroughly to issues of anti-Judaism in New Testament interpretation.[26] Joseph Marchal, meanwhile, warns of the dangers of replacing a view of Paul's letters as resistant to Jewish "legalism" with a view of them as "represent[ing] resistance against the Roman imperial cult or more generally, 'paganism,'" given the insidious ways in which the category "pagan" has been deployed to legitimize colonizing, "civilizing," and missionary enterprises directed toward the non-Christian natives of Africa, Asia, and the Americas.[27]

How did Horsley hit on this strategy in the first place? Where did *Paul and Empire* come from? Horsley's own implicit answer is that it arose from influences both external and internal to the field of biblical studies. Here it is instructive to compare Horsley's introduction to *Paul and Empire* with Laura Donaldson's introduction to *Postcolonialism and Scriptural Reading*. Donaldson, then an associate professor in the Department of English, Women's Studies, and American Indian/Native Studies at the University of Iowa, writes of the previous decade having "witnessed a veritable explosion of publications and conferences about 'postcolonialism' and its importance as an analytical and political tool."[28] Although she is apparently too modest to say so, she herself participated fully in that development throughout the decade, publishing articles with a postcolonial focus in literary studies and cultural studies journals, along with an important monograph entitled *Decolonizing Feminisms*.[29] Without in any way diminishing its significance, then, one might accurately describe *Postcolonialism and Scriptural Reading* as a spillover phenomenon. It exists primarily because of the fact that postcolonial studies had, by the mid-1990s, reached a boiling point in the field(s) of literary studies, as we noted earlier, and had begun to spill over into contiguous fields.

Horsley, too, adduces the postcolonial studies irruption in his introduction to *Paul and Empire*. In contrast, however, to Donaldson, who methodically discusses certain of the key, field-constituting works of postcolonial theory and criticism,[30] Horsley gestures in passing to a thoroughly random handful of examples from the field.[31] This hardly matters in the context, because Horsley is presenting the empire-attuned version of Pauline studies showcased in *Paul and Empire* not as spilling over from literary studies but rather as bubbling up from within biblical studies itself. The ultimate antecedents of *Paul and Empire*, he implies, are the "few recent studies of the historical Jesus [that] have made a point of beginning with the Roman imperial context," the first of which was his own *Jesus and the Spiral of Violence*.[32] More recently, however, "[a] few . . . studies of Paul have finally drawn attention to his opposition to the Roman empire."[33] The studies that he lists are Dieter Georgi's *Theocracy in Paul's Praxis and Theology* and Neil Elliott's *Liberating Paul*.[34] They are excerpted in what appears to be the central section of *Paul and Empire*, "Paul's Counter-Imperial Gospel," where they are joined by Helmut Koester's "Imperial Ideology and Paul's Eschatology in 1 Thessalonians." Instead of the "Holy Trinity" of postcolonial theory, then—Said, Spivak, Bhabha[35]—*Paul and Empire* presents us with a rather different trinity—Georgi, Elliott, Koester.

Does the tale of origins that Horsley spins in his introduction to *Paul and Empire* remain undisturbed in *Paul and Politics*? It does not. It is not extrabiblical postcolonial studies but intrabiblical feminist studies that forces a retelling of the tale. The latter field is represented in *Paul and Empire* only by an excerpt from Elisabeth Schüssler Fiorenza's *In Memory of Her*.[36] In *Paul and Politics*, which contains contributions by Schüssler Fiorenza, Antoinette Clark Wire, Cynthia Briggs Kittredge, Sheila Briggs, and Pamela Eisenbaum, feminism moves from the wings to center stage, and so does attention to issues of race and ethnicity, most of all in Sze-kar Wan's contribution. In his introduction to the collection, Horsley rises gamely to the challenge of describing the multipronged political hermeneutic that ensues. He rightly notes, however, that such a hermeneutic was anticipated by Schüssler Fiorenza, whose 1987 SBL presidential address he quotes as calling for attention to "the complex multiplicative interstructuring of gender, race, class, and colonial dominations and their imbrications with each other."[37] Already in the mid-1980s, then, Schüssler Fiorenza had expanded feminist biblical criticism so that it extended into terrain that would later be termed "postcolonial" (yet a further "beginning" to which we shall later return). Simultaneously, as we saw earlier, and independently, Gayatri Chakravorty Spivak was expanding postcolonial theory so that it extended into feminist terrain. More precisely, Spivak was exploring the complex, multiplicative interstructuring of colonialism, gender, race, and class. These two parallel developments are not brought into dialogue, however, anywhere in the Horsley "trilogy." There are, indeed, no further references in *Paul and Empire* to the extrabiblical field of postcolonial studies after the introduction, and even in the remaining two volumes of the trilogy such references are few and far between.[38]

This is not to say, however, that the Horsleyan brand of empire-attuned Pauline studies has no real interdisciplinary dimension. It is simply that the crucial interdiscipline is not postcolonial studies but rather classical studies, the oldest interdiscipline of all for New Testament studies. Parts I and II of *Paul and Empire* ("The Gospel of Imperial Salvation" and "Patronage, Priesthoods, and Power") feature essay-length excerpts from the work of no fewer than six classicists.[39] The most significant of these classicists for Horsley, it would seem, is S. R. F. Price, author of *Rituals and Power*, the standard study of the Roman imperial cult in Asia Minor.[40] Price shows up once again in the third volume in *Paul and the Roman Imperial Order*, where he is given the last word as general respondent.⁴¹ All of this makes for a version of postcolonial biblical criticism (if that is indeed the proper term for it; more on this below) that barely stretches the traditional New Testament scholar, absorbed as he or she is already with the ancient Mediterranean world in all its dimensions and hence accustomed to grazing in the field of classics.

This brings us to yet another significant "beginning" for postcolonial biblical criticism. In 2007, the first ever article in the *Journal of Biblical Literature* (*JBL*) with the term "postcolonial" in its title made its appearance, David A. deSilva's "Using the Master's Tools to Shore Up Another's House: A Postcolonial Analysis of 4 Maccabees."⁴² The Society of Biblical Literature Web site modestly dubs the *Journal* "[t]he flagship journal of the field,"⁴³ and certainly one would be hard-pressed to name a more representative icon of mainstream biblical scholarship than this hugely oversubmitted periodical. What does it take for postcolonial biblical criticism to move from the margins to the mainstream—from the *Asia Journal of Theology*, say, site of the first postcolonial biblical critical article,⁴⁴ to the *Journal of Biblical Literature*? Mainly it appears to take a strategic bracketing of all contexts but the ancient one. In fairness to deSilva, it should at once be said that his article is superb on many levels. His analysis of 4 Maccabees is incisive and original and will likely open up productive new paths of research on the book. But it is not on the details of his analysis that I wish to comment here so much as his framing of it, together with his choice of subject matter. DeSilva observes in his introduction that the postcolonial lens "has most frequently been employed to examine the use of the Bible and its interpretation as a means of advancing Eurocentric agendas and legitimating the hegemony of Western Europe and its partners, both in situations of formal imperialism and in the lingering aftermath of 'empire.'"⁴⁵ How striking, then, not to say symptomatic, that postcolonial criticism's arrival, announced by name,⁴⁶ in the most closely guarded sanctum of mainstream biblical scholarship should find it coupled with a text that is not part of any biblical canon,⁴⁷ and hence not a text laden with any of the soiled colonialist baggage to which deSilva gestures. Fourth Maccabees is a text that stands entirely outside the history of modern Western colonialism and its neocolonial aftermath, and few contemporary Jews or non-Orthodox Christians even know that it exists, apart from the elite cadre of specialist scholars.⁴⁸ Is contemporary relevance the first casualty of postcolonial criticism's assimilation to the ethos of mainstream biblical scholarship?

Consideration of that question brings us back once again to *Paul and Empire*. Not all of the influences flowing into that volume are so reassuringly mainstream. Neil Elliott's *Liberating Paul*, the only work to be represented by two selections in Horsley's anthology, has its ultimate sources elsewhere than in historical criticism.⁴⁹ Essentially, *Liberating Paul* is an exercise in liberation hermeneutics. In the preface to the second edition, Elliott notes how certain reviewers of the book were "scandalized" that so much of it went "beyond historical reconstruction to draw theological and political connections regarding the imperial order in our own day."⁵⁰ He proceeds to explain how the book "had its origin in a very specific historical moment." The first President

Bush "had launched a catastrophic and virtually unilateral war in Iraq; his administration had supported a bloody coup d'état that had removed the democratically elected president of Haiti . . . ; his tax breaks for the richest Americans fueled budget deficits and accelerated the growing divide between rich and poor."[51] Against this troubling geopolitical and domestic backdrop, Elliott takes on the task of liberating Paul from his long-standing role as "the voice of the sanctified status quo."[52] He notes how "[f]or centuries the apostle's legacy has been systematically manipulated by human structures of domination and oppression, from the conservative interpreters of Paul who found their way into the New Testament itself, down to the legitimation of the 'New World Order' or the sonorous waves of antifeminism backlash in our own time."[53] Thus, Elliott is in no hurry in *Liberating Paul* to slip back into the ancient world and join the hordes of other Pauline specialists happily scurrying about their arcane business. The book's first chapter, "Paul in the Service of Death," takes the reader on a dismal but enlightening tour from colonial South Carolina to the Massachusetts Bay colony, and on to the Nazi death camp at Chelmno and the Reagan-backed civil war in Guatemala. For Elliott, Paul must be liberated so that Paul can liberate. A liberatory Paul is the goal of *Liberating Paul*.

Elliott's book thus suggests another beginning for empire-attuned Pauline studies, a beginning in liberation theology and hermeneutics,[54] though only a beginning, since empire is not yet his unrelenting central focus. For that one must turn to Elliott's recent *The Arrogance of Nations*, a reading of Romans "in the shadow of empire," as the subtitle has it, or rather in the shadow of two empires, the ancient Roman Empire and the contemporary American Empire.[55] Explicit reflection on the far-flung operations of the latter empire frames Elliott's engagement with the former empire. The book's five exegetical chapters are devoted to demonstrating a productively counterintuitive proposition that perfectly encapsulates the Elliott-Horsley brand of empire-attuned Pauline studies, namely, that it is "anachronistic to read Romans as an early specimen of Christian theology. The letter is rather one expression of the range of Judean responses to the Roman Empire."[56] Apart from an occasional reference to the work of Edward Said, however, the extrabiblical field of postcolonial studies is as absent from *The Arrogance of Nations* as it was from *Liberating Paul*. Elliott's principal "secular" resource in *The Arrogance of Nations* is not postcolonial theory but rather the neo-Marxist cultural theory of Fredric Jameson, supplemented by the neo-Marxist power analytic of James C. Scott—more fitting influences, apparently, for a liberationist.[57]

But if Pauline studies as empire studies might be said to have its (other) beginning in Neil Elliott's extension of liberation hermeneutics to Paul in 1994, biblical studies in general as empire studies might also be said to have begun that year, and also in a liberationist register. For 1994 also saw the publication of R. S. Sugirtharajah's "From Orientalist to Post-Colonial," making Sugirtharajah, in his own estimate, "the first to introduce postcolonial criticism to biblical studies."[58] As the title of his article suggests, Sugirtharajah begins that task in dialogue with postcolonial theory, and Edward Said's *Orientalism* remains a significant point of orientation for him in his 1998 monograph, *Asian Biblical Hermeneutics and Postcolonialism*.[59] Yet extrabiblical postcolonial studies is not the primary impetus for postcolonial biblical criticism in the Sugirtharajah mold. That impetus would seem to issue instead from Sugirtharajah's complex relations with liberation theology and hermeneutics, relations characterized by obvious debt and partial estrangement. A defining feature of his work is his extensive internal critique of the liberationist tradition from a postcolonial perspective. Liberation hermeneutics, for Sugirtharajah, is largely prevented by its Christian presuppositions and investments from seeing the Bible as at once a source of emancipation and a source of oppression, and from respecting the truth claims of other religious traditions, even when those traditions are the characteristic religious expressions of the poor. It also conceives of oppression in turn in terms that are too exclusively economic, neglecting other forms based on gender, sexuality, or race/ethnicity.[60] Sugirtharajah's highly influential version of postcolonial biblical hermeneutics, then, is largely a critical reworking of liberation hermeneutics.

Is it possible to construe the biblical texts as at once emancipatory and oppressive and to read them in ways intimately attuned to issues of gender, sexuality, or race/ethnicity—as well as to issues of colonialism, imperialism, and neocolonialism—and still see oneself as situated comfortably within the liberationist tradition? Musa Dube's *Postcolonial Feminist Interpretation of the Bible* would seem to suggest that it is.[61] Indeed, the very combination of the qualifier "postcolonial" with the qualifier "feminist" in its title has the effect of framing Dube's postcolonial project as a project of liberation, as is evident from her own definition of feminist practice: "What distinguishes feminist biblical practice from its male counterpart is its insistence on reading for social liberation."[62] And it is no accident that Dube's analysis of the pericope about the Matthean Canaanite woman in the book, as both a postcolonial *and* a feminist analysis, has her plunging elbow-deep into the oppressive gender ideology of the text. Even without trying, then, Dube avoids being tarred by Sugirtharajah's brush: she does not shrink "from seeing the Bible as at once a source of emancipation and a source of oppression," nor "from respecting the truth claims of other religious traditions," since among the reading strategies of the women of the African Independent Churches celebrated by Dube in her book is "the wisdom of a creative integration of different religious traditions."[63] Yet she seems to feel no estrangement from the liberationist tradition: "The quest of this book owes its birth to some of [the] major liberation currents of the twentieth century, particularly the Two-Thirds World postcolonial and feminist liberation movements."[64]

What of the "first-world" feminist liberation movement? In one of the most arresting chapters of her book, Dube takes a series of white Western New Testament scholars—even (or especially) feminist scholars—severely to task for alleged blindness to issues of colonialism and imperialism in their Matthean scholarship.[65] Elsewhere in the book, Elisabeth Schüssler Fiorenza's feminist reconstruction of Christian origins is singled out for special censure. Schüssler Fiorenza's reconstructive efforts, notwithstanding her ethical commitments, "have bracketed imperial prescriptions and constructions of the biblical texts; hence, they have maintained the violence of imperial oppression against non-Western and non-Christian biblical feminists."[66]

Schüssler Fiorenza responds briefly to Dube in her own recent "empire" book, *The Power of the Word*, arguing that Dube has failed to recognize certain fundamental features of her work.[67] This occurs in the context of Schüssler Fiorenza's own critique of what she perceives as a tendency in postcolonial feminist biblical scholarship generally "to construct a Manichean dualism between wo/men in the Third World and wo/men in the First World, which homogenizes and essentializes wo/men in either world."[68] Schüssler Fiorenza presents herself, quite compellingly, as having been engaged for decades in postcolonial—or to use her preferred term, "decolonizing"—biblical criticism *avant la lettre*[69]—a claim that gives us another, still earlier, "beginning" for postcolonial biblical criticism, as I noted above. Schüssler Fiorenza's key concept of *kyriarchy*[70] does merit more attention from postcolonial biblical critics than it has received, since it equips her to intervene effectively in certain of the debates around empire currently under way in New Testament studies, not least Pauline studies. In "Empire and Ekklēsia," the Pauline chapter of her book, she succeeds in running rings around certain of the prominent (male) contributors to the Paul and empire debate, showing how an empire-critical approach to Paul that is not also a feminist approach limps on one leg. Casting off the "apologetic" approach to Paul that she associates with the empire-critical approach, she navigates deftly "between a rejectionist and an apologetic reading."[71] And yet it might be argued that she also hobbles herself unnecessarily, as her long-standing antipathy to poststructuralist modes of thought delimits in advance her capacity to engage with the extrabiblical field of postcolonial studies (so much of which is infused with a generic poststructuralism, as we saw earlier) and employ it as a catalyst to extend her familiar lines of approach to early Christian literature.[72]

If feminist criticism poses one kind of threat to the "anti-imperial Paul"—the Paul whose fundamental stance vis à vis imperial hegemony in all its manifestations is one of unequivocal opposition—postcolonial theory poses another kind of threat to him. This is particularly evident when the brand of postcolonial theory being employed is that of Homi Bhabha, with its trademark emphases on colonial ambivalence, mimicry, and hybridity.[73] In his book *Competing Identities*, Robert Seesengood recasts Paul as a radically hybrid figure.[74] Extrapolating from Bhabha's deconstructive concept of hybridity, Seesengood argues that there were no "isolated, discrete, cultural (or subcultural) identities within the Roman Empire," while the notion "of a host of potentially describable cultural streams (religious groups, philosophical schools, ethnicities, etc.) converging into a single, 'Hellenized' whole" is equally untenable.[75] Relocating Paul in this hybrid cultural matrix entails recognizing and analyzing a complex coexistence of compliance and resistance in his relations to imperial culture. The most notable facet of Seesengood's analysis is the positive value that he ascribes to such coexistence (although his reliance on Bhabha would lead us to expect no less).

> [P]erhaps the most fruitful (and least attended?) implication of hybridity is not merely *resistance* to power, but the positive *construction* of the "in-between" identity and its potential alteration of alterity itself.... Colonial encroachment and hegemony are ambivalent; they bring both oppression and opportunity. Readings that cast the subaltern

only as deviant (and not simultaneously compliant and transformative) become a two-dimensional liberationist (or Marxist) campaign that sees only categories of suppression and revolt and neglects hybridity's possibility for mutual alteration and mutual coproduction of colonizer and colonized.... "Jews" may be forced to become more "Greek," yet they also alter, via mimicry and hybridity, "Greekness" and coproduce in the process the resulting culture of the colonial exchange.[76]

Paul, on this reading, does not leave the empire as he found it. Of course, neither does this Bhabha-retooled empire leave Paul as *it* found *him*, least of all the anti-imperial Paul.

When postcolonial theory combines with feminist theory, as it does in Joseph Marchal's *The Politics of Heaven*, the anti-imperial Paul finds himself in a perfect storm. Even Bhabha does not survive the encounter unscathed. If Seesengood is primarily interested in Pauline hybridity, Marchal is primarily interested in Pauline mimicry—that is, Paul's exhortations to his *ekklēsiai* to imitate him as he himself imitates Christ. Marchal is not content, however, simply to reframe these exhortations with Bhabha's theory of colonial mimicry. Instead, Marchal draws on alternative theories of mimicry and critiques of Bhabha's theory that have been advanced by feminist postcolonial critics such as Rey Chow, Meyda Yeğenoğlu and Anne McClintock.[77] More important even than feminist postcolonial theory for Marchal, however, is feminist liberation hermeneutics, exemplified for him by the diverse decolonizing projects of Elisabeth Schüssler Fiorenza, Kwok Pui-lan and (above all, it would seem) Musa Dube. This cumulative critique makes for the severest challenge yet to the anti-imperial Paul. For example, Marchal concludes his analysis of the two Philippians passages that have most often been harnessed for anti-imperial readings of the letter—2:9-11 and 3:20-21—by arguing that they both "collude with a comprehensive order of subjection (every knee bowing, every tongue confessing, all things subject)."[78] Thus,

> Paul is not just repeating imperial images in his letters; he is also mimicking imperial-style power arrangements in an effort to consolidate his own authority.... Though he might be competing with the Roman Empire, or qualifying some of the particulars (such as whose rule it is and his place within it), ultimately his arguments mark his attempts to reinscribe imperial relations. The arrangements are neither leveling nor inclusive, but hierarchical and exclusive.... In the end, even if one can manage to argue that all this time Paul is working to overthrow the exploitative Roman Empire, it becomes hard to deny how easily adaptable Paul's rhetorical methods are to an imperial agenda. Unfortunately, this kind of accommodation or collusion will be a significant part of the history for those who claim Paul's texts as their own.[79]

All of this brings us back to the opening scene in *Liberating Paul*. Elliott vividly describes the event that gave rise to the book—a gathering of peace activists against the backdrop of the first Gulf War. He recalls being struck by one insistently reiterated question, posed "with real anguish, by [these] Christians committed to peacemaking in a violent society: 'But what do we do with the Bible?'"—a question that was regularly reduced to another question: "But what do we do with Paul?"[80] "For it was Paul's voice that we heard most often when our churches debated war, or when they discussed domestic violence, or economic injustice, or a number of other 'peace and justice' concerns."[81] *Liberating Paul* emerged as "an attempt to answer the question."[82] But Elliott's (re)construction of an anti-imperial Paul eventually, if indirectly, gives rise to Marchal's (counter-)construction of an imperial Paul,[83] one whose writings all too easily enable us to make sense of a history in which (to employ Elliott's terms) "the apostle's voice has again and again rung out like iron to enforce the will of slaveholders or to legitimate violence against women, Jews, homosexuals, or pacifists."[84] Imperial Paul summons forth anti-imperial Paul, who in turn summons forth imperial Paul in a reciprocal dance of utopian (re)construction and corrective deconstruction.

Anti-imperial Paul does not, however, remain unchanged in the process (a far more complex process than my simple sketch would suggest, needless to say, and involving far more players than Elliott and Marchal).[85] There are now signs that the anti-imperial Paul, at least as a pure type, will become an increasingly rare species. Elliott himself modifies his earlier claims for Paul's anti-imperial credentials in his recent *The Arrogance of Nations*:

> Though I intend to show that some aspects of Paul's rhetoric in Romans were subversive of some of the claims of imperial propaganda, I recognize that Paul never provides a systematic or comprehensive critique of the emperor (whom he never names) or of the empire as such. The empire as such is never his direct target: his goal is to lay a claim on the allegiance of his listeners with which the rival claims of empire inevitably interfered. It is not just that his argumentation is occasionally oblique. Paul's own thinking and rhetoric also was shaped by the ideological constraints of his age.... To borrow an apt phrase from Schüssler Fiorenza, Paul's thought was as fully *kyriarchal*, in its own way, as that of any imperial propagandist.[86]

Elliott's softening of his earlier claims for Paul's anti-imperialism is part of a wider tendency now evident in New Testament scholarship that is attuned to empire. When I first surveyed this subfield in 2000,[87] I drew a sharp distinction between work such as that of Richard Horsley, on the one hand, who read the Gospel of Mark (and, of course, the letters of Paul) as unequivocal anti-imperial resistance literature, and work such as that of Tat-siong Benny Liew, on the other hand, who read Mark as insidiously reinscribing imperial ideology even while appearing to resist it.[88] On surveying the field again in 2006,[89] I still did not feel any need to qualify that distinction. By now, however, that sharply drawn line would no longer map onto the shifting contours of the field. If, for example, Warren Carter's 2001 study *Matthew and Empire* read Matthew as consistently, unequivocally, and exemplarily anti-imperial,[90] his 2007 essay on Matthew for the *Postcolonial Commentary on the New Testament Writings* does not— now Matthew "mirrors imperial realities, even while it contests them," and "protests imperial power, even while it imitates imperial structures."[91] And by 2008 we find even Horsley himself conceding in his introduction to *In the Shadow of Empire*: "Biblical books are not unanimously and unambiguously anti-imperial or pro-imperial. They speak with different and sometimes ambivalent voices."[92]

Interrogating the "Postcolonial" in Postcolonial Biblical Criticism

How much of the work surveyed thus far warrants the label "postcolonial"? This question, too, has been present from the beginning. In the response essay that she contributed to *Postcolonialism and Scriptural Reading*, literature professor Susan VanZanten Gallagher noted that "[f]or some postcolonial literary theorists, several of the essays in this volume would have little, if any, critical validity." For such theorists, the term "postcolonial" acquires its meaning only in relation to the specificity of European colonialism and its post–World War II aftermath, and "[w]ithin this definition, applying postcolonial theory to the Babylonian, Persian, or Roman conquests, the Johannine community's expansionist vision, or any biblical pericope is anachronistic and ahistorical."[93] South African biblical scholar Gerald West has more recently raised similar questions while taking issue with Fernando Segovia's articulation of a three-dimensional "postcolonial optic" for biblical criticism, the first dimension of which would entail analyzing the biblical texts in their ancient imperial contexts.[94] This project has received the lion's share of attention from New Testament scholars attuned to empire, as we have seen, and is also the project that is taking root in the mainstream of the discipline.[95] It is all the more important, then, to take note of West's reaction to the project from an African context:

> [I]t is clear that Segovia is here focusing on the ancient context of production, not current postcolonial readings and actual postcolonial readers (the other two aspects of postcolonial biblical criticism he delineates).... But it is precisely, I would argue, these other two aspects that constitute "postcolonialism proper"! Postcolonial studies emerges from *the reality of the actual lived experiences of particular forms of colonialism*.[96]

West worries that "extending postcolonialism backwards into biblical history ... smooths and 'flattens out' ... the particulars of different colonial experiences and the specifics that gave rise to postcolonialism in our era."[97]

A similar challenge has been sounded from within Pauline studies. "As a politically engaged African American, I cannot ignore the contemporary empire," Brad Braxton states in a recent essay outlining a postcolonial approach to 2 Cor 3:12-18.[98] He notes that the focus of much recent political reading of the Pauline letters "has been upon the ancient world," yet postcolonial studies, as he understands it, is ultimately an invitation to acknowledge "current manifestations of imperialism."[99] He continues: "To read Paul against the backdrop of ancient Rome is intellectually profitable, but the Roman Empire crumbled centuries ago.... What happens if postcolonial critics begin to engage Pauline texts more fully with respect to the neo-imperialism of the twenty-first century?"[100]

Paradoxically, one thing that happens is that the term *postcolonialism* itself is stretched to its breaking point.[101] Whatever chance the term had of capturing the geopolitical complexities of the post–World War II era, it has far less chance of capturing those of the early twenty-first century. The term now in use all over the planet to name the new geopolitical reality is, of course, *globalization*. The field of postcolonial studies is at present visibly engaged in catching up and coming to grips with globalization[102]— and in the process, arguably, is transmuting into something other than "postcolonial studies."

Postcolonial biblical criticism, in the interests of continued relevance, cannot afford to lag too far behind these developments. Yet nothing in the professional training of the average biblical scholar equips him or her to lock analytic horns with the Behemoth and Leviathan of neocolonialism and globalization.[103] (Braxton's own iconoclastic essay sits rather forlornly in a Festschrift dedicated to his Doktorvater Carl Holladay that is otherwise composed almost entirely of ultratraditional historical criticism.) That is not the least important reason why the "X and Empire" brand of postcolonial biblical criticism ("Paul and Empire," "1 Peter and Empire," "4 Maccabees and Empire"), in which the empire in question is reassuringly ancient and remote, is the brand currently poised for the widest circulation, as it represents the smoothest, least taxing, and least threatening extension of historical criticism.

Yet we should beware of dismissing empire studies too lightly, for it is not without teeth. What makes the current preoccupation with ancient empires in biblical studies genuinely significant is its concern with the question of whether or to what extent biblical texts can be said to *resist* empire. All of the texts that would eventually make up the biblical canons were produced in the margins of empire, but with the Christianization of Rome and the Romanization of Christianity the margins moved to the center. Locked in the crushing embrace of the Vulgate, the first official Bible of imperial Christianity, the primary function of the biblical texts became that of legitimizing the imperial status quo, a function that, covertly when not overtly, continued into the modern period. Even the invention of critical biblical scholarship coincided with—and in ways yet to be adequately analyzed was intertwined with—the inexorable expansion of the modern European empires to their outermost limits. Empire studies is united with other forms of postcolonial biblical criticism in the task of disengaging the biblical texts from an imperial embrace that spans the centuries, and to that extent stands in solidarity with an exceedingly long tradition of anti-colonial biblical reading issuing from the margins or the underside of empire.

Meanwhile, the liberationist variant of postcolonial biblical criticism will continue to ride in the slipstream of contextual hermeneutics and continue to counter the inherent inclination of the "X and Empire" variant, as a quintessential academic enterprise, to coagulate into an esoteric discourse herme(neu)tically sealed off from the extra-academic world.[104] In principle, university or seminary classrooms are not sealed off from the larger society or wider world but are linked to them by multiple arteries.

These arteries, however, can become clogged. While the locus of lived Christianity has moved decisively to the global South, the North continues to be the sanctioned training ground for academic biblical scholars, but students from the South in European or North American universities all too often experience their training in terms of arid irrelevance and even continued colonization.[105] Making biblical scholarship more relevant to a large portion of the planet's population is not the least significant benefit of postcolonial biblical criticism, whatever it is destined to become.

CHAPTER TWO

Critical Perspectives on Postcolonial Theory

Susan B. Abraham

This essay offers a critical introduction to academic postcolonial theory. Such an introduction is fraught with difficulty, since academic postcolonial theory is a vast and contested field escaping easy definition or simple thematic and theoretical delineations. Various introductions to postcolonial theory exist, but each presents a refraction of the discipline through the lens of history, cultural studies, intellectual history, economic or political concerns, philosophical questions, literary analyses, or a meld of any or all of these. Instead of a simplistic descriptive reading of these discrete foci, I propose an analytical approach that will complicate any singular and pat presentation of academic postcolonial theory.

Unsurprisingly, the analytic interconnections within the field cause some in academic contexts to fear "postcolonial theory." Rumors of difficulty and abstractions abound, and anxious insistence on "simplicity" of theme and style result in responses that are both dismissive and derogatory. Postcolonial theorists and thinkers are accused of being "impenetrable," "incomprehensible," "elitist," and "masculinist" with regard to their analytic contributions. In a perceptive and deeply insightful foreword to Gayatri Chakravorty Spivak's *In Other Worlds: Essays in Cultural Politics*, Colin McCabe argues that the "rumor of difficulty" is circulated in the interest of control and mastery: "Difficulty is, as we know, an ideological notion. What is manually difficult is just a simple job, what is easy for women is difficult for men, what is difficult for children is easy for adults. Within our ascriptions of difficulty lie subterranean and complex evaluations."[1] McCabe argues that one of the key advances of postcolonial theory and theoretical perspectives is the reorienting of pedagogy in light of cultural politics. Thus, the "rumor of difficulty" with regard to postcolonial theory sheds light on the manner in which academic conventions construct frameworks of meaning and the resistance of conventional academic contexts for exploring the privileged milieu from which such frameworks are produced. Complexity does come at a price, but then, so does simplicity.

Second, postcolonial theory has a complex story of origins as a critical perspective in the academy. Many readers of postcolonial theory have not progressed beyond a shallow grasp of its political intentions and mobilizing these perspectives as part of an older style of liberation politics or philosophy. Such an older style of politics was evident in the identity politics of race, class, and sexuality in the 1980s and early 1990s. These forms of political thought, based in highly dubious binary frameworks, persist within the academy. One way in which such a method functions is to identify this or that minoritized group (racial, cultural, or sexual) and present incoherent assertions aimed at amelioration and recompense by "applying" postcolonial theory. That postcolonial theory continues to be associated with such a form of liberal methodology has been a significantly difficult issue for a number of postcolonial theorists. Gayatri Chakravorty Spivak, for example, as far back as 1991 argued that what goes by the "name of postcoloniality is just bogus."[2] The persistence of binary frameworks for politics is aimed at simplification and rests squarely on an evasion of the epistemological issues presented by a complex analysis engaging multiple foci of domination and oppression. Simplification, in other words, is achieved at great cost because it undermines the kind of political project that postcoloniality attempts to achieve. It is only when such multiply intersecting axes of oppression are simultaneously analyzed that postcolonial theory escapes its theoretical bind to become a politically viable framework, a framework more amenable to the name *postcoloniality*.

Another issue arising from the identity politics of the 1980s and 1990s concerns the category of "culture," which theorists continue to associate problematically with geographic or ethnic identifications while ignoring or tokenizing gender dynamics as intrinsic to "cultural" assignations. "Culture" is not just ethnic, political, or geographical identification; culture consists of a web of interconnected and mutually influencing race, gender, class, and heteronormative relationships on both a local and a global scale. Postcolonial theory asserts that we cannot mobilize the category "culture" unless we are able and willing to examine the manner in which these mutually influencing relationships are constructed and sustained, specifically in the context of neo-liberal capitalism as it reorganizes local and global relationships. When we do so, we discover the power dynamics and power differentials sustaining local and global systems and how power constructs relationships based on race, class, gender, and sexuality. The call for simplification egregiously ignores such a complex analysis of power, often because such an analysis would reveal that the call for simplification rests on binary frameworks that are more easily managed and sustained by a *colonial* logic of domination and subordination.

It is disheartening and bemusing to note the extent to which liberal thinkers in the academy continue to marginalize feminist perspectives as if feminism is a limiting and narrow discourse, disparaging it as a case of "special pleading." Cultural analyses of politics, for example, reveal the extent to which masculinist privilege constructs disciplinary frameworks. In such a view, it is impossible to deploy postcolonial theory without paying adequate attention to contemporary feminist political concerns, particularly as they mesh with issues of race, class, gender, and sexuality. Much of the theoretical work of postcolonial feminist theorists is an attempt not only to peel away layers of masculinist privilege but also to point to ways in which political thinkers from the North rarely examine their own privilege in terms of race, class, and heteronormativity.

As a critical introduction, therefore, this essay presents postcoloniality as the investigation of how an older colonial logic is recreated in the aftermath of decolonization. Two analytical frames will guide this critical enterprise as it grapples with the complexity of postcoloniality's political and ethical commitments. The first, the feminist frame, attempts to chart productive conversations about identity, ethics, and civic polity in a postcolonial context by resolutely signifying the category of "gender" as the lynchpin of its interpretive protocols. To use a feminist frame is not simply to argue for a singular focus on gender issues when attempting to think about postcoloniality; it is rather to say that the feminist frame deconstructs those political proposals that are charted by the more cultural or ethnic dimensions of postcolonial theory. The second frame, the pedagogical, argues that the manner in which we construct meaning and knowledge is one of the most important contributions of postcolonial studies. In its deconstructive mode, it examines the co-opting of postcolonial theory in the Western academy and the consequent loss of the critical edge of postcolonia*lity*.

The Feminist Frame

Postcolonial theory as a critical enterprise can be historically distinguished from the analysis of gender issues. Nevertheless, feminist theory and postcolonial theory developed in a parallel way and converged often in their shared concern for marginalized "Others." Precisely because they are "disciplinary siblings,"[3] a number of rifts have opened up between these two academic strategies. Leela Gandhi points out three areas of controversy between the two forms of critical thought: (a) who or what is the "third-world woman"; (b) the history of the (Western) feminist as imperialist; and (c) the neocolonial mobilization of feminist criteria and rescue missions by neo-imperialism. Arguably, rifts between feminism and postcolonial theory point to the unease with which the academy views both critical forms of nondominative thought.

It is important to note that postcoloniality cannot set gender apart as if it were a separate analytical category. Postcoloniality necessarily engages the category of gender as it shores up imperial logics, whether in the context of historical colonialism or in the context of neo-imperialism. Thus, postcolonial feminist theory is *not* simply an application of either postcolonial theory or feminist theory. It is instead an interaction between the two that does the work of peeling away the dominative logics of colonialism and the more subtle forms of neocolonial tokenism.

As Raina Lewis and Sara Mills assert in their influential anthology, it was feminist concerns that animated many of the initial critiques of colonialism, imperialism, race, and power.[4] Of course, they are not referring to the anticolonial rhetoric of thinkers such as Gandhi or Fanon. They are referring specifically to the concerns of academic postcolonial theory as developed in the Western academic context and the particular framing of race, sexuality, and class concerns as they intersect with gender issues.

Lewis and Mills identify a number of themes that reveal the dynamic relation between postcolonial theory and feminist concerns. In the first place, postcoloniality nuances critical gender theories. One of the original moves in this direction was the attempt to racialize mainstream feminist theory. A key thinker who influenced postcolonial feminist theory was Audre Lorde. For Lorde, the relative privilege enjoyed by white women comes at a dehumanizing cost to black or brown women. Her deconstructive stance is aimed at the false universalism of white feminist theory. Any critical method that cannot examine the universalized category "woman" in a nuanced and historical way ignores the very real differences that shore up social and political power through the unearned privilege of race, class, and sexuality domination. The feminist movement, Lorde argues, has coalesced around a politics that actively dismisses dominative "difference" as it sustains these forms of unearned privilege. Lorde's approach complicates commonsense categories such as "gender" and "women" and so makes thinking and doing critical theory difficult, since one can no longer rest on one's "common sense" when deploying these categories for politics. Her internal critique of racial privilege does not, however, mean that postcolonial thought supersedes feminist thought. In fact, it is a testimony to the vitality of both critical frameworks that they interact in such a manner as persistently to point out the tensions in their political endeavors.

Racializing feminist theory led to the development of another complex of critical ideas, the politics of rethinking "whiteness." It has long been an acceptable commonplace to think of "race" in terms of color, just as it was commonplace and commonsense to think of women when thinking about the category of "gender." When thinking of race, however, the color "white" is rarely scrutinized for its implicit position of having no color, that is, no marker of race. The erasure of whiteness as a racial marker is performed across the board, and white feminists are often guilty of such erasure. Postcolonial feminists, by contrast, seek to explain the complex interconnections between white women's privilege and their complicity in imperializing agendas. Whiteness, they argue, is not only normative in all forms of academic theory, but also performs a sleight of hand in thoroughly mystifying and obscuring its social, cultural, and political privilege relative to blackness or brownness, which are marked as having little or no privilege. The critical project of rethinking whiteness has led to white feminists self-consciously speaking of their race and color as a material reality rather than simply deploying the categories of race and color to identify black or brown feminists. They have begun to examine how they themselves are complicit in framing systems of exclusion by presenting black and brown as markers of "difference" without considering the power that they have in structuring the conversation around difference. In this regard, a deeply challenging essay by Ien Ang argues that the very framework of "inclusion" within white feminism is saturated with a problematic politics of difference.[5] Note here the move to nuance and complicate the already complex terrain inaugurated by a thinker such as Lorde. Whereas Lorde argued for a politics of difference to nuance the categories of "gender" and "woman," Ang makes the case that the very framework of difference ought to be carefully scrutinized.

Both Ang and Lorde point out that early feminism's universalist posture as representative of all female experience was simply an "interested universalism."[6] Their criticism is even more pointed in the context of global capitalism. While Lorde argued for a politics of difference, that mode of politics has been criticized by thinkers such as Ang because the politics of difference rarely questions the way in which ethnic, racial, or sexual identities are constructed by global capitalism. In other words, the politics of difference does not examine the manner in which "difference" is constructed, whether along racial, ethnic, class, or sexuality lines, nor does it examine who deems what qualities or attributes as "different." When one examines "difference" politics carefully, it becomes clear that unequal power—that is, Western, capitalist power—defines difference solely in relation to itself. Well-meaning attempts to address the structure of the politics of difference only exacerbate the issue when a benevolent attitude of "recognition, understanding, and dialogue"[7] is mobilized.

Further, white feminism has not taken seriously the "fundamental sense of permanent dislocation"[8] that, though a common experience of all human life, is intensified in the racialized, ethnicized, and "othered" experience. For Ang, such a world of "white-dominated, Western, capitalist modernity" is the result of a global colonial movement and economic development in one direction that has resulted in the subsumption of other people and cultures into a specific mode of economic and political control. "Difference" is constructed and maintained within such a global system in the service of domination, control, mastery, and hegemony. The knotty politics of inclusion so dear to Western academics, social theorists, and political thinkers only exacerbates the problem by accommodating all differences under the aegis of who wields the power to include. Since "difference" is controlled and managed by liberal capitalist policies, Ang argues that feminist theory and other political forms of thought should engage in a conscious analysis of the *limits* of the fields of intervention and present a politics of partiality that acknowledges the complex continuities and discontinuities in various feminist projects. Her proposal of a politics of partiality in relation to ethics and politics poses a challenge to those who expect easy and immediate solutions. In fact, it confounds the mentality of seeking for solutions and argues instead for a persistent critique of political action that does not rest with providing simple solutions to contemporary political problems.

Alongside categories such as "gender," "woman," and "race" is another category that deserves attention, that of the "third-world subject." One theorist who offers a complex reading of this category is Spivak. In her essay entitled "Three Women's Texts and a Critique of Imperialism,"[9] Spivak examines the assumptions surrounding this term, which implicitly reinforces white, Western, capitalist supremacy. In her view, labeling all third-world women as "generically subaltern," on the one hand, and generating the "unquestioning heroicisation" of third-world women, on the other, are both strategies of control and domination.[10] In order to perform the kind of liberating politics we imagine for the subaltern, academic contexts must rigorously engage in a politics of reading. As Ang has indicated, liberation politics cannot be oriented solely toward thinking about "solutions"; the hard work of ethics and politics demands that we teach ourselves how to *think* differently, particularly about the third-world subject. To do so, Spivak presents postcoloniality as the development of the critical faculty and reading as a deeply political act rather than as a framework to be "applied" to disciplines and contexts.

For Spivak, as for Lorde and Ang, old-style feminism examined a particular kind of women's agency, but postcoloniality complicates this agency by tracking the manner in which women are accorded agency relative to privilege. A text is never innocent of such moves, so one must examine the context in which a text arises. For example, Western feminists rarely examine the cultural, social, and political frame in which literature is produced. For Spivak, by contrast, literature plays an important role in consolidating imperial power. Much of nineteenth-century English literature was complicit in the imperial enterprise by constructing a very specific idea of England for English people.[11] Such literature also consolidated the imperialist project by "worlding" the third world. That is, not only was England represented in a particular way, but the colonized were also represented in relation to the construction of "England." Unless we examine even the sacrosanct classics for their complicity in creating and sustaining imperial logic, we are simply reproducing colonialism. Consequently, the politics of reading introduces a critical stance vis-à-vis texts, a more difficult task than simply seeking to understand their "meaning" or "authorial intent."

In summary, I have argued that doing postcolonial theory leads inexorably to postcoloniality, a critical stance that examines the intersection of gender, race, class, and sexuality. Further, each of these categories is internally differentiated and context-specific. I have also suggested that the complex interconnections between these categories must be closely examined in light of present day global economic frameworks.

The Pedagogical Frame

Postcolonial theory is not simply a method of doing politics; it also involves a normative discourse on subaltern subjectivity, identity, and politics. The method of politics advocated in postcolonial theory resists the liberal and constructive agendas of the academy embodied in terms such as *pluralism* and *multiculturalism*. In fact, the cultural politics of postcolonial theory is of a different order than the earlier identity politics of pluralism and multiculturalism. Thus, postcolonial theory cannot be mobilized as some kind of anthropology. Consider this personal cartography of identity by Chandra Talpade Mohanty:

> Growing up in India, I was Indian; teaching high school in Nigeria, I was a foreigner (still Indian), albeit a familiar one. As a graduate student in Illinois, I was first a "Third World" foreign student, then a person of color. Doing research in London, I was black. As a professor at an American University, I am an Asian woman—although South Asian racial

profiles fit uneasily into the "Asian" category—and because I choose to identify myself as such, an antiracist feminist of color. In North America I was also a "resident alien" with an Indian passport—I am now a U.S. citizen whose racialization has shifted dramatically (and negatively) since the attacks on the World Trade Center and the Pentagon on 11 September 2001.[12]

The cultural politics in which such a complex of identifications and racializations is performed deals with difference, diversity, multiculturalism, colonization, globalization, and nationalism. These contexts reveal the fissures of sexism, racism, heterosexism, and xenophobia, as well as the ethnic, class, academic, and religious elitism that have been important for those invested in critical politics. Education in such a complex context must advance beyond the mere accumulation of disciplinary knowledge in order to interrogate the systems that create and sustain exploitation and to present oppositional alternatives to these systems. The mode of thinking that goes by the name of "postcolonial theory" is not a single type of critical methodology arising out of a specific historical reality (that is, European colonization) but a multiply situated way of thinking critically within the academy. It is not an anthropological account of subjectivity and agency, but rather an investigation of how systems and structures create conditions of subaltern subjectivity. At its heart, the method of postcoloniality is deconstruction.

In Leela Gandhi's words, postcolonial theory has "inherited a deconstructive bias against Enlightenment humanism"[13] and revealed the "epistemological poverty"[14] that informs Western humanism. This deconstructive stand against Western humanism informs all of postcolonial theory. In this regard, Spivak argues that while the task of contemporary politics is indeed to undermine the story of the "ethical universal," that is, "the straight, white, Judeo-Christian, heterosexual man of property," also known as "the hero," the alternative is "not to constantly evoke multiplicity."[15] The impetus to incorporate postcolonial theory into academic contexts to produce the kind of pluralism and multiculturalism embraced by the liberal academy in the West is antithetical to the political intention of Spivak and others. The method of postcolonial theory instead is "to know and to teach the student the awareness that this [initial or partial evocation of multiplicity] is a limited sample because of one's own inclinations and capacities to learn enough to take a larger sample." In other words, postcolonial theory ought to be a critical reflection on the limits of knowledge production, including its own knowledge.

Some postcolonial theorists have consequently traced the development and use of the term *postcolonial* itself. Ella Shohat points out that the academic opposition to U.S. military involvement in the (so-called) Middle East mobilized terms such as *imperialism, neocolonialism,* and *neo-imperialism* in describing the emerging new world order, but not the term *postcolonial*.[16] In her view, the absence of the term *postcolonial* from academic critiques of Western militarized contexts and the accompanying media narratives throws into relief many of the ambiguities of the term, since it reveals how academics themselves are guilty of limiting "postcolonial" to academic frameworks. The term's usefulness does not seem to extend into more popular contexts that are often implicated in endorsing the use of militarized policies toward particular parts of the world. In fact, as she argues, the placement of postcolonial theory and its endorsement in academic institutional settings reveals the extent to which it is apprehended in an ahistorical and depoliticized manner.[17] Such domesticating moves go against the grain of the oppositional and political intent of postcolonial theoreticians.

In arguing for a more limited, historically and theoretically specific use of the term, Shohat presents one of the clearest analyses of how the term *postcolonial* functions in academic contexts by erasing the geographical and temporal markers of race and class exploitation. First, she points out, postcolonial theory "did not emerge to fill an empty space in the language of political-cultural analysis."[18] Its emergence was dependent on and continuous with what was called "third world" studies. Once the term *third world* fell out of favor, the term *postcolonial* emerged. What was lost in this switch, however, was that the more spatially meaningful term *third world* was replaced by *postcolonial* as an adjective to describe the production of third-world scholars working in first-world academic contexts. This erasure of space produces an ambiguity—who or what do the third-world academics in first-world contexts represent? How is their intellectual production received? Recall, for example, the complex of identity charted by Mohanty earlier in this section. The term *postcolonial* does not grapple with the racist and exploitative frameworks under which third-world intellectuals labor. In fact, "postcolonial" here deracinates third-world intellectuals and renders them acceptable in first-world contexts.

Not only is spatiality blurry, but the term *postcolonial* also introduces a fuzzy temporality. *Post* in this context is ordinarily taken to signify the demise of colonialism. If this is the case, the argument can be made that since most of the world is now living beyond the period of European colonialism, *postcolonial* can be applied as a universal category. As Shohat argues, however, such universalization "neutralizes significant geopolitical differences between France and Algeria, Britain and Iraq, and the United States and Brazil."[19] Such a lack of historical specificity leads to diverse chronologies being lumped together, erasing the multiplicity of locations and temporalities. In other words, what goes by the name of postcolonial theory too often gives in to "the globalizing gesture of the postcolonial condition ... [that]downplays multiplicities of location and temporality as well as the possible discursive and political linkages between postcolonial theories and contemporary anticolonial and anti-neocolonial struggles and discourses."[20] For Shohat, as for Spivak, Mohanty, and others, the use of postcolonial theory must be accompanied by a rigorous analysis of (a) what pasts, presents, and visions of a future are being mobilized; (b) what identities, hybridities, and representations are being deployed; and (c) what political vision and goals are in view. In the end, all ahistorical and nonpolitical forms of postcolonial theory are simply instantiating the domesticating agenda of Western academia.

According to Kalpana Seshadri-Crooks, the field of postcolonial studies as it is constituted at present is tinged with a sense of melancholy.[21] Paradoxically, such a sense arises even as the field has gained a foothold in the teaching of the humanities. This sense of melancholy arises precisely because postcolonial theory's critique of imperialism is in effect now institutionalized and therefore rendered "conciliatory."[22] Moreover, postcolonial theorists are painfully aware that they are speaking largely within and to the first world, that it is next to impossible to represent the "third world" in these contexts, and that the very visibility of the field of postcolonial studies renders it toothless in arguments for curricular changes in British and American academic contexts. Postcolonial theory is therefore decidedly not marked by any sense of triumphalism.

For Seshadri-Crooks and others, postcolonial theory must necessarily "rehearse the conditions for the production of its own discourse or be doomed to fall into a form of anthropology."[23] Postcoloniality is not simply a description of subjectivity, even subaltern subjectivity. Postcoloniality is a questioning of the conditions under which subjectivity is claimed, on the one hand, and under which conditions of recognition are fostered and sustained, on the other. Consequently, Seshadri-Crooks is correct in saying that postcolonial studies "has no theory to speak of, concerned as it is with local cultural practices and political issues in the context of transnationalism."[24] What postcoloniality advances for critical thinking is an analysis of conditions of unequal power that is not limited to the historical phenomenon of European colonialism over the past five hundred years. Consequently, postcolonial theory cannot be said to have a clearly identifiable object of analysis, since it engages in local and global critiques of power while seeking to represent, recognize, or subordinate agency. Precisely because it presents materialist critiques of power, postcolonial studies must remain both oppositional and self-critical.

Recent scholarship has attempted to sharpen the self-critical mode of postcolonial studies by arguing that it is time to move beyond some of its established conventions. The editors of the volume *Postcolonial Studies and Beyond* assert that the "project of postcolonial studies is a much larger and more variegated set of intellectual enterprises than might have been presumed thus far."[25] The move advocated in this significant volume is critical to the fields of theology and religious studies because it is precisely postcolonial studies' keen use of interdisciplinarity that can bring to light the ideological and material dimensions of neo-imperialist religiosity. It is critical, therefore, to move away from a narrow culturalist frame for postcolonial studies, which has been its most prominent face in institutionalized frameworks. Postcolonial "keywords" such as "migrancy," "liminality," "hybridity," and "multiculurality" must give way to a more comprehensive analysis of Enlightenment concepts such as "development," "modernity," "globalization," "nationalism," "tradition," and other ideas that have acquired a new and radical cachet in the context of neo-imperialism.

As a final word, I draw on Spivak's incisive analysis of the dependence of postcolonial studies on the method of deconstruction in her *A Critique of Postcolonial Reason: Toward a History of the Vanishing Present*.[26] In her analysis, Spivak argues for "the setting to work of deconstruction"[27] for ethics and politics. Following Derrida, Spivak asserts that a "critical intimacy" is both the requirement for and the upshot of deconstruction. Postcolonial studies, or postcolonial reason, is precisely not the invention of a new and exotic theory outside of a complex intellectual, cultural, and political history braiding together insights from fields that hitherto seemed discrete and disparate. Instead, its theoretical complexity engages in a close study of the critiques of the modern and Enlightenment frameworks, sharpened by the Derridaean insight that radical alterity needs to be cast as a "concept-metaphor"[28] as "the experience of the impossible." Otherness cannot be simply an academic idea. Otherness has to be an experience, an (im)possible experience. Ethics and politics—the frames in which we engage in the service of justice and wholeness—are not just *complicated* by otherness; they call us to *experience* otherness. This is deconstruction's "setting to work" mode. Entering into the experience of otherness cannot be tracked by linear thought. It requires a suspension of the manner in which academic discourses are conducted. It requires a stringent examination of the categories routinely used in political work. This is the difficulty of postcolonial theory, but it is also its unique, though partial gift to ethics and politics. This is what Spivak means when she writes:

> [Deconstruction] in its "setting to work" mode may be of interest for many marginalized cultural systems as a development form within the aftermath of the Kantian Enlightenment, whereby their own calculuses, dominant in reaction, have become as compromised (especially gender compromised) and stagnant as anything perceived by Heidegger in the Kantian line itself. Of course, the possibility of these connections remains dubious as long as the "setting to work" mode remains caught within the descriptive and/or formalizing practices of the academic or disciplinary calculus. And as long as the othering of deconstructive philosophy remains confined to discourses at least accessible to related academic disciplines (such as literature, architecture, theology or feminism), it gives rise to restricted but useful debates.[29]

CHAPTER THREE

Marxism and the Postcolonial Study of Paul

NEIL ELLIOTT

> The originality of Marxist criticism . . . lies not in its historical approach to literature, but in its revolutionary understanding of history itself.
> —Terry Eagleton[1]

> Those of us for whom the Bible's operative vision is of a divine "option for the poor" must confess that only Marxism and its offspring have given political form to that vision.
> —David Jobling[2]

Marxist interpretation of any part of the Bible has been a rarity. Even today, after the end of the Soviet Union and the dramatic dissolution of the Soviet bloc in Eastern Europe, we might expect the name "Marxist" to appear less inflammatory than before those events and even, at least in some academic circles, to enjoy a certain éclat. Yet only a few brave Hebrew Bible scholars, notable among them Roland Boer and David Jobling, routinely identify themselves in their work as Marxist critics.[3] Elements of Marxist criticism may be more widely known as they have passed, perhaps unrecognized by readers, under other names, such as "socio-literary" or "ideological criticism."[4]

The case is similar in New Testament studies, where those scholars who attempt a serious engagement with Marxist theory and methods have generally demurred from identifying their work as Marxist or from any explicit, sustained engagement with Marxism. More often such engagements are presented under the headings of "political" or "liberative" or "materialist" interpretation, or as readings "from the margins" or "from below."[5] So, for example, Richard Horsley has done much to advocate and to advance political, counter-imperial, and "people's history" interpretations of various aspects of early Judaism and Christianity, yet so far as I know, he nowhere describes his own work as Marxist in orientation.[6] Again, although Steven

Friesen has offered a sustained critique of the ideological blind spots in "capitalist criticism" of the New Testament, he does not suggest Marxist criticism as an alternative; instead he pleads that we "move beyond the capitalism/Marxism argument," without pausing to describe what the Marxist side of such an argument might sound like.[7]

Those interpreters who have called most explicitly for a full complement of analytical methods that include distinctively Marxist categories of class and mode of production (whether or not they are identified as such) speak from what continue to be regarded, in mainstream (or in Elisabeth Schüssler Fiorenza's trenchant phrase, "malestream") North American biblical scholarship, as "contextualized" or "perspectival" approaches that combine feminist, gender, and postcolonial criticism.[8] Schüssler Fiorenza's neologism *kyriarchy* is increasingly recognized as an apt way to conceive of the overlapping systemic hierarchies of class, gender, race/ethnicity, colonialism, and sexuality in the ancient world and our own.[9] Yet as she and others observe, such pleas for complex, "multi-axial" methods have most often been met with a studied silence or marginalization by a discipline more interested (as we should expect, in late capitalism) in the proliferation of difference than in concerted thinking and action in terms of class solidarity.[10]

Elements of Marxist Interpretation

Given the relative unfamiliarity with Marxist themes in the field of biblical studies, it might be useful to distinguish Marxist historiography, with which this essay is concerned, from Marxist philosophical theory and Marxist political action, with which it is not. (Many contemporary Marxists in the "New Left" would urge a similar distinction between the Marxist legacy as mobilized in democratic socialist movements and the legacy of Leninism-Stalinism.[11]) I follow G. E. M. de Ste. Croix in understanding "Marxist" historiography as a way of describing past (and present) societies that gives foremost attention to the dynamics of *class* and *class struggle*. By *class* I understand the pattern of relationships between human beings in a society as they are mutually involved in the process of production, whether the relationships involve property or labor. *Class struggle* consists in the exploitation that characterizes those relationships and resistance to that exploitation.[12] Though Marx's particular focus was the industrial capitalism of nineteenth-century England, he was also keenly interested in tracing the dynamics of class struggle throughout history.[13] Following Marx's insights, de Ste. Croix had no trouble describing those dynamics in the Roman world. The propertied class derived the economic surplus that "freed them from the necessity of taking part in the process of production"—not from wage labor, as in contemporary industrial capitalist society, but from unfree labor of various kinds, such as slavery.[14] Imperialism, whether in the undeniably different forms of ancient Rome or in the modern world, is but "a special case" of extraction and exploitation, involving "economic and/or political subjection to a power outside the community."[15]

Quoting liberally from Marx's writings, de Ste. Croix provides helpful correctives to the popular misrepresentation of Marx's ideas as imposing a strict "economic determinism"[16] and to the erroneous assumption that class struggle can be said to exist only when and where self-conscious classes are engaged in explicitly political struggle.[17] The correctives are important. As de Ste. Croix observes, the nearly "complete . . . lack of interest" displayed by English-language historians of the Greco-Roman world issues as much from ignorance or misunderstanding of Marx's ideas as from overt rejection of them.[18] He takes care nevertheless to observe that, to scholars satisfied with the present order, there is reason enough for avoidance of the sorts of questions Marxism raises:

> Whereas descriptions of ancient society in terms of some category other than class—status, for instance—are perfectly innocuous, in the sense that they need have no direct relevance to the modern world . . . an analysis of Greek and Roman society in terms of class, in the specifically Marxist sense, is indeed . . . something *threatening*, something that speaks directly to every one of us today and insistently demands to be applied to the contemporary world. . . .[19]

It is one thing to identify aspects of class struggle in the ancient world and another to describe what a Marxist investigation of the New Testament writings might look like. Obviously, for such an investigation the role these writings subsequently played as the sacred Scriptures of the Christian religion must in no way be allowed to limit or qualify the application of historical methods. As Fredric Jameson declares in his essay on Marxist interpretation, "The convenient working distinction between cultural texts that are social and political and those that are not"—for example, religious texts—"becomes something worse than an error: namely, a symptom and a reinforcement of the reification and privatization of contemporary life" that is "the tendential law of social life under capitalism." By contrast, Marxist interpretation insists that "there is nothing that is not social and historical—indeed, . . . everything is 'in the last analysis' political."[20]

Marxist interpretation of texts makes use of accepted historical- and literary-critical methods, but with a clear conception of the ideological character of cultural texts. Jameson describes three distinct operations in such interpretation. In the first, narrowly historical phase, a text is understood as a symbolic act, an attempt to resolve specific contradictions in a historical situation. Because Marxism understands culture to be generated by the deep contradictions inherent in class struggle that correspond to a particular mode of production, and because these contradictions are evidently still unresolved in the history of which we, too, are a part, the situational character of the text cannot be the final object of our interpretation. Thus Marxist criticism does not end where some applications of historical criticism leave off. Rather, in a second phase, we must regard the text as an attempt at ideological closure, at resolving the unresolvable—those deeper material contradictions that have generated the ideological framework in which a text necessarily operates. The text "maps the limits of a specific ideological consciousness and marks the conceptual points beyond which that consciousness cannot go."[21] So understood, the text points to a broader semantic horizon, the social order that is the expression of class struggle in a particular period. In this second phase of interpretation, the object of investigation is "the great collective and class discourses" of that period, of which the text "is little more than an individual *parole* or utterance."[22]

But because the text inheres, as we do, in "a single great collective story, . . . a single vast unfinished plot," the final horizon of interpretation is nothing less than "the ultimate horizon of human history as a whole."[23] The text as *parole* and the class discourse or *langue* of which it is an utterance point, in a particular place and time, to "the coexistence of various sign systems which are themselves traces or anticipations of modes of production," which are themselves always in flux and tension. The final phase of Marxist interpretation points to the historical possibilities for transformation and "cultural revolution" latent in those tensions.[24]

Marxist Interpretation of Early Christianity

What now appears as a virtual "dividing wall" between New Testament scholarship and Marxism was not a fixed barrier from the beginning. Frederick Engels was keenly interested in early Christianity as "a movement of oppressed people" with "notable points of resemblance with the modern working-class movement"—including its power to attract both the dispossessed and a variety of charlatans eager to prey upon them.[25] Karl Kautsky applied Marxist principles to a much more expansive discussion of the "foundations of Christianity."[26] According to Kautsky's account, Jesus mounted an abortive rebellion that the Gospel writers subsequently covered up; his execution makes sense only on that basis.[27] The organization that Jesus established before his death—an incipient communism among the free proletariat of Jerusalem—survived him: indeed it was "the vitality of the community" that "created the belief in the continued life of their Messiah."[28] Once the movement spread beyond Palestine into the Diaspora, it immediately attracted non-Jews among the lower classes, but the tension between the movement's originally Jewish nationalist impulses and its proletarian appeal across ethnicities became acute.

The figure of Paul was central for Kautsky's account. Paul represented the dynamic that accelerated the spread of Christianity as a proletarian movement unmoored from its Jewish character.[29] This was ultimately a short-lived moment, however, for a number of reasons. First, the destruction of Jerusalem "stifled the last popular force in the Empire" so that afterwards "there was no longer any basis for an independent class movement of the Jewish proletariat."[30] Second, the urban poor and slaves could never achieve a community of production like that which enabled the Jerusalem movement to thrive. Their movement—deprived of any meaningful way to practice the community of production or of goods beyond common meals[31]—became increasingly "subservient and even servile" after the destruction of Jerusalem. It declined into "the budding

Christian opportunism of the second century" which would, at last, "raise the spineless obedience of the slave to a moral duty."[32]

Aspects of this remarkable account of Christian origins find definite, albeit diverse, echoes in more recent works, such as Gerd Theissen's distinction of the "radical theocratic" ethic of the Palestinian Jesus movement from the "familial love-patriarchalism" of the urban Hellenistic mission, where the itinerant ideal "retreats almost completely."[33] Another example is Justin Meggitt's description of the economic "mutualism" that Paul encouraged as a valuable "survival strategy" at the subsistence level for the urban poor, who could not otherwise draw on collective resources as peasants could.[34] Though we find very different estimations of the material circumstances of the Pauline assemblies in Theissen ("a certain degree of prosperity") and Meggitt ("a bleak existence"), both sustain Kautsky's focus on how those material circumstances differed from the situation of the Palestinian Jesus movement.

Since Kautsky's work, however, we have not seen a similarly comprehensive account of the rise and fall of early Christianity as a social revolutionary movement. Nor have we seen as incisive a discussion of the Pauline mission as a fateful tactical blunder in that movement's advance. By advancing too quickly toward a *symbolic* unity of urban proles across ethnic and provincial boundaries, Kautsky argued, the movement overreached its *material* base. Without the clear example of a community of goods that Jerusalem had provided, these communities quickly lost their character as a class movement.

The Curious Absence of Marxist Concerns in New Testament Scholarship

Kautsky represents the keen interest among some early Marxists in the origins of Christianity. If his account is not immediately familiar to New Testament scholars today, it is not because it lacks either coherence or currency with the critical scholarship of his time. The explanation lies elsewhere.

James Crossley describes a general "fear of and hostility to Marxism" in a discipline that remains dominated by Christian theological interests.[35] Karl Barth's dialectical theology and his general suspicion of any socialism that was not avowedly "Christian" certainly played a role in this outcome.[36] So did the powerful influence of anti-Communist ideology, manifested both as pressure on the churches and as dissension within the churches. As a result, although in the last forty years scholarship on the social circumstances of the Pauline assemblies has developed into a robust field, it has done so despite the almost complete neglect of questions of class and class struggle. The fact that New Testament scholars routinely sound warnings against the "danger" of Marxist approaches even though such analysis remains virtually nonexistent should alert us to the presence of ideological currents within the discipline.[37]

As Steven Friesen has shown, Adolf Deissmann's generalizations at the beginning of the twentieth century about the "mixed" social makeup of Pauline Christianity, which he described as a "cross-section" of society drawn from "the middle and lower classes," have exercised a disproportionate influence on subsequent scholarship.[38] Although Wayne Meeks and Abraham Malherbe have hailed a "new consensus" since the 1970s that has replaced the older views of Deissmann, Friesen has shown that their views in fact represent the mainstream consensus of twentieth-century New Testament scholarship, a view that is essentially a continuation of Deissmann's thesis.[39] This mainstream consensus has mostly marginalized the topic of poverty, whether by (a) ignoring it completely, (b) trivializing it by extolling the virtues of a putative first-century economic expansion, or (c) elaborating sophisticated social-scientific models that simply erase class from consideration.[40] The last strategy, dominant since the 1970s, has paid more attention to "social status," but, as Friesen has observed, "economic inequality . . . never gained a foothold as a significant topic of conversation."[41] To the contrary, "our preoccupation with 'social status' is the very mechanism by which we have ignored poverty and economic issues."[42] To Friesen's critiques of social-status modeling we might add a critique of cultural-anthropological scholarship that has advanced a static, functionalist view of first-century society at the expense of any attention to class or class struggle.[43]

Common to these discussions of social realities in the Pauline churches is the refusal "to engage in economic analysis."[44] There are sufficient data to carry out such analysis, as Friesen, Meggitt, and Peter Oakes have recently shown in important studies.[45] But apart from these and similar efforts, the general pattern in scholarship on Paul's communities is clear: if poverty is generally ignored, oppression and class conflict are unmentionable.[46] Friesen relates this mind-set to the broader formation of academic disciplines in the twentieth century, when Fordist industrial capitalism created the need for an educated professional-managerial class. The progression of scholarly discussions of poverty in the Pauline churches (or the systematic avoidance of such discussion) is, Friesen suggests, only one instance of a larger pattern: "Higher education taught future professionals to accept and to overlook economic inequality, and Pauline studies did so as well."[47] Friesen calls this pattern of interpretation "capitalist criticism."

Marxism and Postcolonial Criticism

In contrast to "capitalist criticism" as practiced and taught in the metropolitan centers of the West, one might expect postcolonial criticism to readily and systematically embrace the tenets of Marxism. After all, imperialism, and especially the "impressive ideological formations" that undergird and impel it, lies at the heart of postcolonial criticism,[48] and Marx (and to an even greater extent, Lenin) had already theorized imperialism as the extension of class struggle. Moreover, early critics of colonialism like Frantz Fanon, W. E. B. Du Bois, and C. L. R. James were avowed Marxists. Fanon called for nothing less than socialist revolution as the only viable path to decolonization.[49] More recently, Aijaz Ahmad has invoked Marxism to raise a similarly trenchant critique of the "mystificatory character" of much postcolonial discourse, which effaces the socialist cause in its celebration of national decolonization.[50] Nevertheless, the postcolonial criticism of the last few decades has so largely ignored Marx and Marxism as to give some observers the impression that its proponents wish to "dump" Marx and "forget Marxism."[51]

In her introductory text on postcolonial theory, Leela Gandhi provides a lucid summary of the intellectual "genealogies" that lie behind this debate.[52] Although a long history of Marxist interpretation has insisted that colonialism is at least "a necessary subplot" in the expansion of European capitalism, postcolonial analysts rarely acknowledge their "genealogical debt" to Marxism, claiming closer affinity to Foucauldian poststructuralism. Because Marxism has generally focused its attention on class struggle as manifested in European industrial capitalism, some postcolonial critics have argued that it fails to do justice to the distinctiveness of the colonial experience in other parts of the world. They also protest that the Marxist claim to have uncovered a single dynamic shaping universal history is but another form of European cultural imperialism. Thus, Dipesh Chakrabarty protests that in Marxism as well as other European philosophical traditions, history remains the discourse through which the West construes the rest of the world in terms of its own narrative: "Europe remains the sovereign, theoretical subject of all histories, including the ones we call 'Indian,' 'Chinese,' 'Kenyan,' and so on."[53]

From their side, Marxists insist that privileging the experience of colonialism obscures the genuine similarities and shared interests among oppressed classes who may not have experienced colonization, or may not have experienced it in the same way.[54] Further, because Marxists regard class solidarity across national and ethnic boundaries as the only possible engine of historical transformation, they see the characteristic postcolonial emphasis on the formation of distinctive subaltern subjectivities as a dangerous distraction from the necessary *collective* resistance to political and cultural domination.

The Marxist protest is occasionally phrased in terms that approach *ad hominem* attacks on postcolonial interpreters, as when Arif Dirlik declares that postcolonialism is what happens "when Third World intellectuals have arrived in the First World."[55] Gandhi and Spivak respond that despite the unavoidable challenges of "positionality," the postcolonial interpreter ensconced in Western academia nevertheless has a genuine "political vocation" to precipitate the sort of dialogue between Western and non-Western academies that can "think a way out of the epistemological violence of the colonial encounter."[56]

Marxism and Postcolonial New Testament Studies

Because the topic of empire is at the heart of postcolonial criticism, it is not surprising that New Testament critic Fernando Segovia has named as the "first dimension of a postcolonial optic" an analysis that contextualizes Jewish and early Christian texts within "the reality of empire, of imperialism and colonialism."[57] One would therefore expect to find postcolonial and Marxist perspectives to be closely allied within the discipline. But here again, much postcolonial New Testament interpretation has shown a striking disinterest in Karl Marx's theories, if not outright hostility to them.[58] As Roland Boer quips, "One is more likely to come across Groucho or Harpo Marx in the writings of biblical critics who have taken up postcolonial theory or, indeed, postcolonial critics who have written about the Bible."[59]

Elaborating much of the same genealogy of postcolonialism that Leela Gandhi has described, Boer laments the eclipse in postcolonial biblical criticism of an understanding of history as the arena of class struggle. Instead, the Bible's historical role in the colonial project of "civilizing" the "native" and the associated indigenous project of "decolonizing the Bible" have been elevated to primary status. As a result, postcolonial critics have occupied themselves with a search for "counter-hegemonic moments in canonical texts" rather than "the kind of work that begins to make sense of the anti-colonial movements and wars of independence." Boer asks whether imaginative textual "interventions" will "remain ultimately futile, absorbed into the dominant system?"[60]

This concern echoes the more general critique of postcolonial critics as third-world intellectuals who "have arrived" in first-world academia.[61] It would be unfair, however, to apply such generalizations indiscriminately to postcolonial feminist theologians like Kwok Pui-lan or Musa Dube, who have repeatedly discussed the intersection of overlapping domains of class, gender, and ethnic oppression and the need for a broad solidarity in interrelated struggles for liberation.[62] It is nevertheless appropriate to pose this concern as a "test," as theologian Catherine Keller does, for postcolonial interpreters. Keller asks whether postcolonial theory is used in such a way as "to relativize any revolutionary impulse, to dissipate the political energy of transformation, to replace active movements of change with clever postures of transgression"?[63]

Of course, the decolonization of the Bible is not primarily a phenomenon of Western academia. It is an integral component also of the praxis carried out in local sites of emancipatory struggle, such as apartheid South Africa, where the Bible was an important part, perhaps the most important part, of the symbolic repertoire. Nonetheless, David Jobling ably characterizes such sites as offering "very limited ideological options." The work of decolonizing the Bible requires distinguishing the message(s) of the Bible from the colonizing project brought by European missionaries, but this work is not usually at the forefront of broad popular movements for liberation. Rather it remains the case that "the Bible's location is often—surely *most* often—some form of church."[64] Churches themselves are sites of "very limited ideological options" because they are often divided in their political commitments (where such commitments are even expressed) and because "the Bible/Christianity has tended heavily to be on the wrong side of the colonial/postcolonial struggle."[65] Both Marxism and those churches that practice the decolonization of the Bible can provide resources for local liberative struggles, Jobling argues, not least because those involved in local struggles often "need some sort of organized view of the outside world which confronts them" such as Marxism and Christianity—"two inveterately globalizing mindsets"—provide. But we should hardly expect them to be adopted in equal measure for the same reason that Alistair Kee noted concerning theologies of liberation: churches will not readily embrace Marx's critique of *religion* while pursuing a *theological* decolonization.[66]

We see, then, that postcolonial biblical critics in Western academia—especially those located in theological institutions—occupy a particularly complex, precarious position. They represent their own decolonized nations to the Western academy, yet their incorporation often hinges on their position as expressions of "exotic culture." They represent peoples who remain politically, culturally, or economically oppressed, yet they do so as faculty members at prestigious Western universities and seminaries. They represent often vibrant decolonized churches to a post-Christendom Western ecclesiastical establishment that is often more concerned about its survival than about political transformation. And even if they embrace socialist politics—something that one should hardly assume—that same Western Christian establishment assimilates them as emblems of institutional commitment to multiculturalism rather than as advocates of class struggle. Given the political economy of Western theological higher education, we should not be surprised to find postcolonial biblical criticism more often emphasizing themes of acceptance across cultural difference than of revolutionary class consciousness. An exception to this pattern can be seen in the many subaltern women who have spoken out courageously against the multiple oppressions of ethnic, colonial, class, and gender discrimination despite the compounded jeopardies that these oppressions place upon them.[67]

Marxist Challenges for the Postcolonial Interpretation of Paul

To date, distinctly Marxist categories of analysis such as *class* and *class struggle* have been mostly marginalized in postcolonial interpretations of Paul in favor of conversations about imperial ideology, colonial identity, and hybridity.[68] Rather than adding another survey of postcolonial literature to those presented elsewhere in this volume, I would like to offer a list of challenges that Marxism poses to postcolonial interpretation as well as to more conventional "capitalist" modes of criticism.

Class, Class Struggle, and Ideology

The cornerstone of contemporary Marxist historiography is the correlation of the ideological representations in a particular culture with the economic relations inhering in the current mode of production.[69] With regard to the early Roman Principate, we are dealing with a transition from an agrarian, tributary mode of production to an increasing reliance on slave labor, as conquests occasioned the incorporation of more and more slaves into an expanding imperial economy. The first mode of production correlates with the temple state, of which "religion" and the prerogatives of (divine and human) monarchy (evoked by the term "sacred kingship") were the indispensable ideological apparatus. But the expanding empire faced a more complex ideological challenge. A society that is based on slave production depends on the careful maintenance of a symbolic system of difference: citizens must be distinguished from noncitizens, free persons from slaves, conquerors from conquered. Bodies that enjoy a presumption of freedom from being shackled, flogged, pierced, and crucified must be distinguished from those that do not. In the Roman era, this distinction was represented visually through an elaborate iconographical system that encoded as natural the power differentials inhering in gender and class relationships as well as those distinguishing Romans from other peoples. The distinction was also rehearsed ritually at various sites including the temple or shrine, the arena, and places of crucifixion.[70]

Symbolic representations of the spectacular violence, invincible military might, and inevitability of Roman hegemony were already abundant during the Republic. Under the Principate, these images expanded to include the elaborate ideological representation of the emperor. Beginning with Augustus, the emperor was portrayed simultaneously as a peace-bringing monarch and devoted high priest (symbolizations appropriate to an agrarian mode of production) and a benevolent householder, guardian of domestic morality, and pious father of his people (legitimizations essential to the slaveholding class in a slave-based mode of production). These crucial innovations in the iconographic, literary-poetic, and ideological representations of Augustus were appropriated and adapted by his successors, who asserted both genealogical and theological claims to his legacy, relying particularly on the symbolization of the emperor as *divi filius*, "son of the divine one."[71]

From a Marxist point of view, the correlation between prevailing economic relationships and dominant ideological representations cannot be sundered. For this reason, discussions of the class position of Paul and the members of his assemblies, class-conscious analyses of particular economic practices—what Justin Meggitt has called "mutualism," the only "survival strategy" left to the urban poor—and examination of Paul's resistance to patronage overtures from higher-class individuals are of primary importance.[72] But the interpretation of these economic practices should not be separated from an ideological understanding of Paul's proclamation of a crucified and risen Christ, as if the former were incidental or merely pragmatic mechanisms for sustaining the assemblies as *religious* groups that were primarily concerned with beliefs in the latter. For Paul to insist that Christ took "the form of a slave" and "became obedient to the point of death—even death on a cross" (Phil 2:7-8), and that God's action in raising this "doulomorphic" messiah from the dead made possible the filiation of a new and free people as the "children of God" (Rom 8:12-21) is an unmistakable expression (in the language of Jewish apocalypticism) of solidarity with the lowest classes, akin to what contemporary liberation theologians call the "preferential option for the poor."[73]

Ethnicity and Imperialism

Recent Western interpretation of Paul—especially under the banner of the "New Perspective"—has emphasized themes of multicultural and multiethnic tolerance and inclusion as Paul's legacy for the contemporary world. After landmark studies in the 1970s showed the traditional theological opposition of Paul's doctrine of justification to a supposed Jewish works-righteousness to be historically untenable and morally bankrupt,[74] many interpreters, chastened by those studies, adopted an alternative exposition of Paul's gospel as a form of advocacy for "the inclusion of Gentiles" and the "legitimization of the Gentile church." A corollary of the emerging "New Perspective on Paul" was a new explanation of "what, in Paul's view, was wrong with Judaism," which focused on circumcision, kashrut, and Sabbath observance as badges of identity and thus as expressions of characteristically Jewish "ethnocentrism," nationalism, or "exclusivism."[75] Ethnic tensions between Jews and non-Jews have been proposed as the chief concern motivating Paul's letters to the Romans and Galatians.[76]

The New Perspective has proven quite popular, in part because of its congeniality to the Western liberal celebration of multicultural difference,[77] but it has also met significant criticism. Even when carefully phrased in terms of a conflict between "universal" and "exclusivistic" trends within Judaism rather than as a wholesale conflict between Pauline Christianity and Jewish religion, some of the interpretations associated with the New Perspective have purchased a contemporary theological or cultural relevance for Paul at a high price. Too often they rely on derogatory (and generally undocumented) characterizations of Judaism—especially when Paul is the only named example of the supposed "universalistic" strain in Judaism.[78] Similarly, Jewish feminist scholars have criticized Christian feminist, liberationist, and now postcolonial interpreters for constructions of early Christianity that end up "blaming the Jews for the birth of patriarchy."[79] Attempts to portray Pauline Christianity as being "non-ethnic" or transcending ethnicity face decisive critiques, first, for being unavoidably supersessionistic,[80] and, second, for failing to give full respect to Paul's own Jewish identity.[81]

It is important to recognize that more is at stake here than the perpetuation of inexcusable stereotypes regarding Judaism. In her essay on decolonizing feminism, Chandra Talpade Mohanty notes that "multicultural" analyses in the metropolitan West often bypass an analysis of power relations. She calls for a "fundamental reconceptualization of our categories of analysis so that [ethnic] differences can be historically specified and understood as part of larger political processes and systems."[82] To similar effect with regard to New Testament postcolonial scholarship in particular, Tat-siong Benny Liew highlights the often hidden role that power differentials play in Western discourse on ethnicity and race.[83]

Marxist interpretation poses an additional challenge to the "universal" Paul, asking whether such interpretations are purchased at the price of a studied silence over issues of class, exploitation, and class struggle and a fully historical contextualization of the constructions of ethnicity in Paul's era. Explicit attention must be given to the scope and contours of "Romanization" in the early Principate as the cultural and political means for assimilating provincial elites into the imperial system, as well as to the ways in which patronage and the civic cultus served that assimilation.[84] Mark Reasoner has described a "Roman ethnocentrism," involving integrated codes of strength and weakness, honor and shame, class and status, and patronage and obligation, as the immediate context of Paul's letter to the Romans.[85] Similarly, but with greater theoretical emphasis on the interplay of imperial, class, and gender inequalities, Davina Lopez and Brigitte Kahl have offered insightful studies of Paul's mission, and of Galatians in particular, as posing an alternative to Romanizing constructions of ethnicity as membership in either conquering or conquered peoples.[86]

Judaism and the Law

The political interpretation of Paul that was pioneered among Latin American liberation theologians has recovered the political dimension of Paul's gospel as the advocacy of *dikaiosynē*, that is, of *social justice*. José Porfirio Miranda declared social justice to be the "revolutionary and absolutely central message of Romans," a message "customarily avoided by exegesis." He argues that Paul's critique of "law" involves a more generalized critique of the effect of sin and idolatry within civilization, "whose most characteristic and quintessential expression is the law."[87] Elsa Tamez has also offered a sustained critique of the doctrine of justification by faith as conventionally understood, declaring it to be "good news more for the oppressors than for the poor."[88] Similar generalized readings of Paul's comments on law, informed by deconstruction rather than liberation theology, have been offered by Theodore Jennings and Alain Badiou.[89]

Although these readings expand Paul's critique to include the oppressive structures of imperial civilization, they do not remove "the Jews" from Paul's rhetorical crosshairs; rather they risk *inflating* the role of "the Jews" into a symptom of a larger societal pathology against which only Paul's gospel of justice is the antidote. For Miranda, the "civilization" that Paul criticizes under the name of law includes Jewish civilization as well, against which Miranda poses "evangelization, begun by Jesus and continued by the Church" as alone "God's instrument for causing faith and therefore justice" in human beings.[90] For Tamez, Paul levels against "the Jews" the accusation of presuming on "the privilege of the law" and thus perverting it, creating an "inversion of values" in society.[91] Badiou for his part emphasizes Paul's "rupture ... with Judaism"[92] and argues that Paul sought to free the gospel "from the rigid enclosure within which its restriction to the Jewish community would confine it."[93]

However unintentional these reinstatements of pejorative characterizations of Judaism may be, they highlight the need for a careful rhetorical-critical analysis of Paul's alleged indictment of "the Jew," which may turn out to be something other than an indictment after all.[94] From a Marxist viewpoint, such analysis at the level of rhetoric or ideology must be joined with careful attention to the social and political options available to Jews in the first-century imperial situation, especially as these changed critically in the course of particular crises. This correlation of ideology with sociopolitical options provides the proper interpretive context for Paul's letters.[95]

Furthermore, there are grounds for reconsidering Paul's categorical repudiation of vindication through "works," traditionally understood as his critique of a characteristic Jewish "works-righteousness," for which historical substantiation has proven elusive. Careful attention to Roman imperial ideology and the ideology of patronage and euergetism has shown that these factors provided the context for a lively "theology of works" in Paul's day. Indeed, the "works" of the divine Augustus were celebrated in monuments across the empire.[96] Scholars have used the term "Romanization" to describe incorporation into (a) the system of euergetism; (b) the people of the Romans, who were destined to rule the world; and (c) filiation to Augustus, who recapitulated the virtue of his pious ancestor Aeneas, the founder of the Roman people. Against this background, Paul's multiple repudiations of patronage, idolatry, and ethnic hierarchy, together with his radical proclamation of filiation to a rival "father" and "lord" through the Jewish ancestor Abraham, seem to cohere as a repudiation of the key elements of Romanization. This in turn suggests a very different context for interpreting Paul's comments on "works." In fact, several recent interpreters have argued that the Roman ideology of euergetism (as an instrument of Romanization), rather than Jewish belief or practice, was the primary target of Paul's critiques of "works" in Galatians and Romans.[97]

Gender, Class, and Empire

Postcolonial feminist interpreters have insisted on the importance of attending to the multiple overlapping and intersecting dimensions of power relations in the Roman world, including gender, class, and status (for example, slave or free, citizen or noncitizen).[98] While Marxist interpretation of the place of women in Pauline Christianity has sometimes focused on the subordination codes in the pseudo-Pauline writings (including the interpolation in 1 Cor 14:34-35) to the exclusion of wider considerations,[99] postcolonial and feminist interpreters have generally been careful to distinguish these texts from Paul's genuine letters. This has not stopped them, however, from identifying and assessing the kyriarchal codes and subordinationist themes in Paul's own letters that became so useful to subsequent shapers of the Pauline legacy.[100]

Antoinette Clark Wire's reconstruction of the social experience of Corinthian women prophets is a landmark work, applying gender and rhetorical criticism to 1 Corinthians as well as a nuanced consideration of social status. Wire describes the early Principate as a period in which the power of the senatorial order was weakened relative to the rise of provincial elites. Drawing on Mary Douglas's model of "grid" and "group" social forces, she characterizes the Principate as a "weak group/low grid" society. As Wire summarizes the situation, "In provincial cities like Corinth, if taxes were paid, external controls were basically absent, and honor fell on whoever could generate wealth and connections. Achieved status bypassed attributed status in importance."[101] In this context, and as an effect of what she describes as Augustus's "liberalizing" reforms of marriage laws, Wire proposes that lower-status women in Corinth would have experienced at least a broadening of opportunities for increased status while Paul—as someone reared in the "relatively 'strong group/high grid' system of councils, courts, and synagogues" of the Hellenistic East—would have experienced a diminution of privilege and status. She correlates the disparity between the women prophets' gain and Paul's loss of status with the difference between their "theologies and ethics." This disparity provoked Paul's restrictive rhetoric in his "first" letter to the Corinthians.[102]

Wire's reconstruction might be challenged on two fronts. First, because she and Elisabeth Schüssler Fiorenza (among others) accept 1 Cor 14:34-35 as genuine, they read the entirety of the letter's rhetoric as Paul's highly nuanced effort to rein in the efforts of independently minded "women of spirit."[103] Others, however, regard the passage as an interpolation and consequently read the letter's rhetoric as directed not against women but against elite *male* members of the assemblies.[104]

Beyond these text-critical and rhetorical-critical issues, the Marxist insistence on class analysis suggests that we must give careful consideration to the multifaceted gender, class, and social-status effects of the Pax Augustana and of Augustus's marriage legislation in particular. While Roman aristocrats may have complained about the *nouveaux riches,* this does not mean that there was a broad democratization of wealth or privilege. Instead, models of Roman patronage suggest that any expansion of opportunities was limited to a relatively tiny elite in the provinces, where such opportunities served as incentives to promote conformity and assimilation to the well-defined expectations of Romanization—even if they did not inculcate in a figure like Petronius's Trimalchio the decorum expected of true nobility.[105] Further, Karl Galinsky has observed that Augustus's reforms of marriage laws "aimed particularly at the governing classes": they were designed to regularize sexual, family, and property relationships, rewarding productive marriages with access to patronage. The laws thus incorporated more wealth into the patronage system and thereby presented a more uniformly "moral" governing class to the provinces. The net effect was to draw ambitious upper-class women more closely into marriages.[106] This understanding of the social effects of the early Principate seems at variance with the "liberalizing" effects of Augustan legislation that Wire posits for the Corinthian women prophets. It also suggests that urban society in the early Principate should be described as "high grid/high group," as described in other studies of Roman patronage (grid) and Romanization (group) in Corinth.[107] Despite these qualifications, Wire's correlation of different social experiences (that of Paul and of others in the *ekklēsiai*) with theological expression is an important advance. Clearly this is an area where more thorough exploration by postcolonial, feminist, and Marxist analysis is desirable.

Empire and Ideology

Kwok Pui-lan observes that "Paul's political stance toward the state and empire has long been a bone of contention among biblical scholars and theologians," who usually turn quickly to Rom. 13:1-7.[108] Some interpreters continue to take this passage as a straightforward endorsement of the Roman Empire (as did Kautsky).[109] More attentive exegesis has long recognized that there are tensions both within this passage and between Paul's statements here and his much less sanguine estimation of the "rulers of this world" in other places.[110] Counter- or "anti-imperial" interpretations of Paul have sometimes pointed to reservations in Paul's language in Romans 13—for example, reading *tetagmenai* (13:1) in a restrictive sense, or suggesting that he regards governing authorities as "servants of God" *only insofar as* they promote the good and punish evildoers (13:4). Others have found Paul's statements so modest, when compared with the effusive claims of imperial propaganda, as to seem like demurrals (my own earlier proposal) or even intentional irony.[111] John Marshall has deployed Homi Bhabha's discussion of the phenomenon of *hybridity* among colonized peoples to propose that we read the passage as evidence of Paul's own cultural hybridity, which leads him to speak here in favor of affiliation with Rome and elsewhere about alienation from the colonizing power.[112] Meanwhile, more theologically oriented interpreters continue to insist that the passage is not problematic if read through an appropriately theological and pastoral lens rather than from an inappropriately political perspective. In their view, Paul was not opposed to Caesar's empire "because it was an empire," but rather because he rejected "paganism in all its shapes and forms."[113] Paul's concern, according to this approach, was fundamentally to safeguard the church.[114]

None of these interpretations of Rom 13:1-7 enjoys consensus, and the tremendous weight that this passage continues to carry in interpretation means that there is no consensus regarding Paul's attitude toward the Roman Empire. I persist in thinking that exegesis of Paul's letters must be combined with the fullest possible understanding of Paul's ideological context, including contemporary Roman ideological themes concerning obedience, faith, the virtues of the emperor, the destiny of peoples, and so on. I have also argued that interpreters of Paul must develop an approach to "intertextuality" that considers Roman imperial ideology and iconography to be as much a part of Paul's rhetorical "context" as Israel's scripture.[115] But the impressive tradition of Marxist theory regarding ideology and what Fredric Jameson calls ideological constraint suggests that we shift the object of our interpretive efforts from "Paul's thought" or "Paul's attitude" or even "Paul's theology"—as if any of these could be explored as a coherent system of representation, free of the constraining force of culture—to the ideological, and more specifically *kyriarchal* texture of Paul's rhetoric. Marxist ideological theory suggests that we should understand Paul's rhetoric as a particular *parole* or utterance within a field of forces determined, ultimately, by the power relations of Roman imperialism. The tensions within those power relations are expressed as tensions and even contradictions within Paul's rhetoric—for example, between a God who subjects the world to futility and a Spirit who agitates within the world against just that subjection

(Rom 8:21-23), or between a declaration that the one who does right has nothing to fear from the governing authority and the exhortation to return fear (*phobos*) to that same authority (Rom 13:3, 7).¹¹⁶ Such a shift away from Paul's thought or theology as the object of attention will likely be resisted or rejected by scholars who are invested in preserving a view of theological discourse as an autonomous domain. It may be welcomed, however, by those who are ready to understand Paul as a full participant in the nexus of material forces that we call history.

A Future for Marxist Criticism? A Christian-Marxist Coda

Given the ideological and institutional limitations that circumscribe much of biblical scholarship in Western academia, there is no reason to expect that Marxist theory will ever take the interpretive world by storm—not even the small portion of that world that is postcolonial-critical scholarship on Paul. Even in secular universities free from ecclesiastical pressures, Marxist theory is usually confined to political science curricula; religious studies programs are conceived without any reference to Marxist categories. Departmental commitments to multicultural, multiethnic, gender-critical, and postcolonial perspectives that emphasize the theorization of cultural difference and hybridity have been hard won; the same level of commitment to applying Marxist theory to class-based analysis is rare.

Even deliberate invocations of Marxist theory, for example, in literary criticism, are inadequate in the eyes of some Marxists. Aijaz Ahmad regards the explosion of "theory" following the radical impulses of the 1960s as the result of efforts

> to domesticate, in institutional ways, the very forms of political dissent which those movements had sought to foreground, to displace an activist culture with a textual culture, to combat the more uncompromising critiques of existing cultures of the literary profession with a new mystique of leftish professionalism, and to reformulate in a postmodernist direction questions which had previously been associated with a broadly Marxist politics.¹¹⁷

The decline (or "defeat" or "collapse") of socialist politics marked a fateful development for Marxist theory. Göran Therborn discusses "Marxism's broken triangle," by which he means the former interrelation under the umbrella of Marxism of "a historical social science, . . . a philosophy of contradictions or dialectics, . . . [and] a mode of politics of a socialist, working-class kind." The last of these, socialist politics, "disintegrated in the course of the 1980s." The future of Marxist theory, Therborn suggests, will be shaped more by the vicissitudes of Western liberal academia than by any future revival of socialist politics.¹¹⁸

There is more than a little irony, then, in the development of a new interest in the figure of Paul as "our contemporary" on the part of Marxist or "dialectical materialist" philosophers in Europe, including Alain Badiou, Giorgio Agamben, and Slavoj Žižek. While *theological* interpreters struggle to find meaningful ways to translate Paul's (evidently failed) apocalyptic vision into the present, Paul is being rediscovered as a kindred spirit by just those thinkers who confront the collapse of socialist politics as a crisis of meaning.[119] They agree that the long twentieth-century experiment in centralized state power has ended in decisive failure. They also freely concede that they do not have the formula for a future without capitalism's pathologies. Their writings speak more of existential ache than of dogmatic certainty. Badiou asks how "the communist hypothesis," the notion that "the logic of class . . . is not inevitable, [that] it can be overcome," can be reasserted. He affirms a single, simple truth—that "there is only one world," of rich and poor, oppressor and oppressed, together. The vision of a world in which capitalism triumphantly unfolds to the betterment of all humanity is a delusion that can be maintained only by walling off the reality of the poor.[120] Similarly, Slavoj Žižek declares that "the defining problem of Western Marxism" has been "the lack of a revolutionary subject," so that Marxists have "engaged in a constant search for others who could play the role." He muses that perhaps "waiting for another to do the job for us is a way of rationalizing our inactivity."[121]

Badiou's and Žižek's readers have been left unsure about how exactly Paul offers the answers to their questions. How, for example, might one appropriate Paul's "revolutionary subjectivity" (Badiou) in the present? Perhaps aspects of Paul's praxis show us the hallmarks of a truly revolutionary community: economic mutualism; resistance of the delusional claims of imperial ideology; and the continual *anamnesis* of Jesus and incorporation into his destiny as one condemned to non-being by the powers of this world but alive to a genuine future.[122] But where are the material conditions for the rise of such a revolutionary community? Theologian of liberation Jon Sobrino writes that such a future is *ou-topia*, an impossible place if imagined as an extension of the present, seen from within "the civilization of wealth." From the perspective of the poor, however, "'utopia' means a dignified and just life for the majorities"; it is *eu-topia*, "that 'good place' that must exist." It emerges, Sobrino declares, from the "civilization of solidarity" practiced among the poor.[123]

Such ruminations might be dismissed as romantic—a dismissal Sobrino himself takes great pains to refute. The question of revolutionary agency nevertheless remains an acute problem not just for the theology of liberation but for all forms of Marxist theory as well and, in fact, for any project that seeks a realistic vision of an alternative to the evident hegemony of capitalism's predatory globalization.[124]

One of the lessons that Christianity must learn from Marxism is to relinquish the evasions and sublimations of these questions that have traditionally been made possible by escape into dogmatic speculation. The most urgent task for those among Paul's interpreters who participate in the struggle to realize "another world"—especially those who work in situations of privilege today—may be, at the very least, to embrace in their work the ancient apostolic imperative to "remember the poor" with some measure of Paul's own eagerness (Gal 2:10).

PART TWO

PAUL AND ANCIENT FORMS OF COLONIALISM

A. Paul and Roman Colonial Rule
B. Paul, Colonialism, and Ethnicity
C. Paul, Colonialism, and Gender

CHAPTER FOUR

Pauline Agency in Postcolonial Perspective

Subverter of or Agent for Empire?

JEREMY PUNT

Introduction: The Problematic Paul

Differences of opinion about the interpretation of the Pauline letters and their reach and effects have been around for a considerable time, as many who encountered them through the ages have found it difficult to come to terms with the letters and legacy of the so-called thirteenth apostle of the New Testament.[1] The scene of discontent with Pauline views was set with the early, euphemistic acknowledgment of 2 Peter's author that in the writings of "our beloved brother Paul" (*ho agapētos hēmōn adelphos Paulos*) "some things are difficult to understand" (*estin dysnoēta tina*, 2 Pet 3:15-16). Many contemporary Bible readers in church and society face similar difficulties with making sense of Paul's letters. Some of these problems stem from sociocultural and doctrinal differences that can be traced to difficulties in the letters themselves, while others are rooted in subsequent generations' interpretations of Paul's writings.[2]

A hermeneutical problem that has emerged in recent years more strongly than before is the question of Paul's perceived political (to use a modern term) stance, particularly his attitude toward the Roman Empire.[3] For some time now, Paul's political stance has been debated by scholars, with contrasting conclusions.[4] For some, Paul is the principal representative of political conservatism, an advocate and maintainer of the status quo: "Paul, the radical innovator and founder of the Gentile church, sowed the seeds of the acceptability of the world order as it is and passivity towards it."[5] Others have emphasized a vastly different reading of Paul, identifying him as a radical apocalyptist who anticipated and actively worked toward a world turned upside-down, including the downfall of the political powers.[6] Such contrasting, uncompromising positions result from focusing strongly on particular sentiments in the Pauline letters to the exclusion of others, and rely on interpretative practices derived from traditional methods of historical criticism or textual analysis.[7]

Framing Paul's political stance in radical, binary opposite positions has proved to be too one-sided and unsustainable.[8] A more nuanced approach, which might better account for the apostle's self-positioning toward his imperial context, would plot Paul's attitudes and actions toward empire on a spectrum ranging from revolution against to support for empire. Such an inclusive, broadly focused approach requires an appropriate theoretical approach or methodology to frame and articulate the investigation of Paul's letters. A postcolonial approach has much to offer here, as it provides a theoretical framework capable of accounting for hegemony while also highlighting the ambivalence and the varied types of agency that are inherent in imperial contexts.

Paul and Empire: Accounting for an Ambivalent Situation

In recent years, some scholars have been calling for investigating not only the perceived insubordinate or noncompliant stance of Paul toward empire but also how his language replicated and endorsed empire and imperial power relations.[9] Further analysis of Paul's stance toward the empire has brought more recognition of the political dimensions of his language as it pertained to the imperial environment in which his communities were situated. Nevertheless, too little attention has been given to the hegemonic effects of Paul's use of political language within and with regard to these communities, as illustrated in Richard Horsley's description of Paul's reinscription of a patronage system in his first letter to the Corinthians as merely an attempt to build "his own network of 'friends.'"[10] The ambivalence of Paul's rhetoric, which simultaneously challenges and reinscribes empire, and the possible results and effects of such ambivalence have not yet received adequate attention. The challenge is not merely to acknowledge but also to account for *both* Paul's reinscription of *and* his challenge to imperial and subordinationist schemes, without relinquishing the tension between the two or absorbing one into the other.[11] What is needed is a language and grammar to describe, explain, and make sense of this ambivalence.

A similar kind of ambivalence can be seen in Paul's treatment of another social hegemony of the time, patriarchy, which is related, if not fully analogous, to the imperial situation. Some feminist scholars have suggested that Paul's letters can be used to construct an "*ekklēsia* of wo/men" built on radical egalitarian relationships as an alternative to the empire with its hierarchy of relationships of domination. The *ekklēsia* of wo/men is posited as a historical and theoretical alternative (not a counter- or anti-space) to the empire.[12] Others see an even stronger interpretive conundrum in Paul's stance toward women and gender matters in a context inscribed by patriarchy.[13] They point to the way in which both his constructive theological positions, such as his emphasis on God as savior of all and the goodness of God's creation, and his destructive positions, including his restriction of gender roles, mirror his stratified first-century society. From this they conclude that Paul's writings are characterized by cautious compromises, rooted often in his unquestioned assumptions, and creative insights. As Paul developed and applied his views, however, his actions often failed to live up to his professed principles or standpoints.[14] Ambivalence toward women can be seen throughout Paul's letters, particularly when he deals with matters of authority and power.[15]

In a similar way, the ambivalence of the imperial setting foregrounds the need for a methodological approach that is capable of accounting for Paul's agency in the context of empire, that is, his capacity to act within or to socially engage empire.[16] When developing a framework for understanding Pauline agency in relation to the Roman Empire directly and more subtly,[17] it is especially important to consider the presence of broader ideological strategies at work in the interpretative endeavor. The supports that propped up empire included not only military conquest, the system of patronage, and the imperial cult but also the rhetorics of peace, prosperity, and concord,[18] that is, the ideology of imperial benevolence. The influence of empire was probably strongest at the ideological level,[19] through which it connected with the other dimensions of first-century life.[20] Subsequent to the success of military conquest, it was the rhetoric of empire that continuously inscribed and replicated the language of power and domination that was required for its continuance.[21] In short, the materiality of empire and imperial ideology fed off of each other and constituted the context, informed by a certain discourse of power, in which Paul became enmeshed, and within which his letters must be read.[22]

A Postcolonial Optic on Paul and Empire: Power and Agency

An approach that holds special promise for allowing modern interpreters to come to terms with the ambivalence of Paul's position with regard to the imperial context while also dealing with his use of power and reinscription of hegemony is the postcolonial optic.[23] It can be framed as an analysis of the texts of early Christianity which considers them within the broader sociocultural context of the omnipresent, inescapable, and overwhelming sociopolitical reality of imperialism and colonialism, that was constituted and exercised in various ways during this time.[24] A postcolonial approach provides a framework for investigating how imperialism and hegemony operated in different forms and at different levels, since as a critical theory it engages the complex aftermath of colonialism or imperialism, which is shaped by a history of both repression and repudiation.[25] Postcolonial interpretation represents a shift in focus, attempting to highlight what was missing in previous analyses while also rewriting and correcting; it involves restoration and transformation as well as exposé.[26]

The hegemonic context in the first century C.E. was dominated by the power imbalance that was imposed and maintained by the Roman Empire and supported by various other social configurations such as patriarchalism and slavery. A postcolonial perspective acknowledges the complexity of cultural and political configurations and structures that form boundaries between the opposing sides of the powerful and the marginalized within a hegemonic context.[27] The postcolonial optic, moreover, acknowledges the inevitable ambivalence of the colonial or imperial condition and thus recognizes that the postcolonial condition is about more than subscribing to either of two extremes. Agency is not reduced to setting up binary opposites, of choosing either submission or subversion, but rather comprises unequal measures of aversion and admiration, resentment and desire, rejection and imitation, resistance and co-option, separation and surrender.[28] In short, a postcolonial optic enables us to reflect in an appropriately nuanced way on complexities such as the ambivalence of agency as they are constituted and reflected in the biblical texts.[29]

Postcolonial criticism theorizes human existence and human society in ways that are necessarily different from contemporary, conventional societal patterns.[30] Indeed, rethinking the conventional is part of the motivation for and purpose of its theorizing activity. In postcolonial theory, identity and agency are linked[31] and subjectivity is fixed in language. This creates a particular ambivalence: the ability of a postcolonial subject to resist imperialism is shrouded in ambiguity, since the very act of resistance entails intervention in the conditions that constructed that subjectivity in the first place.[32] Agency is therefore a crucial category in postcolonial theory, as illustrated in the work of Mary Douglas, James C. Scott, and others. While Homi Bhabha insists that any resistance to a dominant culture requires agency of one kind or another, in postcolonial theory the agency of resistance comes from a "hybrid inter-subjectivity."[33] A postcolonial approach would not claim hermeneutical privilege for framing, analyzing, and interpreting such positions, but it certainly offers a hermeneutical advantage.

When speaking of the Roman Empire with its overpowering military force, the language of oppression and subjection accurately describes the nature of empire in the first century C.E. At the same time, empire was made possible through a series of ongoing choices and negotiations between subjects and rulers. Amid the political maneuvers and overtures of the imperial authorities, subalterns were constantly involved in actions that involved the renegotiation of their own positions.[34] By training a postcolonial optic on Paul's letters—represented here by a small section of his first letter to the Corinthians—we can see something of Paul's ambivalence regarding the reigning discourse of power and his own agency amid the push and pull of empire.

Paul, Power, and Agency: The Corinthian Community

Paul wrote two letters to the Corinthian community of Jesus-followers who found themselves in what Paul regarded as a tenuous position in a relatively new city. After the city's complete destruction in 146 B.C.E., Julius Caesar rebuilt the new Corinth in 44 B.C.E. as a colony for the potential dissidents of urban Rome, which resulted in Corinth being populated with freed slaves, retired soldiers, and displaced peasants (Strabo, *Geogr.* 8.6.23). With its strategic position as far as trade was concerned, Corinth became an important and prosperous commercial center by the middle of the first century, inhabited by a multitude of different peoples and cultures. Within this city, Paul founded a community of Jesus-followers that was evidently informed by a Jewish, anti-imperial, apocalyptic strain as well as by a Hellenistic-philosophical concern for personal, spiritual transcendence.[35]

The imperial context was an integral part of the lives of Paul and the Jesus-followers in Corinth whom he addressed. Regardless of whether, as has been suggested, the imperial cult was Paul's primary opponent in the Corinthian correspondence,[36] the Roman presence was tangible in Corinth. Empire and religion could in any case not be untangled in the first century C.E., since the "divinity" of the emperor was obvious and uncontroversial in most of the Roman world. The military success and the worldwide power and control of the emperor and his legions underscored for many his god-given right to rule. It was in a world constituted by these notions that Paul proclaimed the *gospel* according to which Jesus Christ, after being crucified by Roman soldiers, had been raised from the dead and was now the world's true Lord, claiming universal allegiance (1 Cor 1:23; 2:2, 8).[37]

Paul's engagement in the discourse of power is particularly evident in the first four chapters of 1 Corinthians, where he argues for unity within the community (cf. 1 Cor 1:10). Here his use of *ekklēsia* is indicative of a body politic and not merely a religious grouping in the modern, narrow sense of the word. In a similar way, his message about Jesus Christ as *euangelion* was meant to claim the inauguration of a new era in history that would see the end of the Roman Empire and its claims to provide "salvation" and "peace and security."[38] But the ambiguity of Paul's language also emerges early in his first letter to the Corinthians, when in the first four chapters he encourages unity among the Corinthian followers of Jesus by utilizing an apocalyptic framework. In fact, Paul's strategy relied strongly on placing another world in opposition to the world of Greco-Roman rhetoric and status, which was accompanied by an upper-class ideology. This was the world of apocalyptic reality proclaimed in the gospel of Christ, a world that had its own alternative system of values and status attribution. In one sense, the apocalyptic world picked up on the conventional values of the time, but in another sense it counteracted and subverted those values.[39]

Challenging Empire? Weakness and Foolishness as Subversion

In recent years, it is probably Richard Horsley who has most consistently and persistently argued for viewing Paul's letters as presenting a direct, persistent, and unambiguous challenge to the Roman Empire. He has been followed closely by Neil Elliott, who has focused on the anti-imperial content of Paul's theology of the cross;[40] N. T. Wright, who has made a strong argument for Paul's "counter-imperial" theology;[41] and Dominic Crossan and Jonathan Reed, who have argued that Paul posited God's kingdom as a replacement for the imperial regime.[42] Even if these valuable studies do not always tell the whole story, they have contributed much toward a better appreciation of Paul's resistance against the pervasive, persistent, and penetrating tentacles of empire in the first century C.E.[43]

Paul's critique of the Roman Empire can be understood from his Jewish background, given the strong opposition expressed against the empire in contemporary documents such as the Wisdom of Solomon, the War Scroll (1QM), 4 Ezra, and *2 Baruch*.[44] Paul used the dualism of Jewish apocalypticism to argue against the dominant Greco-Roman ideology of the time, positing an "alternative realm to oppose to the apparently seamless, irresistible unity of the dominant Greco-Roman ideology."[45] But Paul's position and agency were compromised by his hybridized identity,[46] as the product of a Jewish background and Hellenistic influences, as well by his religious views, which envisaged neither a new religious movement nor a static appropriation of any one form of Judaism of his day.[47] Paul, as a freeborn and educated Jewish male who willingly compromised his status as a Pharisee and who advocated submission to Christ, would have found it difficult to maintain or extend his position within the Roman Empire.[48]

According to Paul,[49] Jesus' position as Messiah and ruler of the world sends a strong message to worldly rulers.[50] The dislodging of the power of death, one of the empire's most threatening weapons, through the resurrection of Jesus meant the annihilation of the real power behind the tyranny (1 Cor 15:20-28; cf. Col 2:14-15). "The resurrection thus functions in Paul's thought both as history, as theology, and (not least) as symbol, the symbol of a power which upstages anything military power can do."[51] In this way, Paul rearticulated an essentially Jewish political theology that "involved not only a radical critique of pagan power . . . focused especially on Rome as the obvious target in his own day, but also a radical restatement of the duty of God's people when living under present pagan rule."[52] This can be seen even in Romans 13, where all power in heaven and on earth is ascribed to God (cf. also Col 1:16-20 and 1 Tim 2:3-6).

In contrast to imperial authority and power, Paul portrayed his own life as modeling authority and power through notions not often associated with these concepts.[53] In the Corinthian correspondence, Paul speaks of "weakness" and "foolishness,"[54] challenging and subverting the conventions and norms that were operative in the current discourse of power. In a sustained critique of the powers of the day, Paul juxtaposed "foolishness" with "power" and the "folly of the cross" with the "power of God" in 1 Cor 1:18-31. In a carefully worded section filled with shrewd contrasts and insinuations, Paul addressed the Corinthians on the topic of wisdom, warning them not to embrace that which the world claims as wisdom, since God has turned the world's wisdom into foolishness and what the world regards as foolishness into wisdom. Any lingering doubt about whether the "world" (1:20-21) and the "people" (1:25) in these verses refer merely to those not believing in God or Christ is dispelled when Paul links these terms in 1:26-31 with "the powerful" and "those of noble birth," confirming that the imperial powers are the target of his rhetoric.

In contrasting the world and its earthly rulers to God, Paul addressed "the [male] brethren" (1:26) about the value of "foolishness," which was widely considered to be a "feminine" characteristic,[55] thus setting the stage for a letter in which gender and knowledge appear often in close proximity. Unlike in his letter to the Galatians, where the recipients are directly accused of being "foolish" (Gal 3:1, 3), Paul in 1 Cor 1:18-31 encourages a different perspective on "wisdom and foolishness," steering his audience away from worldly standards and toward those of God.[56] Nevertheless, in the hierarchical first-century world, where even the insinuation of foolishness (as a stock trait ascribed to women) could have contributed to downward slippage for the men of the community, something of Paul's ambivalent agency begins to show.

Wisdom was evidently an important concern for Paul in his letters, a concern that continued into the deutero-Pauline tradition (Col 1:25-28; 2:2-4, 8).[57] In Romans, for example, Paul flattered his audience for their wisdom (Rom 1:12, 14; 15:14) while also encouraging them to hold on to the teaching that he had given them (Rom 16:17-20). But 1 Corinthians 1–4 remains the classic text for Paul's high regard for wisdom. Especially noteworthy in this passage is how he links wisdom to the subversion of the sages, the orators, and the rulers "of this age," as well as his insistence (reinforced by quotations from the Jewish Scriptures: cf. Jer 9:22-23 in 1 Cor 1:31)[58] on the supremacy of God's wisdom over the conventional.[59]

Paul's language of "weak" and "strong" in this passage situates him within the ideological grammar of the Roman elite, for whom strength and power were equated with honor and wealth, while weakness was identified with the shamefulness of the lower classes.[60] As in the rest of 1 Corinthians, however, Paul consistently sided with the group whom he labeled "weak" (cf. 1 Cor 2:1-5), even though he actually agreed with (or at least conceded) the arguments of the those he called "the strong" concerning the celebration of the Lord's Supper and the eating of meat offered to idols.[61] Again, an ambivalent agency is at work here, since Paul's acknowledgment of the validity of the "strong" position, not faulting their assessment of the issue but warning them about the practical, ecclesial implications of following through on it, aligned him socially with views of the upper class.[62] In short, Paul's rhetoric of foolishness became his rhetoric of weakness, and the two functioned together in the Corinthian correspondence to challenge the internal problem of dissension and infighting which took place within and was shaped by the external reality of empire.[63]

Paul, Agent for Empire? Asserting Power and Strength

From a postcolonial perspective, it is especially the stabilization of relationships between the powerful and the powerless, the oppressor and the subjugated, the emperor and the subaltern, that attracts attention. The way in which (and the extent to which) the interrelationship between these two parties contributes to the identity and consciousness of both often leads to anxiety. Not only do the subalterns find themselves in a precarious position, where their sense of being is co-determined by imperial design in what Gramsci called "consensual hegemony," but the level of competitiveness and the potential for conflict are vastly increased as they jostle for what is left of power while yearning to secure the support of empire. In short, the internal situation of dissenting groups, including divisions in the Jesus-follower community in Corinth, cannot be understood apart from their broader imperial environment.

Given that language constructs reality, Paul's use of imperial language at the same time subverted and reinscribed the imperial system.[64] According to J. R. Hollingshead, "Again and again Paul places himself in a position of rhetorical power in order to advocate a community based on weakness. There is thus an irony here, both textual and historical. Paul's writings are rich in almost every way, including ambiguity. How can one use the power of persuasion to argue against the exercise of any power?"[65] Paul regularly claimed a position of power over the communities he addressed in his letters,[66] as seen particularly in his calls to the Corinthians to imitate him.[67] As a skilled rhetorician, he also employed various strategies in his letters to claim authority and exercise power, and he did not shrink from applying negative strategies such as silencing, othering, shaming, sarcasm, and even ridicule toward those with whom he disagreed.[68] Good examples of how Paul employed these strategies are found in 1 Corinthians 3, where ridicule accompanies his use of the metaphor of milk, and in the series of rhetorical questions in 1 Corinthians 4, where he sarcastically berates the community for its exaggerated claims while simultaneously seeking to secure his position in the community (vv. 14-16). "Though Paul may have rejected Rome and the prevailing imperial order, at the same time he adopted the hierarchical sex-gender-status cultural presuppositions that had previously served to uphold imperial, not Christian, claims to legitimacy."[69] Notwithstanding his promotion of and insistence on restraint, he frequently refused to acknowledge the validity of the perspectives and positions of his conversation partners and often took up immutable positions for himself, and even more dubiously, for "his gospel."[70]

In 1 Cor 1:18-31, Paul challenges the ideology of the powerful and the dominance and hegemony of the framework of what he calls "this world" or "this age," but it soon becomes clear that he does not intend to challenge the fiber of its constitution. Paul did not do away with high status; he did not attack hierarchy; he did not urge equality. He did, however, advocate a shift in the power balance from Greco-Roman upper-class ideology to a Jewish-apocalyptic, turning-the-tables ideology, that is, a shift from the Roman Empire to God's empire.[71] For Paul, therefore, the problem was not so much the prevailing structure as who populated which parts of it. His message called for replacing social and hierarchical positions and arrangements without doing away with the social hierarchy itself. In the process, Paul reinforced the language of subordination that was typical of the patronage system with its asymmetrical exchange relationships.[72]

In the first-century imperial context, patronage formed the broader framework for understanding agency. The entire empire was a network of obligations characterized by patronage, which regulated people's perceptions of the world and the empire itself

Pauline Agency in Postcolonial Perspective　　　　　　　　　　　　　　　　61

while also regulating the activities of communities and individuals. The dominance of imperial culture and its societal workings, expressed in the form of household ethics and patronage, was understood to be sanctioned by the gods.[73] The materiality of Roman social practices was the external manifestation of an intangible morality (that is, the patronage practices within the traditional sanctity of the household) that offered a holistic perception of the world in which Roman religion and society were intimately connected. Paul's constructions in 1 Cor 3:23 (cf. 3:5-6), where the relationship between the Corinthians and God was seen as mediated by Christ, and in 4:14-15, where Paul as spiritual "father" mediated between his Corinthian "children" and being "in Christ," exemplified these patronage relations.

On the one hand, Paul's critique of empire is evident and poses a challenge to the patronage system, regardless of whether the spiritual elite of the Corinthian congregation aspired to high-status values, thus merging Paul's criticism of empire with his opposition to internal opponents.[74] Yet questions remain as to whether Paul's position toward the system of patronage was characterized by uncompromising opposition or whether his letters also reveal a degree of complicity with the patronage system, even if he was not "fundamentally shaped" by it.[75] According to R. S. Sugirtharajah, "Paul, a genuine immigrant by current political standards, gives the impression in his writings that he has been fully co-opted into the imperial system."[76] In short, one cannot talk about the political dimensions of Paul's language without also attending to the roles, functions, and consequences of political language in the internal arrangements of his communities. A postcolonial optic is useful here, perhaps more than other heuristic schemes, as it provides the tools and perspectives to account for the complexity and interpenetration of relationships in such hegemonic situations.

Conclusion

Perhaps Shawn Kelly goes too far in claiming that "if we wish to understand the essence of Christianity, then we must turn to Paul's theology" and that "Paul, properly understood, becomes, and will remain for a long time, the standard for reading and evaluating the New Testament."[77] But in view of the relative importance of the Pauline corpus in the New Testament and its influence over the centuries, the challenge to situate Paul appropriately with regard to the Roman Empire—without discounting other elements of his first-century context—is clearly important. We have seen how Paul's letters provide evidence of his ambivalence toward the discourse and setting of empire. Does this mean that Paul was an agent of empire working against it from the inside, or that he was a partially co-opted resister of empire? How deeply was Paul's hybrid identity inscribed by his imperial context? Is it possible that he was simultaneously a victim and a perpetrator of consensual imperial hegemony? The answer to all of these questions is yes. From this we can see that a postcolonial approach provides a valuable optic for framing and interpreting the complexity of Paul's letters in their first-century imperial setting.

CHAPTER FIVE

The Politics of Paul

His Supposed Social Conservatism and the Impact of Postcolonial Readings

GORDON ZERBE

Only this: ensure that your politics [*politeuesthe*] be worthy of the saving news [*tou euangeliou*] of the Messiah. (Phil 1:27)

But our political identity [*politeuma*] resides in heaven. (Phil 3:20)

"The problem with Paul is that he never renounced his Roman citizenship." With this assertive interjection, a student effectively interrupted a seminar I was leading at the Ecumenical Theological Seminary in Baguio City, Philippines. The sharp remark came near the end of my opening lecture surveying issues pertaining to Paul's apparent social conservatism in regard to gender, economics, politics, and class.

What followed were a few moments of silence that seemed like an eternity. In the back of my mind, thoughts raced: (1) Do I immediately raise the historical question about whether or not Paul was really a Roman citizen, a datum claimed only by the author of Luke-Acts, Paul's hagiographical biographer some thirty to forty years after his death, and doubted by some biblical scholars?[1] (2) Do I confess right away that, while masquerading as a benign Canadian, I am actually a citizen of "the world's only remaining superpower," the self-reference that Americans are fond of?[2] But to what end? My Filipino colleagues had already reminded me enough that Canada, as a member of the G-7, was among the group of "imperialist countries" complicit in the newer and more subtle and insidious form of colonialism, market globalization. The irony was huge—one of those rare occasions when I had to place myself in Paul's shoes. As the course proceeded, impassioned engagement emerged among many participants who were inclined to disregard, demote, or reject Paul's legacy, particularly in respect to his social and political perspective.

62

Back in the so-called first world, where we have the luxury of theorizing about things that others experience as immediate struggles, it became possible to put a label to the kind of critique that my student employed, evident not only in his identifying Paul's perspective as a problem but also in identifying it in connection with an attitude toward empire, namely, postcolonialism. The term *postcolonialism* emerged in the mid-1980s when, as Arif Dirlik quips, "Third World intellectuals... arrived in First World academe,"[3] especially in the fertile territory of the emerging discipline and polemics of "cultural studies." The term itself has been the subject of considerable debate; in general it is used to describe not a historical period or epoch but either a condition involving a subject position or a critical discourse.[4] The explicit use of postcolonial (or decolonizing) criticism within biblical studies can be seen in recent publications and programs devoted both to methodological perspectives[5] and to substantive interpretation.[6]

Briefly, postcolonial discursive criticism, despite its variety,[7] addresses the overlapping issues of empire, race and ethnicity, diaspora, marginality, and hybridity. It aims to (1) deconstruct the texts, interpretations, ideologies, labels, forms of knowledge, symbolic practices, and definitions of the situation that have been authored by the dominant group in order to unmask the way they legitimize and reinscribe colonial interests; (2) treat once-colonized "others" as historical subjects, giving people of all subordinated groups their voices back, while taking seriously and celebrating new identities and hybridity and rejecting "binarisms," and (3) be emancipatory by linking, through varied discursive interventions, the experiences of diverse so-called others, potentially brokering new alliances, and (in a field such as biblical studies) by rehabilitating various foundational texts through rereadings that are relevant to postcolonial interests. As R. S. Sugirtharajah puts it:

> Postcoloniality is a critical enterprise aimed at unmaking the link between ideas and power which lies behind Western texts, theories, and learning.... [It] is not about the territorial ejection of imperial powers or about learning, Caliban-like, the art of cursing the evils of empire.... It is a discursive resistance to imperialism, imperial ideologies, and imperial attitudes and to their continual reincarnations in such wide fields as politics, economics, history, and theological and biblical studies. Resistance is not simply a reaction to colonial practices, but an alternative way of perceiving and restructuring society.[8]

Postcolonialism shares with postmodernism a reaction against the Enlightenment belief in universal reason and objective textual interpretation and truth, but it sees postmodernism as essentially Eurocentric and devoid of a theory of resistance and a transformative agenda due to its detached attitudes and its skepticism of any grand narrative, including liberation as an emancipatory meta-story. Postcolonialism sees itself in continuity with earlier liberationist interrogations, whether informed by nationalist or Marxist paradigms, but calls into question their use of Western master narratives that perpetuate Eurocentrism.[9]

What, then, of Paul? Primarily a rhetorician and not a systematician, Paul wrote letters as "instruments of his apostolic praxis."[10] Yet the quest for an underlying coherent thought system has continued, despite the complexity and tensions (even contradictions) within the rhetoric of his letters, even as the quest has confounded interpreters.[11] But the tensions remain. And so, on the one hand, Paul is interpreted as championing the sociopolitical status quo, perceived either as its rightful guardian or savior or as the one to blame for repression in the name of Christianity. Others continue to see Paul as one whose vision of a transformed world, and of an alternative community now emerging in the corrupted world, motivates liberating, world-transforming action.

Between the cultural and theological tensions undoubtedly residing within the historical person himself, between Paul the visionary and Paul the pragmatic pastor, Paul's restrictive, cautionary, and conservative words seem most apparent and have been preached most loudly.[12] Indeed, Paul's words are more easily used and manipulated by systems of domination than any other parts of the New Testament, perhaps of the Bible. While social conservatives have held up Paul's advice as warrant to maintain the current social order, and while some rest content in merely explaining his social conservatism, others have decried what they see as Paul's "limited application" or "failure of nerve," suggesting that Paul's own theology should have led him to more radical steps in the real world.[13] Not surprisingly, Paul's apparent and assumed social conservatism has led many interpreters in situations of domination to reject, demote, or disregard his legacy in this area.[14]

In contrast to these interpreters, still others have argued that Paul's texts reveal a posture more liberating and radical than often thought, albeit one that focuses on the emergence of an "alternative society" or "communities of resistance" in anticipation of God's final transformation. For instance, Neil Elliott has argued that it is Christian interpretation that has both depoliticized and then repoliticized Paul.[15] It has depoliticized Paul's gospel by mystifying his understanding of the cross and resurrection, losing sight of his rejection of all imperial rule except for God's rule and leaving merely a gospel of private, spiritual salvation. It has then repoliticized Paul's gospel by taking it as a weapon against Judaism and using it to support empires of every stripe. It has accomplished this by reading Romans 13 as a piece of pro-Roman ideology and making it the canonical center of Paul's political perspective while also misreading his comments on slavery and women, so that Paul has for centuries been in the service of death. Precursors of this alternative reading include the works of Klaus Wengst and Dieter Georgi.[16] Further examples can be found in the works edited by Richard Horsley, and in other recent publications.[17]

In contrast to the traditional interpretation of Paul, which not only assumes that Paul was largely pro-Roman in perspective[18] but often reads the imperial situation itself as providing the favorable and necessary context for the emergence of Christianity,[19] these interpreters have suggested that Paul should be read as more critical, challenging, and antagonistic toward the Roman Empire—perhaps even as fundamentally anti-Roman or anti-imperial—which in turn would explain, among other things, his execution (most likely on the grounds of treason).

What, then, are the main lines of evidence for such a reading of Paul's political perspective? Paul's critical stance with regard to the Roman Empire is evident from three lines of evidence: (1) the underlying millenarian script in his letters; (2) the use of politically loaded words to describe liberation and deliverance (salvation), the Messiah,

The Politics of Paul

and the Messiah's community; and (3) Paul's own experience of arrest, imprisonment, torture, and eventually execution at the hands of the Roman *imperium*.[20] As a final topic (4) we will revisit Romans 13 in the light of these three lines of evidence and try to make some sense of the tension that emerges. It will become clearing this discussion that it is best not to start with Romans 13 when trying to understand Paul's overall political perspective.[21]

The Underlying Millenarian Script

Undergirding all of the extant and authentic[22] Pauline texts and his entire life's work is a comprehensive millenarian script, one that comes to explicit expression from time to time, that is often evident implicitly but never far from the surface.[23] I deliberately use the term *millenarian* (or millennial), instead of the term *apocalyptic,* which is normally used in biblical scholarship, for three reasons. (1) It points to the broader cultural phenomenon of millennialism as entailing a variety of modes of reaction and resistance to imperial, colonial, and cultural domination across time and place.[24] *Millennialism* and *millenarianism* are the preferred terms for the anthropological study of similar phenomena of world-transforming mythologies, based on the reference in the book of Revelation to an idyllic future period of a thousand years ("the millennium") when the Messiah will reign on earth. Using the term *millennialism* links biblical and Pauline millennialism with millennialism throughout history, at least analogically and sometimes causally. (2) It highlights the strange and scandalous nature of Paul's ideological framework and language relative to that of the educated Western academy and theology. Millennialism is usually assumed to be irrational, irresponsible, and escapist. Christians have become accustomed to the notion of a "crucified Messiah," which Paul thought to be the major unintelligible scandal, but in our time it is the millennial moorings of the New Testament writings, if truly understood, that constitute the true scandal for those who seek to follow Jesus as Messiah. (3) The term *millenarian* heightens the potential political valence of this sort of mythology. This is not to say that all millenarian groups are necessarily political in some sense,[25] but many are. For example, various forms of Christian millennialism have energized (and continue to energize) pockets of resistance in the Philippines for over 150 years, first to Spanish and then to American colonial domination.[26] In the same way, a new reading of Jewish apocalypticism in the first century C.E. suggests its close connection to historical action.[27] The scandal of millennialism for us is perhaps not so much a matter of its intelligibility as of our own social and political location.

So what, then, is this underlying script of Paul?[28] It is the story of God's sovereign, imperial faithfulness from creation to re-creation, whereby God will soon triumph throughout creation, signaled by the resurrection of the Messiah, himself victimized by the powers of darkness and death embodied in the empire (1 Cor 2:6-8). Whereas the universe was created good, it has suffered the entry of mysterious, created, yet rebellious powers that oppress God's creation. Among these disparate powers Paul includes, for instance, Error, Death, Law, Satan, Rulers, and Authorities. But beginning with and through the Messiah, God is in the process of reclaiming all of creation for God. Paul's script expresses this by speaking of the "age to come" versus the "age that now stands," a dualism that is at the same time cosmic (God versus Satan, and their respective forces), anthropological (each individual embodies the tension), historical (the dualism has a *telos*, goal), and epistemological (God's wisdom versus worldly wisdom). In Paul's understanding, his own generation is on the verge of a cataclysmic world transformation (cf. 1 Cor 10:11; 7:26, 29, 31), which emerges by what Judith Kovaks has aptly called "God's war of liberation."[29] This framework provides much of the foundation of Paul's ethics, including, for example, his idea of nonretaliation. As Krister Stendahl has remarked in explaining Paul's perspective, "Why walk around with a little shotgun when the atomic blast is imminent?"[30]

The meaning of the "powers" in Paul has been the subject of considerable debate, and the problem is complicated by the fact that Paul's language in this area is not univocal. It is clear, however, that the "powers" are not primarily or exclusively spiritual and heavenly.[31] Rather, as Walter Wink suggests, they are visible and invisible, representing the interiority and exteriority of human structures and institutions, both personal and social in character.[32] While some texts imply that the powers are benign and redeemable, arranged under God's ultimate lordship (for example, Phil 3:21), other texts indicate that the powers, who were responsible for the unjust death of the Messiah, are paradoxically also unmasked by that death (Col 2:15) and will be both conquered and destroyed (1 Cor 2:6-8; 15:21-28).[33]

A crucial text for understanding Paul's millennial and political perspective is 1 Cor 2:6-8, which is part of a broader section (1:18—2:16) that parodies aspects of the social and political order[34] and shames "the pretentious elite questing after power, wealth, wisdom, noble birth, and honorific public office."[35]

> Yet among the mature [lit. "perfect"] we do speak wisdom, though it is not a wisdom of this age or of the rulers [*archontes*] of this age, who are doomed to perish. But we speak God's wisdom, secret and hidden, which God decreed before the ages for our glory. None of the rulers of this age understood this; for if they had, they would not have crucified the Lord of glory. (1 Cor 2:6-8 NRSV)

Some exegetes claim that the "rulers" here are essentially demonic powers;[36] others argue that the reference is primarily to earthly political rulers (or the imperial system), as we see elsewhere in the New Testament,[37] while still others argue that the reference is paradoxically to both cosmic (mythological) and earthly powers.[38] Paul's language is abrupt and elliptical, but in the context of his rhetoric, readers could not have missed hearing something about the doom of the Roman imperial system at some level. References to the powers in 1 Corinthians come to a climax in 15:24-28, where Paul asserts that all of the enemies and powers of this age will be destroyed. At "the end," the

Messiah will "reign" (*basileuein*) and hand the kingdom (*basileia*) over to God, "after he has destroyed every rule [*archē*] and every authority [*exousia*] and power [*dynamis*]," so that "God may be all things in all things (or, among all people)." While the final "enemy" is Death, readers once again must have considered also the political implications of this kind of rhetoric.

Since the life, death, and resurrection of Jesus the Messiah, then, the world is at the edge of the new age. Throughout the history of Christendom, the death of Jesus has been mystified[39] and thus robbed of its political dimensions as an act of faithful solidarity in the face of imperial terror against God's power of good. Granted, Paul's language about the death of the Messiah is not univocal. He also carries on the tradition that was handed on to him that sees Jesus' death as an atoning sacrifice dealing with the problem of Error residing in and having mastery over each person.[40] But even more significantly, Paul also presents Jesus' death in all of its raw, accursed victimization (see Gal 3:13), seeing the cross as an unmasking of the powers and their imperial terror, as an act of solidarity with the lowly, and as a disruption (*skandalon*) in the scheme of things.[41] The resurrection of Jesus is for Paul final proof of the imminent defeat of the powers, proof of the dawning of the new age. And the imminent return of Jesus will accomplish the final defeat (expressed sometimes in military terms) of all the powers and satanic corruption, so that "God will be all in all" (1 Cor 15:28). Paul describes the goal of history using images of the supreme, imperial, and cosmic reign of God and God's Messiah.[42]

But someone might ask, Is not the apolitical character of Paul's rhetoric confirmed by his symbolization of final salvation as transcendent, heavenly, personal, and spiritual? The response to this is that all of these adjectives are inadequate. There are indeed a few places where Paul's comments seem to imply a final salvation that is spiritual and heavenly.[43] Nevertheless, Paul's millennialism is not fundamentally world-ending or world-denying, but world-transforming; it is far more terrestrially next-worldly than vertically other-worldly. It envisions the goal not as a disembodied form of individual immortality but as corporate re-embodiment (especially Rom 8:29) in the context of a restored creation (Rom 8:18-25). Final salvation does not entail the departure of the righteous from earth to heaven, but an ultimate merging of earth and heaven, so that God's imperial reign, now supreme only in heaven, will be universal. "Heaven," actually a rather rare word in Paul's writings when compared with the rest of the NT,[44] is the source of deliverance[45] and the place where salvation is now reserved[46] until the time when it emerges with a renovated earth (Rom 8:18-25); it is not the final destination. Quite apart from being interested in the spatial landscape of final salvation, Paul describes it in social and political terms as God's universal reign following an embattled victory;[47] as implying the relational solidarity of believers with Messiah Jesus;[48] as a realization of peace, justice, and true joy (Rom 14:17); and as the immediate participation in God's splendor (glory).[49]

The millennial moorings of Paul's vocabulary also shape his understanding of the corporate body of believers now united with the Messiah. As J. Christiaan Beker put it:

Because the church has an eschatological horizon and is the proleptic manifestation of the kingdom of God in history, it is the beachhead of the new creation and the sign of the new age in the old world that is "passing away" (1 Cor. 7:29).... The vocation of the church is not self-preservation for eternal life but service to the created world in the sure hope of the world's transformation at the time of God's final triumph. The last judgment is not only a judgment on the world outside the church but also a judgment that will assess the church's faithfulness to its mission in the world (cf. Rom. 14:10; 2 Cor. 5:11; cf. also 1 Pet. 4:17).[50]

Moreover, this community is pictured as participating in the final battle of God's triumph,[51] wearing as its attire and weaponry for war "faith," "love," "hope," and "justice/righteousness" (1 Thess 5:8; 2 Cor 6:7; Rom 6:13; cf. Eph 6:15). As Tom Yoder Neufeld suggests, Paul has democratized and pacified the holy war imagery of Israel.[52] As for the methods to be used in the cosmic war, Paul advises, "Do not be conquered by evil, but conquer evil with good" (Rom 12:21)[53] and observes that "the weapons of our warfare are not fleshly but are powerful in God to destroy strongholds" (2 Cor 10:4).[54] This language implies not a conforming function in relation to the current sociopolitical structures, but a critical function (cf. Rom 12:1-2; Gal 1:4). Yet far from tacitly endorsing actual military conduct, it actually precludes it.[55]

The Use of Politically Loaded Terms

In connection with this basic millennial script, scholars in recent years have identified a number of texts in Paul's letters where there appear parodies or challenges of imperial claims and ideologies. An often-cited example is 1 Thess 5:3, where Paul parodies Roman imperial rhetoric while announcing doom, presumably on the prevailing power structures (which are tied to the community's distress; cf. 1:6—2:2; 3:3): "When they say, 'Peace and security,' then sudden destruction will come upon them."[56] Other examples can be seen in texts where terms of explicit political identity or connotation are applied to the community of the Messiah: the implicitly alternative "[political] assembly [*ekklēsia*] of God" in Thessalonica is exhorted "to lead a life worthy of God, who calls you into *his own* kingdom [*basileia*] and glory" (1 Thess 2:12); the "consecrated" and "faithful ones" in Colossae are reminded that God "has delivered us from the authority [*exousia*] of darkness and transferred us to the kingdom [*basileia*] of the son of his love" (Col 1:13); and the "consecrated ones" in Philippi are advised that their "politics" [*politeuesthe*] should be worthy of the saving news [*euangelion*] of the Messiah" (1:27) and that their true "political identity [*politeuma*] resides in heaven" (Phil 3:20).[57] These texts indicate that for Paul the civic and political authorities have, at most, only a penultimate character, and that their reality has been fundamentally subverted.[58] The political connotations of such terms as *ekklēsia* and *euangelion* have also been highlighted. Paul's usage of *ekklēsia* is linked to the language of political assemblies of Hellenistic city-states and the corporate identity of Israel's past,[59] while that of

The Politics of Paul 69

euangelion (gospel, good news) finds its closest counterpart in the rhetoric proclaiming the deliverance brought by the imperial order.[60]

> Numerous titles of honor applied to the Messiah also appear to have significant political connotations, and some seem to directly challenge titles ascribed to the emperor. These include Son of God, *Christos* (Messiah as a title, not a name), *Kyrios* (Lord), and *Sōtēr* (Deliverer).[61] Commenting on Paul's remark in Phil 3:20 that it is from heaven (where their political identity resides) that believers "await the Saviour, the Lord Jesus, the Messiah," N. T. Wright remarks, "These are Caesar-titles. The whole verse says: Jesus is Lord, and Caesar isn't. Caesar's empire, of which Philippi is the colonial outpost, is the parody; Jesus' empire, of which the Philippian church is a colonial outpost, is the reality."[62]

Corresponding to this is Paul's use of enthronement imagery, which directly rivals that of Hellenistic rulers and the Roman *imperium*, as in Phil 2:5-11:

> Messiah Jesus
> who, though he was in the form of God,
> did not count equality with God [*isa theō*] a thing to be grasped ...
> Therefore God has highly exalted him
> and bestowed on him the name that is above every name,
> that at the name of Jesus every knee should bend, in heaven and on earth and under
> the earth.... (Phil 2:5, 9-10)

When read against the honorific discourse of the ruler cults in the Greek East, features of this hymn (for example, *isa theō*) appear as an ironic appropriation of terms central to the Greco-Roman patronage and imperial system.[63] In addition, Paul's rhetoric of *fides Messiah*, literally *pistis Christou* (faithfulness of the Messiah), in reference to the coming deliverance, is meant to rival the Roman rhetoric of *fides Augustus*.[64] Paul's references to the *parousia* ("coming") of the Lord Messiah[65] likewise mimic the formalized Roman references to the royal *adventus* of the emperor in deliverance, judgment, and celebration.[66]

Other claims of implicit anti-imperial rhetoric have been made for the letter of 1 Corinthians as a whole, as an argument for the realization of an alternative society over against the Roman patronage system;[67] for the opening chapter of Romans, read as a "defiant indictment of the rampant injustice and impiety of the Roman 'golden age,'" and "a direct challenge to the ritual and ceremony of empire";[68] and even for Paul's work in collecting a pool of funds from the relatively more wealthy urbanites of Macedonia and Greece for the poor of Jerusalem.[69] Finally, Paul's attempts to preclude the use of civic courts for settling disputes within the Messiah's community illustrate a rather negative view of the civic judicial system:[70]

> Does a brother ... dare go to law before the unjust [civic courts] instead of the consecrated ones [*hagioi*, saints]? Do you not know that the consecrated ones will judge the world [*kosmos*]? Do you not know that we are to judge angels? (1 Cor 6:1-3)

Paul's Experience at the Hands of Roman and Civic Authorities

Paul's own experience of arrest, torture, and imprisonment seems to confirm that he held a critical posture toward the empire, contradicting the presentation in Luke-Acts of the Roman authorities as protectors of the persecuted believers, a theme that seems intended to improve either the reputation of early Christians in the eyes of the Romans or the reputation of Rome in the eyes of Christians. Some scholars have even doubted the veracity of Luke's repeated claims regarding Paul's Roman citizenship (Acts 16:37-38; 21:39; 22:25-29; 23:27). Paul himself testifies to having been tortured at the hands of both Jewish authorities (2 Cor 11:24, 26; cf. Gal 5:11; 6:12) and Gentile authorities (2 Cor 11:25-26, "three times beaten with rods"; cf. 11:32-33). He was also imprisoned by Roman or provincial authorities at least four times: (1) probably at Ephesus (Phil 1:13; cf. 2 Cor 1:8), the likely setting of Philippians, Philemon, and Colossians (if authentic); (2) in Philippi (see 1 Thess 2:2 and Acts 16:23);[71] (3) in Jerusalem and Caesarea (Acts 21:27-26:32); and (4) in Rome (Acts 28), where he was probably executed (cf. *1 Clement*).

Paul claims as an honor the fact that he has been imprisoned, tortured, and near death (2 Cor 1:8; cf. 4:16-5:5) far more than rival apostles of Jesus (2 Cor 11:23; cf. "prisons," 2 Cor 6:5). He thinks it especially important that he was imprisoned as one who proclaims the gospel of the Messiah (Phil 1:9, 12-17), and he repeatedly presents his experiences as "a paradigm for ... his communities generally" (Phil 1:29-30; 1 Thess 1:6; 2:14).[72] In Paul's view, no human tribunal should be feared (Rom 8:33-34). Klaus Wengst reasons that Paul's flogging, imprisonment, and execution do not invalidate the possibility of his Roman citizenship, especially since the extra-judicial torture of even Roman citizens is known to historians (cf. Josephus, *Jewish War* 2.306-8). Even so, Paul's experiences suggest that Roman citizenship probably meant nothing to Paul (perhaps because he preferred not to identify with the elite, but deliberately chose a loss of status),[73] or to the Romans, or both. Wengst contends that Paul "did not have these experiences because he had committed some illegalities in the moral and legal sense but because as a Christian [*sic*][74] his loyalty was suspect and because he continued to propagate being Christian, which was evidently felt to be a disturbance of the public order."[75] Once Paul's millennial ideology is decoded, however, it is not hard to understand why he might be executed on grounds of treason. Paul had already prefigured his execution in sacerdotal ways, as a participation in the path of the Messiah (Phil 2:17; 2 Cor 1:3-7; 2:14-16; cf. Col 1:24).

Romans 13 and the Monumental Contradiction

What, then, do we make of Romans 13? We seem to be left with a monumental contradiction. Here it seems that the Roman authorities as such are exalted, albeit as "ordered" under God's ultimate sovereignty, while the text appears to teach a virtually blind obedience to the authorities through the imposition of an apparently absolutist subordination scheme.

> Let every person be subject to the prevailing authorities [*exousiai*], for there is no authority [*exousia*] except from God, and those that exist have been ordered [*tassomai*] by God. So that the one who resists/revolts [*antitassomai*] against the authority [*exousia*, that is, *imperium*], resists/revolts against the arrangement [*diatagē*] of God; and the ones who revolt [*anthistēmi*] will incur judgment upon themselves. The rulers [*archontes*] are not a terror to good conduct but to bad.... The authority [*exousia*] is God's minister [*diakonos*] for your good ... to execute wrath on the evildoer. (Rom 13:1-4)[76]

Whereas Rom 12:19-20 presented God as having the sole prerogative for executing justice ("wrath"), here in Romans 13 the Roman *imperium* is portrayed as "God's minister" for the maintenance of order and justice. And whereas elsewhere Paul parodies the Roman *imperium* and predicts its doom, here its legitimacy is apparently certified using the commonplaces of Jewish and Hellenistic political rhetoric.

Most contemporary interpreters have rejected the notion that Paul presents here a formal theory of the state that can be used as a basis for Christian dogma, whether by legitimizing all forms of political authority or by laying the foundation for an ideal Christian political authority. While some would argue that the point of Romans 13 is to highlight God's supreme authority (implicitly subverting that of Rome), others recognize that "Paul's ideological defense of the state [is] difficult to understand, especially his appeal for subjection to the state and his way of describing the state and its officials in the traditional laudatory language of Hellenistic politics."[77] At a minimum, we see expressed here "the conventional prophetic-apocalyptic affirmation that God disposes the rise and fall of empires and gives the power of the sword into the hands of the ruler,"[78] which need not imply divine approval of the rulers' actions or their fundamental legitimacy.

Those who wish to give priority to the more radical stance toward the authorities that Paul expresses elsewhere highlight the situational and historical nature of his rhetoric and the alienation of Jesus-followers from the corridors of imperial power. Alternate explanations of Romans 13 suggest that Paul may have been seeking (1) to preempt violent revolution among some who had joined the ranks of Messiah's community and had not understood the nature of its "warfare of love"; (2) to preclude further repercussions against the Roman Jesus-believing community (whether the Gentile majority, the threatened Jewish minority, or both); (3) to rehabilitate Paul's own reputation within the Gentile-dominated community as being fully loyal to Rome;[79] or (4) to ensure that Paul's plans to make Rome a base of operations for his missionary campaign in Spain are not thwarted.[80] In Romans 12, Paul appears to apply the ethic of nonretaliation and peace (12:13-14, 17-21) to a politically volatile situation, leading some to argue that Rom 13:1-7 is essentially an exhortation for caution and its warrants are auxiliary.[81] A similar tension between practical guidance and theological warrant can be seen in

1 Corinthians 11, where Paul calls the Corinthian community to be cautious regarding people's scruples over women's head attire, even telling the women to cover their heads in worship, while introducing warrants that affirm a hierarchical order in the cosmos that has legitimized Christian misogyny across the centuries.

> The head of every man is Messiah, the head of a women is her husband, and the head of Messiah is God.... The man is the image and glory of God, but woman is the glory of man. For man was not made from woman, but woman from man; neither was man created for woman, but woman for man. (1 Cor 11:3, 7-9)

For Christian interpreters who seek to take seriously the voice of Paul, Romans 13 is only meaningful in the context of a broader biblical dialogue, for example, with Revelation 13, a book written forty years later, in which the Roman *imperium* is presented as the embodiment of the Great Dragon, Satan. Just as one would not go first to 1 Corinthians 7 to develop a Christian theology of marriage, so also one might not want to go first or exclusively to Romans 13 for a Christian approach to the political authorities, let alone a theory of the state itself.

Other interpreters are more inclined to challenge both Paul's rhetoric and its ideological underpinnings. While applauding the new anti-imperial or anti-Roman readings of Paul as explicated especially by Horsley and Elliott, many on the liberationist side still have difficulties accepting their approach to Romans 13. Elisabeth Schüssler Fiorenza, for instance, decries the implicit identification with Paul in these readings and the privileging of "the authorial master-voice of Paul" that valorizes Paul's rhetoric over (against) the pluriform voices within the first-century assemblies of Jesus-believers. In particular, she finds little comfort in embracing an anti-imperial Paul while overlooking Paul's own "politics of 'othering'" within the community itself, as seen in his vilifying of rival missionaries and teachers, his silencing of the voices of those who would differ with him (especially women, such as the Corinthian women prophets), and his reinscribing of hegemonic subordination schemes within the alternative community.[82] Readers like Schüssler Fiorenza see little value in a possibly misleading attempt to "rescue" the political discourse of Romans 13, since such an effort invariably "revalorizes" and "reinscribes Paul's rhetorics of subordination."[83]

Conclusions

What conclusions might we draw from this study?

(1) Texts within the Pauline corpus display considerable tension, ambivalence, and even contradiction on the topic of Paul and politics. For instance, we find two perspectives on the "powers": on the one hand, they are to be redeemed and reconciled; on the other, they are to be conquered and destroyed. Undoubtedly this reflects to a large degree the situational character of Paul's instrumental rhetoric. At the same time, it

The Politics of Paul

may be construed as a consequence of Paul's own ambivalence and internal tension. On one side are texts that seem to indicate that Paul is caught up in the imperial system, lauding its benefits, and unwittingly using and legitimizing its themes and subordinationist ideology. On the other are verses in which Paul appears far more critical of the imperial powers than is often granted by interpreters. Under either reading it is clear that Paul's rhetoric is certainly not apolitical.

A similar tension can be seen in Paul's perspectives on gender and social order (slavery). While Paul understandably perpetuated the endemic patriarchy of his day, his language contrasts with that of other gender moralists, and he included numerous women in his network of leaders. One explanation of this paradox is the interplay between "charisma" and "order" that is apparent in his assemblies.[84] Perhaps Paul's political perspective is fraught with a similar dynamic.[85] Beker speaks of a tension between Paul's apocalyptic "passion" and his practical "sobriety."[86] One could also point to his hybridized cultural identity and status inconsistency as explanations.

(2) Given the diversity of Paul's rhetoric and the primacy of his millennial horizon, Romans 13 cannot (and should not) be seen as the hermeneutical center or sole text for assessing Paul's political perspective. First Corinthians 2:6-8 and 15:24-28 could equally well be identified as hermeneutical starting points.

(3) Paul's practical political vision focuses on the emergence of an alternative society in local communities marked by character and resistance in anticipation of God's coming triumph, not on extending the "ecclesial revolution" to society at large.[87] Yet even here, Paul's vision of a new humanity in which old distinctions based on gender, class, and ethnicity are subverted (cf. Gal 3:26-28), is not applied consistently or comprehensively.[88] It seems that Paul was unyielding on the matter of ending distinctions (but not differences) based on ethnicity, but was willing to compromise when it came to the ending of distinctions based on gender and social class/status. He made steps in these latter areas, but he chose the first as his main arena of battle. The legacy of the church after Paul was to go back on even the small strides made by Paul in those areas.

(4) In view of the tensions in Paul's rhetoric, multiple readings of his political perspective are inevitable. Yet one can still argue that some readings should be given greater priority based on whether the interpretation is in harmony with the overall biblical drama of God's reclamation of all creation toward peace and justice (cf. Rom 14:17), that is, the extent to which they are emancipatory. While some subordinationist and "othering" texts may not be easily rescued, the overall thrust of Paul's rhetoric, in my opinion, is still amenable to—and even demands—an emancipatory reading. In contexts where Paul's authorial voice is venerated, it will be natural to highlight Paul's anti-imperial perspective, reading against the grain of received interpretations. On the other hand, in contexts where readers are open to placing Paul in broader dialogue with other voices in the Christian canon and in the emerging Christian assemblies (including those that were silenced), it will be appropriate to highlight how Paul both challenges and reinscribes imperial and subordinationist schemes.

CHAPTER SIX

Visualizing Significant Otherness

Reimagining Paul(ine Studies) through Hybrid Lenses

DAVINA C. LOPEZ

A State of Postcolonial Affairs

It has become fashionable in certain strands of recent New Testament scholarship to apply concepts from postcolonial literary theory to the study of early Christian literature. Central to this intersectional approach is the identification of the New Testament as a complex collection of texts produced, collected, and disseminated under colonial conditions, in particular the imperial context of the early Roman Empire. Such observations are frequently cast in revelatory terms, as though the entire history of New Testament scholarship until the last decade or so was undertaken by imperial subjects and colluders who, under the banner of methods such as "historical criticism,"[1] have been woefully and willfully ignorant of ancient and modern political configurations as well as contemporary critical theory. Proponents of postcolonially informed biblical scholarship are thus invested in positioning themselves as a departure from "business as usual" in exegetical performances and discourses. It is vital for them to characterize dominant histories of New Testament scholarship as intimately intertwined with, and therefore shaped by, histories of colonization and empire building (including the "empire building" of academic disciplinary formation in institutional settings), since such observations allow scholars to move forward with their eyes trained on the mechanics and technologies of power on a grand scale. It is also important for them to interrogate the tools and methods that are taken for granted in "traditional" New Testament exegesis, since these, too, were developed and deployed in a complicated, multifaceted relationship with colonial power constructs.

Applying postcolonial vocabularies and frameworks to the interpretation of the New Testament has clearly produced positive results. By highlighting the effects of colonizing processes on biblical literature and its interpretation, postcolonial scholars have brought much-needed attention to questions of race and ethnicity and generated renewed interest in the imperial contexts of sacred texts. Yet it is not entirely accurate to credit this relatively new strand of scholarship with pioneering a hermeneutic that exposes imperial resonances between texts and contexts. While it might be true that the dominant history of New Testament exegetical scholarship has been too complicit in Western colonialism to be able to talk honestly about empire, it is also methodologically naïve to believe that attention to empire began with the recent proliferation of publications applying postcolonial studies to the New Testament, or that the history of what has been called "traditional" scholarship is a monolithic entity that has completely ignored issues of politics and power differentials. Long before the concepts of colonial mimicry and ambivalence came onto the theoretical scene, Adolf Deissmann was shedding light (from the "east," of course) on what he called the "polemical parallelism" between the texts of the New Testament and the environment of the Roman Empire.[2] And long before Paul was heralded as a hero or a villain—or a hybrid hero-villain—in relation to imperial rhetorics and processes,[3] Deissmann, along with several other scholars standing on the narrow divide between classical philology and biblical theology, insisted,

> It must not be supposed that St Paul and his fellow-believers went through the world blind-folded, unaffected by what was then moving the minds of men in great cities. . . . The New Testament is a book of the Imperial age. We may certainly take it for granted that the Christians of the early Imperial period were familiar with the institutions and customs that the Empire had brought with it.[4]

In a similar way, Karl Kautsky, one of the leading theoreticians of Marxism's Second International, treated Pauline literature and ancient Christianity as fully situated within—indeed, as a product of—a dehumanizing Roman imperial slave-holding society. He noted that the New Testament texts, in relation to their colonial context, evoked oppositional class-hatred sentiments that would put the "modern proletariat" to shame.[5]

The argument that Paul and other emergent Christian writers were responding to the (imperial) world in which they were situated is not necessarily a methodological innovation that arose in hermeneutical alignment with (post)modern postcolonial theories.[6] Indeed, it stands to reason that the important contributions of postcolonial New Testament scholars, in exposing the submerged histories of (mostly colonized) people whose voices have been absent from dominant theological discourses, might be (contrary to their intentions) genealogically linked to submerged histories of the discipline itself.[7] In this way, both "objective" and "ideological" incarnations of New Testament scholarship have provided valuable insights into the relatedness of early Christian texts to empire, even when the scholars themselves must be categorized as products of their time, that is to say, colonially collaborative and imperially inclined. In some forms of postcolonial New Testament scholarship, such collaborations and inclinations are treated as grounds for indictment and dismissal. But engaging the history of the discipline in light of postcolonial sympathies does not necessarily require a rejection of that history. In fact, such engagement can help to provide critical interventions into, and reimaginations of, the discipline in the present.

Even if the idea that the New Testament's early Christ-followers were engaged in negotiating the Roman Empire in which they lived and to which they were subject is not all that new, scholars have only recently started coming to terms with the ways in which the field itself and its patterns of knowledge production are implicated with colonial and imperial politics, a recognition that represents an important contribution of postcolonial New Testament studies to an assessment of the discipline as a whole. The New Testament's implication in imperial and colonial contexts did not end in ancient times, as Deissmann realized. As part of the Christian Bible, it has also been used as a tool of missionary expansion in the service of religio-political colonial rule and the rise of modern nation-states and empires, especially during the time when the field of biblical studies was developing as a post-Enlightenment academic endeavor.[8] Moreover, as R. S. Sugirtharajah has articulated, the study of the New Testament through historical-critical methods, otherwise known as "higher criticism," has also functioned as a colonizing force, particularly in graduate seminaries that exported theological education from Europe to places like India, where the missionized were taught how to be proper Protestant ministers among their own people.[9] In its most trenchant forms, postcolonial New Testament studies pushes beyond a recognition of ancient imperial contexts and colonial appropriations of the canon, underscoring the idea that hierarchical power relations and social locations have shaped all of the interpretative methods and strategies adopted by biblical scholars past and present, even those that purport to be liberationist in orientation.

Whither Postcolonial Paul(ine Studies)?

While there appears to be a consensus concerning the utility of postcolonial studies for New Testament interpretation in general, a cursory survey of postcolonial works reveals that comparatively little scholarship has been conducted in relation to Paul, Pauline literature, and Pauline studies.[10] One area where a certain amount of work has been done involves using postcolonial concepts such as "mimicry" and "hybridity" as lenses through which to reevaluate Paul's rhetoric, sociotheological positioning, and self-representation in his letters. Such analytic efforts seek to move beyond simplistic attempts to sort out the strands of Judaism, Hellenism, and Romanness in Paul's discourses. In this respect, hybridity appears to be a useful category for bringing postcolonial studies to bear on Paul and his letters, if we can trust the frequency with which the term has been invoked in recent attempts to situate Paul in his Roman imperial/colonial context. As a descriptive category, the term "hybridity" has its roots in the writings of literary theorist and cultural critic Homi Bhabha, whose work is cited

Visualizing Significant Otherness 77

regularly (though often through secondary sources) in current postcolonial research on Pauline literature.[11] The concept of hybridity enables scholars to highlight empire's effects on both colonizer and colonized, positing that the author called "Paul" fits into the categories of both and neither through his ambivalent mimicry of colonial language.[12] Such analyses produce a Paul who is neither consciously using nor avoiding anti-imperial rhetoric in his epistles, but rather is negotiating empire as someone who has an ambivalent relationship with it and an unclear social status within it. This Paul is a hybrid figure who uses a hybrid rhetoric while writing to and dwelling among similarly hybrid communities.

Recent readings of Paul through the categories of postcolonial studies appear to be concerned primarily with the social construction of individual and collective identity and self-definition, locating the apostle as an "in-between" character and narrator—not exclusively Jew, Greek, or Roman, neither colonizer nor colonized. Frequently absent from these readings is not only a familiarity with the nuanced history of imperially interested scholarship, as noted above, but also attention to the usability of a hybrid Paul in struggles over Paul and Pauline studies in the present global religiopolitical context. In other words, recent readings of Paul that claim postcolonial rhetorics tend not to engage questions about Paul's afterlives. One potent example is the question raised by feminist interpreters concerning whether and why it is politically and ethically viable to continue reading Paul at all.[13] Perhaps this absence of reflection on reception can be attributed to the structural, political, and ethical effects that (implicitly at least) result from appropriating Bhabha's terminology in attempts to read Paul postcolonially.

It is critical to note that Bhabha's work is quite distinct from the ways in which it has been adopted and utilized in New Testament studies, especially in recent postcolonial readings of Paul. "Hybridity" is deployed in much of postcolonial New Testament studies as a catchall category to signify a particular pattern of socially constructed identity and culture that takes place through colonial contact in a "third space." Behind such readings lies the hope of overcoming the imaginary binaries of essentialist thinking. Bhabha's idea of hybridity is, however, a highly contestable category that has its roots in Lacanian psychoanalytic theory,[14] a tradition that is characterized by anti-Marxist essentialism and a lack of clear implications for collective social transformation.[15] It is not surprising, then, that proponents of a hybridized ancient Paul say very little about the implications of their work for contemporary rereadings and reapplications of Paul's letters. Such appropriations of hybridity in the service of reconfiguring Paul are unintentionally carrying over and applying potentially undesirable aspects of Bhabha's analysis even when their proponents are committed to liberationist (or even liberal) agendas. Chief among these is Bhabha's proposition that, even though all identity and culture are liminal and located in the sphere of hybridity,[16] the primary symptoms and effects of identity and culture are linguistic. Because postmodern biblical scholarship is so heavily indebted to the linguistic turn, discussions of points of affinity between Bhabha's concept of hybridity and New Testament studies frequently assume that hybridic elements within a text represent the discursive symptoms of an underlying social construction. While hybridity might be useful as an indicator of the irreducibility of all culture to a pure, original state (e.g., there are no "original" English, Indians, or, for that matter, Christians), it remains to be seen how such an observation might foster critical consciousness and ethical action vis-à-vis Paul's letters and the field of Pauline studies.

Hybridity as a Complex, Contestable Signifier in Postcolonial Paul(ine Studies)

Given these general observations, one possibly productive way forward in postcolonial engagement with Paul would be to move beyond discussions of the hybridity of Paul or his ancient communities into an interrogation of contemporary analytical methods themselves from a hybridic interpretative position. Prior to any discussion of hybridity in Paul's letters or in the ancient world in general, a much clearer assessment of methodology itself is needed. Methods are shaped by modern contexts, and hybridity is a recently constructed category that might have more to do with the processes of globalization under late capitalism than anything purely "cultural." One of the critical questions that must be raised about current applications of hybridity to Pauline literature relates to the overdetermination of literary materials as the sole arbiters of identity construction and meaning making in the ancient world, not to mention our constructions of that world through the optics of our own. No matter how much is gained from using hybridity as an analytical tool to reconfigure ancient identities as supposedly reflected in ancient literature, interpreters would do well to attend also to nonliterary representations as a resource for thinking about identity and social and cultural relationships in Paul's context.

By overemphasizing the importance of literary materials as (re)sources for postcolonial engagement, New Testament scholars have inadvertently overlooked much of what we can learn about the matrices of Roman imperial power in the ancient world as a context for Paul and Pauline literature. One of the reasons for this might be our neglect of Marxist and Foucaultian analyses of power, which are less ambivalent and liminal than those of postcolonial theory. Simply put, while power can be located in places both great and small, focusing on those sources of power that represent and hierarchically structure the ancient and modern world leads to a more nuanced engagement with those worlds while also supporting a concern for imagining and then building the world we wish to inhabit on different terms. My questions as a student of New Testament interpretation are structural in nature and, I trust, forward-looking in scope. To this end, and in order to further explore hybridity and its utility as a category for postcolonial Pauline interpretation, I believe that it is important to interact with ancient modes of visual representation, which offer a complex and complementary set of (re)sources for thinking not only about Paul's identity and negotiation of the Roman imperial world that he inhabited but also about power relations in the past, present, and possible future worlds of Paul, Pauline communities, Pauline studies, and beyond.

Visualizing Significant Otherness 79

Resourcing Visual Representation for Potentially Hybrid Postcolonial Reimaginations of Paul(ine Studies)

While scholars of the New Testament have made use of material culture in our disciplinary formations for quite some time, we have tended to do so in narrowly scripted ways, at least since Deissmann invited his audience to read about and gaze upon aspects of the visual environment of the ancient world. Material culture—that which is commonly called "art" and "archaeological remains"—is strategically deployed in New Testament studies to fill in the details of a past that is already "there." Its value is limited to providing a "background" for biblical literature or serving as evidence to "prove" the historicity of biblical texts and figures. In other words, material culture is studied primarily as a means to help us understand literary texts. A related strand of scholarship uses archaeological remains as a means to explain or illuminate certain theological concepts thought to be present in the New Testament and early Christian literature or to defend an already-determined Christian literary identity (as evidenced in texts such as the Acts of the Apostles) in light of those of the visually obsessed "pagans." Such an approach positions ancient (and modern) Christian theology as a by-product of literary materials, leaving visual materials in the background as fodder for doctrinal development through the elite program of words.

When visual representation is used as illustration or background, it functions methodologically as the "colonized other" in relationship to the "colonizing self" of literary representation, occupying the inferior position in a hierarchical structure that places literary forms at the top. In this schema, visual representation has no value in its own right, or is defined in terms of its relationship to words, which are understood to have been there "in the beginning." Literary representation remains a closed semantic system that refers only and endlessly to itself in the service of its own legitimation, justification, and naturalization.

If we are serious about deploying concepts such as hybridity in thoroughgoing ways to think through important issues in the study of the New Testament and early Christianity, and if we desire to come to terms, even if partially, with the imperial and colonial context of Paul's life and work, including the ways he was shaped by that context and the ways we have been shaped by both Paul and his contexts, then we must avail ourselves of the opportunity to realign the sources available to us and to engage as many different resources as possible in order to assess more fully the complex interrelations and interactions that take place within colonial structures, insofar as those can be delimited and determined. Whatever value we find in the terms and categories of postcolonial theories, we must be willing to embrace a messy, irreducibly complex view of power relations that attends to the ways in which ethnic, racial, social, and cultural forces comingled, interacted, and mutated in the process. The modern scholarly focus on historicism has resulted in an obsession with textuality and literary representation (including the "texture" of texts) in New Testament scholarship that has further obscured complex understandings of the past, training us to "see" the ancient world in a linear way and not in the multifaceted, multilayered manner that a concept like hybridity might ultimately demand. Attention to visual representation provides a way of thinking beyond elite literary forms that pushes us also to rethink the nature of social and cultural relations under imperial rule.

In short, New Testament scholarship needs to move beyond an exclusive focus on literary formations as the loci and mediators of meaning to a more fluid and complex set of relationships that views literary texts as part of an inseparable, relational web of residues and artifacts that hang together in ways that are not always easily comprehensible and that might, because of their irreducible nature, be impossible to understand at certain points. Visual representations, while often used as backgrounds or ornamentation for literature, can exhibit a language and grammar of their own, capable of being read and understood on multiple levels as part of a communicative system.[17] As a result, they can provide us with lenses through which to read texts, as opposed to the usual practice of reading images through the prism of texts. In short, images should be central to our methodological efforts to problematize configurations of identity and power relations in Pauline literature and the rest of the New Testament.

Dichotomies and binaries can be destabilized when we bring visual representations into conversation with the subtexts that, as postcolonial readings have noted well, drive contemporary uses of the Bible and its production as text and cultural artifact. These subtexts include colonizer/oppressor and colonized/oppressed (that is, those on top and those below) as well as the hierarchical intersections of gender, race, class, and sexuality that the Romans (and we) are so adept at delineating and naturalizing. Using visual representation allows us to think further about the complex, hybridized encounters between colonizer and colonized that characterized the Roman Empire, whose incredible desirability the Pauline literary record challenges, negotiates, and perhaps also transforms.

Until recently, New Testament scholars and classical historians have not thought of the Romans as a theologically oriented people who might belong in the same discursive space as Paul and his people. Yet Paul and the Romans shared the same rhetorical and material world. The Romans' theological destiny, which they called *providentia* and which they imagined to be determined in heaven among the chief gods, enabled them to envision and define an imperial self characterized by rule over all the nations under force and law, their god-given "arts." Beginning with Augustus, we see a conception of world empire as a mode of disciplining and caring for the self that explicitly rests on the defeat of enemies. Allegories of this ideology were scripted through visual representation in a variety of media.[18] The colonized "others" and the Roman selves were never allowed to occupy the same visual space except in opposition to one another. The "others" could also be shown dying at their own hands, as in the case of the Dying Gauls, Giants, and Amazons. Such images of "peace" accomplished through victory over the enemy served both to represent and to naturalize Roman world power, creating an adaptable notion of what counts as "normal" within this ideology. Augustus and the Julio-Claudians imagined themselves as uniquely fit to rule a world of nations whose two poles, the ruler and the ruled, defined the whole cosmos in gendered and racialized

Visualizing Significant Otherness 81

terms. The nations in turn were envisioned as being opposed to one another in addition to being under Roman rule.

At one end of the Roman-defined world stood the pale and hairy northern and western barbarians, such as the Gauls and their distant relatives the Spaniards, who were imagined as completely uncivilized but defeatable and ultimately tameable through "putting on the toga."[19] At the other end of the Roman imaginary cosmos stood the outrageously luxurious, intemperate, and effeminate eastern peoples, such as the Parthians and Armenians, who were at once despised and respected. The establishment and maintenance of Roman peace through victory over the vanquished borderlands (and everything in between) is represented widely in narrative historical reliefs, statuary, and coins of the early imperial age.[20] Such representations served as a vital channel for communicating an imperial ideology to which Paul and his communities likely responded. A careful examination of a single public monument, Trajan's Column in Rome, will show how attention to ancient visual representation complicates engagements with Paul and with the concept of hybridity as it is currently used in postcolonially invested Pauline studies.

Trajan's Column: Visualizing Romans and Paul as Unstable, Hybrid Figures

Representing imperial relations between colonizer/self and colonized/other by images of sexualized and often violent bodily contact constitutes a significant trope in Roman visual representation. The conquered others in these images are identified as female, uncivilized, peripheral, and racially inferior, as opposed to the male, civilized, centralized, and racially superior conquering selves. This dichotomy can be seen in an important series of visual representations from the Roman empire's capital city, especially Trajan's Column (fig. 1), which is a monument that expresses a particular vision of power relationships between enemies that is rooted in the totalizing narrative of the Roman Empire. It maps stability and universality onto Roman rule over all the nations by depicting as emblematic the conquest of one nation, the Dacians. Trajan, who ruled near the beginning of the second century, represented the Roman imperial ideology of peace through divinely accompanied victory, while significantly broadening its scope. After the disgraces of Domitian, this new emperor—Rome's first non-Italian *pater patriae* (Trajan was from Spain)—sought to make empire desirable again. If we are to believe the literary and visual record, he intended to bring hope and change to a Roman citizenry disheartened by endless wars and economic depression. Trajan was not known for numerous victories over foreign nations, as his imperial ancestor Augustus was, nor was he remembered for self-aggrandizement and corruption, as Nero was. Following the standard trope, however, he was celebrated for uniting and saving the whole world by eliminating the terrorist threat posed by the Dacians. It took Trajan two wars and substantial resources to accomplish this feat. The commemorative building program

Fig. 1. The Column of Trajan, second century C.E. *A likeness of Peter has stood at the top since the sixteenth century. This column, the inspiration for others in colonial France, Germany, and England, currently stands in what was once Trajan's Forum and now is part of the nearly excavated and restored Imperial Fora, a project undertaken during Mussolini's reign. Photo by Davina C. Lopez.*

that he initiated in Rome from the war spoils, fueling the economy after his decisive victory at the turn of the second century C.E., is worthy of a substantive discussion in its own right. The Forum of Trajan was so massive that previously erected imperial fora, such as those of Julius Caesar and Augustus, could fit inside this expansive and expensive public space.[21] Trajan's Column occupied a central location within this imperial space.

There is significant debate among art historians about how to approach Trajan's Column, as well as particular questions about the function of the continuous reliefs that spiral up toward the top. Nearly everyone agrees, however, that the images should be "read" as an uninterrupted narrative that runs from left to right as one moves up and around the column.[22] More than twenty-five hundred bodies are represented along the way, performing all types of roles in the service of war and peace. However, the column, which is also a funerary monument—Trajan's ashes were once located inside the base, which is decorated with a pile of weapons and laurels—cannot in fact be read from the ground. Some of its scenes may have been legible from various vantage points in the surrounding buildings, such as the Greek and Latin libraries that may have flanked the outer edge of the Forum in the column's viewing area. But one cannot simply pick up and hold this "scroll." It is easy to overlook this fact, since our reading of the column today is typically based on the casts and molds of its reliefs that have been placed on display in museums. As a result, we tend to retroject our ability to read the narrative "from the ground" (viewing the column on its side) onto the ancient viewer who, of course, could only view the massive structure standing upright, in which position most of it was likely indecipherable by the naked eye.

No matter where one's eye first catches this straight and yet not-so-straight monument, reading it as a narrative in the proper order is not the issue.[23] The overall message is clear and overwhelming: Trajan is "the man." His *Res Gestae*, his Acts, would have been familiar to the viewers, including the conquered and enslaved viewers who would have entered this public space and walked around it. It is significant that this monument tells the story of war and its aftermath using visual images. While Augustus's achievements were inscribed with words on columns outside his mausoleum (according to the sources) and on temples in Asia Minor, his Acts were most intelligible to those who could understand letter forms. Trajan's achievements, by contrast, were inscribed using pictures, making them readable by many more people, since most of the ancient populace was not functionally literate.[24] We must keep in mind also that the monument is only a part of a broader visual display, as the whole Forum (built on the spoils of war) provides the context that shapes the significations of the column itself.

The main thrust of this column as a reflection of imperial accomplishment is that no one will surpass this man. His deeds are miraculous; his help comes from the gods, whom he joins in death; his virility is solid and unchallenged. He has the power to move more people than previous emperors; he has the wisdom to use technology to build bridges across rivers and roads through mountains into heretofore unreachable northeastern territories; he possesses the virtues and the strength to bring a most tenacious and effeminate barbarian nation to its knees through both battles and "civilizing" projects (figs. 2 and 3). Also noteworthy is the fact that this fatherland shaft reaches up and up into the sky. Beyond the obvious gendered shape of the monument, the column reflects the systemically gendered and sexualized grammar of imperial violence as depicted in Roman art, architecture, and literature. Roman peacemaking is portrayed as a patriarchal activity that includes the sexualized subjugation of the feminized national "other." Such subjugation serves to render *natural* particular patterns of colonizer/self-colonized/other relations that are predicated on violent encounters involving penetration, assimilation, and annihilation of a stable "other" by a similarly stable "self." The meeting ground for "self" and "other" is the battlefield, which in this case is the homeland of barbaric alterity that is razed and rebuilt on terms dictated by the stronger, more solid imperial "self." Imperial self–other relationships are represented as a matter of national and cosmic destiny: it must be this way now because the gods willed it so at the beginning. Such an ideology brooks no challenge; there is no deconstruction, only legitimation, justification, and eternalization.

Despite their centrality to imperial ideology, however, such machinations are not always obvious or stable. For example, while it is common to say that Trajan's Column tells a story of war, there are in fact relatively few scenes of combat on the reliefs. To be sure, there are battle scenes, most of which show a civilized/uncivilized hierarchy of power, with the orderly Romans marching rightward toward the opposing, downward-spiraling barbarians. More often, however, the soldiers are shown in roles other than fighting. In fact, as exemplified by fig. 2, Trajan himself is depicted in more than thirty scenes as

84   Paul and Roman Colonial Rule

Figs. 2a and 2b. Trajan, who appears more than thirty times on the column's reliefs in various poses displaying his virtues, is depicted several times in one of two recurring scenes in the visual narrative: (a) showing fides through regular sacrifice and (b) showing clementia through receiving Dacian barbarian subjects. Cast of the reliefs, Museo della Civiltà Romana. Photos by Grace Lewis and Davina C. Lopez.

Visualizing Significant Otherness

engaging in activities that do not entail explicit, violent conquest. Perhaps the industrious activities of the people who conquered the barbaric "other" are meant to show the benefits that war can bring, thus visually minimizing the distance between the soldiers and civilians who would comprise a viewing community in the empire's capital city.

Most suggestive of the monument's commemorative function are the scenes at the top, well out of plain sight. There the penetration of the intemperate Dacians is shown as being completed not through brute force alone but by what appears to be a mass self-destruction involving the taking of their own lives through the ingestion of some sort of poison taken from a common pot, the burning of their own towns, and the suicide of their king, Decabulus, as Roman soldiers rush in (fig. 4). The message appears to be that the enemy would rather destroy its entire civilization than live enslaved to empire. One has to ask, of course, whether these scenes render the Romans or the Dacians weaker or stronger. Does their apparent act of killing themselves make the Dacians a worthy opponent or an even more outrageous barbarian race? The column leaves this as an open question.

Reading the column through the lens of hybridity, one notes that this conquest is depicted not as the action of the Romans, the master race, fighting alone, but as an

Fig. 3. When not preparing for battle with the Dacians and their multi-national allies, the Roman army is shown engaged in various "civilizing" building projects, often using the wood they cut from indigenous Dacian forests. At the bottom of the column, and thus visible to the naked eye from the ground, the army crosses the Danube river, personified as a male body, over a bridge they apparently built for the occasion. Above the crossing, Roman soldiers build fortifications. Trajan's Column is one of the main visual sources for contemporary reconstruction of Roman architecture of the first and second centuries C.E. Photo by Grace Lewis.

Figs. 4a and 4b. Near the top of Trajan's Column is a set of reliefs suggesting that the Dacians took their own lives rather than submit to Roman rule, a sentiment echoed elsewhere in Hellenistic and Roman visual representation as well as in ancient literature. In (a), Dacian men appear to be drinking a poison from a common pot and dying; in (b) the Dacian King Decabulus puts a dagger to his own neck while Roman soldiers rush in to capture him. Cast of the reliefs, Museo della Civiltà Romana. Photos by Davina C. Lopez.

Visualizing Significant Otherness

Figs. 5a and 5b. Various nations fight on the side of both Romans and Dacians, rendering the war a multi-national endeavor. In (a), the Sarmatian cavalry, distinguishable by the scaly armor covering both riders and horses, aids the Dacians; and in (b), Trajan deploys a band of Numidian warriors, identifiable by their ethnically specific dress and corkscrewed hair, to assist his army in battle. Cast of the reliefs, Museo della Civiltà Romana. Photos by Grace Lewis and Davina C. Lopez.

Fig. 6. At the beginning of the second campaign against the Dacians, Trajan (on the right, facing left) extends his right arm to receive a delegation of several non-Roman nations, identifiable by their dress, hairstyles, and attributes. Photo by Davina C. Lopez.

international endeavor with complicity from other ethnic groups such as the long-conquered and assimilated Numidians. The Dacians also do not fight alone, receiving assistance from their fellow barbarians, the Sarmatians (fig. 5). At one point, in what looks like the beginning of the second Dacian war, Trajan receives delegations from at least six different conquered nations, each identifiable by their dress and attributes (fig. 6). This image of collaboration between nations to defeat a common terrorist threat is supported by the subsequent depictions of battle between Dacians and various ethnic warriors who are shown in service to Rome, many representing nations that had fought against the Romans themselves and lost. Germans (north), Africans (south), Parthians (east), and Spaniards (west) constitute an ancient "Coalition of the Willing," working together to bring Roman freedom to the hinterlands. In other words, the column shows colonized others using violence not only as a defense against empire but also on behalf of empire against a common enemy. Trajan's Column can thus be read as a complex representation of a universalizing, assimilationist, multiethnic, patriarchal structure, which in turn renders the embedded hierarchies complex and convoluted.

Representations like those found on Trajan's Column provide an opportunity for raising critical questions concerning the roles and functions of power, gender, sexuality, and status with respect to the totalizing and universalizing frameworks and hierarchies that shape, reconfigure, and indeed create meaning. Trajan's Column is a penetrating example of an attempt to stabilize a Roman narrative of national identity and destiny

Visualizing Significant Otherness 89

that is characterized by aggression and violence toward both people and land. Through its depictions of both "Romanness" and "otherness" as impure, intertwined, and multicultural, such visual narratives could have rendered empire more desirable to Romans and "the nations" alike. Non-Romans, represented as ethnic outsiders, are invited to take a place at the imperial table, helping the imperial selves to carry out the subjugation of yet more "others." Such a complex visual pattern invites a series of questions. Is imperial prowess only about the acts of individual bodies? Is such violence always perpetrated by the (masculine) figure on top? Does the representation of the collectively conquered as female, as disheveled and powerless, mean that the defeated could not turn and do the same to others in an endless spiral of domination and subordination? How do we analyze the structures of violence when the "others," those already colonized and defeated nations forced into servitude to the Romans, are shown fighting for (a vision of) Rome against a common enemy in the name of peace, abundance, stability, and faith? What do we make of the seemingly innocuous and casual elements on the column, such as the Roman-style bridges, tunnels, roads, plazas, and so on, all now placed in the context of conquest and subsequent devastation? And, importantly, what difference does it make to take the column and the questions it generates seriously as New Testament scholars? Could we open (or close) our eyes and think about Paul and the various groups represented in the New Testament alongside such representations of imperial hybridity? Why or why not? I am proposing that we should do exactly that as part of a conscious and strategic realignment of the primary sources available to us, wherein images are not arranged hierarchically but reconfigured as a complementary semantic system to letters and words.

Yet the question remains: What might we do with Paul in light of a sustained consideration of Roman imperial visual representation, particularly when those representations appear to undermine our assumptions that identity and power relations are stable and fixed, or that they belong to stable and fixed binary oppositions under which, according to many modern readings of Bhabha's work, hybridization takes place? It is important at our particular historical and social moment—fraught as it is with military and political violence, social and economic instability, and fears of many different kinds—to come to terms with the diversity of ways in which the people whom we call "early Christians," some of whom may be represented in the array of texts that eventually came to be known as the "New Testament canon," interacted with their Roman world. It is also important to realize that such figures might have engaged with that world on less-than-friendly and perhaps even oppositional terms, regardless of their potentially hybridic condition and context. Viewed in this way, the New Testament, as a collection of traces and remembrances of now lost and unrecoverable experiences of "others" in the Roman imperial period, offers a locus of signification in which "others" are arranged in relation to the Roman imperial "self." In the process, Paul and his colleagues become the heroes who turn Caesar upside down.

Paul (or at least the images of Paul in his letters) offers a way to illustrate the complex dynamic for which I have been arguing above, opening up a (perhaps third) space for alternative readings and renderings of hybridity and power in relation to modern postcolonial applications. Here the methodological value of reading Paul and his letters in conversation with Roman imperial visual representations such as Trajan's Column will become evident. While there are numerous avenues into this discussion of (re)imag(in)ing Paul, one issue that is particularly worthy of our attention is the manner in which Paul's own body is depicted in his letters. The utility of this focus is that it helps to situate particular kinds of assumptions in relationship to one another. For instance, given the logics of colonizer/self and colonized/other that were pervasive in Roman imperial images, it is tempting to make a pronouncement here about Paul's hybridized body and rhetoric being "neither Roman nor Dacian," always negotiating (and being negotiated by) and mimicking empire. Most scholarship on Paul readily moves in that direction. Yet one could also posit another set of questions that would open up an entirely different range of meanings and significations. For example, we could ask: Whom do we desire Paul to be? Given all that we know, how do we frame an image of Paul's body? What do we think about his self-identification program and his relationships with others? What kind of relationship do we want to have with the apostle? Is it possible that Paul is just like Trajan—that the "apostle to the conquered" is himself a conqueror from start to finish, a stable, authoritative, self-dominating, annihilated other? Or is he some kind of anti-imperial hero, as the last decade of scholarship in what is increasingly being called "empire-critical New Testament studies" would have it? Perhaps these configurations tell us more about us (and our world) than they do about Paul and his.

At the very least, neither of the above two options seems adequate. Paul presents his own "crucified" body as the communicative and pedagogical vehicle for his articulation of relationships that are different than what we might want or need him to have. Paul's shift in consciousness, sometimes called his "conversion," resulted in a radically new configuration of knowledge and a renunciation of his previous affirmation of the power relations that Roman imperial prowess had made to seem natural and inevitable. In so doing, Paul became more conscious of both the particularity of his Jewishness and his commonalities with the other conquered and colonized peoples of the Roman Empire. In other words, Paul came to consciousness not as a conquering self, even though he may have started out that way, but as a marginalized "other" among many others who had been marginalized. Such an understanding of Paul will invariably reshape the way we configure his possible interaction with Jewishness and maleness in the Roman context of impenetrable masculine selfhood. It will also require us to reconsider the opposition between "self" and "other" as a means by which to articulate power relationships.

If such an understanding leads us to think of Paul as a hybrid figure, we must also take into account that this does not preclude the possibility that he represents himself as broken and human. While some interpreters see Paul's brokenness as a sign of his ability to "take it like a man,"[25] I question the stability and impenetrability of the apostle's masculinity. In view of the kinds of images that I have discussed above, I would say that Paul's "manhood" is stable neither in legend nor in letter.[26] Paul is vulnerable in a manner that he would not have been as a Roman citizen, a manly soldier and persecutor imitating Roman hierarchical patterns, or a colonized "other" fighting for the empire. He has "died to the law" and "been crucified" with Christ (Gal 2:19) so that he might live to God, producing a life of compromised masculinity that signifies vulnerability.[27] Paul likes to talk about the pains that he experienced from excessive beatings; clearly these do not indicate elite male status or military success. In fact, such bodily dangers and traumas, particularly whippings and floggings, are common to slaves.[28] Roman men, even ethnic Spaniards who became emperors, would never be portrayed as having been beaten. Paul models a *defeated*, not a heroic, male body, one that is identified with the lower status of enslavement and humiliation.[29] Paul makes a structural move from colonizer/self to colonized/other, which, in the logic of a monument like Trajan's Column, is a move from Roman to Dacian, from empire to terrorist, from civilized to uncivilized.

Paul also envisions this consciousness as transferable, as seen in his use of the rhetoric of mimesis.[30] Such an injunction to become "like" another is not a message of assimilation or a "call to sameness,"[31] but an acknowledgment of similar experiences among the peoples under Roman rule and a movement to engage the colonized others on their own terms. We must ask, then, what does it mean to "become like" Paul's body, which is unheroically broken? What kind of ethics does such a move produce? What kind of power relationships does it engender? Imitating "weakness" and a dominated, penetrated Jewish (or "Jewgreek") male body in the context of Roman imperial ideology does not offer reinforcement to a vertical hierarchy and upward assimilation, nor does it indicate a hybrid impotence. Instead, it requires downward mobility, away from the division established by the conquerors and toward a solidarity with the conquered.

In Galatians, Paul transforms his compromised masculinity into the suffering of a woman in labor (4:19). The brokenness that characterized Paul a few verses earlier is here manipulated into an act of creation. But this creation is *ex nihilo*, from the margins, by a defeated man/woman. Whether it is correct to speak of Paul's identification with laboring motherhood as a "metaphor squared,"[32] the image of Paul having birth pains symbolizes his labor for a new creation based on the desire for a different configuration of relationships between Jews and others, echoing his scriptural context (especially the prophetic tradition) and challenging his "exilic" situation under Roman rule. Such a critical consciousness involves a death to the way the world works at the same time as it gives life to another kind of world.

Paul's critical consciousness insists that imperial violence, as exemplified by the cross, no longer carries the power to threaten and destroy lives. If we want to call this consciousness "hybrid," then we might suggest that to be constituted by hybridic interactions is to constantly say no to the ordinary, oppressive way of doing things and to insist that threatening structures and death machines have no power to define the lives of the colonized and marginalized—even if the marginalized are accustomed to participating in their own continued domination, and even if the colonizers are also complicated and even compromised figures through their encounters and interactions with the colonized. It means also that marginalized people working with each other in relationship, in the service of overcoming that which seeks to divide and conquer, can nullify the power of subjugation and death. The potential for reimagining Paul as a hybrid figure lies in the possibility that he learns, and tries to teach, the idea that structural change—a new creation—is possible and necessary. Such a desire is itself sufficient to reshape the world. Whether Jew or Greek or something in between, Paul represents himself as someone who puts down his own weapons and starts to ask the hard questions about his tradition(s) in light of his prior collaboration with and imitation of dominant imperial realities. Through his mission to the nations, the "significant others" of his letters, he encourages a host of "selves" to do likewise.

Visualizing Hybridity and Honesty: Reimagining Relationships, Then and Now

My point in making these observations is not to claim that Paul is perfect or that his project was ever realized. His ideas might not even be the product of "hybridity." I will say, however, that a reimagination of the apostle and his communities, particularly if we wish to continue to utilize a postcolonial analytic, requires us to visualize and reimagine different relationships. The study of Paul is, ultimately, about relationships: bad relationships and good ones, abusive relationships and loving ones, lost relationships and found ones, impossible relationships and real ones, regrettable relationships and transformative ones, relationships that make us uncomfortable and ones that sustain us, relationships that we do not know we have and ones whose existence we continue to deny. The professional and, should we desire, postcolonial study of the New Testament, Christian origins, and early Christian literature is also about relationships between people, communities, and ideas across time, and perhaps primarily—for better or worse, in sickness and in health—about the relationships between ancient and modern worlds, including the modern world of scholarship. Despite gestures and institutional machinery to the contrary, the field of Pauline studies has, like the discipline of classics and other historically oriented configurations, always been not only about the discovery of an ancient world but also about defining and debating our relationship to that world.[33] The ancient world that we seek to discover and uncover, that which we desire to exegete so closely and precisely, that which we claim to be discovering and uncovering, is alien and even dead to us.

And yet that world is anything but dead, as anyone paying attention to the way biblical texts are deployed and redeployed in our culture can attest. We blame an alien world and its alien inhabitants for problems and injustices that belong to us and rest on our shoulders. And when it is convenient (as it often is), we use that same alien world as origin-story for defining our own contemporary identities, for justifying the good things that we want and getting rid of the bad. The relationship between ancient and modern is complicated, fraught with baggage, and difficult to negotiate. Concepts like hybridity, however, offer us at least one mode of negotiating that relationship, though often at the cost of displacing our own fractured selves onto a distant, stable (even if in complicated ways) past. And herein lies the contradiction, the challenge, and the hope of postcolonial studies, insofar as we begin to understand that our "selves" are caught up (methodologically and personally) in the very hybridic structures that we identify as being part of the alterity (perhaps even the barbarity) of the "other"—in this case, the world of the Roman empire and early Christians.

In other words, the ancient world functions as a (colonized) other, even as we, the (colonizing) selves, are shaped by it, or shaped by our shaping of it under the banner of discovery and, in the case of Pauline studies, bringing it to life through exegesis. We desire it to be this way; we want to justify being alive in the way we are by making the ancient world alive in the way we so deeply desire it to be. The problem with this approach is that no matter which theoretical trajectories we find compelling, we are not consistently honest with ourselves about what we imagine the horizon of our labors to be. Entering into Pauline studies honestly need not entail rejecting exegetical methods or attention to antiquity because such issues and methods became prominent in the nineteenth century through Protestant, mostly German, influences and designs. I see no need to dismiss exegesis or to reject thinking about and with the ancient world as a dusty, antiquarian, pointless exercise designed to keep myself, a female body who questions the naturalness of capitalist, United-States-centric, heteropatriarchal empire and all of its trappings, in an unconsciously subordinate social position. Nor do I see my insistence on reading and rereading Paul as a reason to give up on liberation, to unconsciously reproduce imperial subjectivity, or to engage in colonial mimicry. To be honest about Pauline studies at this point in time is not to ignore histories of interpretation that have been far from kind and affirming toward people who have been historically neglected. As someone who has willingly chosen to bear the stigmata of professional New Testament interpretation, it is precisely my relationship with these histories that engenders a responsibility, even a mandate, to intervene by reconfiguring and reimagining the texts, the field, and the world. This commitment also entails a task of reimagining postcolonial concepts such as hybridity.

Being honest about the kind of work that New Testament scholars should be doing means that we must entertain the possibility that the desire to uncover an ancient world that is already there, waiting to be discovered, is and should be dialectically related to our defining and debating our relationship to that world, particularly in light of our long histories of colonial contact and imperial rule and our attendant responses to those political realities, then and now. How we define ourselves in relation to the "others" of the ancient and contemporary worlds does in fact define the contours of what we can discover about those ancient worlds while also managing their ranges of signification and meaning. What happens, then, if we acknowledge that the way we desire to frame ourselves, including our role as interpreters of Paul at this particular time and place, has more impact than we are willing to admit on the range of significations that we map onto the ancient world that we are ostensibly discovering and uncovering? When and how will we learn that most of what we say about the ancients is also, and probably mostly, about us—and particularly about our relation to imperial and colonial legacies?

I cannot claim to have the answers to such questions, but I will say this: in a time when most of my undergraduate students have grown up experiencing an expensive "war on terror" as completely ordinary, without limits in time or space, it is vital that we reimagine justice-making as something besides international vigilantism and the continued alienation of whole peoples and lands. At this moment of blaming, scapegoating, and destroying the other in defense of self-interest and preservation, no matter who we are, we must examine and be honest about our own complicity in a worldwide story of empire that we keep telling ourselves and in which we continue to have faith.

In recent years, with the help of postcolonial approaches, it has begun to seem almost ordinary to say that individuals in antiquity who resonated with people like Paul negotiated, mimicked, and possibly mocked the pretensions of Roman imperial power and prowess in and through forms of hybridity. Yet the question of empire also has immediate links to our own context. The challenge is to figure out how we get beyond simply noticing the obvious clash between Rome and Jerusalem—and all the other "nations," whom I have suggested elsewhere are the New Testament's "Gentiles"—and move from conceptions of upside-down oppositional resistance to reimagination, not only about the politics and nuances of the ancient world, but about our own. This is not to say that engagement with the ancient world is a futile exercise, for, as Karl Kautsky has said, "The study of the past, far from being mere dilettante antiquarianism, will become a powerful weapon in the struggles of the present, in order to hasten the attainment of a better future."[34] Reimagining Paul and his communities in his Roman imperial context through the postcolonial optic of hybridity is not about Paul or his Roman imperial context. Critical reimagination is about us and our desires for particular relationships with the ancient, contemporary, and future worlds.

Ultimately, our task as hybridized, globalized people is to wrestle with our old friend Paul in light of such possibilities—and to get on with the business of making the world in which we want to live. In this respect, it is worth noting that the image of Trajan that sat atop his column was eventually replaced by a statue of Peter, the "founder" of the Catholic Church. In a similar way Mussolini, by including casts of Trajan's Column in his Museum of Roman Civilization, intended to celebrate this monument, alongside others, as a testament to a new era of power, conquest, and domination. To read all of this from a postcolonial position is in some sense to acknowledge that Trajan himself is a conquered "other," that the emperor can be a victim even as his monument appears to attest otherwise. In some way, a truly hybridic lens, if prismed through a reimaginative project such as the one that I have proposed here, would have to read Trajan and Paul as compatriots, as a "self" and an "other" indistinguishable from the other/self. This is not a "third space"—it is a wholly "new space," one that does not seek to relegate change to an imaginary world. Positing Trajan and Paul as comrades results in a way of seeing that has truly revolutionary potential for this world—and the one to come. And what of the Dacians? They are the haunting memory—the trace, the reminder—that resistance might not be so futile after all.

CHAPTER SEVEN

Reading Romans 7 in Conversation with Postcolonial Theory

Paul's Struggle toward a Christian Identity of Hybridity

L. ANN JERVIS

At the best of times, and in the best of circumstances, human identity is a difficult construct to conceptualize and articulate; and whether that identity is personal, cultural or religious, defining and describing it are always challenging—particularly when it encounters external and uninvited intrusions that disrupt personal, social, and religious patterns and self-understandings. Significantly, this is a problem that is addressed by both postcolonial theory and by the apostle Paul in Romans 7. Accordingly, this essay will take advantage of postcolonial categories as an aid to clarifying Paul's struggle with identity in this notoriously difficult passage—a venture that seems particularly appropriate given the original venue of this paper.[1]

My approach will be to work analogically by identifying similarities of function between actors in both postcolonial theory and Romans 7, although with the understanding that the related discourses and situations are essentially different.[2] In so doing, the controlling principle of my reading of Romans 7 will not be postcolonial categories but exegesis of the passage. Issues in postcolonial thinking will serve to *illustrate* the meaning of Romans 7. Postcolonial categories will be woven into the interpretation of Romans 7, but only for the purpose of serving a secondary function in the process of meaning making. Romans 7 will be mined for analogies to postcolonial issues, not postcolonial issues for analogies to Romans 7. In the process a sharper picture of what Paul was expressing will, it is hoped, come into view.

Identity in Postcolonial Theory

Postcolonial theory recognizes that a fundamental problem created by the forceful imposition of one culture on another (either militarily or economically) is the sense of alienation and confusion of identity that inevitably result. In his book *Black Skin, White Masks*, Frantz Fanon explored this process and noted the psychological challenges of a colonized people.[3] In order to survive, and in order to achieve even a measure of success in the colonized environment, indigenous people are forced to accept, or, at the very least recognize, the European perception of their race—namely, that they are subordinate. The colonized start to define themselves in the context of the colonizer and unwittingly acquire what Leela Gandhi would describe as a "derivative identity."[4]

Using Hegel's study of the master–slave relationship, Fanon describes the problem as one of reciprocity: the master needs the slave and vice versa. The only way out of this damnable reciprocity is for the colonized to begin to understand themselves apart from the categories and values of the colonizers, and to define their identity in terms of their own categories. In other words, they must think themselves out of the box in which they have been imprisoned.[5]

The crisis of identity created by colonization is often compounded by well-meaning postcolonial attempts to remedy the situation. Unfortunately, the offering and bringing of economic, social, and educational aid often unwittingly become simply another, more implicit form of colonization. The aid creates dependence on foreign attitudes and skills and devalues indigenous knowledge. Thus, the desire to help often creates or exacerbates problems.

There are, then, potentially two stages of colonizing activity: first, the foreign invasion of an existing culture; and, second, the attempt to remedy the problems created by this foreign invasion. Obviously, the identity of the colonized culture is affected at both stages. In regard to identity, the goal for the postcolonial cultures is the achievement of a new identity of freedom—an identity that is no longer defined by the master–slave relationship.[6]

Hybridity

Many postcolonial theorists have offered the concept of *hybridity* as a necessary and potentially positive means by which previously colonized cultures can begin to understand themselves as new entities.[7] Generally speaking, the hybrid identity is one that seeks to integrate features of a culture's precolonial past with features of the colonizer's identity in order to come up with a new, hybrid identity.[8]

Homi Bhabha describes hybridity as a "third space" where prior histories are displaced so that a new identity can be formed.

> The importance of hybridity is that it bears the traces of those feelings and practices which inform it ... so that hybridity puts together the traces of certain other meanings or discourses. It does not give them the authority of being prior in the sense of being original: they are prior only in the sense of being anterior. The process of cultural hybridity gives rise to something different, something new ... a new area of negotiation of meaning and representation.[9]

Bhabha represents those postcolonial thinkers who understand hybrid identity as a means capable of subverting the structures of domination that result from the colonial experience.[10] As such, hybrid identity redefines the past in light of the present, rather than the other way around. It rejects the notion that the past, whether of colonialism or an imaginary paradise prior to colonialism, can effectively define the new identity.[11]

Among those who share a positive view of hybridity is postcolonial biblical scholar R. S. Sugiratharajah, who states:

> One of the legacies of colonialism is an intermingling of people and cultures, and the result is a hybridized identity.... Previously ... attempts by the "natives" to redraw their identity by fusing indigenous and imported values was labeled syncretism and dismissed as a disruptive and negative project. Such criticism was grounded in Western Christian exclusivity and expansionist perspectives. Hybridity, however, is a wider and more complex web of cultural negation and interaction, forged by imaginatively redeploying the local and the imported elements. It ... involves a new found independence, achieved not simply by rejecting provincial, national, and imperial attachments, but by working through them.[12]

Others such as postcolonial literary critic Patrick Hogan maintain a negative view of the concept of hybridity and argue that the move to combine into one story aspects of both the colonized and the colonizer is a dangerous process, as it necessarily results in alienation—a state of being in which one has no true home.[13]

Analogical Relationships between Romans 7 and Postcolonial Theory

This essay enters the contorted fray of discussions on identity in Romans 7 in conversation with postcolonial theory. In order properly to engage such a conversation, we will need to find appropriate analogical relationships between players in the colonial drama and those in Romans 7. We will, of course, also need to clarify whether the discourse of Romans 7 refers to Paul's pre-Christian or Christian experience.

We have identified two stages in the colonial drama: colonization and postcolonization. In the first stage there are two actors: the *colonizer*, a foreign force that disrupts and subordinates an existing culture; and the colonized, whose culture and identity are disrupted and subordinated against their will. Accordingly, it seems reasonable to understand Paul's description of sin analogously to the colonizer, and the world and humanity as the colonized: sin came into the world and reigned over humanity (Rom 5:12-14).[14]

The second stage of colonization occurs after the colonial powers have left or been defeated. Typically, as noted above, aid givers seek to remedy the situation. At this stage, a state of dependency often ensues that, perhaps unwittingly, prohibits the previously colonized culture from gaining its own identity and flourishing.

With regard to Romans 7, we may suggest an analogous relationship between the law and postcolonial aid givers. As Paul puts it, the law had a benevolent motive that allowed for self-understanding and the capacity to recognize the oppression caused by sin (7:7). This awareness of the problematic situation indicates a new stage that is analogous to postcolonialism. It is not the stage from Adam to Moses (5:14) but the stage when there is a remedy offered for the horrific consequences of sin's invasion. Yet the law (in a way analogous to postcolonial aid givers) could not take away the fundamental problem created by the colonization of sin. In fact, the well-intentioned law only exacerbated the problem (7:8; cf. 5:20).

The discourse of Romans 7 thus presupposes certain events analogous to events in colonization and the accompanying struggle for a new identity of freedom. The speaker in Romans 7 is aware of the destructive experience of both stages of colonization and is now exposing the challenges of shaping a new identity. To this end, he graphically describes here the cost of and struggle toward wholeness, health, and freedom.

While Paul's depiction of the intense battle to become a new person is often considered to be a negative portrait,[15] it might be preferable to see in Romans 7 the honest heroic fight for freedom. Turning to postcolonial thinkers, we encounter Frantz Fanon's understanding of the failure of "the Negro" as due to the fact that he or she was set free by the master rather than having had to fight for freedom.[16] Underlying Fanon's understanding is Hegel's position that struggle is necessary for the attainment of true freedom: "The individual, who has not staked his life, may, no doubt, be recognized as a person, but he has not attained the truth of this reception as an independent self-consciousness."[17] Accordingly, it might be said that an identity free of the colonial past is forged at a price. And I would suggest that it is this price that Paul describes in Romans 7.

New identity comes from the recognition that the old system of colonization no longer defines one's identity, and that receiving of aid is not necessarily equivalent to independence. In other words, a new identity comes from denying power to both the colonizer and the subsequent aid-givers. It means finding a new story in which to live and by which to be defined, in addition to being careful about aspects of that new story that have the potential to re-enslave one to the colonial past.

In light of this analogy, Romans 7 may be viewed as a description of the profound challenges of shaping a new identity in the aftermath of colonization. After exegeting

Romans 7, we will ask whether the identity that Paul is describing struggling toward is analogous to the hybrid identity described by postcolonial thinkers.

The Identity of the Speaker in Romans 7

Before proceeding, it is necessary to determine the fundamental exegetical issue in any reading of Romans 7—whether the speaker is one who has encountered Christ or one who has not. Even though the latter option is currently the most widely held among scholars,[18] my position is that the speaker is a believer in Christ.[19] My rationale is based in part on the absence of any sort of signpost in Romans 7 indicating that Paul has turned his attention away from the description of the Christian life that he began in 3:21, and that he continues to the end of chapter 8. Unlike instances in chapters 4 and 5, where Paul makes clear that he is discussing events prior to Christ,[20] chapter 7 gives no indication that Paul is referring to a time before the coming of Christ. It is my contention that statements in Romans 7 that seem to be at odds with Paul's convictions about the Christian life are not necessarily de facto signposts.[21] Arguments based on specific words and phrases of Romans 7 for the view that the speaker is a believer will be made in what follows.

At this stage it is important to emphasize that the speaker is not simply a believer in Christ but a Jewish believer in Christ. As such, Paul speaks to, and identifies with, those who know the law (7:1) and have died to the law (7:4). This identification with his fellow Jews who also believe in Jesus can be seen when Paul uses the first person plural (7:5-7). Moreover, when he begins to use the first person singular (7:9-25; with the exception of 7:14a), Paul is referring to an "I" that is representative of the Jewish believer. With this understanding of the identity of the speaker we now turn to the task of reading Romans 7 as a description of the struggle to grasp a new identity of freedom. The following exegesis will make a case for this understanding in the process of reading chapter 7 in conversation with postcolonial thinking.

Romans 7:1-8a: Positioning the Past

In the opening verses of chapter 7, Paul is speaking to Jewish believers (v. 1) who are on the road to a free identity. Drawing them to recognize their potential for freedom through the example of marital law, Paul describes their situation as one in which they have died to the law (v. 4). Significantly, Paul does not say that the law is dead, but rather that they are dead to it. The focus, therefore, is on the Jewish believers' self-understanding and the way in which they position themselves in relation to their colonial past.

The means by which they have this new and liberated stance to the law is "through the body of Christ" (v. 4). Their identity is now derived from the fact that they belong to Christ, "the one who was raised from the dead" (v. 4). Accordingly, Paul stresses the distinctiveness of their new identity from the one they once had: they no longer bear fruit for death but now bear fruit for God (vv. 4-5). To this end, he describes their previous subjugation to the law and urges them to recognize that they have been released from its power (*katērgēthēmen*, v. 6). In other words, Paul describes the law's effective (although perhaps unintended) collusion with the colonizer (sin) in order to clarify for Jewish believers that they should no longer feel dependency on the law.

Paul makes it unmistakably clear that, despite this collusion between the law and sin, they are separate entities: "What shall we say? That the law is sin? By no means!" (v. 7a). This clarification may be important not only to honor the law's good motives (cf. v. 12) but also in order to clarify the distinction between the colonizer (sin) and the aid-giver (the law). For if sin were identified with the law, then Paul's claim that Jewish believers had been discharged from the law could be taken to mean that they had been discharged from sinning. As we will come to see, however, Paul is fully aware that in the struggle for a free identity the colonial past continues to resurface periodically. As chapter 6 makes plain, the colonial past continues to remain a challenge even after one has been incorporated into the body of Christ.[22] The good news, however, is that with a free identity, sin no longer has power, only influence.

The important thing at this point in Paul's argument is that Jewish believers should recognize a distinction between the law and sin, and so acknowledge that sin used the law for its own purposes (v. 8a). In other words, the colonizer effectively remained in charge, even after the aid-giver came. For this reason, Jewish believers cannot be truly free under the law; they need to redefine their identity as one shaped not by the law, which was necessarily shaped by sin (and by extension death), but by Christ.

An analogous move can be found in several postcolonial thinkers, such as Frantz Fanon, as they struggle toward a free identity by imagining identity apart from the values and characteristics assigned by the colonial past.

> As I begin to recognize that the Negro is the symbol of sin, I catch myself hating the Negro. But then I recognize that I am a Negro. There are two ways out of this conflict. Either I ask others to pay no attention to my skin, or else I want them to be aware of it. I try then to find value for what is bad—since I have unthinkingly conceded that the black man is the color of evil. In order to terminate this neurotic situation, in which I am compelled to choose an unhealthy, conflictual solution, fed on fantasies, hostile, inhuman in short, I have only one solution: to rise above this absurd drama that others have staged round me, to reject the two terms that are equally unacceptable, and, through one human being, to reach out for the universal.[23]

In the same way, Paul challenges Jewish believers to define themselves entirely by their newfound position as part of the body of Christ (7:4).

Romans 7:8b-13: The Colonial Past in the Liberated Present

In Rom 7:8b-13, Paul returns to the ideas he expressed in chapter 6 concerning the fact that after faith in Christ sin does not disappear. Even though in the initial enthusiasm over the possibilities of the new identity it may have appeared as though sin were dead (v. 8b), sin still has the capacity to come to life again (v. 9). In fact, sin can use the commandment inherent in faith in Christ (v. 9), just as it used the law.[24] The colonial past, in other words, is not obliterated once a free identity is found. The challenge in shaping a free identity is to set the past in a new perspective so that its inevitable presence no longer captures attention but rather is contextualized by the positive, life-giving, and liberating features of the new identity. Paul's description of the struggle for a free identity is realistic about the capacity of the colonizer (sin)—even though it is no longer in power—to use even the best of the new life.

The interpretation just offered for vv. 8b-9 requires some justification. I am arguing not only that Paul is referring to the lives of Christians but also that in v. 9b he is referring to the commandment (*entolē*) not of the Torah, but of the requirement inherent in the Christian life. These two interpretive decisions must be defended.

Death in the New Life. One obstacle to understanding 7:8b-13 as referring to the life of Christian believers is Paul's statement that once sin revived, "I died" (v. 9b). This statement appears to many as incongruous in a Pauline description of the Christian life. How can he speak of death in the Christian life?

The answer is that, of course, Paul *does* speak of death in the believer's life. He speaks of death to the law (7:4), and of death to sin (6:11). At first glance, however, these deaths seem different from the death about which Paul speaks in 7:9-10. Death to the law and death to sin have beneficial results; dying to the law allows the believer to bear fruit for God (7:4), and being dead to sin allows one to be alive to God (6:11). The dying to which Paul refers in 7:9 seems to lead only to death as such (7:10). Moreover, whereas death to the law and death to sin are deaths to entities apart from the one who dies, in 7:9-10 Paul speaks of *himself* dying (*egō apethanon*).

Broadening our view to 7:13, however, reveals that the death about which Paul speaks in 7:9-10 also has a beneficial result. Sin's character, and the extent of its reach, is revealed through the death that occurs. Sin's use of the good to produce death serves to make sin's activity and character public (7:13). Using the good, sin works death, but this death results only in revealing sin's riotous wickedness (*hyperbolēn hamartōlos*). The capacity of sin to deceive (v. 11) is limited by the good which, though used by sin, nevertheless is capable itself of exposing sin (7:13). The death that sin produces has a further positive result; it maintains the holiness of the law and the holiness, righteousness, and goodness of the commandment (cf. *hōste*, 7:12). Like the other deaths in the Christian life, then, this death too results in good. Consequently, it is not comparable to the death to which Paul refers in chapter 5—a death that led only to death, with no accompanying benefits (5:12, 21).

We should note also that, while the death spoken of in 7:9-13 is death to the *egō*. the self is not terminated. If we do not separate 7:9-13 from 7:14-25,[25] we see that the "ego" continues, capable of recognizing its fleshliness (7:14), its desire for the good, its inability to fulfill that desire (7:15-24), and its wretchedness and need for Jesus Christ (7:24-25).

A further indication that Paul is speaking of the Christian experience is that he says that death occurred because of sin's *revival* (7:9). In 7:8b Paul says "apart from law (*chōris nomou*) sin is dead," which introduces his statement that with the coming of the commandment sin lived anew (*anezēsen*).[26] In Romans, the distinguishing characteristic of God's work in Christ is that it is "apart from law" (*chōris nomou*, 3:21). The phrase *chōris nomou* does not indicate a time *before* the giving of the law, but presumes the existence of the law.[27] It is, then, in the context of life with Christ that sin is dead. Moreover, the very idea of sin being dead is incongruous in a description of anything other than the Christian life. Paul understands believers to be those who are free from sin (6:22). He is convinced that prior to Christ all people were under sin's rule (3:10; 5:12). Consequently, sin's revival (7:9) must occur in the life of one in whom it has previously been defeated—the life of one who is in Christ.[28]

The Commandment in 7:9b-13. The second pertinent matter is the meaning of "commandment" (*entolē*) in 7:9b-13. I have suggested above that in these verses Paul is referring not to a commandment of the Torah but rather to a commandment inherent in the Christian life.

Whereas Paul's first reference to *entolē* in Romans 7 is undoubtedly to a commandment of Torah (7:8), scholars regularly allow Paul's mention of the tenth commandment in 7:7 to define his subsequent uses of the word *entolē*. That is, from the outset of their interpretation of Rom 7:7-25 scholars presume that *entolē* is a command of Torah. It is my contention, however, that Paul transmutes the meaning of the word *entolē* in 7:9. The interpretive principle guiding my suggestion and my reading is that the same word can be used to signify different entities. Paul exemplifies this in chapter 7 with his use of the word *nomos*. The word is used to refer to Torah (7:1, 7, 12, 14, 16), to a principle (7:21),[29] to the inner person (7:23) and to the dictates of sin (7:23). The different referents for the word *nomos* result from the different arenas in which it is placed. When the context is Torah, it refers to Torah; when the context is the experience of seeking to do good, it refers to a principle (7:21) or to aspects of the inner person or the demands of sin (7:23). Given Paul's demonstrated capacity for using, without warning or fanfare, the same word to refer to different entities, we may entertain the possibility that Paul uses *entolē* with similar flexibility. Just as *nomos* has meaning in relation to the context of the discourse, so may *entolē*. While the word invariably means a commandment or order, its meaning is determined by the code or law to which the commandment belongs.

There are several reasons to consider the possibility that at 7:9 Paul *does not* use the word *entolē* to refer to a commandment of Torah. The most important is the fact that Paul qualifies this commandment with a phrase about its having life as its goal—"the commandment which is for life" (7:10). This qualification suggests that the commandment about which Paul is speaking is related to Christian existence. In this regard we must notice that Paul does not speak of the purpose of the law, apart from Christ, as life.[30] In fact, in Galatians Paul emphasizes that the law is not capable of producing life (Gal 3:21).[31] For Paul the concept of life is related only to Christ. Believers are those who are brought from death to life (Rom 6:13). What believers in Jesus know is the word of life (Phil 2:16). While Christians share mortality with the rest of humanity, they know and are promised life both in this time (2 Cor 4:10; Phil 1:21; Gal 2:11) and in eternity (Rom 6:23; 2 Cor 5:4). Paul begins his letter to Rome with the statement that the gospel reveals the righteousness of God, which promises life (Rom 1:17).[32] Furthermore, the words "life" and "living" in the context surrounding Rom 7:9-13 refer to the gift and experience peculiar to the Christian (Rom 5:10, 17, 18, 21; 6:4, 22, 23; 8:2, 6, 10, 38; cf. Rom 6:2, 10, 11, 13; 7:1, 2, 3, 9; 8:12, 13). The fact that Paul should describe the commandment as focused on life both raises a caution about assuming that he is still speaking of a Torah commandment and invites the thought that he may be using *entolē* to refer to a commandment inherent in life in Christ.

This thought is strengthened when we note that Paul elsewhere uses the word *entolē* to refer to requirements intrinsic to the Christian life (1 Cor 7:19; 14:37). It gains further credibility by noticing that other passages in Romans speak of the requirement of obedience for the believer. Paul describes his commission as one focused on "the obedience of faith" (1:5). The interpretation of the ambiguous grammar in this phrase has produced a variety of readings.[33] As D. B. Garlington notes, however, there are really only two viable options: either "the obedience which is faith," or "the obedience which proceeds from faith."[34] These two options amount, in the end, to much the same meaning: faith entails obedience.[35]

Paul describes the necessity of obedience in Romans 6. The person freed from sin can recognize and achieve righteousness by being obedient to teaching about the life of righteousness. Deliverance from bondage to sin is achieved by obedience to "the standard of teaching [*typon didachēs*]" (6:17). The phrase "standard of teaching" indicates not doctrinal instruction but the manner of life required of those who are slaves of God (6:22).[36] Obedience to teaching about behavior appropriate to the Christian life is essential for those freed to be servants of righteousness (6:18). In other words, even though Paul rarely uses the word *entolē* to describe the righteousness required of the Christian (the occurrences in 1 Corinthians noted above being the only examples), he clearly does recognize that there is a requirement of righteousness involved in being "in Christ."

I propose, then, that the "commandment" that comes (7:9b), and is focused on life (7:10), and is holy and just and good (7:12), and is used by sin with the result that sin's character might be revealed (7:13), is not a commandment of Torah but the commandment inherent in faith in Christ.

Shaping a New Identity in Spite of the Colonial Past. One of the clearest indications that Paul is speaking of the experience of seeking to shape a new identity apart from the domination of sin, that is, that he is speaking of the Christian life, is, as noted above, that he says that death occurred because of sin's *revival* (7:9). Paul describes in 7:9a the initial stage of the Christian life: the speaker says that he was alive apart from the law (7:9a).[37] Paul has spoken of this in the previous chapter. At the beginning of life "in Christ" (apart from law), at baptism, there is the recognition of the possibility of walking in newness of life (6:4). There is the knowledge that slavery to sin has ended (6:5).[38] This experience of liberation and life was, however, temporary. It ended when the commandment came (7:9b). The honeymoon period of faith ends when one recognizes that faith entails obedience to righteousness. The length of the honeymoon may be extremely brief, perhaps as long as it takes to be baptized, or, as in the case of some in Corinth, it may be much longer.[39] The moment the commandment of righteousness inherent in the Christian life enters a believer's purview, sin revives (7:9b). Romans 6:12-23 is an impassioned exhortation to believers to be aware of the activity of sin. Paul has said that baptism means that sin no longer controls the believer (6:6). This state of grace becomes, however, a situation requiring vigilance against sin's attempt to reassert control (6:12). Whereas before sin used the Torah, now sin seeks to use the commandment that promises life.

The commandment inherent in the Christian life comes (7:9b), then, with the result that sin reawakens and kills the liberated person (7:9b-11). This death is metaphorical for, as noted above, in the subsequent verses it is clear that the speaker (the "ego") continues his existence. We have also noted that this death is beneficial; it ends in establishing the goodness of the law and the commandment (7:12). The purpose of this death is to reveal the extent of sin's reach. In this scenario, neither the self nor the commandment is defeated by sin. The self is given light to see sin for what it is: "it was sin, working death in me through that which is good, in order that sin might be shown to be sin, and through the commandment might become sinful beyond measure" (7:13). The result of this death is, then, a new perspective on sin. Sin is revealed in all its ugliness (7:13).

Here again we find analogies to colonial categories. Paul is describing stages in the struggle for a new and free identity. At first, after liberation from both the colonizer and the aid-givers, the culture feels completely free of the past ("apart from the law sin is dead"). Unfortunately, however, the story does not end here, for the free identity is not free of its own requirements. There is the need to regulate a new life. Postcolonial cultures require government. This requirement, intrinsic to the free identity, carries with it its own dangers. It is not the requirement itself that is dangerous (provided, as Paul assumes, that the requirement is good). What is potentially harmful is the way the requirement's objectives can be contaminated by the colonial past. The colonial past can rear its ugly head and infect the attempt to create a new identity. The forging of a truly free identity involves intense attention to the capacities of the colonial past to distort even the best of the new situation. Whether through invading the mindsets of previously colonized people and provoking a sense of incompetence or anger or defeatism, or through misshaping government structures and procedures, the colonial heritage can disrupt the attempt to take a liberated place in the world.

Moreover, the achievement of a liberated stance in the world does require aid. The sting of postcolonial contexts is that freedom cannot be won without help. It is impossible for a previously colonized culture to progress to its goal of a free identity without aid from economically viable countries. In order to use this aid well, postcolonial cultures must dissociate the aid's benefits from the aid's colonial ties. It is necessary to honor and accept aid but always as a benefit serving the goal of a new identity rather than as a remnant of the past.

There are peculiar and profound challenges in the postcolonial struggle for a free identity. These challenges are graphically portrayed in the rest of Romans 7.

Romans 7:14-25: The Struggle to Be Free

The struggle facing those who wish to appropriate a free identity is twofold: first, they must recognize that the colonial past continues to attempt to distort their attempts to live liberated lives; and, second, they must find a way to accept necessary aid without becoming dependent on it, and thus be recolonized.

Paul begins his description of this struggle with the remarkable statement: "we know that the law is spiritual; but I am carnal, sold under sin" (7:14). Paul's affirmation of the law's holiness is not a surprise, since he has already stated this in 7:12. What is surprising, though, is that he should use the word "spiritual" (*pneumatikos*) to describe it, since earlier in the chapter Paul differentiated the Spirit from the law (7:6).

When we look ahead, however, we see that Paul is working toward incorporating the law into the Christian life. In Christ the law's goal is honored, although Paul stresses that that goal is accomplished *in Christ*. In 8:4 Paul says that believers fulfill the requirement of the law in themselves on account of the Spirit, and in 13:9 he states that "love is the fulfilling of the law." The affirmation in 7:14 that the law is spiritual, then, fits well alongside Paul's other statements concerning the law in the life of the believer. In fact, it foreshadows the thought of 8:4 that the just requirement of the law is fulfilled by those who walk according to the Spirit; 8:4 is the logical result of Paul's statement that the law is spiritual (7:14).

When, in the struggle for a free identity, the law can be recognized as of the Spirit, it loses its capacity to recreate dependency and enables one to be free of it. Its good work can be incorporated into the Christian life, by seeing it as beneficial in the context of the Spirit, that is, in an arena no longer defined by the law.

Likewise, previously colonized cultures must accept help in order to establish their liberated identities, but they can maintain their freedom only if they do so on their terms, by viewing such help in the context of their new freedom rather than as an extension of the colonial past. In other words, this achievement of a free identity in a situation of postcolonialism requires the redefinition of the identity of the aid-giver in the context of the liberated present. When this happens, the aid received will constructively serve the goals of the free identity, rather than perpetuating subservience.

The flip side of Paul's statement that the law is spiritual is his confession that "I am of the flesh [*sarkinos eimi*], sold into slavery under sin" (7:14b). Some Pauline scholars have argued that this statement conclusively proves that Paul is here referring to life apart from Christ;[40] however, what has not (to my knowledge) been noticed is the difference here in the relative positions of law and sin from passages that are clearly about the non-Christian life. Paul considers that in the person apart from Christ, sin uses the law (7:7-8a) and increases trespasses of it (5:20). In other words, for the nonbeliever the law and sin are in the same arena, so that sin can command the law to do its bidding. This is not the case in 7:14. Sin does not use the law; it uses the person: "I am ... sold under sin." The law is allowed now to be spiritual. The relationship between sin and the law has been realigned.

Furthermore, the speaker *recognizes* that he is fleshly, sold under sin. This recognition is not possible for one whose slavery to sin is such that righteousness is a foreign entity. Paul describes life apart from Christ as one of being "slaves of sin ... free in regard to righteousness" (6:20). The recognition that "I am of the flesh, sold under sin" is possible only for one who thinks of obedience as a goal. It is a statement impossible for one condemned to disobedience (5:18-20).[41]

It is to be noted that the speaker does not say "I" am *in the flesh*, but "I" am *fleshly*. That is, rather than saying that he is in the sphere of the flesh, the speaker uses the adjective *sarkinos*. Paul, of course, claims that believers in Christ have been liberated from the flesh. At the same time, however, he recognizes that they are tempted to *choose* the flesh. For Paul, flesh is a state of being for those who live apart from the Spirit of Christ (8:9); it is a temptation for Christians (8:12-13). It is to this temptation that Paul refers in 7:14—believers are drawn to the flesh.[42] The speaker in 7:14 describes himself as one whose chief characteristic is fleshliness, which is another way of saying that he is sold under sin. Presentation in the first person calls the hearer to recognize that the speaker is aware of his condition. Again, this awareness indicates that Paul is depicting a Christian experience, in contrast to those apart from Christ whom Paul describes as slavishly (6:20) and ignorantly (3:18) living in the flesh.

The speaker in 7:14 says that the reason he, while desiring to be obedient, makes fleshly choices, is that he has been "sold under sin." Paul recognizes here, as he does throughout his letters, that sin remains a problem in believers' lives. What occurred in the past—humanity's bondage to sin—continues to affect the present (note the perfect participle). Although for those "in Christ" sin's power is defeated, its influence remains. Consequently, having once been sold under sin, the believer still has a tendency toward things of the flesh. At the same time, however, the believer is no longer bound by the past. The speaker is now capable of recognizing what is spiritual (7:14).[43] It is to be noted that, in contrast, Paul does not describe sinners as recognizing anything (Rom

5:12, 21). In the same voice, the speaker says later that he desires the good (7:19), even the law of God (7:22).

Romans 7:15-23 plays out the drama involved in shaping a new identity in the shadow of the colonial past. Those attempting this monumental task must recognize that they do not start with a clean slate but are marked by the past to their very core. In these verses, the speaker recognizes that the ensuing struggle toward wholeness is entirely the fault of sin, and that the law should not be blamed. In fact, it is only when the speaker recognizes the capacities of sin that he also recognizes the goodness of the law (7:16).

In postcolonial terms, this remarkable and mature ability to distinguish between entities that formerly worked together can be seen when those who are wrestling for a free identity begin to perceive the aid-giver as dissociated from the colonial past. Accordingly, by regarding aid as a positive contribution to a postcolonial culture rather than as an extension of the past, those struggling to find identity can potentially resist the luring of their culture back to dependency and instead progress toward true freedom.

It is important to acknowledge, however, that the past does not disappear completely. The struggle for a free identity is successful only when it is honest about the continuing influence of the past. Paul's way of struggling with this issue is to reposition the aid-giver in the eyes of the one struggling for a free identity. Rather than perceiving the aid-giver as part of the past, it may be understood as a player connected to and defined by the new identity. The law now, rather than a servant of sin, is liberated to be the law of God (7:22). It is part of the new life but does not define that life. The new identity now defines the law,[44] and as such is no longer threatened by the presence of the law (the aid-giver).

In 7:23, Paul writes that he sees (*blepō*) the struggle that is taking place within himself. This capacity to be self-aware and to be able to recognize colonialism's remaining destructive influence is vital to the battle for a free identity. The struggle to be free of the colonial past requires not rejection of aid but attention to the abiding influence of past colonization, which must be recognized and combatted.

In the end, the only way to be liberated from the past is by focusing on the new story by which one defines oneself. As Paul puts it: "Wretched man that I am! Who will deliver me from this body of death? Thanks be to God through Jesus Christ our Lord!" (7:24-25). The struggle for a liberated identity primarily requires openness to the new drama in which one has put one's trust. It is achieved by countering the destructive remnants of the past with faith in the power of the new identity.

Faith in the power of a new identity is anything but passive. As Paul portrays it, it requires engaging in a struggle for the very core of one's being. Though a defeated force, sin still seeks to manipulate, control, and destroy. Since sin cannot now use the law, it uses the commandment that is focused on life. Thus, the new life is won by trusting that "there is now no condemnation for those who are in Christ Jesus" (8:1). Likewise, it is also won by the intense struggle to recontextualize the past in light of the new story.

The old story is changed because its ending has changed. The challenge, therefore, for the previously colonized, is continually to remember that and act upon it.

Conclusion: The Hybrid Identity Described in Romans 7

It has been argued that in Romans 7 Paul addresses Jewish believers for the purpose of describing a conflict with sin inherent in the obedience of faith. It has also been suggested that this sort of struggle is analogous to a postcolonial situation where intense effort is required to find a new identity that is not defined and limited by the legacy of the colonial past. It is not enough for liberated cultures, and believers liberated by Christ, to accept with gratitude their liberated state. Both must do their part in refashioning an identity that deals constructively with the past.

The new identity that Paul encourages Jewish believers to recognize and actualize in Romans 7 may be understood as "hybrid." Paul challenges his Roman hearers to define their past in light of their new story of being in Jesus Christ (7:25—8:1). Accordingly, Paul offers his hearers a way to deal with the continuing influence of the colonial past (sin), by challenging them to face up to the fact that, though sin no longer has authority over them, it nonetheless remains an influence and has the potential to derail their new identity of freedom. The fact that sin (the colonial past) has shaped believers to the very core (7:14-24) is not changed by liberation. What is changed is that the new and wondrous ending to the colonial story has the power to transform. The colonial past will not disappear, but its capacity to oppress can now be contained by a redefinition of the past in the context of the new and liberated present. Moreover, when the goal of freedom is kept in the forefront, the destructive remnants of the past have less opportunity to infect the present. Likewise, in this context, it also becomes possible to receive the requisite aid without that aid becoming a further extension of the colonial legacy.

Romans 7 offers a riveting depiction of the battle to allow the liberatory conclusion of colonialism's horrific tale to control the negative effects of oppression. In this passage Paul dramatizes the importance of recognizing the damage that the past has done while trusting in the power of the new ending to save him from the ever-present threat of further corruption (7:9b-10). He also emphasizes the need to distinguish between sin and the law (between the colonial power and the aid-giver), and between the law and the wonderful ending of the colonial story. The aid-giver (law) can be useful in the establishment of a free identity if it is dissociated in believers' minds from the colonial past (cf. 7:7: "Is the law sin? By no means!"). As such, it serves not its own function but the function of the new life (8:4).

Paul's description of the struggle for new identity is, therefore, comparable to aspects of the positive hybrid identity discussed by postcolonial thinkers. The identity Paul dramatizes faces up to the past without being dictated by the past. It is aware that the past can distort even the best intentions of the new chapter of freedom (the commandment focused on life can be used by sin, 7:9b-11) unless the past is reckoned with and disempowered through full commitment to the liberated ending ("Thanks be to God through Jesus Christ our Lord," 7:25). The identity that Paul describes believes itself to be more powerful than the damage caused by the past. It uses aspects from the past (the law) for its goal of freedom. It does not allow the law (the aid-giver) to dictate terms, but incorporates the law into the new life (8:4; 13:10).

The identity for which Paul struggles in Romans 7 subverts the negative aspects of the past through the power of the liberated present and future while using the positive aspects of the past for the goal of a free identity. Thus, Paul's exposure of the cost of forging a new identity serves as an appropriate model for redefining the past in light of God's present gift of freedom.

CHAPTER EIGHT

Paul the Ethnic Hybrid?

*Postcolonial Perspectives on
Paul's Ethnic Categorizations*

CHRISTOPHER D. STANLEY

Introduction

Whatever one thinks about the "New Perspective" on Paul, most would agree that it has performed a salutary service by directing attention to the "ethnic" dimension of Paul's thought and writings. Prior to the New Perspective, scholarly discussions of Paul's language regarding "Jews" and "Gentiles" were invariably framed in theological terms, focusing on the question of how Paul viewed the positions of these two groups (and the nascent "Christian" community) in God's plan of salvation. Both the problem and Paul's solution(s), which in the eyes of most scholars centered on "justification by faith," were defined in intellectual terms. Little was said about how Paul's rhetoric might relate to any concrete interactions between real-world "Jews" and "Gentiles" in the communities to which Paul was writing.

Under the New Perspective, by contrast, the problem of social relations between Jews and non-Jews moved to center stage as scholars began to talk about the role of ethnic boundary markers, such as circumcision and the sharing of common meals, in promoting ethnic tensions and separatism within Paul's congregations. In the process, Paul's language about "Jews" and "Gentiles" came to be viewed in more instrumental terms as a strategy for overcoming actual divisions that were hindering the unity of the socially diverse communities of Christ-followers. Despite this shift in thinking, however, the discussion of interethnic relations in Paul's churches has remained curiously abstract, as though such tensions were peculiar to the followers of Jesus (whose identity as a Jew has suddenly become more salient) rather than being endemic to Greco-Roman culture.

A related issue that has been neglected by the New Perspective is the political context of Paul's language about ethnicity. Ethnic conflict is not merely a matter of cultural difference; it also has a profoundly political dimension. Contemporary social scientists see "ethnicity" not as a fixed quality that inheres in an objectively identifiable population group, but rather as a fluid aspect of individual and group self-definition that can be highlighted or ignored as circumstances warrant.[1] Questions of social and political power play a vital role in determining when and where people are categorized in "ethnic" terms, whether by themselves or by others. In some cases the political element is subtle and relatively benign, as when people choose to identify with a group to which they claim ancestral links in order to share in the social benefits that come from that affiliation. At other times the effect is more overt and harmful, as when a ruling authority adopts a policy of categorizing people by their supposed ethnicity and then grants some groups more power than others. In view of the recent "political turn" in Pauline scholarship, one would think that this relationship between political power and ethnicity would have drawn the attention of at least some of the supporters of the New Perspective. Yet the influence of broader sociopolitical factors on interethnic relations has received little attention in their writings.[2]

To explore all of the issues that might be raised by these observations is too large a task for a single article.[3] Instead, I have chosen to focus my attention on two preliminary questions that have received relatively little attention in recent Pauline scholarship. The first concerns Paul's ethnic worldview. What kind of "mental map" did Paul use when thinking about ethnicity? How did he categorize the diverse inhabitants of the Greco-Roman world? How does his categorization schema compare with that of others in his day? A second, related question concerns Paul's ethnic self-categorization. How does Paul represent his own ethnicity in his letters? What role does ethnicity play in his identity as a Christ-follower? How does his ethnic self-presentation compare with his views of others?

In this essay I have chosen to explore these questions through the lens of postcolonial theory. Several reasons can be cited for this choice. In the first place, Paul was both a subject and—if the book of Acts is to be believed—a citizen of a multiethnic colonial empire in which interethnic relations were both complex and contested. The Roman Empire was similar enough to its modern counterparts to raise questions about whether a mode of analysis that focuses on the strategies and effects of colonial rule might improve our understanding of Paul as an ethnic minority colonial subject. Second, postcolonial theory calls attention to the close links between the broader sociocultural mechanisms of colonialism and its effects on the psyches of both dominant and subordinate parties in a colonial context. As a result, it offers a powerful theoretical tool for uncovering any possible links between Paul's social position as a colonial subject, his "mental map" of the ethnically diverse society around him, and his own ethnic self-understanding. Finally, a number of postcolonial theorists have raised critical questions about the meaning and validity of terms such as "ethnicity" and "ethnic identity," including some who assert that these categories are rooted in strategies of colonial domination and ought therefore to be discarded in favor of terms such as "hybridity" and "creolization." Whether these categories are more helpful in Paul's case than the language of ethnicity is one of the questions to be explored in this essay. The results of this admittedly limited analysis should help us to gauge both the possibilities and the limits of using postcolonial theories to analyze the letters of Paul.

Setting the Stage

The overarching goal of postcolonial studies is to identify and counteract the many and diverse ways in which the experience of imperial domination/colonial rule affects both the ruling powers and those over whom they seek to exercise control.[4] According to postcolonial theorists, the effects of colonialism extend to every area of life, from economic and political institutions to social and cultural practices to literary and artistic products to the individual psyche. Neither the colonizers nor the colonized can escape the transformative influence of their mutual but unequal relationship.

Questions of power and identity lie at the heart of postcolonial studies. According to postcolonial theorists, colonial authorities invariably construct negative images of the people whom they colonize, defining them as the barbarian "other" who must be tamed and civilized by the good graces (and military might) of the "enlightened" and "beneficent" forces of empire. The purpose of these binary constructions is not merely to salve the consciences of the colonial authorities but also to enable them to establish psychological control over the inhabitants of the colonized territory by instilling in them a negative image of their own history and identity so that they will embrace colonial rule as a natural and positive development. Control of the educational system and the public media is thus vital for the effective management of a colonized population.

In reality, things do not work out as the colonial rulers plan. Years of close contact and interaction lead to changes in the identity and culture of both the colonizers and the colonized. The effect is more obvious in the case of the colonial subjects, since they are forced to deal with the intrusive presence of an outside authority that challenges their sense of identity and disrupts their culture and institutions. Some try to hold on to their old ways, but all become "hybridized" to a greater or lesser extent. This hybridized identity is simultaneously compliant and resistant. Both of these attitudes are on display in the behavior known as "mimicry," which involves the colonized subject adopting enough of the colonizer's language and practices to get along in the colonial system while tweaking the adopted elements in a way that converts them into a subtle form of mockery.[5]

Colonial domination has especially deleterious effects on women, since they typically become victims of "double colonization" under the patriarchal gaze of both the colonial power and the men of their own culture. Relations between ethnic groups are also disrupted by the presence of colonial rule as the governing authorities seek to reinforce their control by playing one group against another or co-opting one group to serve as their agent in maintaining control over the others. Western powers usually prefer lighter-skinned natives over those with darker skins, leading to the inscription of Western forms of racism onto non-Western cultures. Similar effects can be seen on the economic side, where the capitalist preference for marketable goods invariably disrupts traditional ways of life and modes of production.

Postcolonial analysis does not end, however, with cataloguing the negative effects of imperialism and colonialism. Postcolonial critics are also concerned to reverse these negative patterns in the pursuit of a political agenda of liberation. Yet while they admire political rebels like Frantz Fanon, it is rare to find them on the front lines of revolutionary struggle. Instead, they tend to focus on exposing and changing patterns of thought and social relations that keep people in positions of domination and subjection long after the official instruments of colonial rule have been dismantled. This includes calling attention to the many ways in which Western culture (including the writings of Western academics and intellectuals) continues to perpetuate the assumptions and thought patterns of colonialism. Some have also made a serious effort to retrieve the lost or suppressed voices of colonized peoples, especially those on the bottom rungs of the social ladder, whether by telling their stories, honoring their accomplishments, or simply creating social and literary spaces where their voices can be heard. Many have joined political movements working for social change, and a few have gone as far as to participate in violent revolutions. Though they may differ over strategy, postcolonial critics agree that the gradual winding down of the formal era of Western colonization has not put an end to the influence of colonialism and imperialism in our postmodern, "postcolonial" world.

The "Hybridity" Debates

The concept of "hybridity," mentioned briefly above, has proved to be one of the most fruitful and controversial formulations of postcolonial theory over the past twenty years. The term is most frequently associated with the writings of Homi Bhabha, the Indian literary scholar who, like many postcolonial theorists from formerly colonized nations, now teaches at a major Western university (Harvard University).[6] Unfortunately, Bhabha's language is highly technical and obscure, and his ideas are presented in a series of articles published in different venues over a number of years rather than in a single location, so it is not always clear how (or if) his various statements can be combined to form a coherent whole.[7] With regard to "hybridity," however, most interpreters seem to share a broad understanding of his basic concepts.

According to Bhabha, "hybridity" is not a condition that affects some people and not others, but rather a process that occurs inevitably as part of the colonial experience. Contrary to centuries of Western colonial thought that assumed an essential difference between cultures and framed their encounter in binary terms of superiority and inferiority, Bhabha insists that both colonizers and colonized are changed (or "hybridized") through the colonial experience as each adopts aspects of the other's culture and mindset. In some instances, hybridization is stimulated by imperial policy as colonial rulers use the institutions of education and media to implant their own beliefs and values into the minds of their subjects. Hybridization also occurs from below as members of the subject population (typically the local elites) strive to internalize and embody the mores of their rulers in order to gain social acceptance and thus share in the power and benefits of colonial rule. Still other types of hybridization take place unintentionally through the natural blending of two cultures in close and consistent contact with one another.

Though Bhabha insists that all parties to the colonial arrangement live in a continual state of flux as a result of the hybridization process, he is primarily concerned with its effects on the colonized population. Central to Bhabha's formulation is the claim that hybridity opens up an "in-between space" of resistance for subject populations as it deconstructs the binary view of reality that lies at the heart of the colonizer's rationale for colonial rule.[8] Where colonial rulers strive to promote and defend a vision of "pure" cultures that would degenerate if mixed, the recognition that all cultures are in fact "hybrid" can free the minds of the colonized to envision reality in a manner not defined by their colonizers.[9] Out of this "third space" emerges both creativity and social liberation, as colonized (or formerly colonized) people recognize the value and prospects of embracing "a cultural hybridity that entertains difference without an assumed or imposed hierarchy."[10] It is through hybridity, not through the preservation of a fictitious cultural purity, that "newness enters the world."[11]

But how exactly does this happen? Bhabha is less than clear this point. He offers no concrete strategies for social change, and he largely ignores the revolutionary political program championed by one of his heroes (and one of the ideological fountainheads of the postcolonial movement), the Martiniquan psychiatrist and philosopher Frantz Fanon, even as he embraces Fanon's analysis of the colonial condition.[12] As a literary theorist, Bhabha's chief concern is to undermine the psychologically harmful (and sociologically false) colonial discourse about the status and value of colonized peoples; he has little to say about social or political questions. In addition to Fanon, whose writings show the effects of his psychiatric training, the thinkers who matter most to Bhabha are Sigmund Freud (as refracted through the psychoanalytic philosopher Jacques Lacan) and the poststructuralist philosopher Jacques Derrida. Thus, when Bhabha speaks about hybridity providing a space for resistance, he is talking primarily about changing the way people think, not transforming society. Some interpreters have argued that Bhabha believed that psychological liberation would lead to the creation of a political agenda, but if that was what he intended, he certainly could have said so more clearly.[13]

The closest that Bhabha comes to discussing how hybridity might affect social relations between colonizers and colonized is in his discussion of "mimicry." According to Bhabha, the racialized discourse of colonialism requires that colonial authorities stop short of forming their colonial subjects into mirror images of the colonizers, since to succeed in that effort would undermine the very discourse of inequality upon which colonialism is based. Instead, colonial rulers seek to create "a reformed, recognizable Other, *as a subject of difference that is almost the same, but not quite.*"[14] The result is a colonial population that "mimics" but does not fully replicate the ways of the colonizers.

But the very existence of such "mimic men" threatens the colonial discourse that led to their creation, since it shows that other modes of being are possible outside of its binary framework. It also opens up a space where the colonized can engage in forms of cultural "mimicry" that veer into subversive mockery, a way of behaving that Bhabha also calls "sly civility." As Bhabha puts it, "The display of hybridity—its peculiar 'replication' [of colonial culture]—terrorizes authority with the *ruse* of recognition, its mimicry, its mockery."[15] But what exactly Bhabha means by this is never explained. The closest that he comes is when he cites examples of natives thinking for themselves and questioning specific elements of colonial discourse.[16] Perhaps a nod toward stronger forms of resistance can be seen in Bhabha's assertion that "mimicry marks those moments of civil disobedience within the discipline of civility: signs of spectacular resistance," as well as his ensuing reference to the possibility of changing the "coercive reality" that is too often embedded in "the words of the master."[17] But even here his focus remains firmly fixed on the master's *words*, not his *deeds*.

Bhabha's discussions of "hybridity" and "mimicry" have been both praised and criticized by other postcolonial scholars. His insistence on the inevitability of hybridization in the colonial encounter and his analysis of the challenges that it presents for the binary and essentialist claims of colonial discourse have gained broad approval, though questions remain. On one side are critics who charge that his particular model of "hybridity" is self-contradictory insofar as it appears to presuppose the existence of "pure" cultures prior to the instigation of colonial rule; on the other side are those who ask whether the concept actually has any analytical validity if hybridity is in fact universal.[18] Still others have questioned whether hybridization is as inevitable as Bhabha supposes; as Floya Anthias suggests, "The acid test of hybridity might be the extent to which the dominant culture is open to elements that may challenge its hegemony."[19]

More important for our purposes is the frequent criticism that has been leveled against Bhabha's failure to engage critically with the concrete realities of social, economic, and political inequality that characterize both the colonial experience and its aftermath.[20] Feminist scholars in particular have called attention to his neglect of the "doubly colonized" status of women under male colonial domination, while others have highlighted the near absence of class and ethnicity as categories of analysis in his writings.[21] As Christian Karner has observed, hybridization does not affect everyone equally in a society that is marked by serious power imbalances: "How one experiences hybridity . . . depends significantly on one's position in [the] matrix of power."[22] The same is true for people who have migrated more or less recently into the society in question, such as immigrants and members of various diasporas. Some in these groups actively resist the effects of hybridization out of a desire to maintain allegiance to the culture of their homeland, while others experience discrimination that prevents them from engaging fully with the broader culture.[23] The presence of multiple ethnic populations within a colonized territory also complicates relations between colonizers and colonized, a point that receives virtually no theorization in Bhabha's writings.[24] Finally, questions have been raised about Bhabha's presumption that "mimicry" of colonial culture by colonized peoples invariably represents a posture of resistance.[25] Several recent ethnographic studies have shown how the residents of formerly colonized nations often choose to mimic the culture and practices of the West in ways that make them complicit in the advancement of Western neocolonialism.[26]

These and other criticisms of Bhabha's work should caution us against moving too quickly to apply Bhabha's theories of "hybridity" and "mimicry" to our study of the apostle Paul and his letters. Instead of relying on a single theorist, we should take the time to familiarize ourselves with the works of others who have addressed these questions in order to ensure that we are not forcing our data into a faulty or limited model. Models can be useful tools for making sense of data, but they can also mislead us if they are absolutized or improperly used.

Paul and Postcolonial Studies

So how might this somewhat simplified analysis of the hybridized state of contemporary postcolonial citizens contribute to our understanding of the life and letters of the first-century diasporic Jewish Christ-follower whom we know by the Roman name of Paul(us)? The answer to this question is less clear than many Pauline scholars might wish. Behind it lie two distinct but related concerns, one broad and the other more focused.

The broader question concerns the appropriateness of applying the insights of postcolonial studies to the ancient world. Some postcolonial theorists have taken a narrow view of this question, insisting that postcolonial theory cannot be separated from its particular setting within the history and institutions of Western colonialism nor from the contemporary social and political contexts in which formerly colonized peoples now find themselves, a world marked by increasing globalization, the dominance of capitalist economic models and practices, and various forms of cultural and political neocolonialism. Others have voiced suspicion of any application of postcolonial studies that limits itself to description, as a purely historical account would tend to do, while avoiding any immediate involvement with the political implications of postcolonial theory, which aims to destabilize and ultimately reverse many of the dominant social, economic, and political paradigms of modern Western society.

These are weighty concerns, and scholars of antiquity would do well to heed them. At a minimum, they caution us against succumbing too quickly to a kind of eclectic methodological parallelomania that simply assumes that all colonial contexts are alike and then "applies" the insights of postcolonial theory to the ancient world while ignoring the social and ideological frameworks of those ideas and the real people whose subaltern experience gave rise to them. From a postcolonial standpoint, this kind of careless appropriation of postcolonialism sounds dangerously like an intellectualized extension of the historic Western pattern of white males abusing their colonial subjects and denigrating their cultures.

On the other hand, there is nothing wrong with asking if there might be cross-cultural parallels between colonial situations in different historical periods that could enhance our understanding of the world in which Paul and his converts lived and thought. Since postcolonial thinkers have devoted substantial energy to investigating the psychological and social effects of modern Western colonialism on native peoples, it makes sense to place their insights alongside those of anthropologists, sociologists, and others who have studied issues of social inequality in an effort to discern whether there might be any broad similarities among colonial societies at various times and places.[27] To the extent that such patterns can be identified, they can serve as heuristic tools to help us raise questions about texts or events from the past and to organize and interpret the data that emerge from those questions.[28] Such an approach does not require any judgments about the relative equivalency of various colonial situations; it entails nothing more than the kind of open-ended comparative analysis that social scientists perform on a daily basis. A heuristic mind-set can also ward off any temptations to absolutize or essentialize the insights of postcolonial scholars, whose ideas should be regarded as models to be tested against the data and either accepted or rejected on that basis. This at any rate is the approach that will be followed in the analysis of Paul's letters below.

The second question that must be addressed concerning the relevance of postcolonial theory to Paul's letters is more subtle. Even if we accept that postcolonial studies might have a heuristic value for the study of ancient societies, where should we situate Paul and his letters within the conflicted world of postcolonial discourse? If postcolonial scholars are divided over the meaning and implications of such a vital concept as "hybridity," how do those of us who labor in other fields determine which scholars and theories to trust? Once again we must avoid the pragmatic temptation to choose theories that support our particular enterprise or agenda and ignore competing ideas. Biblical scholars are rightly upset when self-aggrandizing amateurs make claims about the Bible or the ancient world based on a limited understanding of one side in a heated scholarly debate. Postcolonial scholars feel the same way when scholars in other fields draw equally simplistic conclusions based on their work. If we wish to investigate the potential relevance of postcolonial studies for a particular historical question, there is no substitute for reading the works of postcolonial scholars who hold differing views on the subject. Only in this way can we gain the breadth of knowledge and the heuristic skills that we need to make reasoned judgments about the validity of various possible applications of postcolonial theory while also doing justice to the integrity of the postcolonial debates.

Paul's Ethnic Worldview

With these points in mind, we will now investigate whether the postcolonial concepts of "hybridity" and "mimicry" can be fruitfully and responsibly deployed to improve our analysis of the apostle Paul's use of ethnic categories. On first glance, such an approach seems promising, since (a) Paul was a subaltern subject of a multiethnic colonial empire; (b) Paul's preoccupation with questions of identity fits what many postcolonial theorists would expect from a man in his situation; and (c) Paul appears to engage in the kind of verbal and ideological destabilization of essentializing constructions of ethnicity that many theorists would credit to a postcolonial mind-set. But do the data fit the theory?

From a contemporary social-scientific standpoint, the world in which Paul and his fellow Christ-followers lived and operated was ethnically diverse.[29] Nearly every city that Paul visited would have included at least four broad classes of inhabitants: (a) the native population, which would have been significantly hellenized by this time; (b) the "Greeks" (*Hellēnes*), a term that included both the lineal descendants of earlier Greek and Seleucid settlers and the hellenized families of the local elites; (c) the Romans, whose numbers would have been small except in Roman colonies like Philippi and Corinth; and (d) immigrants from other lands, whether long-term or temporary residents, representing a variety of ethnic communities from across the Mediterranean world.[30] The identity of the native population would have varied from region to region, but they would have been the majority in most areas.[31] The "Greek" element would have been more visible in some communities than others, reflecting the uneven hellenization of the Roman Empire, while certain towns and cities would have attracted more immigrants and foreign guests than others, due in part to the variability of business opportunities. The nature and extent of the Roman presence likewise varied from place to place, ranging from permanent residents to occasional visitors.[32] But these local variations do not undermine the essential fact that natives, Greeks, Romans, and people from other lands, including those designated as *Ioudaioi* because of their ancestral ties to Judea,[33] would have lived and worked together on a daily basis in virtually all of the towns and cities in which the apostle Paul carried out his missionary activities. The only significant exception was the cities of Greece, where the bulk of the native population consisted of *Hellēnes*, or "Greeks."[34]

When we turn to Paul's letters, however, the ethnic diversity of the Greco-Roman world is largely obscured. Though he varies his terms from passage to passage, Paul consistently uses binary terms when referring to ethnic differences.[35] For him, the world is divided into *Ioudaioi* and non-*Ioudaioi*, as can be seen in the following summary of Paul's ethnic terminology.

Terms Referring to Ioudaioi

Ioudaioi ("Jews" or "Judeans") and cognates	27 times
Israel	14 times
the circumcision	6 times
my kinsmen	2 times
unbelievers in Judea	1 time

Terms Referring to Non-Ioudaioi

ethnē ("Gentiles" or "nations") and cognates	45 times
Hellēnes ("Greeks")	12 times
unbelievers	12 times
the uncircumcision	7 times
barbarians	2 times
the lawless	1 time

Even when Paul uses the term *Hellēnes*—a title that any audience member would have recognized as an ethnic self-designation of a particular group of people—he invariably couples it with *Ioudaioi* to form a binary pair. The only exceptions to this pattern are Gal 3:1, where *Galatai* appears to retain its ethnic sense, and 2 Cor 9:4, where *Makedones* ("Macedonians") could be taken in a similar way.[36] (The mention of *Skythēs*/"Scythian" in Col 3:11 could be added to the list if we accept Colossians as Pauline.) Other groups, even *Romanoi*, are absent from the ethnic world of Paul's letters.

If asked to explain the narrow range of Paul's ethnic language, most scholars would probably attribute this pattern to the influence of Paul's Jewish heritage. Anyone who knows ancient Jewish texts could cite passages where the in-group is given an ethnic title (*Ioudaioi*) while outsiders are lumped together under a generic designation (often but not always *ethnē*). Closer inspection, however, reveals a number of problems with this explanation.

In the first place, it is not at all clear that Paul conceived of "the nations" in monolithic terms. Eleven times in his letters he sets up a contrast between the ethnic terms *Hellēn/Hellēnes* ("Greeks") and *Ioudaios/Ioudaioi* ("Judeans" or "Jews"), and in one text he evokes the standard Greek contrast between *Hellēnes* and *barbaroi* (Rom 1:14; cf. 1 Cor 14:11, Col 3:11). This latter verse poses problems for the common scholarly practice of interpreting "Greeks" in all of these texts as a synonym for *ethnē*.[37] Paul's passing references to "Galatians," "Macedonians," and possibly "Scythians" also suggest that he was aware of ethnic diversity among "the nations."[38]

Second, it is simply untrue that Jews in Paul's day routinely divided humanity into two camps without remainder. Philip Esler lists over forty people-groups to which Josephus refers in his treatise *Against Apion*,[39] and both Josephus and Philo describe social conflicts that pitted people whom they label as "Egyptians" or "Syrians" against *Ioudaioi* and/or *Hellēnes*.[40] Both also make repeated use of the standard Greek division of the world into *Hellēnes* and *barbaroi*.[41] Paul's ethnic terminology seems remarkably restrained when compared with these Jewish near-contemporaries.

Third, Paul's ethnic language is too varied and creative to support the assertion that he unreflectively adopted the worldview and terminology of his Jewish peers. Even when he speaks in binary terms, he regularly varies the expressions that he uses to identify the two parties, as can be seen in the list below.

Ioudaioi/Hellēnes: Rom 1:16; 2:9-10; 3:9; 10:12; 1 Cor 1:22, 24; 12:13; Gal 3:28
Ioudaioi/ethnē: Rom 3:29; 9:24; 11:14; 1 Cor 1:23; Gal 2:12-14; 1 Thess 1:14-16
Israel/*ethnē*: Rom 9:30-31; 11:11-25
circumcision/uncircumcision: Rom 2:26-27; 3:30; 4:11-12; 1 Cor 7:18
circumcision/*ethnē*: Rom 15:8-9; Gal 2:8-9
those under law/the lawless: 1 Cor 9:20-21
Hellēnes/barbaroi: Rom 1:14
saints (that is, Christ-followers)/*ethnē*: Rom 15:27; 1 Cor 5:1 (cf. 1 Thess 4:5)

Thus, it appears that Paul's handling of ethnic categories is more complex and situational than our initial analysis might have suggested. His preference for binary modes of categorization is real, but so is the dexterity with which he applies those categories to concrete situations. The same can be said, surprisingly, for Paul's ethnic self-designations. If there is one point on which nearly all Pauline scholars today would agree, it is that Paul was a devout Jew who remained (in his own mind at least) a Jew throughout his life—that is, he did not "convert" to a new religion called "Christianity." The fact that Paul took a rather flexible attitude toward obeying the laws of Torah (1 Cor 9:20-23) and challenged the hereditary place of *Ioudaioi* as the people of God is not usually seen as a problem for this position, since he still makes a consistent effort to ground his thinking in the Scriptures and traditions of Israel. A similar explanation is offered for Paul's occasional appropriations of Greek thought and practice: such references do not undermine his "Jewishness," since similar language can be found in the writings of other Jews of his day.

Certainly it is true that Paul normally positions himself as a (hellenized) Jew when crafting his letters. But there are also many passages in which Paul depicts himself (whether directly or indirectly) in terms that are more consistent with a non-Jewish ("Gentile") identity.[42] The evidence can be summarized under three broad headings.

1. Here and there in Paul's letters we find verses in which he criticizes *Ioudaioi* as though he were an outsider pronouncing judgment on the group as a whole (Rom 2:17-24; 9:30-33; 10:1-3; 1 Thess 2:14-15). The most famous of these texts is Rom 2:17-29, where Paul attacks a hypocritical *Ioudaios* in language that echoes many of the negative images of *Ioudaioi* that were prevalent in Greco-Roman culture. The effect is enhanced by placing in the mouth of the *Ioudaios* a series of claims that mimic a stereotypical Jewish attitude of superiority toward non-Jews. Had the same passage been found in a Greek or Roman author, we would not hesitate to characterize it as a one-sided and prejudicial attack on *Ioudaioi* and their religion by a non-Jewish author.

The same point can be made about 1 Thess 2:14-15, where Paul speaks in darkly negative tones about "the *Ioudaioi* who killed both the Lord Jesus and the prophets, and persecuted us, and are displeasing to God and hostile to everyone," who in this way "fill up the measure of their sins" and now stand under God's wrath. A reader who did not know the author of these words would probably conclude that they were penned by a non-*Ioudaios* who held prejudicial views of *Ioudaioi*.⁴³ In particular, Paul's language about *Ioudaioi* being "hostile to everyone" recalls one of the standard accusations voiced by Greek and Roman authors who could not understand why many *Ioudaioi* would not participate in the normal social life of their communities.⁴⁴ Few ancient readers would have guessed that such a text could be penned by a *Ioudaios*.

2. A second type of passage in which Paul comes across as a "Gentile" can be seen in places where he applies to himself language that he uses elsewhere for non-*Ioudaioi*. Many examples can be cited from his letters. In Rom 5:6-8, for example, Paul presents himself as part of a group ("we") whom he describes as having once been "ungodly" and "sinners." The first term recalls his opening salvo in Rom 1:18 against the "ungodliness and wickedness of those who by their wickedness suppress the truth" and turn to idolatry (that is, "Gentiles"), while the second term ("sinners") is ubiquitous in Jewish descriptions of non-*Ioudaioi*. Similar language can be seen in Romans 7, where Paul uses first-person speech to narrate the experience of an individual whom he describes as ruled by "sinful passions" (v. 5) and "sold under sin" (v. 14) and therefore unable to live up to God's righteous requirements. While most scholars have taken this chapter as referring in some way to the experience of a *Ioudaios* (whether Paul or a hypothetical person), the reference to "sinful passions" echoes his description of the idolatrous "Gentiles" in Rom 1:26, and his language about being "sold under sin" recalls his characterization of the "Gentile" Romans in Rom 6:20-21. An astute member of the audience might well conclude that Paul is at least hypothetically presenting himself in the guise of a "Gentile" in this text.

Other places where Paul temporarily adopts a "Gentile" persona include Rom 13:11-14, where he calls on "us" to "lay aside the deeds of darkness" and avoid various forms of behavior that *Ioudaioi* typically associated with non-*Ioudaioi* (such as carousing, drunkenness, and sexual immorality); 1 Cor 10:6-10, where he speaks of "us" being warned by Scripture to avoid behaviors that no *Ioudaios* would seriously contemplate (idolatry and sexual immorality); 1 Cor 10:22, where he asks whether "we" are trying to provoke God's jealousy by engaging in idolatry; and Gal 4:3, where he classes himself among those who were once "enslaved by the *stoicheia tou kosmou*." In all of these cases the reference is jarring enough to be evident to an astute listener.

3. A third type of passage in which Paul's language could be taken as that of a non-*Ioudaios* involves texts where he describes *Ioudaioi* in third-person terms (using the pronouns "they" and "them) as though he is speaking as an outsider. This is especially evident in places where his language seems to undercut some of the traditional ideas of Judaism. Examples abound. In Rom 2:5-16, 25-29, Paul speaks of God's attitude toward *Ioudaioi* and *ethnē* in a way that consistently paints the *ethnē* in a more positive light than the *Ioudaioi*. He ends with a statement that undercuts the value of circumcision as a marker of the people of God: "A person is not a Jew who is one outwardly, nor is true circumcision something external and physical" (v. 28). Similar language can be found in Gal 5:6, where Paul asserts that "in Christ Jesus neither

circumcision nor uncircumcision counts for anything" (cf. 1 Cor 7:19), and Phil 3:3, where he insists that "it is we [Christ-followers] who are the circumcision," and not "those who mutilate the flesh [referring to either *Ioudaioi* or Judaizers]." Paul's negative attitude toward the physical act of circumcision in these texts recalls similar criticisms by Greek and Roman authors against this (to them) odd and disgraceful practice.[45]

Equally relevant are the many passages in which Paul seems to suggest that the *ethnē* now have a higher status with God than the *Ioudaioi*. In Rom 9:30-32, for example, Paul claims that the *ethnē* have obtained righteousness while "Israel" has not (cf. 11:7). In 2 Cor 3:14-18, he asserts that "the sons of Israel" are incapable of understanding the meaning of their own sacred Scriptures, a meaning that is available only to a person "who turns to the Lord" [that is, Jesus]. And in the allegory of Gal 4:21-31, Paul turns the biblical story of Sarah and Hagar on its head in an effort to depict a radical disjunction between "us" (Paul and the Galatian Christ-followers, vv. 26, 31), whom he describes as the "free" beneficiaries of God's covenant with Abraham, and the "enslaved" children of Jerusalem (apparently the *Ioudaioi*), who are to be "cast out" of their father's inheritance. Here and elsewhere Paul comes quite close to the kind of supersessionist language that would be used later by "Gentile" Christians to displace the Jews as the people of God.

In short, a careful investigation of Paul's ethnic self-representations reveals a more complex picture than scholars have generally supposed. This is exactly what we found in our earlier examination of Paul's "mental map" of human diversity. But what do these observations tell us about the way Paul conceptualized ethnic difference? Is there anything from our earlier discussions of "hybridity" and "mimicry" that might help to shed light on Paul's language?

Postcolonial Musings

If there is any validity at all in applying Homi Bhabha's analysis of modern colonialism to the ancient world, then we must think of Paul as a "hybridized" subject of the Roman Empire, since according to Bhabha the process of hybridization unavoidably affects everyone involved in the colonial enterprise. Such a conclusion might seem banal, but it is not without significance. Robert Seesengood draws out the implications of this observation for Paul and his world.

> Hybrids disrupt notions of any isolated, discrete cultural (or sub-cultural) identities within the Roman Empire. There were no "pure" Romans or Greeks or Jews. Further, a single, systemic taxonomy of cultural tropes portraying any of a host of potentially describable cultural streams (religious groups, philosophical schools, ethnicities, etc.) converging into a single, "Hellenized," whole is impossible. We can not say any particular impulse, idea or theme in Paul's writings arises, un-modified, un-hybridised, from Paul's "Jewishness," his "Hellenism," or his status as a Roman citizen.[46]

These comments suggest that we should not be surprised at the flexible language of Paul's ethnic self-designations or his failure to adhere to a consistent pattern of terminology when speaking about ethnic differences. Nor is there any reason for us to search for some uniquely "Christian" explanation for Paul's linguistic practice. Bhabha's theory suggests that Paul was probably quite ordinary in this respect. It is certainly possible that there were others in Paul's day who were more consistent in their language than Paul was, but our default expectation should be diversity, not uniformity.

But can we go further than this? Does Paul's use of ethnic categories lend support to Daniel Boyarin's claim that "Jewish" and "Greek" patterns of thought are so closely intertwined in Paul's mind that they form a seamless whole—"the very organic mode of his thinking"—so that for Paul, "Jewgreek is Greekjew"?[47] Here we must be careful to avoid the common methodological error of overlooking the rhetorical dimension of Paul's letters. Despite their intensely personal tone, Paul's letters do not give us unmediated access to his psyche. He says what he believes is needed to achieve his rhetorical ends, a task that could entail hiding as well as revealing his underlying thoughts and motives. Ancient rhetorical practice involved not only rational argumentation but also various techniques for manipulating an audience to identify with and feel sympathy toward a speaker and his views. As a *Ioudaios* writing to audiences made up primarily of non-*Ioudaioi* who would have been exposed to negative views of *Ioudaioi* at various points during their lives, Paul had to work hard to negate or overcome any prejudicial opinions that audience members might have held toward him as a result of his ethnic status.[48] As a Christ-follower, he also believed that God had done something new through Jesus that had altered the status and relations of *Ioudaioi* and non-*Ioudaioi*. As an apostle of Christ, he was convinced that he had a special role to play in God's plan to bring *Ioudaioi* and non-*Ioudaioi* together in a new social entity that he referred to as the *ekklēsia* of God. To think that we can discern which of these motives is at work in a given passage and then decide which of his statements should be dismissed as a momentary rhetorical strategy and which represent his underlying view of reality is a fool's errand. The "real Paul" has veiled himself too carefully to allow this.

Yet this does not mean that we can say nothing. With regard to the issues before us, Paul's use of binary categories when speaking about ethnic difference is so pronounced and consistent across his letters, continuing even as he varies the actual terms that he employs to describe the different groups, that we can be reasonably confident that this pattern of speech reflects his standard way of interpreting human diversity, the mental template that guided his thinking about ethnic issues. When we ask how he understood his own ethnic identity, on the other hand, we must cast our net more broadly, since Paul's language is less consistent here. As we noted earlier, Paul's thinking is deeply rooted in the Scriptures and traditions of Israel. This is evident not only from his many explicit references to the Jewish Scriptures but also from the nearly unconscious way in which he appropriates biblical ideas and language as a framework for understanding and communicating the significance of the Christ-event and its implications for Christian conduct, even when writing to people from non-Jewish backgrounds. The importance of this observation becomes apparent when we compare Paul with Philo, who refers frequently to the writings of Greek philosophers and engages regularly with their ideas. Bhabha's model of hybridization is clearly applicable in his case; for Philo, Greek and Jewish texts and traditions have merged to form a single "symbolic universe" that frames his thought. In Paul's letters, by contrast, explicit references to non-Jewish thinkers are virtually absent, even when he is writing to the non-Jewish residents of Greek and Roman cities. This suggests that Paul's thought-world remained tethered to a more traditional interpretation of Judaism.[49]

What then do we do with those texts where Paul seems to present himself in the guise of a non-*Ioudaios*? Space does not allow for a careful examination of these texts, but a strong case can be made in every instance that Paul's choice of words has been influenced by his rhetorical or theological interests.[50] In Rom 2:17-29 and 1 Thess 2:14-15, Paul is arguably playing on the anti-Jewish prejudices of a typical Greco-Roman audience in order to elicit their support for his arguments. In the many texts where he speaks of himself in language that he elsewhere reserves for non-*Ioudaioi*, he is momentarily identifying with his audience in order to create a sense of solidarity that he hopes will enhance their receptiveness to his message. In those passages where he speaks of *Ioudaioi* in the third person as though he were not one himself, or where he cites the failure of the *Ioudaioi* to recognize and embrace the revelation of God through Jesus, he is either polemicizing against "Judaizers" in an effort to persuade his audiences to reject their teaching or trying to convince them to adopt a new way of thinking—a "Christian" theological perspective—in which all forms of ethnic identity are subordinated to a new identity "in Christ."[51] In none of these cases is Paul's adoption of a non-*Ioudaios* persona more than a temporary strategic device. It would thus be wrong to use these statements as evidence for the presence of a truly "hybrid" mind-set as posited by Homi Bhabha.

Another problem with applying Bhabha's "hybridity" model to Paul concerns his rigid adherence to binary categories when speaking about ethnicity. One of the chief benefits of the hybridization process, according to Bhabha, is its ability to break down binary thought patterns that rank humans according to ethnicity. In Paul's letters we see precisely the opposite. This is strange in view of the looseness with which he treats other aspects of ethnic identity, as when he tries to undermine the value of circumcision as an identity marker for *Ioudaioi* while at the same time loosening the boundaries of the *Ioudaioi* so that it can include members of the *ethnē*. Why should he still hold onto a binary mode of thinking in this case? Perhaps this should be viewed as an example of the "dark side" of colonial mimicry that has been cited by some of Bhabha's critics but neglected in Bhabha's own formulation of the concept. As we saw earlier, mimicry involves a substantial (though not complete) internalization of the worldview and values of the colonial rulers. In theory this should not extend to the colonizer's negative thought patterns toward the subject population, but in practice such attitudes are often so pervasive that they exert an almost irresistible influence on the minds of the colonized. In Paul's case, however, it is unlikely that he derived his binary view of human differences from contact with the immediate colonial rulers (the Romans), not only because their direct presence was fairly diffuse throughout the empire but also

Paul the Ethnic Hybrid? 125

because the Romans were more aware of human diversity than many other peoples of antiquity. While Roman authors do sometimes refer to non-Romans as *barbaroi*, the practice was by no means universal, and the use of such terminology was more often associated with perceived cultural deficiencies (as with the "barbarian hordes" of Europe) than with ethnic difference per se. In fact, some Roman authors betray a degree of anxiety about their own status in relation to other peoples, especially the Greeks and Egyptians, whose ancient cultures they admired even while they disparaged the contemporary holders of those revered names.[52] The special legal rights that *Ioudaioi* enjoyed from Roman officials in many parts of the empire were also rooted at least partly in a genuine respect for the antiquity of their culture, the sublimity of their ideas, and the uprightness of their morals. In short, binary thinking about ethnicity was not typical of the Roman colonial authorities. Binary thought patterns were well established, however, in the ideology and rhetoric of the prior colonial rulers, the Greeks. From at least the fifth century B.C.E., when the residents of *Hellas* were forced to rally together against the threat of Persian invasion, the idea of a sharp distinction between *Hellēnes* ("Greeks") and *barbaroi* ("barbarians") was a vital element of "Greek" ethnic identity.[53] Even after the cities of the Hellenistic Diaspora opened the door for members of the native elites to cross the ethnic boundary and become "Greeks," the traditional bifurcation of humanity into "Greeks" and "barbarians" remained dominant in Greek culture.[54] Similar patterns prevailed among the people known as *Ioudaioi*. In their sacred Scriptures, texts that recognized a variety of ethnic and political entities coexisted uneasily with verses that drew a sharp distinction between "Israel" and "the nations." The latter view grew steadily in influence through centuries of foreign rule in both the homeland and the Diaspora. The fact that Diaspora *Ioudaioi* were viewed negatively by many of the non-*Ioudaioi* among whom they lived further strengthened this tendency to draw a sharp binary line between themselves and people outside the group.

Thus, it seems likely that Paul, as a *Ioudaios* growing up in a Greek city, would have been trained from infancy to interpret human diversity through a binary lens. With such pervasive and consistent societal influences, he could hardly have adopted any other view. Nor would it have been easy for him to shift into a more nuanced and universalist vision of human difference, even when his own theological principles seemed to demand it. In fact, binary thinking was probably so natural to him that the idea of rejecting it never crossed his mind.[55]

Whether this should be labeled as an example of colonial "mimicry" is less clear. The fact that the influence came simultaneously from the colonial power (of Greece, not Rome) and his own ethnic community is not an argument against such a view, since a successful "top-down" expression of mimicry ought to result in the colonial subjects not only absorbing but also replicating (in full or in part) the values of their colonial rulers. But binary thinking among *Ioudaioi* seems to have predated the coming of the Greeks (cf. the many references in their Scriptures), so at best their interaction with Greek ideology would have only reinforced a pattern that was already present. Thus it seems that in this case, as in our earlier discussion of Paul and "hybridity," Bhabha's theories are less than helpful as heuristic tools for explaining Paul's use of ethnic language.

Conclusion

This relatively negative judgment about the relevance of Bhabha's theories should not discourage us from using other modes of postcolonial analysis to interpret the letters of Paul. As we saw earlier, other postcolonial theorists have offered similar criticisms of Bhabha's views, and some of them have offered their own versions of hybridity theory that might prove more useful than Bhabha's model for analyzing the data described in this essay.[56] Yet this study also shows the importance of maintaining a critical attitude toward the theories and models that we derive from postcolonial studies. Like most of the other methods and approaches that have been applied over the years to the letters of Paul, postcolonial theory offers many valuable insights that can help us better to understand Paul and his world. But it is not a magical key that opens every door. We must therefore be judicious in the way we use postcolonial theory and resist the colonial impulse to wrestle it into subjection to Western critical models. Postcolonial criticism, if it is to remain true to its origins, must always sit uneasily with the dominant discourses of Western culture, including those of contemporary biblical criticism.

CHAPTER NINE

Redressing Bodies at Corinth

Racial/Ethnic Politics and Religious Difference in the Context of Empire

TAT-SIONG BENNY LIEW

With the growing reliance on science in the early twentieth century came a political ideology representing the nation of the United States as a body threatened by infection. During this time, in the words of David Palumbo-Liu, "[a] particular discursive formation evolved that blended science with politics, economics with sociology, national and international interests, within which the nation was imagined as a body that must, through fastidious hygienic measures, guard against what passes from the exterior, excise the cancerous cells that have already penetrated it, and prevent any reproductive act that would compromise the regeneration of its species in an increasingly massified and mobile world."[1] Since the "science" that Palumbo-Liu is referring to includes eugenics, this ideology clearly involves not only the national body but also physical bodies of people who populate the world. As a "medium of culture," a human, physical body is often the site on and through which various cultural and ideological forces compete for inscription and promulgation.[2] By virtue of various factors such as race, ethnicity, sexuality, gender, and religion, bodies are also marked, ranked, normalized, and/or pathologized. Deemed to be as undesirable and harmful as viruses or parasites, certain human bodies must be eradicated out of existence or at least erased out of sight and out of mind if the national body is to remain healthy.

One of the groups that this ideology aims to exclude from the national body—both literally and symbolically—has been Asian-raced bodies. Racialized to be "foreign," "immigrant," "feminine," and/or "sexually deviant,"[3] Asian bodies are also often linked with being religiously different or deficient. Two recent books—one on Cambodian Americans[4] and the other on Korean Americans[5] respectively—have pointed to the challenging dynamics faced by Asian American Buddhists for being a racial/ethnic as well as a religious minority simultaneously.[6]

My point is not to imply that all Asian Americans share the status of being a religious minority. Neither is it my intention to suggest that racial/ethnic differences can be transcended through a shared religion, minority or otherwise. Instead, I have a threefold purpose. First, I want to argue that undesirable bodies often also become disembodied and/or undetectable despite becoming simultaneously marked.[7] Bodies abjected by dominant cultures have a way of becoming insignificant and invisible in general societal discourse and in scholarship in particular, whether American or biblical.[8] Since bodily abjection often involves projections of racial/ethnic "others" in stereotypes, Roland Barthes' description of stereotypes as "emplacement[s] of discourse *where the body is missing*, where one is sure [that] the body is not,"[9] should give us much food for thought. Second, I want to focus on the importance of interstices, particularly the intersection between body politics and imperial politics, and the connections between race/ethnicity and religion for those living in diaspora. Third, I want to show how experiences of Asian Americans may help inform a different reading of difference in 1 Corinthians.[10]

Embodying Corinthian Rhetoric and Politics

Scholars have long suggested that Paul wrote 1 Corinthians to build up the church body in Corinth because its unity or harmony had been torn up by differences that existed within and/or without. These differences were first understood to be mainly doctrinal or theological.[11] Now scholarly trends have for the most part shifted to incorporate a material difference, particularly in terms of class or status.[12] I do not need to renew the dated debate about theological ideas or sociomaterial conditions, as if the two are mutually exclusive. Dale B. Martin's book on Corinthians helpfully points to the "more serviceable concept" of ideology,[13] since ideology—especially in its Althusserian and Gramscian versions—is an interpretive activity that informs and invents one's existence, inclusive of both thought and practice. I do need to point out, however, that Martin's thesis—namely, that the differences between Paul and (some of) the Corinthians may boil down to their different social status positions, and the corresponding assumptions about the human body—can use greater specificity and further embodiment.[14]

What Martin seems to have overlooked is the fact or factor that Paul and the Corinthians have different racialized/ethnicized bodies, though he does make a brief mention of racial/ethnic differences to illustrate the Greco-Roman hierarchies of individual and social bodies.[15] The same is true of those who attribute the division of the church body at Corinth to class or status difference. If one should prefer the term "status" to "class" because of the latter's modern lineage and its overdetermined association with material wealth,[16] then one should be even more mindful of what race/ethnicity meant to the sociopolitical hierarchization of the Greco-Roman world. Ramsey MacMullen, for example, lists four factors in the Roman status equation: time, money, place, and culture.[17] Although MacMullen does not employ the term "race" or "ethnicity," one can see its traces in Plutarch's decision to use a foreigner to illustrate someone who does not quite know his place (*Mor.* 615D [*Quaest. Conv.* 1.2]), or in MacMullen's own statement that Roman urban elites "opposed not only *rusticitas* but *peregrinitas* [foreign manners]."[18] In other words, one's distance from Rome may be more than just a geographical measurement (what MacMullen calls "place"); it may also involve a racial/ethnic differentiation (my conflation of MacMullen's "place" and "culture").[19] As a colonized people, Jews of the first century were at best clients, and at worst abjects of their colonial masters, as evidenced by what Peter Schäfer calls "Judeophobia" in the ancient world, or Benjamin Isaac's chapter on attitudes against Jews in his recent work on "racism" in classical antiquity.[20] Significantly, the Corinthians were not just any Gentiles or non-Jews. According to most Corinthians scholars, the population of Corinth was mostly made up of Greeks and perhaps some Romans.[21] The Corinthians might not have originated from noble or aristocratic families, but in terms of race/ethnicity, they still belonged to the peoples who succeeded each other in colonizing the Jews of Paul's time.

It is therefore surprising that scholars who talk about the status differences among the Corinthians have failed to mention the status difference—particularly the racial/ethnic difference—between Paul and the Corinthians.[22] It is equally surprising that, for all the talk about the prominence of body in 1 Corinthians (even those who dwell on theological difference refer to the letter's theologies of the church body and the resurrected body), the body of knowledge that has been generated by scholars of 1 Corinthians has paid very little attention to any knowledge about the physical body, particularly the racial/ethnic difference that is written on the human body. This phenomenon has, of course, much to do with the Europeanization of Paul in particular and the politics of racialization and negation in biblical scholarship in general,[23] but the dematerialization of Paul's *Jewish* body is especially ironic given Howard Eilberg-Schwartz's description of Jews as "people of the body."[24] Viewed from the perspectives of contemporary Asian Americans, the power dynamics between Paul and the Corinthians are intriguing enough to warrant investigation and interpretation, since the one who founded, fathered, and now hopes to counsel the mainly Gentile Corinthian church happens to be a Jewish "no-body" (that is, one who is insignificant, invisible, and hence disembodied because his racial/ethnic or bodily inscriptions have been made stereotypical by the dominant culture). This difference becomes even more acute if one pays attention to the status inconsistency facing the Corinthians. While most scholars talk about this in terms of economics, I would like to—again, from the perspectives of contemporary Asian Americans—highlight the importance of religious difference. As Mark D. Nanos insightfully proposes in his work on Galatians, it was not a simple thing for first-century Gentiles to follow the tiny Jewish sect under the name of Jesus Christ.[25] To do so was to leave the religious majority and become part of a religious minority. Their religious difference, in other words, might bring about a status reduction if not inversion.[26] Studies of both Korean American Buddhists and Korean American Christians have shown that people experiencing a status inversion in the larger sociopolitical world—particularly men who find themselves marginalized by their immigrant status and racial/ethnic difference, notwithstanding their being part of a religious majority or minority—become even more anxious about and aggressive in competing for status in a smaller religious setting.[27] According to Young In Song:

> [T]he internal conflicts which lead to schisms [in many Korean American churches] are directly correlated with the heterogeneity of characteristics of the congregation, *status alienation of the immigrants*, and the vested interests of Korean clergymen and lay leaders.... Competition for lay leadership positions among Korean men usually evolves into fierce struggle among candidates which frequently accompanies f[r]ictional exaggerated strife within the congregation.[28]

What I would like to suggest is that the status inversion suffered by the Corinthians because of their conversion might not only help to explain their well-acknowledged status anxiety but also give reasons for Paul's problems with them, or their problems with Paul.[29] Their conversion, and hence their status inversion and anxiety, caused them to become even more sensitive and hostile to Paul because of Paul's stigmatized racial/ethnic body as a colonized Jew. This is especially important since in Paul's time race/ethnicity and religion were "constitutively interrelated" even if they should not be collapsed into being one and the same.[30] Going back to MacMullen's Roman status equation, Cicero, for example, singles out religion and cultic/religious practices as *the* "national characteristic" in which Rome is "superior" to "foreign peoples" (*Nat. d.* 2.3.8). If Greco-Roman abjection of Jews has much to do with Jewish religion, hostility against Jews will only intensify in view of what is perceived to be "successful" Jewish proselytism.[31] After all, Roman writers consistently link the two "expulsions" of Jews from Rome (139 B.C.E. and 19 C.E. respectively) to the threat of proselytism, albeit in different degrees (Valerius Maximus 1.3.3; Tacitus, *Ann.* 2.85; and Suetonius, *Tib.* 36). Tacitus, in addition, sees proselytes as "the worst rascals among other [non-Jewish] peoples" (*Hist.* 5.5), and Domitian will lead a "witch-hunt" targeting both Jews and Jewish proselytes to pay the two *drachmae* of *fiscus Iudaicus* (Suetonius, *Dom.* 12.1-2).[32] In Greco-Roman eyes, the Corinthians' conversion through Paul is likely to be understood as a case of partial if not (yet) full Jewish proselytism, and thus be a cause of anxiety for the Corinthians. This is evident in Juvenal's narration of the proselytizing progression from Sabbath observance to circumcision, as well as Juvenal's conclusion that proselytes "have been wont to flout the laws of Rome" (14.96-104). In contrast to Nanos's reading that the Galatians are anxious to become full proselytes through circumcision, I propose that the Corinthians are becoming anxious to distance themselves from Paul. In other words, I am suggesting that these Gentile Christ-followers are beginning to try to separate religious affiliation from racial/ethnic filiation. Paul makes it clear, however, that he will not accept such a separation.[33]

Paul's Rejected Body

Both feminist hermeneutics and ideological criticism have taught us that what is assumed is as important as, or perhaps even more important than, what is said, since what is said needs to be read in the context of the unsaid. What Paul does say in his letter has already led many to propose that Paul's status might be shaky in the eyes of the Corinthians.[34] His decision to preach the gospel "without charge" (9:18), for example, seems controversial enough to warrant an elaborate exposition or explanation (9:1-18). While many have read this as solely Paul's illustration, or even a self-modeling of what he is trying to teach the Corinthians (namely, to be willing to give up one's rights for the sake of others, 8:1-13; 9:19-23; 10:23-11:1), it is nevertheless important to keep in mind how Paul himself characterizes this drawn-out account. He calls it his "apology" or "defense" (9:3).[35]

Perhaps the icy relationship between Paul and the Corinthians is better seen in an earlier part of the letter. Despite his rhetoric that he considers it "a very small thing" to be judged by the Corinthians or any other human being (4:3), Paul immediately goes on to instruct the Corinthians that they should not judge prematurely because, as God's "attendant" and "steward," Paul will be judged by God when his "master" or "lord" comes at some time in the future (4:4-5). But much more than that, Paul goes on to inform the Corinthians, in a rather sarcastic or even bitter tone, that they are "puffed up" (4:6, 18-19). Rather than judging Paul, they are only qualified to "imitate" him, since Paul is after all not just another one of their numerous pedagogues or child-sitters but a spiritual "father" from whom they have received the gospel (4:6-21).

I would suggest that this chapter not only provides a lens to (re)view the first three chapters of 1 Corinthians but also presents a clue to the fundamental problem between the correspondents. After his customary thanksgiving prayer (1:4-9) and an unmistakable statement of his stance against "divisions" (1:10), Paul pits the "foolish" proclamation of the cross against "the wisdom of the world" (1:11-25). Then he reminds the Corinthians of their being called and chosen by God despite their own humble beginnings and asserts the inappropriateness of self-boasting by any human beings (1:26-31). Next Paul goes back—in both literary and historical sense—to acknowledge his own rhetorical deficiencies when he brought the gospel to the Corinthians (1:17a-b, 2:1-2, 4a), though he quickly offers two reasons or remedies for such deficiencies. First, Paul's deficiencies serve to place the attention properly on God's rather than any human's power (2:4b-5). Second, Paul's deficiencies must be read with spiritual instead of physical sense and sensibility (2:6-16). Failing to grasp both of these points (3:1-9, 18-23), these carnal Corinthians, as Paul's spiritual children or posterity, must be careful how they continue to build God's church after Paul, the "wise builder" (3:10-17). I am suggesting therefore not only that the "anyone" in 3:12-15 is referring to the Corinthians, but also that "divisions" (1:10) or "strife(s)" (1:11; 3:3) exist among the Corinthians as well as between Paul and the Corinthians. That is what Paul seems to indicate with that enigmatic statement: "Now these things, brothers, I made into a figure of speech with respect to myself and Apollos for you all, so that through us you may learn" (4:6). In other words, what he has said in the first three chapters about himself and Apollos, as 4:7-21 will help make clear, is actually about the differences between himself and the Corinthians.[36] Of course, the Corinthians' (mis)handling of the(ir) communion shows that these mainly Gentile converts are anxious and competitive about status among themselves (11:17-34). It is at the same time important to see that at least some if not most of them are also anxious and competitive about status against Paul.[37] From Paul's perspectives, both sets of competition are damaging to the harmony and health of the church body.

Likewise, I will argue that 1 Corinthians 4, particularly when read as the continuation and culmination of 1 Corinthians 1–3, alerts us to the focus of the Corinthians' anxiety about and hostility against Paul. Coming after Paul's admission of figuration, what follows 4:6 can be read as the main point of Paul's object lesson—namely, the apparent status difference between the Corinthians and the apostles (inclusive of Paul [and Apollos?]). While the Corinthians "became rich," "became kings," are "wise" and "strong" and "honorable," the apostles seem "last," "foolish," "weak," and "dishonorable" (4:8-10). In a way that reflects the Roman stereotypical image of Jews as poor beggars (Martial 12.57.13; Juvenal. *Sat.* 3.10-18; 6.542-47), Paul adds other detailed descriptions of the (Jewish) apostles. Besides another reference to their manual labor (4:12a), the apostles are also "condemned to death" (4:9). Furthermore, they "hunger and thirst and are naked, and are beaten and unsettled" (4:11). They are "reviled," "persecuted," and "defamed" (4:12b-13a). As "rubbish of the world," they "became the refuse of all things" (4:13b-c). If Paul is done with using figures of speech in 4:6, he has not exactly given up on using word pictures or emphasizing what is visual in what follows. Paul says that the apostles have become "a spectacle to the world" (4:9), and the lesson he wants to teach the Corinthians is partly one of reading and interpreting ("the saying, 'Not beyond what has been written,'" 4:6). The issue, I contend, concerns how the Corinthians would look on the lowly-looking and abjected (Jewish) bodies of the apostles, particularly that of Paul.

Remember at this point that Paul's first indication of his "deficiencies" refers to his rhetoric (1:17a-b; 2:1-2, 4a), but then he seems to link his rhetorical inadequacy to his physical weakness (2:3; see also 2 Cor 10:10). Ancient Greek rhetoric is, after all, inseparable from the orator's physical or bodily stature, which explains Quintilian's advice that aging and ailing orators should retire to avoid ridicule (*Inst.* 12.11.1-3).[38] Keeping Paul's Jewish body in sight may help to explain several things in these first four chapters of 1 Corinthians, such as (1) his emphasis on spiritual (in)sight; (2) his repeated accusation of the Corinthians as being "carnal" (3:1, 3); and (3) his references to "flesh" (1:26, 29) and "birth" (high or low, 1:26, 28) in his first specific attempt to cut down the "boasting" Corinthians a size or two (1:26-31). Doing so will also provide greater nuance to later chapters, as in Paul's somewhat unexpected comment about his "punished" and "enslaved" body that concludes his "defense" of his manual labor (9:24-27), or his peppered references to racial/ethnic constructions in various parts of the letter (1:22-24; 5:1; 7:18-19; 9:20-21; 10:18, 31-32; 12:2, 13; 14:11, 21). Perhaps most pertinent to my purposes is how Paul clearly described the Corinthians as being "puffed up" (5:2) while at the same time making desire for "wisdom" a Greek or Gentile characteristic (1:22).

Body Building over Jesus' Dead (Jewish) Body

Let me recapitulate my main arguments before I go any farther. I am making a case that because of Paul's ministry, his Corinthian converts experienced a status inversion in joining a religious minority, and thus became even more zealous in their competition for status. As a result, they did not just mishandle the communion of their local church, but they also became more sensitive to and despising of the abjected status of Paul's diasporic Jewish body within the imperial ideology of the Roman Empire. How then does Paul negotiate these difficult dynamics in 1 Corinthians?[39] I propose that he does so by lifting up Jesus. Or, more precisely, Paul lifts himself up through and over Jesus' dead (Jewish) body.

It is by now a common scholarly assumption that the opening thanksgiving prayer, if present, is a good place to locate Paul's major concerns in writing a given letter. In 1 Corinthians, Paul's opening thanksgiving "sets a tone for the whole letter by focusing on Christ."[40] One should not forget, however, that this Christ of Paul will not only return in future, but was also once crucified by the Romans. Jesus on the cross, in the context of the Roman Empire, is perhaps the most abjected spectacle of an already abjected Jewish body.[41] For Paul, it is precisely in this other rejected Jewish body that the Corinthians have been enriched in everything and in every way (1:4-5a). After this all-inclusive statement, Paul mentions three specific things that turn out to be main themes of the letter: "words" or "speech," "knowledge," and "gift" (1:5b, 7a). How does Paul relate the crucified and returning Christ to these three things throughout 1 Corinthians?

Words or Speech

Very quickly after the thanksgiving prayer, Paul talks about the contrast between wise words and Christ's cross (1:17). One finds in Jesus' dead (Jewish) body God's greater power and greater wisdom (1:18-25; 4:20). As we have already mentioned, this difference between divine and human power/wisdom changes both the meaning and the merit of Paul's "foolish" and "faulty" speech. If rhetoric is about the body of the orator as much as the body of a speech, the meaning and merit of Paul's Jewish body may also be viewed differently in light of the greater divine power and wisdom being revealed in the crucified Christ. For Paul, the cross reveals God's preferential choice of the less and the least (1:21, 27-28; 3:18-20). Not only does Paul use the Corinthians themselves as an example of this (1:26), but he also claims that the same preferential choice should be made for the "weaker," "dishonorable," "shameful," and "lacking" members of the body (12:22-24). Rather than just emphasizing "diversity and interdependence of the body's members,"[42] I think Paul is giving a much more aggressive triple-talk here, since what he says seems applicable to (1) any physical body; (2) the Corinthian church body; and (3) his own abjected Jewish body. Notice how he has previously used the same or very similar vocabularies to describe himself (2:3; 4:10-13). The contrast or change between a dead Jewish criminal and God's Christ is the kind of inverted relationship or reversal that enables Paul to transform from being a persecutor of the church to being the "last" and "least"—but then finally the hardest working—apostle (15:9-10).

This divine power or grace not only changes the (spiritual?) status of the Corinthians and Paul, but also alters their relationship with each other within the body of Paul's letter. While the early chapters give the impression that Paul is defending or explaining himself against the judgment of the Corinthians, he performs a great rhetorical reversal in 4:14-21, where he transforms himself from the one being judged to a father to be imitated. He then completes this reversal when he exercises judgment over the Corinthians and instructs them on several issues: (1) fornication and proper judgments within the church body (5:1—6:20); (2) marriage and divorce (7:1-40); (3) the relationship between body (through food and fornication) and idolatry, as well as the relationship between one's own freedom and one's love for others (8:1—14:40); (4) the credibility and consequences of Christ's bodily resurrection (15:1-58); and finally, (5) the offering for the Jerusalem church (16:1-4), which is, for Sze-kar Wan, itself a symbol of Paul's anticolonial project.[43] Even Paul's "defense" of his own manual labor is part of this great reversal (9:1-27). Showing himself as one who models the relinquishment of rights for others' benefits, Paul further establishes himself as a strong person who can discipline his own body. Intimating thus negatively the Corinthians' comparative selfishness and lack of strength, Paul is able to claim for himself a moral high ground that trumps their superior standing in terms of both status and race/ethnicity.

Knowledge

The way in which Paul's words gain both substance and volume over Christ's crucified (Jewish) body is in itself already an illustration of how the same rejected body has enriched "knowledge" (1:5c). Rather than repeating myself on God's greater power/wisdom and newly available spiritual (in)sights (1:17—3:23), let me talk about how Christ's death also brings about knowledge of the other world—or more precisely, knowledge about bodily resurrection. For Paul, it is without question that the dead (Jewish) body of Christ has been raised. This "fact" will, according to Paul, ensure not only the bodily resurrection of all of Christ's followers, but also the continuities and discontinuities between this life and the next life, or the earthly body and the heavenly body (6:13c-14; 15:20-57). If his emphasis on continuities functions to bring about bodily discipline (15:29-37), his talk of discontinuities seems to serve a different purpose. It is important to note here that Paul is well aware of and openly acknowledges the markings and rankings of different bodies. Not only does he talk about the differences among different types of (animal and heavenly) bodies (15:39-41a-c); he further mentions the differences that exist within each type ("for star from star differs in glory," 15:41d). In other words, Paul is not only arguing for the existence of what he calls "natural/perishable" and "spiritual/imperishable" bodies before and after death (15:42-54a), but he also admits that people do not all have the same "natural/perishable" bodies in this life. His, for example, is racially/ethnically marked "Jewish," and hence ranked as having a lower glory that those marked "Greek" or "Roman."[44]

It is most interesting at this point to see how Paul uses a second strategy to redress his abjected Jewish body. If the cross of Christ implies a reversal that accords greater honor to Paul's "lesser" body, the bodily resurrection of Christ means that Paul's own inscribed body will one day be literally transformed into one with greater glory and power (15:42-44, 51-52). On the one hand, Paul demands that the Corinthians reevaluate his present body; on the other hand, Paul himself seems to have internalized the negative messages about his racialized body to the point that he desires a changed body. Frantz Fanon suggested years ago that within the "soul" of the colonized is "an inferiority complex [that] has been created by the death and burial of local cultural originality."[45] Paul shows here, however, that this "inferiority complex" goes even deeper. Even when Paul insists on the resurrection of Jesus' and his own (Jewish) body *after* death and burial, he still longs for a different body. Let these "dishonorable," "weak," and "perishable/natural" Jewish bodies die, so that they may be raised again alive and anew (15:36, 54-57). Even as Paul writes to resist and reverse Greco-Roman racial/ethnic hierarchies, he is simultaneously subjected to or subjectified by the fantasized and racialized Jewish body as something that is not desirable.[46]

I will return to Paul's mixture of desire and denigration in 1 Corinthians, but let me proceed now to one final thought about resurrection "knowledge," since it will give us a smooth transition to talk about the relationship between the crucified Christ and "gifts." It is the transformation of Christ's dead body and the appearance of this postmortem body to Paul that turn this Jewish "no-body" into Paul the ("last," "least," but "hardest working") apostle (9:1-2; 15:1-11). According to Paul, the office of "apostles" is the "first" that God has appointed in the church body (12:27-28c). Again, one can see here how Paul's abjected body is being lifted or built up over Christ's body, which seems to effect all kinds of changes by occupying what Fanon calls a "zone of occult *instability*."[47]

Gifts

Along with various office(r)s (apostles, prophets, and teachers), Paul states that this crucified, risen, and returning Christ has also given to the church body various "gifts" (12:28d-h). Just as different bodies are marked and ranked, Paul goes on to rank these "gifts," naming "love" and "prophecy" in particular as the "greater gifts" (12:31—14:40). In Paul's eyes, these two "gifts" are clearly "greater" because of what they mean to the harmony of the church body, which is perhaps an even more basic "gift" given by the crucified Christ.[48] Over Christ's dead (Jewish) body comes a new body, namely, the church community made up of individual bodies of those who follow Christ (1:9-13; 5:4; 6:15a; 12:27). This new (or interim?) body of Christ not only is given by Christ, but it also belongs to Christ exclusively (4:1-4; 6:19-20a; 7:23; 10:21-22).[49] Paul's explicit employment of slavery language implies the Greco-Roman understanding that slaves are but "surrogate bodies" of their lord or master.[50] Like any Greco-Roman body, the church body is also concerned with issues like internal harmony and external integrity. For Paul, the church body and its many individual bodies must be disciplined, even "enslaved," to achieve both ends (9:24-27; 15:30-34, 58). Internally, in a passage that sounds like Galen's *On the Usefulness of the Parts of the Body*, Paul plays the role of an ancient physician (if not exactly a dissector) who, with the privilege of (in)sight on the human anatomy, leads the Corinthians in a meditation on the body's divinely designed harmony (12:12-21).[51] To preserve this internal harmony, members of the church body must learn, following another aspect of divine design as revealed in Christ, to love and look out for one another's benefit, particularly the less and the least (8:1—9:23; 10:23—11:1; 12:22-26; 13:5b). Doing so will bring out unity, since Christ (his body?) is not divided. Doing so is also necessary, since the promise of resurrection body implies that even death will not remove one from social relations. Externally, church members must not associate themselves with idolatry, which may take the form of food and/or fornication, since either will open the body up for undesirable entries or penetrations (5:1-2, 5-13; 6:12-20; 10:1-22). As he has done throughout the letter, Paul supports his arguments with Christ's body. Divisions and strifes because of status difference within the church do not just tear up this body that is given by and belongs to Christ. They are actually murderous acts that crucify Christ's physical body all over again, and these destructive acts on Christ's (physical and church) body will result in the bodily destruction of the offenders (8:11-12; 11:17-30; 15:3-4).[52] As I have intimated, Paul's equating of idolatry with food and particularly fornication is rather (ideo)logical. In a way that parallels physical combat or competition, opening up one's bodily orifices to another's penetration, in terms of Greco-Roman ideologies, is a submissive act that pronounces one's defeat by a more powerful competitor.[53] For Paul, this simply cannot be, because God, upon seeing Christ's crucified body, has already turned Christ into a victor and conqueror (15:24-28).[54]

Paul's Body-Building Projects

One should see that, with his emphases on these church disciplines, Paul is in effect addressing and redressing the Corinthian church body.[55] Nor should one lose sight of Paul's own stake in all this. As founder and father of the Corinthian church body, Paul is also one of its members. All the rhetoric on love, being considerate of one another, honoring the weak, unity, and harmony means that the Corinthians must learn to look upon Paul's Jewish body with a different pair of eyes. They must learn to see that Jews and Greeks were all baptized in one spirit and into one body (12:13), and that within Christ's church body, "circumcision is nothing and uncircumcision is nothing" (7:19).⁵⁶

It is significant that both times Paul makes these statements about racial/ethnic "oneness" within the church, he immediately links them with similar statements about the differences between slaves and free persons (7:20-24; 12:13). Dale Martin has argued that most interpreters have under-read or inadequately interpreted Paul's statements about slavery.⁵⁷ Slaves becoming freed and free persons becoming slaves is, within Greco-Roman household ideologies, not an erasure of difference but a status reversal, since those being freed occupy a middle rung between those who are free and those who are enslaved. Given what Greeks and Romans thought of Jewish bodies in the first century, as well as what Paul himself says about God's preferential choice for the less and the least in Christ, I would suggest that Martin's argument about status reversal is also applicable to Paul's view of racial/ethnic differences within the church body. After all, it is an-other rejected Jewish body (Christ) that has been the all-sufficient source for the Corinthians when it comes to "speech," "knowledge," and "gift."⁵⁸ This reversal of racial/ethnic hierarchy is especially likely if Martin is correct that when Paul argues that greater honor be given to the "weaker," "dishonorable," "shameful," "uncomely," "lacking" but "necessary" body parts (12:22-25), Paul is in fact employing a wordplay and referring to the genitals.⁵⁹ If the "necessary" body part was a euphemism for the penis in Hellenistic writings,⁶⁰ the circumcised penis was also the shameful necessity that stigmatized the Jewish (male) body in the Greco-Roman world (1 Macc 1:41-49, 60-61; 2:42-48; 2 Macc 6:7-11; Tacitus, *Hist.* 5.5; Suetonius, *Dom.* 12.2; Petronius, *Sat.* 102).⁶¹ As Paul persuades the Corinthians to honor the penis and look out for an-other's interests, Paul the Jew—with his circumcised penis—is actually one of these "others" who stand to benefit. His rhetoric or address to redress the Corinthian church body is also a site through which he might redress his own body and his own authority as their esteemed founder or respectable father. Ethos and logos feed off each other.⁶² Just as an audience would find the words of a credible orator more convincing, the Corinthians—should they find Paul's rhetoric agreeable—would also find Paul's person more appealing. This is particularly so since his "judgments" on various issues serve to edify and build up the church body. In other words, Paul is clearly presenting himself as occupying all three of the church offices that he mentions (12:27-28c; 14:21-22, 31). He is an apostle, a prophet, and a teacher; he is also not shy about telling the Corinthians that he speaks "in tongues more than all of you" (14:18).

In light of the difference in race/ethnicity and thus power dynamics, one may also proceed to read Paul's claim to become a Jew with Jews and a Gentile with Gentiles with a different nuance (9:19-23).⁶³ Rather than taking Paul's claim simply as Paul's "assimilation" or, worse, his "transcendence" over race/ethnicity, I contend that it comes across more as a threat. One must keep in mind that within the body of 1 Corinthians, there are all kinds of references to Jewish priority alongside these "all things to all people" statements (9:22c; 10:32-33). Not only does Paul use "Gentile" negatively to refer to those who do not follow Christ (5:1; 12:1-2), but he also makes his argument on the basis of Hebrew Scripture (1:19, 31; 2:9, 16; 3:18-23; 9:8-9; 10:7; 14:21;

15:45, 54), and presents Moses and "Israel according to the flesh" as the Corinthians' authority and "ancestors," as well as examples of/for his arguments (10:1-4, 18-22). This simultaneous insistence on Jewish priority and fluidity is comparable to the "chameleonism" that was identified with the Jews of the early twentieth-century United States.[64] Not only does this ability and willingness to transform and pass as another race/ethnicity—that is, an "otherness" that can change into another "other" that is the self—*not* dilute Jewish difference, but it may also become the very identification of Jewish difference. Claiming an identity that is "marked at once by indistinguishable sameness and irreducible difference,"[65] Paul arouses an anxiety caused by the unclassifiable, or what Zygmunt Bauman calls "proteophobia."[66] Paul becomes in effect a vexing and menacing figure to the Corinthians, especially in light of the sociocultural mixing, rhetorical self-fashioning, and yet colonial racial/ethnic markings that characterized the Greco-Roman world. Paul claims for himself a reproducible body that is simultaneously a double agent that can disrupt, if not exactly dissolve, the scripted performativity of race/ethnicity by performing its contingency, changeability, and convert-ibility.[67]

In his discussion of the "stereotype," Homi K. Bhabha begins by emphasizing that "[a]n important feature of colonial discourse is its dependence on the concept of 'fixity' in the ideological construction of otherness. Fixity, as the sign of cultural/historical/racial difference in the discourse of colonialism, is a paradoxical mode of representation: it connotes rigidity and an unchanging order as well as disorder, degeneracy and daemonic repetition."[68] One can understand the importance of "fixity" not only by recalling what Martin says about the threat of social mobility in terms of status or class in 1 Corinthians,[69] but also by extending Martin's discussion to consider the fury over fluidity in terms of race/ethnicity. If Paul can turn Gentile and infiltrate the Corinthian world, the Corinthians can also slide down the racial/ethnic scales and become stigmatized Jews. This haunting is even made explicit by Paul. After repeating a similar emphasis on being "all thing to all people" (10:32-33), Paul immediately follows up with a call for the Corinthians to "become imitators of me, as I also am of Christ" (11:1; see also 4:16). The mostly Gentile Corinthians are told, in other words, to become chameleons; that is, they are to become (like) Jews. To the horror of the Corinthians but the advantage of Paul, the differences between Gentiles and Jews are, in the space of one letter, simultaneously solidified and dissolved.[70]

Starting from the cross of Christ, Paul promises a resurrection body, disciplines the church body in Corinth, and in the process also redresses his own rejected body as another colonized Jew. Over Christ's dead (Jewish) body, Paul gives not only a glimpse into the future but also a "spiritual" perspective for the present that destabilizes status and identity in order to establish a stable order of a different sort (14:33, 40). Paul does all of this through the textual body of this letter that he wrote to the Corinthians. In different parts of the letter, Paul seems to present himself practically as Christ's spokesperson. While he makes this rather explicit in his statement against divorce (7:10), Paul also makes a more general statement equating his writing with the Lord's commandment (14:37). Although he seems to make a distinction between his own words and those of Christ a couple of times (7:12, 25), he nevertheless concludes with the affirmation that he is speaking as one who has "the spirit of God" (7:40b). In contrast to the carnal Corinthians, Paul has "the mind of Christ" (2:16—3:3). As a "spiritual person," Paul "discerns all things," but "he is discerned by no one" (2:15), particularly not by the carnal Corinthians. In light of his self-representation as Christ's apostle and spokesperson, when he says that "no one speaking by the spirit of God says, 'Let Jesus be cursed'" (12:3a-b), one wonders if he is not also implying that those who curse or judge him are by definition also not speaking by God's spirit.

(Other) Bodies Feminized and Sexualized

In his various works, Frantz Fanon has consistently contended that since colonial power colonizes the geographical space of a people as well as the internal space of a person, one must pay attention to psychic dynamics in thinking about resistance.[71] Because of this form of internal or psychic colonization, a colonized person is often siding *with* as well as siding *against* his or her colonizer. As Steve Pile points out, Fanon's twin concerns (the ambiguity of resistance and the psychic process of colonization) come together in the work of another diasporic Jew, Sigmund Freud of Vienna, since Freud refers to resistance in terms of his patients' *avoidance* of receiving psychoanalytic therapy or his talking cure.[72] Writing about Freud's psychoanalytic ideas as well as Freud's life as a diasporic Jew, Sander L. Gilman argues that psychoanalysis itself was Freud's way of dealing with or "resisting" his own racially/ethnically inscribed body as a European abjection.[73] The problem, according to Gilman, is that Freud's own "resistance" was—in a way that is true to his own theorization—also one that maintained repression or sustained oppression, because Freud ended up deflecting all of his undesirable marginalization as a diasporic Jew onto the female body. Gilman's thesis about race/ethnicity and gender in Freud has been further extended by Daniel Boyarin, who argues that Freud deflected his racial/ethnic abjection as a diasporic Jew onto not only female bodies but also onto homoerotic bodies and relations.[74] In what follows, I will briefly suggest that what Gilman and Boyarin say about Freud's psychoanalytic writings are also applicable to Paul's own body-building project in 1 Corinthians.

Questions of Gender

We have already seen hints of Paul internalizing colonial ideologies in his desire for a new and transformed resurrection body (15:36, 42-44, 51-57). The fact that Paul insists on Christ having a bodily resurrection may be a good indication of what Paul thinks of masculinity. Christ is, after all is said and done, standing erect as a masculine conqueror and victor of all (15:20-28).[75] As colonized Jews, however, Jesus' masculinity and Paul's masculinity were culturally suspect. Because of its "reputation" for attracting mainly women as proselytes, Judaism was attacked in the Greco-Roman world as a religion of and for women.[76] I have already commented on the connection between

Greco-Roman rhetoric and the body of the orator; Maud W. Gleason has further demonstrated a link between rhetorical and masculine competitions, or more precisely, how rhetoric may signify legitimate and illegitimate males.[77] Greco-Roman teachers of rhetoric like Cicero and Quintilian talk also about the need to gesture and posture in a dignified—meaning masculine—manner. Here a single citation from Quintilian will have to suffice. Quintilian suggests learning from dramatic actors who perform distinctions among "slaves, pimps, parasites, farmers, soldiers, prostitutes, maidservants, old men (stern and mild), young men (moral or loose-living), married ladies, and young girls" (*Inst.* 11.3.74).[78] We can therefore observe further subtleties in the relations between Paul's rhetorical deficiencies and his bodily abjection. His bodily abjection as a diasporic and colonized Jew has to do with Paul's racial/ethnic inscriptions as well as his "feminization" by the dominant culture of the Roman empire.[79]

Writing about racial relations in the United States, Robyn Wiegman explains: "In the context of white supremacy, we must understand the threat of masculine sameness as so terrifying that only the reassertion of a gendered difference can provide the necessary disavowal. It is this that lynching and castration offer in their ritualized deployment, functioning as both a refusal and a negation of the possibility of extending the privileges of patriarchy to the black man."[80] Even if the racial/ethnic groups and the exact practices might differ, the underlying ideology of Wiegman's analysis is still transferable back to Paul's world. It was a binary imposition so that Greco-Roman males would have hegemony and monopoly over every masculine privilege, and the racialized Jew would be pushed into what Wiegman calls the "corporeal excess of a racial feminization."[81] Not to be lost or forgotten here is how Roman ideologies also identified Jewish bodies with sexual excess or deviance (Martial 7.30, 35, 82; 11.94).[82] In fact, the connection that elite males made between "foreign cults" and women, sexual immorality, and state subversion is well documented in the Greco-Roman world.[83] The intersecting dynamics of race/ethnicity, gender, sexuality, and questions of national loyalty are, of course, also familiar to many Asian Americans.[84] It is in resistance or reaction to these dynamics that Frank Chin attempts to (re)masculinize Asian America by not only attacking Maxine Kong Kingston's "woman warrior" but also targeting Fu Manchu as a "homosexual menace" and Charlie Chan as an "effeminate closet queen."[85]

Since many feminist readings of 1 Corinthians have—from various perspectives and with different methodologies—done much to critique the masculinist biases of 1 Corinthians, I have no need to duplicate their helpful and insightful critiques here.[86] I do agree with Kittredge that the gender question should never be subsumed or deflected by any other differential relations of power, including imperialism and race/ethnicity.[87] Let me nevertheless emphasize a need to read Paul's masculinist positions alongside his own "feminization" as a diasporic and colonized Jew. I do so not to excuse or, worse, justify Paul's positions. My hope is to promote a contextual reading that refuses to account for certain gender and/or sexuality problems by simply essentializing a minority person and/or culture (Jewish, Asian American, or whatever) as patriarchal and/or "homophobic," and thus letting the dominant and imperial cultures completely off the hook. The dynamics, deflections, and reduplications of bodily abjection must be teased out and scrutinized.[88] In struggling against this process of racialization *and* feminization, Paul (con)fuses sociopolitical agency with "manhood" and ends up becoming hysterical about those who are female and what is considered "feminine." In other words, Paul does wrong (regarding women) even or perhaps especially when he is right (about resisting Roman abjection). As anticolonial resistance takes place in the form of an antagonistic masculinity between Greco-Roman and Jewish males, this competing masculinity also turns into a complementary masculinity in which both groups of men are making and marking their claim through their domination over women.[89] Paul's displacing of his own abjection onto other "others" not only foreshadows Freud and many other colonized and/or racial/ethnic minorities but also echoes those closer to his own time and place. Josephus, for instance, contrasts a high-ranking female convert to Judaism (Fulvia) with an immoral freedwoman who is familiar with the Isis cult (Ida) to deflect the charges that Jews attract people from the lower classes onto another (*Ant.* 18.65-84).[90]

Inseparable from how Paul may have felt "feminized" is perhaps his own ambivalence about masculinity. His "advice" that the Corinthians should put the lesser other first is in a sense an alternative to the agonistic and competitive ethos of the Greco-Roman masculine ideal. One may add to this Paul's consistent emphasis on the believer's body belonging to the Lord (6:19-20a). This belonging and the subsequent union that exists between Jesus and a follower of Jesus, as Hays points out on the basis of 6:16-17, is for Paul comparable to or even deeper than the sexual union between a man and a *female* prostitute.[91] Since Paul thinks that the bodies of husband and wife belong to each other (7:4), his adamant insistence on the Lord's exclusive rights to his followers (7:23; 10:21-22) may well explain Paul's preference for not taking a wife (7:1-9; 9:5). Paul's "heterosexist" assumption regarding sexual union, however, implies that he himself will have to occupy a female or feminine position in his "union" with his Lord. What I am getting at is how Paul's own ambivalence about masculinity (in terms of his nonagonistic advice, his "holy union" with Jesus Christ, and his "feminization" as a colonized Jew) may lead to a haunting anxiety over gender failure that causes Paul to further solidify gender identity in (re)turn.

Questions of Sexuality

Regardless of whether Paul's list of wrongdoers (5:10-11; 6:9-10) originates from Jewish or Hellenistic sources and what its specific terms may be referring to,[92] there is no question that Paul sees—to play on Jonathan Dollimore's book title[93]—"sexual dissidents" and Christ-following bodies (both collective and individual) as mutually exclusive (6:13c-20). This stigmatization of sexual dissidence as deviance (however defined), when read in light of Greco-Roman degradations of Jews as sexually deviant bodies, becomes triply intriguing. First, Paul seems to suggest that the mostly Gentile Corinthians are actually the ones who are sexually deviant.[94] Not only is this true of them before their conversion to follow Christ (6:11), but, to Paul's great amazement and disappointment, their deviant sexuality continues after their participation in the church (5:1-8). Second, Paul's "reversed condemnation" of the Corinthians makes him, though a diasporic and colonized Jew, come across as more Greco-Roman than the Greco-Romans when it comes to matters of sexual "purity." This is especially so since Cicero, for example, has condemned similar incestuous relations (*Clu.* 5.14—6.16).

Writing about the Jews in Algeria in the 1960s, Albert Memmi observed:

> Their constant and very justifiable ambition is to escape from their colonized condition.... To that end, they endeavor to resemble the colonizer in the frank hope that he may cease to consider them different from him. Hence their efforts to forget the past, to change collective habits, and their enthusiastic adoption of Western language, culture, and customs. But if the colonizer does not always openly discourage these candidates to develop that resemblance, he never permits them to attain it either. Thus, they live in constant and painful ambiguity.[95]

Extending Memmi's observation, Bhabha suggests that the "almost-White-but-not-quite" dynamic of colonial ideology actually drives both colonizers and colonized to become more and more white.[96] Studies have shown that Asian Americans, finding themselves in the position of being a racial/ethnic *and* religious minority in diaspora, are also driven to employ this strategy. Many Korean American Buddhists, for instance, stress the compatibility between "American values" (particularly being independent, self-reliant, open-minded, and democratic) and Buddhist teachings (especially the need and ability to "find and know one's mind"), and claim as a result that they are indeed "more American" than, say, their Christian counterparts.[97] Todd Penner's reading of Acts, particularly how Luke depicts the Christian community as living up to, modeling, and/or fulfilling various Greco-Roman ideals for the *politeia* (in terms of membership, ethos, constitution, polity, and result), shows that this strategy is not just a modern invention by Asian Americans.[98] One can easily say the same of Philo, who tries to justify Judaism to Greco-Roman audiences in Greco-Roman terms. Gregory E. Sterling, for instance, has also shown how diasporic or Hellenistic Jews like Josephus, Demetrius, Artapanus, Pseudo-Eupolemus, and Eupolemus are "national historians—*tout-à-fait*—who claim the superiority of the Jewish nation over both other Oriental people and Greeks" by depicting Moses or Abraham as *Kulturbringer* or benefactor to cultures that had become dominant powers of the historians' own time.[99] In the words of Elizabeth A. Castelli, "one of the important rhetorical strategies of early Christian apologists was to argue for their movement's superior embodiment of the highest virtues from the classical world."[100]

One can see Paul employing a similar strategy regarding "wisdom." After characterizing "wisdom" as a Greek thing (1:22), he proceeds to talk about his own (more) "mature" wisdom that is from God (2:6—3:3, 10) and to needle the Corinthians for resorting to the "wisdom" of "worldly" judges (6:1-6). Likewise, the fact that it is now Paul who reminds the Corinthians to prefer suffering over pursuing prosecution (6:7-8)—a lesson taught by Greek and Roman sages like Plato, Epictetus, and Musonius

Rufus[101]—implies again that Paul is the one who is indeed more "Greco-Roman." Given (1) the Stoic-Cynic emphasis on "freedom," (2) the history of Corinth as "Aphrodite's city,"[102] and (3) the dominant Roman sensibilities about industry and efficiency and the related criticism of the Sabbath rest as a habit of an idle people worshiping an equally idle God,[103] one may well say the same thing regarding Paul's teaching of the Corinthians on "freedom" (7:21, 32; 8:9—9:22; 10:23-30) and "love" (8:1-4; 13:1—14:1; 16:14, 24), as well as his insistence on manual labor (9:1-18) and hard work (4:11-13; 15:9-10, 58). Similarly, given the dominant opinion that Jews are unsocial and peculiar not only because of their dietary regulations and circumcision practice but also because of "their belief in a God who does not take human form,"[104] Paul's insistence on Jesus' bodily resurrection (15:1-58) and the Corinthians as the very (interim?) body of Christ on earth (12:12-30) seems to be just another version of the same strategy.

Third, much like his emphasis on a transformed body in the future, Paul's stigmatization of sexually dissident bodies (whether Jewish or Greco-Roman) in particular and his claim to be "more Greco-Roman" than others only end up reduplicating and reinforcing colonial ideologies, whether it is the cult of sexual purity or something else.[105] Dionysius of Halicarnassus, the first-century B.C.E. historian, also used this two-pronged strategy of "appropriation" and transference.[106] Writing against the anti-Roman sentiments that were popular among elite Greeks, Dionysius tries to show in his *Roman Antiquities* that (1) Romans are really Greeks; (2) Roman institutions and morality are similar if not superior to Greek ones; and (3) Rome's power in the world is well deserved (see, for example, 1.4-5, 89; 2.17; 7.66.4-5). Yet in *On the Ancient Orators*, he makes a point of pitting Greeks against "Asians" rather than Romans.[107] Cautious and defensive about what he perceives to be external, foreign, and polluting agents attacking the personal and/or collective body, Paul's attitude resembles the political ideology that represents a nation as a body threatened by infection (for example, Plutarch, *Lyc.* 27.4).[108] In other words, what Gilman and Boyarin suggest Freud did, Paul also does as he projects his own abjection and stigmatization as being "feminine" and "morally corrupt" onto women and other sexual dissidents. By duplicating and displacing colonial abjection onto people who were also in different ways already abjected, Paul greatly compromises his resistance against colonization and racialization. He has, in a sense, become like those who oppress him or what he hates. He is building community on the backs of those whom "everyone" can agree to marginalize and stigmatize. His political view of Jews might well be different from that of others, but his political practice ends up duplicating and reinforcing a larger ideological imperative to establish and eschew abject bodies.

Conclusion

Asian Americans are not only familiar with racial/ethnic and religious difference but also well aware of duplication and deflection in our attempts to redress and/or masquerade our own differences. We do this by highlighting, gloating over, and hiding behind other differences. In Hisaye Yamamoto's short story "Wilshire Bus," a Japanese American woman, Esther Kuroiwa, rides a bus up and down Wilshire Boulevard in post–World War II Los Angeles twice a week to visit her husband, who is hospitalized because "his back, injured in the war, began troubling him again."[109] The plot of the story turns on a chance encounter on the bus between Esther and an elderly Chinese American couple, focusing particularly how Esther changes from acknowledging her similarity with them as "Orientals together on a bus" with a smile[110] to "detaching" herself from them in silence and by "pretending to look out the window."[111] What causes this change is the verbal assault of a male passenger in the back of the bus against the Chinese American woman, because she—though a "nobody" in terms of race, gender, and generation—dares to turn around and give the man "a quick but thorough examination" upon hearing his loud diatribe against a local sports figure in a public space.[112] As expected, the man's assault consists of his opinion that the Chinese American woman should "get off the bus" and "go back to China."[113]

What is pertinent to our purposes here is Esther's own reflection of the incident. Esther realizes that her "saving detachment"[114] has led to her "gloating over the fact that the drunken man had specified the Chinese [rather than the Japanese] as the unwanted."[115] The human tendency to duplicate and deflect abjection onto others becomes clear to Esther as she remembers a man with a placard around his neck in a time of anti-Japanese sentiments during World War II that read "I AM KOREAN."[116] In other words, Esther realizes that she is deflecting abjection onto others on the bus just as Chinese and Korean Americans had done toward Japanese Americans during the war and internment.

This deflection of one's own abjection onto others is analogous to the projection or expulsion of what is unpleasant or undesirable within oneself to the external world. According to Freud, this projection or deflection is known as the psychic process of splitting. Splitting also signifies for my reading of 1 Corinthians what Abdul R. JanMohamed calls a "cleaved subjectivity," in which the subjectivity of a colonized person (like Paul) is bifurcated into two parts, one collaborating with and the other contending against his colonizers.[117] Homi Bhabha has also fittingly compared this splitting process, as a strategy of disavowal, to "a discrimination between the mother culture and its bastards."[118] What must not be forgotten is that while a mother may disown her own as bastards, she is nonetheless unable to have bastards on her own; it takes the involvement of a third party. In Yamamoto's story, this third and "indispensable" party would be the male passenger in the back of the bus who disrupts a public space with his loud commentary and believes that he (alone) has the right to do and say whatever he pleases without public scrutiny, especially not by an elderly Chinese American woman. One must not focus only on the two Asian American women in reading "Wilshire Bus" and forget that there is another subjection *behind* splitting. As splitting itself is a subjecting act, it "disturbs the visibility of the colonial presence and makes the recognition of its authority problematic."[119] One must consider and challenge *both* conditions of subjection, the one behind as well as the one begun in the process of splitting. In Paul's case, this means that one needs to trace, track, or historicize rather than simply essentializing or naturalizing his subjection of others. As one rightfully critiques Paul's marginalization of women and sexual dissidents in 1 Corinthians, one must also not fail to account for the absent presence of Roman colonization and racialization of Jews like Paul. Only by doing so will one be able to "show the levels at which opposition can be both contestatory and complicit, and yet still constitute a subversion that matters."[120] If not, one will easily end up—as Spivak has shown in her famous statement about the imperial excuse of "saving brown women from brown men"[121]—abetting and advancing more imperial violence.

CHAPTER TEN

Imperial Intersections and Initial Inquiries

Toward a Feminist, Postcolonial Analysis of Philippians

JOSEPH A. MARCHAL

Recent developments in the field of biblical interpretation necessitate a reevaluation of the process for and import of interpreting Pauline letters. Indeed, the persistent and pernicious conditions of globalized injustice demonstrate the urgency with which this reevaluation should occur. This urgency presses upon biblical interpreters in particular because the contents of our work have been utilized not only historically but also in recent imperialistic situations. In response, a growing body of work on postcolonial, anti-imperial, and/or decolonizing approaches is emphasizing the relevance of biblical rhetorics within colonizing and colonized discourse.[1] Running parallel to and occasionally overlapping with these approaches, a number of Pauline scholars are more carefully attending to the political context of the letters written to communities within the Roman Empire.[2]

Feminist interpretation has made significant contributions to both of these "strands," though it has too often been decentered in the process. In a similar way, postcolonial feminists from both within and outside of biblical studies have noted how frequently white and/or Western feminists have ignored or elided imperialism in their analyses. These gaps, conflicts, and erasures in and between approaches will be further explored below in preparation for a specifically feminist, postcolonial analysis of Paul's letter to the Philippians. Since this article offers an initial pursuit of this task, I begin with an awareness of the dynamics that prompt such an analysis while seeking to learn how to proceed from the contributions of postcolonial feminist work by biblical interpreters, especially Musa Dube and Kwok Pui-lan.[3] I argue

Imperial Intersections and Initial Inquiries 147

that feminist and postcolonial analyses can and should work toward mutual goals, even as we recognize both the difference between and the intersections of sexism(s) and imperialism(s). The procedures and goals of feminist, postcolonial analysis will prove to be particularly relevant for an examination of Paul's letter to the Philippians.[4]

Prompting Need: Gaps, Erasures, and Conflicts

As I noted above, biblical scholarship that addresses postcolonialism or Roman imperialism should be relevant to the task of analyzing Paul's letter to the Philippians. It also seems that these pursuits would have rather clear connections to the goals of feminist biblical interpretation. Yet feminist contributions have been largely elided and/or decentered in both postcolonial and Roman imperial studies. Additionally, much of white and/or Western feminist scholarship fails to acknowledge or (worse still) implicitly colludes with the imperialist tendencies of biblical studies and the dominant culture.

Postcolonial feminist work in biblical studies and in the wider circles of postcolonial studies has highlighted how the colonial subject has often assumed a specifically male character. Women's roles in historical movements for decolonization have been minimized or erased, while an analysis of colonial dynamics that is particularly and even centrally gendered has rarely been taken up. Gayatri Chakravorty Spivak has pointed out how colonized women have been used as rationales for the "saving action" of colonists, because "white men are saving brown women from brown men."[5] Examining women's circumstances under colonization highlights not only their double or triple colonization but also the difference(s) among various forms of patriarchal oppression.[6] Chandra Talpade Mohanty has been particularly influential in this regard, demonstrating how the categories "woman" and "Third World woman" have been homogenized "under Western eyes." Producing such monolithic pictures erases the complex roles of women and gendered argumentation in colonialism and anticolonialist struggle. Despite efforts by colonial interests to cast women as passive victims or territories to claim, women have been active participants in economic, political, and military struggles in colonized locales.[7]

These gaps and erasures are unfortunate, not only for the work of a feminist scholar but also for a coherent and comprehensive decolonizing project, since "gender inequalities are *essential* to the structure of colonial racism and imperial authority."[8] Even in our contemporary situation, the gendered differences within neocolonialism are apparent in both "the global militarization of masculinity and the feminization of poverty."[9] In a context where women are seen as boundary markers for empire and distant lands are "virgin territory" (under what Anne McClintock has dubbed the "porno-tropics" of empire), it is clear that sexuality as a domain must also be considered in an interconnected but independent fashion along with gender.[10] Treating women, gender, and sexuality in a peripheral fashion or appending the subject of women's colonization as a supplement to the "primary" task only increases the disconnect.[11] By not engaging with an analysis of gender in colonial and anticolonial contexts, postcolonial theory runs the risk of replicating elements of the colonial system.

In some ways, the critiques made by Spivak, Mohanty, and McClintock (among others) of postcolonial theory and anti-imperial work have been incorporated into these fields. It is notable that feminist and/or gender critiques are now acknowledged in the field, so that most introductions must now include such work. However, such contributions are more often listed in their own subsections or chapters, rather than integrated into the whole of the argument.[12] Nevertheless, to an increasing degree postcolonial scholars are aware of the role of their feminist predecessors and feminist advocates within their ranks. The beginnings of postcolonial biblical interpretation are not divorced from these previous tendencies. For whatever reasons—the initially androcentric nature of postcolonial theory at large, the still androcentric character of biblical studies, and/or its still burgeoning condition—postcolonial biblical interpretation has not foregrounded feminist contributions or focused on gender en route to "decolonizing biblical studies."[13]

Scholars such as Ali Mazrui have noted how the three g's—"God, gold, and glory"—were used to justify the imperial regimes of the West.[14] But as Musa Dube has noted in her discussions of biblical interpretation, a great deal is lacking in such an analysis, since women in colonized locales are doubly or triply oppressed (under multiple patriarchal systems),[15] while gendered representations are "central to the narrative strategies of imperialism."[16] As a result, Dube argues compellingly that "gender" should be added to the "three g's" informing colonial analysis of biblical texts.[17] Kwok has also noted how interpreters "have left out the gender dimension" when analyzing the connections between religion and colonialism.[18] This is particularly problematic in biblical studies, given the prominent role of biblical argumentation in ancient and more contemporary forms of colonization.[19] Kwok maintains that postcolonial feminist methods must aid in analyzing and negotiating any kind of "postcolonial bible," since such a collection "must also be seen as a political text written, collected, and redacted by male colonial elites."[20]

In a similar fashion to their colleagues in postcolonial hermeneutics, scholars focused on the Roman imperial context for the study of the Second Testament have also failed to incorporate feminist insights and methods adequately. The "Paul and Politics" section of the Society of Biblical Literature has been the "home base" for the production of several remarkable volumes of collected papers of immediate import for the topic at hand.[21] However, in spite of a range of critiques, cautions, and concerns that feminist scholars have raised in these sessions (and in the volumes that have resulted from them), few of the participants have addressed the topics of gender or sexuality or implemented feminist practices. Far from recognizing the key role of gendered rhetorics in Paul's letters and in the Roman Empire, these volumes include feminist and/or female voices only to ignore or implicitly dismiss them.[22] One striking example involves the series of concerns raised by Elisabeth Schüssler Fiorenza, Cynthia Briggs Kittredge, Sheila Briggs, and Antoinette Clark Wire in the second volume of papers edited by Richard Horsley, titled *Paul and Politics*.[23] Schüssler Fiorenza noted how Paul's violent rhetorics are not very different from imperial discourse, while Briggs demonstrated how ignoring sexuality when discussing slavery in Paul also evades the coercion of Roman imperial institutions.[24] Wire's responses questioned how including women would alter the liberating picture presented by some of the articles.[25] Echoing the parallel insights of postcolonial feminist work, Kittredge pointed out how feminist interpreters treating gender as a central category have already provided important qualifications to such views that had not been taken into account to that point.[26]

An awareness of gender relations or feminist analyses, then, seems crucial to any construction of the imperial system of Paul's time.[27] Yet most of the entries in the two volumes that followed *Paul and Politics* simply pass over or seem unaware of these qualifications and reservations—or, for that matter, of the development of feminist biblical interpretation in the past thirty years.[28] Aside from the final article of the next volume in the series (*Paul and the Roman Imperial Order*),[29] gender constructs and feminist approaches are never considered, while the roles of particular women are treated briefly in only two places (the volume's introduction and Efraín Agosto's article).[30]

Even when insights of feminist scholars are permitted within the bounds of these examinations, these works and those of earlier feminist thinkers are rarely footnoted and even more rarely taken seriously.[31] In a similar way, Richard Horsley insists in *Hidden Transcripts and the Arts of Resistance* that the "resistance" aspects of Paul's letters were "previously unnoticed" until scholars turned to James C. Scott's work.[32] These comments offer a sadly ironic commentary on malestream biblical scholarship, since scholars could only make such comments if they failed to notice how years of feminist scholarship on Pauline literature had already offered a number of strategies for "reading against the grain" using a hermeneutics of suspicion or listening for the submerged voices of the oppressed.[33] Such comments are even more surprising given Kittredge's contribution toward the end of the volume, where she highlights previous feminist contributions to the task at hand while cautioning about the politics of choosing Scott's theoretical model.[34]

Even as feminist (and postcolonial feminist) scholars have been making such arguments to their malestream colleagues, however, the bulk of feminist scholarship on biblical literature has yet to address these same dynamics. Even relatively recent feminist work on Pauline letters foregrounds neither the phenomenon of colonialism nor the conditions of empire that shaped the creation and reception of these letters. Two brief examples should suffice to make this point. In Sandra Hack Polaski's recent *A Feminist Introduction to Paul* (2005), Roman emperors and bits of Roman law are in fact discussed.[35] Yet even as Polaski optimistically presents Paul's letters as standing in contradistinction to the structures of his day, she offers no indication that Roman imperialism might have been an important or even a fundamental agent behind such structures. Of the ten contributions to the *Feminist Companion to Paul* collection (2004), only Luzia Sutter Rehmann's article considers the particularly *imperial* context of Paul's letters.[36] The only entry to critique imperialism is Luise Schottroff's analysis of the anti-Judaism of modern Christian views of "law-free Christianity."[37] This might be an important connection for postcolonial feminist approaches in light of Shawn

Kelley's work that traces how both anti-Judaism and Orientalism were combined in the racialized discourse of the Western colonialist project, with problematic results for the field of biblical studies.[38]

This brief overview of some of the gaps, conflicts, and erasures involved in articulating a feminist, postcolonial analysis of a Pauline letter is not meant to repudiate the work of certain scholars or to attain some "pure" method or vantage point from which to proceed.[39] As Kelley has also already pointed out, embracing any concept of a pristine method or pure origins would only further implicate my own work in the racialist hierarchy that was used to align Paul with civilization, universalism, and existential authenticity.[40] In fact, this colonial and racialized heritage went unacknowledged in my own earlier attempt to work out a feminist analysis of Paul's mutuality rhetorics.[41] This sketch, then, is not meant to be a game of academic "gotcha." Rather, it should be taken as an effort to indicate some of the gaps in recent interpretations of Paul's letters, including my own, and to highlight some of the reasons why postcolonial feminist interpretation is needed.

To be sure, feminist critiques preceded postcolonial analysis and, in some ways, opened up practical and disciplinary spaces for it to proceed. At the same time, we must avoid being overly triumphant about this precedence in view of the complicated historical interconnections between feminism, religious power, and colonialism.[42] Gayatri Spivak has analyzed some of the ways in which Western or "first world" feminists have appropriated the history of two-thirds world women. By claiming the authority to speak for their "others," Spivak argues, feminists like Julia Kristeva have mimicked the role of the imperialist.[43] Unfortunately, this is not a new role for women in the West, as studies of "colonial feminism" have made clear.[44] The role of women as missionaries highlights the fraught nature of this territory. As Kwok notes, "Judging from the magnitude of women's participation in mission and the amount of money raised to support such activities, the women's missionary movement must be regarded as the largest women's movement in the nineteenth and early twentieth centuries."[45]

Thus, we must be careful even when using helpful analytic concepts like *kyriarchy*.[46] Such a concept is instructive for our purposes, as it underscores how colonialism and sexism intersect. However, both Dube and Kwok have raised concerns about situations where analyses of kyriarchy have conflated dominating structures and so "bracketed" or played down the effects of imperialism.[47] Their comments coincide with Laura Donaldson's critique of the homology "man = colonizer, woman = colonized."[48] Challenging this homology should clarify the difference between identifying forms of oppression and treating all forms as identical.[49] For this reason, in the following analysis I argue that we should attempt to recognize how imperialism and sexism intersect with each other as well as with heterosexism, ethnocentrism, racism, anti-Judaism, poverty, nationalism, and militarism (among others).[50] Yet even as I foreground gender in my discussion of colonialism, I recognize that we must also comprehend each of these structures in their distinct functions.

Imperial Intersections and Initial Inquiries 151

Procedure and Precedent

Having briefly contextualized this study within some of the intersecting dynamics between different segments of biblical studies, we still need to establish a procedure that will address these dynamics as part of a feminist, postcolonial analysis of Philippians. Indeed, as the preceding comments should make clear, a number of rich resources already exist for decolonizing or postcolonial feminist work, as biblical scholars have already drawn and could draw still further on the insights of such postcolonial feminist scholars as Gayatri Chakravorty Spivak, Laura Donaldson, Chandra Mohanty, Anne McClintock, and Trinh T. Minh-ha, among many others.[51] In many cases, biblical scholars such as Gale Yee, Judith McKinlay, Hisako Kinukawa, Sharon H. Ringe, and Kathleen O'Brien Wicker have been instructive pioneers and predecessors to this project.[52] However, due to the exigencies of time and space, I will draw primarily from the work of Musa Dube and Kwok Pui-lan for a number of reasons. First, both are pioneers in these areas and have written widely and effectively.[53] Second, both have examined Second Testament texts with at least some allusions to Paul's letters.[54] Third, and most important for the purpose of this section, both have provided guidance for how to proceed with such an analysis.

There is no single way to engage in this task, as Dube makes clear by introducing us to at least eleven different procedures for a postcolonial feminist interpretation.[55] Kwok is careful also to delineate that there is no overarching method or approach for feminists who engage with postcolonial criticism, just as there is no singular feminist method. Nonetheless, Kwok does helpfully sketch five "common concerns" of postcolonial feminist interpretation, most of which this essay seeks to address.[56]

Kwok first highlights the concern to "investigate how the symbolization of women and deployment of gender in the text relate to class interests, modes of production, concentration of state power, and colonial domination."[57] The interrelation of imperialism(s) and sexism(s) plays a foundational role in articulating postcolonial or transnational feminisms.[58] This point is particularly relevant in view of the fact that at least some Pauline interpreters have failed to recognize such interconnections when positing an "anti-imperial Paul."[59] Second, Kwok explains that "postcolonial feminist critics pay special attention to the biblical women in the contact zone and present reconstructive readings as counternarrative."[60] Thus, our analysis should address the role of Euodia and Syntyche in the community as well as the context of ancient Philippi, since it fits Kwok's articulation of a contact zone as "the space of colonial encounters where people of different geographical and historical backgrounds are brought into contact with each other, usually shaped by inequality and conflictual relations."[61]

In some ways, what I have said above has already initiated a consideration of Kwok's third area of concern, which is to "scrutinize metropolitan interpretations, including those offered by both male and feminist scholars, to see if their readings support the colonizing ideology by glossing over the imperial context and agenda, or contribute to decolonizing the imperializing texts for the sake of liberation."[62] Simply identifying the imperial context does not necessarily lead to decolonization.[63] While I do not take up here Kwok's fourth task, that is, "in order to subvert the dominant Western patriarchal interpretations, postcolonial feminist critics, especially those in Africa, emphasize the roles and contributions of ordinary readers," the resulting gap should be critically engaged so that its results can be tested and measured against its import for "flesh and blood readers."[64] Finally, Kwok highlights the importance of "what Mary Ann Tolbert has called the politics and poetics of location."[65] Biblical scholars need to recognize the central shaping role of our complex social backgrounds in terms of gender, ethnicity, race, status, sexual orientation, and other factors (politics) while also striving to assess our texts and interpretive results for their ethical or theological impact (poetics). Though the remainder of this essay addresses primarily Kwok's first two areas of concern, we should expect her other concerns to influence this inquiry and any that might, in turn, develop from it.

Perhaps the most direct way to begin to address Kwok's first two areas of concern is to assess Philippians through some of the more pointed questions that Musa Dube has raised. On more than one occasion, Dube has listed four questions that may be used to evaluate ancient texts on literary-rhetorical and postcolonial grounds:

1. Does this text have a clear stance against the political imperialism of its time?
2. Does this text encourage travel to distant and inhabited lands, and if so, how does it justify itself?
3. How does this text construct difference: is there dialogue and liberating interdependence, or condemnation of all that is foreign?
4. Does this text employ gender and divine representations to construct relationships of subordination and domination?[66]

In the final section of this article, these questions will prove to be particularly useful for an assessment of Philippians and some of the scholarly observations about the letter.[67]

Interpreting Philippians: A Postcolonial Paul?

Engaging with and implementing postcolonial feminist work can provide a new perspective on the question of Paul's place in the Roman imperial world. Indeed, in comparison to most analyses of Paul by postcolonial and Roman imperial scholars, this set of questions will provide a rather different sense of the arguments presented in Philippians.[68] Many reading Paul's letters in the light of Roman imperialism dispute the answer to Dube's first question ("Does this text have a clear stance against the political imperialism of its time?"). Perhaps the best way to answer this first question, then, is to examine the letter's rhetorics through the other three.

Imperial Intersections and Initial Inquiries 153

Does this text encourage travel to distant and inhabited lands, and if so, how does it justify itself?

By beginning with Dube's second question, we address a topic rarely covered in studies that seek to place Paul in his Roman imperial context: Paul's justification for his movement in the empire.[69] In fact, all of Paul's letters presuppose travel to address an audience at often densely inhabited, colonized locales. Paul always writes from a distance, and the letter to the Philippians is no exception. In fact, Paul reflects on this matter with some regularity. For example, early in the letter he seeks to clarify for his Philippian audience that his imprisonment ("my chains," 1:13) somewhere else does not prevent his success.[70] Rather, he has advanced or made "progress" (1:12) even from within the confines of Roman imperial power, the praetorian guard (1:13). Perhaps contrary to expectation, the message that travels to Philippi is that Paul has traveled somewhere else and has successfully won many for Christ.

This message precedes Paul's next journey to Philippi, a return anticipated and echoed throughout the letter. Though he considers being with Christ to be a better option (1:20-23), Paul maintains that the Philippian community needs him: it is "more necessary because of you [pl.]" (1:24). This action should bring "progress and joy" (1:25) for the community, as the letter explicitly connects this benefit to Paul's *parousia* (1:26), a term describing the arrival of a victorious emperor or the visit of an imperial administrator. The fact that Paul twice justifies his travels in the name of progress echoes the historical rationale for colonization: empire is for the good of the subjects, a paternalistic, civilizing force of advancement. The imperial resonance of Paul's *parousia*, then, may not be entirely coincidental.[71] This resonance would be especially striking for an audience at Philippi, given the city's prominence in the history of Rome's civil wars, its subsequent establishment as a *colonia* in the Roman Empire, and the accompanying development of the colony's imperial cult.[72]

The issue of Paul's continuing absence and the possibility of his return shape a number of appeals in the letter. His instructions on how to live properly as citizens (1:27) are given to emphasize the importance of pleasing Paul. What Paul hears about the Philippians should be sufficient reason for their proper behavior, whether Paul is "coming and seeing you or being away" (1:27). The obedient attitude that he extols later in the letter is also expected whether he is absent or among them ("my presence [*parousia*]," 2:12). When Paul cannot be present, he discusses his plans to send emissaries, such as Timothy and Epaphroditus, in his place (2:19-30). One of the conditions of Paul's work seems to be his ability to commission people to travel to other locations. Yet even when Paul explains whom he is sending to Philippi and why, the topic of his presence and his desire to travel also crops up (2:24). In each of these instances, whether Paul travels to see the Philippians or not, he still expects certain reactions from the audience. The persistence of the topic of travel indicates that Paul seeks to position the Philippians' acceptance according to the recurrent possibility of his arrival/return.[73] That all of these travel contingencies involve divine approval ("gospel of Christ," 1:27; "this from

God," 1:28; "on behalf of God's approval," 2:13; and "in the lord," 2:24) is a topic that I will examine further below.

Not only does Paul's letter to the Philippians discuss travel, but it also presupposes travel to distant, inhabited, and colonized locales. The significance of the letter's circulation could be a fruitful avenue to consider given the colonized settings of these communities within the Roman Empire and the particulars of the colonized community at Philippi. Regardless of how ancient letters circulated, however, one must recognize that the letters' messages travel as well. By writing, Paul seeks to transfer his way of thinking or acting from one location to another. Nowhere is this clearer (in Philippians and other letters) than when Paul argues from his own model.[74] Though it is most explicit in Phil 3:14-17 and 4:8-9, Paul uses model argumentation throughout the letter, typically to highlight his own prominence.[75] Indeed, the "progress" that Paul brings with him wherever he goes demonstrates his quality as a model, as does his close association with the divine. Paul's call for the Philippians to imitate him resonates with the colonizing practice of mimicry, a topic that Tat-siong Benny Liew has applied to the Gospel of Mark but which has yet to be considered for its impact on the exhortations in Philippians.[76] Such calls to imitate are ambivalent, however, as Paul's argument mimes imperial discourse by claiming its supreme authority as model at the same time that it opens up possibilities for resistance to the claims made by either Paul or the empire.[77]

Thus, our initial survey finds that Paul not only depends on but also explicitly argues for the practice of traveling to a distant place. Dube's and Kwok's suspicion of the "mission to the Gentiles" as a justification for imperial travel seems well founded here.[78] The letter depicts Paul as the bringer of "progress" to the communities he visits, while casting the audience as in need of his unique authority and model. Though there are clear indications of how this travel is justified in the letter, such justification can be easily explicated by addressing Dube's third and fourth questions.

How does this text construct difference: is there dialogue and liberating interdependence, or condemnation of all that is foreign?

When we ask how Paul constructs difference in Philippians, the oppositional tenor of his arguments comes squarely into view. Paul's attitude toward difference frames how he justifies his activity as well as the specific contents of the letter. Just as he argues from his own model, so also he expresses his view of difference by arguing from a series of anti-models. When people think differently from him at the site of his imprisonment, he depicts them as envious and divisive (1:15-17). To make clear how his Philippian audience should be unified by acting according to his model, he highlights as an anti-model some "opponents" ("those who stand against you," 1:28) who will meet with destruction. If the community accepts Paul's argument, they will act in unity, unlike those others who "seek their own things" (2:21) "according to divisiveness" (*eritheian*, 2:3; 1:15, 17).

Some might object that Paul's stance of violent opposition to those "outside" the community can still be suitably anti-imperial, especially if Paul is cast in an apocalyptic mode.[79] Though there are many reasons to have reservations about such an objection, Paul's own arguments indicate that he is far from calling for dialogue and interdependence, even among those who seem to "belong" in the community. As mentioned above, Paul seeks obedience from the community, with "fear and trembling" no less (2:12). This obedience is not a qualified "love command" but is to be enacted "without grumbling or questioning" (*dialogismon*, 2:14).[80] Paul specifically rules out arguing, questioning, or dialogue between the community and himself. The purpose of this prohibition is that the audience "might be blameless and pure, children of God without fault, in the midst of a crooked and twisted generation" (2:15). The dualistic trajectory of Paul's argument is highly compatible with the standard colonizer's narrative about the value of "civilization." The community can become one with the pure "lights in the world" (2:15) by becoming silent, compliant, obedient subjects in opposition to the base, perverted, and savage surrounding world.[81]

Applying such strong language to those outside or "foreign" to his community is not an unusual practice for Paul, but rather a persistent feature of his argument. In order to develop a contrast with his own model status (3:2-11), Paul famously and viciously warns the Philippians against those who are dogs, evildoers, and mutilators (3:2).[82] Paul continues this dualistic and violently condemnatory argument even in 3:18-21, a favorite passage for those who seek to uncover a postcolonial or anti-imperial Paul.[83] Those who disagree with Paul are described as "enemies" (3:18) who are doomed to destruction since their minds are on the wrong (earthly) things (3:19). That safety and destruction are doled out along absolutist lines of obedience and loyalty makes this letter compatible with, rather than contrary to, imperial thinking. Even in the final section of the letter (4:10-20), Paul works prodigiously to show how he is neither dependent on nor "interdependent" with the Philippians. Unlike the community, which is depicted as in need of Paul's presence and the resultant progress that he brings, Paul has received aid but is still "self-sufficient," since he did not "speak according to need" (4:11).

Far from encouraging dialogue and interdependence, then, Paul argues violently and oppositionally against those whom he considers "outside" the community. An even greater challenge for the recuperation of a "postcolonial Paul," however, is his attitude toward the Philippian community. His letter argues that the community can attain the right kind of unity only through obedience and fear—not by questioning or considering their relation to Paul but by acknowledging his authority and adhering purely to his exclusive, absolutist vision. Though Paul implies that there are other stances and responses that differ from the arguments that he presents here, the tenor of the letter's arguments highlights the perils of some modes of resistance, and specifically the need for interdependence in decolonization, as highlighted in Dube's work.[84] Rather than replicating global capitalism's form of interconnectedness or valorizing the disconnectedness of nativist independence movements or early Western feminism, liberating interdependence seeks to theorize solidarity apart from exploitative colonial and gendered foundations.[85] Too often, the experience of "independence" after colonization belies the continuation of economic dependence and the preservation of the colonial thinking on nationalism and sexism.[86]

Does this text employ gender and divine representations to construct relationships of subordination and domination?

Following Dube's fourth query, the deployment of gender and divine representations in Philippians must now be examined. As one might expect, Paul refers to the divine with regularity in this letter. The pertinent issue, however, is not whether but how he does so. The letter works to affiliate Paul with the authority of the divine, often using God as a "witness" (1:8) or guarantor of his argument (1:28; 2:13; 3:9, 15; 4:7-9, 13).[87] Paul frequently places himself between the community and the divine so that any possible benefit that the Philippians might receive from the divine is because of Paul, their intermediary (1:26; 2:17-18; 3:17-21; 4:7, 9). As N. T. Wright has argued, "Paul, in other words, was not opposed to Caesar's empire primarily because it was an empire, with all the unpleasant things we have learned to associate with that word, but because it was Caesar's."[88] If Paul is arguing in terms of a divine empire, then it seems that he is positioning himself as a provincial governor or colonial administrator for the divine imperator. Another related possibility, highlighted by Kittredge's analysis of 1 Corinthians, is that Paul is reshaping Roman patronage language in his attempt to establish interconnected hierarchies of patrons and clients.[89]

Many who argue for Paul's anti-imperial stance stress that he uses specifically political language in this letter, often in order to explain the relation of the community to the divine. The letter exhorts its audience to "live as citizens [*politeuesthe*] worthy of the gospel of Christ" (1:27). Unlike the aforementioned enemies, those who join Paul will be part of the *politeuma* (commonwealth,[90] citizenship, or polity, 3:20), from which Jesus as *kyrios* and *sōtēr* will come.[91] However, on both occasions when Paul uses terms derived from the Greek political root *politeu-*, the opposed fates of destruction and safety are also emphasized (1:28; 3:19-20). In both cases, moreover, this violence comes from a divine source. Paul represents the divine as ruling through the threat of destruction and the dominating power of violence. To the extent that the divine is linked to the dense use of military language in this letter[92] or to patronage,[93] the representation is particularly gendered, as these institutions were maintained by and for elite, imperial males. In fact, patronage and the military were densely intertwined in the Roman Empire and were among the more effective means used for social control of Roman subjects.[94]

Paul's use of divine threats might be somewhat mitigated as a dominating argument if it could be shown that such relations are meant only for those "outside" the community. Yet these same passages (and others) show that what characterizes the divine is the power of subjection. Community members show their unified spirit when they accept that they are meant to "suffer on his [Christ's] behalf" (1:29). The community is in a

Imperial Intersections and Initial Inquiries 157

debased position in this *politeuma* (*to sōma tēs tapeinōseōs hēmōn*, 3:21), while Christ's body is one of glory (*tēs doxēs*, 3:21). Even if they can somehow be transformed by the divine, it is only achieved because Christ has the power "to subject all things to himself" (3:21). This order of subjection coincides with the terminology of unequal power relations not only in political contexts but also in the realm of household management. As Kittredge has shown, this language of subordination is specifically gendered, as it defines elite male authority over wives, children, and slaves.[95] Even the Christ hymn in Philippians 2 emphasizes God's power to "exceedingly exalt" Christ with a "name over *all* names" (2:9), so that "*every* knee might bend" (2:10).[96] Since the unity that Paul describes in this letter involves the subservience of all to a kyriarch (*kyrios*, 2:11; 3:20), the universalism expressed in the letter is enlisted in an order of domination. Given the role of universalist claims in the racialist discourse of European colonialism, this confluence of domination, universalism, and violently enforced boundaries should trouble our engagement with Philippians.

While the latter part of the hymn serves Paul's subordinationist rhetoric by highlighting Christ's power, the first part is also put to effective argumentative use. The exhortation that immediately follows the hymn makes clear that Paul wants the community to apply the first half to their own lives. Just as Jesus adopted a stance of obedience (*hypēkoos*, 2:8) and humility, so also they should act in an obedient fashion (*hypēkousate*, 2:12) toward Paul.[97] If this obedience is to imitate Christ's "taking the form of a slave" (2:7), then it also participates in establishing a dominating order. The communal obedience is compulsory, with "fear and trembling," as in a slave/master relationship.[98] Paul is again in the intermediate authoritative position: they should obey him whether he is present or not (2:12), and the establishment or continuation of this hierarchical relationship is meant for God's own pleasure (*hyper tēs eudokias*, 2:13).

Though Paul is in the intermediate place in a hierarchy of authority in this letter, the argumentative use of himself as a model predominates (1:3-11, 12-14, 24-26; 2:16-18; 3:7-11, 14-17; 4:2, 8-9). Some of these model rhetorics draw their authority from the way Paul depicts his actions as echoing the pattern presented in the hymn. He is a model because he is willing to suffer or give up status in order to gain something greater (1:12-14, 23-26; 3:7-11).[99] Timothy, Epaphroditus, and Jesus are each used as models in the letter to provide argumentative support for the primary model of Paul. In all of these cases, the model's actions involve neither leveling nor participatory dynamics, but an effort to ascend in a hierarchical arrangement. Since all of these models are male, these arguments also reflect hierarchical gender dynamics. In fact, the terminology used to describe the community is itself phallocentric, since Paul insists that "we ourselves are the circumcision" (3:3).[100] The "we" of Paul's discourse is not only masculine but also someone with status. If the pattern extolled by Paul (and his supporting models) is to give up some kind of status in order to gain something greater, the argument is geared toward those who have status to spare. This raises the question, What about the majority of people in the Roman Empire, most of whom are of lower status? Since Paul is a man with relatively higher status (3:4-6), he casts the paradigm of belonging on his own terms. To accept his view would require those members of the community who are unlike Paul in the imperial and kyriarchal system to identify with a task that they cannot complete: voluntary loss of status.[101] This observation highlights the fact that Paul's position and point of view were not the only options available to the community receiving the letter and underlines how there were other possibilities for resistance both to the empire and to Paul.

If the exhortation to Euodia and Syntyche (4:2-3) is not an afterthought, as scholars are increasingly willing to admit, it becomes easier to recognize here a continuation of these gendered, hierarchical arguments. Paul's argument for these two women leaders to "think the same thing in the Lord" (4:2) builds upon the letter's dualistic and subordinationist tendencies. The appropriate state of mind follows the model qualities that Paul claims to demonstrate (1:7; 3:14-17) and attempts to establish in the community (2:1-5), over against others (2:3; 3:18-19). Those who accept Paul's mindset ("think this," 3:15) and his authoritative model ("become co-imitators of me," 3:17) are "mature" (3:15) and will gain safety (from a *sōtēr* and *kyrios*, 3:20). Those who "think anything other" (3:15) receive a foreboding divine *apokalypsis* (3:15) and are painted as enemies doomed to destruction (3:18-19). In short, Paul argues that safety is gained through loyalty to a *kyrios* who has the power to subject all (3:21). Paul's authority is strongly linked to divine authority, which explains why he feels he can call the community his "crown" (*stephanos*, 4:1). Since these claims appear in the immediately preceding chapter, the exhortation to Euodia and Syntyche is most likely Paul's effort to convince them to adopt his imperially gendered mind-set, accept his authority within a subordinating chain of models, and be on the "right" side of this *kyrios*.[102]

Throughout Philippians, then, Paul develops and intertwines gendered and divine representations in order to establish relations of subordination and domination. These arguments ensure an elevated position for Paul in an imperial and patriarchal hierarchy. According to the letter, the only way to gain safety and peace is by obeying Paul as an expression of loyalty to a divine lord (see also 4:9, where doing what Paul does earns the presence of the "God of peace").[103] Even Paul's closing greetings, highlighting "Caesar's household" (4:22), indicate his place in this order of domination. However this allusion is to be interpreted in terms of personnel or geography, the terms place him unmistakably in the nexus of imperial and patriarchal power—the "household"— where effective emperors learned to claim their mastery over all realms in their role of "father" over all.[104]

Connections and Conclusions

By examining Paul's letter to the Philippians through Dube's three questions, we can develop a nuanced answer to her first question: *Does this text have a clear stance against the political imperialism of its time?* Paul argues for and from his ability to travel while presenting his message and model to those who support him. The letter is Paul's opportunity to characterize the community as in need of his authority and the progress that it can bring to them. This attitude is justified by the violently dualistic way in which Paul conceives of difference in the letter. He condemns enemies and requires obedience from those who "belong." Paul casts the community in the dependent, subordinate role of a hierarchical system, a system he explains and maintains by reference to gendered power dynamics endorsed by the divine.

Even if one could argue that Paul is making these claims over against the empire, his language is not significantly different from the imperialism of his day. In Philippians, Paul argues and thinks imperialistically, so that he might "both subvert and reinscribe the imperial system."[105] Such patterns indicate that even if Paul is trying to subvert the Roman Empire through the letter, his rhetoric could easily be reassimilated or co-opted to serve an imperialist or colonialist agenda.[106] Though Kwok would situate this tendency in the period of Constantine and Nicaea, her words aptly describe Paul's efforts in Philippians "to maintain its symbolic unity and to marginalize ambiguous and polarized differences."[107]

Significant portions of this analysis would have been more difficult to develop if the role of gender in colonized and colonizing discourse were not recognized, if the activities of women in colonial and anticolonial movements were not considered, or if feminist approaches were not engaged. In fact, attention to the gendered dynamics of the letter might further explain why Paul makes such arguments in competition with the empire. Contributions from feminist, postcolonial, and queer theory all highlight how conflicts that are depicted as contests between men or male-coded entities situate women as the site of battle.[108] If conquered space is figured as female, it is not surprising that Paul's exertions against other imperial contenders would be interwoven with gender resonances.[109] Paul strains to code the community as colonized and feminine and therefore in need of his divinely approved model and authority. To prove his elevated position, like the emperor who proves his mettle in his household, he must also demonstrate how he can command obedient responses and control the behavior of women in his community. Thus, Paul's exhortation to Euodia and Syntyche to "think the same thing" is not only a patriarchal gesture but also an attempt to prove his imperial manhood.[110]

In short, I am suggesting that Paul reinscribes and mimics the imperialism of his time in the letter to the Philippians. A more comprehensive feminist, postcolonial analysis would require an assessment of Paul's imitation rhetoric in light of the elusive colonizing strategy of mimicry.[111] For now, however, we can note that Paul's mimicry may be at least partially similar to the surge of nationalism experienced by peoples striving to throw off colonial governments and mentalities.[112] This should cause us at least some suspicion, as Dube notes: "Because the imitations or reversal models hardly offer liberative alternatives, the literature of both groups tends to be characterized by sharp dualisms, rigid cultural boundaries, vicious racisms, heightened nationalisms, and hierarchical structures that would license any power to victimize other nations."[113] Even so, the pains taken to extol colonial mimicry underscore its fundamental instability ("almost the same, but not quite white") and its distinct potential for seditious resistance.[114]

This last point might prove important in the consideration of the role of women and/or the colonized peoples in and around Philippi, an ancient imperial "contact zone." As a *colonia* of the Roman Empire on an important route for travel, Philippi brought people of disparate ethnic, cultic, political, and geographical origins together. Given the Roman imperial control of the city, their mixing, like the argumentation in Philippians, would have been "shaped by inequality and conflictual relations."[115] As in colonial attempts to enforce cultural mimicry, however, the conditions of the contact zone would have provided other possibilities besides fearful obedience. These possibilities offer fruitful avenues for considering how we might construct the potential historical situation of this letter and the roles of women in this community. They also give us new incentives for investigating the kind of unity that Paul promotes in Philippians. Ultimately, they pose relevant questions not just about the letter but also about feminist and biblical studies. What kinds of approaches do we wish to see in Pauline studies? What intersections can be found or what connections made in feminist interpretation? What coalitions are still possible between those who study feminism, postcolonialism, and Roman imperialism? What kinds of inquiries are still to come?

CHAPTER ELEVEN

Beyond the Heroic Paul

Toward a Feminist and Decolonizing Approach to the Letters of Paul

MELANIE JOHNSON-DEBAUFRE
AND LAURA S. NASRALLAH

In 1963, Krister Stendahl attempted to divert scholars from reading Paul as the quintessential Western individual and the Pauline letters as "documents of human consciousness."[1] Since then, Paul's communal orientation and social-political goals have come to be a focal point of interest and debate. These days, Paul is not an introspective conscience—the characterization with which Stendahl wrestled—but a cultural critic, a community organizer, a political philosopher, or a hybrid subject under empire. Yet these very characterizations show that an interest in Paul-the-individual persists. Paul frequently still functions as a paradigmatic human, so that explorations of his theology, politics, and even his subjectivity become the grounds for contemporary meditations on the same.

Let us juxtapose this interest in Paul's thought and actions with two stories that dramatically decenter him and thus begin to *change the subject/s*. In his discussion of Paul and African American interpretation, Brian Blount recounts the report of Rev. J. Colcock Jones, a nineteenth-century Methodist missionary, to his missionary board: "I was preaching to a large congregation [of slaves] on the *Epistle to Philemon*: and when I insisted on fidelity and obedience as Christian virtues in servants, and upon the authority of Paul, condemned the practice of *running away*, one-half of my audience deliberately rose up and walked off with themselves."[2] In her chapter on postcolonial and feminist biblical interpretation, Kwok Pui-lan tells a similar story about an early-twentieth-century Chinese woman who could barely read, yet who nonetheless "used a pin to cut from the Bible verses where Paul instructed women to be submissive and remain silent in the church."[3]

In both examples, the hearers of Paul's letters take center stage as thinkers and actors. They interpret Paul (and those who try to interpret Paul for them) for themselves, voting with their feet and hands. Some of the slaves in Rev. Jones's audience stayed to debate. They did not question what Paul really meant, but whether there was such an epistle in the Bible or whether what they had heard was in fact the gospel.[4] Kwok similarly reclaims the interpretive agency of the uneducated woman who edits Paul's text. She notes that remembering the Chinese woman's interpretation can "enliven the historical and moral imagination" of feminist postcolonial interpreters because it "demonstrates how oppressed women have turned the Bible, a product introduced by the colonial officials, missionaries, and educators, into a site of contestation and resistance for their own emancipation."[5]

In this chapter, we will suggest that there is much to gain from reading the letters of Paul—in their writing, reception, and afterlives—as sites of debate, contestation, and resistance rather than as articulations of one individual's vision and heroic community-building efforts.[6] Such an approach takes seriously Paul's own writings, where he presents himself as one among many other apostles, teachers, and siblings who struggled together to puzzle out the meaning of being assemblies in Christ. Focusing on Paul alone often replicates his self-authorizing rhetoric and Acts' heroic depiction of him, rather than presenting him as one significant voice among many.[7] By shifting the lens from Paul alone to Paul among others, we gain a better understanding of differences of opinion and perspective, thereby opening debates and productive collaborations both ancient and contemporary, rather than limiting our understanding of the political vision and practices of the Christ-assemblies to whatever Paul alone meant or means.

Our discussion proceeds in two stages. First, we explore how politically engaged Euro-American Pauline scholarship[8] has focused largely on Paul, whether as an anti-imperial hero, an imperial collaborator, or, now, something in between.[9] Despite the attention given to diverse voices in feminist and postcolonial scholarship, Paul's identity, politics, and voice remain the focus of both theological-philosophical engagement and historical reconstruction. Second, we demonstrate the potential of decentering Paul by exploring one theme from postcolonial biblical studies—the idea of travel—and by questioning the constructions of Paul as a heroic traveling missionary in 1 Thessalonians and Acts. At the end, we propose some fruitful areas of inquiry for a decolonizing feminist[10] approach to a politically and communally focused Pauline studies.

The Heroic Political Paul

The persistence of a heroic Paul and the magnification of his voice as *the* voice of the Christ-assemblies with which he was associated result not only from a Western predilection for individualism but also from a process of identification spurred by Paul's rhetoric. From epistle to epistle, Paul offers himself as a model for imitation,[11] even as his self-presentation shifts from community to community—sometimes within a single letter. He is father and nurse (1 Cor 4:15; 1 Thess 2:7), apostle and slave (Gal 1:1; Rom 1:1), both under the law and outside the law (1 Cor 9:20-21). This Paul mediates self and other while negotiating his own particularity and his universal connection to others. Paul offers this rhetorically constructed in-between self as a model for, and an argument to, his inscribed audiences. In this larger context, the *hōs mē* injunctions in 1 Cor 7:29-31, where Paul talks about how to live "as if not" in a particular condition, and the self-wrestling *egō* speech in Rom 7:13-25, in which Paul seems tortured about his own actions, can be and have been read as simultaneously Paul and not Paul. That is, they have been read both as windows onto Paul's religious and/or ethnic subjectivity and as compelling expressions of human subjectivity in any place and age.[12]

Several contemporary discussions about power, difference, religion, and politics have taken up this theme of Paul-as-subject. Despite their differences, we find that the books emerging from the Paul and Politics section of the Society of Biblical Literature and those of continental philosophers thinking about unity and diversity share a tendency to think with and about Paul in the context of contemporary politics. This interest is apparent also in certain scholars from the "New Perspective" on Paul. Such approaches are not necessarily problematic. As we will show, they use Paul to think about challenging contemporary issues such as diversity and inclusion. But by centering on Paul rather than situating Paul among those to whom he wrote, they—and we—miss an opportunity to engage with true diversity and the multiple struggles concomitant with it. Such works tend to emphasize one aspect of difference or to whitewash difficult and exclusionary passages in Paul's letters that function in churches today to condemn Judaism as a sin,[13] to deny women's leadership, and to exclude gays and lesbians from full participation in Christian community.

As is apparent from the title, Paul takes center stage in Pamela Eisenbaum's *Paul Was Not a Christian: The Real Message of a Misunderstood Apostle*. Building on the New Perspective on Paul, Eisenbaum explains how Paul's writings make more sense if one reads him as a Jew called to apostleship and not as a converted Christian. At the heart of her project is an effort to plumb Paul's logic of how, with the pressure of the end of time, individual salvation is not a key issue but rather the means by which both Jews and Gentiles alike can enter into God's redemption. Paul's particular struggles have contemporary resonance for Eisenbaum: "I have come to regard Paul as a Jew who wrestled with an issue with which many modern American Jews wrestle: how to reconcile living as a Jew with living in and among the rest of the non-Jewish world."[14] Focusing on Paul's own relation to difference, Eisenbaum suggests that his writings can provide insights for contemporary engagement with religious difference and pluralism.[15]

In a similar way, Daniel Boyarin's earlier book, *A Radical Jew: Paul and the Politics of Identity*, takes seriously the New Perspective on Paul, resituating him as a first-century Jewish thinker. Boyarin also finds that Paul's rhetorical stance between particularity and universality helps him to think about the challenges of contemporary identity politics.

> In his very extremity and marginality, Paul is in a sense paradigmatic of "the Jew." He represents the interface between *Jew* as a self-identical essence and *Jew* as a construction constantly remade. The very tension in his discourse, indeed in his life, between powerful

self-identification as a Jew ... and an equally powerful, or even more powerful, identification of self as everyman is emblematic of Jewish selfhood.[16]

For Boyarin, the Jewish dilemma of the self is one that is characteristic of both our time and Paul's.[17] The particularity of the figure of Paul thus connects the past and present, so that contemporary politics are engaged through a reading of the life and thought of Paul. Boyarin's Paul is complex but also politically heroic, as we see in much of the politically attuned Pauline scholarship of today. Conceding that "in the reception history of Paul, his texts have generally served what might be broadly called conservative cultural-political interests; they have been used as props in the fight against liberation of slaves and women as well as major supports for theological anti-Judaism," Boyarin argues, like many other recent scholars, that "Paul need not be read this way, indeed, ... his texts support, at least equally well, an alternative reading, one that makes him a passionate striver for human liberation and equality."[18] In a similar way, much of the recent empire-critical scholarship on Paul presents him as resisting or reversing imperial discourses and structures.[19] The four volumes emerging from the Paul and Politics section of the Society of Biblical Literature, for example, feature several explications of Paul's subversive efforts to overturn the logic and power relations of empire.[20] Many scholars have taken as the hermeneutical key to all of Paul's writings the pre-Pauline baptismal statement in Gal 3:28 ("there is neither Jew nor Greek, there is no longer slave or free, there is no longer male and female") rather than Romans 13, in which Paul appears to urge quiescence to empire, or 1 Corinthians 11, where women's voices in prayer or prophecy are circumscribed by the act of veiling.[21] In this way Paul is read as a cultural-political visionary who is relevant to those of us with a particular political bent—not perfect, but still savvy, a subtle revolutionary in the midst of a hierarchical empire.[22]

Where New Testament scholars generally privilege Paul's historical particularity and sometimes draw larger analogies between Paul's writings and contemporary identity politics or struggles with/against American empire, European scholars like Slavoj Žižek, Alain Badiou, and Giorgio Agamben approach the themes of Paul's thought as timeless philosophical categories.[23] Thus, Paul the solitary political subject moves beyond the fields of biblical studies and Christian theology to engage with continental philosophy and cultural criticism, where he becomes a heroic philosopher of universalism and love.[24] For Žižek, for example, Paul argues for a nation- and culture-transcending *agapē*, a love "that enjoins us to 'unplug' from the organic community into which we were born—or, as Paul puts it, for a Christian, there are neither men nor women, neither Jews nor Greeks."[25] While these conversations aim to energize new communal secular-political visions, they do so without the chorus of New Testament scholars who have worked to expose the Christian supersessionism and anti-Semitism of many interpretations of Paul.[26] Such a decontextualization allows secular authors to rehabilitate an authoritative (Christian) Paul as a loving Everyman who successfully and rightly supersedes his (Jewish) particularity.

In our opinion, these varied depictions of a political Paul and his politics, whether created by biblical scholars or European cultural critics and philosophers, fail to articulate adequately the fact that Paul was and continues to be one among many, part of a community that is diverse and multicentered.[27] Where political debate is theorized, it is most often framed as a dialogue either between the historical Paul and his (usually wrongheaded) epistolary audiences or between a political Paul and contemporary beliefs about religious exclusivism/capitalism/empire.[28] As Boyarin notes, "When Paul says, there is no Jew or Greek, no male and female in Christ, he is raising an issue with which we still struggle. Are the specificities of human identity, the differences, of value, or are they only an obstacle in the striving for justice?"[29] We could extend this discussion to the ancient *ekklēsia* that first heard the letter or even to communities today by imagining that they might debate the issues raised in Paul's letters rather than simply accepting or rejecting Paul's words on the subject.

To some extent our critique—the belief that we should turn the scholarly focus from a reconstruction or use of Paul alone to consideration of Paul's letters as sites of contestation and debate—has already been enacted and heard. In each of the SBL's Paul and Politics sessions, a feminist scholar has disrupted or mitigated the focus on a heroic anti-imperial Paul by calling for serious consideration of the perspectives and contributions of his comrades and interlocutors in both the ancient *ekklēsiai* and the history of interpretation.[30] Some of the hearers have acted on these constructive critiques.[31] For example, in *The Arrogance of Nations: Reading Romans in the Shadow of Empire*, Neil Elliott—a longtime champion of the anti-imperial Paul—engages some feminist interpretations of Paul and draws on the writings of Fredric Jameson and Antonio Gramsci to map both the context and the limitations of Paul's political discourse. Elliott concludes that Paul's hierarchical and messianic political solution is the only thinkable or utterable counterpoint to the extreme violence and claims to universal sovereignty that characterize imperial rule. His approach thus helps to trace the inscription of kyriarchal logic in Romans—that is, how Paul's vision of God's victory is a political counterpoint to Roman imperial systems of domination that simultaneously replicates aspects of imperial logic. However, *Arrogance of Nations* does not explore whether any nascent or alternative political responses to empire might have been present in Paul's communities or activated by diverse interpreters of Paul.

Elliottt's Judean political Paul disrupts imperial and capitalist Euro-American Christianity.[32] Paul's Gentile audience in Romans is loosely correlated with "modern, comfortable, more-or-less secularized first-world Christians who remain the primary consumers of Pauline scholarship."[33] With important prompting from Latin American liberation theologians and the struggles against poverty and injustice in Haiti, Elliott reads Paul's God-talk in Romans as giving voice to the human struggle for justice and freedom, what Fredric Jameson calls the "single vast unfinished plot" of history.[34]

Elliott makes an important step forward by beginning his book with Haitian women and Latin American martyrs and theologians. Yet these figures do not play a role in the main part of the book, with the result that their multivocality is made univocal: within the *ekklēsiai* of Christ, Paul alone becomes the voice of those struggling under empire. In the end, it seems the arrogant Gentiles and the political Paul are the worst and best sides of (white, liberal) U.S. Christianity.[35]

How might these contemporary figures—the voices of Haitians, Latin Americans, others—be foregrounded in the project of historical reconstruction so that they add to our understanding of how the letter to the Romans might have been heard in the imperial metropole?[36] Incorporating such voices does not mean that historians necessarily risk having less precision in their reconstructions of the ancient world; such voices rather "enliven our historical imaginations," as Kwok suggests, regarding the possible range of responses of those who first received Paul's letter. Such voices also disrupt a center-and-margins view of contemporary political discourse; they open up the possibility that the women in Haiti might have political visions that complicate, contest, reframe, or even discard Paul's vision (and thus Elliott's and our own). The meaning of Romans might then be varied and its possibilities and limitations more fully unfolded.[37] Such an approach takes Paul's letters as partial inscriptions of the political visions and debates of the Christ-assemblies rather than as a repository for Paul's thought alone.

The persistence of the Paul-centered habit in politically engaged Pauline studies is apparent even among postcolonial feminist and gender-critical scholars. Both Davina Lopez and Joseph Marchal, for example, situate their work in a complex nexus of empire-critical, postcolonial, feminist, and gender-critical interpretations of Paul. Each is clear about the need to confront the intertwined sexist, racist, and colonialist legacies of the Pauline tradition. Reading them side by side, however, does not produce a unified feminist or postcolonial view of Paul. Instead, two different portraits of Paul emerge: the rhetorical-textual Paul is either the organizer of the empire's subjugated nations or their imperial subjugator. Paul either undermines or wields dominant notions of masculinity.

In her preface, Lopez states, "this book seeks to re-imagine Paul's consciousness and communities as critically liberationist in orientation and transformative in potential."[38] She situates her project as intervening in contemporary debates that draw on an authoritative figure of Paul in order to exclude and dehumanize society's marginalized. She asks:

> Who can claim Paul as authoritative? ... With whom does Paul side? I re-imagine Paul as occupying a vulnerable, subversive social position of solidarity among others and as part of a useable past for historically dominated and marginalized peoples in the present.[39]

The framework of *Apostle to the Conquered* is thus defined by an intentionally Paul-centered approach that sees Paul's solidarity with the conquered and marginalized as part of "building a more just human and earth community."[40]

Lopez's book does not explore the complexities of Paul's self-construction across his letters,[41] nor the possibility that the "nations" to which he wrote might not desire or uniformly appreciate his particular form of rescue and resurrection. In reality, they might have debated with him or even ignored him, as it appears some did in Galatians. In addition, this authoritative Paul functions importantly as a model for political conversion (or, more accurately, consciousness raising) in the U.S. context, that is, for those who need to recognize and repent of their complicity with imperial politics. If

Beyond the Heroic Paul 167

we ignore Paul's conversation partners and his shifting self-presentation in response to them, the diverse subjects in the Pauline assemblies become the recipients of Paul's mission rather than subjects with political agency and imagination.

Marchal's Paul is defined with similar sharpness.[42] In his view, however, Paul did not offer liberation to the communities to which he wrote, but rather a new form of colonialism. Marchal's intersectional analysis shows clearly that empire-critical work cannot sidestep the fundamental hierarchical structures of gender, sexuality, race, and nation that are embedded in imperial discourse on their way to an anti-imperial Paul. Throughout the book, Marchal applies to Paul's letter to the Philippians the four broad questions posed by Musa Dube in *Postcolonial Feminist Interpretation of the Bible* for identifying the influence of imperial and/or colonial ideologies ([1] Does this text have a clear stance against the political imperialism of its time? [2] Does this text encourage travel to distant and inhabited lands, and if so, how does it justify itself? [3] How does this text construct difference: does it promote dialogue and liberating independence or condemnation of all that is foreign? [4] Does this text employ gender and divine representations to construct relationships of subordination and domination?).[43] He concludes that "both Paul's letters and Pauline interpretation are the results of imperially gendered rhetorical activities."[44] Marchal thus locates the political-rhetorical Paul and his interpreters on an undifferentiated trajectory stretching from Roman to Euro-American Christian imperialism. Marchal writes in order to challenge the empire-critical scholarship discussed above, so that the scholarly production of the singularly anti-imperial Paul births its opposite: a singularly imperial Paul. This single-minded focus on Paul is not Marchal's intent;[45] the application of Dube's questions to Paul functions primarily to enact a feminist, postcolonial critique of the heroic political Paul. Thus, while it makes sense to begin with Dube's questions, developing them with a concern for multiple contexts and interpretations of imperial rhetoric might tell a different story (or complicate a single one). In short, we need to ask whether Paul's self-authorizing rhetoric (and its reinscriptions) might be better understood in the context of debates within the *ekklēsiai* of Christ and the history of interpretation rather than as a general will to imperial power.

Empire-critical approaches to Paul confront imperialist and capitalist Euro-American Christianity either by opposing it with Paul's obscured and now revealed anti-imperial gospel or by exposing the complicity of Paul's rhetoric with imperial ideologies. At the same time, they construct Western Christianity and U.S. politics as religious-political monoliths, obscuring the ways in which each has been and continues to be a complex site of oppression, liberation, and local contestation. As Schüssler Fiorenza has argued, a Paul-centered approach accepts Paul's self-construction as founder and authoritative teacher, thus limiting our ability to imagine the diverse communities of women and men that supported, shaped, and even differed from Paul without thereby being imperialistic themselves.[46]

We propose that an approach that is both feminist and decolonizing should interpret the letters of Paul as embedded in a contested, complex, and shifting context that includes both ancient empire and modern neocolonialism, thus allowing an engagement with the present to revise our approach to the past and vice versa. These epistles—produced, read, and debated by multiple voices and dialogical in their very nature, even if we lack half of the correspondence and all of the oral communications—inscribe a variety of communities that were engaged in negotiating, contesting, and colluding in the context of empire. An approach that decenters Paul requires that we interrogate Paul's arguments in light of their silenced or elided counter-arguments, interpreting Paul's self-construction as reacting to and against various other self-understandings. Such an approach also allows us to recognize the diversity of Pauls after Paul, as letters written under Paul's name and narratives that feature Paul the heroic Christian missionary add to the diversity and richness of our understanding of the contestation and debates that took place in early Christian communities.

Disrupting the Heroic Traveling Missionary: 1 Thessalonians and Acts as Test Cases

How can we begin to enact such a program of feminist and decolonizing interpretation? Following Marchal, let us consider one of Dube's programmatic questions for bringing postcolonial analysis to bear on biblical studies: "Does this text encourage travel to distant and inhabited lands, and how does it justify itself?"[47] Putting this question to 1 Thessalonians produces some interesting observations for an *ekklēsia*-focused interpretation. Ostensibly, the letter narrates the travels of Paul and his co-workers from Philippi (2:2) to Thessalonica (2:2-13) to Athens (3:1), while constructing Paul's imitative readers (1:6) as self-sufficient (2:9), heroic travelers who bravely face danger (2:2, 15; 3:7). The justification and the measure of Paul's success are sacralized: "We have been approved by God to be entrusted with the gospel, so we speak not to please people but to please God" (2:4). Such a missionary needs no invitation. God wills his territorial presence, and his aggressive persistence (2:18) is coded as perseverance against sinfulness (2:14-16) and godlessness (1:9).

We need not search far to trace some possible effects of Paul's self-construction.[48] In a sermon entitled "The Qualities of a Great Missionary," the popular American evangelical preacher John MacArthur draws on the brief description of Paul's experience in Philippi in 1 Thessalonians 2:2 to claim Paul's missionary boldness as a "quality with no substitute" for both Paul and contemporary Christians:[49]

> Even after they had been beaten up and were treated shamefully, they were still bold. Paul could never be daunted, there just wasn't any way to stop him.... When you want to start something for God, you get organized first and then say, "Here I go, God. I'm doing this for you." But as soon as you take one step, Satan is there. Now you have a test. If you have boldness, you go right through to *victory*. Boldness is essential to *victory* because it is the quality that makes you go through the test when you're being resisted.... If you have the opportunity on your job to share Jesus Christ, and your supervisor says, "Shut up or you'll be fired," in your heart say, "Good," and then continue to declare Jesus Christ. If you are

fired for sharing Christ, go to a new job and you will have some *new territory* for declaring Jesus Christ. And if your neighbor can't stand your testimony, she will move away and a new one will come. Boldness makes for greater opportunity, and it always did in the Book of Acts. They were bold and people got upset. They would be thrown out of places and they would go to new places. . . . Don't be ashamed. Boldness is basic because there will always be resistance. Boldness is the only capacity that says, "I will not succumb to the resistance." Now that doesn't mean that you should be a bull in a china closet, stomping all over people's necks and becoming terribly offensive.[50] But it does mean that nobody should be allowed to stop you in a ministry that you believe the Spirit of God has called you to.[51]

This interpretation of Paul as a heroic missionary is not being used for authorizing a foreign missionary society.[52] Yet the language of competing for territory—the job and the neighborhood—and the expectation of victory easily evoke that history and locate the daily struggles of the addressee—the emboldened "you"—within it.

Regardless of Paul's context or intent, the heroic Paul takes on a life of his own with the help of the book of Acts and contemporary interpreters who shape bold and territorially minded Christians through an identification with the figure of Paul. Many New Testament scholars could easily provide an effective and even convincing historical counterpoint to MacArthur's reading of Paul. For example, they could critique MacArthur's individualizing, religious, self-authorizing reading with a reading of Paul as "other" with a communal outlook and a countercultural politics. This process, however, would also replicate the tendency to cast Paul as a hero and to draw on his life and thinking to address contemporary social, political, and religious issues.[53]

First Thessalonians' construction of Paul as a heroic, tramping traveler is, however, just that: a construction. Thus we might also think about the letter's image of Paul as a suffering and triumphant apostle in relation to the text's construction of the ancient *ekklēsia* in Thessalonica, asking what such a construction attempts to produce or hide and how it might take on different force in different contexts.[54] The heroic apostolic traveler contrasts with the construction of the Thessalonians in the letter. It is Paul and his co-workers who faced trouble in Philippi, and Paul who is lonely in Athens but prevented by Satan from returning. The community members are not called to be imitators of Paul by actively traveling and preaching; rather, they imitate Paul and Jesus when they *receive* the word (1:7). Combined with Paul's advice to the community to live quietly and mind their own affairs, the narration of the traveling Paul rhetorically renders the Thessalonians passive, localizing them to smaller spheres of movement and influence and minimizing their suffering by smoothing their relations with the larger society. While *Paul* appears as the counter-cultural persecuted hero for the gospel, the *community* should "command the respect of outsiders" (4:11).

But perhaps the community was not so insular. The letter does not describe how the word about the Thessalonians had spread through the region. But by mentioning that they already love all the communities throughout Macedonia, the letter points to existing networks of information and economic exchange. Such connections were likely maintained not by traveling apostles or missionaries but through the travel of various ordinary men and women—slave messengers, poor artisans and agricultural laborers seeking work in the cities, and members of households connected by various informal and formal familial ties such as marriage, adoption, inheritance, and other factors.[55] As the rhetoric of the self-sufficient traveler draws on imperial discourses, so also these communal networks emerge from the realities of empire, including the system of Roman roads and the increase in mobility and urban populations that resulted from economic and social displacement.[56] If we privilege the apostolic traveler, we hear the prelude to ideologies of colonization and the centralization of leadership around a few heroic men. If we privilege a much wider range of travelers and social networks, we see structures of economic survival and diverse efforts to create distinctive communities in Christ in the context of an expanding empire.[57]

Despite Paul's construction of apostolic independence and lonely suffering, he himself is fully a part of these networks of support. He has received financial support from the Philippians (Phil 4:16), and he must *make the case* that he supported himself while he was living among the Thessalonians (1 Thess 2:9). Paul's economic dependence is problematic for him because it can easily be spun as greedy and self-promoting (2:5). Moreover, in the context of hegemonic imperial constructions of masculinity, it also signals his weakness. Thus, in 1 Thessalonians Paul masks his economic need through claims to economic self-sufficiency and imagery that speaks of caretaking rather than dependence—"we were gentle among you, like a nurse taking care of her children" (2:7) and "like a father with his children" (2:11). In this gender-slipping self-presentation, we see an example of community leaders in colonized positions constructing their own relative weakness as power. But Paul's rhetoric also serves to infantilize the community and thus to subordinate any community leadership to his own.[58]

Paul's status and authority with the community are evidently at stake. Although 1 Thessalonians is widely characterized as a letter of encouragement or consolation, it is Paul who sends Timothy to confirm that the community has not lost its regard for Paul in light of the afflictions he faced when among them (3:1-5). If anything, *their* message (sent through Timothy) was a message of encouragement to Paul. This reading of Paul among others restores Paul to sociality as a participant in networks of women and men who promote, resist, or ignore him while he is away.[59]

Thus, the Pauline letters represent the *creation* of structures of interdependence and identity among competing but subordinated subjectivities in the context of empire. They also contribute to the construction of powerful configurations of outsiders and foreignness that drew new maps in the context of Western territorial expansion.[60] The "mission to the gentiles" in the Pauline letters is not the same as the nineteenth-century Western missionary movement.[61] If we fail to see these complex negotiations of identity in the particular context of the Roman Empire, then Paul-the-Jew becomes a colonizer of the Gentiles (despite their being the dominant culture) and our interpretations replicate the anti-Judaism that has long characterized triumphalist Christianity.[62] When this happens, we are effectively reading Paul's letters through Acts.

Despite more than a century of cautions about using Acts to read Paul, scholars continue to do this in an effort to make sense of the order and content of Paul's epistles. Frequently Acts 16–17, the account of Paul in Philippi and Thessalonikē, is used to explain both 1 Thessalonians and Paul's stance toward the Roman Empire. We suggest that a decolonizing feminist analysis should take into account not only "the genuine Paul" but also his afterlife in pseudepigraphical letters and narrative representations. Investigation of the politics and rhetoric of Paul-after-Paul can sensitize us to what is occluded and revealed when we read Paul through these later lenses. Viewed in this framework, Acts is one of the earliest interpretations of the Pauline traditions, an interpretation that famously ignores the weak and letter-writing Paul while weaving from various strands in Paul's own rhetorical self-construction a larger-than-life hero.

The issue of space and geography, introduced so powerfully in Acts 2,[63] recurs throughout the book as the narrative moves from Jerusalem to Rome with Paul collecting cities for the Christian Way.[64] Acts participates in a kind of urban and imperial network building that was common at the time as subjected Greek cities sought to find their place in the *oikoumenē* ("inhabited world") of the Roman Empire. The Roman emperor Hadrian, for instance, sponsored and encouraged such coalitions of Greek city-states in the form of a Panhellenion, centered in Athens, that engaged in religious and judicial activities, maintaining that they had ancient ethnic ties to Athens, on the one hand, and current ties to Rome through politics and benefactions, on the other.[65]

Luke uses a logic similar to that of the Panhellenion to craft a coalition of Christian cities from across the *oikoumenē*, most of which were brought into this network by the mapping movement of Paul's body. In Paul's own letters we see a plurality of apostles; in other New Testament texts, including the beginning of Acts, we see a diversity of co-workers and theological ideas within earliest Christianity. Yet the narrative of Acts funnels the reader's focus ever narrower. This is similar to other stories of travel from this period, which reflect Rome's interest in geographical expansion and conquest, on the one hand, and the model of ancient Greek travelers, on the other. Men are cast in the mold of the Odysseus of old, bravely making their way through exotic regions with different customs, wealth, and dangers. Acts likewise narrows its focus from an initial interest in various apostolic (and other) travelers to center increasingly on Paul as a quintessential traveler. Philologically and ideologically, Luke effectively reduces the plural Christian *ekklēsiai* or civic assemblies of Paul's letters (the plural appears only once in Acts) to a singular *ekklēsia* (mentioned twenty-two times in Acts) and thus to one univocal church. Local networks of support and contested leadership are erased by the attention on Paul's dangerous, heroic, relentless move across much of the Roman *oikoumenē*.

In the sections of Acts that are set in Philippi and Thessalonica, there seem to be tensions between Paul and the Roman Empire. In Philippi, Paul and his cohort are accused of being Jews (*Ioudaioi*) who are disturbing the city: "They advocate customs which it is not lawful for us Romans to accept or practice" (16:20-21 RSV). Yet Paul the traveler, despite being accused of sedition against the empire, uses the standards of empire to trump the acts of empire: he asserts his Roman citizenship to humiliate local officials who have imprisoned and humiliated him. In Thessalonica, too, Paul's cohort is dragged into the street and accused: "These who have turned the world (*oikoumenē*) upside down have come here also, and Jason has received them; and they are all acting against the decrees of Caesar, saying that there is another king, Jesus" (Acts 17:6-7). Yet Paul slips off safely even while under threat, though the threat involves Jewish violence toward Jewish followers of Christ, not Roman injustice or even judicial proceedings. When Paul and Silas are accused by Jews in Thessalonica, they slip away by night to Beroea, where high-status Greek women as well as men, along with Jews more noble than those in Thessalonica, accept their message (17:10-13).

In creating this heroic and unifying Paul, the writer of Acts seeks to distance the one true *ekklēsia* and the one true Paul from contemporaneous Jews who might be seen as seditious toward the empire, especially after the events of 70 C.E. and in light of the upcoming Bar Kokhba revolts.[66] Luke crafts Paul in the image of contemporary elites who seamlessly combined Greek and Roman identities while appealing to both. As Lawrence Wills and Shelly Matthews have shown, the majority of Jews in Acts are portrayed as chaotic and moblike, while Roman justice is generally straightforward and fair. Paul is able to rehearse the narratives of ancient Judaism while remaining different from rabble-rousing contemporary Jews; he is embraced by Romans and by those of high status. In a similar way, Luke's Paul, unlike the Paul of Romans 16 and other Pauline texts, has no female traveling companions and meets no female co-apostles, troublesome authoritative women who might disturb the *oikonomia* of empire.

Luke is one of the earliest sources to frame the question that is still contested in Pauline scholarship: Was Paul a rebel against Rome and thus a postcolonial hero? For Luke, the answer is no. Nothing comes of the accusations of sedition against Rome. Luke carefully constructs a Way that has no place for sedition, and charges of resistance and rebellion eventually melt away. Paul and his cohort never agree that such accusations are true, and the canonical Acts suggests that the Roman authorities actually *like* Paul. As we know, the end of Acts leaves the reader hanging and Paul involved in what seems to be a pleasant house arrest.

Acts must therefore have been written in response to a lively conversation—argument, really—about the relationship of emerging Christian communities to Jewish communities and to the Roman Empire. In response, Luke chose to foreground not the communities that housed and supported Paul, but Paul himself. In 1 Thessalonians, Paul's rhetorical focus on his own brave body and its travels does not fully mask the possibility of resistance to that focus. Acts, building on Paul's rhetorical self-construction, goes beyond Paul's own letters, further limiting what we know about early communities in Christ. Once we see how Acts narrows its focus primarily to Paul, we are in a better position to recognize and oppose the genealogy of interest in Paul's heroic identity.

Conclusions

Empire-critical, postcolonial, and feminist work in Pauline studies has too often become stuck in individualistic debate—replicating the historiographical model of great men who stood alone to change history—over whether Paul was a liberator or an oppressor of women, slaves, and Gentiles. Scholars disagree over whether his letters attest a creative and radical subversion of imperial discourse and structures or whether they appropriate imperial language and logic and thus collaborate with empire. Decolonizing feminist scholarship can and should interrogate and disrupt this legacy through various strategies.

One such strategy is to recenter attention on Paul's letters as sites of vision *and* debate. Such work begins with privileging the ancient communities to which Paul wrote—groups that struggled with, alongside, and sometimes against him—while simultaneously tracing the diverse communities that have interpreted Paul throughout history. Such an approach can imagine and articulate both the ancient "in Christ" assemblies and contemporary sites of interpretation as *contested spaces* more readily than an approach that begins with Paul himself.

Another strategy is to turn away from the question of whether the ancient Paul was a hero or a villain and instead to imagine him and his interpreters as fully engaged in the messier political subjectivities of the diverse communities to which he wrote and those that have subsequently interpreted him. Taking seriously the differences, the rifts, and the discontinuities between our own identities and those of our contemporaries (as well as the overlaps and the possibilities for solidarity) can facilitate our reconstruction of similar differences in antiquity. Conversely, a disciplined intimacy with ancient texts and contexts provides an ethical and intellectual pattern that can facilitate a similar attentiveness to the politics, conditions, and textures of situations and persons in the present. Feminists often speak of the importance of reading texts in community or in the "contact zone" where an awareness of our differing perspectives can both challenge and expand our readings. Focusing on the diversity within and around the Pauline assemblies both then and now can provide a site for such engagement.

A third strategy is to trace the effects of different reconstructions of Paul. A story of Paul the ancient hero (masked as an authoritative, historical account) can weave into community life Paul's justifications of his subordination of women or his apparent disregard for transforming the master–slave ideology of the ancient world. Similarly, a story of Paul the collaborator (masked as the only historically viable reading) can also silence the survival, movement, vision, vitality, and open dissent and debate that occurred in the Pauline *ekklēsiai*, as well as the struggles that various men and women, ancient and modern—including Paul—have faced as unwelcome or imprisoned travelers.

When we examine Paul's letters alongside his afterlife in the Acts of the Apostles (as well as other texts such as the *Acts of Thecla*), we enact a decolonizing feminist historiography that interrogates not only the Pauline correspondence and its earliest interpretation but also the legacy of the Pauline tradition as a "base text" for Western imperialism and diverse patriarchies. We do not seek to exonerate or free Paul's letters from Acts and its legacy of imperial collusion. Instead, we assume a history of resistance and rereading of Paul through time and in different contexts. Stories of resistant Georgia slaves and uneducated Chinese women are fully a part of this history and can be used to imagine a similar agency and voice for the members of Paul's audiences and for early Christians in the time of Acts. This sort of feminist and decolonizing historiography recognizes the complex and diverse strategies of resistance, adaptation, and transformation that characterize individual and corporate negotiations of subjectivity and survival in the context of empire. It also takes up the dual task of articulating an ethics of interpretation,[67] on the one hand, and working for liberating interdependence and justice, on the other, even if it is difficult to determine precisely what those might be in a given context.

Engaging the Pauline letters as rhetorical instruments that construct both Paul and his audience in various ways might leave us less certain about what Paul the individual thought or accomplished. But it will give us more clarity about how a particular construction of Paul serves to authorize, valorize, or erase particular agendas and voices. More importantly, if we place the assemblies at the center and hear Paul's letters as one voice among many, we can imaginatively reconstruct and reclaim a richer history of interpretation of Paul, a history populated with subjects struggling in different ways within the varied contexts of empire.

CHAPTER TWELVE

To What End?

*Revisiting the Gendered Space of
1 Corinthians 11:2-16 from
a Feminist Postcolonial Perspective*

JENNIFER G. BIRD

In this essay, I will employ a critical feminist postcolonial hermeneutics to engage with 1 Cor 11:2-16 and several scholars' contributions on this passage in order to discuss three points of interest. I will begin by discussing how, when a scholar engages in a "hermeneutics of identification with Paul," the power and authority that are granted to a Pauline passage are transferred to or claimed by this scholar.[1] Next, I will suggest that there is a direct connection between this particular text's potential to control and constrain females/wives and the need among biblical scholars to proclaim a "correct" interpretation of the passage. Finally, I will bring these two points together to show how Paul and his writings are, in effect, being colonized by biblical scholars in a way that makes Paul's writings useful for programs of colonization, domination, and control.[2] In this case, that means authorizing restrictive proclamations directed toward females.[3]

As a feminist scholar interested in postcolonial theories and their engagement with biblical texts, I find 1 Cor 11:2-16 and the scholarship focusing on it to be remarkably fertile ground. Not only is this passage one of two or three that are consistently invoked for insight into the proper roles of females in the church, thus making it an incredibly powerful text, but it is also one over which there is great contention in terms of what Paul actually thought or meant regarding the matters discussed in the passage. Such an ongoing lack of consensus raises the question of what is at stake in the "correct" interpretation of these verses.

Briefly, this passage asserts that Christ is the head of man and man is the head (or source) of woman (v. 3), then deals with the propriety of head coverings for males and females while praying or prophesying (vv. 4-5), then makes a correlation between the (culturally determined) shame associated with a woman praying uncovered and a woman with a shaved head (vv. 5-6). Then comes that tricky business about males being the glory of God and females being the glory of males, as confirmed by the order of creation in the second creation account (vv. 7-9), followed by the ever-confusing reference to angels in worship (v. 10); a claim about the interdependence of males and females that directly contradicts v. 3 and vv. 7-9 (vv. 11-12); an appeal to "nature" regarding gender expectations for the length of a person's hair (vv. 13-15); and finally a claim that "we" have no other practice (as opposed to what is not made clear) (v. 16). What is certain about this passage is that we cannot make conclusive claims about what Paul is actually declaring, or even what the primary underlying issue is. In spite of this awkward situation, scholars continue to offer conclusive mandates based on this passage.

With these points in mind, it should not surprise us that the scholarship on this brief passage is highly diverse, comprising a range of meanings that sometimes contradict and sometimes complement one another.[4] Of the many points of disagreement on how to read this passage, the division that is most salient to our interest in the politics of interpretation is between (a) those who say that Paul was in part quoting what he had heard that the Corinthians were saying and then countering it[5] and (b) those who insist that all of the statements in this passage reflect Paul's own beliefs.[6] This division among scholars is no small matter, since for the first group the text's message of subordination is ultimately trumped or denounced by Paul, while for the second group subordination is precisely what Paul recommends.[7] There is also a third group of scholars that has arisen in the past decade who maintain that all of the content in 1 Cor 11:2-16 is Pauline, including its tensions, yet they still assert that Paul was essentially egalitarian.[8] It is not coincidental that we see such tensions among the scholars who have studied this passage, since the differences are symptomatic of the ambivalence within the text itself.

It is worth noting that a number of points can be cited in favor of the first position listed above. (1) When the passage is read as a dialogical exchange instead of reflecting entirely Paul's views, much of the tension and difficulty within the passage disappears.[9] (2) The two most difficult passages in Paul's letters for anyone who prefers to believe that Paul was more or less egalitarian (this one and 1 Cor 14:33b-36) can be handled in the same manner, thus making sense of both texts while also leaving Paul without contradicting himself. (3) If Paul was as educated as I have been led to believe he was, it seems likely that he would have been aware of such blatant contradictions within his own thought and rhetoric and would have corrected them. (4) If Paul was seeking to counter a gendered veiling requirement, as some have argued, the problem becomes even more acute, since in that case nearly two thousand years of church tradition, teaching, preaching, and social convention have actually perpetuated what Paul sought to discredit.[10]

In spite of these substantial points in favor of a dialogical reading, most scholars have read this passage as entirely Paul's own ideas. Whatever the reasons behind this reading strategy, it is clear that many scholars continue to feel a need to make sense of this "Pauline directive." This need highlights not only the authority that many scholars ascribe

To What End? 177

to Paul and the trust that they have in his words but also the political importance that Paul's insights continue to have today.

Mapping the Method[11]

I am endlessly fascinated by how many scholars, pastors, and laypeople look to Paul and his writings as their primary source for instruction on women's roles and activities in the church and how consistently their readings perpetuate the "otherness" of females.[12] Yet there is also an implied admission by many of these same readers that the "subordination passages" present something of a problem. Everyone seems to agree that there are texts in Paul's letters that endorse the subordination of women to men, but they differ over whether this implication should be excused owing to Paul's sociopolitical location (he could not help himself), justified because of its agreement with other biblical claims that endorse the subordination of females to males, or challenged as not worthy of being considered "the word of God."[13] In the case of a passage in a genuinely Pauline letter such as this one, the first two options are the norm, even among some feminist scholars.

By contrast, one of the primary assumptions underlying my own feminist postcolonial approach to analyzing biblical texts[14] is that both the texts and the scholarly works written about them are the "results of imperially gendered rhetorical activities."[15] Employing a hermeneutics of suspicion,[16] I analyze the different voices within the scholarly material in order to discover what kinds of gendered discourse or power struggles they (knowingly or not) are engaging in or are engendering for those who take their insights seriously. To do this, I first look for essentialist descriptions and assumptions made by scholars about the females who are addressed in a particular passage. Such language is quite common, since many of the biblical texts that have attracted scholarly attention (including 1 Cor 11:2-16) are full of essentializing rhetoric. Second, I look for conclusions or assumptions that use gendered terms in a way that establishes or perpetuates hierarchies, thereby justifying the domination of one group over another. Third, I examine whether the scholar's representations of women's sexuality and/or bodies function so as to leave the scholar in a position of structural and relational control, particularly when the interpretation benefits kyriarchal[17] and imperial systems. To put this point another way, is the scholar making essentialist assumptions about what roles a female can fill that focus on her bodily capacities? Claims based on such assumptions have the potential to limit a female to maternal roles and household realms. All such gendered assumptions about who females are, what they can do, and the hierarchies that "keep them in their place" maintain and benefit imperial voices and agendas.

Another set of questions that informs my approach concerns how a scholar positions her-/himself in relation to females and what kind of language s/he uses to do so. Is the scholar speaking on behalf of or to all females? Do the scholar's comments arise from a position of power over women rather than a perspective that desires their empowerment? Does the scholar use malestream[18] language, knowledge, and power that mimic imperial methods of control and relational structures? Does the scholar's language imply that being male is normative and/or endorse interpretations that perpetuate this fallacy? If any of these practices is present, the scholar is contributing to suppressing peripheral and non-normative voices and simultaneously (re)investing with power those who uphold androcentric kyriarchal views. In other words, the scholar is complicit in using Paul to justify the control of females for the sake of godliness or for orderliness within faith communities.

These interrogations invariably lead us back to the text itself. At that point the question becomes not simply whether the scholar reads "with the text" (positivistically) or "against the grain" (critically), but also to what extent the scholar is influenced and affected by the rhetoric of the text, that is, whether the scholar mimics the rhetoric of the text in his or her writing. Elizabeth A. Castelli, Jorunn Økland, and Caroline vander Stichele and Todd Penner have all contributed important works dealing with the rhetorical effects of Paul's writings.[19] All of them agree that it is not enough to ask "what did Paul say" or "what did Paul mean," not only because "meaning" is found only when a person or group engages a text (as opposed to the idea that it is contained in the words themselves), but also because leaving the discourse at the level of "meaning" ignores and thus leaves unchallenged the implications of those meanings when put into practice. This does not mean that efforts to find "what Paul meant" are not well intentioned, but far too often these efforts end up perpetuating oppressive or unjust systems and dynamics simply because scholars do not consider the *implications* of these claims. When the focus is on finding what Paul meant, the materiality of his letters—how they come to be realized in people's lives—is viewed as secondary and is even presumed by many to be what is best for all involved.[20]

My intention in this chapter is to invite readers to question more than to conclude. Chief among the points to be considered is the authority attributed to Paul and his writings, followed closely by the power dynamics implied in Paul's rhetorical activities. These points will lead us in turn into a broader discussion of the power of texts to define, circumscribe, and control the beliefs and behaviors of people today, particularly when those beliefs and behaviors stand in opposition to another's best interest.[21]

To What End?

Now that I have outlined my particular feminist postcolonial methodological approach to the study of Paul and his letters, I will explore how it might be applied to 1 Cor 11:2-16. My discussion is divided into three sections that address three intriguing elements in Pauline scholarship: scholarly identifications with Paul; the creation of contested space (territory) as a result of the implications that this passage has for non-males; and the colonizing effect of Paul's writings.

Identification with Paul

Scholars who engage in a hermeneutics of identification with Paul claim his authoritative voice, and their interpretations of Pauline material are also frequently ascribed this same authority.[22] What many scholars resist admitting is that making this association or identification with Paul and his rhetoric is just as much an ideological choice as is a stance counter to Paul.

As I noted earlier, the same kind of tension that can be seen in the passage at hand shows up in the scholarship on it. The tension in the passage comes primarily from reading 11:3, 7-9, in juxtaposition with 11:11-12.

> 11:3, 7-9 But I want you to understand that Christ is the head of every man, and the man is the head of a woman, and God is the head of Christ.... For a man ought not to have his head covered, since he is the image and glory of God; but the woman is the glory of man. For man does not originate from woman, but woman from man. For indeed man was not created for the woman's sake, but woman for the man's sake.

> 11:11-12 However, in the Lord, neither is woman independent of man, nor is man independent of woman. For as the woman originates from the man, so also the man has his birth through the woman; and all things originate from God.

I have yet to discover a scholar who denies that there is a contradiction between 11:3, 7-9 and 11:11-12. Why, then, does it seem appropriate to so many scholars to go on and find a way to say that these two ideas actually form a coherent whole?[23] What is at stake for them (or for Paul) if someone were to claim that either some of this content is not from Paul or that Paul himself was not fully rational? Too often the scholarly discussion remains at the level of making sense of the text in its first-century context, as if this is all that modern readers need. One can quite easily "make sense" of a passage and decline to endorse the implications of it when applied, but it is this second step that is startlingly rare within Pauline studies.[24]

For scholars who see the dissonance in this passage yet want to resolve the tension, the solutions that they offer not surprisingly end up with a dissonance similar to what we see in the passage itself. Not only is the need to smooth over such an irruption or dissonance in the fabric of the text worthy of analysis, but the fact that scholars often repeat the confusion or ambivalence within the text in their effort to resolve it, *without seeming to realize it*, raises the question of why such allegiance to Paul and his words pervades Pauline scholarship. In the process of these painful acrobatic maneuvers, the voice and authority claimed by Paul are transferred to or implicitly claimed by the scholar. The voice of the scholar is simultaneously authoritative and ambivalent.

Judith Gundry-Volf, one of several scholars who attempt to "account for the tension in Paul's thought" in this passage,[25] does so in such a way that the tension ultimately remains. Her innovative approach suggests that Paul was working with three separate yet interdependent realms: his own culture, the eschatological life in Christ, and the creation story. According to Gundry-Volf, "Paul adopts a patriarchal reading of creation in 11:7-9 that suits the goal of integrating the Corinthian pneumatics into their wider social context; in 11:11-12 he reads creation in a way that bursts out of a patriarchal framework and prefigures the gender equality that characterizes the cultic context of Corinthian worship."[26] I see two primary problems with Gundry-Volf's "resolution" of the tension in this passage.

First, Gundry-Volf does not address the issue that the "patriarchal reading of creation" in 11:7-9 builds on the theologically grounded ideas in 11:3: "But I want you to understand that Christ is the head of every man, and the man is the head of a woman, and God is the head of Christ." She also claims that for Paul to depart from the traditional gender roles/expectations of his culture would be a source of shame for anyone in the faith community, as suggested by his statements regarding the "head" in 11:3-4. In short, she seems to be saying that the culturally respectful patriarchal message in 11:7-9 applies only when the Corinthians are engaged in social settings. Paul has, however, given these sociocultural standards a theological grounding, which invites these kyriarchal roles and expectations into the religious setting.

Second, Gundy-Volf claims that in 11:11-12 women "have the priority" and that it is based on a woman's role in procreation.[27] But does this not simply flip the hierarchy on its head and thus maintain a form of inequality? Does she really intend to give women "the priority" based on a female body's capacity to bear a child, thereby essentializing females as mothers? This very passage that Gundry-Volf claims "bursts out of a patriarchal framework and prefigures the gender equality" in the Corinthian community has actually been a useful tool for promoting male dominance over females and controlling females by privileging only their maternal role. As Cynthia Briggs Kittredge reminds us, a paradigm that involves accommodating any of the conventional social scripts will consistently work against egalitarian visions.[28] I am hard-pressed to see any equality in Gundry-Volf's rendering of this passage.

Thus, the question remains: By what standard are the Corinthians to conduct their worship—by their well-established, culturally defined gender roles, or by their freedom from the standards of this world that Paul describes elsewhere as a defining mark of any community that gathers in the name of Christ? Gundry-Volf offers no help for modern readers in making sense of the passage as an argument for a particular practice or in applying it in their faith communities today. In spite of what I imagine was her intention, Gundry-Volf privileges Paul's words as authoritative, identifies with Paul, and leaves her task at the level of "making sense" of this passage. Just as we do not know what Paul is actually advocating, so also we do not know what Gundry-Volf would have us do with this passage.

Gendered Contested Space

Those who are invested in women's roles in the church know that 1 Corinthians 11 is an important part of the conversation. This initial move, however, which privileges texts that specifically mention females as the most relevant ones in this discussion, is the epitome of an androcentric, malestream perspective. It is another way of saying that general directives are for males, while non-males must be addressed separately. While this might have been the case at the time the biblical texts were written, the continuation of this assumption today upholds the "other" status of females while also implying that the male writers of the first century had definitive insights into such matters.

The struggle over this passage is ultimately about controlling meaning, which in turn "controls" lives. It is precisely because this passage is about controlling the power and voices of women/females rather than males that this passage is such a contested space. There is a great deal at stake in having "the" correct meaning to put into practice today. Thus, this passage is constituted as a gendered space of control and power, which in turn makes it fertile ground for maintaining and perpetuating kyriarchal relations and agendas. It should not surprise us, then, that what is being said in a passage about women lays a hand of control on them, or that it defines the realms and roles available to females in negative, restrictive, or circumscribing terms. Just as we see a top-down, God–Christ–male–female hierarchy in 1 Cor 11: 3-4, where females are to relate indirectly to God through the males they glorify, so we see the parameters that females are "allowed" to inhabit being mediated through Paul and his interpreters. The social control of females in the text continues to play out in our modern context every time a scholar reads "with the text."

Pointing to Paul's use of *philoneikos* ("argumentative, contentious") in 11:16, Margaret Mitchell suggests that the primary issue behind this passage is that there are two different opinions regarding how women should appear in worship. In 11:3-9 and 11:13-16, Paul issues strong pleas in favor of the more conservative position, but in 11:10 he seems to suggest that "women have the *exousia* to do what they want with their heads." While acknowledging their "rights" or "powers," Paul pleads with them to renounce their rights for the sake of the greater good, as he does himself in 1 Corinthians 8–9. It is all about avoiding *philoneikia* in the church, "in union with the custom of the church universal."[29]

Mitchell includes no discussion on the sociopolitical difference between Paul's renouncing rights that have always been available to him and women renouncing newfound "rights" within these communities. She reads with Paul's argument and, in doing so, elides the deeper ramifications of this seemingly understandable concession that Paul requests of the women. Mitchell's voice rings out authoritatively because she identifies with Paul and simultaneously positions herself over or against females, since she too suggests that they renounce their freedoms for the sake of a greater unity.[30]

In a similar vein, Andrew Perriman's word study on the term *kephalē*, which surveys the works of Philo, Plutarch, and the Septuagint, offers a fantastically positivistic interpretation of Paul's metaphorical use of "head" in 11:3-4.[31] His conclusion is that, while matters of "source" or "origin" may be part of the argument, the main point Paul was trying to make has to do with women's behavior as judged by what they do with their bodies in worship, which ought to bring honor to the men. He concludes by observing, "We might almost say that 'man is the head of woman' and 'woman is the glory of man' are reciprocal statements."[32] While the terms "head" and "glory" are not specifically gendered on their own, the application of them in this manner makes it clear that the male's role is to lead, while the female's purpose and identity are defined by her connection to the male. The male has specifically active roles and responsibilities, while the female is called to an abstract role of highlighting the male. Perriman's interpretation clearly echoes a stereotyped view of gender that assigns action to males and passivity to females.

Additionally, the metaphor or image expressed in the top-down hierarchy of God–Christ–male (or husband)–female (or wife) reflects the relational expectations that dominated the social and familial realms at that time, so that to apply such a hierarchy unquestioningly to anything related to "newness in Christ" or to read it alongside Gal 3:28[33] is nothing short of laughable. Perriman does not offer any disclaimer, however, but seemingly agrees with this image and its application. Thus, Perriman condones the dominant place of male over female. In choosing to focus on the issue of "headship," which reflects a kyriarchal norm, he is able to speak from a position of power by drawing on the authoritative status of Paul's words and thus to justify the domination of females by males. Given that the idea is contained in the Christian canon, then, it is all theologically justified as well.

In stark contrast to Perriman's contribution, Jouette Bassler offers an exquisite example of scholarship for our consideration. While she thinks that Paul is responsible for the entire passage and acknowledges that Paul's argument is "inarticulate, incomprehensible, and inconsistent," she explains this ambivalence by observing that "where reason fails, emotions and traditions take over."[34] She does not, however, indicate how people today should handle statements like this that reflect the influence of emotions and traditions rather than Paul's reasonable mind. If we are to see this passage for what she claims it is, does this mean that we should simply forgive Paul for this understandable misstep and ignore his statement? Since the passage remains in the Christian canon, an explanation of where its content came from is simply insufficient.

Bassler takes Paul's application of Gen 1:27 in 11:7-9 to be a "misreading," since the Genesis passage speaks of male and female with no indication of one preceding or ruling over the other, whereas Paul's application makes the primacy of males clear. One might ask why she thinks 1 Cor 11:7-9 is an application of Gen 1:27 and not of Gen 2:7-25, which is usually read as an affirmation that the male came first.[35] Her suggestion does not exonerate Paul from his "misreading," but it does suggest that, had he not been influenced by the pull of emotions or tradition, he would have offered a more egalitarian interpretation. She then addresses the idea in 11:7 of woman being the glory of man, which she takes to mean that the woman is the *reflection* of man. While this clarification of the word *glory* might soften the edges of Paul's claim, it still does not eradicate the secondary status of women implied by this passage.[36]

It is somewhat unfortunate that Bassler has chosen to critique Paul's argumentation without taking the next step of addressing what modern faith communities ought to do with such a faulty text. Regardless of whether this is a game of semantics, it is noteworthy that even a contributor to the *Women's Bible Commentary* does not critique the assumptions of a first-century male perspective regarding the roles of females. Because she does not directly address the implications of Paul's thought, Bassler manages to perpetuate the authoritativeness attributed to Paul's voice and the (false) assumption that his ideas are universally relevant. This move is all the more striking coming from a female scholar who is seeking the empowerment of females.

The Colonizing Effect of Paul's Writings

Since identifying with Paul infuses a scholar's interpretation with authority, it is not surprising that the gendered space of 1 Cor 11:2-16 has produced contention among scholars who wish to pronounce the definitive word from Paul regarding women's roles and practices. But it is because his rhetoric functions in an authoritative manner that the ongoing application of his letters, unchallenged, perpetuates a colonizing, "power over" worldview. Two final examples will show that even self-proclaimed feminist scholars can engage this passage in a way that seemingly redeems Paul from disparaging accusations yet employs his ideas to normalize kyriarchal practices.

Ann Jervis begins her article by declaring that if it were possible to identify "the myth that informed Paul's way with women," we would be able to see that the "conflicting pieces of his words and actions may, in fact, rest comfortably together."[37] Is this not an attempt to resolve the irresolvable? But beyond this startling announcement, she too fails to problematize the implications of Paul's theologically grounded subordination of women to men.

> With God as the head of Christ, and Christ as the head of every husband, whatever else being head of a wife meant for Paul, it must have meant reflecting the self-sacrificial character of God and Christ. Likewise, Paul's words to the women to be silent in church and his direction that they should ask their husbands at home, occur in a context where he is teaching the Corinthians that the greatest spiritual gift is love, and that even in the moment of greatest spiritual ecstasy, considerate love should reign.[38]

In spite of the patriarchal nature of "headship" terminology, Jervis does not seem interested in taking on that discussion. Even more disturbingly, she implies that whatever "being head of a wife" might mean pales in comparison with self-sacrifice, which is in turn compared with "considerate love." Given that patriarchal societies are already dependent on the self-sacrifices of females, it strikes me as theologically irresponsible to tell these same females that their subordinate position is actually an expression of the ultimate form of love. According to this perspective, submitting to and perpetuating a patriarchal society would be the ultimate Christian duty.

We could also come at this issue from the angle of differentiating between, on the one hand, what Christian theology asserts that Jesus sacrificed, as a member of the Trinity, in his self-emptying and death and, on the other, the self-sacrifice of any "normal" human being, especially the non-male members of society. The former actually had a status and an identity to give up; the latter are people who were already disenfranchised and who, prior to becoming members of Christ's body, knew nothing but emptiness and sacrifice. However well-intentioned Jervis is in her interpretation, she still manages to suggest that patriarchy is theologically justified and that those attracted to the empowering aspect of the gospel can legitimately be asked to give up this newfound life for the sake of proper behavior in worship. According to Jervis, Paul's "way with women" is not very different from that of others in his first-century context.

Luise Schottroff's chapter in *Distant Voices Drawing Near: Essays in Honor of Antoinette Clark Wire* focuses on purity and holiness in 1 Corinthians as a whole, so she addresses the passage in question only peripherally. The reference she makes to 1 Cor 11:10, however, is quite telling. Schottroff suggests that it is a "complete parallel" with 11:29,

> because he lines up the behavior of women refusing symbolic subordination to men with the behavior of the rich during Eucharist. He wants women to cover their heads "because of the angels." I really do not know the meaning of these words. I am not convinced that what Paul has in mind is the sexual desire of the angels. Perhaps he presupposes that the holiness of the angels requires women's subordination: otherwise their holiness and that of the communities could be endangered. The time of prayer, of prophecy, and of Eucharist is both a time for celebrating holiness and a time of vulnerability and danger. Holiness can be injured, and people can be damaged.[39]

Suggesting that women submit to "symbolic" subordination, it seems, is supposed to be understandable or bearable for the females in the Corinthian communities in light of social codes and expectations. The question I have for Schottroff is whether she finds any power or meaning in symbols. Not only are they used precisely because of their power, but they are also quite helpful in perpetuating an idea for generations beyond the one in which they were initially employed. That is why we see the continuation of their usage to this day.

It is one thing to try to "explain" where an idea might have come from but another entirely to suggest that this explanation justifies putting this idea into practice and that we should continue to maintain such ancient cultural standards today. Since Schottroff does not problematize this scenario, the latter is, in effect, what her reading of the passage accomplishes. If Schottroff would have us endorse the first-century practice of veiling for the sake of the purity of the communities, then she is condoning faith communities, both then and now, choosing to uphold cultural norms instead of reflecting the "newness in Christ" that Paul elsewhere proclaims. She is simply following in the path of the many other biblical scholars who perpetuate Paul's authoritative voice, justify or explain away problems in his writings, and thus end up endorsing messages that resonate with kyriarchal and imperial methods of control.

Conclusion

A feminist and postcolonial reading of Paul's letters (and the scholarship on them) includes asking questions about the authority of Paul and the power dynamics within his letters in general. It also probes the role the biblical texts have in forming the identities and practices of faith communities, including why such an ancient text continues to have such a stronghold on us and our perceptions of women in the twenty-first century. It queries what is at stake for a scholar who seeks to redeem a text, since this move usually implies that these writings or the intentions behind them are somehow inerrant. A feminist postcolonial critic of Paul wonders why there is a *need* to have his writings understood in one way or another at all. What are we doing when we take up one or two privileged passages from Paul's letters and make so much of them? In the present case, why is it so pressing to know what Paul meant or was trying to do in these fifteen verses? These are questions that must be faced by biblical scholars, clergy, and laity alike.

It is simply astounding to me that the gender roles and expectations that are depicted in first-century writings and worldviews are still, in the twenty-first century, allowed into the conversation regarding male and female roles in the church. In fact, they are not only allowed in, but they predominate over the session. In spite of repeated denials by both experts and laypeople, Paul's first-century ideas about gender and sexuality in this passage still play a part in informing and defining our ideas today.

Ultimately, the issue here is broader than what Paul thought about the veiling of females as they participated in worship in first-century Corinth and how we ought to apply this belief today. Behind this debate lies the question of why Paul continues to hold such power and authority over us that we cannot challenge his claims and assertions. We ought to do some serious soul-searching to figure out why a church body would look for, and often find, a way to justify upholding the androcentric and kyriarchal worldview expressed in 1 Cor 11:3-4 because they believe it is what Paul's endorses, then breathe a sigh of relief when they become convinced that this is no longer necessary because such an androcentric worldview is in fact the idea that Paul was refuting.

In light of the authority that is attributed to all directives received from Paul and the subsequent reinscription of an arbitrary ancient cultural norm of subordination of women to men that results from granting such authority to 1 Cor 11:2-16, I suggest that Pauline scholars would do well to attend more carefully to the ethics and politics of their own interpretations. This is truly a matter of life and death that affects the well-being of all members of faith communities that embrace passages such as 1 Corinthians 11. Since the nature of Paul's writings lends itself to such varied applications, our task cannot end with simply interpreting his writings. It is incumbent upon us as biblical scholars to be aware of these realities and to "cease and desist" such harmful, oppressive, and controlling applications of biblical content and to render empowering, egalitarian, and liberating messages in their place.

PART THREE

PAUL AND MODERN WESTERN COLONIALISM

CHAPTER THIRTEEN

Wrestling with the "Macedonian Call"

Paul, Pauline Scholarship, and Nineteenth-Century Colonial Missions

ROBERT PAUL SEESENGOOD

We have heard the Macedonian call today,
"Send the Light! Send the Light!"
—Charles H. Gabriel, "Send the Light" (1890)

Introduction: Another Look at Hybridity and the Pauline Writings[1]

In 2005, I published an essay using Homi Bhabha's models of hybridity, mimicry, and mockery to read Paul.[2] In that essay, I argued that postcolonial criticism could prove fertile for the analysis of Paul's writings, given Paul's context in the Roman imperial world and his ethnic ambivalence. My essay was an attempt to take up the challenge posed by one of Fernando F. Segovia's "postcolonial optics" where he claimed that biblical scholars were not yet attending to the colonial contexts of New Testament writings.[3] At the time of that writing, postcolonial criticism was an established but still marginal methodology for biblical critics. Very little work was being done to analyze the colonial context of the first followers of Jesus; even less work had been done examining the colonial context of Paul.

Over the past five years, the situation has dramatically changed, as the present volume demonstrates. Postcolonial readings have become a substantial voice in biblical criticism, and several studies have been written that dwell heavily, if not exclusively, on the tensions of alterity and subalterity in the Roman world and the

189

development of Christian confession and literature. These studies are now making significant inroads into Pauline criticism.

At present, most of the work of postcolonial Pauline criticism has focused on later colonial reception of biblical texts and, more recently, on the subaltern and colonial context of the biblical writers—two of the "optics" proposed by Segovia. Still, little or none of this work has engaged the "left hand" of Bhabha's thesis: the claim that colonization alters *both* the colonized (via hybridity and the hybrid's enforced "mimicry") *and* the colonizer (via the forces of control and the required rhetorics of domination). Segovia's third "optic" is relevant here. In addition to calling our attention to the colonial context of the earliest followers of Jesus, he also calls for "analysis of the readers of the texts of ancient Judaism and early Christianity that takes seriously into consideration their broader sociocultural contexts in the global sphere, whether in the West or outside the West."[4] Bhabha speaks of the moment of colonization as one that produces a "third space" for identity.[5] In this "space," both colonized and colonizer are altered; the transformation is mutual.

Marxist criticism, apart from its structuralist assumptions, constructs a rigid separation between the classes. Critiques of the colonial engagement have tended to do the same. To be sure, a fundamental assumption of postcolonial critique is that the colonial encounter is fundamentally unequal. But this does not mean that the subaltern alone is modified by colonial engagement; indeed, a recognition of this mutual inter-alteration (along with a general tendency to avoid binaries found in most poststructuralist critique) is part of what sets postcolonialism apart from Marxism. Of course, there is an understandable hesitancy to give even *more* attention to the hegemonic colonial voice. Yet failing to see the colonizer as equally altered by the colonial engagement borders on implicit racism: the subaltern is regarded as both radically Other and radically malleable, lacking in its Otherness the immutable substance of the altern class. As Sara Suleri notes,

> If colonial cultural studies is to avoid a binarism that could cause it to atrophy in its own apprehension of difference, it needs to locate an idiom for alterity that can circumnavigate the more monolithic interpretations of cultural empowerment that tend to dominate current discourse. To study the rhetoric of the British Raj in both its colonial and postcolonial manifestations is therefore to attempt to break down the incipient schizophrenia of critical discourse that seeks to represent domination and subordination as though the two were mutually exclusive terms. Rather than examine a binary rigidity between those terms—which is an inherently Eurocentric strategy—this critical field would be better served if it sought to break down the fixity of the dividing lines between domination and subordination. . . . Diverse ironies of empire are too compelling to be explained away by the simple pieties that the idiom of alterity frequently cloaks.[6]

The following essay will explore the transformations of Western biblical scholarship during the nineteenth century, an era marked by the pressures arising from colonial engagement with the "third world." European colonization, once the initial martial conflict was ended, became an ongoing attempt to bring the colonized nations into cultural harmony with the colonizing West. One aspect of this cultural rescript was the introduction of Christianity via the explosion of Protestant Christian missionary movements. The Christian missionary was a force for cultural hegemonic expansion.[7] Much of the fuel for Christian mission work came from interpretations of Paul's life and letters. These texts, however, required particular strategies for reading in order to function appropriately as goads (or models) for Christian missions. Critical to that reading strategy was an insistence on the "historicity" of both Acts and the Pastorals.

At the dawn of the nineteenth century, scholarship from Europe was arguing that many of the Pauline letters in the New Testament were pseudepigraphic. The book of Acts was considered both historically unreliable and tendentiously biased in Paul's favor. Paul, as constructed by the higher critics, was more earnest than credentialed, more passionate than qualified, more zealous than successful. This scholarship was largely German and Dutch in origin.

During the nineteenth century, England, America, and Australia began active programs of mission work in India, Africa, China, and Southeast Asia. At the same time, major voices in Anglophone Pauline scholarship argued for Pauline authorship of all thirteen letters assigned to Paul in the New Testament, including the Pastorals and Philemon. Paul was considered the ideal, paradigmatic missionary. Acts was regarded as historically reliable. Pauline texts (and the Pauline biography drawn from Acts) served as the foundations of Protestant Christian missions during this era.

Using Segovia's neglected "third optic," I will argue that the colonial impulse factored strongly, if not centrally, into the constructions of Pauline theology in Protestant Anglophone congregations of the period. Such readings of Paul created, reinforced, and guided colonial expansion. These mutual and interdependent processes are especially evident in nineteenth-century debates over Paul's authorization of slavery (the most "colonial" of colonial encounters), as we will see when we examine nineteenth-century readings of Philemon. Opinions regarding the historicity of the Bible often dovetailed with the needs and social location of the scholars involved, and these needs were in turn influenced by colonialism. In other words, the colonial moment produced hybridized scholars among the altern who, in turn, constructed ways of reading Paul that enabled the colonial process. In this way, colonization and hybridity altered the way the Bible was read by Western scholars.

The Bible and Nineteenth-Century Missions

Christian missions underwent considerable changes in the nineteenth century. The use of the word "mission" or "missionary" as a term primarily indicating Christian proselytism dates to the late sixteenth or early seventeenth century.[8] Initially, Christian missions were carried out primarily by the Roman Catholic Church, particularly the churches in Spain and Portugal. By the nineteenth century, however, Christian missions were largely Protestant and originated in Anglophone nations. These missions were organized by industrious para-church societies that raised and administered funds and maintained exacting records while also carefully vetting and training missionaries. As the century progressed, leading Christian theorists argued increasingly that the most effective means of world evangelism was to foster indigenous modes of Christian expression. These mission campaigns were supported by a growing number of ambitious "Bible societies."

The Era of Modern Missions is said to have begun with the work of William Carey in 1793. His ideas were expressed most famously in his notable sermon "An Inquiry into the Obligation of Christians to Use Means for the Conversion of the Heathens."[9] The sermon was printed as an eighty-seven page tract and circulated widely in the English-speaking world. Its message was based on Isa 54:2-3 and was permeated with images from the Acts of the Apostles, focusing particularly on Paul's three "missionary journeys," which were viewed as fulfillments of Jesus' command in Acts 1:8 to "be my witnesses in Jerusalem, in all Judea and Samaria, and to the ends of the earth." Carey was the author also of a key tract, appended to later copies of his sermon, that presented various "Christian evidences" and included "unassailable" arguments for the Bible's infallibility. Similar arguments had been put forward by William Paley in tracts circulated in 1791. The view underlying these tracts was that the truth of Christianity and the inspiration of the Bible could be demonstrated by defending the Bible's infallibility. Among the texts that Carey used to defend this view were 2 Tim 3:16-17 and the book of Hebrews, which he argued was Pauline. These arguments did not aim merely to legitimate Christian evangelism and dissemination of the Bible; they made both practices morally obligatory. Carey's summons was quickly answered. In the next century, translations of the Bible exploded from fifty to two hundred fifty and missionary societies increased from virtually none to over a hundred.

Among the first missionaries sent from North America was Adoniram Judson. He and his wife, Ann, focused their energies on Burma. Judson was educated at Andover Theological Seminary and, as a student, had forged his zealous plans for missionary work as a member of a student group called "the Brethren" (the normal term for believers in Acts). The book of Acts and the letters of Paul provided critical elements of his vocabulary. In his reports, Judson denied that his plan to win the Burmese interior for Christ was unreasonable; he repeatedly appealed to God's greater wisdom, echoing 1 Corinthians 2.[10] He even called his first, pivotal converts "apostles." James Thoburn quotes the famous missionary advocate and early missiologist George Smith as suggesting that "Adoniram Judson ... is surpassed by no missionary since the Apostle Paul in selfless devotion and scholarship, in labors and perils, in saintliness and humility and in the results of his trials on the future of an empire."[11]

The Yorkshire-born Hudson Taylor spent fifty-one years of his life during the latter half of the nineteenth century doing missionary work in inland China. His work resulted in more than eighteen thousand conversions, the construction of well over a hundred schools, and the importation of over eight hundred fellow missionaries through the China Inland Mission, which he founded. This success was not without substantial personal cost. Yet when Taylor's wife, Maria, died from childbirth while in the mission field, Taylor responded to this loss in letters filled with overtly biblical language, focusing particularly on Paul's assertions about the hope of the resurrection in 1 Corinthians. Taylor's ambitions imitated those of Paul, a fact not lost on Ruth Tucker, a scholar of the history of Christian missions. Echoing Dr. Smith's assessment of Judson, she argues that Taylor's organization, territorial coverage, and methods were matched by no other Christian missionary except Paul, whom Taylor used as his model.[12] Taylor was particularly adept at learning indigenous languages and culture, following local cultural norms even to the details of his dress. He based his behavior on Paul's assertion that he had "become all things to all people so that he might, by any means, win some" (1 Cor 9:22). His strategy became the model for many Christian missionaries after him.

The nineteenth century also saw the blossoming of "Bible societies."[13] Among the first of these was the British and Foreign Bible Society. This organization was founded in 1804, largely through the work and advocacy of Thomas Charles, a Bible seller in Wales. He told the story of a young woman named Mary (Jacob) Jones who, at the age of sixteen, had saved her meager income for six years to purchase a Bible translated into her native Welch. To purchase the text, she had to walk more than twenty miles barefoot to Rev. Charles's shop. According to one version of the tale, when she arrived, she found that all of the copies had been sold or promised to others, so she waited an additional two days for her copy. Rev. Charles was deeply moved (though apparently not enough to simply give her a copy, appropriate one of the reserved copies for her, or even offer her a ride back home) and founded the Religious Tract Society, whose primary purpose was to disseminate Bibles in indigenous dialects and languages.

Charles's program eventually became the British and Foreign Bible Society. Its mission was to spread Bibles, free of charge, in indigenous languages, throughout the world. No other campaign of evangelism was to be undertaken and no additional doctrinal materials were to be circulated. The reason for the proscriptions was twofold: it ensured that monies and participation could be drawn from various and divergent Protestant groups, and it echoed the view of many Protestant groups that a legible Bible was all that was needed to bring the sincere seeker to a saving faith. Despite their differences, nearly every Protestant denomination was united in the belief that sincere seekers, if left alone to simply read the Bible, would believe "correctly." The root of this belief was "Paul's" statement in 2 Tim 3:16-17, "All scripture is inspired by God and is useful for teaching, for reproof, for correction, and for training in righteousness, so that everyone who belongs to God may be proficient, equipped for every good work."

By 1808 similar societies were being founded in the United States, the earliest being the Pennsylvania Bible Society. These societies combined in 1816 to form the American Bible Society. Other societies rapidly developed. The Edinburgh and Glasgow Societies were founded in 1809 and 1812 respectively and merged in 1861 to form the Scottish Bible Society. The Australian Bible Society was formed in 1817. The Bible Society of New South Wales began in 1817, and similar societies began in Colombia in 1825 and New Zealand in 1846. The multiple societies often found themselves at cross-purposes, providing double coverage in some regions while neglecting others. In time, these societies came together under the auspices of the United Bible Societies, an organization that currently gives away tens of millions of Bibles each year and publishes the standard scholarly texts of the Bible in Greek and Hebrew.

The Protestant orientation of these societies, whose practices were expressly rooted in Protestant readings of Paul's theology, produced controversies among some of the Bible societies as well as between the Bible societies and the Catholic establishment. The Scottish Bible Society formed because the British and Foreign Bible Society began to circulate Bibles that included the Apocrypha, which was recognized by Roman Catholics but not by Protestants. On the Catholic side, Pope Gregory XVI issued an encyclical in 1844 titled *Inter Praecipuas* ("On Biblical Societies") that condemned the widespread dissemination of the vernacular Bible. American Protestants saw this as an implicit acknowledgment by the Catholic Church that Catholic doctrines were not biblical. The Bible societies' insistence on the power of *sola scriptura* was rooted in Lutheran beliefs, which, of course, were in turn were rooted in Paul's theology. According to nineteenth-century Protestants (and more than a few modern Bible readers), Paul's letters indicated that the Bible was the inspired (and many argued, inerrant) word of God. This status made its circulation not only critical but also singularly urgent. No other action was so important or so necessary. Indeed, in the eyes of many Christians, any activity beyond this was dangerously close to the introduction of "human doctrines."

Another controversy among the Bible societies concerned the practice of translation. Several groups refused to simply render Greek and Hebrew words literally into their target languages during translation. One of the most contentious issues was the treatment of *baptizomai*, which could be translated either "washed" or "immersed." Translators disagreed over whether this meant that new Christians should be "washed" or fully "immersed" in water when they were "baptized." Translations that used the word *immerse* were viewed by many as violations of the Bible societies' charters, which stated that nothing but the simple word of God—no human doctrine or creed—was to be disseminated. Responding to this concern, the Baptist theologian W. H. Wyckoff wrote an impassioned plea under the title *The American Bible Society and the Baptists, the Question Discussed, Shall the Whole Word of God be Given to the Heathen* (1842).[14] Wyckoff's title echoes Acts 20:21 and 18:11, both of which pertain to Paul's missionary activity, showing how deeply the notion of spreading the written word of God was associated with the Pauline mission. In this particular case, Wyckoff argued that the literal translation ("immerse") was the only genuinely unbiased option. Such dissension over the boundaries of the canon and the relation between translation and interpretation reveals both the limits of Bible society ideology and the pressures that mission society agendas placed on biblical criticism in the nineteenth century.

The nineteenth century was also an era of European colonization accompanied by intellectual and cultural hegemony. For example, British control of India resulted in the adoption of English as the official legal language of the country, together with the construction of British-style schools, civic processes, courts, and industries. Colonialism also introduced religious innovations. Often these secular and religious transformations were imposed as a set: English literacy was produced by training students to read the Bible, while the goal of literacy was to enable economic and political engagement on the part of the natives. The missionary programs of organizations such as the American Bible Society and the British Bible Society played a vital role in this process of colonization.[15] In fact, Bible societies began at roughly the same time that Christian missions shifted toward more "indigenous" methods of communication and expansion.

As we saw earlier, the central concern of the Bible societies was to promote the spread of "the word of God." In this they relied on several key components of the New Testament depiction of Paul. In the first place, their emphasis on "the word alone" as the means of salvation was rooted in a Lutheran/Protestant interpretation of the theology of Paul. Second, Paul is the missionary par excellence in the New Testament. Many of these missionary societies and Bible societies based their work directly on the characterization of Paul in the book of Acts. Third, arguments upholding the authenticity and history of the letters of Paul helped to reinforce Protestant images of the Bible as inspired and inerrant. This belief in turn helped to promote the cultural hegemony of colonial Christianity.

In the letters of Paul, one place where we see particular attention to the missionary activity of Paul and the power of "the word" is in the Pastoral Epistles. In these letters, Paul is presented as actively engaged in the mission field and advising his protégés on missionary expansion. In addition, 2 Tim 3:14-17 presents the sine qua non argument for the authority and transformational power of Scripture. It should come as no surprise, then, that as Paul's letters and activities came to be regarded as foundational to the missionary enterprise, the historical reliability and Pauline authorship of the Pastoral Epistles also became a matter of vital concern.[16] In a similar way, the pressures and needs of colonization and the hegemonic expansion of Christianity forced scholars into arguing for the historical reliability of other New Testament texts. In this way, the dynamic of colonization and the construction of "hybridized" missionary communities altered the way in which the altern West argued about the proper interpretation of the Bible and used the Bible in missionary activity.

These movements toward missionary expansion did not occur in a political vacuum. As we noted earlier, the strident expansion of Anglophone missions was accompanied by an equal expansion of Anglophone colonization. It is no accident that the major areas of missionary work in the nineteenth century—China, Africa, India, North America, Southeast Asia—were also the primary sites of British, American, and Australian colonization. As a result, the political changes of the era were accompanied by background conversations regarding the validity and historicity of biblical literature associated with Paul.

Historicity and Paul: Two Competing Views

The theory, practice, and makeup of Christian missions changed during the nineteenth century. Many of these changes were dependent on readings of Paul and required arguments for the (inerrant) historicity of Acts. Missions became more "indigenous," yet they also became more focused on the Bible as a near talisman or cipher for Christian authority. Anglophone Protestant missions dramatically increased.

Scholarship on the letters of Paul also changed markedly during the same period, as evidenced by the opposing voices of F. C. Baur and William Ramsay at the beginning and end of the century. Baur was remarkably critical of New Testament ideology, Pauline authorship, and the historical reliability of Acts, while Ramsay positioned his own work in conscious contrast to Baur. The differences between Baur and Ramsay mirror many of the century's changes in the conduct of Christian missions.

In the early decades of the nineteenth century, no scholar of Paul was more influential than F. C. Baur.[17] For Baur, Paul's message of inclusion through repudiation of Torah put him squarely at odds with Jesus' earliest followers. Relying on Jesus' own assertions that he did not come to "destroy the law, but to fulfill it," these followers of Jesus, led by apostles such as James and Peter, advocated that non-Jews could come to God via Jesus, but only if they also adopted Jewish ritual practices. Paul, on the other hand, claimed that adherence to Jewish laws was no longer necessary. The showdown between these two parties occurred in Galatia. According to Baur, some teachers who were loyal to James had come to visit Paul's churches in his absence and told the new believers there that everyone needed to obey the Jewish ritual law, including food laws and circumcision. On hearing news of this, Paul dashed off his angry letter to the Galatians. For Baur, then, Paul was an angry, troubled, confrontational, self-appointed missionary of apocalyptic doom to the Gentiles who was squarely at odds with James and Peter.

The historicity of Acts was also challenged by Baur. In 1827, after being appointed professor of New Testament and ancient Christianity at the University of Tübingen, Baur began to search for some "universal" element of Christian identity that was not rooted in traditional textuality. His insistence that the Bible could and should be read according to the standards of any other book led him to ask hard questions about the historical reliability of the texts. Comparisons between Paul's letters and the book of Acts revealed substantial chronological and contextual disparities. On this basis, Baur concluded that several letters identified as Pauline were in fact pseudepigraphical.

Such questions were hardly new or unique. Much critical study had already been done, for example, on the historical context of Jesus of Nazareth. The Gospels had clearly been written some time after the death of Jesus, and (as John 20:21 overtly notes) were written by and for believers in order to create (or reinforce) the faith of new believers. In other words, the writings had a clear theologically motivated tendency (Baur's term) and ideological agenda. This agenda, many argued, clouded the historicity of the works, obscuring any objective history that they might have contained.

Baur raised similar questions about the canonization of the New Testament writings and the career of Paul. Prior to Baur, Paul had seemed a more "historically stable" figure. Thirteen letters of the New Testament explicitly identify Paul as their author, and several stress that they are written or signed in Paul's own handwriting. Jesus had left no direct historical witness, but Paul left an abundance of material. Paul also frequently described personal encounters, inner thoughts, and specific events and people in his letters, which made him seem more accessible to modern historians. Finally, the narrative of Acts seemed to provide a good framework for understanding Paul's work and travels. In short, it seemed that a historian had much more to work with regarding Paul than regarding Jesus.

Baur's work shattered this confidence in the historicity of Paul and his letters. Baur began by critiquing the process of manuscript preservation and collection, asking whether other documents related to first-century Christianity might have been lost, or perhaps suppressed or destroyed for theological reasons. He also questioned whether some of the New Testament documents might have been altered or forged to create a "document trail" for a particular ideology or to silence its critics. In other words, he posed questions about whether the New Testament collection was complete, how it reached its present form, and whether it represents the entirety of first-century Christianity. Baur also questioned whether the book of Acts accurately represented Paul's career, pointing to numerous discrepancies between Paul's letters and the narrative of Acts. As a result of these comparisons, Baur came to doubt the authenticity of several of Paul's writings. In time, he would reject the Pauline authorship of all but Romans, 1 Corinthians, Galatians, and Philippians, and he argued that even these letters had been altered. By comparing Paul's letters with Acts, Baur also deduced that Acts was written well after Paul's death as an attempt to soften and redeem Paul's reputation. To promote harmony within the new religion, believers had first altered, then forged, letters in the names of both Paul and Peter to gloss over their initial conflicts. They subsequently wrote the Acts of the Apostles to present this hybridized harmony as a historical fact, stressing the unity of the early Christian community and blaming all of its conflict on "the Jews." Finally, they omitted or erased (whether actively by suppression or passively by nonpreservation) documents that depicted the conflict in terms that were too sharp for later consumption.

The picture of ancient Christian thought and practice that resulted from Baur's analysis was marked by open conflict, hostility, and dissension. The writings that the early Christians left behind could hardly be described as "infallible" or inspired. They were tendentious, spurious, and riven with conflict. The compromise that they fostered became the foundation for second-century Christian theology, a hybridized system of thought that would over time become the voice of orthodoxy.

Baur's research awakened major debates regarding the "center" of Paul's theology, the nature of his opponents, and the potential for variations within ancient Christianity. Implicitly, he also raised questions about who bears the "burden of proof" behind claims regarding the New Testament and ancient Christian history. Should the New Testament be taken at face value as a historical work that presents a reasonably accurate picture of ancient Christianity, or must its historicity be defended? In short, Baur (and the students who followed after him, later known as the "Tübingen School") raised a series of profound questions about the reliability of Acts and the image of Paul that appears in his letters. Baur's reconstruction of early Christianity (including Paul) provoked a heated debate in which agreement or compromise became increasingly unlikely.

It is easy to see how the Tübingen School's reconstructions, if true, would have had a devastating effect on missionary ideologies that were dependent on Pauline models and doctrines. To put the matter simply, if Paul's letters had been both altered and placed in an artificial historical context, they could no longer be reliably used to construct Paul's original ideology. This in turn means that they would lose their value as central texts for missiology. Missions and proselytism require confidence, if not certainty, about one's central ideology.

Defining the book of Acts as a historically spurious document also had devastating effects on conventional reconstructions of Pauline biography. The very foundation of missionary activity (not to mention the theology of most forms of Protestant Christianity) was rendered unstable. The founding father of Christian missions was now shrouded in historical mist. And to make matters worse, Baur and his followers were building their arguments largely on the biblical text. One could certainly argue (as many did) that they were engaging in too much conjecture and that they were cynically predisposed to mistrust the Bible's veracity. But Baur's followers pointed out that they were simply noting discrepancies found in the Bible itself and deriving solutions that were based on the most rational possibility. Certainly no one could demonstrate that their readings were *prima facie* impossible. Baur, for his part, contended that his opponents were the ones who were biased, relying on faith rather than sound historical judgment.

In many ways, this conflict defined the competing positions in the major debates in biblical criticism for the next century. Not surprisingly, those who advocated on behalf of Christian missions and defended the Bible as the core text for Christian teaching under the influence of figures like Carey and Paley responded vigorously to Baur's challenge. Those who argued that the Bible was the inspired word of God were particularly incensed at Baur's assertion that 2 Timothy was a forgery; they had a vested interest in sustaining a "historical" Paul and the potential for these documents to lead to reliable historical data. Those who did not affirm this view (mostly scholars who sought to uncover the "essence" or "idea" of Christian "philosophy") were more interested in criticizing Baur's positivist assertions. The divergence of views on the historicity of the New Testament that arose from these conflicts continues to shape biblical scholarship to this day.

Working in the latter part of the nineteenth century, Sir William Ramsay devoted the bulk of his career to the study of Paul and his message as a historically reliable and coherent body of work.[18] Ramsay sought to establish the intellectual "soil" of Paul's ancient world. He began his work on Paul as a classical studies scholar who was trained in "German techniques" and uninterested in Christian theology. Indeed, he began his work with the assumption that the biblical accounts were so theologically motivated they could not be used to provide a reasonable historical account of early Christianity.

After doing archaeological work in Turkey, he began to study the Acts of the Apostles, reading the text in its original Greek and comparing it with other ancient historical documents. As a result, he became more and more convinced that the book contained reliable history. In the end, he found himself "intellectually compelled" to accept Acts' picture of Paul. The rest of Ramsay's scholarly work following that pivotal moment centered on the study of Paul's message and missionary career and the political and cultural world in which Paul worked.

For Ramsay, Paul was the consummate ancient intellectual, a brilliant and innovative scholar of the Jewish Bible. Paul had been schooled (formally, in Ramsay's view) in Greek philosophy and rhetoric. Paul brought these skills into his mission work and used them to frame his beliefs about Jesus. The passion that Paul derived from a direct encounter with the risen Jesus led him to traverse the major cities of the eastern Mediterranean, where he encountered communities of interested Jewish and Gentile intellectuals and engaged them in debate about Jesus. Ramsay's prodigious skills in Greek and his vast knowledge of the archaeology of Asia Minor enabled him to argue that Paul was in fact, as the book of Acts indicated, an active and ambitious missionary who presented an overwhelming case for the messianic identity of Jesus. Any opposition that he encountered arose from the insincere (and threatened) minds of his (Jewish) audiences. Confronted with a Paul whom they could not best in debate, his opponents turned their frustrations into violence.

Ramsay's reading of Paul was obviously far more congenial to Christian missions than that of Baur. It would be too much, however, to say that Baur wrote with deliberate antagonism toward the Protestant mission project, since much of it postdated his work. More accurately, he wrote with complete indifference toward the usefulness of the Pastorals or Acts for Christian missions; he was simply following the "scientific" approach to biblical scholarship begun by Erasmus and Hugo de Groot (Grotius). Baur's concern was to read the Bible as a "rational" historian, analyzing the text without the "encumbrances" of faith or confession. If the climate of the academy (and perhaps even popular sentiment in Germany) was indifferent or even hostile to the idea of missions, Baur was certainly comfortable in that milieu.

By contrast, Ramsay frequently positioned his own work against that of Baur. In his later works, Ramsay often spoke autobiographically or philosophically about the implications of his research. In the revised edition of *The Bearing of Recent Discovery on the Trustworthiness of the New Testament,* Ramsay argued that "no one can comprehend Luke or Matthew so long as his mind is clogged with the old ideas about [the] trustworthiness of these episodes."[19] What was transcendent, what was true about the New Testament could be understood only if the documents could be viewed as historically "intact."[20] Only such a reading could reveal the "breadth and dignity" of the New Testament.[21] Ramsay saw his work, including his scholarly transformation (a form of hybridity?) as a refutation of German exegesis, which "fetter[ed] great and moral truths ... with the precise, hard and wholly inadequate expression of dull logical conception."[22] His self-analysis was deeply influenced by evangelical and nationalistic (anti-German) convictions.

Ramsay's work quickly became a bastion for evangelical and conservative biblical scholars.[23] In their view, if the Bible was historically unreliable, it was also unfit for faith, which meant that it could not be used as a basis for missionary work nor be disseminated abroad to "the heathen." If some of Paul's letters were not written by Paul, then traditional claims about their textual inspiration and spiritual value were void. If the book of Acts was not historically valid, then it was useless; an errant Bible would not do. If the Bible could not be trusted, missionary work and Bible societies were in vain.

Paul and Arguments for (Colonial) Enslavement

While it is certainly plausible to argue that political and colonial needs (including missionary ideologies) influenced the methodologies and conclusions of nineteenth-century research into the validity of Acts and the letters of Paul, this is not the only area where political arguments spilled over into Pauline criticism. Similar influences can be seen in scholarship on Paul's letter to Philemon.[24]

Philemon is a notoriously difficult letter for scholarship. On first review, it seems to be a simple document. Philemon is less than a chapter in length, containing only around three hundred words. Not only is it brief, but it also seems remarkably specific. The letter presents itself as being written to a single individual, Philemon, to address a particular set of concerns relating to another individual, Onesimus, and his relationship with Philemon. For such a short letter, it contains a remarkable number of references to specific individuals; indeed, the density of proper names is among the highest in the Pauline corpus. The letter mentions (in addition to Jesus) Timothy, Philemon, Apphia, Archippus, Onesimus, Epaphras, Mark, Aristarchus, Demas, and Luke. Several of these names can be found in Paul's other letters or Acts. Paul also refers to his imprisonment and asserts that he is writing this letter in his "own hand" (v. 19). In short, there is a surprising amount of specific data in this brief letter. It would seem, then, that Philemon is one of the few Pauline letters for which scholars should be able to establish a firm setting and context to aid in defining its meaning.

The "meaning" of the letter, too, seems relatively clear on first reading. Paul is writing from prison to recommend a man named Onesimus who is returning to Philemon after some dispute. Paul tells Philemon that both men are believers in Jesus and therefore "brothers" in Christ. Philemon, who owes some moral debt to Paul, is being asked to receive Onesimus in love. Paul promises to repay any debts incurred or to make good any damage done (out of what funds, given that Paul is in prison, we cannot know) by Onesimus. Paul's rhetoric is both cautious and ornate, but he succeeds nonetheless in communicating at least the spirit that he wants Philemon to display, even if he stops short of telling him explicitly what to do.

In reality, however, the letter is phantasmagoric. The specific cause of the harm done to Philemon is never stated, nor is the exact identity of Onesimus, though there are hints. Paul encourages Philemon to "receive back" Onesimus. The name "Onesimus" may itself be a clue, as it means "useful" or "beneficial." (Paul puns on the name in v. 11.) It is most likely the name of a slave. In the Roman Empire, slaves who were enslaved from birth were not considered full "people," so they did not need "real" names. Instead, they were named in much the same way that people today might name a working animal. Many scholars, following early traditions, have argued that Philemon had once owned a slave named Onesimus who had escaped, an offense that could result in a severe beating, maiming, or even death if he were caught. The escaped slave somehow encountered Paul while Paul was a prisoner, perhaps in Rome, and the incarcerated apostle preached to Onesimus and converted him to following Jesus. At the time of the letter, Paul is sending Onesimus back to Philemon, Paul's own close friend and convert, and urging him to accept Onesimus back without punishment, even hinting that Philemon should go further and set Onesimus free. Paul's language, according to this interpretation, is necessarily artful, since he is interfering with a delicate matter of Philemon's household management and is thus cautious about causing undue disruption. At the same time, Paul cagily addresses the letter to Philemon's entire household (tradition holds that Apphia is his wife and Archippus his son) as well as to the church that meets in his home, thus ensuring that many eyes will be observing Philemon's response.

Further reflection, however, renders this reading problematic. In the first place, how would a fugitive slave have encountered the imprisoned Paul? One obvious answer would be that Onesimus was captured and incarcerated along with Paul. Yet this kind of coincidence would strain credulity. Moreover Paul, in sending Onesimus back of his own accord, would be directly violating Deut 23:15-16, which forbids the return of an escaped slave. Even more troubling is the fact that the letter never openly asserts that Onesimus is a slave; in fact, it refers to Onesimus as Philemon's "brother." The letter is also cagey in other ways about the relationships among those named; the family portrait that scholars have sometimes drawn from v. 1 is entirely conjectural. Verse 22 also seems to suggest that Paul either expects to be freed soon or has a degree of latitude regarding his travel and lodging.

Several contemporary scholars have constructed alternate readings of Philemon that begin with very different assumptions. For example, Onesimus the slave may have been sent by Philemon to care for Paul during Paul's incarceration. On this reading, Paul is in effect refusing the gift but being cautious in his language so that he neither offends Philemon nor implies any displeasure with Onesimus. Other scholars have explored different possibilities for the identities of Apphia and Archippus. For example, it is quite possible that Apphia is the matron of a house church and has no relationship to Philemon at all. The only real reason to think otherwise is the preconceived notion that women would not normally be leaders of congregations, despite similar references to Chloe and Phoebe in Paul's other letters (1 Cor 1:11, Rom 16:1).

Behind all these textual ambiguities looms the biggest problem of all: if Onesimus is a slave, then Paul is upholding the institution of slavery by sending Onesimus home to Philemon. Such a reading is not necessarily inconsistent with other parts of the Pauline canon. Despite his pronouncement in Gal 3:28 that there is neither "slave nor free" in

Christ, Paul writes in 1 Corinthians 7 that slaves are to "remain as you are" and not be obsessed with achieving freedom. In the disputed letters of Colossians and Ephesians, slaves are commanded to obey their masters. Paul also uses "slave" as a metaphor to describe his own service to the cause of Jesus (Rom 7:24) and Jesus' submission to God's will (Phil 2:7).

While this is surely uncomfortable for contemporary interpreters, it was an even more acute problem in the nineteenth century, which was marked by heated arguments over slavery as an institution. Since most of those engaged in these debates were Christians, the New Testament, and specifically Paul's letter to Philemon, was a vital battleground in the conflict. Several writers argued that slavery was permissible (even if unpalatable to some) because the New Testament does not explicitly condemn the institution. Certain ways of treating slaves are criticized as immoral, but nothing is said about the institution itself. This allowed for the possibility that there was, at least theoretically, a morally correct way to own a slave. Many of those who argued for this position were themselves slave owners. In the American South, many dedicated Christians roundly attacked those who advocated for the abolition of slavery for sitting in moral judgment over the Bible. Reading the Bible literally, they took the absence of condemnation as a tacit form of endorsement.

If such arguments were less than convincing, they turned to Philemon. Supporters of slavery pointed out that nowhere in this letter does Paul condemn slavery; on the contrary, he sends the slave Onesimus, a convert, back into servitude. This was as good as a clear statement by Paul that slavery, as an institution, was perfectly permissible for Christians. Even scholars who personally opposed slavery reached the same conclusion. Despite his own objections to the practice, Moses Stuart, a venerated professor of theology at Asbury Seminary,[25] wrote that, after examining the Greek text of Philemon in close detail, he was forced to conclude that the letter tacitly endorsed slavery.

The key point of controversy in the interpretation of Philemon was the absence of any specific language asserting that Onesimus was an escaped slave owned by Philemon. Philemon 15-16 reads, "Perhaps this is why [Onesimus] was parted from you for a while, that you might have him back forever, no longer as a slave but more than a slave, as a beloved brother, especially to me but how much more to you, both in the flesh and in the Lord." Abolitionists argued that Paul's use of "slave" here was a metaphor; his use of both "brother" and "in the flesh" indicated that Onesimus and Philemon were siblings, physical brothers parted by some form of domestic dispute. Paul therefore wrote Philemon to resolve this dispute. Given that it was a matter of conflict between close kin, Paul had to be very careful in his language.

Against this view, Moses Stuart insisted that the Greek text of Philemon could not support this argument. Stuart argued that the most natural way to read the passage was to assume that "slave" was to be taken literally while "brother" was metaphorical (or spiritual, referring to "brothers in faith"). The phrase "in the flesh," Stuart argued, was best understood as a reference to Onesimus's impending physical return to Philemon. Stuart was hardly alone in this reading. He went on to develop his ideas in later publications, citing the uniform tradition regarding the biographical context of Philemon as his primary defense (that is, that Onesimus, the escaped slave, had met Paul and been converted to Christ). This biography was taken as "obvious" and even necessary despite our earlier observations about the many places where interpreters were forced to read into and behind the actual text to reach this conclusion. Regard for the reliability and authority of the Bible, Stuart argued, forced one to admit that Paul had endorsed slavery; the possibility of other readings being valid was simply unthinkable. The same was true for Paul's statements that appeared to be endorsing—in fact, by example, requiring—the return of escaped slaves.

Yet the literature of the nineteenth century is also replete with examples of abolitionist ridicule and horror in the face of such readings. Moses Roper, an escaped slave who later wrote a memoir, waged extensive and aggressive combat against the view of Onesimus as a slave. Roper argued forcefully that Onesimus was in reality an estranged brother of Philemon.[26] Frederick Douglass famously (and frequently) savaged the morality of Christians who would use the Bible (a text they regarded as inspired and inerrant) to support slavery. Douglass pointed out how pro-slavery readers were constructing hypothetical biographies of Philemon to produce arguments from silence that supported their immoral position while arguing that they were "compelled" to do so by the text itself. Abolitionists told horror stories of slaves who had sought refuge in local churches only to be handed over to slave hunters by clergymen who argued that the authoritative Bible enjoined them to act in this way. One of the boldest voices opposing pro-slavery readings of the Bible was Harriet Beecher Stowe, who wrote extensively about the evils of slavery and the immorality of its perpetuation. Against those who asserted that slavery was compatible with biblical revelation, she stated that if this were true then the Bible itself was immoral.

As in our earlier discussion of the debates over the historicity of the Pauline narrative in Acts and its implications for missionary societies, larger social issues shaped the interpretation of Paul and his letters. And once again these interpretations hinged on hypothetical reconstructions of Paul's biography. On one side were the defenders of an "orthodox" history of Paul, who based their views on a dogmatically literal reading of Scripture. These people claimed to be compelled by the biblical text read, in light of conventional and received Pauline biographies, to allow, if not outright defend, the institution of slavery. Many did so "despite their own feelings"; they were bound, they argued, by the "simple truth of the Bible."

Others, however, rejected these claims. A handful agreed that Paul did not oppose slavery, but they regarded this as a moral failing on his part, so that Paul need no longer be consulted on the matter. Some went so far as to reject biblical authority altogether. Most, however, continued to wrestle with the text of Scripture in an effort to find a more plastic means of interpreting the Bible. For some, this meant rewriting Paul's biography. As we noted earlier, supporters of slavery had to create a hypothetical biographical context for Paul's letter to Philemon before they could use it to defend their position, since the language of the letter is vague at best. But those who sought to reconstruct an alternate Pauline biographical context for Philemon were likewise led by a firm conviction that slavery was wrong. The Bible simply could not be read as endorsing slavery, despite the fact that this was a plausible or even likely reading of Paul's text.[27]

In the end, the letter to Philemon is ambiguous; it cannot, if read on its own, "compel" anyone to take a particular position regarding American slavery. The texts of Exodus and Deuteronomy are much more explicit about the bounds and propriety of slavery. How one reads Philemon is a product of the assumptions that one makes about its context. The same is true for debates over how the Bible relates to other moral questions; much depends on one's assumptions about the authority, inspiration, inerrancy, and relevance of the Bible. Without question, the colonial moment of slavery influenced the way Philemon was read and what people thought about how biblical scholarship ought to be conducted. Here we see clearly how political and colonial needs arising from that most "hybrid of hybrid" encounters—slavery—affected the way in which altern communities read their Bibles.

Conclusion: Hybridity in the Reading of Paul

In *The Location of Culture*, Homi Bhabha, addressing the tensions surrounding Christian mission expansion as a means of colonial control, writes:

> The historical "evidence" of Christianity is plain for all to see, Evangelists would have argued, with the help of William Paley's *Evidences of Christianity* (1791), the most influential missionary manual throughout the nineteenth century. The miraculous authority of colonial Christianity, they would have held, lies precisely in its being both English and universal, empirical and uncanny.[28]

We might also add to the last sentence, "historically reliable and paradigmatic." The Bible, in its role as the colonizer's authority and talisman, drew power from its "unassailable truth," its historicity.

In many ways, the arguments laid out in this essay are very conventional. To argue that Christian missions were an element of European (and American) colonial control is almost axiomatic. It is also only sensible that those who would affirm a need for Christian missionary endeavor would hold a high view of Scripture, while those who did not have a high view of Scripture would be less mission minded. But such positions are certainly not automatic. Albert Schweitzer, for example, did not believe that critical views on the historicity of the Synoptics (including the impossibility of discovering the "historical Jesus") precluded a life of missionary engagement. He saw the questions of biblical historicity and the power of Christian missionary work as quite separate.

More often than not, however, Christian missions (and Christian views of slavery) were linked to the needs of Western colonization and thus required particular reading strategies. The way that the Bible was read, critiqued, and taught in the colonial West was shaped by the dynamic of colonization, even as the colonizers insisted that their readings were "natural" or even compulsory. These readings in turn fueled and legitimated colonial missionary expansion and constructed a notion of biblical authority and voice that enabled the Bible to become one of the major tools for hegemonic control of the colonized. Much of this activity was rooted in readings of Paul. The resultant debate over whether the Bible should be viewed as one of many books making historical claims or as a historically trustworthy document continues among New Testament exegetes to this day. Yet few recognize how deeply these debates are rooted in the soil of nineteenth-century colonial needs, nor how the colonial moment transformed the very discourse of the colonizing West regarding the scholarly discussion of its sacred texts.

CHAPTER FOURTEEN

Galatians and the "Orientalism" of Justification by Faith

Paul among Jews and Muslims

BRIGITTE KAHL

B inaries are omnivores and ravenous. Once in place, they devour everything in their reach—fowl and fish, men and mice—metabolizing them into one big polarity of *us* versus *them*. Vastly diverse identities are homogenized under the defining rubric of inferior, outlandish, evil; they become "the same" in bizarre configurations as they are turned into "Others" by a dominant Self that has set out to order the world in its own image. Adolf Hitler managed to bundle together such heterogeneous entities as Jews, financial capitalism, bolshevism, and Eastern/Asiatic barbarism as "the" enemy of the German people and the Occident, thus mobilizing a surprisingly broad spectrum of support for his total war that in the end left over seventy million dead.

The pattern goes back to the very roots of our civilization. The ancients started with mythological abnormities of striking variety that eventually morphed into a long list of historical foes: Centaurs, Cyclopes, Giants, Titans, Amazons, Persians, Gauls/Galatians, Carthaginians, Egyptians, Orientals—in short, "barbarians." Warmaking, power politics, and colonialism were the driving forces in these classifications from their onset. Othering as a means of ideological colonization predates, accompanies, and follows the physical conquest of foreign territories and peoples.[1] Greeks versus barbarians and West versus East are two of the most influential antithetical stereotypes that have shaped the self-definition of our civilization since its origins, providing a toxic presence even when seemingly dormant, always ready to reappear in new mutations of the old pattern—anti-Judaism morphing into anti-Islamism, anti-communism into anti-terrorism—and always carrying the latent possibility of sparking a new total war or total power claim where nothing counts but *we* and *they*. *We* the civilized, the righteous, the advanced part of humanity; *they* the primitive, irrational, destructive others, the threat. *We* the victims who are justified by our innocence; *they* the culprits and perpetrators. Eventually this hierarchical binary became Christianized; the Occident was Christian and stood against the non-Christian Orient that was populated by Muslims and other peoples or powers antithetical and inferior to *us*.[2]

The question at the heart of this essay is this: In the global war zone of the present-day encounter between the dominant Euro-American Self and the territory, religion, culture, and economy of people who are other-than-us, what are the spiritual and moral resources that Christianity has to offer toward new practices of peacemaking and reconciliation?

The apostle Paul seems at first sight to be an unlikely ally in this quest. "Justification by faith," the signature doctrine of Galatians and Romans and later of Protestantism, is undoubtedly deeply implicated in the Western politics of othering. Irreconcilable polarities—faith versus law, grace versus works, justification by faith rather than by law or by works—are the most prominent features of the theological argument throughout Galatians, the most polemical letter that Paul ever wrote. Already in the opening section of the letter he hurls a twofold anathema against his "opponents" (Gal 1:8-9). As it turns out, these "falsifiers" and "perverters" of the gospel of Christ (Gal 1:6-9) had advocated for circumcision among the Galatian *ekklēsiai* (Gal 2:3, 7-9; 5:1-12; 6:12). On this basis, their "Jewishness" seemed to be an established fact, although Paul himself never discloses their precise identity and hints at a more complex background (6:12-13). But the simplifying power of Occidental binaries left little space for nuance, and Paul's passionate plea against circumcision morphed with ghastly ease into the overarching antithesis of Christian faith versus Jewish works-righteousness, making Galatians the Magna Carta of Christian (and specifically Protestant) anti-Judaism. But this binary core construct proved capable of assimilating a long and diverse list of "adversaries" of Christian faith and grace justification. Martin Luther, for example, in the introduction to his commentary on Galatians names no fewer than six groups of enemies that are aligned with law, works, works-righteousness, and Satan: Jews, Turks, papists, sectarians, fanatical spirits, and Mohammedans.[3] The seemingly natural coexistence of Jews and Muslims/Turks on this list of anti-Christian protagonists of "law" and "works" will be considered further below.[4]

While the cooptation of Paul and his most influential theological concept for the master narrative of the Christian Occident is beyond doubt, the normativity of this reading is in urgent need of being reexamined. From a postcolonial and empire-critical perspective, the theology of justification by faith deserves to be scrutinized through a bifurcated lens: on the one hand, as a powerful source for the binary Western construct of Self and Other during centuries of Christian empire-building and colonization; on the other hand, as an even more powerful antidote whose original thrust toward justice seeking, peace building, depolarization and conflict resolution has been widely suppressed.

Edward Said: Decolonizing Orientals and Occidentals, Muslims and Jews

Edward Said's *Orientalism*, published in 1978, is a foundational text of postcolonial studies.[5] It analyzes how the Occident has systematically fabricated and produced the Orient as an inferior Other that it was entitled to colonize and rule. Orientalism, as the deep-rooted essentialist and stereotyped dichotomy in Western-centric perceptions of the Oriental Other, is profoundly linked to imperial and colonial power politics. Drawing insights from the early Michel Foucault, Said demonstrated the extent to which these power relations are inscribed into the very fabric of Western knowledge in all its dimensions, even where it seems most objective and neutral.[6] Among the inferior characteristics that were included in an allegedly coherent body of knowledge about the "Orient" are degeneracy, lack of logic and accuracy, lethargy that is devoid of energy and malleability, fatalism and indifference, sensuality, splendor and eccentricity, and cruelty and despotism. To a large extent these characteristics intersect with the classic features that were attributed to barbarians in antiquity. All of them serve as markers of backwardness that establish the binary typology of an advanced Occidental civilization facing a retarded and uncivilized Orient that is ready to be educated, developed, and dominated: "Since the Oriental was the member of a subject race, he had to be subjected: it was that simple."[7]

When postcolonialism somewhat belatedly crossed over from literary criticism and cultural studies into departments of religion and Bible, it stimulated a far-reaching inquiry into the history and constructs of Western biblical interpretation and its complicity with colonialism and imperialism, focusing especially though not exclusively on Christian missionary endeavors. Intersecting to a large extent with empire-critical studies, postcolonial criticism reexamines biblical texts in their synchronicity and entanglement with imperial and colonial contexts from the ancient world to the present day.[8] This approach now constitutes an indispensable dimension of critical biblical scholarship.

As a result of these studies, the concept of Scripture and scriptural authority has become a highly contested territory. The "innocence" of the biblical texts vis-à-vis their later colonial and imperial interpretations is often vehemently disputed by postcolonial and postmodern interpreters, marking a fine line of distinction between their approaches and the allegedly less critical viewpoints of the empire-critical and liberationist paradigms, which are accused of implicitly affirming and reinscribing the established conservative readings of Scripture.[9] It is needless to say that Paul, who has long been regarded as a bastion of theological and social conservatism and whose writings have been intensely implicated in the missionary enterprise with all of its imperial and colonial ramifications, is at the center of these debates, emerging with some predictability as an obvious target of postcolonial scriptural criticism.[10]

My aim in the present essay is to chart a path that avoids the self-defeating alternatives of viewing postcolonial criticism as a denial of scriptural authority or scriptural authority as a denial of postcolonial criticism. Taking up Paul's core concept of "justification by faith" in its historical Galatian setting, on the one hand, and Said's category of "Orientalism," on the other, I intend to demonstrate the analytical fecundity of postcolonial and empire-critical tools for scrutinizing the "Orientalizing" effects of the established (Protestant) interpretations of justification theology. In a next step, I will use these same tools to deconstruct the dominant reading paradigm, showing that the "colonizing text" of Paul is in reality a "colonized text" that has been domesticated and co-opted by Western exegetes and is in need of decolonization. "Scripture" has to be read against "tradition" and Paul against established modes of Pauline interpretation without at the same time postulating the "innocent text" as a given. Claiming Paul's justification theology as a radically decolonizing and empire-critical concept does not imply that Paul himself was not shaped by dominating thought patterns, for example, with regard to gender constructs. At the same time, "colonizing" readings of Paul within the New Testament canon (particular Luke's depiction in Acts and that of the Pastoral Epistles) must be critically examined.[11]

Interestingly, the concept of Orientalism itself so far has received relatively little attention in Pauline postcolonial and empire-critical scholarship.[12] From his perspective as a Palestinian American, Edward Said himself was particularly concerned about the anti-Muslim implications of Occidental thinking that he saw closely connected to anti-Judaism as its twin concept.[13] In the 1994 edition of *Orientalism*, he expressed serious concern about not only the murderous escalation of the Israeli–Palestinian conflict but also the "rush by some scholars and journalists to find in an Orientalized Islam a new empire of evil" in the aftermath of the demise of the Soviet Union, thus lumping together "Islam and terrorism, or Arabs and violence, or the Orient and tyranny" and replacing "Cold War bipolarism" with Samuel Huntington's "clash of civilizations."[14] These observations point to the need for a critical look at the history of Pauline interpretation. While the "New Perspective" has done invaluable work over the past few decades to establish a critique of traditional anti-Judaism in Pauline scholarship, the related complicity between anti-Judaism and anti-Islamism has so far received little attention. As an introduction to the Orientalizing tendency in Pauline interpretation, a pattern that is simultaneously anti-Jewish and anti-Muslim, Sir William M. Ramsay's work on Galatians appears as a model example.

Galatians Colonizing Phrygians, Turks, Jews, and Muslims: William M. Ramsay

William M. Ramsay (1851–1939) was more knowledgeable about the historical context of the Galatian correspondence, including its imperial and colonial ramifications, than virtually any other scholar. An explorer, archaeologist, and professor of humanities at the University of Aberdeen in Scotland, he traveled extensively in Asia Minor and became an eminent expert on the history and archaeology of the region, making significant contributions to the study of the New Testament and Christian origins as well as to the history of the Roman Empire.[15] Even after the ideological underpinnings of his scholarship are understood, his work is still an invaluable source of information about first-century Roman Galatia and its inhabitants, with whom Paul had his most dramatic and theologically consequential disagreement about the need of circumcision.

Ramsay was well aware that the Galatians, who entered Asia minor in 278 B.C.E., were part of the vast Celtic migrations of the fourth and third centuries B.C.E. that originated from central Europe, where the Celts inhabited portions of today's Austria, Germany, Switzerland, France, Britain, and Spain as early as the fifth century B.C.E., and affected northern Italy, the Balkans, Greece, and Turkey. On this basis, Ramsay asserted categorically that the Galatians were Occidentals who were "still a western people at heart, essentially unlike the Greek and Asiatic peoples around them"; indeed, "a deep gulf still separated these Occidentals from the Asiatics."[16] Their inherently Occidental character was evident, according to Ramsay, in their power to conquer and rule. The Galatians had the "qualities of an aristocracy, proud of their own individual superiority"—qualities that they preserved as long as they "continued to be a nation of warriors" who kept themselves away from the manners of their subjects.[17] A certain loss in their Occidental superiority occurred, however, when the Galatians took over the religion of their Phrygian subjects and became a "mixed race."[18]

According to Ramsay, the Phrygians had themselves entered Asia Minor as a noble warrior race (Phryges) of European origin that brought "a love of war and a love of freedom, an energy and pertinacity and self-assertiveness which always seems to be stronger and more deep-rooted in the north and west than in the south and east."[19] Later, however, they amalgamated with the "peaceful and unenterprising" indigenous peoples and "sank to that placid level of character which belonged to the older subject population."[20] As they lost their distinctiveness and thus their dominance, they degenerated into slavishness. The Phrygian was seen in antiquity as "the slave *par excellence*," wholly unfit for war, and together with the Thracians they were the "least honoured of mankind."[21] It is noteworthy that "peace" in this taxonomy marks inferiority; what we today might see as a desirable demilitarization of the Occidental Self was in Ramsay's view what made the ex-conquerors prone to be righteously subjugated by the invading Galatians.

Gender and racial stereotypes are closely interwoven in Ramsay's Orientalizing discourse of conquest and colonization, and not surprisingly the inferior Other is tied to the Other of earth and nature as well. The Phrygians' slavelike nature is manifest in their effeminacy: they wore earrings like women[22] and worshiped the mother goddess Cybele, who among other things was a manifestation of the Earth Mother and the life of nature.[23] The Phrygians thus adhered to a religion that was "a glorification of the female element in human life." This lack of masculinity corresponds to their national character as "receptive and passive, not self-assertive and active." While the ancient Phrygian warriors followed a masculine religion, they eventually surrendered to the "genius of the land on which they lived" and to the lure of "Anatolian religion." Cybele worship represented "the female element as the nobler development of humanity, while the male is secondary and on a lower plane. The Goddess-Mother was represented in the mystic ritual as the prominent figure; the God comes in only to cause the crisis in her life." This is the essence of the Orient that is destined to be ruled by the Occident, since, as Ramsay emphatically states, "among the peoples of the west it was very different."[24] The adequacy of Ramsay's description of Oriental inferiority was confirmed (in his mind) by the people that he encountered in his own travels: the "slow, dull, contented Turk," the famous "Mevlevi or dancing Derwishes of modern Turkey" whose actions echo Cybele worship, and the feminine and thus "Phrygian" art of embroidery that is still skillfully practiced in contemporary Anatolia.[25]

Next to the Galatians and the Phrygians, the Jews are the third party in Ramsay's scenario. An outspoken proponent of the so-called South Galatian hypothesis, Ramsay argued for a strong affinity between Jews and Phrygians/Lycaonians, that is, a union of Semites, Orientals, and Asiatics. The people of Lycaonian Lystra and Derbe to the south of the Roman province of Galatia, where Paul, according to Acts 14:5-20, was first hailed as Hermes and then stoned at the instigation of hostile Jews, were not only "much more Oriental in type than Greek" (making them like the Phrygians), but they also depicted their god in a way that looks like an "almost typical Semite." There is "no natural antipathy" and "no strong racial antipathy" between the Oriental/Asiatic type and "the Semite," which also explains why "the Jew" in modern times has been "better treated before Turkish law than before the law and government of most European countries."[26] In this setting, it is self-evident that Paul's circumcision-free (and thus non-Semitic) form of Christianity was highly contested in Phrygian South Galatia, where the people had a natural preference for the more Semitic version that was propagated by Paul's opponents.

Thus the Galatian conflict becomes in Ramsay's reading the grand clash between Orient and Occident as the defining moment at the root of Christianity.

> Asia Minor is the Debatable Land, in which Orientalism and Occidentalism have often striven for mastery. Under the early Roman Empire, and again at the present day, a vigorous Occidentalism is striving, apparently with every prospect of success, to subdue the plateau.... The deep lying Orientalism always recurs. The Western conqueror triumphs, and before he is aware, when he turns his back for a moment, his results have melted into the old type.... Such was Paul's experience.... Such was the experience of every century in the Christian time. Every heresy in Anatolia recurred to a more Oriental and specially Judaistic type; and at last Phrygia and Galatia reverted to Semitic Mohammedanism.[27]

Paul's battle against Phrygian, Lycaonian, and Asiatic Orientalisms, all of which were embodied in Judaism, finally merged for Ramsay into its contemporary counterpart, "Semitic Mohammedanism." The ease with which Ramsay transitions from Pauline anti-Judaism to anti-Islamism is striking and confirms Said's observation that both Jews and Muslims are at the core of the Occidental construct of the Oriental enemy and Other. The superior forces of the West are in this case represented by Paul—and by imperial Rome. When he was describing the indelibly Occidental character of the

Galatians as "still a western people at heart," Ramsay cited this as a reason for their natural inclination to align themselves with Rome.[28] The Galatians are caught in a tug-of-war between Orient and Occident; they have to make a decision between Phrygia and Rome, past and future, Western progress or Eastern-Jewish-Asiatic backwardness. According to Ramsay, "The fundamental fact in central Asia Minor at that time was this: to be educated, to be progressive, to think, to learn, was to become Romanised or Hellenised. To be a Phrygian, was to be rude, ignorant, unintelligent, slavish."[29]

We are reminded of Said's statement that the inferiority of the conquered justifies their conquest by the superior and makes colonization a benign and beneficial act of education and social advancement. On this reading, Paul as a Christian missionary would be the advocate of Romanization as self-submission of the East to the superior Occidental culture, calling people to a decision against the complacent, earthly, and effeminate "spirit of Orientalism, of stagnation, of contended and happy ignorance, of deep-rooted superstition"[30] that was embodied in Judaism and circumcision. In addressing his audience as "Galatians" (Gal 3:1), Paul was challenging their old Oriental, Asiatic, and pro-Semitic identity as Phrygians or Lycaonians and reminding them of their newly-won Romanness as "men of the Roman province of Galatia." It is as if someone in Ramsay's day were to address another person as "British" rather than "English."[31] Thus, for Ramsay, Paul speaks as "the Roman" in the same way that Ramsay himself speaks as a proponent of the British Empire: Paul's "Roman point of view and his imperial statesmanship" must be fully taken into account if we wish to understand him.[32] Not surprisingly, this new Christ-religion was from Ramsay's perspective ideally suited to be the religion of the Roman Empire, superior to Judaism, the "emasculated" religion of Anatolia, and all the other existing religions (even the emperor cult) in its capacity to transcend national boundaries and become a unifying imperial world religion.[33]

Thus, Ramsay has inscribed the battle of Occident versus Orient into the Galatian conflict of foreskin versus circumcision. Though he candidly states at the outset of his Galatians commentary that he is not concerned with the "dogmatic or doctrinal value" of the letter,[34] he has made Paul's plea for justification by faith at least implicitly a justification of Roman imperial conquest and colonization. The Pauline mission among the nations becomes a call for submission to Rome. It enables its newly converted subjects to pride themselves on being members of the conquering Western civilization that rightly subdues and enslaves its Eastern Others. Ramsay mobilizes the full spectrum of sexist, racist, imperialist, and colonialist dichotomies that are deposited in the conscious and subconscious of the Western Self to construct an epistemology of Christian faith-righteousness versus Jewish works-righteousness: masculinity versus effeminacy, active versus passive, civilized versus barbarian, aristocratic versus slavish, educated and enterprising versus ignorant, superstitious, and complacent. Paul is the Christian embodiment of the self-assertive Western warrior who represents the Roman law of conquest while standing in triumph over inferior Easterners, Jews, Muslims, Turks, Asiatics, non-men, and ultimately earth/nature.

The Dying Galatian and the Justification of the Occidental Self: Critical Reimagination I

Ramsay's unabashedly colonial reading of "justification by faith," with its explicit focus on the Orient–Occident binary, might seem peculiar to his stance as an advocate of the British Empire in the late nineteenth/early twentieth century, but he is by no means an anomaly in the broader pattern of Protestant interpretation of Paul with its intrinsically dichotomous structure. The question that presently marks the cutting edge of Pauline scholarship, however, is whether this justification of the colonizing Roman Self accurately renders the original thrust of Paul's Galatian controversy or, on the contrary, represents its irredeemable distortion. Recent work on Paul that has integrated a focus on his Jewishness with an exploration of his Roman imperial context as his defining hermeneutical framework has unearthed a profoundly empire-critical (rather than Torah-critical) and anticolonial framework within which the apostle conceptualized the core terms of his justification theology, such as Jews and Gentiles/nations, righteousness and justification, boasting, law, faith, and grace.[35] A different image of Paul is emerging that shows him laboring to give birth to a new kind of human being (cf. Gal 4:19) that would reject the deeply ingrained tendency of the old Self to establish an inferior and unjustifiable Other in order to construct its own superiority and justification—a new creation of humanity "in Christ" where the Other is no longer condemned to justify the status, distinction, privileges, and power claims of the dominant Self.[36]

A visual image might offer some assistance for understanding this far-reaching subversion of the dominant logic of Self and Other that is encapsulated in Paul's antithesis of faith versus law/works. The sculpture of the *Dying Gaul* (see image below), which in its countless copies and numerous variations has captivated European imaginations for centuries, is one of the most famous pieces of Self-assertive Occidental victory art. It is also an invaluable "time capsule" that has preserved the normative perception of "Galatians" as Others in the first-century world where Paul, Romans, Jews, and non-Jews interacted on a daily basis. Showing a Celtic warrior in the moment of his defeat, the sculpture tells a story of the Galatians different from the one told by William Ramsay and the majority of interpreters of Paul's Galatian correspondence. By engaging in *critical reimagination*, an approach that draws on the "power of images"—to borrow the title of Paul Zanker's highly influential book[37]—we can grasp the "unseen" and unread or misread elements of a New Testament text. Examining visual sources such as images, spaces, architecture, performances, and rituals can help us to deconstruct and reconstruct our perception of the ancient world in its interaction with the words of the text and open up new dimensions of understanding by making specific aspects of the vanished everyday realities behind these texts visible again.[38]

The *Dying Gaul* is at home in many places of the ancient Mediterranean—he is Roman, Greek, Pergamene. He is also a Galatian, a person from the New Testament known to us through Paul's letter, although scholars have rarely noticed this fact. The oval shield with the protruding central boss on which he has fallen, the torque around

The Dying Gaul, marble; commonly described as Roman copy of a Pergamene original from 230 to 220 B.C.E.; Musei Capitolini, Rome. Photo: Erich Lessing, Art Resource, N.Y.

his neck, the moustache and spiky hair, the nakedness and whiteness of his wounded body, the broken war trumpet—all of these are, in the commonly understood *koinē* of the images, clearly legible markers of Gaul, Galatians, Celts. We might as well call him a *Dying Galatian*, especially if we keep in mind that, in the ancient languages, the designations of Gauls and Galatians are similar: Latin *Galli* (Gauls) are *Galatai* (Galatians) in Greek. In order to "read" this sculpture, we have to understand some of the history behind it, a dramatic history that reaches over many centuries and across nearly the entire Greco-Roman world, where Gauls/Galatians had a ubiquitous presence as settlers, soldiers, migrants, mercenaries, and, if we trust the ancient sources, vicious enemies of civilization.[39]

Although the statue of the *Dying Galatian* is believed to be a Roman copy of a lost third-century B.C.E. Pergamene original, he is at the same time an "original" Roman creation. In 387 B.C.E., an army of Gauls attacked, conquered, and burned down the city of Rome. This was a disastrous defeat that Rome would never forgive, though Rome was eventually able to convert it into a doctrine of justified preventive strikes. Foreshadowing Julius Caesar's brutal campaign in Gaul (58–52 B.C.E.), for example, Manlius Vulso in 189 B.C.E. carried out a wholesale massacre of the three Galatian tribes of Asia Minor at Mount Olympus (near Gordium) and Mount Magaba (near Ancyra). These were the direct ancestors of the New Testament Galatians. They had done nothing against Rome and were unprepared for the terrible onslaught. Forty thousand people died in Manlius's murderous campaign that, according to Livy (*Ab urbe condita*, 38–39), was justified as a legitimate preemptive act of self-defense against the notorious enemies not only of Rome but also of the divine order and of humanity as a whole.

The *Dying Galatian* is also Greek. Not only did the Gauls conquer Rome, but a hundred years later, during their massive migration movements, they appeared at Delphi in 279 B.C.E. They tried to raid the sanctuary of Apollo with its proverbial treasuries, despite its status as the supreme religious center and "navel" of the Greek world. This was another unforgivable act that solidified the Gauls' image as blasphemous barbarian raiders and robbers. Galatians/Gauls thus became the "universal barbarians" against which the Greco-Roman world united as the "common enemy," a lawless and relentless foe marked by a truly terrifying nature. In fact, the term "terror" is frequently used when ancient authors talk about Galatians.[40] Their depravity made the violence used against them moral and righteous. Defeating them was not simply an ordinary victory over an enemy somewhere but an act of salvation for humanity everywhere.

No one was able to exploit this ideology as masterfully as the Pergamenes, who around 240 B.C.E. defeated the three Anatolian tribes of the Galatians in a series of violent clashes at the sources of the river Caicus. One of the smaller Diadochean states, Pergamon was nevertheless able to use the "power of images" to communicate its victory over the Gauls as a major world-saving triumph of cosmogonic dimensions. This moment is the birth of the *Dying Galatian*. He is the forerunner of a visual program that was exhibited later on a much larger scale at the Great Altar of Pergamon (ca. 180–160 B.C.E.). An artistic and intellectual achievement of unprecedented dimension and beauty, the Great Altar shows the Galatians, mythologically disguised as Giants and sons of the Earth Mother Gaia, in rebellion against the Olympic gods. Their defeat is the archetype of the foundational world battle against chaos, lawlessness, and barbarism that gave rise to Western civilization and the Occidental self-construct.[41]

As we know from Karl Strobel's groundbreaking work in reevaluating the stereotype of the "Galatian barbarian,"[42] not only Pergamon but also all the other successor states of Alexander's empire—Macedonians, Seleucids, Ptolemies—exploited the image of the Galatians as notorious invaders and enemies of civilization (an image that is still common in scholarship today) for their own ends. It is not at all clear whether the Galatians/Gauls were indeed so much more rapacious and predatory than the civilizations that needed to stigmatize them as the evil Other in order to justify their own violence and power claims. According to this view, conquering the world was not an act of imperial expansion but rather a meritorious deed on behalf of civilized humanity, as long as it could be presented as a triumph over lawless Galatians. In the post-Alexander world of would-be empire builders, every victory in an anti-Galatian campaign could be presented as an act of euergetism and salvation on a universal scale, an achievement of cosmic dimensions that held the promise of entitlement to rule the world.[43] With his bent back, the *Dying Galatian* thus became a stepping-stone to world power.

The winner in this competition for world power was not Pergamon, nor the Antigonids, Seleucids, or Ptolemies, but Rome. Already in 133 B.C.E. Rome had "inherited" the kingdom of Pergamon, including all of its images, and turned it into the Roman province of Asia. A hundred years later, shortly after Augustus defeated Antony and the Ptolemaic queen Cleopatra at Actium as his last remaining competitors in the competition for world rule, he likewise appropriated the kingdom of the last Galatian ruler, Amyntas, and founded the Roman province of Galatia (25 B.C.E.). In Paul's day, then, the *Dying Galatian* was a profoundly and entirely Roman image that communicated the worldview and triumph of the colonizers and conquerors of the world.

The *Dying Galatian* is a vanquished warrior. Blood is dripping from a gash on his right side, and his arm can barely hold up his sunken body. The victorious antagonist who dealt the deadly blow stays out of the picture. What made this sculpture so appealing? Perhaps it is the silent invitation that it conveys to the spectator to step into the role of the invisible victor and to imagine himself in the moment of triumph over an enemy of such fortitude. Perhaps it is the lure of an aesthetics of violence that turns the pain of the Other into an art object of supreme beauty. What is especially noteworthy, however, is the apparent compliance of the dying warrior with his destiny. He does not indict the victor, nor does he plead for mercy, compassion, or solidarity. His gaze does not meet ours; instead, he dies all by himself, totally confined to his own space and the heroic solitude of his dying. As he has detached himself from our space, so we can stay detached from the space of his Otherness. His suffering, bloodshed, and death all remain at the Outside of what we have demarcated as our Inside. He makes no effort to challenge our Self-detachment, as if he were sure that his time had run out and his cause was lost, that he indeed had to give way to the superior.

Images are not merely depictions of the world as it is, especially an image like the *Dying Gaul/Galatian* that was a prominent subject of public art and a hard-to-miss visual paradigm in the world of Paul. Instead, they show the world as it is meant to be seen. In cultures with low levels of literacy, like those that existed around the ancient Mediterranean, visual representations served as tools of "perception management" and communicated a particular worldview. Images often speak more plainly about the dominant ideology and its perceptions of the proper order of things than written sources. Representing the ideology of the conquerors and colonizers of Gaul and Galatia, the *Dying Gaul/Galatian* reassures his victors that they are justified in their victory and righteous in their warfare with its ensuing casualties, pain, and suffering. The violence and extreme brutality that were the signature of both Julius Caesar's Gallic War and Manlius Vulso's campaign against the Galatians are characterized as justifiable means toward the higher end of establishing law among the barbarians, just as enslavement, exploitation, and oppression are the lawful and legitimate results of the barbarian defeat.

In a way, the *Dying Galatian* himself represents a "work of law." Law, *nomos*, is written in large letters all over his body, invisible yet clearly readable by anyone in the ancient world. He is dying for his transgressions against the law of the cosmos, the laws of heaven, the laws of civilization, the law of Rome. Lawlessness (*anomia*), as opposed to Greek "righteousness" and "justice" (*dikaiosynē*), was one of the fundamental barbarian vices.[44] The Galatian dies as a sinner, and whoever conquered him can boast of the righteousness that is exhibited in his "works of law"—works of conquest and colonization. Wherever this sculpture was displayed, it was a justification of the victorious Self as superior and therefore entitled to subjugate the inferior and lawless Other. This is the message that was communicated in the language of the victors about the law and order of Western civilization; it made the *Dying Gaul* an immortal presence in the imagination of the Occident.

Christ Crucified and the Justification of the Other: Critical Reimagination II

O foolish Galatians! Who has bewitched you? It was before your eyes that Jesus Christ was openly portrayed [*proegraphē*] as crucified. (Gal 3:1)

Paul, in his passionate polemic against the first-century Galatians of Asia Minor, uses a powerful counterimage that fundamentally subverts and contradicts the ideological effects of the *Dying Gaul*. Undeniably, the image of *Christ crucified*, which he reminds them he has publicly painted or portrayed before their eyes, is at the core of the justification theology that he has just outlined in the immediately preceding passage (Gal 2:15-21). In a way, one could describe Paul's entire theology of faith-justification as an act of irreverent noncompliance with the established imperial and colonial rules for dying Gauls, dying Galatians, dying Jews, and dying Others in general.

Dying Galatian versus Christ crucified—the antithetical correspondence between these two images, first observed by David Balch,[45] requires some further exploration. In the imagination of empire and imperial colonization, the image of a crucified man of whatever ethnicity is a twin image of the *Dying Gaul*, only not in the sanitized and aestheticized rendering of an art object but in the raw and unrefined real-life image of a most brutal and dehumanizing form of capital punishment. Crucifixion was used by Rome on a large scale to keep "the lower classes, i.e., slaves, violent criminals and the unruly elements in rebellious provinces" at bay.[46] Crucifixion exhibits the gruesome details of the Other's body being destroyed minute by minute, hour after hour, under unspeakable torture and pain, visibly staged before everybody's eyes as a form of public entertainment, political education, humiliation, and deterrence.[47] Crucifixion was imposed on the rebellious territories of vanquished Otherness on the underside of empire as a draconian restatement of Roman law, the inscription of the colonizers' *nomos* into the colonized provincial and slave body, whether in Gaul or Judea or elsewhere. For spectators, the "show" or "spectacle" (*theōria*) of crucifixion, as it is called in Luke 23:48, is a visual lesson in subordination and Self-distancing from the transgressive Other.[48]

Paul radically violates these rules of perception. He does not comply with the normative way of seeing a *Dying Jew*, or a *Dying Galatian* for that matter. His presentation of Christ crucified turns the hierarchical binaries of superior versus inferior, Self versus Other, law versus lawlessness, justification versus unrighteousness upside down. First, the image of Christ crucified closes off any escape route for the Self to remain distanced from the suffering of the Other. In a powerful inversion, the transgression that causes the lawful punishment and death of the Other is no more seen as the Other's transgression, but as our transgression, the sin of the Self. Jesus did not die for himself and for his own sins but for our sake (Gal 1:4; 2:20). The polar construct of a superior, righteous, law-abiding, justified Self standing over against an inferior, unrighteous, lawless, sinful Other collapses, and with it the law of the dominant order that justifies crucifixion, imperial warfare, and colonial subjugation. The Self can be justified only if it accepts its unjustifiable complicity with the Other's death and thus its own status as sinner.[49]

Second, with the collapse of the established binary, the image of God undergoes a profound transformation as well. While the dominant order always aligns the divine with the superior Self and its law, making the Other by implication godless and lawless (as the construct of the "blasphemous" Galatian barbarian vividly demonstrates), Paul shows that God-Self has stepped up in solidarity with the lawless crucified Other and justified him as God's son. God is thus reimagined on the side of the *Dying Galatian*, that is, on the side of the enemy-Other, subverting any notion of God-willed and lawful violence that the Self can impose on the Other for God's sake and in alliance with God. With the justification of the Other, the sinner, the loser, the defeated, the justification of victory, conquest, and colonization as "divine" provision falls apart. *Christ crucified*, as the image of God-with-the-Other, is the scandalous challenge to the "natural" theological conviction of the Self that God must be on "our" side.

"God, I thank you that I am not like other people . . ."—the Pharisee's competitive effort in Luke 18:9-14 to demonstrate his own distinction and alliance with God by pointing to the clearly undeserving Other, consisting of lawless thieves, rogues, adulterers, and tax collectors, sounds like a narrative explication of Paul's justification language: "We ourselves are Jews by birth and not sinners from the Gentiles" (Gal 2:15). In referring to the sinfulness of the Other (Gentiles), in the established binary semiotics of the time, Paul, automatically and without even explicitly mentioning it, attributes righteousness to "us" (Jews). Yet this Self-justification through the degradation of an Other, which Paul in Galatians and especially in Romans describes as "boasting," is not specific to Jews. Instead, as Robert Jewett has convincingly shown, it was an integral part of the whole Greco-Roman culture of honor and status competition, with Rome standing at the top of an all-encompassing culture of "boasting."[50] Justification by faith rather than by boasting (Rom 3:27-28; Gal 6:13) therefore means the renunciation of "works" that can be presented to distinguish the Self as superior from its less accomplished Other, thus pulling the rug from under the whole edifice of hierarchical dichotomies. With this, the focus of Paul's law criticism irrevocably shifts from criticism of Jewish Torah—still the dominant interpretational paradigm—to a much more general criticism of Greco-Roman *nomos* and any subsequent law construct that justifies "our" Selves as dominant and superior over and against *them*, the unjustified.

Yet as we know that a human is not justified by works of the law, rather by faith in Jesus the messiah-Christ, we too have come to be faithful in Jesus the messiah-Christ so that we may be justified by faith and not by works of law. (Gal 2:16)

Faith in the messiah Jesus means that the one who died as a sinner and Other is God's son; he did not die for *his* sins, thus justifying *our* righteousness derived from our self-righteous law and its "works," but he died for *our* sins, thus unmasking our false claims to righteousness. It is not *they* who are the demonstrable sinners (even if they are), but *we*. Shockingly, as in the parable of the Pharisee and the tax collector, it is not *we* who can claim God's righteousness for ourselves and go away justified but *he*, the Other, the tax collector who repents (Luke 18:14). This is the challenge and scandal of a faith-justification that is rooted in the cross (cf. 1 Cor 1:18, 23). Only if *we* put ourselves on the same level with *them* before God, and on the same level as Jesus, who "otherized" himself, can we become justified, not over against but together with *them*. This in turn points toward the emergence of a new, decolonized community that entirely dismantles the combat order that lies behind the Occidental binaries.

Galatian Foreskin as Sign of Noncompliance and Nonconformity: Critical Reimagination III

The *Dying Gaul* is the quintessential image of imperial and colonial control. His dying is clearly under control. His Gallic/Galatian territory is also under control, the territory of lawless barbarian Otherness with all its wealth and natural resources that his fallen body can no longer defend. His life—whatever is left of it after the disciplinary strokes of the master race, and whatever life means for the conquered and enslaved—is under control. The wound on the *Dying Galatian's* right side shows how his body is bleeding out, perpetually donating its vital energy to the victorious Rome in the form of taxes, tributes, slaves, and warriors. Economically, he and his kin provide the life-blood that circulates in the veins of Rome's colonial empire. And if his first-century C.E. descendants in Roman Gaul or Roman Galatia are allowed to live, it is clear that they have to live in accordance with Roman law. Step by step, the Galatians of Asia Minor were co-opted as subjects and soldiers of Rome after the devastating onslaught of Manlius Vulso in 189 B.C.E.[51] In the process, they were compelled to perform all of the required "works" of subordination to the Roman world order, including Roman religion, and to be mindful at all times that it was the divine Caesar alone who by his grace and righteousness justified their right to live or their condemnation to death.

Christ crucified, in its plain historical setting, is an image of imperial control as well, one that is not much different from the *Dying Galatian*. The resurrection of Christ, however, turns this image upside down. Pointing to an alternative divine ruler who can justify the lawless Other and bring the dead and dying back to life, undoing the works of Roman law enforcement, it ridicules all of the colonial masters' control fantasies. As Paul began to "see" after Damascus, this subversion cannot be confined to the image of a dying Jew alone; it transforms the dying of the other vanquished nations (*ethnē*) as well, the so-called Gentiles. The body of the crucified and resurrected Christ becomes for Paul a new social sphere in which both Self and Other are reborn, rectified, resurrected. Jews and non-Jews become "one" in Christ as they are collectively drawn into the transformative process of co-dying and co-living with the crucified Other (Gal 2:19-20). A deep structure of solidarity is established within the collective body of the conquered that challenges colonial and imperial law in all its variations: the law of Self versus Other, Jews being superior to Gentiles/Galatians, Greeks higher than barbarians, free on top of slave, male in charge of female, and so on (Gal 3:28; Rom 1:14).

Paul points to this new order of solidarity when he reminds the Galatians of their earlier encounter when he himself was in a position of extreme weakness and vulnerability, a Jewish Other in precarious circumstances that would have given the Galatians every reason to distance themselves from the foreigner. Yet, as he states, they acted differently: "You did not scorn or despise me, but welcomed me as an angel of God, as the messiah/Christ Jesus" (Gal 4:14). In so doing, they crossed the decisive boundary into a new commonality and solidarity "in Christ"—a solidarity between Self and Other, between Jews and nations/Gentiles—that is no longer defined by the colonizer's law of conquest and its works of Self-justification that rely on the binary mechanisms of "othering." In stark contrast to William Ramsay's colonial imagination, it was "through the weakness of the flesh" and the peaceful force of solidarity, not through the strength of a powerful and conquering Self, that Paul first proclaimed and successfully rooted the gospel in Galatia (Gal 4:13).

Yet as the Galatians obviously had come to understand in the meantime, Paul's Jewish-ecumenical practice of an inclusive and nonhierarchical "body of Christ" that incorporated, and re-corporated, both Jews and Galatians was irreconcilable with the body politics of Caesar that are so vividly monumentalized in the sculpture of the *Dying Galatian*. Claiming the Galatians as Abraham's children and children of the Jewish god (Gal 3:29; 4:7), declaring them to be adopted or reborn into a new mode of being in which Self and Other stand in mutual support rather than incessant competition (Gal 4:5, 19), submitting them to the law of Christ (Gal 6:2) and the law of love (Gal 5:14), defining as a fulfillment of Torah what essentially was the law of a crucified outlaw—all of this clashed with Caesar's exclusive and inalienable property rights. For this very reason it would also raise concerns on the side of Jews who were not affiliated with the Pauline Jesus movement. The Galatian body was already and permanently marked by Roman *nomos*, a branding that was not negotiable and could not be replaced by the tattoos of an Other law like Paul's *stigmata tou Iēsou* (cf. Gal 6:17). The Galatians were not free to live by the grace of a god other than Caesar, especially if this God claimed sole allegiance in a way that clashed with the expectations and requirements of emperor religion. Paul claimed for the Jewish God what belonged to Roman Caesar.

This is probably the point where the circumcision debate entered the scene. Of all the vanquished nations of the Roman Empire, only the Jews had the precarious privilege of being exempted from certain practices of Roman religion and law that allowed them to be Other within the established civic order with regard to food laws, Sabbath regulations, table community, and the worship of civic or imperial gods. Paul, however, had created a social, political, and religious anomaly: uncircumcised Galatians who lived as if they were circumcised Jews (Gal 4:8-9). As Paula Fredriksen observes, "By insisting both that they not convert to Judaism (thus maintaining their public and legal status as pagans) and that they nonetheless not worship the gods (a protected right only of Jews), Paul walked these Gentiles-in-Christ into a social and religious no-man's-land."[52] They subscribed to Israel's one God alone, no longer worshiping the gods of the city or the god Caesar as they used to, and they formed communities where they followed the law of love rather than the law of competition and Self-distinction. This could not be tolerated, since it was an open declaration of nonallegiance to the gods and the Roman imperial order on the part of the colonized nations. It was an act of civil disobedience that restored the Galatians to their old, rebellious, barbarian Otherness. And the image of the *Dying Galatian* vividly reminded them of what the consequences of their foolish involvement with Christ crucified could be.

In this context, the suggestion to have the Christ-Galatians circumcised makes sense. Presenting them as proselytes would restore at least a minimal appearance of normalcy and conformity for the sake of both the Galatian and Jewish communities—an "evasive action," as Bruce Winter, followed by Mark Nanos, has proposed.[53] Paul himself indicates clearly that his "opponents" are driven not by any specifically "Jewish" concerns for a strict interpretation of Torah per se but by fear of persecution from an outside party: "It is those who want to make a good showing [*euprosōpēsai*] in the flesh who force you to be circumcised, only that they may not be persecuted for the cross of Christ" (Gal 6:12). Paul, however, fiercely refused this kind of pragmatic realism and developed his theology of justification by faith to affirm the righteousness of Galatians and Jews being co-resurrected into the body of Christ and living a new commonality of Self and Other in which the old binaries were transformed through a continuous negotiation of conflicts, hierarchies, and competitions based on their horizontal mutuality "in Christ": bearing one another's burdens (Gal 6:2), practicing freedom as slave service toward one another (Gal 5:13), and fulfilling Torah by obeying the single commandment to love one's neighbor and (br)Other as oneSelf (Gal 5:14).

From a Roman viewpoint, this border-transgressing, transnational community consisting of members of the colonized nations looked dangerously like a worldwide insurrection against Roman law and order, especially as the Galatians were involved. Paul had made the Galatians' foreskin the sign of their nonconformity, not primarily to Jewish Torah but to the Roman *nomos* and its works. "Justification by faith" is, on this reading, the most radical intervention into the order of Occidental binaries that is conceivable, a theology that anathematizes not the Other of Judaism but the colonial and imperial order itself, specifically its inherent polarity between Self and Other (Gal 1:8-9).

Conclusion

In the crisis- and war-ridden world of today, Paul's depolarization of Self and Other is a potent spiritual resource for transformation and renewal that deserves to be revitalized. One of the most burning theological questions at the beginning of the third millennium is whether the Christian Occident will recognize and renounce its complicity in the colonial and neo-colonial enterprise and allow this transformative power to reemerge and interfere with the deadly and ultimately self-destructive logic of warfare, revenge, and power politics. The confession of guilt that German Christians formulated at Darmstadt in 1947, responding to twelve years of tacit or explicit complicity of their churches with Hitler's regime, sounds very timely: "Not the slogan: Christianity and Occidental culture, but turning back to God and turning towards the neighbor through the power of the death and resurrection of Jesus Christ is the one thing which ... we as Christians need."

CHAPTER FIFTEEN

Paul, Nation, and Nationalism

A Korean Postcolonial Perspective

JAE WON LEE

Although historians and interpreters try to avoid anachronisms, neither can get along without the well-known criterion of analogy: interpreters assume that events in antiquity took place in ways that correspond to the ways in which they occur today. Against the Enlightenment assumption that understanding reality requires suppressing subjectivity, one strategy of minority criticism is to name subjectivity up front and thereby to challenge dominant interpretations by unveiling the subjectivity concealed in what claims to be objective. This brief reflection on theory indicates how my experiences of the Korean situation today feed my interest in Paul and how I cannot disengage my reading of Paul from concrete realities of Korea and the global context today.

In 1945, when the Korean peninsula gained independence after thirty-six years of Japanese colonization, it had little chance to breathe fresh air. External powers of the United States and its allies, on the one hand, and the Soviet Union and its allies, on the other, divided Korea into North and South along ideological lines. Painfully and shamefully, people with the same ethnic identity were socialized to hate fellow Koreans on the other side of the (arbitrary) thirty-eighth parallel, and the two regimes enforced separation by violence and imprisonment for their citizens who dared to cross the boundary. Oddly, proponents of reunification have been named traitors and have suffered political persecution—and some have even lost their lives. Clearly, the conflicts between the two Koreas and the repression of attempts at reunification within each regime cannot be separated from the context of global imperial powers.

The Western representation of a vibrant South Korea and an impoverished North Korea hides both minuses and pluses. For example, only a small percentage of the population has reaped benefits from the economic growth in South Korea. At the same time, North Korea has achieved and maintained a degree of autonomy for over fifty years in contrast to U.S. military and economic dominance in South Korea. But from the perspective of either North or South, *reunification would be an anti-imperialistic move*. It is with this kind of context of my own political reality that I turn to Paul with the question of his relationship to his nation.

The dominant reading of Paul in Western biblical interpretation is that he set the Jesus movement free from Israelite nationalism so that it could become a universal movement without boundaries, as if transnationalism is the opposite of nationalism. This has been shown to be a consequence (unintended?) of the New Perspective on Paul, which envisioned Paul moving from Israelite particularism to universalism. Further, the traditional interpretation of Rom 13:1-7 makes Paul a supporter of the state as a God-given institution (an obvious anachronism, since the nation-state emerged only with the Enlightenment), so that ironically Paul is supposed to have left behind his Israelite nationalism while simultaneously becoming a supporter of the imperial state. Paul certainly carried out his mission across cultural barriers and national frontiers. But based on analogies from my Korean perspective and the testimony of Paul's letters, I find it impossible to believe that Paul embraced the Roman Empire and abandoned his own people. In what follows, I will develop an interpretive context for Paul's letters by discussing theories about nations, postcolonialism, and empires, and I will locate Paul's commitment to his mission to the nations in the context of his commitment to his own nation. My overarching thesis is that transnationalism is not antithetical to nationalism[1] and in fact cannot get along without it.

Paul and Nation

Any consideration of Paul and nation has to face the dilemma of trying to define what is meant by the term "nation." A nation cannot be identified by phenomena of the present moment, because it includes both its past and its future, that is, the purposes that its people supposedly seek to achieve in the future. But the past is invariably confused by selective memories, expressed in myths of origin, which turn a blind eye to the violence and injustice that inevitably occur in the founding and maintaining of nations.[2] Further, the lack of national unity that occurs when different interests collide with each other leaves future goals uncertain. For these reasons, Homi Bhabha describes national identity as liminal and ambivalent.[3] National identity lies on the threshold between a past that is complex and uncertain and a future that is fragmented and unfocused. Like the proverbial pot of gold at the end of the rainbow, it is unattainable.

Though associated with territory, a nation is not defined by the land that it inhabits. Even though folk songs and poetry extol the beauty of mountains and rivers, persistent migrations and forced resettlements have repeatedly disrupted people's attachments to the earth. The inadequacy of defining nations by territory is apparent in the case of citizens who are imprisoned: they live within the nation's territory but are nevertheless excluded from it.[4]

The issue of territory was even more complex before the modern nation-state emerged with the Enlightenment, since only then did borders become so fixed that they could be determined with precise geographical surveys. Someone living in proximity to the "border" between ancient Galilee and Syria might identify with one or the other on the basis of heritage rather than location, while nomads, like their sheep, know nothing of borders. Even walled cities were not easily defined by territorial limits. To take Jerusalem as an example, the Mount of Olives, though outside the walls of the city, was considered by the rabbis to be part of the temple precincts (*m. Parah* 3:6, 11; *m. Šeqal.* 4:2; *m. Yoma* 6:4; *b. Roš Haš.* 31a). The urban system also included the surrounding regions, where many poor and non-elite people lived outside the walls.[5] All of this cautions against bringing in modern notions of nation and nationality to make sense of antiquity.

Theorists tend to deal with what a nation is at an abstract level. Even when they acknowledge that one definition will not fit all, they seldom weave together specific cases to form a concrete definition of what it means to be not simply a nation but a particular nation.[6] What, for instance, might Paul have claimed as his nationality? Even if, as the author of Acts reports, he was a Roman citizen, would he ever have identified himself as Roman? Would he claim to be from Cilicia, and, if so, would he call himself Cilician? Or in a world where major cities outshine provinces, was he "Paul of Tarsus" as in Acts? Or did ethnicity trump territory, as when Paul three times calls himself an "Israelite" (Rom 11:1; 2 Cor 11:22; Phil 3:5)?

Bringing ethnicity into the picture only complicates the problem since, according to Jonathan Hall, determining ethnicity in antiquity was fraught with difficulty. Though ancient sources such as Herodotus (*Hist.* 9.122.3) and Pseudo-Hippocrates (*De aere* 24) associate ethnic character with geography and climate, and though modern researchers have tested hypotheses linking ethnicity with kinship, language, religion, and special cooperative existence (as in the Greek city-states), exceptions undermine all of these proposals. According to Hall, ethnicity in antiquity is a subjective construct[7] that defies objective criteria. In the end, however, Hall finally settles on a putative shared ancestral heritage as the most prominent criterion for ethnicity.[8] This places a premium on the coincidence of being born into relationships established long before birth in which socialization occurs.[9]

In contrast to Hall, Davina C. Lopez challenges the scholarly presumption that Paul uses the term *ethnē* in the sense of ethnicity. In her view, *ethnē* is a reference to "the nations."[10] In relation to Hall's criterion of putative ancestry, Lopez is obviously correct insofar as Paul could not have assumed a common ancestry for the various *ethnē* that he encountered in his mission. On the other hand, Paul both parallels and contrasts the *ethnē* with *Ioudaioi* in situations where ethnic tension is obvious.[11] He also manifests a concern to include the *ethnē* in the putative ancestry of Abraham.

How exactly Paul construes ethnic identity is not important for the present discussion, but these attempts to conceptualize nation and ethnicity offer entrances into the way Paul thought about these subjects. In the final analysis, however, national identity is not merely a mental construct; it is also expressed in concrete behavior,[12] as in Paul's persecution of God's *ekklēsia* and his mission to the *ethnē*.

Postcolonialism and National Relationships

Postcolonialism initially found a potent expression in literary criticism, from which position it exercised influence on New Testament studies. Postcolonialism circumscribes the hegemonic center of the Western world with an alternative perspective from the margins. The margins allow for multiple lifestyles. The marginalized may simply acquiesce as the dominant culture entices them to emulate the center, luring them by the possibility of accruing power and privilege. If they do not flow toward the center, it is taken for granted that they will remain "undeveloped." Politically, they may be designated "aliens"—if not illegal aliens, then resident aliens.

In postcolonialism, on the other hand, this table is turned upside down. The margin is no longer a place defined by the Western center but a place from which minority critics can engage Western hegemony with a different way of construing reality.[13] The margin can be a place for enhancing the values of people whom the center considers to be unenlightened because their values differ from Western norms.[14] Postcolonialism does not call those on the margins to separate from the dominant center, since in that case the margin would still be defined by the hegemonic center from which it derives its orientation, even if in opposition. Instead, following Mikhail Bakhtin's claim that "the most intense and productive life of culture takes place on the boundaries,"[15] the margin can be a place of creative, critical engagement with hegemony, a place of communication and exchange.[16]

On the other hand, the margin should not be romanticized as a Garden of Eden.[17] Its creative character offers no incentive to move to the margin, since it is also a place of injustice. The margin exists because winners with power displace subdominant people. Nevertheless, the margin can refuse to be defined by the dominant center, whether by submission or retaliation, producing the paradox in which terrorism is defined by its adversary. In this sense, the margin is a creative space to seek meaning by unveiling injustice and formulating its own values and purposes.

Homi Bhabha appropriated the term "hybridity" to describe the relationship of the margin to the center. Hybridity dismantles "the binary logic through which identities of difference are often constructed—black/white, self/other," while the "interstitial passage between fixed identifications opens up the possibility of a cultural hybridity that entertains differences without an assumed or imposed hierarchy."[18] Hybridity involves a mutual influence of cultures that forms a synthesis from which there is no return. A return to nativism is not possible, because relationships of power still control the conditions under which a movement toward nativism would take place.[19] Moreover, nativism perpetuates identity by reinforcing the binary oppositions between colonizer and colonized while simultaneously overestimating the ability of the colonized to ignore the consequences of colonialism that they have appropriated into their own reality.

According to Bhabha, cross-fertilization among cultures enriches the new synthesis. Yet Bhabha also sees hybridity as disruption.[20] For one thing, it disrupts the fiction of the cultural homogeneity of the dominant culture. Hybridity is a process that takes place beyond what parades as hegemonic culture, revealing that it, too, was produced by a hybridization of cultures.[21] Hybridity also disrupts subdominant cultures, since it often means a loss of such things as language and homeland. For them, however, hybridity is a strategy for engagement with the dominant culture, a creative space where experiences of loss stimulate the generation of fresh signification.[22]

As valuable as postcolonialism's revaluation of the margin as a place for creativity is, I share the reservations of Aijaz Ahmad and Simon During, who state that the tendency of postcolonial thinkers to consider all nationalism as (un)founded in distorted myths of origin and as fostering false claims for homogeneity restricts their efforts at political action. To resist imperialism and act positively against it requires commitment to, rather than detachment from, aspects of national socialization that refuse to acquiesce.[23] Contrary to the poststructuralist toleration of difference adopted by some postcolonialists, many colonized peoples do not wish simply to be tolerated by those who are willing to value their third-world difference; they want to make specific demands for justice.

Tat-siong Benny Liew describes his intriguing Asian approach to Mark's Gospel as "reading with yin yang eyes." He views Mark as a hybridized text that challenges colonialism at the same time that it serves as a site of neocolonial domination.[24] Although he insists that his dual reading does not produce a meaningless ambiguity but rather serves as a source of both liberation and oppression, a careful reading suggests that the eyelids of his dual reading are heavy with the hybridity of Asian yin yang philosophy and poststructuralist indeterminacy. In fact, the "site" for his dual reading is the hermeneutical mind of the modern reader and not Mark's concrete social location. I agree with Liew that no book stands completely on the side of liberation,[25] yet I also note that, in affirming this, Liew presupposes a notion of liberation as a norm without any criteria for adjudicating what is liberating. My concern at this point is not to complain about the absence of criteria but rather to observe that (a) norms such as "liberation" do not materialize out of nothing but are produced by some form of socialization, and (b) any commitment to such norms requires going beyond a tolerant recognition of diversity in values. Aijaz Ahmad points out the implications of such an ambivalent position when he criticizes the ideological stances of some postcolonial theorists:

> The dismissal of class and nation as so many "essentialisms" logically leads towards an ethic of non-attachment as the necessary condition of true understanding.... [B]reaking away from collective socialities of that kind inevitably leaves only the "individual"—in the most abstract sense epistemologically, but in the shape of the critic/theorist concretely—as the locus of experience and meaning, while the well-known poststructuralist

skepticism about the possibility of rational knowledge impels that same "individual" to maintain only an ironic relation with the world and its intelligibility.[26]

Christine DiStefano raises similar questions about postmodern deconstruction: "Why is it, just at the moment in Western history when previously silenced populations have begun to speak for themselves and on behalf of their subjectivities, that the concept of the subject and the possibility of discovering/creating a liberating 'truth' become suspect?"[27] Ahmad suggests that conscientious efforts should be made to distinguish between "progressive and retrograde forms of nationalism with reference to particular histories"[28] if we intend to engage in constructing liberation as resistance to the historical violence of imperialism from the past to the present. These observations point toward the need for an empire-critical approach.

Empire Criticism

What difference does an empire-critical approach make to New Testament studies? One of the central concerns of postcolonialism is to unveil the distortions that characterize myths of origin and the disunities that underlie fictions of national unity. Empire criticism, by contrast, emphasizes imperial systems as the overarching context of the New Testament. A few further remarks in dialogue with Liew will demonstrate the value of this additional dimension. Liew sees Mark's Gospel as a site for contemporary hermeneutical readings. But if Mark is viewed as a local, concrete phenomenon in history, is it credible to see the author as writing from any site except the margins of imperial culture?[29] Liew cautions that to focus on Mark's imperial context neglects Mark's portrayal of Jewish leaders and women, as if these two groups were somehow separate from the empire.[30] From an empire-critical perspective, however, the empire is the context for understanding all of these characters. For example, the Jewish leaders about whom Liew speaks function as a part of imperial systems that trickled down from the emperor through provincial governors, client kings, and local elite collaborators. Thus, Mark's portrayal of local leaders cannot be separated from imperial systems. Even if Mark reinscribes imperial values in a display of colonial mimicry, his words reveal something of the inevitable complicity of anyone who seeks to coexist in the empire, a complicity that Liew also recognizes.[31]

With regard to Paul, Richard A. Horsley initiated a dramatic shift in perspective by locating Paul's rhetoric not merely in the context of Greco-Roman rhetorical forms and political functions but also in relation to Paul's historical context in the Roman Empire.[32] Horsley has shown how Paul, because of his national socialization in a Jewish apocalyptic worldview and his experience of Christ, filled popular rhetorical forms with a quite different content. Rather than serving the interests of elite benefactors who used their wealth to support and maintain the empire, including the imperial cult,[33] Paul used conventional rhetorical forms to revalue the marginalized, counter the system of imperial patronage, and oppose dominating powers within the unavoidable imperial context.

Horsley's approach undermines the view that Paul advocated universalism at the expense of his own people, since behind this position lies the untenable assumption that Paul wrote from the middle of the dominant culture. When Paul calls himself an Israelite, he identifies himself as a member of a colonized people, which pushes him far down the imperial social hierarchy. The Arch of Titus in Rome, erected shortly after Paul's presumed death, glorifies Titus's sacking of Jerusalem and demeans the conquered Jews.[34] Tacitus expresses a similar view when he calls the Jews "the most degraded out of other nations" (*Hist.* 5.5). Israelite identity also immerses Paul in a history of imperial conquests and domination from time immemorial. (A history of sacrifice and suffering is a recurring mark of ethnic identity.) Conquests, exiles, oppressions, and liberations are part of the ancestral heritage to which Paul appeals.[35] Thus, when Paul claims to be an Israelite, he is identifying with a people who were marginalized not only geographically but also ethnically as God-forsaken losers.[36] This is why Paul can say, "The name of God is blasphemed among the nations because of you" (Rom 2:24) and "For your sake we are being killed all day long; we are accounted as sheep to be slaughtered" (Rom 8:26). Paul also adopts a marginalized position within the Roman social hierarchy when he interprets the crucifixion of Jesus as part of the history of Israelite suffering: "The insults of those who insult you have fallen on me" (Rom 15:3, recalling Ps 69:9 [68:10 LXX]).

In 2 Cor 11:23, Paul claims to have suffered imprisonments, and he wrote Philippians from a Roman prison. As I noted earlier, no matter what the territory, imprisonment removes prisoners from the nation, so writing from prison is writing from the extreme margin of Roman society. Paul also claimed as a major part of his identity his discipleship to a man who had been crucified under the imperial system. As Joel Marcus has shown, not only was crucifixion reserved for the marginalized (such as insubordinate slaves and defiant foreigners), but it was itself an attempt to shame the victim.[37] To be a follower of one who was crucified is to locate oneself on the remote margins of imperial culture.

In addition to writing from the margin, Paul also writes to communities consisting largely of conquered and vanquished nations, as Brigitte Kahl and Davina Lopez have recently shown. Against the New Perspective's claim that Paul's Christian universalism replaced his earlier Jewish ethnocentricity, Kahl locates Paul within the historical realities of imperial systems.[38] By foregrounding the imperial context, Lopez also shows how the *ethnē* are historically and politically the nations "defeated by and incorporated into Roman imperial territorial rule."[39] Thus Paul, the Israelites, and the *ethnē* stood as conquered people whose political reality was complicated by the adoption of different positions of collaboration, negotiation, and resistance.

The existence of competing positions is especially evident when local elite collaborators are compared with the populace at large. Like modern global powers, Rome promoted differences among the conquered nations in order to sow seeds of disunity, diffuse solidarity, and fortify their hegemonic superiority. Disunity was guaranteed by local elite collaborators who were separated by status and function from the populace at large. Such imperial collaboration may be reflected in Paul's reference to "the present Jerusalem" in Gal 4:25. By contrast, Paul's gospel of the cross with its creation of "hybrid" communities made up of both Jews and *ethnē* subverts the imperial pluralism of the Roman hierarchy without losing sight of the restoration of Israel. These are the kinds of insights that arise from viewing Paul as a conquered Israelite who wrote to readers from vanquished nations.

Paul and Nationalism

The image of Paul that has been painted thus far stands in opposition to two popular views: (1) the conventional belief that Paul moved beyond his Israelite nationalism to a universal view of God's power of salvation, that is, the perspective that nationalism and transnationalism contradict each other; and (2) the tendency in postcolonial thought to abandon the nation to ambiguity because of the fallacies in national myths of origin, the lack of any unity of purpose, and the presence of phenomena such as hybridity and diaspora identity that for many signify the end of nationalism.[40] My own perspective is that the kind of nationalism that Ahmad classifies as "progressive" (in contrast to "retrograde nationalism"[41]) and transnationalism are not mutually exclusive either in Paul's day or in ours. Without attempting to bring Paul into the twenty-first century, I find in his letters a commitment both to nationalism and to a wider transnationalism that is relevant to situations like the division of Korea today. But since nationalism can wear different faces, as Ahmad has shown, it is necessary to make distinctions regarding what nationalism means.[42] Paul's letters can help us to make such distinctions.

If the term "nationalism" is restricted to extremists, most scholars would concede that the early Paul was a nationalist.[43] According to his own account, he was extremely zealous for a national culture that he calls *Ioudaismos*. He also claims to have exceeded his peers in his devotion to his ancestral traditions. His extremism, moreover, is attested by his persecution of God's *ekklēsia*. What then happened to his nationalism when he experienced the revelation of God's son? Did his nationalism come to an end?

Michael Billig argues convincingly that it is misleading to restrict nationalism only to extremists (like the early Paul) to the neglect of habitual ways of expressing national identity.[44] Billig begins his discussion of nationalism by speaking of that for which citizens are willing to sacrifice their lives.[45] Two texts in Paul's letters appear to fit this criterion: (1) Paul's vow in Rom 9:3 that he is willing to become anathema from Christ for the sake of his people, and (2) Paul's remarks about taking the collection to Jerusalem (which also carried implications for the way "the nations" are related to his own nation) at the risk of his life (Rom 15:25-27, 31).

Paul's willingness to become anathema for the sake of his people (Rom 9:3) shows his commitment to Israel's restoration. Elsewhere he affirms that God is irrevocably committed to Israel's restoration (Rom 11:26-32). Is Paul's concern for Israel part of a pattern that can be described as "ethnocentric"? According to Denise Kimber Buell and Caroline Johnson Hodge, in spite of his mission to Gentiles, Paul invariably gives preference to Jews. In Rom 1:16, salvation is for everyone who believes, "to the Jew first and also to the Greek." Here Paul assigns Israel priority over the Gentiles. Although Paul later unites Jews and Gentiles under Abraham's ancestry, "to the Jew first and also to the Greek" is a hierarchical order.[46]

Paul's language about Israel's restoration in Romans 11 appears at the end of a long argument that starts in 1:16 and passes through chapter 4. Paul's commitment to Israel's restoration (11:26) is closely linked to his earlier statement about the power of God for salvation "to the Jew first and also to the Greek" (1:16) as well as his explication of God's promise to Abraham in Romans 4. According to Paul, the promise of descendants has two distinct but related facets: Abraham is the ancestor of "many nations" as well as those descendants who bear the mark of circumcision (4:17-18). It is this latter assertion that carries forward into Paul's argument in chapter 11: "For the gifts and the calling of God are irrevocable" (11:29).

Elsewhere I have considered whether "first" and "also," as in Rom 1:16, are to be understood in hierarchical terms.[47] Here I emphasize three points. First, in the broader context, Paul asserts the equality of Jews and Gentiles before God on the basis of monotheism (3:29). Second, for Paul this God is also the Creator (1:20, 25; 8:19-23), which is to say that God has a history of dealing with humanity prior to Abrahamic paternity. Third, Rom 1:16 is not Paul's final comment on the relation of Jews and Gentiles.

Read on its own, Rom 1:16 seems to confirm a hierarchy, as Kimber Buell and Johnson Hodge assert. But the same sequence also appears in two other passages. Romans 2:9 speaks of a startling reversal in God's dealings with the problem of evil: "Tribulation and distress are upon the life of every human being who does evil, the Jew first and also the Greek." Insofar as the hierarchy here pertains to priority in judgment, this is an inversion of Paul's earlier statement about God's power for salvation.

The reversal in Rom 4:10-12 is equally startling. Paul asks why Abraham was circumcised. In his answer, he first asserts that Abraham is the ancestor of Gentiles who have faith like his. The act of circumcision then makes him also the ancestor of the circumcised who have faith like his. Because Abraham had faith before he was circumcised, Abrahamic heritage belongs to Gentiles first and then to Jews. Clearly in this context, "to the Jew first and also to the Greek" should not be understood in terms of an ethnic hierarchy. Instead, as Lopez has shown, the hierarchy that impinges on Paul's mission is that of Roman imperial claims to cultural and political superiority over the conquered nations, including the Israelites. The latter belong to "the underside of a Romans/nations hierarchy as one of many defeated and incorporated peoples."[48]

Nevertheless, Paul's commitment to Israel's restoration is nationalistic in Billig's sense, as he is willing to offer himself as a sacrifice for his people. At this point, a brief personal reflection might be helpful, since I find myself in a situation that is similar to Paul's commitment both to his nation and to a transnational mission. Without equating my own situation with Paul's, I cannot help but see analogies between my longing for the reunification of Korea and Paul's commitment to the restoration of Israel. At the same time, my nationalism does not negate my commitment to a transnational global peace.

The second case of Paul's willingness to risk his life for a national cause concerns the collection. When describing how the so-called Jerusalem council made a division of labor between a mission to the circumcised and a mission to the uncircumcised, Paul mentions a stipulation from the leaders in Jerusalem that the Pauline mission should remember the poor (Gal 2:6-10). Paul's strategy for fulfilling this stipulation is commonly called the collection. As Sze-kar Wan correctly argues, this collection was not limited solely to meeting the needs of the poor but also had a symbolic function for expressing how Gentiles are related to Israel.[49] (1) The collection presented a distinct alternative to unequal exchanges between elite benefactors and their clients in the imperial patronage system. The collection symbolized mutuality rather than patronage. This made it an alternative to imperialistic economics. (2) The collection spoke symbolically of crossing the boundaries between Israelite and non-Israelite ethnicity.

Under this second point, Wan implies the erasure of Israelite identity by claiming that Paul constructs a "new ethnos."[50] If Wan means that Paul envisions a single community embracing both non-Israelites and Israelites, then of course he is correct. Traditional Israelite boundary markers such as circumcision no longer determine who is inside and who is outside this community. The new community, however, does not dispense with ethnicity. Members of the new community maintain embedded identities that do not cease. The new community includes Israelites and non-Israelites, slaves and freeborn, male and female. Paul makes Abraham the father of both by drawing a line between his status before and after he was circumcised. In this way, Paul maintains the distinct ethnicities of the circumcised and the noncircumcised. Thus, the boundaries of the people of God are enlarged, but not the boundaries of Judaism, as Wan alleges. In Romans 4, Abraham is the father not of one new *ethnos* but of many *ethnē*, one of which is Abraham's descendants who bear the mark of circumcision.

Still, Paul fears that he is risking his life by taking the collection to Jerusalem, which means that the relationship between Jerusalem and the Gentiles is too important for him to abandon. If Jerusalem should not accept the gift, it would be a cause of severe disappointment, but it would hardly entail the risk of his life. As Wan has shown, however, Rome prohibited the transport of gold from the provinces toward the east, away from Rome, but made concessions for Diaspora Israelites to pay the temple tax.[51] Paul's statement thus raises questions about whether the collection was a legal transport of wealth toward the east. At this point, Wan separates the symbolic meaning of Jerusalem from resistance to the empire. Should the Jerusalem authorities not accept the collection as analogous to the temple tax, Paul would be at the mercy of Roman agents. Against this background, a passage from Josephus that Wan himself quotes betrays the influence of the imperial system of the time. In this passage, the Roman general (later emperor) Titus addresses the Israelites whom he has conquered, saying, "We [Romans] allowed *you* to occupy *this* land and set over you *kings of your own blood*; then we maintained the laws of your forefathers . . . ; above all we permitted *you* to exact tributes for God and to collect offerings . . . " (*War* 6.335-36 [my emphasis]). In the imperial system that Titus's speech presupposes, client kings and local collaborators were granted such concessions under the condition that they, not the Roman agents, should enforce decorum and legality. Thus, Paul would have been at risk from Roman collaborators who in the interest of not losing status and permission to collect the temple tax would themselves have enforced Rome's prohibition against transporting gold away from Rome. Whether Paul's risk arose from fear that Roman agents or collaborators in Jerusalem would enforce the prohibition against transporting wealth to the east makes little difference when it is a matter of the imperial system.

The symbolic meaning of the collection, however, is not merely that Jerusalem will recognize the nations. It is often overlooked that the collection also means Jerusalem's recognition of its relationship to the nations, that is, the relationship between nationalism and transnationalism, which is precisely what Paul's mission is about.

In a critique of Wan's article, Calvin Roetzel expresses difficulty in squaring the subversive nature of the collection with Rom 13:1-7, which he takes as Paul's position on the imperial structure as a useful institution.[57] But Romans 13 is not a statement on the institution of the state as such. It is rather a particular strategy for how Roman Christ-followers could coexist in the empire. By means of the collection, marginalized Pauline communities embedded in the empire could work out an alternative not only to imperial values but also to the system itself. Coexistence within an imperial system is no hindrance to an alternative way of life that offers a different form of distributing resources than imperial patronage. Paying taxes to the empire was part of a broader strategy of coexistence for a transnational movement that was also engaged in gathering a collection for Jerusalem.

As I noted earlier, Billig also speaks about other forms of nationalism that stand at the opposite extreme from what people are willing to die for. He calls these attitudes "banal nationalism." Banal nationalism is so pervasive at a barely conscious level that people fail to notice that it is embedded in the very language that is used for expressing ordinary thoughts.[53] What kind of nationalism is expressed in Paul's language? Paul's references to Jerusalem in the autobiographical section of Galatians indicate a particular "geopolitical" perspective, as Mark Nanos puts it.[54] In antiquity, national identity was more strongly oriented toward major cities than to provinces. Inasmuch as Paul in Galatians 2 makes casual references to Jerusalem that are secondary to his rhetorical purpose, these references occur at the barely conscious level. His perspective is that he goes "up" to Jerusalem (1:18 [cf. v. 17]; 2:1, 2), the center of the Israelite temple state, the point where heaven meets earth, the center of the world. Jerusalem is also the location from which Paul begins his mission as the center of the circle (*kyklō*) of his activity (Rom 15:19). These subtle indicators point to Jerusalem and the Israelite people as Paul's "natural" nationalized identity.

In keeping with Billig's attention to what language expresses about one's relation to the nation, it is noteworthy that Paul does not write in imperial Latin. Instead, he sticks to Greek. But even this practice manifests a kind of hybridity, since it goes back to a series of earlier conquests of his people from the time of Alexander the Great. Paul also preserves two bits of Aramaic in his letters, the words *Abba* and *maranatha*. He would not have written these words had it not been for an earlier imperial conquest of his people by the Babylonians. He claims to be a Hebrew, but he never writes a single word of Hebrew. The irony of a Hebrew writing in Greek with two Aramaic ornaments is the product of a long history of imperial conquests.

Is this to be understood from the romantic perspective that cross-fertilization invariably produces a new synthesis? Or is it more like Bhabha's idea of disruption? Paul's use of Greek signals a loss of the mother tongue of his own tradition due to his isolation from his homeland and its ancient culture. Greek overwhelms Paul to such an extent that he engages his own Hebrew Scriptures in the form of the Greek Septuagint. If the rhetorical critics are correct, Paul uses Greek rhetorical commonplaces that presume polytheism to proclaim his monotheism, a monotheism that ties Jerusalem and the nations together beyond the divide of Israel and the Gentile world. In the process, he produces a discourse in the context of an imperial presence that sets Israelite traditions both within and against imperialism.[55] His discourse claims a heritage that is incompatible with the polytheistic syncretism of the Roman Empire.

Paul also uses images that are strikingly different from what appears on Roman statues, coins, and monuments. Among his images is the olive tree, which dominates Romans 11. Of course, the metaphor presupposes the presence of a tree, but, contrary to much commentary, Paul does not actually describe a tree but rather paints a picture of the root and branches. The root consecrated to God stands in continuity with the branches. Because of this consecration, the image is theocentric, as Ernst Käsemann puts it, "stressing the continuity of God's hidden faithfulness in Israel's history."[56] Of course, it must be understood that God's dealings with Israel include the nations, toward whom God has also made promises. When the wild olive branches are grafted onto the tree, it signifies that God's faithfulness moves beyond Israel to the nations. If Paul had left the image at this point, it would have spoken primarily about God's promises to the nations. But Paul goes on to talk about a relationship between the unnatural branches and the natural branches that have been broken off, affirming that the latter will be grafted in once again so that one root supports all of the branches. At the end, it is still possible to distinguish the natural branches from the wild ones. At this point Caroline Johnson Hodge introduces the idea of hierarchy: Israel comes first as the "natural branches" linked to the root by natural descent, while the Gentiles are secondary, as "wild branches" incorporated by adoption.[57] Hodge and I are in agreement that the difference remains, but difference does not mean hierarchy. In fact, Paul's exposition of the metaphor speaks about difference without touching on the question of hierarchy. In both cases the relationship of the root to the branches is the same, and in both it rests on divine promises. The Gentiles do not enter the image only after the fact, as ingrafted branches. They enter at the root, as beneficiaries of God's promises. Thus, the metaphor of the ingrafting of the wild olive branches gives expression to Paul's internationalism, but only in the context of the consecration of the root to God and the ingrafting again of the broken branches, images that are fundamentally nationalistic. The two images hang together on the basis of God's fidelity to the promises.

Conclusion

Postcolonial criticism has invited us to interrogate imperialist colonial discourses in biblical texts as well as in dominant biblical interpretations. Postcolonial literary-critical and empire-critical studies of the New Testament have also directed our attention to the intersection of identity, culture, and gender in imperial constructions of the relationships between imperialist domination and (post- and neo-)colonial subordination. I have sought to show that Paul, as a diasporic Jew, committed his life and practice to forming alternative communities comprising the subordinate people-groups of Jews and Gentiles ("the nations") and that his vision had both national and international horizons. Once again, Paul challenges New Testament scholars to relocate historical questions for biblical texts and scrutinize our own ideological positions in dealing with the historical political dynamics of Roman imperial domination over the defeated and conquered nations, including Israel.

While acknowledging the difficulties associated with theorizing about nation and nationalism in the contemporary global political economy and making correlations between Paul's colonial context and the Korean context in today's imperial globalization, I find myself uneasy with certain tendencies in both postcolonial theory and postcolonial biblical interpretation, especially in discussions of the category of "nation." My reading of Paul among Jews and the nations is influenced by my experience of the struggles of the Korean people and my aspirations for the reunification of Korea, including Koreans in diasporic communities, as viewed from the perspective of the people (*minjung*) who have suffered from the historical and political reality of our divided nation, namely, the poor (mainly urban laborers and farmers) and the marginalized (including foreign laborers).

In postcolonial and empire-critical readings of Paul, conflicting claims have been made as to whether Paul's letters should be read as offering liberation from imperial domination or as more ambivalently reinscribing colonial and imperialist discourses. We should be cautious of any totalizing tendency in either direction, since the current politics of interpretation seems to lack any theoretical (subject) position for adjudication. Is it possible that this ambiguity in postcolonial readings of Paul's letters reflects the ambivalence of contemporary interpreters toward the imperialist domination system that is embedded in late capitalist globalization?

CHAPTER SIXTEEN

Constructions of Paul in Filipino Theology of Struggle

GORDON ZERBE

The apostle Paul continues to be a challenge for those who seek to appropriate his legacy in contemporary contexts, not least in settings where Christians are committed to some form of social transformation. As an example of the latter, this paper explores the ways in which Paul has been appropriated in Filipino theology of struggle.

Theology of struggle (ToS),[1] the preferred way since the early 1980s to speak of the distinctive form of liberation theology in the Philippines, denotes both a location and mode of theologizing: "in" and "of" struggle.[2] While difficult to circumscribe or define neatly, generally speaking theology of struggle is aimed at grounding, sustaining, and motivating Christian participation in and solidarity with the Filipino people's aspirations for radical social transformation. Emerging out of the situation of authoritarian rule under Ferdinand Marcos (martial law, 1972–86), but drawing on earlier roots, theology of struggle has persisted to today. While the nature of the struggle for social transformation, and of Christian participation in it, has been the subject of vigorous rethinking and debate since the early 1990s, the momentum of theologizing from the standpoint of struggle is not likely to wane.[3]

At least three responses to the figure of Paul can be observed in writings associated with the theology of struggle: (1) overt criticism, especially of Paul's sociopolitical perspective; (2) polite avoidance and disregard; and (3) sympathetic and critical appropriation. An example of overt criticism is found in the following comments by Oscar Suarez published in 1985 in regard to Paul's political perspective:

> We cannot ignore the obvious *ambiguity* in the Pauline doctrine of state-power as accounted for in Romans 13. In this particular passage, Paul (and let me make a few accusations here) sounds to be a little outdated in his politics. Paul's political-

ideological understanding is quite incomplete, if not all wrong.... But perhaps we should not blame him too much, after all he himself was a Roman citizen.[4]

Overt criticism, however, is rare in printed works and is usually followed by some extenuating explanation or off-setting factors.[5] The relative infrequency of overt criticism may be due in part to (a) the high formal authority ascribed to Scripture in the Philippines; (b) the goal of the rhetoric, namely, to appeal to church people for support and participation in the struggle, for which attacks on the formal authority would be counterproductive; and (c) the prominence of a "hermeneutics of appreciation."[6] These three factors are probably also behind the seemingly more common response of polite avoidance in cases where Paul's perspective is found to be problematic or embarrassing. Paul, it seems, has been mostly sidelined as a benchwarmer in the theology of struggle, used at best as a backup or support player.[7]

Nevertheless, Paul has also been claimed by some as a powerful resource for the theology of struggle, appropriated sympathetically, even if critically. This paper focuses on these appreciative, albeit critical, appropriations of Paul, which I group according to five thematic rubrics based on the major emphases of particular writers: (a) an emphasis on Paul's vision of a new world coming, that is, of cosmic transformation; (b) an emphasis on *kenōsis* ("emptying") and the unmasking of and victory over powers, along with an emphasis on human depravity as bondage; (c) the theme of Paul's work involving the dismantling of oppressive structures (of law) and freedom from bondage, along with claims of transcendence as the basis for a critique of all human projects; (d) the appropriation of the classic Reformation themes of tortured conscience, justification by faith, and the dialectical separation of realms, including gospel and law; and finally (e) the emphasis on Paul as a model of contextual theologizing, for which his conversion provided illumination, while stressing his vision of a transformed world.

Perhaps not surprisingly, the group of writers who have given sustained attention to Paul includes only men. While women have made significant contributions to the theology of struggle in the Philippines,[8] with rare exceptions they seem to have politely avoided Paul.[9] Nevertheless, the following sample of comments on Paul by Filipina authors exemplifies some critical themes. Mary John Mananzan emphasizes the abolition of distinctions in Gal 3:28 and the presence of Gentiles, slaves, and women in leadership roles, including Prisca, Lydia, and Thecla. But she also observes the pervasive "ecclesiastical partriarchalization" in Paul, drawing on the work of Elisabeth Schüssler Fiorenza, Rosemary Radford Ruether, and others.[10] Virginia Fabella also relies on the work of Schüssler Fiorenza to highlight the presence of women leaders (Junia, Phoebe, Nympha) in early Christianity, which went against the grain of the prevailing patriarchy.[11] Elizabeth Dominguez challenges irresponsible uses of Romans 13, analyzing it alongside Matthew 2, Luke 1 and 4, and Acts 4.[12] Sharon Rose Joy Ruiz-Duremdez argues that Paul is "one of the most misunderstood biblical authors" whose writings have been wrongly "used to legitimize sexist and spiritualized theology." Instead, "Paul's concern was for the whole world. He believed that God was seeking to establish a 'new world' in which all former distinctions between Jew and Gentile, slave and free men, men and women have been abolished (Galatians 3:28)." She also draws attention to the theme of equality in Paul's fundraising campaign (2 Corinthians 8–9) and to the liberating social significance of the sacraments of baptism and Eucharist.[13] Arche Ligo contextualizes the "anti-woman" texts in Paul, giving him the benefit of the doubt: "Paul's preoccupation in maintaining social order and distinctions between men and women was a reaction against Hellenizing influences that tended to blur many of the traditional social distinctions and role. It was not originally intended to dominate women." Even in the household codes, she says,

> Submission . . . is framed in a wider discourse in which women are urged to advance freedom in the world through a revolutionary charity drawn from their own strength as women. . . . The Pauline . . . ethics of love, forgiveness and submission on the part of slaves and wives remain ideal behavior for subordinated peoples as critique against domination and oppression. Patriarchal culture subverted their deeply critical content and turned them around as a martyr complex idealizing subordination. By the time of the second and third generation Christianity, women were dislodged from positions of leadership (1 Cor 11:2-16), silenced (1 Cor 14:33-35) and subordinated (Eph 5:21-23; Col 3:18-25; Tit 2:3-9 and 1 Pet 3:1-7). . . . As women reading the sacred texts, we are advised to read with critical eyes, as one who is subject to class, race, ethnic and gender discrimination.[14]

As a final example, Jurgette Honclada includes a section on feminism reclaiming the Bible, noting the New Testament models of women who overturned stereotypes (Martha, Mary of Magdala, Phoebe, Mary) and concluding that Christianity is not necessarily supportive of patriarchy. In regard to Paul's inconsistencies, she observes, "Paul's seemingly inconsistent regard for women is explained" in terms of "his own background as a former Jewish rabbi, the apocalyptic temper that gives rise to the unparalleled egalitarianism of Gal 3:28, and a later slowing down when the second coming does not transpire and the early Christian community had to come to terms with the socio-cultural milieu."[15]

We turn, then, to a review of sympathetic and critical appropriations of Paul in the theology of struggle, following the five key themes outlined above.

The Vision of a New World Coming
(Emerito Nacpil, Julio X. Labayen, O.C.D., and Carlos H. Abesamis, S.J.)

Emerito P. Nacpil

Emerito P. Nacpil[16] is not typically grouped among representatives of the theology of struggle, since he has displayed a more reformist than radical outlook since the 1980s.[17]

I include his essay from 1972 here, however, since he draws heavily from the writings of Paul, and since it anticipates themes of the later theology of struggle.

In "A Gospel for the New Filipino," written shortly before the declaration of martial law in 1972, Nacpil stresses the need for "systematic and adequate exposition" of the "human meaning and social content of the Christian faith."[18] He complains about the legacy of Protestant missionary activity in fostering a religiosity that focuses on personal and otherworldly salvation, individualistic conversion, and the separation of the spiritual and material concerns. Protestant interest in schools, hospitals, and development projects, he argues, was an instrument of its evangelistic focus on individual conversion and not an expression of the "social meaning of the Gospel."

In his exposition of the "social meaning of the Gospel," Nacpil appeals to Paul more than any other biblical writer. He stresses that the gospel must be understood (1) as liberation, (2) as a summons to responsibility, and (3) as a horizon of hope.

First, noting that "liberation" is a key element in biblical notions of salvation and appealing to the Ephesian notion of God's salvific purpose as "uniting all things in Christ" (Eph 1:9-11), Nacpil proceeds to articulate the various levels of liberation that the gospel entails. While salvation includes deliverance from God's wrath, sin, condemnation, and death, it also means "deliverance from structures of cruelty and injustice and the building of a society of shalom" (p. 129). Drawing on texts and images from Paul, Nacpil observes that the goal of salvation is that all oppressive dominion and power be abolished (1 Cor 15:24), including metaphysical bondage (Gal 3:23-24; 4:1-5). "Paul sees the death and resurrection of Jesus as God's struggle with, and the glorious triumph over, the cosmic powers" (p. 131, citing Col 1:13-14; 2:15; Eph 1:20-21).

Second, Nacpil goes on to explicate the gospel as a summons to responsibility, both to care for the earth (Gen 1:26-28; Psalm 8) and to "transform and humanize society" by promoting "peace and order, economic development, social justice and integrity in public office, quality of life for the masses, and health" (p. 138).

Third, Nacpil presents the gospel as a horizon of hope. He observes that there is no separate hope for Israel, the church, and humankind (appealing to Eph 1:10; Revelation 21; and Romans 9–11), and that the mandate of the church is not just for social welfare work but for the pursuit of the "glorious *liberty* of the children of God" (Rom 8:21) and a "new heaven and earth where *justice* is at home" (p. 143, citing 2 Pet 3:13; his emphasis). This hope has a clear social and historical dimension: "It is in its social content and in its power to heal human lives and to renew society and redirect history toward attainment of mankind's liberty and maturity that the kingdom of God is the horizon of hope" (p. 143). The kingdom of God thus "joins with social change in the Philippines in her groaning effort to bring forth the new Filipino." As a result, "attempts at social reform, no matter how feeble, receive messianic significance." Echoing a common theme in the theology of struggle, Nacpil continues (p. 143):

> But the hope of the kingdom of God is not born in human history, not even in Filipino history, without committed struggle, patient suffering, and vicarious sacrifice. As Paul portrays it, the whole of creation as well as first fruits of the Spirit—that is, the church—

inwardly groan in travail together while waiting patiently for the fulfillment of this hope (Rom. 8:22-25).

The crucifixion of Jesus he views as the result of the reaction of the status quo, the establishment, while the resurrection is the outcome of the struggle and the confirmation of the truth of Jesus' historical ministry (pp. 143-44):

> The outcome of the struggle is what the resurrection of Jesus is all about. For the resurrection is the "hinge" on which the future destiny of mankind turns, the victory of the Crucified One, over the powers of the old order in world history. By this victory, world history itself is redirected to its final goal in the kingdom of God, for through it, God vindicates the messianic ministry and vicarious death of Jesus.[19]

Julio X. Labayen, O.C.D.

Julio Xavier Labayen, who retired as bishop of the Prelature of Infanta, Quezon Province, in August 2003, a position that he had held since 1966, has been a longtime advocate for social justice and human rights as well as for the rights of the weak and vulnerable in the context of imperialism and globalization.[20] His passion has been for the church to become "the Church of the Poor," and he has sought to promote the theology and spirituality needed to sustain its ministries in solidarity with the poor toward social transformation.[21] The Second Plenary Council of the Philippines (1991) made a commitment to this notion largely as a result of Labayen's continuing advocacy.[22]

Labayen's 1995 book *Revolution and the Church of the Poor* seeks to expound the notion of the "church of the poor" in the context of revolutionary change and people's struggles. In contrast to the church of the poor stands the Christendom model of the church, inherited "from a Euro-centric Christianity during an era of Euro-cultural imperialism and colonialism" (p. 14). Crucial for Labayen is the fact that the church of the poor is based not on economics, status, or ideology but on faith; its foundation is God's predilection for the poor. Punctuating his presentation are citations and references to ecclesiastical documents and to biblical texts on which his exposition is grounded.

His book proceeds to take up questions such as how the mission of the church of the poor intersects with historical revolutions, where past revolutions went wrong (including the national democratic revolution in the Philippines),[23] whether Jesus sought to proclaim or initiate a revolution, and how religions can be truly liberating, beyond their domestication and use as legitimations.

Defining revolution as "comprehensive and radical change," Labayen argues that insofar as "revolutions are the expressions of the restless longings of the imprisoned human heart and the disturbing protest of an oppressed and suppressed human spirit, revolutions have to be a continuing historical occurrence until the day dawns when our restless longings and unfulfilled aspirations will have been fulfilled." He emphasizes that cultural change (the creation of an alternative consciousness) and attention to the human factor, the human heart, the psychological dimension, are just as crucial as the political and economic components of revolution (p. 88). In his view, "revolutions will be a continuous dramatization of the Paschal Mystery of Jesus Christ.... Genuine revolution... will bear lasting fruits of justice, love, compassion, and peace, and integrity of creation" (pp. 161–62). The church of the poor is committed to this task of personal, social, and cosmic transformation and seeks to create the conditions for its realization (p. 163).

In the course of this exposition, Labayen appeals to numerous New Testament texts, including nearly as many from the Epistles as from the Gospels. Labayen's use of Pauline texts can be grouped into three categories. A first set serves to explicate the vision and hope of radical cosmic transformation, "God's dream of universal interwovenness and complementarity." Here Labayen cites or quotes Eph 1:10 (5x) and Col 1:15-20 (2x), alongside 2 Pet 3:13 (8x) and Rev 21:4-5 (5x). It is this vision that motivates and sustains "revolutionary fervor and commitment to the Church of the Poor" (p. 168); it is toward the realization of this vision that the church of the poor is to prepare the way as a prophetic church (p. 157); it is toward this end that Jesus' followers are to become co-creators (p. 58) and to write their own history (p. 100); it is through the alternative consciousness that comes with this hope that the poor will opt for radical social change (p. 135); it is a world beyond the reach of the rational and scientific mind (p. 112); it is the destination toward which God walks with his struggling people within historical processes (p. 115); it is the goal to which the church, as the sacramental sign of Christ's definitive and dynamic presence in history, is called to shape and direct history (p. 60). In other places he adds Gal 3:28 to the litany of his citations.[24]

A second set of Pauline texts focuses on the experience of the suffering and servant Jesus, the crucified Christ: Phil 2:6-8 (3x); 2 Cor 8:9 (3x); 1 Cor 1:18-25 (5x). For Labayen, these texts also illustrate the church's path of solidarity with Christ in humility, poverty, and oppression, as it moves toward a servant model of church as opposed to a triumphalistic and self-confining Christendom model of church (pp. 9–10, 158). They exemplify the church's servant vocation for the life of the world (p. 54); they reveal the path of selfless and heroic love required of all disciples (p. 96); and they show God's point of view, seeing things from the perspective of the "victims of oppression and exploitation," the proper point of view of all revolutions (pp. 139–40).

A third set of Pauline texts is used to highlight the inner resources that enliven, motivate, make whole, and sustain disciples in the struggle: Gal 2:20; Rom 8:10-11, 14-17 (2x); Gal 4:6-7; 1 Cor 2:6-16; 10:4; Col 2:3 (pp. 26, 80, 101, 115, 116). This theme is consonant with Labayen's concern for the "spirituality" of the struggle.[25]

Carlos H. Abesamis, S.J.

Longtime professor of biblical and contemporary Asian theology at the Loyola School of Theology and a founding member of EATWOT (Ecumenical Association of Third World Theologians) and CATS (Conference of Asian Theologians),[26] Carlos Abesamis, who died in January 2009, can easily be regarded as the dean of New Testament scholarship among Filipino theologians of struggle.[27] Although he has published a number of books and articles,[28] he is most widely known for the many seminars and workshops he conducted around the Philippines in the last four decades.

Abesamis's writings display his twin interests in careful biblical scholarship and the contextualizing of theology. These are not two unrelated steps; in his view, biblical scholarship must not only use the tools of historical-critical, literary, and sociological analysis but must also take up a particular set of lenses, viewing the world through the eyes of the poor.[29] His work is marked by a dialogue with current realities, an orientation to the grassroots, a commitment to the poor and oppressed, a participation in the struggle for justice and full humanity, and an openness to contemplation of the mystery of the cosmic Christ that transcends rational knowledge.[30]

In his own Catholic circles in the Philippines, he is a forceful exponent of the need for the study of Scripture to be liberated from its constricted role as a mere servant of dogmatics and systematic theology.[31] While fully aware of the technical minutiae of biblical scholarship and debate, he prefers to focus on the core of the biblical story and its preoccupation with people and life, which cannot be "cut up."[32]

In writings spanning three decades, Abesamis has consistently emphasized that the biblical vision of salvation is historical and total, focusing on the hope of a new world (through various images and terms), and that the meaning of Jesus is to be found not first in the paschal mystery (his atoning death and resurrection) but in his mission statements centering on the kingdom/reign of God and on the good news of liberation and justice for the poor (one of the blessings of the kingdom).

While Absesamis's published biblical expositions focus on the ministry of Jesus especially as framed in the Synoptic Gospels, his exposition of the early Christian hope for a new world and the early Christian understanding of the life, death, resurrection, and *parousia* of Jesus is replete with references to other New Testament writers, including Paul. Though Paul is still regarded as the "prime theologian" of the belief in Jesus' death as atonement for sin, Abesamis holds Paul's theology in high regard. When commenting on the character of a proper contextual Christian theology, he notes that "theology should have the hallmarks of the simplicity and concreteness of Jesus, and the depth and the cosmic reach of Paul and John."[33] He continues in regard to Paul:

> How ironic that Pauline theology, in the hands of traditional systematics, has become a smorgasbord of doctrines and dogmas. Paul's more important concern is to offer a table, an altar-table really, where the contemplative is invited into a personal union with Christ and the Spirit (Gal. 2:20; 4:6) which grows into a human (1 Cor. 15:20ff.) and cosmic transformation ... and oneness with that tremendous Mystery which unites all things in heaven and on earth (Col. 1:15-20; Eph. 1:9-10; 1 Cor. 15:24-28; Rom. 8:19-23).[34]

Abesamis's citation of these same texts elsewhere in his writings confirms that they represented for him a sort of core for appropriating Paul's significance.

The following key points can be observed in Abesamis's approach to Paul:

(1) He presents Paul's theology in continuity with what he sees as the core theme of the entire Bible, namely, the hope for a present and coming new world—final, total, integral, and definitive salvation. This includes the defeat of the "powers" (Col 2:15; 1:15-20; 1 Cor 15:24-28; Eph 1:9-10), whose incarnations in our own time include the current "neo-liberal ideology of globalization" and its "minions."[35] It involves the hope of resurrection, which is still within the orbit of Semitic conceptuality.[36] Even in Paul, however, the blessings of the new age are experienced already, and corporeality is affirmed.[37] Summarizing New Testament affirmations of Jesus' resurrection with regular reference to Paul, Abesamis concludes that it is primarily to be seen as (a) God's vindication of Jesus' ministry and mission (Phil 2:8-9), (b) the guarantee and pledge of believers' own resurrection and basis of the risen Christ's sanctifying spirit in people's lives (Gal 4:6; 2 Cor 3:18; Eph 3:17; Rom 8:9-11; Phil 1:19; 1 Cor 15:45), and (c) the dawning of the new world (Eph 1:23; 4:10; 1 Cor 15:28), insofar as Jesus is the firstborn and firstfruits of that new world (Col 1:18; 1 Cor 15:20).[38] Ultimately, however, the primary horizon of hope is the *parousia* (admittedly not a regular part of Filipino Catholic religiosity), not individual life after death.[39] It is a vision of the unity of all things (Rom 11:36)—indeed, "a universe soaked in God" (1 Cor 15:24-28; Eph 1:9-10). As a vision of the reconciliation and harmony of all creation (Rom 8:19-23), it entails an interconnectedness in line with ancient, Asian, and modern wisdom.[40]

(2) Abesamis finds in Paul (especially in Romans and Ephesians) support for the notion that the Bible's core narrative is that of salvation in history, a drama concerned with the story of humankind and of the world.[41]

(3) As the "prime theologian" of Jesus' death as atonement (Gal 2:20; Romans 5), however, Paul (along with John, the author of Hebrews, the author of 1 Peter, and to a lesser extent Matthew and Mark) displays an "incomplete" and thus "inadequate" understanding of the life and death of Jesus. The focus of Paul's "gospel" is the death and resurrection of Jesus (1 Corinthians 15);[42] Paul says next to nothing about Jesus' pre-crucifixion life, much less about the historical causes of Jesus' death.[43] Paul thus displays secondary reflection on Jesus, beyond the sequentially first meaning, that of the pre-crucifixion Jesus. While Jesus himself may have attached atoning meaning to his death at the end, he certainly did not set out to die.[44]

(4) Nevertheless, this insight of Paul regarding the death of Jesus is not to be debunked and remains a "sure constituent of our faith." It is only problematic to the extent that it is made into an item of dogma for cerebral analysis or assent and regarded as the total biblical view.[45] Abesamis argues that one must "play it fair with the biblical data," giving attention to both historical and theological aspects of Jesus' death.[46] While it is true that Paul seems most responsible for popularizing and initiating the move toward later dogmatic formulations, once a broader biblical view is taken, Paul's statements on Jesus' death become a special "treasure," a personal testimony of his mystical insight (Gal 2:20) and an expression of his cosmic reflection (Col 1:17-20).[47] Galatians 2:20 in particular is cited frequently and is likened to drinking in the spirit of a rebel, "an open side from whose juices we slake our thirst"; it is to be appropriated sacramentally, not cerebrally.[48]

(5) Paul provides support for the notion of the priority of justice versus worship without justice (1 Cor 11:20-22).[49]

(6) Abesamis also deals with Pauline texts that appear to stand in contradiction to the proclamation of Jesus, particularly his apparent rejection of "food" as a constituent interest of the kingdom of God (1 Cor 6:13; Rom 14:17). He offers a variety of possible explanations: (a) one cannot harmonize all texts; Paul's theology is perhaps just "different" from that of Jesus; (b) for Paul, the image of the kingdom of God as banquet was perhaps used more symbolically, in the manner of other rabbis; (c) these texts have to do with contextual matters, namely, debate about food offered to idols and pagan temples; the point is that the kingdom of God is not concerned with "debates" about food.[50]

(7) Finally, Abesamis explains the imminence of the hope for the new world as the basis for the early church's passivity on matters of social transformation. Imminent expectation is thus the key difference between the spirituality of the NT generation and our own. Today it is necessary to "actively participate in the building of a world order that is just and humane." The necessary struggle now is to "move history" toward the goal that God has promised, an aspect not seen in the New Testament because of its sense of nearness. The hope of the *parousia* is thus today a summons to action.[51]

Kenōsis and the Unmasking of and Victory over the Powers (Levi Oracion)

Systematic theologian Levi Oracion is the author of numerous short articles and two recent books.[52] Oracion finds the clue to God's saving work, and the supreme criterion for necessary and inevitable Christian participation in sociopolitical struggles,[53] in the logic of the gospel given in the incarnation, crucifixion, resurrection, and second coming of Jesus.[54] His theology is replete with biblical images and themes, but usually without explicit citation or exposition of biblical passages. His use of the Bible is often rather more allusive and analogic.[55]

Nonetheless, the Pauline provenance of three dominant emphases in his writings is readily apparent. These are (1) the notion of human fallenness and depravity as a form of bondage to principalities and powers; (2) the notion that "the struggle against evil powers characterizes the very essence of divine activity in human history";[56] and (3) the centrality of *kenōsis* ("plunging") as the manner of divine and human action in the struggle against evil and injustice.

(1) Oracion discusses human depravity in regard to bondage and domination, both in its personal dimensions (citing Rom 7:18-24) and in its sociocultural significance.[57] In connection with Rom 1:21, he observes that "in the era of globalization human beings are much more creatures of the powers of the global village than of the Creator himself."[58] Elsewhere he states that "powers of domination and injustice are still the pervasive and dominant reality in the historical life of struggling communities."[59]

Accordingly, Paul's words counseling obedience to the state (Romans 13), which serves an ordering function for the benefit of an entire society, do not apply in cases in which there is manifest the fallen human proclivity to absolute power which destroys all forms of human communities.[60]

(2) Oracion's writings regularly draw on the Pauline imagery of the struggle against principalities and powers. In one place he refers specifically to Col 1:15-16, explaining that God's creative act in Jesus, which embraces all creation, is founded on the reality that God's being is opposed to all injustice and evil in creation.[61] This struggle for the poor and oppressed, for truth, righteousness, and life against the powers of sin, injustice, and death, can be observed in the historical ministry of Jesus, where it provides the meaning of the incarnation. The cross is God's ultimate demonstration of solidarity with human suffering, but it is also a shattering of the security of the powers, an exposing of the unjust powers and the depth of human evil. The resurrection signifies the triumph of the kenotic struggle and provides empowerment in that struggle, while the second coming signals the consummation of God's purposes for the whole of creation. All of this is seen as parallel to the current situation and struggle in the Philippines.[62]

(3) It is especially the *kenōsis* of the incarnation of Jesus (including his historical ministry) and the cross that provide the ultimate clue to the center of the gospel. Philippians 2:5-11 is the most frequently cited New Testament text in Oracion's writings, and its images can be found at many turns.[63] This "divine metamorphosis" revealed in Jesus is in fact the key to the title of his major work, *God with Us*.

Along with this text, the imagery of "plung[ing] into the struggle" occurs frequently to explain the meaning of Jesus' work of solidarity with the poor and its violent consequences, and accordingly also Christian discipleship. Citing Pauline texts, Oracion observes that the same pattern is the mark of Christian obedience (Phil 2:4-5; 3:8-11), even as Christ's work endows the believer with courage (Rom 8:31-39).[64] Acts of obedience are even more revelatory than the tomes of armchair theologians, while "people's movements for justice are, in our time, the unknowing bearers of God's liberating grace," the "true doers of theology."[65]

The participation in the struggle can be explained by direct reference to Pauline texts, albeit by analogy:

> St. Paul had to go against the law in order to bring out more clearly and forcefully the liberating and life-giving power of the Gospel. Some perceptive Christians of our time [similarly] had to expose the bankruptcy of democratic liberalism in order to give rise to new forms of socio-political arrangements that are more just and more responsive to human need.[66]

Thus, Oracion can call Paul the "theologian par excellence,"[67] and treat him with considerable approval. But he still has a major demurrer. Citing Rudolph Bultmann, he argues that a "fateful shift" occurred between Jesus and Paul: "a momentous shift from the poor to the sinner." With Paul, the message and work of Jesus were transposed onto a radical eschatological horizon, such that the political struggle of Jesus is ignored.

Oracion posits that the imminence of Christ's second coming, implying a cessation of world history, may have caused the political dimensions of the gospel to be repressed in Paul's preaching.

> Firstly, the Christian struggle shifts from the socio-political to the moral and spiritual realm, and the theological struggle gets largely confined within the personal individual soul. Secondly, the Gospel's bias for the poor is superseded by a universalist perspective that offers the poor and the non-poor equal access to the grace of God. And thirdly, the revolutionary dynamic of the Gospel that is so pronounced in the Gospel story disappears and a gospel of peace without justice takes its place.... Paul failed to make a full-bodied transmittal of the wholeness of the ministry of Jesus whose central focus is to declare the kingdom of God as good news to the poor.... A theology that shows no bias for the poor has assumed preeminence in the life of the church over that of a theology where the poor [are] the central focus in the divine redemptive action.[68]

At the same time, Oracion states that he trembles for fear that he might somehow be speaking against the central New Testament affirmation of sinners saved by grace through faith, which he does not wish to challenge. He also admits that Paul did not abandon Jesus' perspective of solidarity with the poor entirely, as illustrated by the counsel that he gives to the Corinthians in the strong words of 1 Cor 1:26-29.

Dismantling Oppressive Structures, Freedom from Bondage, and Transcendence as a Critique of All Human Projects (Benito Dominguez)

As with other Filipino biblical scholars and theologians, most of the writings of Benito M. Dominguez are products of presentations for particular audiences and events.[69] His writings demonstrate a wide range of concerns and textual interpretation. Consistent themes include Christ's triumph over the principalities and powers; liberation of people from all kinds of bondage; solidarity with the poor and oppressed; the degradation of human and natural life by the powers of this age; and the agency of humanity through the church for God's work to redeem all creation. Philippians 2:5-11 and Col 1:15-20 are cited repeatedly. The latter, along with Rom 8:19-23, is used to promote ecological responsibility, according to God's purpose for all creation. But Col 1:15-20 is employed also to stress God's sovereignty over all other claims of power and lordship and to demonstrate the proper exercise of power to fulfill God's purpose in creation, which is to "enhance life" in the manner that Jesus did, from serving the needy to seeking to transform structures.[70] Philippians 2:5-11 is used to emphasize God's solidarity with the afflicted, but also God's power over all forces that negate life, even the forces of death. Along with Phil 3:10 (and 2 Cor 4:7-12), Phil 2:5-11 is employed to promote Christian solidarity with suffering while relying on the sufficiency of God's grace. Yet

Dominguez also emphasizes with regard to the sufficiency of grace in suffering, "This is not taking belief in God as 'opium' for the suffering masses; rather it is that stubborn insistence of the Christian that God takes the side of the afflicted—to empower and liberate them—in the here and now.[71]

In an essay exploring the encounter of the human and the holy, Dominguez chooses Paul as a paradigm expressly because Paul embodies a hybrid cultural heritage and its accompanying struggles, not unlike many Christian Asians. He shows special interest in Paul's "creative use of tradition" in addressing the problems of his own time, a practice that he sees as a model for doing theology in Asia. This contextual feature of Paul's theologizing enhances the seriousness with which one ought to read Paul and other biblical texts. The Bible is to be taken seriously not as a deposit of the Word but as the channel by which the "Word springs out of the printed page." Dominguez can do careful exegetical work, dealing with the Greek text and with European and American scholarship in footnotes, but his interest lies elsewhere. The goal of serious textual interpretation is "so that we may be enabled to get the message for our time and situation."[72] The traditions of which creative use might be made includes Asian cultural and religious traditions, although he cautions against "extreme" contextualization.[73]

A further Pauline theme that holds significance for Dominguez is the move from slavery (bondage) to freedom (liberation). While this is applied (for example, in an exposition of Phil 3:1-11) to the enslavement of humans questing for false security through achievements and illusory pretensions in the encounter with the holy, it is also brought to bear on the sociopolitical witness and work of the church. In a 1986 article, Dominguez clarifies his own understanding of a "theology of struggle" toward social transformation and explains its biblical mandate and foundations for the sake of church people. He presents five models from the New Testament: Jesus, Paul, John, Luke, and Revelation. He summarizes Paul's contribution to a theology of struggle as follows:

> Paul's ministry could be summarized as a dismantling of an enslaving tradition (the Jewish Law) which was backed up by a very strong institution (Judaism-Temple) and supplanting it with the Good News of God's liberating/transforming grace. His letters, especially Romans, illustrate the dismantling-supplanting act of God. For Paul, manipulating God through wealth, power and even self-assumed righteousness and classifying people into "saints" (good) and "sinners" (bad on the basis of "performance") imposed by those in authority (who acted like gods!) had no place in a social order where every person is treated as an heir to the Kingdom, which in our parlance means, living like a true human being![74]

In the same article, he applies the imagery of the "principalities and powers" indirectly to Americans, who propped up of the dictatorship of Ferdinand Marcos and in the process were "able to appear as benefactors even if in reality they [were] beasts!" This anticipates a later comment in which, summarizing the relevance of the book of Revelation for a theology of struggle, he observes that Revelation 13 provides a necessary contrast to Romans 13.[75]

Tortured Conscience, Justification by Faith, and the Dialectical Separation of Gospel and Law (Everett Mendoza)

A prolific writer of short theological reflections who has been active in ecumenical and people's organizations, systematic theologian Everett Mendoza has stressed that the church must be faithful to its Christian heritage and yet relevant in the face of contemporary challenges, including being open "to new and untried forms of Christian discipleship" as mandated by those challenges.[76] For Mendoza, no theologizing is relevant or useful without a thorough and prior analysis of the situation in which one finds oneself.

As a Protestant by choice, Mendoza shows a consistently high regard for the value of Paul's legacy, especially in its classic Reformation and Lutheran interpretation. The entire belief system of Christianity, he avers, rests on the foundation of justification by faith.[77] In a 1980 essay, he summarizes his estimate of Paul and his relationship to Jesus.[78] Whereas Jesus preached a salvation from bondage to Satan, articulated in specifically materialistic and holistic terms, Paul preached a spiritual and individualistic gospel of salvation from God's wrath that led to peace with God. Salvation for Paul, he says, is largely a private relationship between an individual and his God through justification. Peace with God does not come through performing pious acts, although genuine fruits emerge through sanctification following the experience of justification.

Embarking on class analysis, Mendoza observes that, though Paul was not rich, he was comfortable enough to be free from economic or political worries; had Paul been a Galilean, Mendoza surmises, he would not have been among Jesus' mass following, given his socioeconomic status. In Paul, rather, we find a "good news to the unpoor, unexploited, and the unoppressed." But Mendoza does not thereby seek to denigrate Paul's legacy. He refuses to consider that Paul either misunderstood or sought to correct Jesus' message. Instead, "Paul understood Jesus and correctly appropriated Jesus' message *to himself*" [my emphasis], providing an example of "theology as biography." Paul, he says, was simply overwhelmed by a different burden: dominated by a sense of guilt and fear, plagued by a tortured conscience, and finding no peace through obedience to the Mosaic law, he sought a gospel by which he could achieve justification and righteousness before God.

In a subsequent essay (1988), which draws especially on Rom 7:13—8:11, 14:17-19, and 6:13, 19, Mendoza identifies a twofold enslavement that reflects Paul's dual Greek and Jewish heritage.[79] From the former come wild and insatiable passions and lust, and from the latter comes a tyrannical and tortured conscience (because of the law). Impotent to extricate himself from this bondage, Paul can rely only on God's free and unmerited gift through justification to bring him liberation. Only in the experience of liberation from this bondage is the human being "enabled to work for justice and peace," having been liberated from being a "servant and weapon for evil, to being the servant and weapon for justice" (Rom 6:13, 19). Liberation through justification is only the beginning; "it must be followed with the positive act of doing the work for justice because freedom is complete and real only when there is justice."[80] The way of the spirit is one in which humanity lives in "justice, peace and joy (Rom 14:17)." Reflecting on Paul's summary of the character of God's reign in Rom 14:17, he concludes: "In Paul's understanding, justice is the ultimate end toward which creation moves. Consequently, [humanity's] historical vocation is none other than to work for justice."[81] He also cites Rom 8:19-25 to highlight the horizon of freedom (liberation) and its interconnection with justice in God's redemption of the whole creation.

In other essays, Mendoza explores on the basis of Pauline texts the necessity of religious encounter with the risen Jesus, which provides "the motivating force that brings us into solidarity with the suffering." Moreover, it is Paul's notion of radical transcendence in particular that can provide the ground for a thorough critique of the present oppressive structures, analogous to Marx's "apprehension of an existence that transcends the present historical condition—oppressive capitalist society."[82] Mendoza is not terribly impressed with nor particularly worried about some of Paul's specific conclusions on moral or political topics. Most significant and valuable for him is Paul's theological method and his experience and affirmation of the transcendent world as the basis for a critique of the present order and as a motivating factor for participating in the struggle against injustice and oppression in the face of ever-present despair and passivity.[83]

The most novel feature of Mendoza's work is his appropriation of Paul's legacy through its Lutheran interpretation, namely, through the doctrine of justification by faith and the radical disjunction of law and gospel, nature and grace. Here he finds the foundation of a theology that grounds and sustains Christian participation in revolutionary struggles.[84] This is the basic theme of his dissertation, completed in 1990 and published in 1999 as *Radical and Evangelical: Portrait of a Filipino Christian*.[85] Mendoza hopes that the historical momentum of the "evangelical solution" to the nature–grace problem, which has hitherto "been disastrous to the interest of social justice," can be redirected or even reversed (pp. 152–53). Instead of abandoning the "evangelical symbols of faith" because they seem to provide no support to the Christian revolutionary, Mendoza seeks to reframe them so that "one can be truly evangelical and politically radical" (p. 19).

Mendoza thus seeks to situate his systematic reflections over against Latin American liberation theology and the Catholic logic of a grand synthesis in which the divine and the human are seen analogously. Instead, he envisions the relationship of theology and politics as dialectical and paradoxical, in the Kierkegaardian sense of the "infinitive qualitative distinction." Thus, he divides reality into polar categories: divine action versus human projects, grace versus law, faith versus works, gospel versus law, spirit and living Word versus letter, salvation versus liberation, inner versus outer, sacred versus secular, eternal versus temporal. Based on the Lutheran notion of two kingdoms, he posits the secularization of politics and the radical interiorization of faith (pp. 152–53), rejecting the "christianization of politics and the politicalization of Christianity" (p. 131; cf. vi, 20–21, 191–94). Faith has no relation to political ideology (pp. 144–46), since politics is determined by "universal standards of justice" (pp. 99–101, 146), not by authoritative theological judgments that lie beyond rational criticism. Only in the careful distinction between these two fields can the (dialectical) relationship be considered; the criteria of one are not applied to the other (p. 154). The payoff for Mendoza is to keep politics from domination by ecclesiastical control, which is the traditional Christendom model in the Philippines, and free from moral inhibitions such as principled nonviolence, which is based on authoritarian theological grounds separate from political ideology.[86] For Mendoza, then, participation in politics is a matter of obedience to God, and yet politics works by the (materialistic) rules of the earthly kingdom: "The Christian Gospel does not justify or endorse any kind of politics, even liberating politics. This exercise is the exclusive right of the Law, of political justice, which is accessible to human judgment without the benefit of theology" (p. 194).

Admitting that the Protestant solution must pass "the bar of biblical fidelity" (pp. 29, 52–55), Mendoza asserts that the biblical scholarship of the Reformers provided them with "a more accurate interpretation of Paul's idea of justification which points to a basically forensic meaning" (pp. 54–55). This means that "the effect of justification is the forgiveness of sins and the imputation of righteousness rather than the attainment of essential righteousness" (p. 55).

In short, Mendoza draws on key theological themes from the Pauline and Lutheran legacies while discarding Paul's and Luther's own specific views on politics (p. 94).

> It is important to be able to recognize the composite nature of Luther's ethical stance and to distinguish his theology from his political philosophy. The latter is a property of a feudal age and should be left where it belonged. But his theology, namely, the dialectical operation of the political and the spiritual orders, remains a lively source of paradigm-building for theological and ethical construction today.

In the process, he argues that God's sword of justice, which in Luther's feudal era was granted to the power of the princes, is now granted to popular struggles for justice, since the granting of the power of God's sword is premised on the commitment to the cause of justice and peace (p. 98).

Finally, the notions of the tortured conscience and meritorious good works are applied specifically to the Philippine revolutionary dynamics. The good works that too easily become the ground of human hubris in the quest for self-justification are paradoxically the very acts of working for justice for which the gospel calls (pp. 199–201). At the same time, the tortured conscience is especially that of the revolutionary: only the experience of justification and grace can keep the tortured conscience of the Christian revolutionary at peace.[87]

Constructions of Paul in Filipino Theology of Struggle 251

Paul as a Model of Contextual Theologizing, Conversion as Illumination
(José de Mesa and Lode L. Wostyn, C.I.C.M.)

In their collaborative work, *Doing Chistology: The Re-Appropriation of a Tradition*, which was intended as a textbook,[88] Catholic scholars José de Mesa and Lode L. Wostyn search for a christology and a soteriology appropriate to the Philippine context.[89] Rejecting the Western conceptions of salvation as individualistic and spiritualized and thus irrelevant (though admittedly pervasive) in the Philippines, they argue that christology and soteriology must be attentive to two key concerns: (1) "the struggle to free ourselves from structural evil and injustice," without neglecting the personal and transcendent dimensions of salvation and personhood (pp. 307, 320); and (2) the "indigenous culture," especially as experienced by the "folk Christian." Using indigenous terms, they articulate a soteriology that focuses on the concrete "well-being" of people while rejecting a historical conceptions of salvation (p. 311). A discipleship in service of life, they conclude, is marked by caring for the earth; caring for the neighbor (seeing the liberational aspect of salvation not as developmentalism but along an oppression–liberation axis);[90] caring for culture (which includes protecting cultural integrity but also the possible modification of worldview, values, and customs toward authentic social transformation and well-being, that is, the evangelization of culture); contemplation (which must be integrated with committed historical action); taking up the cross (which is not private devotion or masochism but suffering-in-hope for the sake of and in solidarity with others); and taking up responsibility for history (working toward the coming together of the ecclesial, mystical, and sociopolitical dimensions) (pp. 314–40).

Following an introductory methodological segment, *Doing Christology* first treats the memory of Jesus, then discusses later reflection on the meaning of Jesus in the New Testament and in the Greco-Roman world. Finally it addresses the matter of reappropriation in the Filipino context. De Mesa and Wostyn take a special interest in Paul, viewing him as "the greatest pastor of early Christianity." They emphasize that he wrote out of and for particular human experience, a fact that confounds dogmatic interpreters and makes the attempt to construct a systematic account of his theology nearly impossible.[91] Instead of providing propositions for dogmatic theology, Paul provides a model for the "process of theologizing," that is, re-expressing the gospel in light of lived experience and appropriating it to new situations (pp. 240, 251, 299).[92] "The rich variety of images in Paul"—including redemption, justification, reconciliation, victory/triumph, and sacrifice (with none given priority)—offers an example of "how the first Christians used the whole field of their religious-cultural experiences-interpretation to express the significance of what they had witnessed in the life and death of Jesus" (p. 245). Possibly in accord with this, Paul's own conversion and resurrection experience and that of other early disciples are interpreted primarily as illumination and enlightenment (pp. 200–201; cf. 2 Cor 4:1-6; Gal 1:15-16).

Beyond this general appreciation of Paul's method, several substantive themes are also given distinctive emphasis. (1) Arguing against the denigration of Paul as responsible for the hellenization, dogmatism, privatization, and spiritualization of the Christian faith, as illustrated in the views of George Pixley (pp. 237–39), they seek to demonstrate that there is actually a marked continuity between the praxis of Jesus and that of Paul. While granting that Paul gives only the barest details of Jesus' life in his letters, they stress that in Paul's action "we see the same fidelity to the rule of God which we see in the ministry of Jesus. . . . Paul did exactly the same as Jesus did, he literally poured his life in inaugurating what Jesus stood for" (pp. 240–41). In the gift of self and in a life of service, which Paul interpreted as solidarity with Christ's suffering for the sake of God's reign (2 Cor 1:5; 4:7-12; 6:9-10; 12:8-10; 1 Cor 4:9-12), "Jesus' experience of the reign was re-lived by Paul in his own apostolate" (p. 241), even though he verbalized this experience differently from Jesus. "In Paul's action, we see how he recovers what was central in Jesus' life: the ministry of inaugurating the kingdom" (p. 240; cf. 336). In a similar way, they argue that the theme of Jesus crucified in Paul is actually shorthand for "Jesus' life in service of the kingdom. . . . Paul believes first of all in the saving significance of Jesus' life which was consummated, notwithstanding curse and execution, in a commitment till death" (p. 243; cf. 246). They argue further that in 1 Cor 12:3 ("nobody can say 'Jesus is cursed'") Paul castigates the Corinthian Christians for ignoring the earthly, crucified Jesus. In their view, "resurrection is not the cancellation of the life and the cross of Jesus, but its confirmation and continuation" (p. 246).

(2) In accord with this emphasis on Paul, as shown especially in his hardship catalogues, they emphasize a discipleship of Christian solidarity with suffering, for the sake of the struggle against suffering (pp. 241, 336).

(3) In regard to Paul's politics, they grant that Paul, like other New Testament authors, sought to make Jesus look politically innocuous and also tried to show that Christians were loyal subjects of Rome, as illustrated by Romans 13. But they explain that this was simply "the only way to survive," and that Paul was merely continuing the tradition of diasporic Judaism. This survival reaction does not imply, however, that the sociopolitical dimension of Jesus was "downgraded." Instead, "because of concrete historical circumstances, they did the only thing they could do," which meant focusing on the renewal of earthly society within their own communities. "These communities of disciples carried on the subversive stance of Jesus by living in a prophetic way a renewed society as a paradigm for what had to happen in the world" (p. 322). They concede that Revelation, where the empire is treated as a monster, is the "only political manifesto" in the New Testament.

(4) A final point of emphasis in their appropriation of Paul is to highlight the value of 1 Corinthians 15 and Romans 8 for ecological consciousness (pp. 318, 337).

Constructions of Paul in Filipino Theology of Struggle 253

Summary and Conclusions

Filipino theologians of struggle, when they draw on Paul, appear to use Paul as he used his own sacred texts, that is, selectively according to the rhetorical needs of particular situations. We might well talk of "echoes of Paul"[93] in the theology of struggle. There are no systematic accounts of Paul in Filipino theology of struggle. Because the authors are concerned with issues of praxis and not primarily with academic and systematic thought, writings associated with the theology of struggle favor a contemporizing, analogical hermeneutic as opposed to an exegetical and historical one. Accordingly, citations from Paul often draw attention to evocative images that provide parallels or illustrations of the author's current situation, often quite unrelated to the presumed original contexts of the texts. But if one were to complain that the biblical texts are taken out of context, these writers could retort that they do nothing other than what their hero did.

At the same time, however, Paul is not used arbitrarily. There is a coherent, though often unstated, understanding of the substantive core of Paul's thought that guides the appropriation of Pauline texts in particular rhetorical contexts. If Paul could refer to "the promise" in connection with his understanding of the substantive core of his sacred texts (as in Romans 4 and Galatians 3–4), so could theologians of struggle use the notion of "promise" as a way to articulate their coherent appropriation of Paul. While there is some variation here, it is striking that the overwhelming majority of writers who appropriate Paul constructively place at the center of Paul's message the "promise" of a coming new world and its guiding vision of cosmic transformation and harmony, repeatedly citing such texts as Eph 1:9-10; Col 1:15-20; 1 Cor 15:24-28; Rom 8:19-25; 11:36 (see Nacpil, Labayen, Abesamis, Dominguez, Ruiz-Duremdez).[94] In continuity with this basic theme are further ideas that appear often: victory over/ defeat of the "powers" (Col 1:13-14, 15-20; 2:15; Eph 1:20-21; 1 Cor 15:24-28; see Nacpil, Abesamis, Oracion, de Mesa and Wostyn);[95] the cosmic Christ who pervades all things (Col 1:15-20; see Abesamis); the sovereignty of God and the Messiah over all forces that negate life and over all human projects (Phil 2:5-11; Col 1:15-20; emphasized by Dominguez);[96] the reality of "principalities and powers" that are "made flesh in the systems and structures of society" (Eph 6:10-20; see Abesamis, Oracion, Dominguez); the coming reign of God as an order of peace and justice (Rom 14:17 [Mendoza]; 1 Cor 11:20-22, [Abesamis]); the implications of cosmic re-creation for caring for the earth (Rom 8:19-25; 1 Cor 15; Col 1:15-20; see Nacpil, Labayen, Abesamis, Dominguez, de Mesa and Wostyn); and the fulfillment of this hope in human history (Romans 4; 9–11; Ephesians 2; Gal 3:28; see Nacpil, Labayen, Abesamis, Mendoza).[97]

One might observe how these Filipino theologians of struggle have discerned the centrality of Paul's millennial vision,[98] including the notion of "God's triumph" throughout the cosmos, an emphasis that is now being "rediscovered" in Western scholarship.[99] This contrasts with the serious limitations of many other accounts of Pauline theology that leave out the cosmic and social dimensions of Paul's salvific vision, limiting salvation to the individual human.

It is perhaps not accidental that only one of the authors surveyed in this paper follows the Reformation claim that the centerpiece of Paul's theology is justification (of the individual) by faith, seen as rescuing humans from the tortured conscience that arises through the quest for human self-justification by good works (Mendoza).[100] A similar but more common theme is the emphasis on Paul's work as centering in the dismantling of oppressive structures (of the law, of Judaism), drawing on the imagery of freedom/liberation from bondage/domination in his letters and reapplying it to a new context (Gal 3:23-24; 4:1-5; 5:1; see Nacpil, Oracion, Dominguez).[101]

Closely tied to the prior themes and texts, the theology of struggle has also appropriated in significant ways Paul's language about *kenōsis* and God's solidarity with suffering, including the sufferings listed in Paul's hardship catalogues (cf. 2 Cor 4:7-12), as a way to understand the work of Jesus and to promote the importance of Christians immersing themselves in people's struggles and suffering. They also use this imagery to explain the suffering and rising up of the Filipino people (Phil 2:4-11; 2 Cor 8:9; 1 Cor 1:18-29; Phil 3:8-11; see Nacpil, Labayen, Oracion, Dominguez, de Mesa and Wostyn).[102]

Paul is also cited regularly to draw attention to the inner (mystical and sacramental) resources that are available to sustain the Christian in solidarity with the struggle (Absesamis, Labayen);[103] the virtues of fortitude or courage that support and guide the Christian (Nacpil, Oracion, Dominguez);[104] the sanctifying work of becoming "weapons for justice" (Romans 6; Mendoza); and the posture of resistance that is required in the face of oppressive powers (Eph 6:10-20; Oracion, Dominguez, Abesamis).[105]

In regard to Paul's conversion, two approaches are evident. One view echoes the classical Lutheran notion of the tortured conscience in the face of impossible ethical demands (Mendoza, the Protestant,), while the other sees it as the dawning of illumination and enlightenment, citing Gal 1:15-16 and 2 Cor 4:16 (de Mesa and Wostyn). Paul's interest in the cross and resurrection of Jesus to the neglect of his life and ministry is a source of embarrassment for some (Abesamis, Oracion), while others argue that Paul did not consider Jesus' historical ministry meaningless, especially as a ministry that led toward death (de Mesa and Wostyn).

On the whole, it appears that Paul is appropriated not so much for the particular results of his situational theologizing but primarily as a model for theologizing, as well as for exemplifying a hybrid identity with its unavoidable inner contradictions (Abesamis, Dominguez, Mendoza, de Mesa and Wostyn).

Finally, in regard to Romans 13, we must recognize that the theology of struggle was born in a context in which Romans 13 was used by the ruling elite to demand compliance with authoritarian rule. As a result, most of the authors surveyed here treat Romans 13 with polite or studied avoidance.[106] Those who do address this text explain it as (a) a survival reaction in line with the approach of diasporic Judaism (de Mesa and Wostyn); (b) a statement about the proper role that the state is to perform in society (Oracion; Suarez); (c) an isolated passage that is meaningful only in dialogue with texts like Revelation 13 and Acts 5:29 (Dominguez, de Mesa and Wostyn); and (d) an understandable self-limitation by a person who held imperial citizenship and therefore enjoyed its benefits.[107]

This last explanation invites a revisiting of the notion of Roman citizenship and the meaning that it held for Paul in connection with issues of identity and loyalty. If we attend primarily to Paul's own writings and not to the construction of Paul in Luke-Acts, we must conclude with Klaus Wengst that Roman citizenship probably meant nothing to Paul (who instead chose the path of the cross) and that Paul's citizenship ultimately meant nothing to the Romans.[108] In other words, Paul considered his imperial citizenship more of a burden than an advantage. Similarly, it would appear that the latter part of Philippians 3, which contrasts enmity toward the cross and treating bellies as gods with citizenship in God's imperial order (vv. 18-21), should be read alongside 1 Corinthians 1. Reading the texts in this way reveals that Paul was challenging not a generic antinomianism nor a particular Jewish identity but rather people who arrogantly display or energetically pursue the status, privileges, and consumerism that come with imperial citizenship. In other words, given the palpable anti-imperial force of the rhetoric in Phil 3:20, we should assume that in Philippians 3 Paul is exposing the dangers of both an exclusivist particularizing identity (vv. 2-11), and a hubristic universalizing imperial identity (vv. 17-21). Paul does not seem to endorse a dual citizenship involving both the temporal and the spiritual order (at least not when the temporal order is imperialist or absolutist); instead, loyalty to God's reign and God's Messiah is exclusive.

Paul is often (and understandably) interpreted as having been co-opted by imperial power, especially in places where Christianity was introduced alongside the colonial enterprise. The image becomes less clear, however, if we reimagine Paul living within the dynamics of our present world. We might, for instance, imagine him being born to a family of Filipino migrant workers living, say, in Hong Kong and being sent back to his homeland for a proper education. There he would encounter a new religious movement that had sprung up in the hills of a remote part of conflicted and impoverished Mindanao and found a foothold in the capital city despite the "salvaging"[109] of its founding prophet. In this reimagining, Paul would first zealously resist the new movement but then embrace it with equal zeal, proclaiming its message of a soon-to-be transformed world to people in the centers of commercial and political power. It should not surprise us that the last time we would hear of such a person is in a place of detention.

Notes

Foreword

1. See Efraín Agosto, "Letter to the Philippians," in *A Postcolonial Commentary on the New Testament Writings*, ed. Fernando F. Segovia and R. S. Sugirtharajah, Bible and Postcolonialism 13 (London and New York: T&T Clark, 2007).
2. See my *Servant Leadership: Jesus and Paul* (St. Louis: Chalice, 2005).
3. For this and what follows on Segovia's description of the "postcolonial optic," see Fernando F. Segovia, "Biblical Criticism and Postcolonial Studies: Toward a Postcolonial Optic," in idem, *Decolonizing Biblical Studies: A View from the Margins* (Maryknoll, N.Y.: Orbis, 2000), 119–32.
4. A recent study of the Albizu Campos years by Osvaldo Torres Santiago is actually entitled *El Evangelio de Don Pedro Albizu Campos* [The Gospel of Don Pedro Albizu Campos] (San Juan: Letras de America, 2008).

Introduction

1. While there is little consistency in the use of terms among "postcolonial" authors, the term "postcolonial studies" will be used here to designate the quasi-discipline (or perhaps better, the sphere of discourse) in which academic scholars discuss, debate, and apply the insights of "postcolonial" analysis, while "postcolonial criticism" will refer to the collection of methods and perspectives employed by various "postcolonial" scholars. Of course, this leaves open the question of what is meant by the term "postcolonial," a question to which the contributors to this volume offer varied answers.
2. Much of the content of this paragraph is drawn directly from Stephen Moore's essay in the present volume. For a more comprehensive survey of the historical roots of "postcolonial studies," see Robert J. C. Young, *Postcolonialism: An Historical Introduction* (Oxford: Blackwell, 2001).
3. The works of both scholars are cited numerous times in the articles that make up the present volume, so there is no need to duplicate the list in this introductory essay. Three books, however, are worth noting because of the light that their titles shed on their authors' perceptions of the place of postcolonial studies within the field of biblical studies from the mid-1990s to the (near) present: R. S. Sugirtharajah, ed., *Voices from the Margin: Interpreting the Bible in the Third World* (3rd ed.; Maryknoll, N.Y.: Orbis, 2006); Fernando F. Segovia, *Decolonizing Biblical Studies: A View from the Margins* (Maryknoll, N.Y.: Orbis, 2000); and R. S. Sugirtharajah, *Still at the Margins: Biblical Scholarship Fifteen Years after Voices from the Margin* (New York and London: T&T Clark, 2008).

4. On the problems associated with viewing postcolonial criticism as a "method" to be "applied" when studying historical or contemporary forms of colonialism, see Susan Abraham's essay in the present volume.

5. Not a single article on Paul is to be found in either the seminal 1996 *Semeia* volume edited by Laura Donaldson entitled *Postcolonialism and Scripture Reading* (Semeia 75; Atlanta: Society of Biblical Literature, 1996), or in R. S. Sugirtharajah, ed., *The Postcolonial Biblical Reader* (Oxford: Blackwell, 2006) that appeared ten years later. Similarly, Stephen D. Moore's 2006 introduction to postcolonial studies tellingly included chapters on Mark, John, and Revelation, but nothing on Paul (*Empire and Apocalypse: Postcolonialism and the New Testament*, Bible in the Modern World 12 [Sheffield: Sheffield Phoenix, 2006]).

6. *Paul and Empire: Religion and Power in Roman Imperial Society* (Harrisburg, Pa.: Trinity Press International, 1997); *Paul and Politics: Ekklēsia, Israel, Imperium, Interpretation: Essays in Honor of Krister Stendahl* (Harrisburg, Pa.: Trinity Press International, 2000); *Paul and the Roman Imperial Order* (Harrisburg, Pa.: Trinity Press International, 2004); *Hidden Transcripts and the Arts of Resistance: Applying the Work of James C. Scott to Jesus and Paul*, Semeia Studies 48 (Atlanta: Society of Biblical Literature, 2004). The handful of articles in these collections that draw explicitly on the work of postcolonial authors are cited in several of the essays in the present volume. The relation between "empire studies" (as cultivated in the SBL "Paul and Politics" section) and "postcolonial studies" is discussed in Stephen Moore's opening essay in the present volume and more briefly in several of the other essays.

7. I reviewed these articles in a paper entitled "Postcolonial Perspectives on Paul" that was presented at the International Meeting of the Society of Biblical Literature in Vienna, Austria, in the summer of 2008. Four of them (the essays by Gordon Zerbe, Ann Jervis, Tat-siong Benny Liew, and Joseph Marchal) are reprinted in the present volume. Several of the articles were authored by scholars with non-European names, but it was unclear how many of them were natives of formerly colonized nations.

8. See, for example, the various essays on Paul's letters in Fernando F. Segovia and R. S. Sugirtharajah, ed., *A Postcolonial Commentary on the New Testament Writings*, Bible and Liberation (Edinburgh: T&T Clark, 2007); Davina C. Lopez, *Apostle to the Conquered: Reimagining Paul's Mission*, Paul in Critical Contexts (Minneapolis: Fortress Press, 2008); Joseph A. Marchal, *The Politics of Heaven: Women, Gender, and Empire in the Study of Paul*, Paul in Critical Contexts (Minneapolis: Fortress Press, 2008); and Brigitte Kahl, *Galatians Rediscovered: Reading with the Eyes of the Vanquished*, Paul in Critical Contexts (Minneapolis: Fortress Press, 2009).

1. Paul after Empire

1. Edward W. Said, *Beginnings: Intention and Method* (New York: Basic Books, 1975; repr., New York: Columbia University Press, 1985), xii–xiii. The quotation is from the preface to the reprint edition.

2. Edward W. Said, *Orientalism* (New York: Pantheon, 1978). I am grateful to Chris Stanley for his editorial labors on behalf of this essay, and to Melanie Johnson-DeBaufre, who critiqued an earlier version of it and saved me from errors that I hope were more serious than any that still remain.

3. For in-depth discussion and differentiation of the concepts of colonialism, imperialism, neocolonialism, and postcolonialism, see Robert J. C. Young, *Postcolonialism: An Historical Introduction* (Oxford: Blackwell, 2001), 13–70.

4. Bill Ashcroft, Gareth Griffiths, and Helen Tiffin, *The Empire Writes Back: Theory and Practice in Post-Colonial Literature* (London and New York: Routledge, 1989); eidem, eds., *The Post-Colonial Studies Reader* (London and New York: Routledge, 1995). They also authored *Key Concepts*

in *Post-Colonial Studies* (London and New York: Routledge, 1998; reprinted in 2001 as *Post-Colonial Studies: The Key Concepts*).

5. For a relatively brief definition of poststructuralism (which, however, is notoriously resistant to brief definition), see Stephen D. Moore, *Empire and Apocalypse: Postcolonialism and the New Testament*, Bible in the Modern World 12 (Sheffield: Sheffield Phoenix, 2006), 79–80 n. 8.

6. Gayatri Chakravorty Spivak, "Can the Subaltern Speak?," in *Marxism and the Interpretation of Culture*, ed. Cary Nelson and Larry Grossberg (Urbana: University of Illinois Press, 1988), 271–313 (a much expanded version of the 1985 original); eadem, *In Other Worlds: Essays in Cultural Politics* (New York: Methuen, 1987); eadem, *A Critique of Postcolonial Reason: Toward a History of the Vanishing Present* (Cambridge, Mass.: Harvard University Press, 1999). For more on Spivak's complex relations to postcolonial studies, see Stephen D. Moore, "Situating Spivak," in *Planetary Loves: Spivak, Postcoloniality, and Theology*, ed. Stephen D. Moore and Mayra Rivera, Transdisciplinary Theological Colloquia (New York: Fordham University Press, 2011).

7. Homi K. Bhabha, *The Location of Culture* (London and New York: Routledge, 1994).

8. Another partial exception is Said's (highly generalized) strategy of "contrapuntal reading"; see his *Culture and Imperialism* (New York: Knopf, 1993), especially 51, 66–67.

9. Biblical-scholarly engagements with Bhabha have been more numerous than with any other practitioner of postcolonial studies; see, for example, Tat-siong Benny Liew, *Politics of Parousia: Reading Mark Inter(con)textually*, Biblical Interpretation Series 42 (Leiden: Brill, 1999); Erin Runions, *Changing Subjects: Gender, Nation and Future in Micah*, Playing the Texts 7 (Sheffield: Sheffield Academic, 2002); Jin Hee Han, "Homi Bhabha and the Mixed Blessings of Hybridity in Biblical Hermeneutics," *Bible and Critical Theory* 1 (2005), http://publications.epress.monash.edu/loi/bc (accessed May 20, 2010); Yong-Sung Ahn, *The Reign of God and Rome in Luke's Passion Narrative: An East Asian Global Perspective*, Biblical Interpretation Series 80 (Leiden: Brill, 2006); Moore, *Empire and Apocalypse*; and Simon Samuel, *A Postcolonial Reading of Mark's Story of Jesus*, Library of New Testament Studies (New York: T&T Clark, 2007), in addition to certain Pauline studies discussed below. Said has been an interlocutor for a handful of biblical scholars; see especially Keith W. Whitelam, *The Invention of Ancient Israel: The Silencing of Palestinian History* (London and New York: Routledge, 1996); R. S. Sugirtharajah, *Asian Biblical Hermeneutics and Postcolonialism: Contesting the Interpretations*, Bible and Liberation (Maryknoll, N.Y.: Orbis, 1998); Steven J. Friesen, *Imperial Cults and the Apocalypse of John: Reading Revelation in the Ruins* (Oxford: Oxford University Press, 2001); Christopher A. Frilingos, *Spectacles of Empire: Monsters, Martyrs, and the Book of Revelation*, Divinations: Rereading Late Ancient Religion (Philadelphia: University of Pennsylvania Press, 2004); and Ahn, *Reign of God and Rome*. For a rare example of biblical-scholarly engagement with Spivak, see Laura E. Donaldson, "Gospel Hauntings: The Postcolonial Demons of New Testament Criticism," in Stephen D. Moore and Fernando F. Segovia, eds., *Postcolonial Biblical Criticism: Interdisciplinary Intersections*, Bible and Postcolonialism 8 (London and New York: T&T Clark, 2005), 97–113; C. I. David Joy, *Mark and Its Subalterns: A Hermeneutical Paradigm for a Postcolonial Context*, BibleWorld (London: Equinox, 2008); and Tat-siong Benny Liew, "Postcolonial Criticism: Echoes of a Subaltern's Contribution and Exclusion," in *Mark and Method: New Approaches in Biblical Studies*, ed. Janice Capel Anderson and Stephen D. Moore (2nd ed.; Minneapolis: Fortress Press, 2008), 211–31.

10. For a profound expression of this older tradition and a searching critique of postcolonial theory on the basis of it, see Benita Parry, *Postcolonial Studies: A Materialist Critique*, Postcolonial Literature (London and New York: Routledge, 2004), and for an earlier study in the same vein, Ahmad Aijaz, *In Theory: Classes, Nations, Literatures* (London: Verso, 1992). And yet the lines are not so simply drawn. Spivak, for example, also situates herself fully in the Marxist tradition. For more

on the relation of Marxism and postcolonialism, see Roland Boer, "Marx, Postcolonialism, and the Bible," and David Jobling, "'Very Limited Ideological Options': Marxism and Biblical Studies in Postcolonial Scenes," in Moore and Segovia, *Postcolonial Biblical Criticism*, 166–83 and 184–201 respectively, as well as the essay by Neil Elliott in this volume.

11. Fanon's work has been the most influential for the subsequent field; see especially his *Black Skin, White Masks*, trans. Charles Lam Markmann (New York: Grove Press, 1967; French original 1952), and *The Wretched of the Earth*, trans. Richard Philcox (New York: Grove, 2004; French original 1961).

12. Moore, *Empire and Apocalypse*, 82–85.

13. Laura E. Donaldson, ed., *Postcolonialism and Scriptural Reading*, Semeia 75 (Atlanta: Scholars Press, 1996). Although I have told the tale myself on more than one occasion, nobody tells it better or in more detail than Fernando F. Segovia. See, most recently, his "Postcolonial Criticism and the Gospel of Matthew," in *Methods for Matthew*, ed. Mark Allan Powell, Methods in Biblical Interpretation (Cambridge: Cambridge University Press, 2009), where he asserts: "The point of origin is the volume entitled *Postcolonialism and Scriptural Reading*" (p. 196).

14. Richard A. Horsley, ed., *Paul and Empire: Religion and Power in Roman Imperial Society* (Harrisburg, Pa.: Trinity Press International, 1997).

15. It is not even cited as forthcoming in his footnote listing works that substantiate his claim that biblical studies is currently "discovering the importance of imperial relations, particularly its own connection with modern empire" (ibid., 2 n. 5).

16. Nor is that beginning merely dual, as we shall see.

17. Richard A. Horsley, ed., *Paul and Politics: Ekklēsia, Israel, Imperium, Interpretation. Essays in Honor of Krister Stendahl* (Harrisburg, Pa.: Trinity Press International, 2000); idem, ed., *Paul and the Roman Imperial Order* (Harrisburg, Pa.: Trinity Press International, 2004). The impression that these volumes are a de facto trilogy is reinforced by the fact that the manifesto-like argument with which Horsley introduces the first volume (and which I summarize below) is repeated point by point in the introduction to the third volume.

18. Horsley, "General Introduction," in *Paul and Empire*, 5.

19. Ibid., 6.

20. Ibid.

21. Ibid., 6–7.

22. Ibid., 6.

23. Ibid., 5.

24. Jacques Derrida, *Positions*, trans. Alan Bass (Chicago: University of Chicago Press, 1981), 42.

25. Here I am adapting (and diluting) Derrida's own account of the second phase in a deconstructive operation (ibid., 42–43).

26. Amy-Jill Levine, "The Disease of Postcolonial New Testament Studies and the Hermeneutics of Healing," *Journal of Feminist Studies in Religion* 20 (2004): 91–99. Levine is not, however, addressing work such as *Paul and Empire* but rather work issuing from formerly colonized regions of the global South.

27. Joseph A. Marchal, *The Politics of Heaven: Women, Gender, and Empire in the Study of Paul*, Paul in Critical Contexts (Minneapolis: Fortress Press, 2008), 119.

28. Laura E. Donaldson, "Postcolonialism and Biblical Reading: An Introduction," in eadem, *Postcolonialism and Scriptural Reading*, 1.

29. Laura E. Donaldson, *Decolonizing Feminisms: Race, Gender, and Empire-Building* (Chapel Hill: University of North Carolina Press, 1992).

30. Donaldson, "Postcolonialism and Biblical Reading," 1-6. She begins with *The Empire Writes Back* (see n. 4 above).

31. Horsley, "General Introduction," 2 nn. 3-4. His sample includes, for example, an essay entitled "After Orientalism," but not *Orientalism* itself, and an essay entitled "Can the 'Subaltern' Ride?" but not "Can the Subaltern Speak?"

32. Horsley, "General Introduction," 3; Horsley, *Jesus and the Spiral of Violence: Popular Jewish Resistance in Roman Palestine* (San Francisco: Harper & Row, 1987).

33. Horsley, "General Introduction," 3.

34. Dieter Georgi, *Theocracy in Paul's Praxis and Theology*, trans. David E. Green (Minneapolis: Fortress Press, 1991; German original, 1987); Neil Elliott, *Liberating Paul: The Justice of God and the Politics of the Apostle*, Bible and Liberation (Maryknoll, N.Y.: Orbis, 1994). Theodore W. Jennings, Jr., has argued that Jacob Taubes's political reading of Romans, published posthumously as *Die Politische Theologie des Paulus: Vorträge, gehalten an der Forschungsstätte der evangelischen Studiengemeinschaft in Heidelberg, 23.-27. Februar 1987*, ed. Aleida Assmann and Jan Assmann (Munich: Wilhelm Fink, 1993), "stands as the forerunner of Georgi's work" (*Reading Derrida/Thinking Paul: On Justice*, Cultural Memory in the Present [Stanford, Calif.: Stanford University Press, 2006], 179 n. 10). The "beginning" of empire-attuned work on Paul thus continues to recede as we advance on it.

35. Robert Young's label for the trio, which quickly became an academic cliché. See Young, *Colonial Desire: Hybridity in Theory, Culture, and Race* (London and New York: Routledge, 1995), 163.

36. Elisabeth Schüssler Fiorenza, *In Memory of Her: A Feminist Theological Reconstruction of Christian Origins* (New York: Crossroad, 1983)

37. Richard A. Horsley, "Introduction: Krister Stendahl's Challenge to Pauline Studies," in *Paul and Politics*, 10 n. 35, quoting Elisabeth Schüssler Fiorenza, "The Ethics of Biblical Interpretation: Decentering Biblical Scholarship," reprinted in her *Rhetoric and Ethic: The Politics of Biblical Interpretation* (Minneapolis: Fortress Press, 1999), 5.

38. The rule-proving exception is Abraham Smith, "'Unmasking the Powers': Toward a Postcolonial Analysis of 1 Thessalonians," in *Paul and the Roman Imperial Order*, 47-66. Sze-kar Wan, "Collection for the Saints as Anticolonial Act: Implications of Paul's Ethnic Reconstruction," in *Paul and Politics*, 191-215, is more tentative: "My reading here is not strictly postcolonial, but in some aspects it does coincide with the goals of postcolonial studies" (p. 192 n. 5).

39. *Paul and Empire* is largely (if not exclusively—this is unclear) an anthology of previously published work.

40. S. R. F. Price, *Rituals and Power: The Roman Imperial Cult in Asia Minor* (Cambridge: Cambridge University Press, 1984).

41. S. R. F. Price, "Response," in *Paul and the Roman Imperial Order*, 175-83.

42. *Journal of Biblical Literature* 126 (2007): 99-127.

43. See http://www.sbl-site.org/publications/Journals_JBL_NoLogin.aspx (accessed November 8, 2009).

44. R. S. Sugirtharajah, "From Orientalist to Post-Colonial: Notes on Reading Practices," *Asia Journal of Theology* 10 (1996): 20-27. I return to this article below.

45. DeSilva, "Using the Master's Tools," 100.

46. DeSilva's titular naming of his analysis as "postcolonial" distinguishes his study from the handful of previous articles in the *Journal of Biblical Literature* that treated the theme of empire but did not claim the label "postcolonial."

47. Although 4 Maccabees does appear as an appendix to the Greek Orthodox canon.

48. It would be disingenuous of me not to confess that I too have published on 4 Maccabees, and even in the *Journal of Biblical Literature*.

49. As does Schüssler Fiorenza's *In Memory of Her*, which is also excerpted, as noted earlier. Schüssler Fiorenza's complex relationship to postcolonial biblical criticism is discussed below.
50. Elliott, *Liberating Paul*, xiv. The second edition appeared in 2006.
51. Ibid.
52. Ibid., ix–x.
53. Ibid., x.
54. I do not apply the label "liberation hermeneutics" lightly to *Liberating Paul*. Much in the book invites that label, not least the fact that one of its sections is entitled "Paul's Preferential Option for the Poor and Oppressed" (pp. 87–88). Of course, Elliott's is a "first world" inflection of liberation hermeneutics, comparable to that of Michael Prior, whose *The Bible and Colonialism: A Moral Critique*, Biblical Seminar 48 (Sheffield: Sheffield Academic Press, 1997) is a smooth extension of his *Jesus the Liberator: Nazareth Liberation Theology (Luke 4.16-30)*, Biblical Seminar 26 (Sheffield: Sheffield Academic, 1995).
55. Neil Elliott, *The Arrogance of Nations: Reading Romans in the Shadow of Empire*, Paul in Critical Contexts (Minneapolis: Fortress Press, 2008).
56. Ibid., 15; cf. 8: "The themes that dominate Romans are *political* topics" (his emphasis).
57. As far as I am aware, Horsley has been more explicit than Elliott about his reservations regarding postcolonial theory. See especially Richard A. Horsley, "Subverting Disciplines: The Possibilities and Limitations of Postcolonial Theory for New Testament Studies," in *Toward a New Heaven and a New Earth: Essays in Honor of Elisabeth Schüssler Fiorenza*, ed. Fernando F. Segovia (Maryknoll, N.Y.: Orbis, 2003), in which he criticizes postcolonial theory in blanket terms for what he sees as "its steadfast rejection of metanarratives, its lack of interest in envisioning an alternative future" (p. 94).
58. See n. 44 above. The quotation is from R. S. Sugirtharajah, "Postcolonial Biblical Interpretation," in *Voices from the Margin: Interpreting the Bible in the Third World*, ed. R. S. Sugirtharajah (3rd ed.; Maryknoll, N.Y.: Orbis, 2006), 72.
59. See n. 9 above.
60. R. S. Sugirtharajah, *The Bible and the Third World: Precolonial, Colonial and Postcolonial Encounters* (Cambridge: Cambridge University Press, 2001), 203–75; idem, *Postcolonial Criticism and Biblical Interpretation* (Oxford: Oxford University Press, 2002), 103–23. These criticisms also find abbreviated expression in his "Postcolonial Biblical Interpretation," 77–80.
61. Musa W. Dube, *Postcolonial Feminist Interpretation of the Bible* (St. Louis: Chalice, 2000).
62. Ibid., 169.
63. Ibid., 192.
64. Ibid., 198. See further Musa W. Dube, "Jumping the Fire with Judith: Postcolonial Feminist Hermeneutics of Liberation," in *Feminist Interpretation of the Bible and the Hermeneutics of Liberation*, ed. Silvia Schroer and Sophia Bietenhard (Journal for the Old Testament Supplement Series 374; London: Sheffield Academic Press, 2003), 60–76, and eadem, "Postcolonialism and Liberation," in *Handbook of U.S. Theologies of Liberation*, ed. Miguel A. De La Torre (St. Louis: Chalice, 2004), 288–94. Neither essay posits any disjunction or tension between postcolonial and liberation hermeneutics.
65. Dube, *Postcolonial Feminist Interpretation*, 157–96.
66. Ibid., 28, part of a five-page critique of Schüssler Fiorenza's work.
67. Elisabeth Schüssler Fiorenza, *The Power of the Word: Scripture and the Rhetoric of Empire* (Minneapolis: Fortress Press, 2007), 124 n. 44, 126 n. 51, 128 n. 58.
68. Ibid., 123.
69. Ibid., 126–29.
70. For more on this, see her *Wisdom Ways: Introducing Feminist Biblical Interpretation* (Maryknoll, N.Y.: Orbis, 2001), 118:

Structures of wo/men's oppression are not just multiple but multiplicative: racism is multiplied by sexism multiplied by ageism, multiplied by classism multiplied by colonial exploitation.... In order to articulate and make visible the complex interstructuring of the conflicting oppressions of different groups of wo/men, I have argued that patriarchy must be re-conceptualized as *kyriarchy*, a neologism which is derived from the Greek *kyrios* (lord, master, father, husband) and the verb *archein* (to rule, dominate).... Kyriarchy is best theorized as a complex pyramidal system of intersecting multiplicative social structures of superordination and subordination, of ruling and oppression.

71. Schüssler Fiorenza, *Power of the Word*, 105 n. 103.

72. Schüssler Fiorenza has now developed her reflections on postcolonialism more fully as part of a complex and important argument for a radical democratization of graduate education in biblical studies; see her *Democratizing Biblical Studies: Toward an Emancipatory Educational Space* (Louisville: Westminster John Knox, 2009), 57–63, 95–106. Her engagement with postcolonial theory, however, is largely second-hand (for example, "Boer charges that Chakravorty Spivak herself, together with Edward Said and Homi Bhabha..." [p. 103]).

73. For references, see nn. 7 and 9 above. It should be added that one of the eleven essays that make up Bhabha's *The Location of Culture* is a reflection on the reception of the Bible in nineteenth-century India: "Signs Taken for Wonders: Questions of Ambivalence and Authority under a Tree Outside Delhi, May 1817" (pp. 102–22). The essay was originally published in 1985. Technically, then, this is the earliest example of "postcolonial biblical criticism" considered thus far, its most remote "beginning," and one arising as far outside the field of biblical studies as can reasonably be imagined.

74. Robert Paul Seesengood, *Competing Identities: The Athlete and the Gladiator in Early Christianity*, Library of New Testament Studies 346 (New York: T&T Clark, 2006), 20–34.

75. Ibid., 23.

76. Ibid. (his emphasis).

77. Marchal, *Politics of Heaven*, 59–90.

78. Ibid., 56.

79. Ibid., 57. Davina C. Lopez engages similarly in a postcolonial feminist reframing of Paul, including a significant recourse to queer studies; see her *Apostle to the Conquered: Reimagining Paul's Mission*, Paul in Critical Contexts (Minneapolis: Fortress Press, 2008). If I focus on Marchal rather than Lopez here, it is only because his position on Paul and empire contrasts more sharply with that of Elliott and Horsley. Lopez's position is more nuanced than Marchal's: "I submit that characterizations of Paul as excessively dominating and irretrievably harmful suffer from a lack of complexity" (p. 15).

80. Elliott, *Liberating Paul*, ix. This time I am quoting from the preface to the first edition.

81. Ibid.

82. Ibid.

83. Somewhat eerily, Marchal's *Politics of Heaven*, notwithstanding its 2008 date, also opens with the first Gulf War and an anecdotal explanation of how the author's "own specific awareness of empire began to emerge" in response to it (p. vii).

84. Elliott, *Liberating Paul*, ix.

85. Other significant studies on Paul and empire include Richard J. Cassidy, *Paul in Chains: Roman Imprisonment and the Letters of St. Paul* (New York: Crossroad, 2001); Efraín Agosto, "Paul vs. Empire: A Postcolonial and Latino Reading of Philippians," *Perspectivas: Occasional Papers* 6 (Fall 2002): 37–56; Jeremy Punt, "Towards a Postcolonial Reading of Freedom in Paul," in *Reading the Bible in the Global Village: Cape Town*, ed. Justin S. Ukpong et al., Global Perspectives on Biblical Scholarship 3 (Atlanta: Society of Biblical Literature, 2002), 125–49; idem, "Paul and Postcolonial Hermeneutics: Marginality and/in Early Biblical Interpretation," in *As It Is Written: Studying Paul's*

Use of Scripture, ed. Stanley E. Porter and Christopher D. Stanley, Society of Biblical Literature Symposium Series 50 (Atlanta: Society of Biblical Literature, 2008), 261–90; John Dominic Crossan and Jonathan L. Reed, *In Search of Paul: How Jesus's Apostle Opposed Rome's Empire with God's Kingdom. A New Vision of Paul's Words and World* (San Francisco: HarperSanFrancisco, 2004); Richard A. Horsley, ed., *Hidden Transcripts and the Arts of Resistance: Applying the Work of James C. Scott to Jesus and Paul*, Semeia Studies 48 (Atlanta: Society of Biblical Literature, 2005); Peter Oakes, "Re-mapping the Universe: Paul and the Emperor in 1 Thessalonians and Philippians," *Journal for the Study of the New Testament* 27 (2005): 301–22; idem, *Reading Romans in Pompeii: Paul's Letter at Ground Level* (Minneapolis: Fortress Press, 2009); Joerg Rieger, *Christ and Empire: From Paul to Postcolonial Times* (Minneapolis: Fortress Press, 2007), 27–67; Tatha Wiley, "Paul and Early Christianity," in *Empire and the Christian Tradition: New Readings of Classical Theologians*, ed. Kwok Pui-lan, Don H. Compier, and Joerg Rieger (Minneapolis: Fortress Press, 2007), 47–62; Gosnell L. Yorke, "Hearing the Politics of Peace in Ephesus: A Proposal from an African Postcolonial Perspective," *Journal for the Study of the New Testament* 30 (2007): 113–27; Mark G. Brett, *Decolonizing God: The Bible in the Tides of Empire*, Bible in the Modern World 16 (Sheffield: Sheffield Phoenix, 2008); Seyoon Kim, *Christ and Caesar: The Gospel and the Roman Empire in the Writings of Paul and Luke* (Grand Rapids: Eerdmans, 2008); Tat-siong Benny Liew, *What Is Asian American Biblical Hermeneutics? Reading the New Testament* (Honolulu: University of Hawai'i Press, 2008), 75–114; Roland Boer, "Resistance versus Accommodation: What to Do with Romans 13?," in *Postcolonial Interventions: Essays in Honor of R. S. Sugirtharajah*, ed. Tat-siong Benny Liew, Bible in the Modern World 23 (Sheffield: Sheffield Phoenix, 2009), 109–22; Theodore W. Jennings, Jr., "Paul against Empire: Then and Now," in *The Bible and the Hermeneutics of Liberation*, ed. Alejandro F. Botta and Pablo R. Andiñach, Semeia Studies 59 (Atlanta: Society of Biblical Literature, 2009), 147–68; Brigitte Kahl, *Galatians Re-Imagined: Reading with the Eyes of the Vanquished*, Paul in Critical Contexts (Minneapolis: Fortress Press, 2009); and Duk Ki Kim, "Cultural-Political Theology and East Asian Biblical Hermeneutics: Postcolonial Identity and Solidarity in Galatians 3:28," in *Mapping and Engaging the Bible in Asian Cultures: Congress of the Society of Asian Biblical Studies 2008 Seoul Conference*, ed. Yeong Mee Lee and Yoon Jong Yoo (Seoul: Christian Literature Society of Korea, 2009), 141–73, along with the nine relevant essays in Fernando F. Segovia and R. S. Sugirtharajah, eds., *A Postcolonial Commentary on the New Testament Writings*, Bible and Postcolonialism 13 (New York: T&T Clark, 2007). Still further examples are listed in the remaining notes. Empire-attuned biblical scholarship has, to date, yielded more work on Paul than on any other biblical author.

86. Elliott, *Arrogance of Nations*, 15. Schüssler Fiorenza's clarion call for a politically engaged biblical scholarship was a major inspiration for *Liberating Paul*, as the latter book made clear (pp. x–xi). This statement in *The Arrogance of Nations* is but one of several in Elliott's work that indicate that he has been disposed to take her criticisms of his reconstruction of Paul with the utmost seriousness.

87. Stephen D. Moore, "Postcolonialism," in *Handbook of Postmodern Biblical Interpretation*, ed. A. K. M. Adam (St. Louis: Chalice, 2000), 182–88.

88. I focused on Horsley's "Submerged Biblical Histories and Imperial Biblical Studies," in *The Postcolonial Bible*, ed. R. S. Sugirtharajah, Bible and Postcolonialism 1 (Sheffield: Sheffield Academic, 1998), 152–73, and Liew's "Tyranny, Power and Might: Colonial Mimicry in Mark's Gospel," *Journal for the Study of the New Testament* 73 (1999): 7–31.

89. Moore, *Empire and Apocalypse*, 3–23.

90. Warren Carter, *Matthew and Empire: Initial Explorations* (Harrisburg, Pa.: Trinity Press International, 2001).

91. Warren Carter, "The Gospel of Matthew," in Segovia and Sugirtharajah, *Postcolonial Commentary on the New Testament Writings*, 73. For more on this shift in Carter's perception of Matthew, see Segovia, "Postcolonial Criticism and the Gospel of Matthew," 221–27, who concludes: "[The]

conflicted reading is the one that I would espouse" (p. 236). Carter's *John and Empire: Initial Explorations* (New York: T&T Clark, 2008) likewise posits a more complex relationship to Rome for John than *Matthew and Empire* did for Matthew.

92. Richard A. Horsley, "Introduction: The Bible and Empires," in *In the Shadow of Empire: Reclaiming the Bible as History of Faithful Resistance*, ed. Richard A. Horsley (Louisville, Ky.: Westminster John Knox, 2008), 7.

93. Susan VanZanten Gallagher, "Mapping the Hybrid World: Three Postcolonial Motifs," *Semeia* 75 (1996): 230.

94. Gerald O. West, "Doing Postcolonial Biblical Interpretation @Home: Ten Years of (South) African Ambivalence," *Neotestamentica* 42 (2008): 147–64; Fernando F. Segovia, "Biblical Criticism and Postcolonial Studies: Toward a Postcolonial Optic," in Sugirtharajah, *Postcolonial Bible*, 49–65.

95. As a further symptom of this development, consider the section "Postcolonial Approaches" in Magnus Zetterholm, *Approaches to Paul: A Student's Guide to Recent Scholarship* (Minneapolis: Fortress Press, 2009), 200–209, which reduces such approaches to a focus on Paul's relations to Rome.

96. West, "Doing Postcolonial Biblical Interpretation @Home," 158 (his emphasis).

97. Ibid., 160. The phrase "flattens out" comes from Sugirtharajah (*Bible and the Third World*, 268), who expresses similar concerns.

98. Brad R. Braxton, "Paul and Racial Reconciliation: A Postcolonial Approach to 2 Corinthians 3:12–18," in *Scripture and Traditions: Essays on Early Judaism and Christianity in Honor of Carl R. Holladay*, ed. Patrick Gray and Gail R. O'Day, Supplements to Novum Testamentum 129 (Leiden: Brill, 2008), 413.

99. Ibid. Davina Lopez also demonstrates awareness of this issue, carefully distinguishing between an "empire-critical" and a "postcolonial" approach to the New Testament in general and to Paul in particular (*Apostle to the Conquered*, 8–11).

100. Braxton, "Paul and Racial Reconciliation," 413.

101. See Vijay Mishra and Bob Hodge, "What Was Postcolonialism?," *New Literary History* 36 (2005): 379–80.

102. See, for example, Ania Loomba et al., eds., *Postcolonial Studies and Beyond* (Durham, N.C.: Duke University Press, 2005), especially part 1, "Globalization and the Postcolonial Eclipse"; Clara A. B. Joseph and Janet Wilson, eds., *Global Fissures: Postcolonial Fusions* (Amsterdam and New York: Rodopi, 2006); Revathi Krishnaswamy and John C. Hawley, eds., *The Postcolonial and the Global* (Minneapolis: University of Minnesota Press, 2008); Sankaran Krishna, *Globalization and Postcolonialism: Hegemony and Resistance in the Twenty-First Century* (Lanham, Md.: Rowman & Littlefield, 2009).

103. Brian J. Walsh and Sylvia C. Keesmaat's popularly pitched *Colossians Remixed: Subverting the Empire* (Downers Grove, Ill.: InterVarsity, 2004) attempts to overcome that handicap and engage centrally with globalization. Especially important, however, is Justin S. Ukpong, "Reading the Bible in a Global Village: Issues and Challenges from African Readings," in idem, *Reading the Bible in the Global Village*, 9–39, to which Musa W. Dube responds in "Villaging, Globalizing, and Biblical Studies," 41–63.

104. Not that postcolonial biblical criticism issuing from the two-thirds world, even when rooted in the liberationist tradition, will inevitably privilege the contemporary imperial context over the ancient. Indian scholar David Joy, for example, in his "Colossians, Paul and Empire: A Postcolonial Reconstruction," *Bangalore Theological Forum* 39 (2007): 89–101, focuses centrally on the Roman context of Colossians.

105. So Musa W. Dube, "Rahab Is Hanging Out a Red Ribbon: One African Woman's Perspective on the Future of Feminist New Testament Scholarship," in *Feminist New Testament Studies: Global and Future Perspectives*, ed. Kathleen O'Brien Wicker, Althea Spencer Miller, and Musa

W. Dube (New York: Palgrave Macmillan, 2005), 189. This problem is also of central concern to Schüssler Fiorenza in *Democratizing Biblical Studies* (see n. 72 above).

2. Critical Perspectives on Postcolonial Theory

1. Colin McCabe, foreword to *In Other Worlds: Essays in Cultural Politics,* by Gayatri Chakravorty Spivak (New York: Methuen, 1987), xviii.
2. Gayatri Chakravorty Spivak, "Neocolonialism and the Secret Agent of Knowledge: An Interview with Gayatri Chakravorty Spivak," *Oxford Literary Review* 13 (1991): 224.
3. Leela Gandhi, *Postcolonial Theory: A Critical Introduction* (New York: Columbia University Press, 1998), 83.
4. Reina Lewis and Sara Mills, eds., *Feminist Postcolonial Theory: A Reader* (New York: Routledge, 2003), 1.
5. Ien Ang, "I'm a Feminist, But . . . : 'Other' Women and Postnational Feminism," in Lewis and Mills, *Feminist Postcolonial Theory,* 190–206.
6. Ibid., 191.
7. Ibid., 192.
8. Ibid., 197.
9. In Lewis and Mills, *Feminist Postcolonial Theory,* 306–23.
10. Ibid., 310.
11. Ibid., 306.
12. Chandra Talpade Mohanty, "Race, Multiculturalism and Pedagogies of Dissent," in eadem, *Feminism without Borders: Decolonizing Theory, Practicing Solidarity* (Durham, N.C.: Duke University Press, 2003), 190.
13. Gandhi, *Postcolonial Theory,* 42.
14. Ibid., 40.
15. Gayatri Chakravorty Spivak; "In a Word/Interview," in eadem, *Outside in the Teaching Machine* (New York and London: Routledge, 1993), 19.
16. Ella Shohat, "Notes on the 'Postcolonial,'" in *The Pre-Occupation of Postcolonial Studies,* ed. Fawzia Afzal-Khan and Kalpana Seshadri-Crooks (Durham, N.C.: Duke University Press, 2000), 126–39.
17. Ibid., 126.
18. Ibid., 127.
19. Ibid., 130.
20. Ibid., 131.
21. Kalpana Seshadri-Crooks, "At the Margins of Postcolonial Studies: Part I," in Afzal-Khan and Seshadri-Crooks, *Pre-Occupation of Postcolonial Studies,* 3–23.
22. Ibid., 3.
23. Ibid., 18.
24. Ibid., 19.
25. Ania Loomba et al., eds., *Postcolonial Studies and Beyond* (Durham, N.C.: Duke University Press, 2005), 3.
26. Gayatri Chakravorty Spivak, *A Critique of Postcolonial Reason: Toward a History of the Vanishing Present* (Cambridge, Mass.: Harvard University Press, 1999).
27. Ibid., 423–31.
28. Ibid., 426.
29. Ibid., 429.

3. Marxism and the Postcolonial Study of Paul

1. Terry Eagleton, *Marxism and Literary Criticism* (London: Methuen, 1976), 3.
2. David Jobling, "Very Limited Ideological Options: Marxism and Biblical Studies in Postcolonial Scenes," in *Postcolonial Biblical Criticism: Interdisciplinary Intersections,* ed. Stephen D. Moore and Fernando F. Segovia (London and New York: T&T Clark, 2005), 192.
3. Roland Boer, "Western Marxism and the Interpretation of the Hebrew Bible," *Journal for the Study of the Old Testament* 78 (1998): 3–21; idem, *Marxist Criticism of the Bible* (London and New York: T&T Clark, 2003); idem, "Marx, Postcolonialism, and the Bible," in Moore and Segovia, *Postcolonial Biblical Criticism,* 166–83; Jobling, "Very Limited Ideological Options," 184–201.
4. Norman K. Gottwald, *The Tribes of Yahweh: A Sociology of Liberated Israel 1250–1050 B.C.E.* (Maryknoll, N.Y.: Orbis, 1979); idem, *The Hebrew Bible: A Socio-Literary Introduction* (Philadelphia: Fortress Press, 1985); Gale A. Yee, *Poor Banished Children of Eve: Women as Evil in the Hebrew Bible* (Minneapolis: Fortress Press, 2003); eadem, "Ideological Criticism: Judges 17–21 and the Dismembered Body," in *Judges and Method: New Approaches in Biblical Studies,* ed. Gale A. Yee (2nd ed.; Minneapolis: Fortress Press, 2007), 138–60.
5. On materialist or "non-idealist" approaches to the Bible, see Brigitte Kahl, "Toward a Materialist-Feminist Reading," in *Searching the Scriptures: A Feminist Introduction,* ed. Elisabeth Schüssler Fiorenza with Shelly Matthews (2 vols.; New York: Crossroad, 1993), 1:225–40; and Davina C. Lopez, *Apostle to the Conquered: Reimagining Paul's Mission,* Paul in Critical Contexts (Minneapolis: Fortress Press, 2008), 7–11. Kahl names 1960s Europe as the formative environment for the scholars whom she discusses.
6. See, among many works, Richard A. Horsley, "Submerged Biblical Histories," in *The Postcolonial Bible,* ed. R. S. Sugirtharajah, Bible and Postcolonialism 1 (Sheffield: Sheffield Academic Press, 1998), 152–73; Horsley, ed., *Christian Origins,* vol. 1 of *A Peoples' History of Christianity* (Minneapolis: Fortress Press, 2006). "People's history" was pioneered by British Marxist historians; see the concise retrospective of James G. Crossley, *Why Christianity Happened: A Sociohistorical Account of Christian Origins (26–50 CE)* (Louisville: Westminster John Knox, 2006), 5–18.
7. Steven J. Friesen, "Poverty in Pauline Studies: Beyond the So-called New Consensus," *Journal for the Study of the New Testament* 26, no. 3 (2004): 323–61; quotation from 336–37.
8. For example, Yee, *Poor Banished Children of Eve;* Kwok Pui-lan, *Postcolonial Imagination and Feminist Theology* (Louisville: Westminster John Knox, 2005); Joseph A. Marchal, *The Politics of Heaven: Women, Gender, and Empire in the Study of Paul,* Paul in Critical Contexts (Minneapolis: Fortress Press, 2008), ch. 1.
9. Elisabeth Schüssler Fiorenza, *The Power of the Word: Scripture and the Rhetoric of Empire* (Minneapolis: Fortress Press, 2007), 1.
10. Marchal, *Politics of Heaven,* ch. 1. Fredric Jameson understands "postmodernism" and the proliferation of difference as a function of capitalism's continuing mutation: see *Postmodernism, or, the Culture of Late Capitalism,* Post-contemporary Interventions (Durham, N.C.: Duke University Press, 1992).
11. See Göran Therborn, *From Marxism to Post-Marxism?* (London: Verso, 2008). The question of "exonerating" Marx for the crimes committed in his name is of course contested; see Leszek Kolakowski, *Main Currents of Marxism: The Founders, the Golden Age, the Breakdown,* trans. P. S. Falla, with a new preface and epilogue (3 vols. in one; New York: Norton, 2005).
12. G. E. M. de Ste. Croix, *The Class Struggle in the Ancient Greek World: From the Archaic Age to the Arab Conquests* (Ithaca: Cornell University Press, 1981), 31–33.
13. A point ably made by de Ste. Croix (*Class Struggle,* 23–25); on the reception of Marx (or lack of it) among classical scholars, see ibid., 19–23.
14. Ibid., 39, 133–47.

15. Ibid., 44; on Roman imperialism, see chs. 6–8.
16. Ibid., 25–28.
17. Ibid., 36, 57–66.
18. Ibid., 19–20.
19. Ibid., 45.
20. Fredric Jameson, "On Interpretation," in idem, *The Political Unconscious: Narrative as a Socially Symbolic Act* (Ithaca: Cornell University Press, 1981), 20.
21. Ibid., 47.
22. Ibid., 76.
23. Ibid., 19–20, 76; see further 83–88.
24. Ibid., 76; see 88–96. On the vexed debates over the category "mode of production," see 89–90; also Boer, *Marxist Criticism of the Bible,* 229–46.
25. Frederick Engels, "On the History of Early Christianity." German original published in *Die neue Zeit,* 1894–95; trans. Institute of Marxism-Leninism, 1957; available online at www.marxists.org/archive/marx/works/1894/early-christianity/index.htm (accessed September 1, 2009).
26. Karl Kautsky, *Foundations of Christianity,* trans. Henry F. Mins (New York: Russell & Russell, 1953), 86; Eng. trans. of *Der Ursprung des Christentums* (Stuttgart: Dietz. 1908).
27. Ibid., 310–14.
28. Ibid., 322–23.
29. Ibid., 328–29.
30. Ibid., 334–35.
31. Ibid., 352–53.
32. Ibid., 354–55.
33. Gerd Theissen, "Legitimation and Subsistence," in idem, *The Social Setting of Pauline Christianity: Essays on Corinth,* trans. John Schütz (Philadelphia: Fortress Press, 1982), 36–37.
34. Justin J. Meggitt, *Paul, Poverty, and Survival,* Studies of the New Testament and Its World (Edinburgh: T&T Clark, 1998), ch. 5 ("Survival Strategies").
35. Crossley, *Why Christianity Happened,* 9.
36. Ibid., 3–5; Gerd Theissen, *Social Reality and the Early Christians: Theology, Ethics, and the World of the New Testament* (Minneapolis: Fortress Press, 1992), 9–13.
37. Crossley, *Why Christianity Happened,* 11, citing Luise Schottroff, "'Not Many Powerful': Approaches to a Sociology of Early Christianity," in *Social-Scientific Approaches to New Testament Interpretation,* ed. David G. Horrell (Edinburgh: T&T Clark, 1999), 278–79; trans. of "'Nicht viele Mächtige': Annäherungen an eine Soziologie des Urchristentums," *Bibel und Kirche* 1 (1985): 2–8.
38. Friesen, "Poverty," especially 326–27. For Adolf Deissmann, see *Paul: A Study in Social and Religious History* (1912; New York: Harper Torchbooks, 1957), 241–43.
39. See Wayne A. Meeks, *The First Urban Christians: The Social World of the Apostle Paul* (New Haven: Yale University Press, 1983); Abraham J. Malherbe, *Social Aspects of Early Christianity* (2nd enlarged ed.; Philadelphia: Fortress Press, 1983); and now Todd D. Still and David G. Horrell, eds., *After the First Urban Christians: The Social-Scientific Study of Pauline Christianity Twenty-Five Years Later* (London: T&T Clark, 2009).
40. Steven Friesen, "The Blessings of Hegemony: Poverty, Paul's Assemblies, and the Class Interests of the Professoriate," pp. 117–23 in *The Bible in the Public Square: Reading the Signs of the Times,* ed. Cynthia Briggs Kittredge, Ellen Bradshaw Aitken, and Jonathan A. Draper (Minneapolis: Fortress Press, 2008), 122–24.
41. Ibid., 124–25.
42. Ibid. For further discussion, see Neil Elliott, "Diagnosing an Allergic Reaction: The Strange Silence of Marxist Criticism in New Testament Interpretation," *The Bible and Critical Theory,* forthcoming.

43. I have in mind Bruce J. Malina and John J. Pilch, *Social-Science Commentary on the Letters of Paul* (Minneapolis: Fortress Press, 2006), especially 393; and Bruce J. Malina, *The New Testament World: Insights from Cultural Anthropology* (3rd ed.; Louisville: Westminster John Knox, 2001), 97. For critiques of their positions, see Elliott, "Diagnosing an Allergic Reaction."

44. Friesen, "Poverty," 357.

45. Ibid. Friesen's work gives statistical precision to the argument of Meggitt (*Paul, Poverty, and Survival*). These ideas are taken up in Peter Oakes's discussion of living space in Pompeii (*Reading Romans in Pompeii: Paul's Letter at Ground Level* [London: SPCK, 2009; Minneapolis: Fortress Press, 2009]). Meggitt's work provoked strong reactions from advocates of the alleged "new consensus"; see Dale B. Martin and Gerd Theissen in *Journal for the Study of the New Testament* 84, no. 1 (2001): 51–64 and 65–84, respectively, and Meggitt's response in the same issue, 85–94.

46. Friesen, "Poverty," 335.

47. Friesen, "Blessings," 125–27.

48. Edward Said, *Culture and Imperialism* (New York: Vintage, 1993), 9.

49. Frantz Fanon, *The Wretched of the Earth*, trans. Constance Farrington, with preface by Jean-Paul Sartre (New York: Grove, 1963).

50. Aijaz Ahmad, *In Theory: Classes, Nations, Literatures* (Oxford: Oxford University Press, 1992), ch. 8; quotation from 317.

51. Boer, "Marx, Postcolonialism, and the Bible," 166–67.

52. Leela Gandhi, *Postcolonial Theory: A Critical Introduction* (New York: Columbia University Press, 1998).

53. Ibid., 24–26, 170–71. Dipesh Chakrabarty, "Postcoloniality and the Artifice of History: Who Speaks for 'Indian' Pasts?" *Representations* 37 (1992): 1–26; quotation from 1.

54. This protest is raised especially against postcolonial critics who fail to distinguish adequately between former colonies like the United States or Australia and other formerly colonized nations: see Gandhi, *Postcolonial Theory*, 167–70, against Bill Ashcroft, Gareth Griffiths, and Helen Tiffin, *The Empire Writes Back: Theory and Practice in Postcolonial Literatures* (London: Routledge, 1989).

55. Arif Dirlik, "The Postcolonial Aura: Third World Criticism in the Age of Global Capitalism," *Critical Inquiry* 20 (1994): 328–56; Ahmad offers similar criticisms in *In Theory*. See also Gandhi, *Postcolonial Theory*, 27–28, 56–57.

56. Gayatri Spivak, *Outside in the Teaching Machine* (New York: Routledge, 1993); Gandhi, *Postcolonial Theory*, 54–63, 176.

57. Fernando F. Segovia, "Biblical Criticism and Postcolonial Studies: Towards a Postcolonial Optic," in Sugirtharajah, *Postcolonial Bible*, 56.

58. Perhaps the most dramatic opposition appears in K.-K. Yeo's postcolonial interpretation of 1 Thessalonians, where he dismisses Marxism as an expression of "the spirit of the anti-Christ" (*Global Bible Commentary*, ed. Daniel Patte [Nashville: Abingdon, 2004], 500).

59. Boer, "Marx, Postcolonialism, and the Bible," 170.

60. Ibid., 170. Boer (pp. 171–74) takes the prodigious work of R. S. Sugirtharajah as a particular example of the eclipse of Marx and the abandonment of Marxist methods as thoroughly dispensable.

61. See, for example, Gandhi, *Postcolonial Theory*, 59–60; Spivak, *Outside in the Teaching Machine*, 56–57.

62. Kwok, *Postcolonial Imagination*; Musa Dube, *Postcolonial Feminist Interpretation of the Bible* (St. Louis: Chalice, 2000).

63. Catherine Keller, *God and Power: Counter-Apocalyptic Journeys* (Minneapolis: Fortress Press, 2005), 103.

64. Jobling, "Very Limited Ideological Options," 187; the phrase comes from Takatso Mofokeng, "Black Christians, the Bible and Liberation," *Journal of Black Theology* 2 (1988): 40. On the role

of the Bible in popular struggles, see especially Gerald O. West, *The Academy of the Poor: Towards a Dialogical Reading of the Bible*, Interventions 2 (Sheffield: Sheffield Academic, 1999).

65. Jobling, "Very Limited Ideological Options," 189.

66. Ibid., 190. Alistair Kee, *Marx and the Failure of Liberation Theology* (Philadelphia: Tirinity Press International, 1990).

67. Keller speaks to these multiple jeopardies and for the necessity of a relational ethic of "just love" rather than of ideological purism (*God and Power*, 107–11).

68. See, for example, the variety of essays on the letters of Paul in *A Postcolonial Commentary on the New Testament Writings*, ed. Fernando F. Segovia and R. S. Sugirtharajah, Bible and Postcolonialism 13 (Edinburgh: T&T Clark, 2007). While economic realities are discussed in several of the essays on Pauline letters, nowhere does the reader encounter a sustained discussion of class relations based in the organization of material production.

69. On mode of production, see Boer, *Marxist Criticism of the Bible*, 244–45; Jameson, *Political Unconscious*, 89–90; de Ste. Croix, *Class Struggle*, 29–35; on the Roman economy, see Peter Garnsey and Richard Saller, *The Roman Empire: Economy, Society, and Culture* (Berkeley: University of California Press, 1987), 3–5. These paragraphs are more fully developed in Neil Elliott, *The Arrogance of Nations: Reading Romans in the Shadow of Empire*, Paul in Critical Contexts (Minneapolis: Fortress Press, 2008), 28–30, 156–59; and idem, "Ideological Closure in the Christ-Event: A Marxist Response to Alain Badiou's Paul," in *Paul, Philosophy, and the Theopolitical Vision: Critical Engagements with Agamben, Badiou, Žižek, and Others*, ed. Douglas Harink, Theopolitical Visions 7 (Eugene, Ore.: Wipf & Stock, 2010), 144–45.

70. On iconography, see Paul Zanker, *The Power of Images in the Age of Augustus*, trans. Alan Shapiro, Jerome Lectures, 16th Series (Ann Arbor: University of Michigan Press, 1988); for application to the interpretation of Paul, see Lopez, *Apostle to the Conquered*, and Brigitte Kahl, *Galatians Rediscovered: Reading with the Eyes of the Vanquished*, Paul in Critical Contexts (Minneapolis: Fortress Press, 2009).

71. I argue that this ideology is the immediate context of Romans in *Arrogance of Nations*, ch. 1.

72. On the location of Paul and the vast majority of his congregations among the poor, see Meggitt, *Paul, Poverty, and Survival*, ch. 4; on mutualism, ibid., ch. 5. I compare Meggitt's argument with analogues in contemporary rural Haiti in "Strategies of Resistance and Hidden Transcripts in the Pauline Communities," in *Hidden Transcripts and the Arts of Resistance: Applying the Work of James C. Scott to Jesus and Paul*, ed. Richard A. Horsley, Semeia Studies 48 (Atlanta: Society of Biblical Literature, 2004), 97–122. On Paul's resistance to patronage, see John K. Chow, *Patronage and Power: A Study of Social Networks in Corinth*, Journal for the Study of the New Testament Supplement Series 75 (Sheffield: JSOT Press, 1992); on his repudiation of the logic of asymmetrical obligation that was the basis of patronage, see Mark Reasoner, *The "Strong" and the "Weak": Romans 14:1—15:13 in Context*, Society for New Testament Studies Monograph Series 103 (Cambridge: Cambridge University Press, 1999). On the collection, see Dieter Georgi, *Remembering the Poor: The History of Paul's Collection for Jerusalem* (Nashville: Abingdon, 1992) (trans. of *Die Geschichte der Kollekte des Paulus für Jerusalem* [Hamburg: Herbert Reich, 1965]); Sze-kar Wan, "Collection for the Saints as Anticolonial Act: Implications of Paul's Ethnic Reconstruction," in *Paul and Politics: Ekklesia, Israel Imperium, Interpretation. Essays in Honor of Krister Stendahl*, ed. Richard A. Horsley (Harrisburg, Pa.: Trinity Press International, 2000), 191–215. On the radicality of Paul's economic practice, see Monya Stubbs, "Subjection, Reflection, Resistance: An African American Reading of the Three-Dimensional Process of Empowerment in Romans 13 and the Free-Market Economy," *Navigating Romans through Cultures: Challenging Readings by Charting a New Course*, ed. K.-K. Yeo, Romans through History and Cultures (New York: T&T Clark, 2004); Lawrence Welborn, *That There May Be Equality*, Paul in Critical Contexts (Minneapolis: Fortress Press, forthcoming).

73. See now Jon Sobrino, *No Salvation outside the Poor: Prophetic-Utopian Essays* (Maryknoll, N.Y.: Orbis, 2008); Elliott, *Arrogance of Nations*, ch. 5 and epilogue.

74. Krister Stendahl, *Paul among Jews and Gentiles, and Other Essays* (Philadelphia: Fortress Press, 1976); E. P. Sanders, *Paul and Palestinian Judaism: A Comparison of Patterns of Religion* (Philadelphia: Fortress Press, 1977); idem, *Paul, the Law, and the Jewish People* (Philadelphia: Fortress Press, 1983).

75. On the "New Perspective," see James D. G. Dunn, "The New Perspective on Paul," *Bulletin of the John Rylands University Library of Manchester* 65 (1983): 95–122, and idem, *The Theology of Paul the Apostle* (Grand Rapids: Eerdmans, 1998); further bibliography and discussion are available online at http://www.ThePaulPage.com.

76. See, for example, James C. Walters, *Ethnic Issues in Paul's Letter to the Romans: Changing Self-definition in Earliest Roman Christianity* (Valley Forge, Pa.: Trinity Press International, 1993); Philip F. Esler, *Conflict and Identity in Romans: The Social Setting of Paul's Letter* (Minneapolis: Fortress Press, 1993); idem, *Galatians*, New Testament Readings (London: Routledge, 1998).

77. See William S. Campbell, *Paul's Gospel in an Intercultural Context: Jew and Gentile in the Letter to the Romans*, Studien zur interkulturellen Geschichte des Christentums 69 (New York: Peter Lang, 1991); John Barclay, "'Neither Jew nor Greek': Multiculturalism and the New Perspective on Paul," in *Ethnicity and the Bible*, ed. Mark G. Brett, Biblical Interpretation Series (Leiden: Brill, 1997), 197–214; Esler, *Galatians*, 235–39 (on "the intercultural promise of Galatians"); Eung Chun Park, *Either Jew or Gentile: Paul's Unfolding Gospel of Inclusivity* (Louisville: Westminster John Knox, 2003).

78. A good critique of the New Perspective can be found in Thomas Deidun, "James Dunn and John Ziesler on Romans in New Perspective," *Heythrop Journal* 33 (1992): 79–84. Interpretations directed in part against it include Mark D. Nanos, *The Mystery of Romans: The Jewish Context of Paul's Letter* (Minneapolis: Fortress Press, 1993); Daniel Boyarin, *A Radical Jew: Paul and the Politics of Identity*, Contraversions 1 (Berkeley: University of California Press, 1994); and Pamela Eisenbaum, *Paul Was Not a Christian: The Real Message of a Misunderstood Apostle* (San Francisco: HarperOne, 2009).

79. See Judith Plaskow, "Anti-Judaism in Feminist Christian Interpretation," in Schüssler Fiorenza, *Searching the Scriptures*, 1:117–29; Susannah Heschel, "Anti-Judaism in Christian Feminist Theology," *Tikkun* 5, no. 3 (1990): 25–28, 95–97; Luise Schottroff, Silvia Schroer, and Marie-Theres Wacker, *Feminist Interpretation: The Bible in Women's Perspective*, trans. Martin Rumscheidt and Barbara Rumscheidt (Minneapolis: Fortress Press, 1995), 55; on the same dynamic in postcolonial studies, see Amy-Jill Levine, "The Disease of Postcolonial New Testament Studies and the Hermeneutics of Healing," *Journal of Feminist Studies in Religion* 20, no. 1 (2004): 91–99; Kwok, *Postcolonial Imagination*, 93–99.

80. See Denise Kimber Buell and Caroline Johnson Hodge, "The Politics of Interpretation: The Rhetoric of Race and Ethnicity in Paul," *Journal of Biblical Literature* 123, no. 2 (2004): 235–51; Caroline Johnson Hodge, "Apostle to the Gentiles: Constructions of Paul's Identity," *Biblical Interpretation* 13, no. 3 (2005): 270–88; Neil Elliott, *Arrogance of Nations*, 47–50.

81. Pamela Eisenbaum criticizes the tendency of some New Perspective scholarship to read Paul as ethnically or culturally Jewish—as a Jew *"kata sarka"*—but as theologically Christian ("Paul, Polemics, and the Problem of Essentialism," *Biblical Interpretation* 13, no. 3 [2005]: 224–38).

82. Chandra Talpade Mohanty, *Feminism without Borders: Decolonizing Theory, Practicing Solidarity* (Durham, N.C.: Duke University Press, 2003), 193.

83. Tat-siong Benny Liew, "Margins and (Cutting-)Edges: On the (Il)Legitimacy and Intersections of Race, Ethnicity, and (Post)Colonialism," in Moore and Segovia, *Postcolonial Biblical Criticism*, 114–65.

Notes to Chapter 3

84. Key studies include Greg Woolf, "Becoming Roman, Staying Greek: Culture, Identity, and the Civilizing Process in the Roman East," *Proceedings of the Cambridge Philological Society* 40 (1994): 116–43; idem, "Beyond Romans and Natives," *World Archaeology* 28, no. 3 (1995): 339–50; Richard Gordon, "From Republic to Principate: Priesthood, Religion, and Ideology," in *Pagan Priests: Religion and Power in the Ancient World*, ed. Mary Beard and John North (Ithaca: Cornell University Press, 1990), ch. 7.

85. Reasoner, *The "Strong" and the "Weak."*

86. Lopez, *Apostle to the Conquered*; Kahl, *Galatians Rediscovered*.

87. José Porfirio Miranda, *Marx and the Bible: A Critique of the Philosophy of Oppression*, trans. John Eagleson (Maryknoll, N.Y.: Orbis, 1974), 152, 160.

88. Elsa Tamez, *The Amnesty of Grace: Justification by Faith from a Latin American Perspective*, trans. Sharon H. Ringe (Nashville: Abingdon, 1991), 20–22.

89. Theodore W. Jennings, *Reading Derrida/Thinking Paul: On Justice*, Cultural Memory in the Present (Stanford: Stanford University Press, 1980); Alain Badiou, *Saint Paul: The Foundation of Universalism*, trans. Ray Brassier, Cultural Memory in the Present (Stanford: Stanford University Press, 2003).

90. "Sin, although it entered the world because of the guilt of one man, has become structured into human civilization itself, whose most characteristic and quintessential expression is the law" (Miranda, *Marx and the Bible*, 182; cf. 174). Miranda declares that Jesus, Paul, and the Gospel writers all perceived the redaction of the Torah to include laws within the exodus theophany as the "artifice of the later legislators" (ibid., 158).

91. Tamez, *Amnesty of Grace*, 101–2.

92. Badiou, *Saint Paul*, 35 (emphasis added).

93. Ibid., 13.

94. Neil Elliott, *The Rhetoric of Romans: Argumentative Constraint and Strategy and Paul's Dialogue with Judaism* (1990; repr., Minneapolis: Fortress Press, 2006); *Arrogance of Nations*, ch. 3.

95. Neil Elliott, "The 'Patience of the Jews': Strategies of Resistance and Accommodation to Imperial Cultures," in *Pauline Conversations in Context: Essays in Honor of Calvin J. Roetzel*, ed. Janice Capel Anderson, Philip Sellew, and Claudia Setzer, Journal for the Study of the New Testament Supplement Series 221 (Sheffield: Sheffield Academic, 2002), 32–42; idem, "Disciplining the Hope of the Poor in Ancient Rome," in Horsley, *Christian Origins*, 177–98; and idem, *Arrogance of Nations*, chs. 3–4.

96. On the importance of "works" (*erga*) as distinguishing "people of exceptional merit, esp. benefactors," see the revised entry in W. Bauer, F. W. Danker, W. F. Arndt, and F. W. Gingrich, *Greek-English Lexicon of the New Testament and Other Early Christian Literature* (3rd ed.; Chicago: University of Chicago Press, 2000), 390; and Frederick W. Danker, *Benefactor: An Epigraphic Study of a Graeco-Roman and New Testament Semantic Field* (St. Louis: Clayton, 1982); on their importance to Augustus's self-presentation, see the *Res Gestae*; on the Augustan ideology of works, Karl Galinsky, *Augustan Culture: An Interpretive Introduction* (Princeton: Princeton University Press, 1996), 93–100; on patronage and cultus as modes of incorporation into the ideology of imperial benefaction, see Gordon, "From Republic to Principate." A marble copy from Lyons of the *clupeus virtutis* given to Augustus by the Senate commemorates his *erga*—the only Greek word in the Latin inscription.

97. See Kahl, *Galatians Rediscovered*, ch. 5; Elliott, *Arrogance of Nations*, 138–41.

98. Marchal, *Politics of Heaven*.

99. De Ste. Croix, for example, devotes most of his admittedly "brief and oversimplified" discussion of women in the Greek and Roman world (*Class Struggle*, 98–111) to a withering critique of "Christian attitudes toward women," for which the pseudo-Paulines are his chief exhibits.

100. See Antoinette Clark Wire, *The Corinthian Women Prophets: A Reconstruction through*

Paul's Rhetoric (Minneapolis: Fortress Press, 1990); Cynthia Briggs Kittredge, *Community and Authority: The Rhetoric of Obedience in the Pauline Tradition,* Harvard Theological Studies 45 (Harrisburg, Pa.: Trinity Press International, 1998); Kwok, *Postcolonial Imagination,* 89–93; Schüssler Fiorenza, *Power of the Word,* ch. 3.

101. Wire, *Corinthian Women Prophets,* 191. Mary Douglas's model of "grid" and "group" forces is presented in *Natural Symbols: Explorations in Cosmology* (New York: Pantheon, 1970).

102. Wire, *Corinthian Women Prophets,* 181–95; 217–19.

103. Ibid., 229–32; cf. Elisabeth Schüssler Fiorenza, "Rhetorical Situation and Historical Reconstruction in 1 Corinthians," *New Testament Studies* 33 (1987): 386–403.

104. See Peter Marshall, *Enmity in Corinth: Social Conventions in Paul's Relations with the Corinthians,* Wissenschaftliche Untersuchungen zum Neuen Testament 2/33 (Tübingen: Mohr Siebeck, 1991); Neil Elliott, *Liberating Paul: The Justice of God and the Politics of the Apostle,* Bible and Liberation (Maryknoll, N.Y.: Orbis, 1994), 52–54, 204–14.

105. See Ramsay MacMullen, *Roman Social Relations 50 B.C. to A.D. 284* (New Haven: Yale University Press, 1974), 44–45, 114; Ste. Croix, *Class Struggle,* 341–43, 364–67, and passim. For Trimalchio, see Petronius's *Satyricon*; for the contemporary challenge of distinguishing true nobility from the "nouveaux riches" under globalized capitalism, Slavoj Žižek (*Living in the End Times* [London: Verso, 2010], 4 n. 3) cites Marcel Proust's reference to the unwritten, informal habits that always mark true nobility, even when the external marks of hierarchy are abolished.

106. Galinsky, *Augustan Culture,* 128–38.

107. In addition to works cited above, see Susan E. Alcock, *Graecia Capta: The Landscapes of Roman Greece* (Cambridge: Cambridge University Press, 1993).

108. Kwok, *Postcolonial Imagination,* 90.

109. So Bruno Blumenfeld, *The Political Paul: Justice, Democracy, and Kingship in a Hellenistic Framework,* Journal for the Study of the New Testament Supplement Series 210 (Sheffield: Sheffield Academic, 2001), 378–94; Kautsky, *Foundations of Christianity,* 336.

110. Ernst Käsemann regarded it as "an alien body in Paul's exhortation," though he did not consider it an interpolation (as others have) (*Commentary on Romans,* trans. Geoffrey W. Bromiley [Grand Rapids: Eerdmans, 1973], 352; see also Leander E. Keck, "What Makes Romans Tick," in *Pauline Theology III: Romans,* ed. David M. Hay and E. Elizabeth Johnson [Minneapolis: Fortress Press, 1993], 3–29).

111. Neil Elliott, "Romans 13:1-7 in the Context of Neronian Propaganda," in *Paul and Empire: Religion and Power in Roman Imperial Society,* ed. Richard A. Horsley (Harrisburg, Pa.: Trinity Press International, 1997), 184–204; T. L. Carter, "The Irony of Romans 13," *Novum Testamentum* 46, no. 3 (2004): 209–28.

112. John W. Marshall, "Hybridity and Reading Romans 13," *Journal for the Study of the New Testament* 31, no. 2 (2008): 157–78. Ronald Charles pursued a similar argument in his paper at the 2009 SBL annual meeting, "A Bhabhaian Reading of Paul as a Diasporic Subject of the Roman Empire."

113. N. T. Wright, "Paul's Gospel and Caesar's Empire," in Horsley, *Paul and Politics,* 364, on the background" of Paul's concern for church unity.

114. N. T. Wright, "Romans and the Theology of Paul," in Hay and Johnson, *Pauline Theology III: Romans,* 62; Dunn, *Theology of Paul the Apostle,* 675. I concur that concern for the safety of the assemblies—but more especially of Jews as a particularly vulnerable population—is Paul's motive in the passage (*Liberating Paul,* 221–26).

115. Neil Elliott, "'Blasphemed among the Nations': Pursuing an Anti-imperial 'Intertextuality'

in Romans," in *As It Is Written: Studying Paul's Use of Scripture*, ed. Stanley E. Porter and Christopher D. Stanley, Society of Biblical Literature Symposium Series 50 (Atlanta: Society of Biblical Literature, 2008), 213–33; idem, *Arrogance of Nations*, 40–43.

116. Elliott, *Arrogance of Nations*, 50–57; on ideology, see Jameson, *Political Unconscious*; Terry Eagleton, *Ideology: An Introduction* (updated ed.; London and New York: Verso, 2007); Jan Rehmann, "Ideology Theory," *Historical Materialism* 15 (2007) 211–39; idem, *Einführung in die Ideologietheorie* (Hamburg: Argument, 2008).

117. Ahmad, *In Theory*, 1. Terry Eagleton provides a similar assessment of theory for its own sake in *Literary Theory: An Introduction* (2nd ed.; London: Blackwell, 1996; Minneapolis: University of Minnesota Press, 1996), 205.

118. Therborn, *From Marxism to Post-Marxism?*, 116–19.

119. Badiou, *Saint Paul*; Slavoj Žižek, *The Fragile Absolute: Or Why Is the Christian Legacy Worth Fighting for?* (London: Verso, 2001). On the debate among philosophers, theologians, and biblical scholars, see Slavoj Žižek and John Milbank, *The Monstrosity of Christ: Paradox or Dialectic?* ed. Creston Davis, Short Circuits (Cambridge, Mass.: MIT Press, 2009); John D. Caputo and Linda Martin Alcoff, eds., *St. Paul among the Philosophers*, Indiana Series in the Philosophy of Religion (Bloomington: University of Indiana Press, 2009); and Harink, *Paul, Philosophy, and the Theopolitical Vision*.

120. Alain Badiou, "The Communist Hypothesis," *New Left Review* 49 (January–February 2008): 29–46.

121. Slavoj Žižek, "How to Begin from the Beginning," *New Left Review* 57 (May–June 2009): 43–55.

122. I have elaborated these suggestions in two lectures to the International Seminar on St. Paul sponsored by the Society of St. Paul in Ariccia, Italy, in April 2009. See "Paul between Jerusalem and Rome: A Political Understanding of His Apostolate" and "Liberating Paul: Pauline 'Evangelization' in the Shadow of Empire," copyright © 2009 Società San Paolo, published online at http://www.paulus.net/index.php?option=com_content&task=view&id=655&Itemid=478.

123. Sobrino, *No Salvation outside the Poor*, 61; Elliott, *Arrogance of Nations*, 161.

124. The question of revolutionary agency is at the heart of Michael Hardt and Antonio Negri's explorations in *Empire* (Cambridge, Mass.: Harvard University Press, 2000) and *Multitude: War and Democracy in the Age of Empire* (New York: Penguin, 2004). Especially in the wake of U.S. wars in Iraq and Afghanistan, the authors have been stoutly criticized for their argument that the role of nation-states is increasingly irrelevant; see Gopal Balakrishnan's review, "Virgilian Visions," *New Left Review* 5 (September–October 2000): 142–48; and Atilio A. Boron, *Empire and Imperialism: A Critical Reading of Michael Hardt and Antonio Negri* (London: Zed, 2005).

4. Pauline Agency in Postcolonial Perspective

1. Russell Pregeant (*Engaging the New Testament: An Interdisciplinary Introduction* [Minneapolis: Fortress Press, 1995], 402–12) points out some of these interpretative difficulties, referring to the ambiguous nature of Pauline positions regarding the status and role of women, homosexuality, and social activism, and achieving limited success in debunking traditional views of Paul as chauvinistic, anti-homosexual, and socially conservative. In a different vein, George Bernard Shaw criticized what he perceived as the Pauline degradation or negation of human dignity: "It was Paul who converted the religion that raised one above sin and death into a religion that delivered millions of men [*sic*] so completely into a dominion that their own common nature became a horror to them, and the religious life became a denial of life" (quoted in Brian J. Dodd, *The Problem with Paul* [Downers

Grove, Ill.: InterVarsity, 1996], 12). Sojourner Truth is reported to have vowed, after being repeatedly adjured from Paul's letters to be obedient as a slave, never to read that part of the Bible should she become free and learn to read (Elisabeth Schüssler Fiorenza, *In Memory of Her: A Feminist Theological Construction of Christian Origins* [New York: Crossroad, 1983], 154). A similar response to Paul was made by Howard Thurman's mother; cf. Amos Jones, Jr., *Paul's Message of Freedom: What Does It Mean to the Black Church?* (Valley Forge, Pa.: Judson, 1984), 6. In the Christian–Jewish dialogue, "Paul emerged as the major stumbling block" (H. Eberhard von Waldow, "The Christian–Jewish Dialogue: In the Footsteps of Markus Barth," *Horizons in Biblical Theology* 17, no. 2 [1995]: 149).

2. Of various studies on the "difficulties" in the Pauline documents and their interpretation, Dodd's work (see n. 1) is representative.

3. The traditional notion that the struggle of the early Jesus-follower communities was directed more against Greek or Hellenistic philosophies and culture than against the politics of the Roman Empire (for example, Lamin O. Sanneh, *Translating the Message: The Missionary Impact on Culture*, American Society of Missiology Series 13 [Maryknoll, N.Y.: Orbis 1989], 50–67) raises the question whether such a distinction between culture and empire is tenable. To what extent can the empire or the ruler cult, so pervasive in Paul's world, be equated with either culture or political power to the exclusion of the other?

4. See Kwok Pui-lan, *Postcolonial Imagination and Feminist Theology* (Louisville: Westminster John Knox, 2005), 86.

5. Christopher Rowland, "Social, Political, and Ideological Criticism," in *The Oxford Handbook of Biblical Studies*, ed. J. W. Rogerson and J. M. Lieu (Oxford and New York: Oxford University Press), 667.

6. Dieter Georgi, *Theocracy in Paul's Praxis and Theology*, trans. David E Green (Minneapolis: Fortress Press, 1991). Ambiguity concerning Paul's engagement with sociopolitical concerns has been denied by some scholars who have been eager to present Paul as consistently critical of and actively opposed to empire. All suggestions of social conservatism on Paul's part—his subordination of his communities to a higher missionary ideal, his sociocultural accommodation and neglect of social justice matters, his notion of love-patriarchalism, his acceptance of a positive role for violence—are deemed to be distortions of Pauline thinking (see Neil Elliott, *Liberating Paul: The Justice of God and the Politics of the Apostle*, Bible and Liberation 6 [Maryknoll, N.Y.: Orbis, 1994], 181–82).

7. Space does not allow fuller discussion of the history of the reception of the Pauline texts. Two typical elements of the interpretive history of normalizing Pauline thinking must suffice. One is his use of a politics of identity and a rhetoric of othering in his letters, as seen especially in his construction of various kinds of binaries, especially regarding gender. The second concerns his essentializing view of reality, which through its focus on differences between the past and the present ensures the construction of sameness between Paul and his communities, as well as "malestream" readerly identification with the apostle and his views (Elisabeth Schüssler Fiorenza, *The Power of the Word: Scripture and the Rhetoric of Empire* [Minneapolis: Fortress Press, 2007], 83–89).

8. The difficulty that many scholars have in dealing with Rome has been framed by Shawn Kelley as an expression of racialized discourse, inherited from centuries of scholarship, in which Rome has become epitomized as the place where "rationality, freedom and mature political power all came together" (*Racializing Jesus: Race, Ideology and the Formation of Modern Biblical Scholarship*, Biblical Limits [London and New York: Routledge, 2002], 44). According to Kelley, "The lengthy rule of Rome, first as a pagan empire and then as a Roman Catholic Empire, will prepare modern, Christian Europe for the emergence of absolute knowledge (in the form of philosophy) and absolute religion (in the form of Christianity)" (p. 62).

9. Cynthia Briggs Kittredge, "Corinthian Women Prophets and Paul's Argumentation in 1 Corinthians," in *Paul and Politics: Ekklesia, Israel, Imperium, Interpretation. Essays in Honor of Krister*

Stendahl, ed. Richard A. Horsley (Harrisburg, Pa.: Trinity Press International, 2000), 108; cf. Antoinette Clark Wire, "Response: The Politics of Assembly in Corinth," in ibid., 127.

10. Richard A. Horsley, "1 Corinthians: A Case Study of Paul's Assembly as an Alternative Society," in *Paul and Empire: Religion and Power in Roman Imperial Society*, ed. Richard A. Horsley (Harrisburg, Pa.: Trinity Press International, 1997), 250. However, more recently Horsley has acknowledged that Paul's use of imperial images in what he calls Paul's "anti-imperial" (though this should probably be "anti-Roman Empire") rhetoric "could only reinforce relations of subordination within the assembly" (*Paul and Politics*, 93).

11. Kittredge, "Corinthian Women Prophets," 105; Gordon M. Zerbe, "The Politics of Paul: His Supposed Social Conservatism and the Impact of Postcolonial Readings," *Conrad Grebel Review* 21, no. 1 (2003): 97 (republished in revised form in the present volume).

12. Schüssler Fiorenza, *Power of the Word*, 69–109. Far from claiming that the Pauline letters embody this vision in full or constantly, Schüssler Fiorenza pleads for constructing "alternative models" or "imaginative designs" through refocusing interpretation and history writing. This process Schüssler Fiorenza refers to as "'quilting,' as piecing scriptural remnants of the gospel of equality, in the debates of the ekklēsia, together in a new design." She explains further: "The past in not simply there in the text, waiting for us to discover how things really were or what Paul really meant. In other words, those biblical interpreters who favor an ekklēsia model of church will emphasize the radical democratic elements inscribed in Pauline texts and those who favor a 'hierarchical' one will stress the authoritative voice of Paul. Those who emphasize an ekklēsia model of church will either identify with Paul or with the members of the communities depending on their social location in the kyriarchal model" (p. 109).

13. See Robert C. Tannehill, "Paul as Liberator and Oppressor: How Should We Evaluate Diverse Views of First Corinthians?" in *The Meanings We Choose: Hermeneutical Ethics, Indeterminacy and the Conflict of Interpretations*, ed. Charles H. Cosgrove, Journal for the Study of the Old Testament Supplement Series 411 (London: T&T Clark, 2007), 203–22. It appears that while Paul advocated for a transformed relationship between Jews and Gentiles, and while he might have advocated some form of resistance against the Roman Empire, he apparently maintained the status quo as far as the subordinate position of women in church was concerned. Similarly, criticism of Paul's failure to address slavery cannot simply be dismissed as anachronistic idealism, since slavery tied in with the Roman imperial order as well as those elements constituting its significant building blocks, namely, the emperor cult, the place and role of the paterfamilias, and the patronage system. These should not be construed as elements of a history of ideas, since they pervaded the entire material and certainly also the ideological domain of the first century C.E. Gender was at any rate securely interwoven with slavery, and both patriarchalism and slavery were important constituent elements of the first-century C.E. Roman Empire. See Sheila Briggs, "Paul on Bondage and Freedom in Imperial Roman Society," in Horsley, *Paul and Politics*, 110–23, and Kwok, *Postcolonial Imagination*, 87.

14. See Sandra Hack Polaski, *A Feminist Introduction to Paul* (St. Louis: Chalice, 2005), 122.

15. In recent times, the intersection of gender issues with political power and control in hegemonic or colonial situations has been pointed out by many scholars. As Kwok Pui-lan notes, "In the study of modern anti-colonial movements, postcolonial feminists have also shown that the struggle against the colonial regime does not automatically lead men to give up their patriarchal privileges, and in many cases they want to reinscribe male-domination norms to protect their 'manhood'" (*Postcolonial Imagination*, 86).

16. L. M. Ahearn's provisional definition is that "agency refers to the socioculturally mediated capacity to act" ("Language and Agency," *Annual Review of Anthropology* 30 [2001]: 112).

17. See N. T. Wright's proposal to use the seven criteria that Richard Hays developed for tracing Old Testament quotations in the Pauline letters as a means of locating "echoes of Caesar" in Paul's letters. The seven criteria are availability, volume, recurrence, thematic coherence, historical plausibility,

history of interpretation, and satisfaction (*Paul: In Fresh Perspective* [Minneapolis: Fortress Press, 2005], 61-62).

18. See Horsley, "1 Corinthians," 87-90; idem, "Rhetoric and Empire—and 1 Corinthians," 74-82 in idem, ed., *Paul and Politics*. Concepts such as "peace" were of course defined differently by those within and outside the empire. Tacitus puts the following words in the mouth of the British rebel commander Calgucus about the Romans: "To robbery, butchery and rapine, they give the name of 'government'; they create a desolation and call it 'peace'" (cited in J. R. Hollingshead, *The Household of Caesar and the Body of Christ: A Political Interpretation of the Letters from Paul* [Lanham, Md.: University Press of America, 1998], 26 n. 16).

19. An empire is generally driven by a sense of moral virtue and operates with a vision of reordering the world's power relations for the sake and betterment of all.

20. The widespread and insidious presence of empire in New Testament texts raises a variety of questions concerning culture, ideology, and power, including the relationship between the center and the margins, the construction of identities and "others," and the ways in which oppression and justice are perceived and construed (Fernando F. Segovia, "Biblical Criticism and Postcolonial Studies: Towards a Postcolonial Optic," in *The Postcolonial Bible*, ed. R. S. Sugirtharajah, Bible and Postcolonialism 1 [Sheffield: Sheffield Academic, 1998], 57-58).

21. Beyond ideology and rhetoric, imperial control was also exercised in a variety of seemingly innocuous ways. For example, coinage was used not simply as a means of trade but also as a commonly accessible and generally agreed yardstick for transactions. "The coins and money changers functioned effectively to control agrarian production through taxes, and populations through debt, although offering the illusion that a hidden treasure or windfall would improve the honor rating and resource base of the impoverished powerless" (Douglas E. Oakman, "Batteries of Power: Coinage in the Judean Temple System," in *In Other Words: Essays on Social Science Methods and the New Testament in Honor of Jerome H. Neyrey*, ed. Anselm C. Hagedorn, Zeba A. Crook, and Eric Stewart, Social World of Biblical Antiquity, Second Series 1 [Sheffield: Sheffield Phoenix, 2007], 171-85, esp. 182). Clearly, Roman imperial policy would have been impressed by the extent to which coinage was successful in drawing labor energy and agrarian produce to the center of power.

22. This point will be developed further in Jeremy Punt, "Empire as Material Setting and Heuristic Grid for New Testament Interpretation: Comments on the Value of Postcolonial Criticism" (forthcoming).

23. See Segovia, "Biblical Criticism," 56, for a discussion of the term "postcolonial optic."

24. See Edward Said's distinction between *imperialism*, which he defines as "the practice, the theory, and the attitudes of a dominating metropolitan city ruling a distant territory," and *colonialism*, a consequence of imperialism, which he regards as "the implanting of settlements on distant territory" (*Culture and Imperialism* [New York: Knopf, 1993], 9-10).

25. Postcolonial theory is revolutionary, as it challenges and pushes against the boundaries of and conventions within society, occupying the liminal spaces of human existence. Appeals against the conventions of society are not unilaterally directed at the concerns of certain groups, but the marginalized are accorded a particular vantage point. As a result, society as a whole stands to benefit from the efforts of the agents in postcolonial theory.

26. See Jeremy Punt, "Postcolonial Biblical Criticism in South Africa: Some Mind and Road Mapping," *Neotestamentica* 37, no. 1 (2003): 59.

27. Cf. Homi K. Bhabha, *The Location of Culture* (London and New York: Routledge, 1994), 173.

28. Stephen D. Moore, *Empire and Apocalypse: Postcolonialism and the New Testament*, Bible in the Modern World 12 (Sheffield: Sheffield Phoenix, 2006), x.

29. One difficulty in accounting for the NT documents is determining their position in relation

to the powers of their day. Some scholars argue that the Bible was written from the perspective of the powerless, that it was part of the "little tradition" because its authors had no real political power, even if they had power in the church (Wayne A. Meeks, "A Hermeneutics of Social Embodiment," *Harvard Theological Review* 79 [1986]: 177–79). Others offer a more qualified approach: "They [the NT texts] were produced by the colonized, yet they subscribe to the ideology of expansion to foreign land based on relationships of unequal power inclusion (Matt 28:16-20; Jn 4:1-42)" (Musa W. Dube, "Reading for Decolonization [John 4:1-42]," *Semeia* 75 [1996]: 41 n. 5).

30. In this sense, it is not unlike queer theory, which actively theorizes and therefore promotes a specific perception of the world and people that challenges and disrupts the more conventional heteronormativity. "The shift from an *epistemological* account of identity to one which locates the problematic within practices of *signification* permits an analysis that takes the epistemological mode itself as one possible and contingent signifying practice . . . the question of *agency* is reformulated as a question of how signification and resignification work" (Judith P. Butler, *Gender Trouble: Feminism and the Subversion of Identity*, Thinking Gender [New York: Routledge, 1990], 144; emphasis in original).

31. In the process, queer and postcolonial theorists often present positions on behalf of those who have been and are presently "othered." Moreover, identity is characterized by a break with the notion of "autonomous human actions" (E. Barvosa-Carter, "Strange Tempest: Agency, Poststructuralism, and the Shape of Feminist Politics to Come," in *Butler Matters: Judith Butler's Impact on Feminist and Queer Studies*, ed. Margaret Sönser Breen and Warren J. Blumenfeld [Aldershot, U.K.: Ashgate, 2005], 175; cf. S. Jeffreys, "Return to Gender: Post-Modernism and Lesbianandgay Theory," in *Radically Speaking: Feminism Reclaimed*, ed. Diane Bell and Renate Klein [London: Zed, 1996], 362–64). In queer theory, gender identity is not "a stable identity or locus of agency from which various acts follow; rather, gender is an identity tenuously constituted in time, instituted in an exterior space through a *stylized repetition of acts*" (Butler, *Gender Trouble*, 139–40). Identity is "performatively articulated as the *effect* of regulatory regimes—a constraint queer theory attempts to transgress, subvert, and disrupt" (John C. Hawley, "Introduction," in *Postcolonial, Queer: Theoretical Intersections*, ed. John C. Hawley, SUNY Series: Explorations in Postcolonial Studies [Albany: State University of New York Press, 2001], 3).

32. As noted by Stephen Slemon in "The Scramble for Post-Colonialism," in *The Post-Colonial Studies Reader*, ed. Bill Ashcroft, Gareth Griffiths and Helen Tiffin (London and New York: Routledge. 1995), 10.

33. Roland Boer, "Marx, Postcolonialism, and the Bible," in *Postcolonial Biblical Criticism: Interdisciplinary Intersections*, ed. Stephen D. Moore and Fernando F. Segovia, Bible and Postcolonialism (London and New York: T&T Clark, 2005), 175.

34. Cf. S. R. F. Price, "Response," in *Paul and the Roman Imperial Order*, ed. Richard A. Horsley (Harrisburg, Pa.: Trinity Press International, 2004), 176. Hegemony in postcolonial thought is often posited as *domination by consent* (Gramsci), "the active participation of a dominated group in its own subjugation" (Moore, *Empire and Apocalypse*, 101). This is true even where those who are subjugated numerically outweigh those exercising power over them, since the oppressor or army of occupation may have the advantage in terms of instruments of subjugation such as sophisticated weaponry and the like. "In such cases . . . the indigene's desire for self-determination will have been replaced by a discursively inculcated notion of the greater good, couched in such terms as social stability . . . and economic and cultural advancement" (cf. ibid.).

35. Discussed by Richard A. Horsley in "The First and Second Letters to the Corinthians," in *A Postcolonial Commentary on the New Testament Writings*, ed. Fernando F. Segovia and R. S. Sugirtharajah, Bible and Postcolonialism 13 (New York: T&T Clark, 2007), 222–30.

36. See R. Saunders, "Paul and the Imperial Cult," in *Paul and His Opponents*, ed. Stanley E. Porter, Pauline Studies 2 (Leiden and Boston: Brill, 2005), 227–38.

37. See Wright, *Paul*, 65. Paul's use of key words and ideas such as *kyrios, sōtēr, parousia, euangelion,* and *dikaiosynē* in his letters is probably indicative of a counter-imperial challenge (ibid., 70), even if subtly so, along the lines of James C. Scott's idea of "hidden transcripts" (*Domination and the Art of Resistance: Hidden Transcripts* [New Haven and London: Yale University Press, 1990]).

38. Horsley, "First and Second Letters to the Corinthians," 227.

39. See Dale B. Martin, *The Corinthian Body* (New Haven and London: Yale University Press, 1995), 57.

40. Elliott, *Liberating Paul* (see n. 6).

41. Wright, *Paul*, 69–79.

42. John Dominic Crossan and Jonathan L. Reed, *In Search of Paul: How Jesus's Apostle Opposed Rome's Empire with God's Kingdom. A New Vision of Paul's Words and World* (New York: HarperSanFrancisco, 2004). Note also Crossan's focus on "justice of equality" in his reading of Paul being anti-empire (*God and Empire: Jesus against Rome, Then and Now* [San Francisco: HarperSanFrancisco, 2007]). See the criticism of their work in Schüssler Fiorenza, *Power of the Word*.

43. Pauline texts that probably represent a fairly explicit challenge to empire include 1 Thess 5:3, with its cynical questioning of reigning imperial notions of peace and security; Phil 3:20, which speaks of another, heavenly commonwealth (cf. also Gal 4:26 on "the Jerusalem above"); 2 Corinthians 8–9, where Paul's hard work on the collection for the church in Jerusalem stands in contrast to prevailing sentiments and structures of the distribution of wealth (see Sze-kar Wan, "Collection for the Saints as Anticolonial Act: Implications of Paul's Ethnic Reconstruction," in Horsley, *Paul and Politics*, 191–215); and Romans 13, which in the context of chs. 12–13 presents a subtle subversion of empire (cf. Elliott, *Liberating Paul*, 217–26; Sylvia C. Keesmaat, "If Your Enemy Is Hungry: Love and Subversive Politics in Romans 12–13," in *Character Ethics and the New Testament: Moral Dimensions of Scripture*, ed. Robert L. Brawley [Louisville: Westminster John Knox, 2007], 141–58; Wright, *Paul*, 78–79).

44. Noted by Wright, *Paul*, 65–69.

45. Martin, *Corinthian Body*, 60–61.

46. As discussed by Kwok, *Postcolonial Imagination*, 85.

47. At a personal level, Paul's refusal to accept money (1 Thess 2:9; 1 Cor 9:1-15; 2 Cor 12:14-17; however, cf. Phil 4:14-20) could have been understood not only as a genuine concern not to be a burden but also as a way to prove a point about status reversal. Paul deliberately undermines the possibility that a congregation might get a grip on him while ensuring that he retains his position of authority over them (cf. Martin, *Corinthian Body*, 80–85). In the process, he sideswipes the patronage system, a key building block of the Roman Empire.

48. In the relationship between empire and NT texts, anachronistic scenarios should of course be avoided. Jesus and his followers were not archetypical freedom fighters who, following modern lines of thinking, had their eyes set on reshaping social realities by removing an oppressive regime. However, claims that "Jesus and the prophetic tradition . . . show no interest in structures, democratic or any other" and that they "are only interested in *how* power is exercised, and *to what end*" (Christopher Bryan, *Render to Caesar: Jesus, the Early Church and the Roman Superpower* [Oxford: Oxford University Press, 2005], 127) are probably too broad. Such claims tend to divorce agency and purpose from institutions in a manner that was foreign to ancient times and, contrary to the author's explicit claim, seem to presuppose contemporary structural change as a possibility, notwithstanding the dictatorial rule of empire in a hierarchical world.

49. Wright (*Paul*, 70) describes Paul's theology with reference to four important themes or foci: (a) creation admits to God's responsibility for and ultimate rule of the world; (b) the covenant stresses God's commitment to freeing his people from pagan oppression; (c) seeing Jesus as Messiah means that he is also king, lord, and savior; and (d) God's apocalyptic justice is unveiled in Jesus' death and resurrection as Messiah.

50. In the Wisdom of Solomon, it is also the defeat of death and the return of the martyred righteous that signals the end of the earthly rulers (Wright, *Paul,* 69).

51. Ibid., 70

52. Ibid.

53. Joerg Rieger, *Christ and Empire: From Paul to Postcolonial Times* (Minneapolis: Fortress Press, 2007), 51.

54. Without suggesting dependence or an authorial link, the quotation from Jer 9:22-23 that appears in 1 Cor 1:31 and 2 Cor 10:17 provides an important intertextual link between the arguments of 1 Corinthians 1-3 and 2 Corinthians 10-13. For a brief discussion of how Paul used the language of weakness and foolishness in 2 Corinthians 10-13 in a manner similar to the postcolonial concept of mimicry, see Jeremy Punt, "Paul and Postcolonial Hermeneutics: Marginality and/in Early Biblical Interpretation, in *As It Is Written: Studying Paul's Use of Scripture,* ed. Stanley E. Porter and Christopher D. Stanley, Society of Biblical Literature Symposium Series 50 (Atlanta: Society of Biblical Literature, 2008), 261-90.

55. Noted in Polaski, *Feminist Introduction,* 5, 19-20, 62, 76.

56. See Jouette M. Bassler, *Navigating Paul: An Introduction to Key Theological Concepts* (Louisville: Westminster John Knox, 2007), 45.

57. Diana A. Swancutt, "Scripture 'Reading' and Identity Formation in Paul: *Paideia* among Believing Greeks" (paper presented at the 2006 Paul and Scripture Seminar, Society of Biblical Literature annual meeting, Washington, D.C., November 2006), 3; available online at http://www.westmont.edu/~fisk/paulandscripture/SwancuttScriptureAndIdentityFormationInPaul.pdf (accessed June 1, 2010).

58. Ibid., 4.

59. On the Greco-Roman setting of Paul's boasting, see Duane F. Watson, "Paul and Boasting," in *Paul in the Greco-Roman World: A Handbook,* ed. J. Paul Sampley (Harrisburg, Pa.: Trinity Press International, 2003), 77-100; with reference to 2 Corinthians 10-13, see ibid., 81-95, 96-97.

60. Discussed by Mark Reasoner, *The Strong and the Weak: Romans 14:1—15:13 in Context,* Society for New Testament Studies Monograph Series 103 (Cambridge: Cambridge University Press, 1999); cf. Neil Elliott, "Political Formation in the Letter to the Romans," in Brawley, *Character Ethics,* 185.

61. See Martin, *Corinthian Body,* 73-76.

62. Later Martin admits that he believes that "Paul was someone originally of high status whose current status was problematic when seen from an upper-class standpoint" (*Corinthian Body,* 85). Cf. Hollingshead, *Household of Caesar,* 193-95.

63. In Acts, Luke's portrait of Paul as not only a Greek philosopher but also a Roman citizen is instrumental in his account of the origin of Christianity. In the context of the countervailing missionary forces of empire and church portrayed in the narrative of Acts, Paul's appeal to Caesar not only shows the hybridity of imperial situations but also marks the decisive break between Christianity and Judaism (see Christopher N. Mount, *Pauline Christianity: Luke-Acts and the Legacy of Paul,* Supplements to Novum Testamentum 104 [Leiden: Brill, 2002], 173).

64. See Kittredge, "Corinthian Women Prophets," 105.

65. Hollingshead, *Household of Caesar,* 242. Whether this tension is resolved for Paul in the death of the Messiah (as Hollingshead contends) or exacerbated by it is another question. Gordon Zerbe ("Politics of Paul," 82) has remarked how, when he was teaching a course on Paul in the Philippines, a student raised the simple but forthright question of why Paul, if he did not curry the favor of the Roman Empire and consciously and otherwise subverted its claims, never renounced his Roman citizenship.

66. Others see a more strategic and innocuous motive for Paul's actions: he claimed a high-status

position for himself in 1 Corinthians in order to be able to persuade a group among the Corinthians to be willing to abandon their own high status and to imitate him in accepting a low-status position (see Martin, *Corinthian Body*, 67). There is also the sociocultural explanation, which argues that accounting for one's deeds, particularly for one's beneficent actions toward others, required an emphasis on one's personality, training, and education as a method of asserting one's identity and reaffirming male status in a public context (Bruce J. Malina and Jerome H. Neyrey, *Portraits of Paul: An Archaeology of Ancient Personality* [Louisville: Westminster John Knox, 1996]).

67. As discussed in Elizabeth A. Castelli, *Imitating Paul: A Discourse of Power*, Literary Currents in Biblical Interpretation (Louisville: Westminster John Knox, 1991).

68. See Bassler, *Navigating Paul*, 72.

69. Jennifer Wright Knust, "Paul and the Politics of Virtue and Vice," in Horsley, *Paul and the Roman Imperial Order*, 173: "His [Paul's] critique of Roman imperial pretensions, framed, in part, in terms of sexual virtue and vice, depended upon and reinscribed hierarchical theories of sex and gender that, historically, had been used by Romans and Greeks to claim their own privileged status while undermining the claims of their rivals." Others have rushed to Paul's defense; see Stephen C. Barton's apology for Paul's harsh tone and position under the heading of "the limits of tolerance": "not even-handed tolerance but zeal for God"; "not rationalistic optimism but apocalyptic hope"; "not 'live and let live' but love with a view to transformation" (*Life Together: Family, Sexuality and Community in the New Testament and Today* [Edinburgh: T&T Clark, 2001], 207–19).

70. See Polaski, *Feminist Introduction*, 122.

71. See Martin, *Corinthian Body*, 59–60.

72. Kittredge, "Corinthian Women Prophets," 108.

73. As far as the Roman Empire was concerned, the social order and the divine order were one and the same, and therefore the ethics of Roman society were sacred and non-negotiable. "The Romans always understood themselves to be the world's rightfully dominant culture, the gods' own people, and they understood the workings of their society, the ethics of household and of patronage, to be sacred" (Hollingshead, *Household of Caesar*, 113).

74. Horsley, *Paul and Empire*, 242–52.

75. Kittredge, "Corinthian Women Prophets," 105, 107–8.

76. R. S. Sugirtharajah, *Asian Biblical Hermeneutics and Postcolonialism: Contesting the Interpretations*, Bible and Liberation (Maryknoll, N.Y.: Orbis, 1998), 20.

77. Kelley, *Racializing Jesus*, 75–76.

5. The Politics of Paul

This article is adapted from a presentation given at Currents in Theological and Biblical Dialogue, a conference in September 2001 at St. John's College, Winnipeg, and was previously published in *Conrad Grebel Review* 21, no. 1 (2003): 82–103. It is republished here with permission.

1. For references, see Hans Dieter Betz, "Paul," *The Anchor Bible Dictionary*, ed. David Noel Freedman (6 vols.; New York: Doubleday, 1992), 5:187.

2. For a recent discussion that eerily appeared just before September 11, 2001, see Lewis A. Lapham, "The American Rome: On the Theory of Virtuous Empire," *Harper's Magazine*, August 2001, 31–38.

3. Arif Dirlik, "The Postcolonial Aura: Third World Criticism in the Age of Global Capitalism," *Critical Inquiry* 20, no. 1 (1994): 329.

4. For example, R. S. Sugirtharajah, *Asian Biblical Hermeneutics and Postcolonialism: Contesting the Interpretations*, Bible and Liberation (Maryknoll, N.Y.: Orbis, 1998), 3–28; Ankie Hoogvelt,

Globalization and the Postcolonial World: The New Political Economy of Development (Baltimore: Johns Hopkins University, 1997), 153–61.

5. For example, R. S. Sugirtharajah, ed., *The Postcolonial Bible,* Bible and Postcolonialism 1 (Sheffield: Sheffield Academic, 1998); Fernando F. Segovia, *Decolonizing Biblical Studies: A View from the Margins* (Maryknoll, N.Y.: Orbis, 2000); R. S. Sugirtharajah, *The Bible and the Third World: Precolonial, Colonial, and Postcolonial Encounters* (Cambridge: Cambridge University Press, 2001).

6. Musa W. Dube, *Postcolonial Feminist Interpretation of the Bible* (St. Louis: Chalice, 2000); Fernando F. Segovia and R. S. Sugirtharajah, eds., *A Postcolonial Commentary on the New Testament Writings,* Bible and Postcolonialism 13 (London and New York: T&T Clark, 2007).

7. Sugirtharajah remarks: "It must be stressed that it is not a homogenous project, but a hermeneutical salmagundi, consisting of extremely varied methods, materials, historical entanglements, geographical locations, political affiliations, cultural identities, and economic predicaments" (*Asian Biblical Hermenuetics*, 15).

8. Ibid., 17.

9. Ibid., 15–16. Thus, to treat postcolonialism as a subspecies of Eurocentric postmodernism is to engage in intellectual imperialism.

10. Neil Elliott, *Liberating Paul: The Justice of God and the Politics of the Apostle,* Bible and Liberation (Maryknoll, N.Y.: Orbis, 1994), 74–75, 83–84.

11. For example, Paul W. Meyer, "Pauline Theology: A Proposal for a Pause in Its Pursuit," in *Pauline Theology,* vol. 4, *Looking Back, Pressing On,* ed. E. Elizabeth Johnson and David M. Hay, Society of Biblical Literature Symposium Series 4 (Atlanta: Scholars, 1997), 140–60.

12. See Rom 13:1-7; 1 Cor 7:17-24; 11:2-16; 14:34-35; Col 3:18—4:1.

13. For a brief review, see Elliott, *Liberating Paul,* 37–40.

14. So Sugirtharajah, *Asian Biblical Hermeneutics,* 20: "Paul, a genuine immigrant by current political standards, gives the impression in his writings that he has been fully co-opted into the imperial system. An example occurs in Romans 13, in which he reinscribes colonial values by asserting that God and history are on the side of the Roman Empire. The sensible thing for Christians, Paul writes, is to live peaceably with the colonial administration and to work within its framework, rather than to revolt. The almighty Roman power was hardly questioned in his epistles, except in teleological terms. Occasionally he censures the evils of the Empire, but offers no political strategy or practical solution for its liquidation." For North American feminist responses, see n. 82 below.

15. See Elliott, *Liberating Paul.*

16. Klaus Wengst, *Pax Romana and the Peace of Jesus Christ,* trans. J. Bowden (Philadelphia: Fortress Press, 1987), especially 79–89; see also his *Humility: Solidarity of the Humiliated,* trans. J. Bowden (Philadelphia: Fortress Press, 1987); and Dieter Georgi, *Theocracy in Paul's Praxis and Theology,* trans. D. Green (Minneapolis: Fortress Press, 1991).

17. Richard A. Horsley, ed., *Paul and Empire: Religion and Power in Roman Imperial Society* (Harrisburg, Pa.: Trinity Press International, 1997); idem, ed., *Paul and Politics: Ekklēsia, Israel, Imperium, Interpretation: Essays in Honor of Krister Stendahl* (Harrisburg, Pa.: Trinity Press International, 2000); idem, ed., *Paul and the Roman Imperial Order* (Harrisburg, Pa.: Trinity Press International, 2004). See Jacob Taubes, *The Political Theology of Paul,* ed. Aleida Assmann et al., trans. Dana Hollander, Cultural Memory in the Present (Stanford: Stanford University Press, 2004; German original, 1993); John Dominic Crossan and Jonathan Reed, *In Search of Paul: How Jesus's Apostle Opposed Rome's Empire with God's Kingdom. A New Vision of Paul's Words and World* (New York: HarperCollins, 2004); Warren Carter, *The Roman Empire and the New Testament: An Essential Guide,* Abingdon Essential Guides (Nashville: Abingdon, 2006); Neil Elliott, *The Arrogance of Nations: Reading Romans in the Shadow of Empire,* Paul in Critical Contexts (Minneapolis: Fortress

Press, 2008); Davina C. Lopez, *Apostle to the Conquered: Reimagining Paul's Mission,* Paul in Critical Contexts (Minneapolis: Fortress Press, 2008); Marcus J. Borg and John Dominic Crossan, *The First Paul: Reclaiming the Radical Visionary behind the Church's Conservative Icon* (New York: HarperOne, 2009); Gordon Zerbe, "Citizenship and Politics according to Philippians," *Direction* 38, no. 2 (2009): 193-208.

18. As argued by Betz, "Paul," 187.

19. In textbook after textbook, the great virtues of the Pax Romana, along with the imperial conquests of Alexander, are celebrated as providing the fertile ground for the spread of the gospel, as if the gospel of the cross really needed such power structures in order to thrive. For an alternative reading of the Roman Empire, see Wengst, *Pax Romana,* 7-54; Horsley, *Paul and Empire,* 10-137.

20. The Latin term for "command," used to refer to the Roman state and its "sovereignty" and "authority."

21. Thus also Oscar Cullmann, *The State in the New Testament* (New York: Scribner, 1956), 50-70.

22. In addition to the letters deemed "undisputed" by biblical scholars (Romans, 1 and 2 Corinthians, Galatians, Philippians, 1 Thessalonians, Philemon), I tend to treat Colossians also as an "authentic" letter of Paul. Once Paul is taken out of a dogmatic straitjacket and freed from the necessity of absolute logical consistency (as when Romans 6 is contrasted with Colossians 3) and from the demand to have his ethics cleaned up (Col 3:18—4:1; cf. 1 Corinthians 7; 11) and treated, moreover, as a rhetorician, the arguments against the authenticity of Colossians become less convincing. The linguistic and stylistic arguments themselves are not decisive, and the more spatially framed millenarianism of Colossians is not absolutely incompatible with that of the undisputed letters. In this essay I address the perspective of Paul as he is available to historical reconstruction, as opposed to the Paul of the canon, or the Paul of history, canon, and legend.

23. See especially the landmark work by J. Christiaan Beker, *Paul the Apostle: The Triumph of God in Life and Thought* (Philadelphia: Fortress Press, 1980).

24. For a helpful typology, see Bryan Wilson, *Magic and the Millennium: A Sociological Study of Religious Movements of Protest among Tribal and Third-World Peoples* (New York: Harper & Row, 1973).

25. Elisabeth Schüssler Fiorenza ("Paul and the Politics of Interpretation," in Horsley, *Paul and Politics,* 40-58, especially 55) refers to both the critical and the conforming functions that are potentially present in millennial ideology.

26. Reynaldo Ileto, *Pasyon and Revolution: Popular Movements in the Philippines, 1840-1910* (Manila: Ateneo de Manila University Press, 1979).

27. Richard A. Horsley, *Jesus and the Spiral of Violence: Popular Resistance in Roman Palestine* (San Francisco: Harper & Row, 1987), 121-45; Elliott, *Liberating Paul,* 141-80.

28. This is the central thesis of Beker, *Paul the Apostle*; for an application of Paul's apocalyptic heritage to his anti-imperial perspective, see Richard A. Horsley, "Rhetoric and Empire—and 1 Corinthians," in *Paul and Politics,* 93-102.

29. Judith Kovaks, "The Archons, the Spirit, and the Death of Christ: Do We Really Need the Hypothesis of Gnostic Opponents to Explain 1 Cor. 2:6-16?" in *Apocalyptic in the New Testament: Essays in Honor of J. Louis Martyn,* ed. Joel Marcus and Marion L. Soards, Journal for the Study of the New Testament Supplement Series 24 (Sheffield: JSOT Press, 1989), 224.

30. Krister Stendahl, "Hate, Non-retaliation, and Love: 1QS x, 17-20 and Rom. 12:19-21," *Harvard Theological Review* 55 (1962): 345. For a discussion of whether Paul's ethic of nonretaliation is merely an apocalyptic restraint or is tied also to the values of love and reconciliation, see Gordon Zerbe, "Paul's Ethic of Non-retaliation and Peace," in *The Love of Enemy and Nonretaliation in the*

Notes to Chapter 5 283

New Testament, ed. Willard M. Swartley, Studies in Peace and Scripture 3 (Louisville: Westminster John Knox, 1992), 177–222.

31. Contra James D. G. Dunn, *The Theology of Paul the Apostle* (Grand Rapids: Eerdmans, 1998), 104–10.

32. Walter Wink, *Naming the Powers: The Language of Power in the New Testament*, vol. 1 of *Powers* (Philadelphia: Fortress Press, 1984); idem, *Engaging the Powers: Discernment and Resistance in a World of Domination*, vol. 3 of *Powers* (Minneapolis: Fortress Press, 1992), 65–85.

33. Discomfort with this last theme is evident among interpreters. It is de-emphasized by Wink (*Naming the Powers*, 59–63); and these last two texts are also absent from the discussion of the "powers" by John Howard Yoder, *The Politics of Jesus: Vicit Agnus Noster* (Grand Rapids: Eerdmans, 1972), 135–62.

34. Georgi, *Theocracy*, 52–57.

35. Richard A. Horsley, "1 Corinthians: A Case Study of Paul's Assembly as an Alternative Society," in idem, *Paul and Empire*, 244.

36. So Gordon D. Fee, *The First Epistle to the Corinthians*, New International Commentary on the New Testament (Grand Rapids: Eerdmans, 1987), 103–4.

37. So Horsley, "1 Corinthians," 244.

38. Wink, *Naming the Powers*, 40–45; Cullmann, *State*, 62–64; cf. Elliott (*Liberating Paul*, 110–13), who interprets the powers in terms of the "mythic symbolism of Jewish apocalypses," so that Pilate's individuality is seemingly dissolved. While not referring to a specific, official miscarriage of justice, the phrase still refers to the cosmic powers who stand behind the earthly actors. "We should marvel, not that Paul can speak of his 'word of the cross' without specifically identifying Pilate, but that his indictment goes beyond Pilate to include all the powers of heaven and earth together that stand hostile to God" (ibid., 113). In other words, Paul refuses to demonize a particular individual but rather invites discernment to see how the powers are embodied.

39. See especially Elliott, *Liberating Paul*, 105–31.

40. For texts and scholarly discussion, see Elliott, *Liberating Paul*, 254 n. 55.

41. On the notion of the cross as God's burlesque, as expressed in the phrase *skandalon tou staurou* ("scandal of the cross"), see Georgi, *Theocracy*, 46–51.

42. Romans 8:18-39; 15:12; 16:20; 1 Cor 2:6-8; 6:2-3; 15:23-29; Phil 1:27-30; 2:9-11; 3:20-21; Gal 1:4; 1 Thess 4:13—5:11.

43. See, for example, 1 Thess 4:13-18, "caught up in the clouds," "meet the Lord in the air"; 2 Cor 4:16—5:10, longing for the building from God, eternal in the heavens; Phil 3:20, "our citizenship is in heaven"; Phil 1:23-26, longing to depart and be with Messiah; Col 1:5, "hope stored up in heaven"; Col 1:12, to share in "the inheritance of the saints in light"; 1 Cor 15:50, "flesh and blood cannot inherit the kingdom of God"; 1 Cor 15:19, pitied if only for this life we have hoped in the Messiah. Cf. the notions of "immortality" in 2 Cor 5:4 and physical transformation in 1 Cor 15:20-28; Phil 3:21; Rom 8:23.

44. Occurring a mere eleven times in the undisputed letters—sixteen times if Colossians is included—compared with 273 in the entire New Testament.

45. Romans 1:18; 2 Cor 5:2; 1 Thess 1:10; 4:16; cf. Rom 11:26 (reading "Zion" as heavenly Zion).

46. Philippians 3:20; Col 1:5; cf. Gal 4:26 ("the Jerusalem above"). See the comments on Phil 3:20 by Andrew T. Lincoln, *Paradise Now and Not Yet: Studies in the Role of the Heavenly Dimension in Paul's Thought with Special Reference to His Eschatology*, Society for New Testament Studies Monograph Series 43 (Cambridge: Cambridge University Press, 1981), 193: "It is not, as has often been thought, that heaven as such is the homeland of Christians to which they, as perpetual foreigners on earth, must strive to return, but rather that since their Lord is in heaven, their life is to be governed

by the heavenly commonwealth." So also ibid., 63: "Paul often conceives of objects and events normally associated with the end-time as existing already in heaven (e.g., the Jerusalem above in Galatians 4:26)."

47. 1 Corinthians 15:20-28; 35-57; 1 Thess 4:16 (trumpet imagery); Rom 8:18-25, 37; 11:25-26, 32, 36; 15:12; 16:20; Phil 1:27-28; 2:9-11; as the "day" (1 Cor 1:8; Phil 2:16) and as involving judgment, destruction and wrath (1 Thess 1:10; 5:1-11; Phil 1:27-30; 3:17-21; Rom 1:18; 2:5-16; 1 Cor 4:5). Cf. the promise that believers are "given all things," Rom 8:32; "inherit the cosmos," Rom 4:13; and judge the cosmos and angels, 1 Cor 6:2-3. On the judgment of believers, see Rom 14:10-12; 1 Cor 4:4-5; 11:27-32; 2 Cor 5:10.

48. 1 Thessalonians 4:13-18; Phil 1:23-26; Rom 8:39; Col 1:12-13; 3:3; Gal 2:19-20; 1 Cor 13:10-12.

49. On "glory" and "glorification," see Rom 8:17, 30; 2 Cor 4:17; Phil 4:20; Col 3:3; on "life" and "age-like life," see Rom 8:13; Gal 6:7. For more on the use of "glory" in Paul, see Carey C. Newman, *Paul's Glory-Christology: Tradition and Rhetoric*, Supplements to Novum Testamentum 69 (Leiden: Brill, 1992).

50. Beker, *Paul the Apostle*, 313.

51. For example, Rom 13:11-14; cf. Paul's reference to fellow "soldiers" in Phil 2:25 and Phlm 2.

52. Thomas R. Yoder Neufeld, *'Put on the Armour of God': The Divine Warrior from Isaiah to Ephesians*, Journal for the Study of the New Testament Supplement Series 140 (Sheffield: Sheffield Academic, 1997).

53. See also Rom 13:11-14 and 2 Cor 10:3-4 for warfare imagery and Rom 8:32, 37 for conquest imagery Cf. Eph 6:10-20.

54. In this text, the divine warfare is directed against the community itself (2 Cor 10:5-6, 8; 13:10), as often in the prophetic holy war texts of Israel.

55. Compare the assertion (without argument) by Michel R. Desjardins, *Peace, Violence and the New Testament*, Biblical Seminar 46 (Sheffield: Sheffield Academic Press, 1997), 82: "The military metaphors so loved by Paul are not his attempts to 'spiritualize' what he considered unworthy of Christianity; rather, they reflect his recognition of the importance and worth of the military—or at least his acceptance of it."

56. See Helmut Koester, "Imperial Ideology and Paul's Eschatology in 1 Thessalonians," in Horsley, *Paul and Empire*, 158-66.

57. See nn. 43-46 above, and the remarks on Phil 3:20 by Schüssler Fiorenza, "Paul and the Politics of Interpretation," 55: "The '*politeuma* in heaven' has usually been understood in dualistic terms as 'pie in the sky' or as otherworldly spiritualized reality that has nothing to do with the reality and politics of the earthly Roman Empire. However, if one understands 'otherworldliness' and 'heaven' not as negation of humanness and creation, but as the site of G*d's justice and well-being that is traditionally called 'salvation,' then one can conceptualize the Divine *politeuma* as the theological location from where a radical critique of oppressive 'earthly' structures becomes possible."

58. On the notion that the messianic community can never legitimate the political order, but can only relativize and ultimately replace it, see Taubes, *Political Theology of Paul*, 13-16, 121-22, 130-31.

59. See Beker, *Paul the Apostle*, 313-17; Georgi, *Theocracy*, 57-58.

60. Georgi, *Theocracy*, 83; see also N. T. Wright, "Paul's Gospel and Caesar's Empire," in Horsley, *Paul and Politics*, 164-65.

61. See esp. Wright, "Paul's Gospel and Caesar's Empire," 166-70, 173.

62. Ibid., 173.

63. Erik Heen, "Phil 2:6-11 and Resistance to Local Timocratic Rule: *Isa theō* and the Cult of

Notes to Chapter 5

the Emperor in the East," in Horsley, *Paul and the Roman Imperial Order*, 125–54. On Rom 1:3-4 as a "declaration of war on Rome," see Taubes, *Political Theology of Paul*, 13–16.

64. Georgi, *Theocracy*, 36–44, 83–84. Cf. Gal 2:16, 20; 3:22; Rom 3:22, 26; Phil 3:9.

65. Notably in 1 Cor 15:23; 1 Thess 2:19; 3:13; 4:15; 5:23.

66. For references, see W. F. Bauer, F. W. Danker, W. F. Arndt, and F. W. Gingrich, *Greek-English Lexicon of the New Testament and Other Early Christian Literature* (3rd ed.; Chicago: University of Chicago Press, 2000), s.v. *parousia*.

67. As argued by Horsley in "1 Corinthians" and "Rhetoric and Empire"; cf. Georgi, *Theocracy*, 52–60.

68. Neil Elliott, "Paul and the Politics of Empire: Problems and Prospects," in Horsley, *Paul and Politics*, 37–39.

69. Sze-kar Wan, "Collection for the Saints as an Anticolonial Act: Implications of Paul's Ethnic Reconstruction," in Horsley, *Paul and Politics*, 191–215. Wan notes Paul's rejection of vertical Roman patronal structures and his emphasis on the new messianic eschatological universalism.

70. Highlighted by Cullmann (*State*, 60–62) as a counterbalance to Paul's positive remarks about the authorities in Romans 13.

71. In 1 Thess 2:2, Paul refers to his flogging (Acts 16:20-24) as "maltreatment."

72. See especially Wengst, *Pax Romana*, 76.

73. Ibid., 75; on Paul's deliberate move down the social ladder, see Elliott, *Liberating Paul*, 57–66.

74. To use the term "Christian" at this stage of the emergence of Christianity is of course anachronistic.

75. Wengst, *Pax Romana*, 75.

76. My translation. Deciding on the translation of this text itself is notoriously difficult and politically charged: are the readers invited to "be subordinate" or to "be subject" (*hypotassomai*)? Are the authorities "ordered/arranged" (*tetegmenai*, v. 1) or "ordained/instituted" (*diatagē*, v. 2) by God? Are the readers called not to "resist" in general or not to "revolt" (*antitassomai*; *anthistēmi*) in some more specific sense?

77. Beker, *Paul the Apostle*, 326.

78. Elliott, *Liberating Paul*, 224. Cf. Isa 44:2-8; 45:1-7 (Cyrus as God's "anointed"); Jer 25:9; 27:6; 43:10 (Nebuchadrezzar as God's "servant"); Dan 2:37.

79. Wengst, *Pax Romana*, 82.

80. See especially Neil Elliott, "Romans 13:1-7 in the Context of Imperial Propaganda," in Horsley, *Paul and Empire*, 184–204.

81. For example, Jan Botha, *Subject to Whose Authority? Multiple Readings of Romans 13*, Emory Studies in Early Christianity 4 (Atlanta: Scholars, 1994), 219–26.

82. Cf. Elisabeth Schüssler Fiorenza, "Paul and the Politics of Interpretation." Classic works on recovering silenced voices in first-century Chrisianity include Schüssler Fiorenza, *In Memory of Her: A Feminist Theological Reconstruction of Christian Origins* (New York: Crossroad, 1983) and Antoinette Clark Wire, *The Corinthian Women Prophets: A Reconstruction through Paul's Rhetoric* (Minneapolis: Fortress Press, 1990). Other helpful studies include Elizabeth A. Castelli, *Imitating Paul: A Discourse of Power*, Literary Currents in Biblical Interpretation (Louisville: Westminster John Knox, 1991); Cynthia Briggs Kittredge, *Community and Authority: The Rhetoric of Obedience in the Pauline Tradition*, Harvard Theological Studies 45 (Harrisburg, Pa.: Trinity Press International, 1998); and Joseph Marchal, *The Politics of Heaven: Women, Gender, and Empire in the Study of Paul*, Paul in Critical Contexts (Minneapolis: Fortress Press, 2008).

83. Schüssler Fiorenza, "Paul and the Politics of Interpretation," 53.

84. That is, the leadership roles for numerous women in Paul's circles (as evidenced in texts like

Romans 16) can be explained as expressions of "charisma," the giftedness of the assemblies which is not distributed by gender and which interrupts prevailing patriarchal norms for ordering communities. In Colossians, however, it appears that the concern for "order" (*taxis*, 2:6; cf. 3:18—4:1) overtakes the democratizing role of charisma. Other texts expressing an explicit concern for communal "order" are 1 Cor 14:40 (*taxis*), 1 Cor 7:35 (*euschēmon*, decorum, good form), 1 Cor 14:33 and 2 Cor 12:20 (contra *akatastasia*, disorder), and 1 Thess 5:14 (contra the *ataktoi*, the disorderly, the out of rank, the insubordinate). Georgi (*Theocracy*, 60–61) claims, however, on the basis of 1 Cor 14:33 that Paul plainly distinguishes between "peace" and "order," favoring the former over against contemporary ideology.

85. Cf. Heikki Räisänen's argument that Paul's remarks on the Jewish Torah are fundamentally incoherent in *Paul and the Law* (Philadelphia: Fortress Press, 1986).

86. J. Christiaan Beker, *The Triumph of God: The Essence of Paul's Thought* (Minneapolis: Fortress Press, 1990), 35–36.

87. For a discussion of this, see especially Beker, *Paul the Apostle*, 325–27.

88. Ibid., 322.

6. Visualizing Significant Otherness

1. For a collection of appraisals of the historical-critical approach to biblical texts from a variety of feminist and postcolonial perspectives, see *Her Master's Tools? Feminist and Postcolonial Engagements of Historical-Critical Discourse*, ed. Caroline Vander Stichele and Todd Penner (Global Perspectives in Biblical Scholarship 9; Atlanta: Society of Biblical Literature, 2005). In their introduction, Penner and Vander Stichele discuss three options for postcolonial and feminist engagement of historical-critical discourse: uncritical use of the tools, outright rejection, or a "third way": "One can engage the dominant discourses and create counter-discourses and communities, reconfiguring and reconstituting traditional tools, methods, and aims in alternative directions and contexts. In the latter case, voices within and without of the guild find each other, and those at the center and the margins can establish (some) common cause. Herein also lies the possibility and prospect for the creation of shifting identities and the development of subversive discourses amidst the employment of alternative ones" (p. 28).

2. Adolf Deissmann, *Light from the Ancient East: The New Testament Illustrated by Recently Discovered Texts of the Graeco-Roman World*, trans. Lionel R. M. Strachan (1910; 4th ed.; repr., Peabody, Mass.: Hendrickson, 1995), 342.

3. See, for example, the now much-cited *Paul and Empire: Religion and Power in Roman Imperial Society*, ed. Richard A. Horsley (Harrisburg, Pa.: Trinity Press International, 1997).

4. Deissmann, *Light from the Ancient East*, 341.

5. Karl Kautsky, *The Foundations of Christianity*, trans. Henry Mins (New York: Russell and Russell, 1908).

6. Specifically, such studies have resonances with (and significant departures from) a significant tradition of non-idealist/Marxist/materialist biblical interpretation, not to mention a considerable body of feminist research. Simply put, not all treatments of ancient and modern empires in contemporary New Testament studies can be traced to an intersection with postcolonial theories. For a discussion and bibliography, see Davina C. Lopez, *Apostle to the Conquered: Reimagining Paul's Mission*, Paul in Critical Contexts (Minneapolis: Fortress Press, 2008), 7–17.

7. For a similar set of observations on submerged or otherwise ignored histories of New Testament scholarship, see Todd Penner, "*Die Judenfrage* and the Construction of Ancient Judaism: Toward a Foregrounding of the Backgrounds Approach to Early Christianity," in *Scripture and*

Traditions: Essays on Early Judaism and Christianity in Honor of Carl Holladay, ed. Patrick Gray and Gail O'Day, Supplements to Novum Testamentum 129 (Leiden: Brill, 2008), 429–55.

8. For a variety of analyses that critically appraise one aspect of New Testament studies in relation to historical constructions of nation-states and state power before, during, and after colonialism, see *Jesus beyond Nationalism: Constructing the Historical Jesus in an Age of Cultural Complexity*, ed. Halvor Moxnes, Ward Blanton, and James G. Crossley, Bible World (London: Equinox, 2009).

9. R. S. Sugirtharajah, "Catching the Post or How I Became an Accidental Theorist," in *Shaping a Global Theological Mind*, ed. Darren C. Marks (Aldershot, U.K.: Ashgate, 2008), 176–85.

10. Within the New Testament canon, the Gospels and Revelation have been prime targets for postcolonial analysis. For recent treatments of Paul, see Robert Paul Seesengood, "Hybridity and the Rhetoric of Endurance: Reading Paul's Athletic Metaphors in a Context of Postcolonial Self-Construction," *Bible and Critical Theory* 1, no. 3 (2005): 1–13; Jeremy Punt, "Paul and Postcolonial Hermeneutics: Marginality and/in Early Biblical Interpretation," in *As It Is Written: Studying Paul's Use of Scripture*, ed. Stanley E. Porter and Christopher D. Stanley, Society of Biblical Literature Symposium Series 50 (Atlanta: Society of Biblical Literature, 2008), 261–90; Joseph A. Marchal, *The Politics of Heaven: Women, Gender, and Empire in the Study of Paul*, Paul in Critical Contexts (Minneapolis: Fortress Press, 2008); and Aliou Cissé Niang, *Faith and Freedom in Galatia and Senegal: The Apostle Paul, Colonists, and Sending Gods*, Biblical Interpretation Series 97 (Leiden: Brill, 2009). Niang in particular describes postcolonial New Testament studies as representing no single approach, but as incorporating a variety of sometimes incongruent methods. The authors in the "Paul and Empire" volumes would not necessarily claim postcolonial orientation, and hardly any of the essays cite postcolonial theories. A notable exception is to be found in Sze-kar Wan, "The Collection for the Saints as an Anti-Colonial Act," in *Paul and Politics: Ekklesia, Israel, Imperium, Interpretation*, ed. Richard A. Horsley (Harrisburg, Pa.: Trinity Press International, 2000), 191–215.

11. See Homi Bhabha, *The Location of Culture* (New York: Routledge, 1994).

12. An example here is Daniel Boyarin's conception of Paul as neither Jew nor Greek, but "Jewgreek" and/or "Greekjew"; such a label is "reminiscent of Bhabha's hybrid" (Seesengood, "Hybridity and the Rhetoric of Endurance," 3). For Boyarin's analysis, which draws largely not on postcolonial theory but on talmudic studies through the lenses of psychoanalytic and Derridean deconstructionist tendencies, see *A Radical Jew: Paul and the Politics of Identity*, Contraversions 1 (Berkeley: University of California Press, 1994).

13. This question appears in feminist New Testament studies as early as Elisabeth Schüssler Fiorenza, *In Memory of Her: A Feminist Theological Reconstruction of Christian Origins* (New York: Crossroad, 1983). Even intersectional approaches that attempt to take feminist agendas and postcolonial theory seriously, together, tend to maintain that attempts to reread Paul for our world are tantamount to "rescuing" or "rehabilitating" a dominating male imperialist Paul. For reviews of such approaches, see Lopez, *Apostle to the Conquered*; and Marchal, *The Politics of Heaven*.

14. See especially Bhabha, *Location of Culture*, 85–92.

15. The work of Fredric Jameson provides useful appraisals of Lacanian analysis in relation to materialist approaches. See especially "Imaginary and Symbolic in Lacan: Marxism, Psychoanalytic Criticism, and the Problem of the Subject," *Yale French Studies* 55/56 (1977): 338–95; idem, *The Political Unconscious: Narrative as a Socially Symbolic Act* (Ithaca: Cornell University Press, 1983); and idem, *Jameson on Jameson: Conversations on Cultural Marxism* (Post-contemporary Interventions; Durham, N.C.: Duke University Press, 2007).

16. Bhabha, *Location of Culture*, 2–5.

17. I develop this argument in relation to the ancient world in "'Before Your Very Eyes': Roman Imperial Ideology, Gender Constructs, and Paul's Internationalism," in *Mapping Gender in Ancient Religious Discourses*, ed. Todd Penner and Caroline Vander Stichele, Biblical Interpretation Series 84

(Leiden: Brill, 2007), 119–62. For a general discussion of visual semiotics, see Jacques Rancière, *The Future of the Image*, trans. Gregory Elliott (London: Verso, 2007); for a discussion of ancient visual semiotics, see Tonio Hölscher, *The Language of Images in Roman Art*, trans. Anthony Snodgrass and Annemarie Künzl-Snodgrass (New York: Cambridge University Press, 2004).

18. For examinations of Roman imperial visual representation in relationship to Paul, see John Dominic Crossan and Jonathan Reed, *In Search of Paul: How Jesus's Apostle Opposed Rome's Empire with God's Kingdom. A New Vision of Paul's Words and World* (San Francisco: HarperSanFrancisco, 2004); Lopez, *Apostle to the Conquered*; Brigitte Kahl, *Galatians Reimagined: Reading with the Eyes of the Vanquished*, Paul in Critical Contexts (Minneapolis: Fortress Press, 2010).

19. Greg Woolf, *Becoming Roman: The Origins of Provincial Civilization in Gaul* (Cambridge: Cambridge University Press, 1998).

20. See the now-classic treatment by Paul Zanker, *The Power of Images in the Age of Augustus*, trans. Alan Shapiro, Jerome Lectures, 16th Series (Ann Arbor: University of Michigan Press, 1990).

21. For an extended discussion and reconstruction of Trajan's Column and Forum, including its excavation history, see James E. Packer, *The Forum of Trajan in Rome: A Study of the Monuments*, California Studies in the History of Art 31 (2 vols.; Berkeley: University of California Press, 1997).

22. For a summary and suggestive argument as to the ritual purpose of the visual program on Trajan's Column, see Penelope J. E. Davies, "The Politics of Perpetuation: Trajan's Column and the Art of Commemoration," *American Journal of Archaeology* 101, no. 1 (1997): 41–65.

23. On the visual problem of Trajan's sculpture program and readability, see Valérie Huet, "Stories One Might Tell of Roman Art: Reading Trajan's Column on the Tiberius Cup," in *Art and Text in Roman Culture*, ed. Jaś Elsner, Cambridge Studies in New Art History and Criticism (New York: Cambridge University Press, 1996), 9–31; see also Caroline Vout, *Power and Eroticism in Imperial Rome* (Cambridge: Cambridge University Press, 2007).

24. For a discussion of the paucity of textually literate individuals in the ancient Greek and Roman worlds, see William V. Harris, *Ancient Literacy* (Cambridge, Mass.: Harvard University Press, 1989); *Orality, Literacy, Memory in the Ancient Greek and Roman World*, ed. E. Anne Mackay, Mnemosyne Supplements 298 (Leiden: Brill, 2008); and *Literacy and Power in the Ancient World*, ed. Alan K. Bowman and Greg Woolf (New York: Cambridge University Press, 2008).

25. For example, J. Louis Martyn states that "[c]onsidering his physique to be a major form of communication, alongside the words of his letter, Paul points literally to his own body. He can do this because his body tells the story of the forward march of the gospel, as do his words" (*Galatians*, Anchor Bible 33A [New York: Doubleday, 1997], 568). For interpreters such as Martyn, the somatic brokenness Paul reports is evidence of his masculine participation in "God's war." More recently, Jeremy Barrier has attempted to argue, using postcolonial approaches, that the "stigmata" in Galatians points to Paul's identification as a slave to Jesus Christ, as a "colonized Jew looking for an alternative language to express his deep need for a master worthy of his loyalty" ("Marks of Oppression: A Postcolonial Reading of Paul's *Stigmata* in Galatians 6:17," *Biblical Interpretation* 16 [2008]: 336–62, here 336). In neither Martyn nor Barrier does the method deployed challenge a desired outcome to see Paul as an early Christian hero.

26. In the second-century *Acts of Paul* we find one of the earliest third-person descriptions of Paul's body: "A man small in size, bald headed, with crooked legs, in a good state of body, with eyebrows meeting, and a rather hooked nose. But full of friendliness, sometimes he seemed like a man, and sometimes he had the face of an angel" (4). See "The Acts of Paul" in *New Testament Apocrypha*, vol. 2, *Writings Relating to the Apostles; Apocalypses and Related Subjects*, ed. Wilhelm Schneemelcher, trans. R. McL. Wilson (rev. ed.; Louisville: Westminster John Knox Press, 1992), 213–70.

27. In 2 Corinthians 11 Paul tells of the "strength out of weakness" of which he can "boast": "among more abundant labors, among more frequent imprisonments, among far more beatings,

among death often. Five times under Judeans I received forty minus one (lashes), I was beaten with rods three times; once I was stoned. Three times I was shipwrecked, for a night and day I was in the deep. On frequent journeys, in danger from rivers, danger from robbers, danger out of (my) race [*ek genous*], danger out of nations [*ek ethnōn*], danger in a city, danger in a desert, danger in a sea, danger among false brothers. By labor and toil, among sleeplessness often, among hunger and thirst, among fastings often, among cold and nakedness" (2 Cor 11:23-27).

28. See Jennifer A. Glancy, "Boasting of Beatings (2 Cor 11.23-25)," *Journal of Biblical Literature* 123, no. 1 (2004): 99–135. Glancy concludes that "many scholars identify Paul's scars as tokens of virtue.... Within a Roman *habitus*, scars that established a man's virtue or virility were typically incurred in battle. Display of war wounds was a common feature of Roman somatic rhetoric. Those habituated to a first-century corporal idiom distinguished between a breast pierced in battle and a back belted by a whip: not every scarred body told a war story. Whippability was a token not of honor, excellence, or virility, but of dishonor, abasement, and servility. In analyzing Paul's boasting of beatings, scholars often cite examples of heroism attested by wounded bodies, although they do not always acknowledge the martial context of those wounds. Scholars have, moreover, passed over the semiotic distinction between a battle-scarred body and a flogged body" (p. 134). On this passage and gender constructs, see also Jennifer Larson, "Paul's Masculinity," *Journal of Biblical Literature* 123, no. 1 (2004): 85–97.

29. Christ also occupies the "slave" position in Phil 2:6-11, the so-called "Christ hymn." Such weakness, however, is exalted by God. The extra worldwide dominion of Jesus expressed in the hymn is reminiscent of the universal reach of Caesar predicted in Virgil's *Aeneid*; however, the dominion of Jesus comes from a position of punishment and weakness and not military strength.

30. Paul calls for "imitation" from his communities (1 Thess 1:6-7, 2:14; Phil 3:17; 1 Cor 4:16, 11:1), but such imitation is not without resultant power relationships and possible hierarchies of its own. When examining Paul's own rhetoric in its Roman imperial context and shelving the overtheologized implications of Paul's "conversion" experience, we must ask what precisely is being imitated and what is at stake in such imitation.

31. For a discussion of the "mimesis" pattern in Paul's rhetoric, see Elizabeth A. Castelli, *Imitating Paul: A Discourse of Power*, Literary Currents in Biblical Interpretation (Louisville: Westminster/John Knox, 1991). Her argument rightly locates Paul's rhetoric as discursively constructing relationships between the apostle and his communities, which are never innocent or unimplicated in the maintenance of power dynamics.

32. Beverly Roberts Gaventa, *Our Mother Saint Paul* (Louisville: Westminster John Knox, 2007), 29–39.

33. For a discussion of how our engagement of the ancient world is ultimately about defining our relationship with that world, see Mary Beard and John Henderson, *Classics: A Very Short Introduction* (New York: Oxford University Press, 1995).

34. Kautsky, *Foundations of Christianity*, 4.

7. Reading Romans 7 in Conversation with Postcolonial Theory

This article was originally published in *Theoforum* 35, no. 2 (2004): 173–94, and is republished here with permission.

1. The paper was presented at a conference at Codrington College, Barbados.

2. The *Oxford English Dictionary* defines *analogy* in the context of biology as the "resemblance of function between organs essentially different."

3. Frantz Fanon, *Black Skin, White Masks*, trans. Charles Lam Markmann (New York: Grove, 1967).

4. Leela Gandhi, *Postcolonial Theory: A Critical Introduction* (New York: Columbia University Press, 1998), 21.

5. Fanon writes: "In no way should I dedicate myself to the revival of an unjustly unrecognized Negro civilization. I will not make myself the man of any past. I do not want to exalt the past at the expense of my present and of my future.... I am not a prisoner of history. I should not seek there for the meaning of my destiny. I should constantly remind myself that the real *leap* consists in introducing invention into existence. In the world through which I travel, I am endlessly creating myself" (*Black Skin, White Masks*, 226, 229).

6. Fanon ends his remarkable book *The Wretched of the Earth* (trans. C. Farrington; New York: Grove Press, 1963), with this call: "For Europe, for ourselves, and for humanity, comrades, we must turn over a new leaf, we must work out new concepts, and try to set afoot a new man" (p. 316).

7. Noted by L. Gandhi, *Postcolonial Theory*, 130.

8. See Robert J. C. Young, *Colonial Desire: Hybridity in Theory, Culture and Race* (London and New York: Routledge, 1995), 1-28, for a history of the idea of hybridity in biology, linguistics, and cultural politics.

9. Homi Bhabha, "The Third Space," in *Identity: Community, Culture, Difference*, ed. Jonathan Rutherford (London: Lawrence & Wishart, 1990), 211. See also idem, *The Location of Culture* (London and New York: Routledge, 1994).

10. Bhabha's understanding of hybridity is complex. I have here alluded to only one aspect of it. See Patrick Colm Hogan's critique of Bhabha in *Colonialism and Cultural Identity: Crises of Tradition in the Anglophone Literatures of India, Africa, and the Caribbean*, SUNY Series, Explorations in Postcolonial Studies (Albany: State University of New York Press, 2000), 24-43.

11. See Stuart Hall, "Cultural Identity and Diaspora," in Rutherford, *Identity*, 222-37.

12. R. S. Sugirtharajah, *Asian Biblical Hermeneutics and Postcolonialism: Contesting the Interpretations*, Bible and Liberation (Maryknoll, N.Y.: Orbis, 1998), 16-17.

13. Hogan, *Colonialism and Cultural Identity*, 2-17.

14. There is no explicit contradiction between this understanding and that of Rom 1:28. Romans 1:28 does not talk about how or when sin entered the world, but deals simply with God's giving of humanity up to it.

15. Perhaps one of the reasons scholars shy away from regarding this passage as Paul speaking in a Christian voice is that they presume that the Christian life should not contain such challenges.

16. Fanon, *Black Skin, White Masks*, 219.

17. Georg F. W. Hegel, *The Phenomenology of Mind*, trans. J. B. Baillie (2nd rev. ed.; London: Allen & Unwin, 1949), 233.

18. J. Louis Martyn rightly describes as "dominant" the view that in Romans 7 Paul is describing the human condition apart from Christ ("A Formula for Communal Discord as a Clue to the Nature of Pastoral Guidance," in *Putting Body & Soul Together: Essays in Honor of Robin Scroggs*, ed. Virginia Wiles, Alexandra Brown and Graydon F. Snyder [Valley Forge, Pa.: Trinity Press International, 1997], 208).

19. Among the contemporary scholars who hold this view are C. E. B. Cranfield (*A Critical and Exegetical Commentary on the Epistle to the Romans*, International Critical Commentary [2 vols.; Edinburgh: T&T Clark, 1975], 1:330-70), James D. G. Dunn (*Romans 1-8*, Word Biblical Commentary 38A [Dallas: Word Books, 1988], 357-412), A. Segal ("Romans 7 and Jewish Dietary Law," *Studies in Religion/Sciences religieuses* 15, no. 3 [1986]: 361-74), D. B. Garlington ("Romans 7:14-25 and the Creation Theology of Paul," *Trinity Journal* 11 [1990]: 197-235), and Mark A. Seifrid ("The Subject of Rom 7:14-25," *Novum Testamentum* 34 [1992]: 314-33).

20. In Romans 4 Paul discusses Abraham, and in Romans 5 he discusses Adam and mentions Moses.

21. Paul Meyer, for instance, views 7:14 as conclusive proof that Paul is speaking about the non-Christian life ("The Worm at the Core of the Apple: Exegetical Reflections on Romans 7," in *The Conversation Continues: Studes in Paul and John in Honor of J. Louis Martyn*, ed. Robert T. Fortna and Beverly Roberts Gaventa [Nashville: Abingdon, 1990], 67).

22. In ch. 6 Paul repeatedly commands his hearers to consider themselves dead to sin (v. 11), to take charge and simply not let sin reign in their bodies (v. 12), to act as if they had been brought from death to life (v. 13) and so give their members as weapons in service of the righteousness of God (v. 13).

23. Fanon, *Black Skin, White Masks*, 197.

24. This interpretation will be argued for below.

25. Even those, like Meyer, who divide 7:7-25 into two parts (vv. 7-12 and 14-25, with v. 13 as a transition) see these verses working sequentially toward what he calls Paul's antithetical climax in 7:25b. Meyer calls these two parts "movements" ("Worm at the Core," 73).

26. Ernst Käsemann makes the curious claim that *anazaō* "*naturally* means 'awake', not 'come to life again'" (*Commentary on Romans*, trans. Geoffrey W. Bromiley [Grand Rapids: Eerdmans, 1980], 197 [italics mine]; cf. the German text: "ἀνέζησεν in 9a meint natürlich 'erwachen', nicht 'wiederaufleben'" (*An die Römer*, Handbuch zum Neuen Testament 8A [Tübingen: Mohr, 1973], 189). Though the Bauer-Arndt-Gingrich-Danker lexicon interprets Rom 7:9 this way, Liddell-Scott-Jones takes the word to mean what I take to be its more natural meaning: "return to life, be alive again."

27. Contra Meyer, who translates *chōris nomou* in 7:8b-9 as, "in the absence of the law," equating the sense to that of 5:13 ("Worm at the Core," 73). In 5:13, however, Paul writes *achri nomou*.

28. See above for discussion about how the kind of death about which Paul speaks in 7:9 is different from the death to which he refers in 5:12-14.

29. So Joseph A. Fitzmyer, *Romans: A New Translation with Introduction and Commentary*, Anchor Bible 33 (New York: Doubleday, 1993), 131, 145; W. Bauer, W. F. Arndt, F. W. Gingrich, and F. W. Danker, *Greek-English Lexicon of the New Testament and Other Early Christian Literature* (Chicago: University of Chicago Press, 1979), s.v. νόμος 2; W. Gutbrod, νόμος, *Theological Dictionary of the New Testament*, ed. G. Kittell and G. Friedrich, trans. G. W. Bromiley (10 vols.; Grand Rapids: Eerdmans, 1964–76), 4:1071.

30. A seeming exception to this statement might be Rom 10:5. This verse, however, is part of the explanation that Paul gives to his statement in 10:4 that the righteousness by faith, as manifested in Christ, is the goal and completion of the law. Leviticus 18:5 is used by Paul as part of his proof that the law's goal of life is realized only by faith in Christ, the one who perfectly obeyed the law. See Cranfield, *Romans;* Richard B. Hays, *Echoes of Scripture in the Letters of Paul* (New Haven: Yale University Press, 1989), 76–77.

31. This fact is noticed by Dunn, who uses the appeal to the Adam narrative to "solve" the problem (*Romans 1–8*, 384).

32. The only possible exception to Paul reserving the concept of "life" for Christian existence is 1 Cor 15:45, where Paul refers to the first man Adam becoming a "living soul."

33. See Cranfield, *Romans*, 1:66, for a summary of the main options.

34. D. B. Garlington, *The Obedience of Faith: A Pauline Phrase in Historical Context*, Wissenschaftliche Untersuchungen zum Neuen Testament 2/38 (Tübingen: Mohr Siebeck, 1991), 1 n. 4.

35. As C. K. Barrett wisely puts it, for Paul "obedience has a place in the system of grace and faith" (*A Commentary on the Epistle to the Romans*, Black's New Testament Commentaries [London: A. & C. Black, 1957], 131).

36. So Cranfield, *Romans*, 1:324.

37. For the purposes of this article we do not need to enter the debate over whether Paul's *egō* statements in Romans 7 are autobiographical or representative. Either option amounts to the same

thing in the context of my argument; if Paul is talking only about himself, he is doing so in order to clarify matters for his fellow Jews. If the *egō* is representative, its purpose is also to clarify matters for other Jewish believers.

38. He describes this experience also in Gal 2:16: "I through the law died to the law, that I might live to God."

39. Paul's task in 1 Corinthians is to announce to some in Corinth that the honeymoon is, in fact, over—while faith in Christ may mean that all things are now lawful, it does not give permission to be selfish. In fact, faith in Christ demands righteousness—putting the good of the other before one's desires (1 Cor 10:23-24).

40. For example, Meyer, "Worm at the Core."

41. It should also be distinguished from Paul's statements judging the human condition, as in 3:9. Romans 7:14 is, rather, a statement of self-awareness.

42. Romans 6 is an extended exhortation on this very problem.

43. So Martin Luther, *Commentary on the Epistle to the Romans*, trans. J. T. Mueller (Grand Rapids: Kregel, 1954), 112.

44. Life in the Spirit is the fulfilling of the decree of the law (8:4); pleasing God is being obedient to God's law (8:7-8); love is the fulfilling of the law (13:10).

8. Paul the Ethnic Hybrid?

1. The seminal work in this area is *Ethnic Groups and Boundaries: The Social Organization of Culture Difference*, ed. Frederik Barth (Boston: Little, Brown, 1969). Other classic studies include Richard A. Schermerhorn, *Comparative Ethnic Relations: A Framework for Theory and Research* (New York: Random House, 1970); Henri Tajfel, ed., *Social Identity and Intergroup Relations*, European Studies in Social Psychology (Cambridge: Cambridge University Press; Paris: Editions de la Maison des Sciences de l'Homme, 1982); Anya Peterson Royce, *Ethnic Identity: Strategies of Diversity* (Bloomington: Indiana University Press, 1982); and Richard Jenkins, *Rethinking Ethnicity: Arguments and Explorations* (London: SAGE, 1997).

2. This is not to say that the political context of ethnic tensions in the early Christian movement has been entirely neglected; many scholars, for example, have sought to explain Paul's letter to the Romans by positing the existence of ethnic tensions between Jewish and Gentile Christians as a result of an earlier (political) expulsion of Jews from Rome. But virtually no use has been made of the theoretical tools and insights of social-scientific and postcolonial analysis in these studies. (For an exception to this pattern, see Philip F. Esler, *Conflict and Identity in Romans: The Social Setting of Paul's Letter* [Minneapolis: Fortress Press, 2003].) More recently, a few scholars have begun to explore the political context of Paul's ethnic language in the letter to the Galatians: see, for example, Mark D. Nanos, "The Inter- and Intra-Jewish Political Context of Paul's Letter to the Galatians," in *Paul and Politics: Ekklesia, Israel, Imperium, Interpretation. Essays in Honor of Krister Stendahl*, ed. Richard A. Horsley (Harrisburg, Pa.: Trinity Press International, 2000), 146–59; Davina C. Lopez, *Apostle to the Conquered: Reimagining Paul's Mission*, Paul in Critical Contexts (Minneapolis: Fortress Press, 2008); Brigitte Kahl, *Galatians Re-Imagined: Reading with the Eyes of the Vanquished*, Paul in Critical Contexts (Minneapolis: Fortress Press, 2010).

3. A broader discussion of these and related questions will be presented in a monograph that I am currently preparing under the title *Neither Jew Nor Greek: Ethnic Rhetoric in the Letters of Paul*.

4. Some postcolonial theorists use the terms "imperialism" and "colonialism" as virtual synonyms, while others apply the former term to systems in which the dominant party exercises its power from a distant territory and the latter to forms of control that involve creating residential settlements

in the homeland of the dominated party. See Edward Said, *Culture and Imperialism* (New York: Knopf, 1993), 9.

5. For more on these themes, see the materials cited in the discussion of "hybridity" below.

6. Despite the common association of the concept of hybridity with Bhabha's name, similar ideas had been voiced by others before him; see the comments in Ulf Hannertz, "Flows, Boundaries, and Hybrids: Keywords in Transnational Anthropology," available for download at http://www.transcomm.ox.ac.uk/working%20papers/hannerz.pdf, 12–15 (accessed January 28, 2010), and especially Vince P. Marotta, "The Hybrid Self and the Ambivalence of Boundaries," *Social Identities* 14 (2008): 295–312.

7. A number of his most important works have been collected into a volume entitled *The Location of Culture* (London and New York: Routledge, 1994).

8. Bhabha offers a trenchant philosophical and psychoanalytic critique of the nature and operation of colonial discourse in his essay, "The Other Question: Stereotype, Discrimination, and the Discourse of Colonialism," in *Location of Culture*, 94–120.

9. As Bhabha puts it, "What is irremediably estranging in the presence of the hybrid . . . is that the difference of cultures can no longer be identified or evaluated as object of epistemological or moral contemplation: cultural differences are simply not *there* to be seen or appropriated" (*Location of Culture*, 163 [emphasis his]).

10. Bhabha, *Location of Culture*, 5.

11. The phrase comes from the title of one of Bhabha's essays ("How Newness Enters the World: Postmodern Space, Postcolonial Times, and the Trials of Cultural Translation"), published in *Location of Culture*, 303–37, which in turn alludes to a statement made by the author Salman Rushdie regarding his novel *The Satanic Verses*: "*The Satanic Verses* celebrates hybridity, impurity, intermingling, the transformation that comes of new and unexpected combinations of human beings, cultures, ideas, politics, movies, songs. It rejoices in mongrelization and fears the absolutism of the Pure. *Mélange*, hotchpotch, a bit of this and bit of that is *how newness enters the world*" (*Imaginary Homelands: Essays and Criticism 1981–1991* [London: Granta, 1991], 393 [emphasis his]). Bhabha makes a similar pronouncement using different terminology: "The borderline work of culture demands an encounter with 'newness' that is not part of the continuum of past and present. It creates a sense of the new as an insurgent act of cultural translation. . . . It renews the past, refiguring it as a contingent 'in-between' space, that innovates and interrupts the performance of the present" (*Location of Culture*, 10).

12. See, for example, his discussion of Fanon in *Location of Culture*, 57–93, which focuses primarily on Fanon's 1952 book, *Black Skins, White Masks* (introduction by Homi K. Bhaba [London: Pluto, 1986]). Elsewhere, Bhabha reveals a principled objection to the model of revolutionary struggle on the grounds that it simply reinscribes the binary mind-set of the colonizer; see his treatment of Fredric Jameson's Marxist analysis in *Location of Culture*, 303–37.

13. Perhaps this is what he had in mind when making statements such as the following: "The language of critique is effective . . . to the extent to which it opens up a space of translation: a place of hybridity, figuratively speaking, where the construction of a political object that is new, *neither the one nor the other*, properly alienates our political expectations, and changes, as it must, the very forms of our recognition of the moment of politics" (*Location of Culture*, 37 [emphasis his]). For a discussion of the problems and prospects of using psychoanalysis as a tool for analyzing colonial and postcolonial cultures, see Ania Loomba, *Colonialism/Postcolonialism* (London and New York: Routledge, 1998), 133–51.

14. Bhabha, *Location of Culture*, 122 (emphasis his).

15. Ibid., 165. Bhabha offers a lengthy discussion of "mimicry" in *Location of Culture*, 121–44,

but he focuses primarily on how it implicitly undermines colonial discourse rather than how it might function as a strategy of resistance to colonial rule.

16. The classic example is his description of Indians questioning the authority of the Bible in the essay, "Signs Taken for Wonders," reprinted in *Location of Culture*, 145–74. Here he speaks of the natives "challenging the boundaries of discourse and subtly changing its terms by setting up another specifically colonial space of the negotiations of colonial authority" (ibid., 169).

17. Bhabha, *Location of Culture*, 172. In a 1989 interview, Bhabha offered a similarly vague assessment of the disruptive potential of hybridity: "This third space displaces the histories that constitute it, and sets up new structures of authority, new political initiatives, which are inadequately understood through received wisdom" ("The Third Space: Interview with Homi Bhabha," in *Identity: Community, Culture, Difference*, ed. Jonathan Rutherford [London: Lawrence & Wishart, 1990], 211).

18. Helpful discussions of the former point can be found in John Hutnyk, "Hybridity," *Ethnic and Racial Studies* 28 (2005): 81–83; Virinder S. Kalra, Raminder Kaur, and John Hutnyk, *Diaspora & Hybridity* (London: SAGE, 2005), 42–45, 88–89; and David Huddart, "Hybridity and Cultural Rights: Inventing Global Citizenship," in *Reconstructing Hybridity: Post-Colonial Studies in Transition*, ed. Joel Kuortti and Jopi Nyman, Text: Studies in Comparative Literature 51 (Amsterdam and New York: Rodopi, 2007), 21–23. On the latter point, see Floya Anthias, "New Hybridities, Old Concepts: The Limits of 'Culture,'" *Ethnic and Racial Studies* 24 (2001): 622, 637. Katharyne Mitchell, who is deeply disturbed by the abstract nature of recent discussions of hybridity, goes so far as to question the very existence of the "third space" that is so central to Bhabha's theorizing: "This space is able to accomplish all of these marvelous things, precisely because it does not actually exist" ("Different Diasporas and the Hype of Hybridity," in *Critical Geographies: A Collection of Readings*, ed. Harald Bauder and Salvatore Engle-DiMauro [Kelowna, B.C.: Praxis (e)Press, 2008]: 258 n. 3; available online at http://www.praxis-epress.org/availablebooks/introcriticalgeog.html [accessed January 28, 2010]).

19. Anthias, "New Hybridities," 638; cf. 630. Anthias presents an alternate model of "translocational positionality" that aims to take seriously the situational elements of colonial and postcolonial encounters and relationships (ibid., 633–35). This model holds significant promise for the study of "hybridity" in Paul's letters, but its potential relevance exceeds the boundaries of the present investigation. A similar sensitivity to the situated nature of hybridization can be seen in Marotta, "Hybrid Self," 305–9, and Mitchell, "Different Diasporas," 257–61.

20. John Hutnyk's criticism is especially trenchant; in his view, "syncretism and hybridity are academic conceptual tools providing an alibi for lack of attention to politics, in a project designed to manage the cultural consequences of colonization and globalization" ("Hybridity," 92). Later he claims that "hybridity lulls us to sleep." Similar types of criticism have been voiced by other scholars, including Anthias, "New Hybridities," 630–31, 637; Marotta, "Hybrid Self," 296–97; and Jin Hee Han, "Homi K. Bhabha and the Mixed Blessing of Hybridity in Biblical Hermeneutics," *Bible and Critical Theory* 1 (2005): 37.1–37.12.

21. Cf. Anthias, "New Hybridities," 626–31; Sabine Broeck, "White Fatigue, or, Supplementary Notes on Hybridity," in Kuortti and Nyman, *Reconstructing Hybridity*, 50–51; Joseph A. Marchal, *The Politics of Heaven: Women, Gender, and Empire in the Study of Paul*, Paul in Critical Contexts (Minneapolis: Fortress Press, 2007), 79–90; and the collection of essays in *Postcolonial Feminist Theory: A Reader*, ed. Reina Lewis and Sara Mills (London and New York: Routledge, 2003).

22. Christian Karner, *Ethnicity and Everyday Life*, New Sociology (London and New York: Routledge, 2007), 95. A number of theorists have argued that the discourse about "hybridity" says more about the experience of displaced native elites who now live in the West than about the everyday experience of real people in formerly colonized countries; see Gayatri Chakravorty Spivak, *A*

Critique of Postcolonial Reason: Toward a History of the Vanishing Present (Cambridge, Mass.: Harvard University Press, 2003), 358–60, 373; Rajagopalan Radhakrishnan, *Diasporic Meditations: Between Home and Locations* (Minneapolis: University of Minnesota Press, 1996), 174; Benita Parry, "Problems in Current Theories of Colonial Discourse," in *Postcolonialism: Critical Concepts in Literary and Cultural Studies*, ed. Diana Brydon (5 vols.; London and New York: Routledge, 2000), 2:731–33; Jonathan Friedman, "Global Crises, the Struggle for Cultural Identity, and Intellectual Porkbarreling: Cosmopolitans Versus Locals, Ethnics and Nationals in an Era of De-Hegemonisation," in *Debating Cultural Hybridity: Multi-Cultural Identities and the Politics of Anti-Racism*, ed. Pnina Werbner and Tariq Modood, Postcolonial Encounters (London: Zed Books, 1997), 70–89; and Kalra, Kaur, and Hutnyk, *Diaspora & Identity*, 101.

23. See the discussions in Ien Ang, "Together-in-Difference: Beyond Diaspora, Into Hybridity," *Asian Studies Review* 27 [2003]: 141–46; Sean Carter, "The Geopolitics of Diaspora," *Area* 37 (2005): 54–63; Sunil Bhatia and Anjali Ram, "Culture, Hybridity, and the Dialogical Self: Cases from the South Asian Diaspora," *Mind, Culture, and Activity* 11 (2004): 224–40; Anthias, "New Hybridities," 622–24, 628–29.

24. The point is discussed briefly in Anthias, "New Hybridities," 624–25. Robert Young raises a parallel point about whether postcolonial critics have oversimplified matters by neglecting the variety of ways in which colonialism was performed by (ethnically) different European powers; for example, the French worked from a much more egalitarian view of humanity than the race-conscious British. See *Colonial Desire: Hybridity in Theology, Culture and Race* (London and New York: Routledge, 1995), 164–65.

25. The same can be said about "hybridity" in general; see Anthias, "New Hybridities," 628: "Hybrid cultural forms are not necessarily more desirable or progressive than others. Hybrids ... may be tied to violence and alienation, as receivers or producers." So also Mitchell, "Different Diasporas," 258; Kalra, Kaur, and Hutnyk, *Diaspora & Hybridity*, 42–45.

26. See, for example, Raka Shome, "Thinking Through the Diaspora: Call Centers, India, and a New Politics of Hybridity," *International Journal of Cultural Studies* 9 (2006): 105–24; Mitchell, "Different Diasporas," 257–77; Bhatia and Ram, "Culture, Hybridity, and the Dialogical Self," 229–38. The reason for this weakness in Bhabha's analysis is not hard to see; as Dimple Godiwala cogently observes, "The previously colonized subject—who is the locus of Bhabha's theory of the mimic—mimics because he or she has internalized the notion that their cultural values are inferior to that of the colonials" ("Postcolonial Desire: Mimicry, Hegemony, Hybridity," in Joel Kuortti and Jopi Nyman, ed., *Reconstructing Hybridity: Post-Colonial Studies in Transition* (Amsterdam: Rodopi, 2007), 61. Similar concerns have been raised about the application of Bhabha's theories on mimicry to the early Christian writings by Joseph Marchal (*Politics of Heaven*, 54–57, 71–73, 78–79), and Tat-siong Benny Liew ("Tyranny, Boundary and Might: Colonial Mimicry in Mark's Gospel," *Journal for the Study of the New Testament* 73 [1999]: 7–31), among others.

27. Even postcolonial analysis that focuses entirely on modern Western colonialism assumes a certain degree of cross-cultural similarity among various colonial/postcolonial situations. The very idea of "hybridity" is rooted in a series of universalizing generalizations about the inevitable effects of Western colonialism on those who participate in it.

28. Cf. Ien Ang: "Hybridity is a heuristic device for analysing complicated entanglement" ("Together-in-Difference," 150).

29. A review of what contemporary social scientists mean by "ethnicity" is beyond the scope of this paper. For more on this topic, see Christopher D. Stanley, "The Ethnic Context of Paul's Letters," in *Christian Origins and Hellenistic Judaism: Social and Literary Contexts for the New Testament*, ed. Stanley E. Porter and Andrew W. Pitts, Early Christianity in Its Hellenistic Context 2 (Leiden: Brill, 2011). Solid introductions can also be found in Esler, *Conflict and Identity*, 19–33, 40–53,

and Denise Kimber Buell, *Why This New Race: Ethnic Reasoning in Early Christianity* (New York: Columbia University Press, 2005), 1–33.

30. For a helpful discussion of the ethnic diversity of Paul's world, see Richard Wallace and Wynne Williams, *The Three Worlds of Paul of Tarsus* (London and New York: Routledge, 1998), though their "three worlds" scenario overlooks the substantial presence of immigrant groups in the Greek *poleis*. As members of the local community of *Ioudaioi* (that is, people who traced their ultimate origins to Judea), Paul's family would have fallen into this latter group, assuming that the book of Acts is correct in placing Paul's origins in Tarsus.

31. For a glimpse into the bewildering ethnic diversity of the native population of Asia Minor in Paul's day as seen by a native of the region, see Strabo, *Geogr.* 12–14; cf. the helpful analysis by Stephen Mitchell in *Anatolia: Land, Men, and Gods in Asia Minor* (2 vols.; Oxford: Clarendon, 1993), 1:171–76. Our familiarity with the native populations is rather limited for many parts of the Greco-Roman world, since most of them left little or no literary remains (the natives of Judea and Greece are obvious exceptions) and much of the information that we do have comes from biased or even hostile sources.

32. Even in Roman colonies, the extent of the Roman presence varied widely, depending on whether the colony was a new foundation or a reorganization of a native or Greek town or city.

33. The Greek word *Ioudaioi* is left untranslated here and elsewhere in order to avoid prejudging the question of whether the term is better translated "Jews" or "Judeans," a question that can be answered only by a careful analysis of individual passages.

34. The distinction here is more apparent than real; the native population of Greece in Paul's day was the product of a long history of ethnic conflict and mixing that is veiled by the designation of its inhabitants as *Hellēnes*, a term that first came to prominence in the fifth century B.C.E. as a rallying point for resistance to the Persian invaders. Regional ethnic identities remained salient for many of the residents of Hellas into the Roman period. A more nuanced study would show that the same was true for many of the other areas where Paul traveled.

35. For a more detailed analysis of Paul's ethnic terminology, see Caroline Johnson Hodge, *If Sons, Then Heirs: A Study of Kinship and Ethnicity in the Letters of Paul* (Oxford: Oxford University Press, 2007), 43–66, though her categorizations and conclusions are not identical to those presented here.

36. For more on the ethnic significance of *Galatai* and *Makedones*, see the first article cited in n. 29.

37. The ethnic significance of Paul's use of the terms *Hellēn/Hellēnes* will be explored further in the book cited in n. 3. A preliminary discussion can be found in the article cited in n. 29.

38. In a couple of instances Paul uses geographic place-names metaphorically to refer to the Christian residents of a region (Rom 15:26; 2 Cor 9:2), but most such references are entirely geographic, with no evident ethnic overtones.

39. Esler, *Conflict and Identity*, 59.

40. Josephus, *Ant.* 18.9.9; 20.8.7; 20.8.9; *J.W.* 1.4.3; 2.13.7; 2.18.2; 7.8.7; Philo, *Leg.* 166, 200–201, 205.

41. Josephus, *Ant.* 1.3.9; 4.2.1; 8.11.3; 11.7.1; 15.5.3; 16.6.8; 18.1.5; *J.W.* 5.1.3; 6.3.3; Philo, *Opif.* 128; *Ebr.* 193; *Conf.* 190; *Mut.* 35; *Abr.* 136; and others.

42. Johnson Hodge speaks briefly about one aspect of this phenomenon, noting that "Paul commonly uses the first-person plural 'we' to indicate that he identifies with his Gentile audience" (*If Sons, Then Heirs*, 71). She explains this practice by pointing to the ancient pedagogical strategy of "adaptability," whereby philosophical teachers would temporarily adapt themselves to "the dispositions, characters, and identities of different types of students" in order to lead them toward a greater apprehension of the truth (ibid., 124–25). This explanation is insufficient, however, insofar as it isolates one aspect of Paul's self-presentation as a "Gentile" and ignores the other data presented here.

43. This is true even if Paul was referring to the contemporary inhabitants of Judea and not *Ioudaioi* as a class, since the ambiguity of his language could allow for either construction.

44. The literature on how *Ioudaioi* were viewed in the ancient world is vast; recent treatments include Erich S. Gruen, *Diaspora: Jews Amidst Greeks and Romans* (Cambridge, Mass.: Harvard University Press, 2002); Peter Schäfer, *Judeophobia: Attitudes Toward the Jews in the Ancient World* (Cambridge, Mass.: Harvard University Press, 1997); and Louis H. Feldman, *Jew and Gentile in the Ancient World: Attitudes and Interactions from Alexander to Justinian* (Princeton: Princeton University Press, 1993).

45. See the studies cited in the previous note.

46. Robert Seesengood, "Hybridity and the Rhetoric of Endurance: Reading Paul's Athletic Metaphors in a Context of Postcolonial Self-Construction," *Bible and Critical Theory* 1 (2005): 16.2-3, repeated with slight variation in idem, *Competing Identities: The Athlete and the Gladiator in Early Christianity*, Library of New Testament Studies 346, Playing the Texts 12 (New York and London: T&T Clark, 2006), 23. Seesengood draws on Bhabha's notion of hybridity to explain the way Paul handled Greco-Roman athletic imagery in his letter; he offers no critique of Bhabha's views.

47. Daniel Boyarin, *A Radical Jew: Paul and the Politics of Identity*, Contraversions 1 (Berkeley, Calif.: University of California Press, 1994), 78-79.

48. This latter point receives extended attention in Benny Liew's article in the present volume.

49. Of course, this does not mean that Paul was somehow a more "pure" Jew than Philo. All Jews in Paul's day had been "hybridized" to varying degrees by their long exposure to Greek political and cultural domination.

50. A full demonstration of the following points must await the completion of the book cited in n. 3.

51. Johnson Hodge makes a similar point about Paul arguing for the precedence of identity "in Christ" over all other forms of identity, including ethnic identity (*If Sons, Then Heirs*, 103-6, 125-34).

52. For a good recent summary of the data on Roman views of non-Romans, see Benjamin Isaac, *The Invention of Racism in Classical Antiquity* (Princeton: Princeton University Press, 2004). A somewhat older study that is still useful is J. P. V. D. Balsdon, *Romans and Aliens* (Chapel Hill: University of North Carolina Press, 1979), 30-71.

53. For a helpful summary of the evidence, see Esler, *Conflict and Identity*, 54-61. More extensive treatments can be found in Edith Hall, *Inventing the Barbarian: Greek Self-Definition through Tragedy*, Oxford Classical Monographs (Oxford: Clarendon, 1989); Jonathan M. Hall, *Ethnic Identity in Greek Antiquity* (Cambridge: Cambridge University Press, 2000), 34-66, and idem, *Hellenicity: Between Ethnicity and Culture* (Chicago: University of Chicago Press, 2002), 173-225; T. J. Haarhoff, *The Stranger at the Gate: Aspects of Exclusiveness and Co-operation in Ancient Greece and Rome, with Some Reference to Modern Times* (London: Longmans, Green, 1938), 6-59; and Aubrey Diller, *Race Mixture among the Greeks before Alexander*, Illinois Studies in Language and Literature 20.1-2 (Urbana: University of Illinois Press, 1937), 14-56.

54. On the gradual redefinition of "Greekness" after Alexander, see Haarhoff, *Stranger*, 60-117. The often-quoted statement of Isocrates on this theme (*Paneg.* 50) is actually earlier than Alexander: "So far has our city [Athens] distanced the rest of mankind in thought and in speech that her pupils have become teachers of the rest of the world, and she has brought it about that the name 'Hellenes' no longer suggests a race but an intelligence." But it would be wrong to take this as a de-ethnicization of the term "Greek," since even Isocrates remained an implacable foe of all things "barbarian": in the very same text he speaks of the need to "reduce all the Barbarians to a state of subjection to the whole of Hellas" (*Paneg.* 131, quoted in Haarhoff, *Stranger*, 60).

55. Joseph Marchal, viewing Paul through a postcolonial feminist lens, has recently called attention to the prevalence of binary thinking in many other aspects of Paul's thought and rhetoric (*Politics*

of Heaven, 48–57, 76–79). In these cases, Marchal argues that Paul is in fact mimicking and reinscribing the rhetoric of inequality and domination that characterized the Roman imperial authorities. This might well be true in the cases that he is analyzing, but it is less likely in the case of Paul's thinking about ethnicity, since there is little evidence that the Roman authorities viewed ethnicity through a binary lens and the influence of Jewish and Greek models offers a simpler explanation. Johnson Hodge (*If Sons, Then Heirs*, 48–65) limits her analysis to Paul's Jewish influences; her book has virtually nothing to say about the broader phenomenon of interethnic tensions and prejudice within Greco-Roman society.

56. See especially Anthias, "New Hybridities," and Marotta, "Hybrid Self." The value of their approaches will be discussed in the book project cited in n. 3.

9. Redressing Bodies in Corinth

This essay is a slightly revised version of chapter 5 of my book *What Is Asian-American Biblical Hermeneutics? Reading the New Testament*, Intersections: Asian and Pacific American Transcultural Studies by Tat-siong Benny Liew, copyright © 2008 University of Hawaii Press. Used by permission.

1. David Palumbo-Liu, *Asian/American: Historical Crossings of a Racial Frontier* (Stanford: Stanford University Press, 1999), 24.

2. Susan Bordo, "The Body and the Reproduction of Femininity: A Feminist Appropriation of Foucault," in *Gender/Body/Knowledge: Feminist Reconstructions of Being and Knowing*, ed. Alison M. Jaggar and Susan R. Bordo (New Brunswick, N.J.: Rutgers University Press, 1989), 13. See also Sidonie Smith, *Subjectivity, Identity, and the Body: Women's Autobiographical Practices in the Twentieth Century* (Bloomington: Indiana University Press, 1993).

3. See Neil T. Gotanda, "Citizenship Nullification: The Impossibility of Asian American Politics," in *Asian Americans and Politics: Perspectives, Experiences, Prospects*, ed. Gordon H. Chang (Stanford: Stanford University Press, 2001), 79–101; Lisa Lowe, *Immigrant Acts: On Asian American Cultural Politics* (Durham, N.C.: Duke University Press, 1996); David L. Eng, *Racial Castration: Managing Masculinity in Asian America*, Perverse Modernities (Durham, N.C.: Duke University Press, 2001).

4. Aihwa Ong, *Buddha Is Hiding: Refugees, Citizenship, the New America*, California Series in Public Anthropology 5 (Berkeley: University of California Press, 2003).

5. Sharon A. Suh, *Being Buddhist in a Christian World: Gender and Community in a Korean American Temple*, American Ethnic and Cultural Studies (Seattle: University of Washington Press, 2004).

6. In addition to featuring two different ethnic groups within "Asian Americans," there is yet another important difference between the work of Ong and Suh. While Suh, comparatively speaking, concentrates on the dynamics between Korean American Buddhists and Korean American Christians, Ong pays greater attention to the dynamics between Cambodian Americans and European Americans. Both, however, use the language of "hiding" to communicate the marginal position occupied and felt by a religious minority group, whether in relationship to a co-ethnic group or an entirely different racial/ethnic group; see Suh, *Being Buddhist*, 4, 165, 187, 195, and note the title of Ong's book (*Buddha Is Hiding*).

7. See the discussions in Iris Marion Young, *Justice and the Politics of Difference* (Princeton: Princeton University Press, 1990); and Linda Schlossberg, "Introduction: Rites of Passing," in *Passing: Identity and Interpretation in Sexuality, Race and Religion*, ed. María Carla Sánchez and Linda Schlossberg, Sexual Cultures (New York: New York University Press, 2001), 1–12.

8. Here is an intriguing irony that can use more exploration. Racial difference is visible, but that

visibility has only made racial minorities undetectable and unseen in this country. Tina Chen has chosen to signify this irony with a strategic use of the term "in/visibilities" (*Double Agency: Acts of Impersonation in Asian American Literature and Culture* [Stanford: Stanford University Press, 2005], 6, 160). In these same pages, she has also suggested that a distinction needs to be made between being "invisible" and being "unmarked," contrary to Peggy Phelan's thesis about the power of being unmarked or unseen (*Unmarked: The Politics of Performance* [New York: Routledge, 1993]).

9. Roland Barthes, trans. Richard Howard (New York: Hill and Wang, 1977), 90 (emphasis original).

10. I trust that my reasons for choosing 1 Corinthians will become clear as I develop my arguments in this chapter. Suffice to state now that one prominent commentator, after describing Corinth as "a city only a few generations removed from its founding by colonists seeking upward social mobility," compares the Corinthians of Paul's days to the commentator's own "American readers" (Richard B. Hays, *First Corinthians*, Interpretation [Louisville: John Knox, 1997], 3). As we will see, what this commentator fails to recognize—as in Todd Penner's introduction to *Contextualizing Acts: Lukan Narrative and Greco-Roman Discourse* (ed. Todd Penner and Caroline Vander Stichele, Society of Biblical Literature Symposium Series 20 [Atlanta: Society of Biblical Literature, 2003], 1–21)—is the racial/ethnic differences that exist between the Corinthians and Paul as well as among his "American readers."

11. John C. Hurd, *The Origin of 1 Corinthians* (2nd ed.; Macon, Ga.: Mercer University Press, 1983), 97–105; Wolfgang Schrage, *Der erste Brief an die Korinther*, Evangelisch-katholischer Kommentar zum Neuen Testament 7 (4 vols.; Zurich: Benziger; Neukirchen-Vluyn: Neukirchener Verlag, 1999–2001), 1:38–63.

12. Gerd Theissen, *The Social Setting of Pauline Christianity*, ed. and trans. John H. Schütz (Philadelphia: Fortress Press, 1982); Peter Marshall, *Enmity in Corinth: Social Conventions in Paul's Relations with the Corinthians*, Wissenschaftliche Untersuchungen zum Neuen Testament 2/23 (Tübingen: J. C. B. Mohr, 1987); Stephen M. Pogoloff, *Logos and Sophia: The Rhetorical Situation of 1 Corinthians*, Society of Biblical Literature Dissertation Series 134 (Atlanta: Scholars, 1992); Dale Martin, *The Corinthian Body* (New Haven: Yale University Press, 1995), 69–79.

13. Martin, *Corinthian Body*, xiv.

14. See also Jennifer A. Glancy, "Boasting of Beatings (2 Corinthians 11:23-25)," *Journal of Biblical Literature* 123 (2004): 99–135.

15. Martin, *Corinthian Body*, 33–34. Martin does mention that Paul's body was an issue to his critics in Corinth. However, he sees this—like the issue concerning Paul's manual labor—as becoming a "real" issue only in 2 Corinthians, and he also limits Paul's bodily problem to "illness, disfigurement, or simply constitutional infirmity" (ibid., 53–55, 83–86). Martin never explains or elaborates on what he means by "constitutional infirmity," but the thought that Paul's body is racially/ethnically marked as Jewish does not seem to cross his mind. Perhaps Martin, in correctly refuting the assumption that so-called Judaism and Hellenism must be mutually exclusive when it comes to Paul's cultural heritage, influence, and repertoire (see "Paul and the Judaism/Hellenism Dichotomy: Toward a Social History of the Question," in *Paul beyond the Judaism/Hellenism Divide*, ed. Troels Engberg-Pedersen [Louisville: Westminster John Knox, 2001], 29–61), has gone too far and ends up (dis) missing Paul's racially/ethnically marked body as a Jew altogether. Again, a helpful corrective might be found in contemporary Asian American experiences: their bodies are still raced and stigmatized as "Asian" even if they are fluent and knowledgeable in things both "Asian" and "American." In other words, Martin's call to rethink "culture" in Pauline studies ("Judaism/Hellenism Dichotomy," 59–61) must be supplemented with a thinking of race/ethnicity. As we will see later in this chapter, influence and resistance are also not necessarily mutually exclusive. Instead of giving an example from Asian America, let me for now point to the wisdom tradition of Ben Sira, a Jewish teacher from the

Hellenistic period, since one can find in that tradition both uses and critiques of Greek thought and rhetoric (see Pogoloff, *Logos and Sophia*, 163–67).

Pauline scholars of earlier generations did talk about Jewish–Gentile difference in 1 Corinthians. However, they did so by completely separating racial/ethnic and religious issues from the context of imperial politics, and by completely subsuming racial/ethnic issues as questions of religious practices in one direction (that is, whether Jewish Christ-followers would or should accept Gentiles who followed Christ without taking on certain Jewish practices like circumcision); see, for instance, F. C. Baur, "Die Christus Partei in der korinthischen Gemeinde," *Tübinger Zeitschrift für Theologie* 5 (1831): 61–206. It is important to note that this trail of scholarship has continued within Pauline studies in general, even if not in the study of 1 Corinthians in particular. More recently, studies of Paul from the "New Perspective" would emphasize Paul's Jewishness to interrogate the continuity and permeability between Jews (who are not followers of Christ) and Christ-followers more than the dynamics between Christ-followers who were Jewish and Christ-followers who were Gentile. These studies have also concentrated less on 1 Corinthians and much more on Romans and Galatians. Two representative scholars to look at in this regard would be E. P. Sanders (*Paul and Palestinian Judaism: A Comparison of Patterns of Religion* [Philadelphia: Fortress Press, 1977] and *Paul, the Law, and the Jewish People* [Philadelphia: Fortress Press, 1983]) and Daniel Boyarin (*A Radical Jew: Paul and the Politics of Identity*, Contraversions 1 [Berkeley: University of California Press, 1994] and *Border Lines: The Partition of Judaeo-Christianity*, Divinations [Philadelphia: University of Pennsylvania Press, 2004]).

Despite the view that "race" is a modern invention and the many attempts to distinguish "race" from "ethnicity," I will couple the terms together as "race/ethnicity" in this chapter for the same reasons that Denise Kimber Buell has identified ("Rethinking the Relevance of Race for Early Christian Self-Definition," *Harvard Theological Review* 94 [2001]: 450 n. 3): (1) to acknowledge the two terms' intricate relationship and implications with each another in ancient and modern times; and (2) to acknowledge that understandings and knowledge of the past and the present inform and influence each other in all intellectual endeavors (regarding anti-Semitism in particular, see also Peter Schäfer, *Judeophobia: Attitudes toward the Jews in the Ancient World* [Cambridge, Mass.: Harvard University Press, 1997], 2–3). On top of that, I also want to honor the work of African-American scholars who argue not only for the presence of blacks in the Bible but also against the assumption that biblical Jews were necessarily "whites" (see, for example, Charles B. Copher, "The Dark Presence in the Old Testament," in *Stony the Road We Trod: African American Biblical Interpretation*, ed. Cain Hope Felder [Minneapolis: Fortress Press, 1991], 146–64, and Cain Hope Felder, "Cultural Ideology, Afrocentrism and Biblical Interpretation," in *Black Theology: A Documentary History*, ed. James H. Cone and Gayraud S. Wilmore [2 vols.; Maryknoll, N.Y.: Orbis, 1993], 184–95). Michael Joseph Brown has recently questioned this practice of identifying black presence by fellow African American Bible scholars because the concept of "race," as I mentioned, is a modern construction (*Blackening of the Bible: The Aims of African American Biblical Scholarship*, African American Religious Thought and Life [Harrisburg, Pa.: Trinity Press International, 2004], 52). Note, however, that a couple of recent works have helpfully indicated that color-coded prejudice was very much alive in antiquity regardless of whether the term "race" is employed (Benjamin Isaac, *The Invention of Racism in Classical Antiquity* [Princeton: Princeton University Press, 2004]) or not employed (Gay L. Byron, *Symbolic Blackness and Ethnic Difference in Early Christian Literature* [New York: Routledge, 2002]; see also J. Albert Harrill, *Slaves in the New Testament: Literary, Social, and Moral Dimensions* [Minneapolis: Fortress Press, 2006], 42–43, 46).

For my immediate purposes, let me point out that if one is willing to grant (1) the association of blackness with Egyptians; and (2) the relevance of Acts for Pauline studies, Paul's mistaken identity as an Egyptian by Lysias in Acts 21:38 might be taken as an indication of Paul's blackness.

In the final analysis, however, my emphasis on racial/ethnic difference in this chapter is not dependent on the actual color of Paul's skin. One must remember, first, from the example of the Irish, who were first deemed to be "black," but later deemed to be "white" (Noel Ignatiev, *How the Irish Became White* [New York: Routledge, 1995]), that skin color is not necessarily "color" (St. Clair Drake and Horace R. Cayton, *Black Metropolis: A Study of Negro Life in a Northern City* [New York: Harcourt, Brace and Company, 1945], 503) but that phenotypical differences are "something that we learn to see" (Viet Thanh Nguyen, *Race and Resistance: Literature and Politics in Asian America*, Race and American Culture [New York: Oxford University Press, 2002], 169). That is to say, color, race, or ethnicity (including "Jewishness" in Paul's time) is like the emperor's "new clothes"; it is a display of power—a fantasy of power and a powerful fantasy—in which physical evidence is secondary to observer compliance. In addition to the extant educational and ideological work on how to see Jews in the Greco-Roman world, it is important to recognize that, aside from the general question of the visibility or readability of Jewish difference, Paul himself is not shy in owning up to his race/ethnicity as a Jewish person (1 Cor 10:1-6; 2 Cor 11:22). For my own understanding of race and ethnicity, see "Margins and (Cutting-)Edges: On the (Il)Legitimacy and Intersections of Race, Ethnicity, and (Post)Colonialism," in *Postcolonial Biblical Criticism: Interdisciplinary Intersections*, ed. Stephen D. Moore and Fernando F. Segovia, Bible and Postcolonialism (New York: Continuum, 2005), 114-21. I would also like to thank here both Randall C. Bailey and Gay L. Byron for pushing me to think through the idea of black presence in the Bible by providing both conversations and bibliographical recommendations.

16. Pogoloff, *Logos and Sophia*, 208; Martin, *Corinthian Body*, xvi–xvii; John R. Lanci, *A New Temple for Corinth: Rhetorical and Archaeological Approaches to Pauline Imagery*, Studies in Biblical Literature 1 (New York: Peter Lang, 1997), 34–38.

17. Ramsey MacMullen, *Roman Social Relations: 50 B.C. to A.D. 284* (New Haven: Yale University Press, 1974), 122.

18. Ibid., 30–31. I will not limit my Greco-Roman references to those that are known to have existed before the time of Paul, since my use of them is motivated not by a search for source or influence but by a desire to understand the cultural sensibilities of the general time period.

19. For example, Romans saw the Greeks as "the world's greatest chatterboxes. Not only did they talk too much, but at the wrong time. The learned Greek ... was often gauche, *ineptus*, a bore.... They talked shop, their own shop, in a manner offensive to polite conversation" (cited in Pogoloff, *Logos and Sophia*, 266). See also Juvenal, who satirizes the Greeks with the preface that they are "the race which is most dear to our rich men" (*Sat.* 3.58–125). What is clear is the existence of a social and racial/ethnic scale in the Roman Empire; see Simon Goldhill, ed., *Being Greek under Rome: Cultural Identity, the Second Sophistic, and the Development of Empire* (New York: Cambridge University Press, 2001). For example, *barbarus* gradually became a negative stigma for all those who were not Greek or Roman in the Greco-Roman world (Byron, *Symbolic Blackness*, 2).

20. Schäfer, *Judeophobia* (see n. 15 above); Isaac, *Invention of Racism*, 440–91; see also Louis H. Feldman, *Jew and Gentile in the Ancient World: Attitudes and Interactions from Alexander to Justinian* (Princeton: Princeton University Press, 1993), 123–76. What I am suggesting here is that the picture of diasporic Jewish communities as one of "people secure in their self-understanding, loyal to their traditions but open to their neighbors and (with the exception of the aristocracy) respected by their Gentile and later Gentile Christian neighbours" (Lloyd Gaston, "The Impact of New Perspectives on Judaism and Improved Jewish-Christian Relations on the Study of Paul," *Biblical Interpretation* 13 [2005]: 253) is skewed and overly optimistic. It (dis)misses underlying and at times explosive racial/ethnic tensions. One should also keep in mind that underlying racial/ethnic tensions are arguably more often and more keenly felt by marginalized racial/ethnic groups, and that in Paul's portrayal, the

Corinthians are longing for status—and thus aristocratic identifications, including a lack of respect for Jews?—even if they were not originally of high birth (1 Cor 1:26-31; 4:6-19; 11:17-34).

Gaston's essay is part of a larger and recent collection of essays and responses on the New Perspective on Paul as a Christ-follower who remains Jewish. While this collection as a whole seems to acknowledge the importance of race/ethnicity for Greco-Roman religion in general and hence for Pauline studies in particular, it very quickly seems to reduce everything to religion and religion alone. Despite the fact that four of seven contributors are footnoted in Shawn Kelley's book, *Racializing Jesus: Race, Ideology and the Formation of Modern Biblical Scholarship*, Biblical Limits (New York: Routledge, 2002), 248 n. 26 (Neil Elliott), 263 n. 32 and 266 n. 38 (Mark D. Nanos), 271 n. 2 (Caroline Johnson Hodge), 306 n. 25 (William S. Campbell), only one gives substantial attention to Paul's ethnicity or racialization (Caroline Johnson Hodge, "Apostle to the Gentiles: Constructions of Paul's Identity," *Biblical Interpretation* 13 [2005]: 270–88). What one finds in this collection is the paradox of referring to race/ethnicity and then just as quickly evaporating race/ethnicity into (almost) nonexistence.

Of immense significance is the fact that neither Schafer nor Isaac sees prejudice against Jews as a merely "Christian" hostility, but rather as a much wider phenomenon of the Greco-Roman world. In fact, Isaac intimates more than once that Greco-Roman hostilities toward Jews tended to be more intense outside than inside Judea (*Invention of Racism*, 442, 456, 467, 478). If that was true, then a diasporic Jew like Paul would have been more vulnerable to racial/ethnic discrimination. Perhaps the best-known attacks on Jews in the Greco-Roman world are those by Tacitus (*Hist.* 5.4–5) and Juvenal (*Sat.* 14.96–106); for an example of a Greek author, see Cassius Dio 37.16.5–17.4.

Of no less importance is Schäfer's thesis that it was Egypt (both before and during its hellenization) rather than Syria-Palestine in the second century B.C.E. that was the "'mother' of anti-Semitism" (*Judeophobia*, 11). Given Schäfer's own German heritage and his admission of the long and problematic relations between Germans and Jews (ibid., 1–2), his thesis reads like an attempt to shift the blame. This is particularly troubling given the link that some African American Bible scholars make among Egypt, Africa, and black persons and presence. Does Schäfer's thesis, whatever his intentions, have the effect of shifting at least part of the responsibilities for "anti-Semitism" from (mainly white?) Europeans to (mainly black?) Africans? I will have more to say about this dynamic of "shifting" or transferring to another vulnerable minority population in a later part of this chapter.

21. Hays, *First Corinthians*, 2–4; Lanci, *New Temple*, 26–30; Richard A. Horsley, *1 Corinthians*, Abingdon New Testament Commentaries (Nashville: Abingdon, 1998), 22–28.

22. Horsley's disregard of racial/ethnic differences in 1 Corinthians is especially problematic, since this disregard leads him to the (con)fusion of Hellenistic Jews and Gentiles, as seen by his rather pervasive use of Philo to illustrate or argue for what he sees to be representative of the Corinthians; see, for example, *1 Corinthians*, 117–21, 181–82, 211–12. As I have tried to point out in reference to Dale Martin, there is an immense variety of social space between complete isolation and total assimilation for racial/ethnic minority groups to operate in any given society. It is equally important to remember that both the area and the approach of that operation are often contested and limited by various dominant cultural forces.

Commenting on the controversial casting of Jonathan Pryce as an Asian or Eurasian in the first performances of *Miss Saigon* in New York, Karen Shimakawa indicates that such "cross-castings" (of whites playing Asian/American-s)—by making Asian/American-s disembodied and invisible—on stage might be a "more comprehensible" and "more pleasurable" experience for dominant audiences, and hence also a "more profitable" setup for producers (*National Abjection: The Asian American Body Onstage* [Durham, N.C.: Duke University Press, 2002], 46, 48). Given the long-standing and perhaps willful anti-Jewish and anti-Semitic practice in biblical studies in general (see Joseph B. Tyson, *Luke, Judaism, and the Scholars: Critical Approaches to Luke-Acts* [Columbia: University of South Carolina

Press, 1999]; and Kelley, *Racializing Jesus*) and in Pauline studies in particular (Martin, "Judaism/Hellenism Dichotomy"), I wonder if the same comment cannot be made of "our" academic research and publishing. Mindful of modern racism and anti-Judaism, Denise Kimber Buell is correct in calling scholars of early Christianity to pay more and better attention to questions of race/ethnicity. Although her earlier article ("Rethinking the Relevance") tends to focus on how early Christians adapted Jewish rhetorical uses of ethno-racial concepts to construct a new race/ethnicity rather than transcended the racial/ethnic particularity or exclusivity of Judaism, her more recent collaboration with Caroline Johnson Hodge ("The Politics of Interpretation: The Rhetoric of Race and Ethnicity in Paul," *Journal of Biblical Literature* 123 (2004): 235–51) does focus more explicitly on Paul's identity as a diasporic Jew or Judean.

23. As discussed by R. S. Sugirtharajah, *Postcolonial Reconfigurations: An Alternative Way of Reading the Bible and Doing Theology* (St. Louis: Chalice, 2003), 104–9.

24. Howard Eilberg-Schwartz, ed., *People of the Body: Jews and Judaism from an Embodied Perspective*, SUNY Series, The Body in Culture, History, and Religion (Albany: State University of New York Press, 1992). Part of the problem has to do, I think, with the conventional understanding that Paul is seeking to "transcend" or "overcome" racial/ethnic divides. Thus, what Theodor W. Adorno says about interpreting in general is applicable to interpreting race in Paul in particular: "The person who interprets instead of accepting what is given and classifying it is marked with the yellow star of one who squanders his intelligence in impotent speculation, reading things in where there is nothing to interpret" ("The Essay as Form," in *Notes to Literature*, ed. Rolf Tiedemann, trans. Sherry Weber Nicholsen [2 vols.; New York: Columbia University Press, 1991–92], 1:4). Perhaps a bigger part of the problem is the fact that many people are simply not comfortable with talking about race. Paul Gilroy makes the insightful observation that many in the twenty-first century have tried to avoid the question of race by making race a distinctively mid-twentieth-century problem (*Postcolonial Melancholia*, Welleck Lectures [New York: Columbia University Press, 2005], 13–14). That is to say, race and racism are really problems of the past, and the present generations should be given the freedom to move on rather than being dragged down, or worse, made responsible for them. This avoidance of race is, however, not done only by burying race in the past; it is also done with the charge of anachronism or, ironically enough given Gilroy's observation, so-called presentism. According to this view, race is a modern fifteenth- or sixteenth-century construct, so any talk about race before that time—for example, during the Greco-Roman world of the first century—is illegitimate. In other words, race is bracketed and safely quarantined within several hundred years of human history. It is a fantasy or a fabrication to talk about race in antiquity, and it is unhealthy nostalgia to talk about it in the present.

Related to this is Judith Butler's reflection on how masculine disembodiment is achieved through the reduction of women to corporeality or bodily forms ("Variations on Sex and Gender: Beauvoir, Wittig and Foucault," in *Feminism as Critique: On the Politics of Gender*, ed. Seyla Benhabib and Drucilla Cornell, Feminist Perspectives [Minneapolis: University of Minnesota Press, 1987], 133). Of course, I need to point out here that what Butler identifies (the rendering of an "other" as "essentially body") happens not only to women but also to people of color. Since the guild of biblical studies is still predominantly white and male, these white male scholars' tendency to identify with Paul often ends up—following Butler's rationale—turning Paul into yet another noncorporeal soul or spirit.

25. Mark D. Nanos, *The Irony of Galatians: Paul's Letter in First-Century Context* (Minneapolis: Fortress Press, 2002). One must not forget, as Pamela Eisenbaum reminds us, that Paul wrote before the twin births of rabbinic Judaism and Christianity as separate "religions" ("Paul, Polemics, and the Problem of Essentialism," *Bibiblical Interpretation* 13 [2005]: 237). While these twin births have traditionally been understood as having taken place at the end of the first century C.E., some are

suggesting now that the so-called "parting of the ways" did not happen until as late as the fourth century C.E.; see, for example, Boyarin, *Border Lines* (n. 15 above).

26. For a brief but helpful survey of the Corinthian "context," including the major Gentile or Greco-Roman religious streams, see Horsley, *1 Corinthians*, 22–28. While this kind of "background" or "contextual" information is routinely given in commentaries on the Corinthian letters, not enough nuanced attention has been given to how religious difference (particularly in majority/minority terms) is played out in the letters themselves. Neither has adequate attention been given to the intersection between race/ethnicity and religion. As I mentioned in an earlier note, questions have pretty much been limited to those about Gentile Christ-followers and Jewish circumcision, though without the kind of sociopolitical framing that Nanos proposes. One scholar who does talk about both ethnic and religious difference in 1 Corinthians is Brad Ronnell Braxton ("The Role of Ethnicity in the Social Location of 1 Corinthians 7:17-24," in *Yet with a Steady Beat: Contemporary U.S. Afrocentric Biblical Interpretation*, ed. Randall C. Bailey, Society of Biblical Literature Semeia Studies 42 [Atlanta: Society of Biblical Literature, 2003], 19–32), but he limits his inquiry to the issue of circumcision in 1 Cor 7:17-24. Moreover, Braxton seems to be reading 1 Corinthians through the lens of Nanos's reading of Galatians in the way he attributes to the Corinthians a desire to be circumcised and the way he accounts for that desire. Finally, Braxton reads (and critiques) Paul as (naïvely) arguing for a transcendence over ethnic differences in 1 Corinthians. I do not think that ethnic issues can be limited to a single chapter or a single issue in 1 Corinthians, nor do I agree with Braxton's reading that Paul is lifting up one's allegiance to Christ to overwhelm or cancel out all other ethnic identities or allegiances, since in my view, Paul continues to see race/ethnicity and religion as closely connected. I would furthermore like to insist that one should read 1 Corinthians in terms of 1 Corinthians rather than through another Pauline letter.

27. See Young In Song, "Critical Feminist View of Patriarchal Structure of the Korean American Christian Church," in *Korean American Women Living in Two Cultures*, ed. Young In Song and Aileen Moon (Los Angeles: Keimyung-Baylo University Press, 1997); Suh, *Being Buddhist*.

28. Song, "Critical Feminist View," 71 (emphasis added).

29. Since we only have the letter(s) of Paul and thus only one side of the conversation, it is practically impossible to know to what extent Paul's rhetoric is an accurate reflection or Paul's own projection of the Corinthian situation. Either way, I am suggesting that paying attention to both racial/ethnic and religious differences will add much to one's reading of 1 Corinthians. For the sake of readability, my language in the rest of the chapter will not make a differentiation between reflection and projection, but readers should nevertheless keep in mind this delicate but decisive distinction.

30. Buell, "Rethinking the Relevance," 459–60; see also Mary Beard, John North, and Simon Price, *Religions of Rome*, vol. 1, *A History* (New York: Cambridge University Press, 1998), 214–15.

31. See Schäfer, *Judeophobia*, 9, 32, 77–81, 106–18; Isaac, *Invention of Racism*, 453–54, 456–57, 459–62, 466–69, 479–81, 488. I am emphasizing Greco-Roman perceptions here because I do not want to imply that Greco-Roman Judaisms were necessarily all zealous in missionary activities and at all times. For a helpful discussion of that topic, see Martin Goodman, *Mission and Conversion: Proselytizing in the Religious History of the Roman Empire* (Oxford: Clarendon, 1994). My interest here has less to do with how conversions by non-Jews to Judaisms took place and more with how Greco-Romans tended to see and respond to the presence of Jews and the conversions of non-Jews. That is to say, I am also paying attention to what might in reality be anticipation or anxiety over *potential* proselytism as well as actual proselytism. While Schäfer is (like me) not concerned with whether Jews of the ancient world were active in missions, he (unlike me) still concerned with whether proselytism had in fact taken place.

32. While Schäfer helpfully suggests how proselytes are part of the "hunted," he is in my view mistaken to conclude that "we have to regard Domitian's vigorous enforcement of the *ficus Iudaicus*

not as a measure against proselytes (he only wanted them to pay the tax)" (*Judeophobia*, 113–16, here 115). Who needs to pay tax and who does not need to pay tax is always a matter of politics and power relations. Again, a look at Asian American history will be helpful here. For example, money was clearly not the only issue when a "Foreign Miners' Tax" was passed in 1850 and reenacted in 1852 primarily against the Chinese, or in 1870—at a time when Chinese laundrymen in San Francisco were known for delivering laundry without using horses—when a citywide stipulation was made to charge laundry shops a higher quarterly fee for laundry deliveries made without horses (see Sucheng Chan, *Asian Americans: An Interpretive History* [Boston: Twayne, 1991], 46).

33. This reading is actually consistent with Boyarin's recent (re)constructionist history of Jewish–Christian relations in *Border Lines*. For Boyarin, the births and more or less simultaneous separation between rabbinic Judaism and Christianity were part of a long process of negotiation that extended from the end of the first century C.E. to the fourth century C.E. What is significant is that on the "Christian" side, Boyarin sees *Gentile* followers of Christ (in other words, not Paul himself) to be the main players in the construction of heresiology and hence the construction of Christianity as a "religion" that is no longer understandable in terms of a race or a *genos* (*Border Lines*, 4, 16–17, 29, 59, 62, 65–67, 72–73). While Boyarin begins his investigation of the process with Justin Martyr, my own reading of 1 Corinthians might see it as an earlier or even pioneering engagement of that long negotiation between race/ethnicity and religion.

34. For example, Antoinette Clark Wire, *The Corinthian Women Prophets: A Reconstruction through Paul's Rhetoric* (Minneapolis: Fortress Press, 1990), 1–11; Horsley, *1 Corinthians*, 43, 61, 67–68; Elisabeth Schüssler Fiorenza, *Rhetoric and Ethic: The Politics of Biblical Studies* (Minneapolis: Fortress Press, 1999), 105–28.

35. I am therefore suggesting that there is no need to read this account one-dimensionally. As I will show in the latter parts of this essay, Paul may well be working on several fronts with this single account.

36. Many others have questioned the factuality of the four Corinthian factions that Paul describes in 1:12, since he seems to focus only on the conflict between the "weak" and the "strong" as he progresses in the letter. See, for example, Margaret M. Mitchell, *Paul and the Rhetoric of Reconciliation: An Exegetical Investigation of the Language and Composition of 1 Corinthians* (Louisville: Westminster John Knox, 1991), 83–86; Martin, *Corinthian Body*, 58; Horsley, *1 Corinthians*, 34–35, 44–45.

37. I am thus arguing that conflicts and divisions in 1 Corinthians not be limited to those at Corinth but, on the basis of race/ethnicity, be extended to problems between the Corinthians and Paul, a colonized Jew. Notice in this regard that the four teachers Paul names (himself, Apollos, Cephas, and Christ) in 1:12 are, if we can trust Acts' account of Apollos, all Jews. The same is also true of the apostles, whom Paul, as we will see, contrasts with the Corinthians in 4:8-13. Nils Dahl ("Paul and the Church at Corinth according to 1 Cor. 1:10—4:21, " in *Studies in Paul: Theology for the Early Christian Mission* [Minneapolis: Augsburg, 1977], 40–61) has suggested that 1 Cor 1:10—4:21 should not be read as (Paul's) "apologetic," because Paul seems to be critical also of those who claim allegiance to himself (1:13; 3:4-9; 4:6). In the next section, I will talk about how Paul argues for his authority not by directly affirming or asking for personal allegiance but by appealing indirectly to an-other Jewish body (that of Christ). In other words, since the conflict involves racial/ethnic difference, Paul is building up for his own apology not only a united Jewish front but also one that is fronted by Christ. One should remember also that Dahl does finally admit that the first four chapters of 1 Corinthians contain "apologetic elements" (ibid., 61 n. 50). Cynthia Briggs Kittredge has made a similar (but more one-sided) revisionary reading of Paul's letter to the Philippians on the basis of gender. Instead of seeing—as scholars used to do—the two women mentioned in 4:2 (Euodia and Syntyche) as opposing each other, Kittredge suggests that they might in fact be presenting a united front

against Paul (*Community and Authority: The Rhetoric of Obedience in the Pauline Tradition,* Harvard Theological Studies 45 [Harrisburg, Pa.: Trinity Press International, 1998], 53–110).

38. See also Pogoloff, *Logos and Sophia,* 147–49; Martin, *Corinthian Body,* 35, 54–55.

39. Scholars who are adamant that 1 Corinthians is a piece of deliberative rhetoric (Mitchell, *Rhetoric of Reconciliation*; Martin, *Corinthian Body,* 38–39) might see my reading here as a plug for taking the letter as a piece of forensic rhetoric, but I am personally less concerned with such deliberations and delineations. Such definitions of rhetorical genres are in my view often too neat, too rigid, and thus too limiting. In practice, types of rhetoric are usually mixed and messy, just as logos, ethos, and pathos are interconnected and inseparable elements of any speech. I would further contend that my reading provides greater continuity between 1 and 2 Corinthians than readings that (dis)miss Paul's "apology" or "defense" in 1 Corinthians as "merely" rhetorical (for example, Martin, *Corinthian Body,* 52–53).

40. Horsley, *1 Corinthians,* 41.

41. Forms of Roman punishment were contingent not only on the nature of the crime but also on the status of the offender. Punishment and status hence were mutually constitutive and "disciplinary" in a most profound manner. See Elizabeth A. Castelli, *Martyrdom and Memory: Early Christian Culture Making,* Gender, Theory, and Religion (New York: Columbia University Press, 2004), 39–41.

42. Horsley, *1 Corinthians,* 171.

43. Sze-kar Wan, "Collection for the Saints as Anticolonial Act: Implications of Paul's Ethnic Reconstruction," in *Paul and Politics: Ekklesia, Israel, Imperium, Interpretation. Essays in Honor of Krister Stendahl,* ed. Richard A. Horsley (Harrisburg, Pa.: Trinity Press International, 2000), 191–215.

44. Buell ("Rethinking the Relevance," 469), commenting on the existence of racial/ethnic hierarchies in the Greco-Roman world, quotes Philo's wish that with the beginning of the Roman imperial period would come "a fresh start" for the Jews (*Mos.* 2.44). The articulation of this wish not only betrayed the low status hitherto suffered by Jews but also turned out sadly to be a wish unfulfilled. For more on such racial/ethnic hierarchies in antiquity, see Byron, *Symbolic Blackness,* and Isaac, *Invention of Racism.*

45. Frantz Fanon, *Black Skin, White Masks,* trans. Charles Lam Markmann (New York: Grove, 1967), 18.

46. Similar dynamics were at work in the attempt among some Jews within the Greco-Roman world to reverse the Jewish practice of circumcision. Paul himself mentions circumcision and uncircumcision in 1 Corinthians (7:18-19). I will have more to say about the Jewish circumcised penis a little later on in this chapter.

47. Fanon, *Black Skin, White Masks,* 227 (emphasis added).

48. According to Martin (*Corinthian Body,* 96–103), Paul's evaluation of these gifts also has to do with his desire for a reversal of status, since prophecy was generally associated with the lower *nous* ("mind") while tongues or esoteric speech was generally associated with the higher *pneuma* ("spirit").

49. Ernst Kantorowicz has suggested that it is from medieval Christology (Christ as having the corporeal duality of human and God) that the English and the French developed the doctrine of the "king's two bodies," namely, the king's body natural and body politic (*The King's Two Bodies: A Study in Mediaeval Political Theory* [Princeton: Princeton University Press, 1957]). I am not sure if one cannot actually attribute this doctrine more directly to Paul's explication in 1 Corinthians on Christ's physical body and church body. The irony in all this is that I read Paul's argument about Christ's dual corporeality as at least partly a challenge to the colonialism of the Roman Caesar, while Kantorowicz proposes that the corporeal duality of the English and French monarch functioned to ensure the indestructibility of the king's sovereign body, and hence the dual idea of sovereign succession and the

Notes to Chapter 9

indestructibility of English and French body politic. Both ideas being suggested by Kantorowicz have, of course, a role to play in the subsequent development of the English and French colonial projects.

50. Jennifer A. Glancy, *Slavery in Early Christianity* (New York: Oxford University Press, 2002), 15–16; see also Harrill, *Slaves in the New Testament*, 19–20, 39.

51. See also the discussion in Shigehisa Kuriyama, *The Expressiveness of the Body and the Divergence of Greek and Chinese Medicine* (New York: Zone, 1999), 123–28.

52. See also Martin, *Corinthian Body*, 190–95.

53. Ibid., 178.

54. Since Paul uses the same "master-and-slave" or "ownership" vocabularies not only to describe the relations between Christ and his followers but also to underscore the (bodily) obligation that Christ-followers have to one another (9:19-27) and the (bodily) obligation that married couples have to each other (7:4), a potential dilemma arises for followers who are married to an "unbeliever." Paul awkwardly dances around this scenario by asserting that within marriage and family, the cleansing power of the follower is greater than the contaminating influence of the unbeliever (7:12-16). Nevertheless, Paul is clear that the best thing for a Christ-follower to do is to remain celibate and abstain from sex altogether (7:5-7, 15). See the discussion in Martin, *Corinthian Body*, 209–19.

55. Hays refers to this as a process of "resocialization" on the part of the Corinthians (*First Corinthians*, 4, 11–12, 63, 98, 111).

56. One must not collapse Paul's various letters together as if what he says in one is unproblematically transferable to another. This means that we should not (*pace* Braxton, "Role of Ethnicity") assume because of Galatians that Paul's statement here about circumcision and uncircumcision being "nothing" implies that the Corinthians were also wanting to be circumcised. Note that Paul's statement in 7:19 is preceded by 7:18, where he discourages the "correction" or removal of circumcision as much as he does the seeking of circumcision. I am therefore suggesting that Paul's statement in 1 Corinthians functions to remedy or correct a negative view that the Corinthians had about Jewish men and their circumcised penises.

57. Dale B. Martin, *Slavery As Salvation: The Metaphor of Slavery in Pauline Christianity* (New Haven: Yale University Press, 1990), 63–68.

58. As Buell and Johnson Hodge have argued on the basis of Romans and Galatians, Paul's incorporation of Gentiles "in Christ" is not racially/ethnically neutral, since he is using a Jewish or Judean rhetorical strategy (regarding racial/ethnic inheritance through generations) to "graft" Gentiles into a Jewish or Judean ancestry under Abraham and thus the God of Israel even if these Gentiles do not necessarily have to become Jewish or Judean in all of their practices ("Politics of Interpretation," 247–50; see also Gaston, "Impact of New Perspectives," 267–68; Johnson Hodge, "Apostle to the Gentiles," 276).

Notice also that throughout the letter, Paul uses Jewish Scripture as yet another weapon to correct or counteract the Corinthians' obsession with "wisdom," which Paul also stereotypes as a Greek or Gentile characteristic. Pogoloff, for example, has suggested, after typifying rhetoric as a(nother) form of (Greco-Roman?) cultural wisdom and thus an index of social status, that Paul cited Jewish or Hebrew Scripture in 1:19 (Isa 29:14); 1:26-31 (Jer 9:22-23); and 3:19 (Job 5:12-13 and Ps 93:11) to recommend a different but good kind of wisdom. This (Jewish) wisdom teaches not exaltation of one's own status but humility before God, which is also commended by Paul through his citing of Isa 64:4 in 2:9 and Isa 40:13 in 2:16 (*Logos and Sophia*, 54, 140, 156–58). Much has been written on the importance of Hebrew Scripture for Paul's letter to the Corinthians; see, for example, Christopher D. Stanley, *Arguing with Scripture: The Rhetoric of Quotations in the Letters of Paul* (New York: T&T Clark, 2004), 75–96; and John Paul Heil, *The Rhetorical Role of Scripture in 1 Corinthians*, Society of Biblical Literature Studies in Biblical Literature 15 (Atlanta: Society of Biblical Literature, 2005).

59. Martin, *Corinthian Body*, 94–95.

60. One may extend Martin's point and further link the "necessary" part to Paul's other adjectives in 12:22-25 as references to the circumcised penis, because Greeks were against the Jewish practice of circumcision as a mutilation of an otherwise perfect body and hence as a crude and ugly violation of beauty; see Kenneth James Dover, *Greek Homosexuality* (Cambridge, Mass.: Harvard University Press, 1989), 124–35.

61. See also Schäfer, *Judeophobia*, 93, 96–99. As Johnson Hodge correctly points out ("Apostle to the Gentiles," 270), Paul himself sees circumcision as the Jewish or Judean identity marker in Gal 2:7-8.

62. For my purposes, let me reiterate what one's body (including one's race/ethnicity) might mean to one's ethos in the Greco-Roman world. Theon, for example, discusses ethos under three main categories: (1) external qualities like education, friendship, reputation, and wealth; (2) bodily qualities like health and beauty; and (3) virtues and deeds (*Prog.* 9.15-24; 10.13-18). Not only does the body of the orator occupy a separate category, but markings of the body can also be found beyond the category of "bodily qualities." For example, included under "external qualities" is one's breeding or birth, which might well involve one's race/ethnicity.

63. Johnson Hodge argues that the "lawlessness" in 1 Cor 9:21-22 refers to a moral deficiency (as in "evil") rather than a racial/ethnic designation (as in "Gentile"). In the literary context of 1 Corinthians, I do not see the two as necessarily mutually exclusive. For Paul, as we will see, Gentiles are also morally suspect.

64. Daniel Itzkovitz, "Passing like Me: Jewish Chameleonism and the Politics of Race," in Sánchez and Schlossberg, *Passing*, 38–63.

65. Ibid., 43.

66. Zygmunt Bauman, *Postmodern Ethics* (Oxford and Cambridge, Mass.: Blackwell, 1993), 164–65.

67. African-American critics have suggested that the practice of "passing" does not only "turn what [is] conceived of as a natural opposition into a societal one" (M. Giulia Fabi, *Passing and the Rise of the African American Novel* [Urbana: University of Illinois Press, 2001], 5), but also indicates a desire "to control the terms of their racial definition, rather than be subject to the definitions of white supremacy" (Gayle Wald, *Crossing the Line: Racial Passing in Twentieth-Century U.S. Literature and Culture*, New Americanists [Durham, N.C.: Duke University Press, 2000], 6). At the same time, I do not deny that "passing" or "chameleonism" may be—for some—a matter of survival, and that it may have both accommodative and subversive effects.

68. Homi K. Bhabha, *The Location of Culture* (New York: Routledge, 1994), 66.

69. Martin, *Slavery as Salvation*, 30–38, 42–44.

70. Johnson Hodge ("Apostle to the Gentiles," 282–85), arguing for a more fluid understanding of ethnic identity in Paul, also discusses 1 Cor 9:19-22, although she does so through the lens of Clarence E. Glad's "psychagogy." The "individual dispositions" and "communal context" of Glad's "psychagogy" (*Paul and Philodemus: Adaptability in Epicurean and Early Christian Psychagogy*, Supplements to Novum Testamentum 81 [Leiden and New York: Brill, 1995]) are in my view inadequate for the Corinthian passage in question because Glad's "psychagogy" does not take into consideration the racial/ethnic rankings at work within the larger imperial dynamics of the Roman Empire. As a result, Johnson Hodge, despite her own reference to how colonization created multiple identities in ancient Sicily (p. 274), presents Paul's desire to live "gentilelishly" to fulfill his hope for Israel's restoration as if the (imperial) power relations within Paul's context were either inconsequential or at most one dimensional. That is to say, in Glad's formulation and hence Johnson Hodge's application of "psychagogic" and pedagogical dynamics, the teacher (Paul) is always already the one who has the power over the students, and hence the emphasis or the burden is consistently on the teacher's willingness and ability to be flexible to adapt and meet the changing "dispositions" of the students ("Apostle

to the Gentiles," 283–85). Power dynamics within a teaching and learning community are, however, often much more complicated and even confrontational. What is not emphasized enough is precisely the power differential between a teacher who is a colonized Jew (Paul) and a student audience made up of mainly Greco-Roman colonizers (the Corinthians). Put differently, Paul's "adaptability" is not necessarily accepted or appreciated by the Corinthians, just as a predominantly white institution is not necessarily ready to adopt a racial/ethnic minority faculty member, even if or perhaps especially because he or she is willing to talk and act white. I also find Johnson Hodge's concluding remarks about Paul's prioritizing "in-Christness" over other available identities a little confusing because it once again sounds like being "in Christ" is subsuming if not transcending other ethnic identities and identifications. It would be helpful to clarify here again that being "in Christ" is, as Johnson Hodge has argued both alone and along with Buell, being incorporated into Israel's larger story or into a Jewish/Judean ancestry ("Apostle to the Gentiles," 276; cf. Buell and Johnson Hodge, "Politics of Interpretation," 247–50). Put differently, the effect of prioritizing "in-Christness" is not the disappearance of racial/ethnic difference; instead, since Christ is Jewish, its effect has more to do with, negatively speaking, not discriminating against Jews or, positively speaking, the endorsing or embracing of Jewish identities. If racial/ethnic identities are multiple and malleable as Johnson Hodge is arguing, I would suggest that in the context of the Roman Empire, the malleability of racial/ethnic identities by a Jew and by a Corinthian carries vastly different significations and implications.

71. Frantz Fanon, *The Wretched of the Earth*, trans. Constance Farrington (New York: Grove, 1963); idem, *Black Skin, White Masks* (see n. 45 above).

72. Steve Pile, "Introduction: Opposition, Political Identities and Spaces of Resistance," in *Geographies of Resistance*, ed. Steve Pile and Michael Keith (New York: Routledge, 1997), 23–24.

73. Sander L. Gilman, *Freud, Race, and Gender* (Princeton: Princeton University Press, 1993).

74. Daniel Boyarin, *Unheroic Conduct: The Rise of Heterosexuality and the Invention of the Jewish Man*, Contraversions 8 (Berkeley: University of California Press, 1997).

75. Elisabeth Bronfen, writing about the pervasive portrayals of women dying in modern narratives and paintings, refers also to Freudian psychoanalysis to suggest that this representation, repetition, or continuation is a simultaneous acknowledgment and denial of the threats of death in life (*Over Her Dead Body: Death, Femininity and the Aesthetic* [New York: Routledge, 1992], 30, 65, 102, 120). By portraying and mourning the death of an-other, Bronfen contends, the speaker or spectator is at the same time able to enjoy a moment of self-congratulatory satisfaction for having survived. This portrait, literary or otherwise, functions therefore in a sense as the survivor's immortalizing self-portrait. For Bronfen, this sense of satisfaction or superiority, as well as the transposing or ciphering act of the surviving speaker or spectator, make and mark the survivor as culturally, even if not biologically, masculine.

76. Shelly Matthews, *First Converts: Rich Pagan Women and the Rhetoric of Mission in Early Judaism and Christianity*, Contraversions (Stanford: Stanford University Press, 2001).

77. Maud W. Gleason, *Making Men: Sophists and Self-Representation in Ancient Rome* (Princeton: Princeton University Press, 1994); see also Erik Gunderson, *Staging Masculinity: The Rhetoric of Performance in the Roman World*, Body, In Theory (Ann Arbor: University of Michigan Press, 2000); and Amy Richlin, "Gender and Rhetoric: Producing Manhood in the Schools," in *Roman Eloquence: Rhetoric in Society and Literature*, ed. William J. Dominik (New York: Routledge, 1997), 90–110. Richard B. Hays gets very close to this idea when he compares Greco-Roman orators to "movie stars and sports heroes" (*First Corinthians*, 30), though he never articulates "masculinity" as an issue in rhetorical competitions; see also pp. 27, 35. For more on masculinity and Paul's Corinthian correspondence in particular, see Jennifer Larson, "Paul's Masculinity," *Journal of Biblical Literature* 123 (2004): 85–97; for masculinity and Pauline studies in general, see David J. A. Clines, "Paul, the Invisible

Man," in *New Testament Masculinities*, ed. Stephen D. Moore and Janice Capel Anderson, Society of Biblical Literature Semeia Studies 45 (Atlanta: Society of Biblical Literature, 2003), 181–92.

78. Quintilian's suggestion shows in my view also the complex relations between rhetoric and masculinity. Actors were generally considered to be part of the undesirable *infames* in Roman society (Catherine Edwards, "Unspeakable Professions: Public Performance and Prostitution in Ancient Rome," in *Roman Sexualities*, ed. Judith P. Hallett and Marilyn B. Skinner [Princeton: Princeton University Press, 1997], 66–95). What this reference points to, then, is what Schüssler Fiorenza calls "the feminine typecasting of rhetoric" (*Rhetoric and Ethic*, 63) vis-à-vis the pursuit of a masculine philosophy (and one can readily include performance in that "feminine typecasting"). If rhetoric and performance were both already suspect in terms of Greco-Roman masculinity, the insistence that rhetoric should become a performance of masculinity might be an attempt to defend or shore up an acknowledged lack or conscious threat. As we will see, I think this dynamic has implications for Paul's own gender understanding in 1 Corinthians.

79. Despite Isaac's statement that Jews "are not usually accused of softness or effeminacy," he does refer to Rutilius Namatianus's comment in the fifth century C.E. that the Jewish God, by reason of the Sabbath rest, must be soft or effeminate (*Invention of Racism*, 464, 471–72). Harrill also reads the Corinthians' attack on Paul's body and rhetoric (2 Cor 10:10) as reflecting their view of Paul as slavish and lacking in manhood (*Slaves in the New Testament*, 35–57). What Harrill seems to have forgotten in that reading is a point that he himself emphasizes repeatedly throughout his larger project on New Testament slavery, namely, that Greco-Roman slavery does not only connect with issues of masculinity, since slaves, women (hence the issue of masculinity), barbarians or foreigners (hence the issue of race/ethnicity), and beasts (hence the issue of humanity or humanness) elide easily into one another (ibid., 37, 41–42, 47, 69, 124, 130, 136–37). In other words, Harrill has overlooked the fact that Paul's body is also "Jewish," even if he cites Cicero's statement that "Jews and Syrians" are "born to be slaves" (*Prov. cons.* 5.10; cited in *Slaves in the New Testament*, 44).

80. Robyn Wiegman, *American Anatomies: Theorizing Race and Gender*, New Americanists (Durham, N.C.: Duke University Press, 1995), 90.

81. Ibid., 98.

82. Schäfer, in his reading of Martial, argues for a particular connection that the Roman writer makes between a circumcised penis and a fantasized sexual potency and lustfulness on the part of the Jews; see *Judeophobia*, 99–102.

83. Matthews, *First Converts*, 72–82.

84. See especially Eng, *Racial Castration* (n. 3 above).

85. Jeffrey Chan et al., "Introduction," in *The Big Aiiieeeee!: An Anthology of Chinese American and Japanese American Literature*, ed. Jeffery Paul Chan et al. (New York: Penguin. 1991), xiii; see also Frank Chin, "Come All Ye Asian American Writers of the Real and the Fake," in ibid., 66). Of course, my point here is not to argue for the portrayals of Fu Manchu and Charlie Chan as positive, but to demonstrate how Chin ends up buying into and collaborating in the abjection of effeminacy and homosexuality in the name of a progressive racial politics.

86. Wire, *Corinthian Women Prophets*; Jouette M. Bassler, "1 Corinthians," in *Women's Bible Commentary*, ed. Carol A. Newsom and Sharon H. Ringe, exp. ed. with Apocrypha (Louisville: Westminster John Knox, 1998), 411–19; Schüssler Fiorenza, *Rhetoric and Ethic*, 105–28; Jorunn Økland, *Women in Their Place: Paul and the Corinthian Discourse of Gender and Sanctuary Space*, Journal for the Study of the New Testament Supplement Series 269 (London: T&T Clark, 2004); Todd Penner and Caroline Vander Stichele, "Unveiling Paul: Gendering Ethos in 1 Corinthians 11.2-16," in *Rhetoric, Ethic, and Moral Persuasion in Biblical Discourse: Essays from the 2002 Heidelberg Conference*, ed. Thomas H. Olbricht and Anders Eriksson, Emory Studies in Early Christianity 11 (New York: T&T Clark, 2005), 214–37. Not only does Paul seem to have intentionally left out the "no longer

male and female" part of the baptismal formula in 12:13, but he also explicitly argues for a "natural" or "divinely ordained" ordering of men over women in 11:3-10, as well as commanding women to silence in 14:33b-36. Others have pointed out the way that Paul, in contrast to what one finds in Acts, places Aquila before Prisca in 16:19, and how Paul interrupts his practice of addressing both men and women when he comes to the question of "virgins" in 7:25-38. For a helpful discussion of this interruption in particular and Paul's treatment of women in 1 Corinthians in general, see Martin, *Corinthian Body*, 227–49.

87. Cynthia Briggs Kittredge, "Corinthian Women Prophets and Paul's Argumentation in 1 Corinthians," pp. 103–9 in Horsley, ed., *Paul and Politics*.

88. This is why I am not satisfied with the otherwise very fine article by Buell and Johnson Hodge, because they simply conclude that Paul's vision on race/ethnicity is not ideal because it "structurally subordinates one ethnoracial group [Gentiles] to another [Jews/Judeans]" like some German Christians did during the Third Reich ("Politics of Interpretation," 250). Read in the imperial context of the first century C.E., Paul's reversal of dominant Greco-Roman racial/ethnic hierarchies does have an element of (anticolonial) protest and resistance; it might even be his strategy of survival. One must not forget the reality of *different* power differentials when one evaluates this admittedly imperfect and inadequate move by Paul (say, between Paul and Greeks/Romans and between Hitler's German Christians and Jews). Differences in social location and in race/ethnicity do make a difference, even if the rhetoric and the concepts seem to be similar. Again, my goal here is not to defend Paul but to insist on a more nuanced reading that teases out the complexities even as one brings out the complicities in one's efforts to resist.

89. James Kyung-Jin Lee, *Urban Triage: Race and the Fictions of Multiculturalism*, Critical American Studies (Minneapolis: University of Minnesota Press, 2004), 134–35.

90. See also Matthews, *First Converts*, 21–28.

91. Hays, *First Corinthians*, 104.

92. Ibid., 87–88, 96–97; Horsley, *1 Corinthians*, 81–82, 86–87. The most controversial terms here are undoubtedly *malakoi* and *arsenokoitai* (6:9), which the NRSV translates as "male prostitutes" and "sodomites" respectively. For a detailed discussion of both terms, see Dale B. Martin, "*Arsenokoitēs* and *Malakos*: Meanings and Consequences," in *Biblical Ethics and Homosexuality: Listening to Scripture*, ed. Robert L. Brawley (Louisville: Westminster John Knox, 1996), 117–36, and Martti Nissinen, *Homoeroticism in the Biblical World: A Historical Perspective*, trans. Kirsi Stjerna (Minneapolis: Fortress Press, 1998), 113–18.

93. Jonathan Dollimore, *Sexual Dissidence: Augustine to Wilde, Freud to Foucault* (New York: Oxford University Press, 1991).

94. This is, of course, part of the stereotypical portrayal of Gentiles by Jews; see Buell and Johnson Hodge, "Politics of Interpretation," 244. In other words, both Jews and Romans used the strategy of "oppositional ethnic self-definition" (Jonathan M. Hall, *Ethnic Identity in Greek Antiquity* [Cambridge: Cambridge University Press, 1997], 47), albeit from very different positions of power. Just as Tacitus attacks the Jews for their dietary and sexual practices (*Hist.* 5.5), Paul is accusing the Corinthians of idolatry in the form of food and/or fornication (5:1-2, 5-13; 6:12-20; 10:1-22).

95. Albert Memmi, *The Colonizer and the Colonized*, trans. Howard Greenfeld (exp. ed.; Boston: Beacon, 1991), 15.

96. Bhabha, *Location of Culture*, 88.

97. Suh, *Being Buddhist*, 119, 166, 189–90. Other early Christ-followers after Paul (including Clement, Athenagoras, and Justin) would continue to use this strategy to justify their following of Christ as they simultaneously worked to negotiate what "being Roman" might mean; see Buell, "Rethinking the Relevance," 460–66.

98. Todd Penner, "Civilizing Discourse: Acts, Declamation, and the Rhetoric of the *Polis*," in Penner and Vander Stichele, *Contextualizing Acts*, 84-100.

99. Gregory E. Sterling, *Historiography and Self-Definition: Josephus, Luke-Acts and Apologetic Historiography* (Leiden: Brill, 1992), 223; see also Carl R. Holladay, "Acts and the Fragments of Hellenistic Jewish Historians," in *Jesus and the Heritage of Israel: Luke's Narrative Claim upon Israel's Legacy*, ed. David P. Moessner, Luke the Interpreter of Israel 1 (Harrisburg, Pa.: Trinity Press International, 1999), 174-97; Erich S. Gruen, *Heritage and Hellenism: The Reinvention of Jewish Tradition*, Hellenistic Culture and Society 30 (Berkeley: University of California Press, 1998).

100. Castelli, *Martyrdom and Memory*, 13.
101. Hays, *First Corinthians*, 95-96.
102. Lanci, *New Temple*, 97-99.
103. Schäfer, *Judeophobia*, 86-88.
104. Ibid., 17; see also Tacitus, *Hist.* 5.5.
105. See also Castelli, *Martyrdom and Memory*, 150-51, and Jennifer Wright Knust, *Abandoned to Lust: Sexual Slander and Ancient Christianity*, Gender, Theory, and Religion (New York: Columbia University Press, 2006).

106. See Emilio Gabba, *Dionysius and the History of Archaic Rome*, Sather Classical Lectures 56 (Berkeley: University of California Press, 1991).

107. Here I am of course only comparing Paul and Dionysius in terms of their strategies, not the purpose or direction of those strategies. That is to say, I am not suggesting with this comparison that Paul is pro-Roman or engaging in an apologetic on behalf of Rome.

108. See also Isaac, *Invention of Racism*, 479. Paul would, however, speak of the influence of a Christ-follower in cleansing rather than contaminating terms (7:12-16). Using a similar language of pollution against the body to explain 1 Corinthians, Martin nevertheless argues that Paul is worrying about a fundamental and internal polluting agent that is more threatening than women who do not follow Christ (since he does allow marriages between followers and non-followers to continue in 7:12-16) and other sexual dissidents (*Corinthian Body*, 198-228). According to Martin, Paul is most afraid of desire, which is also assumed to be particularly dangerous and tempting for women.

109. Hisaye Yamamoto, *Seventeen Syllables and Other Stories* (rev. and exp. ed.; New Brunswick, N.J.: Rutgers University Press, 2001), 34.

110. Ibid., 35.
111. Ibid., 36.
112. Ibid., 35.
113. Ibid., 35-36.
114. Ibid., 37.
115. Ibid., 36.
116. Ibid.
117. Abdul R. JanMohamed, *The Death-Bound-Subject: Richard Wright's Archaeology of Death*, Post-contemporary Interventions (Durham, N.C.: Duke University Press, 2005), 91.

118. Bhabha, *Location of Culture*, 111.
119. Ibid.
120. Dorinne Kondo, *About Face: Performing Race in Fashion and Theater* (New York: Routledge, 1997), 11.

121. Gayatri Chakravorty Spivak, "Can the Subaltern Speak?" in *Marxism and the Interpretation of Culture*, ed. Cary Nelson and Lawrence Grossberg (Urbana: University of Illinois Press, 1988), 297.

10. Imperial Intersections and Initial Inquiries

My thanks to the editors of the *Journal of Feminist Studies in Religion* for permission to reprint this slightly revised version of an article that appeared in vol. 22, no. 2 (Fall 2006): 5–32, as well as for all of the support and feedback I received from colleagues before and after its publication.

1. On (not explicitly feminist) postcolonial biblical interpretation, see, for example, Fernando F. Segovia, *Decolonizing Biblical Studies: A View from the Margins* (Maryknoll, N.Y.: Orbis, 2000); R. S. Sugirtharajah, *Asian Biblical Hermeneutics and Postcolonialism: Contesting the Interpretations*, Biblical Seminar 64 (Maryknoll, N.Y.: Orbis, 1998); idem, *The Bible and the Third World: Precolonial, Colonial, and Postcolonial Encounters* (Cambridge: Cambridge University Press, 2001); idem, *Postcolonial Criticism and Biblical Interpretation* (Oxford: Oxford University Press, 2002); idem, *Postcolonial Reconfigurations: An Alternative Way of Reading the Bible and Doing Theology* (St. Louis: Chalice, 2003); and collections from the Bible and Postcolonialism series, including R. S. Sugirtharajah, ed., *The Postcolonial Bible* (Sheffield: Sheffield Academic Press, 1998); idem, *Vernacular Hermeneutics* (Sheffield: Sheffield Academic Press, 1999); Fernando F. Segovia, ed., *Interpreting beyond Borders* (Sheffield: Sheffield Academic Press, 2000); Roland Boer, *Last Stop before Antarctica: The Bible and Postcolonialism in Australia* (Sheffield: Sheffield Academic Press, 2001); Musa W. Dube and Jeffrey L. Staley, eds., *John and Postcolonialism: Travel, Space, and Power* (London: Continuum, 2002); and Stephen D. Moore and Fernando F. Segovia, ed., *Postcolonial Biblical Criticism: Interdisciplinary Intersections* (London: T&T Clark, 2005). For the roots of postcolonial theory, most refer to Edward W. Said's 1978 book, *Orientalism* (rev. ed, with new preface and afterword [New York: Vintage Books, 1994]), as well as idem, *Culture and Imperialism* (New York: Vintage Books, 1993); Gayatri Chakravorty Spivak, *In Other Worlds: Essays in Cultural Politics* (New York: Routledge, 1988); eadem, *The Post-Colonial Critic: Interviews, Strategies, Dialogues*, ed. Sarah Harasym (New York: Routledge, 1990); eadem, *A Critique of Postcolonial Reason: Toward a History of the Vanishing Present* (Cambridge, Mass.: Harvard University Press, 1999); and Homi K. Bhabha, *The Location of Culture* (London: Routledge, 1994).

2. Richard A. Horsley, ed., *Paul and Empire: Religion and Power in Roman Imperial Society* (Harrisburg, Pa.: Trinity Press International, 1997); idem, ed., *Paul and Politics: Ekklesia, Israel, Imperium, Interpretation. Essays in Honor of Krister Stendahl* (Harrisburg, Pa.: Trinity Press International, 2000); idem, ed., *Paul and the Roman Imperial Order* (Harrisburg, Pa.: Trinity Press International, 2004); idem, ed., *Hidden Transcripts and the Arts of Resistance: Applying the Work of James C. Scott to Jesus and Paul*, Semeia Studies 48 (Atlanta: Society of Biblical Literature, 2004). Some of the work of scholars represented in these volumes reflects the aforementioned overlap between postcolonial analysis and political readings of Paul's letters; see Richard A. Horsley, "Submerged Biblical Histories and Imperial Biblical Studies," in Sugirtharajah, *Postcolonial Bible*, 152–73; idem, "Feminist Scholarship and Postcolonial Criticism: Subverting Imperial Discourse and Reclaiming Submerged Histories," in *Walk in the Ways of Wisdom: Essays in Honor of Elisabeth Schüssler Fiorenza*, ed. Shelly Matthews, Cynthia Briggs Kittredge, and Melanie Johnson-DeBaufre (Harrisburg, Pa.: Trinity Press International, 2003); Sze-kar Wan, "Collection for the Saints as Anticolonial Act: Implications of Paul's Ethnic Reconstruction," in Horsley, *Paul and Politics*, 191–215; idem, "Does Diaspora Identity Imply Some Sort of Universality?: An Asian-American Reading of Galatians," in Segovia, *Interpreting beyond Borders*, 107–31; and Abraham Smith, "'Unmasking the Powers': Toward a Postcolonial Analysis of 1 Thessalonians," in Horsley, *Paul and the Roman Imperial Order*, 47–66.

3. See, for example, Musa W. Dube, *Postcolonial Feminist Interpretation of the Bible* (St. Louis: Chalice, 2000); and Kwok Pui-lan, *Postcolonial Imagination and Feminist Theology* (Louisville: Westminster John Knox, 2005).

4. In this argument, feminism(s) is/are many things, but could be defined in terms of the

common aphorism: "Feminism is the radical notion that women are people," or by the fact that, "at the very least, feminism, like other liberation movements, attempts a critique of the oppressive structures of society." For the latter, see Mary Ann Tolbert, "Defining the Problem: The Bible and Feminist Hermeneutics," *Semeia* 28 (1983): 115. For the former, as well as a range of definitions for feminisms, see Elisabeth Schüssler Fiorenza, *Wisdom Ways: Introducing Feminist Biblical Interpretation* (Maryknoll, N.Y.: Orbis, 2001), 54–64; Phyllis A. Bird, "What Makes a Feminist Reading Feminist? A Qualified Answer," in *Escaping Eden: New Feminist Perspectives on the Bible*, ed. Harold C. Washington, Susan Lochrie Graham, and Pamela Thimmes, Biblical Seminar 65 (New York: New York University Press, 1999), 124–31; Pamela Thimmes, "What Makes a Feminist Reading Feminist? Another Perspective," in ibid., 132–40. Debates about the term "postcolonial" are typically centered on whether to focus on its temporal or political meaning, colonialism's historical or ongoing existence, or a primarily material or discursive analysis. This argument seeks to hold all these options in tension and will follow Dube, who explains, "The term *postcolonial* does not denote that colonialism is over, since the latter did not simply consist of geographical and political domination but also included cultural and economic structures that persist to this day. Postcolonial, therefore, refers to an overall analysis of the methods and effects of imperialism as a continuing reality in global relations" (Dube, *Postcolonial Feminist Interpretation*, 48). For reservations about the term, with some reflections on gender, see Anne McClintock, "The Angel of Progress: Pitfalls of the Term 'Post-Colonialism,'" *Social Text* 31/32 (1992): 84–98; and Ella Shohat, "Notes on the 'Post-Colonial,'" *Social Text* 31/32 (1992): 99–113.

5. Gayatri Chakravorty Spivak, "Can the Subaltern Speak?" in *Colonial Discourse and Post-Colonial Theory: A Reader*, ed. Patrick Williams and Laura Chrisman (New York: Columbia University Press, 1994), 92. Reprinted from *Marxism and the Interpretation of Culture*, ed. Cary Nelson and Lawrence Grossberg (Urbana: University of Illinois Press), 271–313. Whereas Spivak was referring to Western reaction to sati in India, Kwok Pui-lan notes the same imperialist rationale about foot binding in China in her "Unbinding Our Feet: Saving Brown Women and Feminist Religious Discourse," in *Postcolonialism, Feminism, and Religious Discourse*, ed. Laura E. Donaldson and Kwok Pui-lan (New York: Routledge, 2002), 62–81. For connections to the complex analysis of discourses on the veil in Muslim contexts, see the entries in that volume as well as the section of six entries on "Harem and the Veil" in *Feminist Postcolonial Theory: A Reader*, ed. Reina Lewis and Sara Mills (New York: Routledge, 2003), 489–609.

6. See Chandra Talpade Mohanty, "Under Western Eyes: Feminist Scholarship and Colonial Discourses," in *Feminism without Borders: Decolonizing Theory, Practicing Solidarity* (Durham, N.C.: Duke University Press, 2003), 17–42; Kirsten Holst Peterson and Anna Rutherford, ed., *A Double Colonization: Colonial and Post-Colonial Women's Writing* (Mundelstrup and Oxford: Dangaroo Press, 1986); Dube, *Postcolonial Feminist Interpretation*, 76, 117, 122–23, 174, 184, 201.

7. For these roles as well as the particular ways women have been figured in nationalist discourses as reproducers, signifiers, and transmitters of ethnic boundaries or difference, see Nira Yuval-Davis and Floya Anthias, eds., *Woman-Nation-State* (Hampshire: Macmillan, 1989), 7–10.

8. Kwok, *Postcolonial Imagination*, 66 (emphasis added). Cf. Anne McClintock: "Gender dynamics were, from the outset, fundamental to the securing and maintenance of the imperial enterprise" (*Imperial Leather: Race, Gender, and Sexuality in the Colonial Contest* [New York: Routledge, 1995], 7).

9. McClintock, *Imperial Leather*, 14. Many of the observations made in the introduction to this volume were first presented in McClintock, "Angel of Progress" (n. 4 above).

10. See McClintock, "The Lay of the Land: Genealogies of Imperialism," in eadem, *Imperial Leather*, 21–74. See also Laura E. Donaldson, "The Breasts of Columbus: A Political Anatomy of Postcolonialism and Feminist Religious Discourse," in Donaldson and Kwok, *Postcolonialism,*

Feminism, and Religious Discourse, 41–61. For an example of how postcolonial, feminist, and queer theory can be profitably linked in theological discourse, see Kwok Pui-lan, "Postcolonial Feminist Theology: What Is It? How to Do It?" in *Postcolonial Imagination*, 125–49.

11. See Kwok, *Postcolonial Imagination*, 80–81; and Dube, *Postcolonial Feminist Interpretation*, 112.

12. See, for example, Williams and Chrisman, *Colonial Discourse and Post-Colonial Theory*, 191–267; Leela Gandhi, *Postcolonial Theory: A Critical Introduction* (New York: Columbia University Press, 1998), 81–101; and John McLeod, *Beginning Postcolonialism*, Beginnings (Manchester: Manchester University Press, 2000), 172–204.

13. Segovia, *Decolonizing Biblical Studies*.

14. Ali A. Mazrui, *Cultural Forces in World Politics* (London: James Curry, 1990), 29; cf. Dube, *Postcolonial Feminist Interpretation*, 10–12.

15. Dube, *Postcolonial Feminist Interpretation*, 20. See also the sources listed in note 3 above.

16. Ibid., 118.

17. Ibid.

18. Kwok, *Postcolonial Imagination*, 7.

19. Ibid., 7–8; cf. Dube, *Postcolonial Feminist Interpretation*, 3–4.

20. Kwok, *Postcolonial Imagination*, 8–9.

21. See the four volumes edited by Richard A. Horsley cited in n. 2 above, particularly the latter half of *Hidden Transcripts*.

22. Recognition and inclusion do not necessarily involve alliance, acceptance, and integration. The inclusion of certain voices in a peripheral manner facilitates malestream scholarly management and disregard for feminist and/or female perspectives. In a similar manner, colonizers often overtly recognized certain injustices caused by colonization and included them in their speech-acts. This was done not to reform, alter, or end colonialism (and the effects explicitly noted) but to further endorse the imperial order, functioning apologetically within their "anti-conquest" claims. See Dube, *Postcolonial Feminist Interpretation*, 64–67. Here she is referring especially to David Quint, *Epic and Empire: Politics and Generic Form from Virgil to Milton*, Literature in History (Princeton: Princeton University Press, 1993), 99–130.

23. Elisabeth Schüssler Fiorenza, "Paul and the Politics of Interpretation," in Horsley, *Paul and Politics*, 40–57; Cynthia Briggs Kittredge, "Corinthian Women Prophets and Paul's Argumentation in 1 Corinthians," in ibid., 103–9; Sheila Briggs, "Paul on Bondage and Freedom in Imperial Roman Society," in ibid., 110–23; Antoinette Clark Wire, "Response: The Politics of the Assembly in Corinth," in ibid., 124–29; eadem, "Response: Paul and Those Outside Power," in ibid., 224–26. For concerns about this group of scholars not being sufficiently engaged with contemporary postcolonial theory, see Stephen D. Moore, "Postcolonialism," in *Handbook of Postmodern Biblical Interpretation*, ed. A. K. M. Adam (St. Louis: Chalice, 2000), 186–88; and Stephen D. Moore and Fernando F. Segovia, "Postcolonial Biblical Criticisms: Beginnings, Trajectories, Intersection," in Moore and Segovia, *Postcolonial Biblical Criticism*, 7–8. Further engagement with feminist practices and postcolonial feminist work could remedy this concern.

24. Schüssler Fiorenza, "Paul and the Politics of Interpretation," 50; Briggs, "Paul on Bondage and Freedom," 114–17.

25. Wire, "Response: The Politics of the Assembly in Corinth," 129; and eadem, "Response: Paul and Those Outside Power," 226. See also Schüssler Fiorenza, "Paul and the Politics of Interpretation," 50, on how the picture changes if "one focuses on the marginal and powerless, such as slaves and/or wo/men."

26. Kittredge, "Corinthian Women Prophets," 103–4.

27. Ibid., 105.

28. Horsley, *Paul and the Roman Imperial Order*, and Horsley, *Hidden Transcripts*, especially the introduction and part 2, 1–26, 97–171.

29. Jennifer Wright Knust, "Paul and the Politics of Virtue and Vice," in *Paul and the Roman Imperial Order*, 155–74. Could the continued physical placement of women's contributions toward the end of these volumes be a further (subconscious?) indication of precisely how peripheral these methods and concerns are to the project of "Paul and Politics"? See also the *Paul and Empire* and *Hidden Transcripts* volumes.

30. Horsley, "Introduction," in *Paul and the Roman Imperial Order*, 17–18; Efraín Agosto, "Patronage and Commendation, Imperial and Anti-Imperial," in *Paul and the Roman Imperial Order*, 118–22.

31. In the first seven entries in *Paul and the Roman Imperial Order*, for example, only twelve of 456 footnotes include references to feminist scholarship, and two of the works are listed only so that the scholar can dismiss them: Neil Elliott, "The Apostle Paul's Self-Presentation as Anti-imperial Performance" (pp. 73–74 n. 20), and Efraín Agosto, "Patronage and Commendation, Imperial and Anti-Imperial" (119 n. 42). On my reading, the only feminist scholar named in the body of these entries is Gayatri (Chakravorty) Spivak, in Abraham Smith, "'Unmasking the Powers,'" 48.

32. Horsley, "Introduction: Jesus, Paul, and the 'Arts of Resistance': Leaves from the Notebook of James C. Scott," in *Hidden Transcripts*, 7, 8.

33. Kittredge makes exactly this point in the beginning of her contribution to this volume, "Reconstructing 'Resistance' or Reading to Resist: James C. Scott and the Politics of Interpretation," in Horsley, *Hidden Transcripts*, 145. See, for example, the previously cited work of Schüssler Fiorenza, Wire, Briggs, and Kittredge, among others.

34. Kittredge, "Reconstructing 'Resistance,'" esp. 145–46, 152–55. As in the 2004 volume, in this collection gender plays a central role only in Kittredge's analysis. Of the 225 works referenced in this volume, feminist scholars wrote only thirteen, eight of which were cited in Kittredge's article.

35. Sandra Hack Polaski, *A Feminist Introduction to Paul* (St. Louis: Chalice, 2005). Neither Polaski's book nor Levine's collection (see n. 36 below) makes any reference to postcolonial feminist work, including that of Kwok Pui-lan, Musa W. Dube, or Laura E. Donaldson, or even to any of the volumes edited by Richard A. Horsley.

36. Luzia Sutter Rehmann, "To Turn the Groaning into Labor: Romans 8:22-23," in *A Feminist Companion to Paul*, ed. Amy-Jill Levine, with Marianne Blickenstaff (Cleveland: Pilgrim, 2004), 74–84, especially 78–80.

37. Luise Schottroff, "'Law-Free Gentile Christianity'—What about the Women? Feminist Analyses and Alternatives," in Levine, *Feminist Companion to Paul*, 183–94. Though it may be coincidental, it should be noted that these were the only two articles written by representatives from outside North America (at least in terms of academic appointment). Could the history of European colonialism or the American denial of its empire be at least partially responsible for these differences in topic?

38. Shawn Kelley, *Racializing Jesus: Race, Ideology, and the Formation of Modern Biblical Scholarship*, Biblical Limits (London: Routledge, 2002). On this particular combination, see especially 7, 148; cf. Said, *Orientalism*, 27–28, 133–48. Further, as Kwok points out: "The persecution of the Other within Europe—the heretics, the witches, and the Jews—was linked with early European expansion and its colonial impulse"(*Postcolonial Imagination*, 16). These intersecting dynamics are not entirely separate from the slave trade or the decimation of Native Americans. For the question of anti-Judaism in (especially feminist) postcolonial interpretation, see the roundtable discussion in *Journal of Feminist Studies in Religion* 20, no. 1 (Spring 2004): 91–132.

39. As Amy-Jill Levine explains about her editorial work on the collection: "We were also deliberate in inviting scholars from outside Western Europe, the USA, and Canada; whereas the response rate from this set of invitations was less than ideal" (*Feminist Companion to Paul*, 3).

40. Kelley, *Racializing Jesus*, 75–79, 145–50. For Kwok and Dube's concerns with universalism, see Kwok, *Postcolonial Imagination*, 36, 48–50, 56, 83, 91; and Dube, *Postcolonial Feminist Interpretation*, 18, 29, 105, 177, 183.

41. A version of this paper has since been published as "Mutuality Rhetorics and Feminist Intepretation: Examining Philippians and Arguing for Our Lives," *Bible and Critical Theory* 1, no. 3 (August 2005). My thanks to Abraham Smith, who graciously responded to my paper and pointed out Shawn Kelley's vital work.

42. See especially Donaldson and Kwok, *Postcolonialism, Feminism, and Religious Discourse*.

43. See Spivak, "French Feminism in an International Frame," in eadem, *In Other Worlds*, 134–53.

44. Kwok, *Postcolonial Imagination*, 18, 49. See, for example, Sara Mills, *Discourses of Difference: An Analysis of Women's Travel Writing and Colonialism* (New York: Routledge, 1992); Mary Louise Pratt, *Imperial Eyes: Travel Writing and Transculturation* (New York: Routledge, 1992); Rana Kabbani, *Imperial Fictions: Europe's Myths of Orient* (London: Macmillian, 1985); and Jenny Sharpe, *Allegories of Empire: The Figure of Woman in the Colonial Text* (Minneapolis: University of Minnesota Press, 1993).

45. Kwok, *Postcolonial Imagination*, 18.

46. Schüssler Fiorenza coined the term "kyriarchy," based on the Greek word for "lord." Rather than a simplified, dualistic analysis of power in gendered terms, kyriarchy highlights how multiple and mutually influential structures of domination and subordination function together, as evident not only in sexism, but also in racism, classism, ethnocentrism, heterosexism, colonialism, nationalism, and militarism. For an introductory discussion of this neologism, see Schüssler Fiorenza, *Wisdom Ways*, 1, 118–19, 211; and eadem, *Rhetoric and Ethic*, ix. See also eadem, *Bread Not Stone: The Challenge of Feminist Biblical Interpretation* (rev. ed.; Boston: Beacon, 1995), 211 n. 6; and eadem, *But She Said: Feminist Practices of Biblical Interpretation* (Boston: Beacon, 1992), 8, 117.

47. Dube, *Postcolonial Feminist Interpretation*, 28–36; Kwok, *Postcolonial Imagination*, 55. Dube ultimately states: "Despite these criticisms, I do believe that Schüssler Fiorenza's theoretical articulations of *kyriarchy* and *ekklesia* of women do go a long way toward counteracting imperialism, if followed" (p. 37).

48. Laura E. Donaldson, *Decolonizing Feminisms: Race, Gender, and Empire Building* (Chapel Hill: University of North Carolina Press, 1992), 5–6.

49. For the further problem of identifying with one's sources, especially the Pauline letters, see Schüssler Fiorenza, "Paul and the Politics of Interpretation," 40–57.

50. Cf. Dube, *Postcolonial Feminist Interpretation*, 43; Kwok, *Postcolonial Imagination*, 66. This recognition includes continuing to use the conceptual term "kyriarchy" in the following analysis; the concerns that have been noted indicate that the potential for problems lies not with the concept but with its potential uses. For more on Schüssler Fiorenza's response to and reflections on these critiques and concerns, see Schüssler Fiorenza, *The Power of the Word: Scripture and the Rhetoric of Empire* (Minneapolis: Fortress Press, 2007), 111–29.

51. See the work of Spivak, Donaldson, Mohanty, McClintock, Mills, Pratt, Kabbani, Sharpe (all cited above), and Trinh T. Minh-ha, *Woman, Native, Other: Writing Postcoloniality and Feminism* (Bloomington: Indiana University Press, 1989); Rajeswari Sunder Rajan, *Real and Imagined Women: Gender, Culture, and Postcolonialism* (London: Routledge, 1993); Ann Laura Stoler, *Race and the Education of Desire: Foucault's History of Sexuality and the Colonial Order of Things* (Durham, N.C.: Duke University Press, 1995); M. Jacqui Alexander and Chandra Talpade Mohanty, eds., *Feminist Genealogies, Colonial Legacies, Democratic Futures*, Thinking Gender (New York: Routledge, 1997); Chilla Bulbeck, *Re-Orienting Western Feminisms: Women's Diversity in a Postcolonial World* (Cambridge: Cambridge University Press, 1998); Ann Laura Stoler, *Carnal Knowledge and Imperial Power:*

Race and the Intimate in Colonial Rule (Berkeley: University of California Press, 2002); and Lewis and Mills, *Feminist Postcolonial Theory*, among others.

52. Gale A. Yee, *Poor Banished Children of Eve: Woman as Evil in the Hebrew Bible* (Minneapolis: Fortress Press, 2003); Judith E. McKinlay, *Reframing Her: Biblical Women in Postcolonial Focus*, Bible in the Modern World 1 (Sheffield: Sheffield Phoenix, 2004); Hisako Kinukawa, "De-colonizing Ourselves as Readers: The Story of the Syro-Phoenician Woman as a Text," in *Distant Voices Drawing Near: Essays in Honor of Antoinette Clark Wire*, ed. Holly E. Hearon (Collegeville, Minn.: Liturgical, 2004), 131–44; Sharon H. Ringe, "Places at the Table: Feminist and Postcolonial Biblical Interpretation," in Sugirtharajah, *Postcolonial Bible*, 136–51; Kathleen O'Brien Wicker, "Teaching Feminist Biblical Studies in a Postcolonial Context," in *Searching the Scriptures*, vol. 1, *A Feminist Introduction*, ed. Elisabeth Schüssler Fiorenza (New York: Crossroad, 1993), 367–80.

53. Works by Kwok Pui-lan include *Discovering the Bible in the Non-Biblical World*, Bible and Liberation (Maryknoll, N.Y.: Orbis, 1995); "Jesus/the Native: Biblical Studies from a Postcolonial Perspective," in *Teaching the Bible: The Discourses and Politics of Biblical Pedagogy*, ed. Fernando F. Segovia and Mary Ann Tolbert (Maryknoll, N.Y.: Orbis, 1995), 69–85; *Introducing Asian Feminist Theology*, Introductions in Feminist Theology 4 (Cleveland: Pilgrim, 2000); "Mercy Amba Oduyoye and African Women's Theology," *Journal of Feminist Studies in Religion* 20, no. 1 (2004): 7–22; and Donaldson and Kwok, *Postcolonialism, Feminism, and Religious Discourse*. Works by Musa Dube include "Reading for Decolonization (John 4:1-42)," *Semeia* 75 (1996): 37–59; "Toward a Postcolonial Feminist Interpretation of the Bible," *Semeia* 78 (1997): 11–26; "Scripture, Feminism, and Post-colonial Contexts," in *Women's Sacred Scriptures*, ed. Kwok Pui-lan and Elisabeth Schüssler Fiorenza (London: SCM, 1998), 45—54; "Postcolonial Biblical Interpretations," in *Dictionary of Biblical Interpretation*, ed. John H. Hayes (2 vols.; Nashville: Abingdon, 1999), 2:299–303; "Consuming the Colonial Cultural Bomb: Translating Badimo into Demons in the Setswana Bible (Matt. 8:28-34; 15:22; 10:8)," *Journal for the Study of the New Testament* 73 (1999): 33–59; as well as O'Brien Wicker, Musa W. Dube, and Althea Spencer-Miller, eds., *Feminist New Testament Studies: Global and Future Perspectives*, Religion/Culture/Critique (New York: Palgrave Macmillan, 2005).

54. For some of their comments on Paul's letters, including the topics of "the mission to the Gentiles" and Paul's views of women, gender, and sexuality in empire, see Dube, *Postcolonial Feminist Interpretation*, 12–14, 181–82; and Kwok, *Postcolonial Imagination*, 77, 89–93.

55. In particular, see the description in her conclusion to *Postcolonial Feminist Interpretation*, 199–201.

56. Kwok, *Postcolonial Imagination*, 81–84.

57. Ibid., 81.

58. I return to this point below. For a work that examines transnational movements as domains of critique and engagement, see Mohanty, *Feminism without Borders*.

59. See Horsley and Elliott, among others, as well as the critiques cited above by Kittredge, Wire, and Schüssler Fiorenza. On the analytic of domination, see also Schüssler Fiorenza, *Rhetoric and Ethic*, 50, and Schüssler Fiorenza, *Wisdom Ways*, 172–75.

60. Kwok, *Postcolonial Imagination*, 82.

61. Ibid., 82. For a definition of "contact zone," see Pratt, *Imperial Eyes*. On the hermeneutics of remembrance and reconstruction, see Schüssler Fiorenza, *Rhetoric and Ethic*, 51–52; and eadem, *Wisdom Ways*, 183–86. For further reflections on the utility of the "contact zone" for historical reflections, see Joseph A. Marchal, *The Politics of Heaven: Women, Gender, and Empire in the Study of Paul*, Paul in Critical Contexts (Minneapolis: Fortress Press, 2008), 91–109, 166–76.

62. Kwok, *Postcolonial Imagination*, 83. See also the examination of previous scholarship on mission patterns in Matthew in Dube, *Postcolonial Feminist Interpretation*, 157–95. For possible

connections to the hermeneutics of suspicion, see Schüssler Fiorenza, *Rhetoric and Ethic*, 50–51; and eadem, *Wisdom Ways*, 175–77.

63. Historically, empires have identified themselves as imperial but rationalized their empire by extolling the beneficent, civilizing, and paternalistic quality of their rule. Thus, identifying could even be the act of the colonizer. As a result, Pauline scholars need to be cautious about how we identify imperial contexts or rhetorics. See Marchal, "Military Images in Philippians 1–2: A Feminist Rhetorical Analysis of Scholarship, Philippians, and Current Contexts," in *Her Master's Tools? Feminist and Postcolonial Engagements of Historical-Critical Discourse*, ed. Caroline Vander Stichele and Todd Penner, Global Perspectives on Biblical Scholarship 9 (Atlanta: Society of Biblical Literature, 2005), 285–86.

64. Kwok, *Postcolonial Imagination*, 83. See also Malika Sibeko and Beverley Haddad, "Reading the Bible 'with' Women in Poor and Marginalized Communities in South Africa," *Semeia* 78 (1997): 83–92; Gerald O. West, *The Academy of the Poor: Towards a Dialogical Reading of the Bible*, Interventions 2 (Sheffield: Sheffield Academic, 1999); and the section titled "Reading With and From Non-academic Readers," in *Other Ways of Reading: African Women and the Bible*, ed. Musa W. Dube, Global Perspectives on Biblical Scholarship (Atlanta: Society of Biblical Literature, 2001), 101–42. On the possible connections to a hermeneutics of experience and social location, see Schüssler Fiorenza, *Rhetoric and Ethic*, 49; and eadem, *Wisdom Ways*, 169–72. For the phrase "flesh and blood readers," see Segovia, *Decolonizing Biblical Studies*, 50.

65. Kwok, *Postcolonial Imagination*, 84; cf. Mary Ann Tolbert, "The Politics and Poetics of Location" in *Reading from This Place*, vol. 1, *Social Location and Biblical Interpretation in the United States*, ed. Fernando F. Segovia and Mary Ann Tolbert (Minneapolis: Fortress Press, 1995), 305–17. On potential connections to the hermeneutics of ethical and theological evaluation or transformation, see Schüssler Fiorenza, *Rhetoric and Ethic*, 51, 53–54; and eadem, *Wisdom Ways*, 177–79, 186–89. For further reflections on the intersections of race, ethnicity, and gender in the interpretation of Second Testament and early Christian materials, see Laura Nasrallah and Schüssler Fiorenza, eds., *Prejudice and Christian Beginnings: Investigating Race, Gender, and Ethnicity in Early Christian Studies* (Minneapolis: Fortress Press, 2009), including especially my entry discussing a feminist postcolonial approach to mimicry in the context of another letter, 1 Corinthians, "Mimicry and Colonial Differences: Gender, Ethnicity, and Empire in the Interpretation of Pauline Imitation" (101–27).

66. Dube, *Postcolonial Feminist Interpretation*, 201, 57, 129. The first listing does not include divine representations in the fourth question (p. 57), but they are discussed in the analysis following it and thus added to the later listings (pp. 129, 201). The third question also alternately discusses "mutual interdependence" and "condemnation and replacement."

67. Dube's repeated stress on analyzing "this text" in these questions indicates that her approaches are geared primarily toward literary-rhetorical assessment rather than historical reconstructions. Nevertheless, as several feminist rhetorical scholars have demonstrated (for example, Wire, Schüssler Fiorenza, and Kittredge), rhetorical analysis of Paul's letters can facilitate an exploration of the various points of view in the potential audience. Thus, in implementing Dube's questions, the following analysis in this study will be most useful for the initial task, with only a few helpful notes for reconstructing these other perspectives.

68. For "aspects of a postcolonial reading" of Philippians, see Efraín Agosto, "Paul vs. Empire: A Postcolonial and Latino Reading of Philippians," *Perspectivas: Occasional Papers* 6 (Fall 2002): 37–56. Agosto's comments focus on Paul's imprisonment and the collection for the poor, yielding some very different results from mine. See the response to Agosto by Hjamil A. Martínez-Vázquez, "Postcolonial Criticism in Biblical Interpretation: A Response to Efraín Agosto," *Perspectivas: Occasional Papers* 6 (Fall 2002): 57–63. For other readings of Pauline letters (besides Philippians) using elements of postcolonial theory, see the other entries in this volume, as well as Khoik-Khng Yeo, "The Rhetorical

Hermeneutic of 1 Corinthians 8 and Chinese Ancestor Worship," *Biblical Interpretation* 2 (1994): 294–311; Wan, "Collection for the Saints"; idem, "Does Diaspora Identity"; Smith, "'Unmasking the Powers'"; Vander Stichele and Penner, "Paul and the Rhetoric of Gender," in *Her Master's Tools?*, 287–310; Robert Seesengood "Hybridity and the Rhetoric of Endurance: Reading Paul's Athletic Metaphors in a Context of Postcolonial Self-Construction," *Bible and Critical Theory* 1, no. 3 (2005): 16.1–16.14. For initial reflections on the consequences of Roman imperialism for Philippians, see also Horsley, "General Introduction," "Introduction" to "Part 3: Paul's Counter-Imperial Gospel," and "Introduction" to "Part 4: Building an Alternative Society," in *Paul and Empire*, 1–8, 140–47, 206–14; N. T. Wright, "Paul's Gospel and Caesar's Empire," in Horsley, *Paul and Empire*, 160–83; and Erik M. Heen, "Phil 2:6-11 and Resistance to Local Timocratic Rule: *Isa theō* and the Cult of the Emperor in the East," in Horsley, *Paul and the Roman Imperial Order*, 125–53. For some paralleled points of analysis on Horsley, Wright, Agosto, and Heen, see also Marchal, *Politics of Heaven*, 37–44, 144–47.

69. The following rhetorical analysis depends on, develops in conversation with, and yet is distinguishable from preceding feminist analyses of Philippians. See especially Carolyn L. Osiek, "Philippians," in *Searching the Scriptures*, vol. 2, *A Feminist Commentary*, ed. Elisabeth Schüssler Fiorenza (New York: Crossroad, 1994), 237–49; Cynthia Briggs Kittredge, *Community and Authority: The Rhetoric of Obedience in the Pauline Tradition*, Harvard Theological Studies 45 (Harrisburg, Pa.: Trinity Press International, 1998); Joseph A. Marchal, *Hierarchy, Unity, and Imitation: A Feminist Rhetorical Analysis of Power Dynamics in Paul's Letter to the Philippians*, Society of Biblical Literature Academia Biblica 24 (Atlanta: Society of Biblical Literature, 2006), idem, "Military Images"; idem, "'With Friends like These . . .': A Feminist Rhetorical Reconsideration of Scholarship and the Letter to the Philippians," *Journal for the Study of the New Testament* 29, no. 1 (September 2006): 77–106.

70. For a different interpretation of Paul's imprisonment, see Agosto, "Paul vs. Empire," 43–46, 48, 50–51. On Paul's imprisonment, see also Craig S. Wansink, *Chained in Christ: The Experience and Rhetoric of Paul's Imprisonment*, Journal for the Study of the New Testament Supplement Series 130 (Sheffield: Sheffield Academic Press, 1996); and Richard J. Cassidy, *Paul in Chains: Roman Imprisonment and the Letters of Paul* (New York: Crossroad, 2001). Whether Paul is imprisoned in Ephesus or Rome changes little concerning the rhetorics about and effects of travel, distance, or the claims of progress.

71. On *parousia*, see Helmut Koester, "Imperial Ideology and Paul's Eschatology in 1 Thessalonians," in Horsley, *Paul and Empire*, 158–66. The source of the Philippians' joy would also be their *pistis*, their loyalty or adherence to this message (now imperially cast).

72. For further historical and material considerations of the multiple colonizations of Philippi and the resulting conditions for the possible citizens, veterans, and their descendants, alongside other inhabitants, see Marchal, "Military Images," 271–80; and idem, *Hierarchy, Unity, and Imitation*, 50–64, 99–112.

73. See also passages like 4:15-16, 21-22, which discuss Paul's travels or situate him in another location offering greetings across some geographical space to the audience.

74. For a helpful, critical, but exploratory investigation of the power dynamics of Pauline imitation, see Elizabeth A. Castelli, *Imitating Paul: A Discourse of Power*, Literary Currents in Biblical Interpretation (Louisville: Westminster John Knox, 1991). For some critical reflections and elaborations upon this work, see Marchal, *Politics of Heaven*, 59–90, 154–66.

75. For Paul as the model, see also 1:3-11, 12-14, 24-26; 2:16-18; 4:2, and perhaps implicitly also 1:30; 2:23-24, 29; 3:7-11, 4:11-13. Markus Bockmuehl maintains that "the theme of imitation recurs as an integrating focus in every major section of Philippians" (*The Epistle to the Philippians*, Black's New Testament Commentaries [Peabody, Mass.: Hendrickson, 1998], 254).

76. Tat-siong Benny Liew, "Tyranny, Boundary, and Might: Colonial Mimicry in Mark's Gospel," *Journal for the Study of the New Testament* 73 (1999): 7–31. For the use of mimesis, mimicry, or

mimeticism in postcolonial work, see Bhabha, *Location of Culture*; Rey Chow, *The Protestant Ethnic and the Spirit of Capitalism* (New York: Columbia University Press, 2002); McClintock, *Imperial Leather*; and Meyda Yeğenoğlu, "Veiled Fantasies: Cultural and Sexual Difference in the Discourse of Orientalism," in Lewis and Mills, *Feminist Postcolonial Theory*, 542–66, reprinted from Yeğenoğlu, *Colonial Fantasies: Towards A Feminist Reading of Orientalism*, Cambridge Cultural Social Studies (Cambridge: Cambridge University Press, 1998), 39–67. On the concept of mimicry as it relates to Paul's hybridity, see Seesengood, "Hybridity and the Rhetoric of Endurance."

77. On the authoritative, hierarchical dynamics of imitation, see especially Castelli's analysis in *Imitating Paul*. For one conceptualization of the ambivalent agency of the colonized who are asked to imitate, see Bhabha, *Location of Culture*.

78. See Dube, *Postcolonial Feminist Interpretation*, 13–14, 155, 181–83, and Kwok, *Postcolonial Imagination*, 65. Dube is concerned with a feminist reconstruction of mission and women's roles in "mission texts," because "it proceeds by assuming that the mission to the Gentiles was and is itself liberating, since it does not scrutinize or problematize the strategies of the mission nor the power relations it advocates" (*Postcolonial Feminist Interpretation*, 183). See also Kwesi Dickson's observations about the exclusivist, anti-indigenous tendency of Paul's argumentation in *Uncompleted Mission: Christianity and Exclusivism* (Maryknoll, N.Y.: Orbis, 1991), 59–69.

79. On the apocalyptic aspect of Paul's anti-imperial arguments, see the various entries by Horsley, Koester, and Elliott (among others) in the collections *Paul and Empire*, *Paul and Politics*, and *Paul and the Roman Imperial Order* (n. 2 above). Even if one accepts their arguments, the question about whether anticolonial apocalyptic rhetoric can still be redeployed as part of a colonizing regime remains to be addressed, especially considering its dualistic argumentation; see Dube, *Postcolonial Feminist Interpretation*, 73. Reading Paul as an apocalyptic thinker also requires reconsidering the potentially threatening elements of passages like 3:15 (God's "revelation" for those who think anything different) and 4:3 (inclusion or exclusion in the book of life).

80. For a series of malestream mitigations as to the hierarchical nature of obedience rhetorics, see the overview and critique in Kittredge, *Community and Authority*, 13–36. Victor Paul Furnish's claim that Pauline obedience is a kind of loving mutuality is particularly susceptible to this critique. See Furnish, *The Love Command in the New Testament* (Nashville: Abingdon, 1972).

81. For the attribution of sexual perversity to outsiders and colonized people as an imperial rationale, see Said, *Orientalism*; Knust, "Paul and the Politics of Virtue and Vice"; and Knust, *Abandoned to Lust: Sexual Slander and Ancient Christianity*, Gender, Theory, and Religion (New York: Columbia University Press, 2005).

82. For N. T. Wright's interpretation of these slurs as a coded challenge to the empire, see Wright, "Paul's Gospel and Caesar's Empire," 174–81. What eludes Wright here is that Paul's argument likely coincides with and reinforces imperial argumentation. Wright seems initially aware of this possibility (p. 164), but his interpretation does not consider it further.

83. See Horsley, "General Introduction," "Introduction" to "Part 3: Paul's Counter-Imperial Gospel," and "Introduction" to "Part 4: Building an Alternative Society," in *Paul and Empire*, 3–6, 140–43, 211–14; Wright, "Paul's Gospel and Caesar's Empire," 164, 173–81; Agosto, "Paul vs. Empire," 45–49; and the analysis in Marchal, *Politics of Heaven*, especially 38–41, 144–46. See also Schüssler Fiorenza, "Paul and the Politics of Interpretation," 55–56.

84. Dube develops the postcolonial feminist value of interdependence based on her work with women in African Independent Churches (AICs) (*Postcolonial Feminist Interpretation*, 184–95). On the importance of solidarity, as opposed to sisterhood, as a paradigm for decolonizing, transnational feminist organizing, see Mohanty, *Feminism without Borders*, especially 7, 40–45, 110–11.

85. See Dube, *Postcolonial Feminist Interpretation*, 184–86.

86. On this phenomenon, Dube comments: "The postindependence experience of many Two-

Thirds World countries has also rudely shown that 'independence' from other nations and cultures, even from those that oppressed them, is neither practical nor the best means for survival" (*Postcolonial Feminist Interpretation*, 185). This raises the question, if Paul *is* anti-imperial, is his position more akin to that of some post-independence authorities than that of an anticolonial revolutionary?

87. For more on how Paul constructs himself in gendered and imperialist terms in another letter (1 Corinthians), see Vander Stichele and Penner, "Paul and the Rhetoric of Gender."

88. Wright, "Paul's Gospel and Caesar's Empire," 164. On the same page, Wright also suggests, "To say that Paul opposed imperialism is about as politically dangerous as suggesting he was in favor of sunlight, fresh air, and orange juice." Is it not "politically dangerous" because there is a lack of acknowledgment of imperial relations within and extending out from the United States and the UK (at least by some of its citizenry)? Or is this an indication of how apolitical our analysis of imperialism has been? Nevertheless, as Wright's comments seem to acknowledge (though his analysis fails to develop), Paul is not against imperialism as a dynamic of dominating rule.

89. Kittredge, "Corinthian Women Prophets," 107–9.

90. That "commonwealth" is an imperial term implying commonality, reciprocity, or equality, while masking the exploitative conditions of colonization(s), should give pause to those who want to claim its use here as liberating. On the origins of postcolonial literature as a terminological replacement for "commonwealth literature," see R. S. Sugirtharajah, "A Postcolonial Exploration of Collusion and Construction in Biblical Interpretation," in idem, *Postcolonial Bible*, 92.

91. For the Roman imperial resonance of these terms, see Dieter Georgi, "God Turned Upside Down," in Horsley, *Paul and Empire*, 148–57; Elliott, "Romans 13:1-7 in the Context of Imperial Propaganda," in ibid., 184–204; and Karl P. Donfried, "The Imperial Cults of Thessalonica and Political Conflict in 1 Thessalonians," in ibid., 215–23, among others.

92. On military images in Philippians, see Edgar M. Krentz, "Military Language and Metaphors in Philippians," in *Origins and Method: Towards a New Understanding of Judaism and Christianity; Essays in Honour of John. C. Hurd*, ed. Bradley H. McLean, Journal for the Study of the New Testament Supplement Series 86 (Sheffield: JSOT Press, 1993), 105–27; Timothy C. Geoffrion, *The Rhetorical Purpose and the Political and Military Character of Philippians: A Call to Stand Firm* (Lewiston, N.Y.: Mellen, 1993); and Edgar M. Krentz, "Paul, Games, and the Military," in *Paul in the Greco-Roman World: A Handbook*, ed. J. Paul Sampley (Harrisburg, Pa.: Trinity Press International, 2003), 344–83. For a summary and assessment of these rhetorics and the scholarly examination of them, see Marchal "Military Images."

93. For a consideration of patronage and friendship in this letter and the Roman imperial context, see John T. Fitzgerald, "Paul and Friendship," in Sampley, *Paul in the Greco-Roman World*, 319–43, and Marchal, "With Friends like These."

94. For interconnections between military and patronage/friendship rhetorics, see Marchal, *Hierarchy, Unity, and Imitation*, 64–70.

95. Kittredge, *Community and Authority*, 37–51; and eadem, "Corinthian Women Prophets," 105–7. If taken seriously, Kittredge's work on the verb *hypotassethai* ("to be subjected") would nuance some of the positive claims made about Paul by Elliott and Agosto. See Elliott, "The Apostle Paul's Self-Presentation as Anti-Imperial Performance," in Horsley, *Paul and the Roman Imperial Order*, 73–74; and Agosto, "Patronage and Commendation, Imperial and Anti-Imperial," in ibid., 114.

96. Here I part ways with the analysis of the hymn offered by Kittredge and other feminist scholars. See Kittredge, *Community and Authority*, 99–100, 110; and Luise Schottroff, *Lydia's Impatient Sisters: A Feminist Social History of Early Christianity*, trans. Barbara Rumscheidt and Martin Rumscheidt (Louisville: Westminster John Knox, 1995), 43–46. Though the hymn might have offered a pattern of reversal as a hope to those oppressed in various ways by the kyriarchal culture, its imagery and vocabulary are still embedded in this kyriarchal matrix of slave–master (2:7) and

subject–ruler (2:9-11). For a similar assertion about the kyriocentric nature of this text, see Sheila Briggs, "Can an Enslaved God Liberate? Hermeneutical Reflections on Philippians 2:6-11," *Semeia* 47 (1989): 137-53.

97. Here Kittredge's argument is clear and decisive about the function of the hymn in extolling obedience. See Kittredge, *Community and Authority*, 83–86.

98. On the connection between "fear and trembling" and the obedience of slaves in the Pauline corpus, see Carolyn L. Osiek, *Philippians, Philemon*, Abingdon New Testament Commentaries (Nashville: Abingdon, 2000), 70.

99. For a fuller explication of this repeated pattern of "descend in order to ascend" and its connections to the rhetorics of sacrifice, see Marchal, "Mutuality Rhetorics and Feminist Intepretation"; and idem, *Hierarchy, Unity, and Imitation*, 141–43, 171–73.

100. For further arguments that Pauline community language (including the body of Christ and brothers/*adelphoi*) is androcentric, see Jorunn Økland, *Women in Their Place: Paul and the Corinthian Discourse of Gender and Sanctuary Space*, Journal for the Study of the New Testament Supplement Series 269 (London: T&T Clark International, 2005), 211–17.

101. Both Craig S. de Vos and Peter S. Oakes maintain that the community to which Paul wrote was likely composed primarily of people with lower status. See de Vos, *Church and Community Conflicts: The Relationships of the Thessalonian, Corinthian, and Philippian Churches with Their Wider Civic Communities*, Society of Biblical Literature Dissertation Series 168 (Atlanta: Scholars Press, 1999), 250–61; and Oakes, *Philippians: From People to Letter*, Society for New Testament Studies Monograph Series 110 (Cambridge: Cambridge University Press, 2001), 57–63. For the impact of relative social standing on the rhetorics of Pauline letters and the communities to which he writes, see Antoinette Clark Wire, *The Corinthian Women Prophets: A Reconstruction through Paul's Rhetoric* (Minneapolis: Fortress Press, 1990), 62–71. On Paul's status, including some initial postcolonial analysis, see Seesengood, "Hybridity and the Rhetoric of Endurance."

102. Most scholarship on Philippians has acquiesced to Paul's division of authority in this manner, assuming that the call in 4:2 to "think the same thing" portrays a conflict between Euodia and Syntyche rather than a difference between Paul and the two women. As on previous occasions, Kittredge's argument that Euodia and Syntyche are not in a conflict with each other but with Paul is unique and convincing (*Community and Authority*, 105–8). Cf. Marchal, *Hierarchy, Unity, and Imitation*, esp. 147–52, 189–90; idem, "Military Images"; and idem, "With Friends like These."

103. That "the lord is near" (4:5) might also be a foreboding hint of the end for those who do not accept the letter's specific message of divine peace (4:7, 9). Peace is the province of the Romans since Augustus's reign established a "Pax Romana."

104. See Mary Rose D'Angelo, "Abba and 'Father': Imperial Theology and the Traditions about Jesus," *Journal of Biblical Literature* 111 (1992): 611–30; and eadem, "Early Christian Sexual Politics and Roman Imperial Family Values: Rereading Christ and Culture," in *The Papers of the Henry Luce III Fellows in Theology*, ed. Christopher I. Wilkins (6 vols.; Pittsburgh: Association of Theological Schools, 2003), 6:23–48.

105. Kittredge, "Corinthian Women Prophets," 105.

106. Even if my argument that Paul's argumentation repeats, reinscribes, or coincides with imperialism proves unconvincing, there is still no assurance that Paul's letters function to decolonize. See, for example, Dube's three questions about rhetorical methods of decolonizing in *Postcolonial Feminist Interpretation*, 97.

107. Kwok, *Postcolonial Imagination*, 10.

108. On "erotic triangles," the homosocial/homoerotic contest for authority, and the maintenance of power, see Eve Kosofsky Sedgwick, *Between Men: English Literature and Male Homosocial Desire*, Gender and Culture (New York: Columbia University Press, 1985), especially 21–27. For the

interweaving of this kind of analysis with postcolonial feminist concerns, see Laura E. Donaldson, "A Passage to 'India': Colonialism and Filmic Representation," in eadem, *Decolonizing Feminisms*, 88-101.

109. For this pattern in ancient visual culture, see Davina C. Lopez, "Before Your Very Eyes: Roman Imperial Ideology, Gender Constructs, and Paul's Inter-nationalism," in *Mapping Gender in Ancient Religious Discourses*, ed. Todd Penner and Caroline Vander Stichele; Bibiblical Interpretation Series 84 (Leiden: Brill, 2007), 115-62; Rene Rodgers, "Female Representation in Roman Art: Feminizing the Provincial Other," in *Roman Imperialism and Provincial Art*, ed. Sarah Scott and Jane Webster (New York: Cambridge University Press, 2004), 69-93; and on imperialism in general, see McClintock, *Imperial Leather*.

110. On the importance of manliness in the empire see D'Angelo, "Abba and 'Father'" and eadem, "Early Christian Sexual Politics"; Craig A. Williams, *Roman Homosexuality: Ideologies of Masculinity in Classical Antiquity*, Ideologies of Desire (New York: Oxford University Press, 1999); Vander Stichele and Penner, "Paul and the Rhetoric of Gender"; and Virginia Burrus, *"Begotten, Not Made": Conceiving Manhood in Late Antiquity*, Figurae (Stanford: Stanford University Press, 2000).

111. Such an assessment would require a longer and more complicated analysis than can be offered at this stage; see the attempt to engage postcolonial and postcolonial feminist work on mimesis, mimicry, and mimeticism, in Marchal, *Politics of Heaven*, 59-90, 154-66.

112. For a feminist engagement with the perils of nationalism and globalization, see the roundtable discussion in *Journal of Feminist Studies in Religion* 21, no. 1 (Spring 2005): 111-54.

113. Dube, *Postcolonial Feminist Interpretation*, 52.

114. For the phrases, "almost the same, but not quite," and "almost the same, but not white," see Bhabha, *Location of Culture*, 86, 89.

115. Kwok, *Postcolonial Imagination*, 82. For further elaborations on the potential historical dynamics in this particular contact zone (Philippi), see Marchal, *Politics of Heaven*, 91-109, 166-76.

11. Beyond the Heroic Paul

1. Krister Stendahl, "The Apostle Paul and the Introspective Conscience of the West," *Harvard Theological Review* 56 (1963): 199-215.

2. Cited in Brian K. Blount, *Then the Whisper Put on Flesh: New Testament Ethics in an African American Context* (Nashville: Abingdon, 2001), 121.

3. Kwok Pui-lan, *Postcolonial Imagination and Feminist Theology* (Louisville: Westminster John Knox, 2005), 77. See also the reaction of Gordon Zerbe's Filipino students to Paul in "The Politics of Paul: His Supposed Social Conservatism and the Impact of Postcolonial Readings," *Conrad Grebel Review* 21 (2003): 82-103.

4. Blount, *Whisper*, 121.

5. Ibid., 77-78.

6. See also Elisabeth Schüssler Fiorenza, *Power of the Word: Scripture and the Rhetoric of Empire* (Minneapolis: Fortress Press, 2007), 69-109; and earlier, the essays of Schüssler Fiorenza ("Paul and the Politics of Interpretation"), Cynthia Briggs Kittredge ("Corinthian Women Prophets and Paul's Argumentation in 1 Corinthians"), and Antoinette Clark Wire ("Response: The Politics of the Assembly in Corinth" and "Response: Paul and Those Outside Power") in *Paul and Politics: Ekklesia, Israel, Imperium, Interpretation. Essays in Honor of Krister Stendahl*, ed. Richard A. Horsley (Harrisburg, Pa.: Trinity Press International, 2000). While Paul remains the primary dialogue partner, there is some opening toward a dialogical and communal engagement with the Pauline traditions in Yung Suk Kim, *Christ's Body in Corinth: The Politics of a Metaphor*, Paul in Critical Contexts (Minneapolis:

Fortress Press, 2008), and earlier, Charles H. Cosgrove, Herold Weiss, and Khiok-Khng Yeo, *Cross-cultural Paul: Journeys to Others, Journeys to Ourselves* (Grand Rapids: Eerdmans, 2005).

7. Our review of a range of politically engaged Pauline scholarship suggests that Elisabeth Schüssler Fiorenza's original assessment of Paul-centered scholarly discourse remains true today: "A full paradigm shift from an individualistic Euro-American malestream framework of interpretation to a fully political and communal paradigm of Pauline studies has not yet been accomplished. The reason for this, I suggest, is the hegemonic politics of interpretation. The rhetoric of Pauline interpreters continues not only to identify themselves with Paul but also to see Paul as identical with 'his' communities, postulating that Paul was the powerful creator and unquestioned leader of the communities of whom he writes" ("Paul and the Politics of Interpretation," 44). See also eadem, *Rhetoric and Ethic: The Politics of Biblical Studies* (Minneapolis: Fortress Press, 1999), 180–88; and *Power of the Word*, 83–89. In an early essay, Randall C. Bailey questioned this process of identification among African-Americans ("The Danger of Ignoring One's Own Cultural Bias in Interpreting the Text," in *The Bible and Postcolonialism*, ed. R. S. Sugirtharajah [Sheffield: Sheffield Academic, 1998], 79).

8. By this we mean scholars who frame their work as informed by and somehow interested in contemporary politics, in contrast to those who have ethical-political concerns but do not foreground them. Insofar as this scholarship articulates political and cultural valences of what has traditionally been read as (purely) religious discourse, it can make an important contribution to the already politically forthright feminist and postcolonial conversations. Richard Horsley and Neil Elliott have been influential in framing a trajectory of Pauline scholarship that articulates the *political* rather than *religious* content and meaning of Paul's letters (now called an "empire-critical" approach).

9. See Robert C. Tannehill, "Paul as Liberator or Oppressor: How Should We Evaluate Diverse Views of First Corinthians?" in *The Meanings We Choose: Hermeneutical Ethics, Indeterminacy and the Conflict of Interpretation*, ed. Charles H. Cosgrove, Journal for the Study of the Old Testament Supplement Series 411 (London: T&T Clark, 2004), 122–37. For a discussion of his "he was both" answer, see Schüssler Fiorenza, *Power of the Word*, 92–94. Zerbe also sees Paul as both reinscribing and challenging empire ("Politics of Paul," 97). For Paul as a fully postcolonial hybrid subject, see Robert Paul Seesengood, *Competing Identities: The Athlete and the Gladiator in Early Christianity*, Library of New Testament Studies 346, Playing the Texts 12 (New York: T&T Clark, 2006).

10. We use "decolonizing" rather than "postcolonial" here to indicate the ongoing nature of the struggle within and against empire and to signal complex connections of this approach to a range of liberationist projects. For discussion, see Musa W. Dube, *Postcolonial Feminist Interpretations of the Bible* (St. Louis: Chalice, 2000), 111–24; Schüssler Fiorenza, *Power of the Word*, 111–29; and Fernando F. Segovia, *Decolonizing Biblical Studies: A View from the Margins* (Maryknoll, N.Y.: Orbis, 2000).

11. See Elizabeth A. Castelli, *Imitating Paul: A Discourse of Power*, Literary Currents in Biblical Interpretation (Louisville: Westminster John Knox, 1991); Joseph A. Marchal, *The Politics of Heaven: Women, Gender, and Empire in the Study of Paul*, Paul in Critical Contexts (Minneapolis: Fortress Press, 2008), 59–90.

12. For two very different examples of using Romans 7 to think about subjectivity in a postcolonial/imperial context, see L. Ann Jervis, "Reading Romans 7 in Conversation with Post-Colonial Theory: Paul's Struggle Toward a Christian Identity of Hybridity," *Theoforum* 35 (2004): 173–93 (reprinted in this volume); and more briefly, Néstor Míguez, Jeorg Rieger, and Jung Mo Sung, *Beyond the Spirit of Empire: Theology and Politics in a New Key*, Reclaiming Liberation Theology (London: SCM, 2009), 137, 139, 161–62.

13. See the first anecdote in Pamela Eisenbaum's *Paul Was Not a Christian: The Real Message of a Misunderstood Apostle* (New York: HarperCollins, 2009).

14. Ibid., 3.

15. Ibid., 4.

16. Daniel Boyarin, *A Radical Jew: Paul and the Politics of Identity*, Contraversions 1 (Berkeley: University of California Press, 1994), 3. For an extended treatment of the politics of difference, see 228–60.

17. Ibid., 9. In a similar way, much recent empire-critical scholarship on Paul's letters regards Roman and American imperialism as comparable contexts that both Paul and contemporary people must navigate. This view of interactivity between the past and the present is valuable and productive, but it also poses challenges both for writing history that takes seriously the otherness of the past and for interpreting the distinctiveness of the present situation.

18. Boyarin, *Radical Jew*, 9.

19. Elliott locates Boyarin within New Perspective scholarship that is still driven by a religious reading of Paul's categories and interests ("Paul and the Politics of Empire: Problems and Prospects," in Horsley, *Paul and Politics*, 20, 33–34). In reality, however, Boyarin's Paul is political insofar as cultural-ethnic-religious-gendered discourses are also political. Equating "political readings" with readings that are attentive to the Roman empire seems a narrow and monolithic understanding of politics—see the response of Simon Price in *Paul and the Roman Imperial Order*, ed. Richard A. Horsley (Harrisburg, Pa.: Trinity Press International, 2004), 182–83. A primary and not insignificant difference between the two is that Boyarin's politics are informed by feminist and cultural criticism while Elliott's are shaped by Marxism.

20. See the three volumes edited by Horsley: *Paul and Politics; Paul and the Roman Imperial Order;* and *Paul and Empire: Religion and Power in Roman Imperial Society* (Harrisburg, Pa.: Trinity Press International, 1997), especially the articles by Elliott, Robert Jewett, Horsley, N. T. Wright, Sze-kar Wan, Abraham Smith, Rollin A. Ramsaran, Efraín Agosto, Erik M. Heen, and Allen Dwight Callahan. Horsley has long been an important advocate for a (re)politicized reading of the New Testament that takes seriously the socioeconomic structures of the Judean temple-state and the Roman Empire. While Horsley rightly criticizes the Lutheran-theological Paul as *homo religiosus* and the "hero of justification by faith," Horsley's Paul frequently looks like *homo politicus*, the hero of anti-imperialism.

21. For a critique of Paul-centered readings of Gal 3:28 (that is, reading it as Paul's theology and not that of the *ekklēsia*), see Schüssler Fiorenza, *Rhetoric and Ethic*, 165–69.

22. Working from an exploration of Paul's ethnically based vision of human unity, Sze-kar Wan calls Paul's vision "subtly anti-imperial." Although he does not explore the topic further, Wan does open a small space for subjects to speak back to this construction of Paul: "Rather than eschew universal claims, a move postcolonial readers would have liked him to make, he unabashedly constructs a metanarrative based on his own ethnicity, an eschatological universalism" ("Collection for the Saints as Anticolonial Act: Implications of Paul's Ethnic Reconstruction," in Horsley, *Paul and Politics*, 209–10). It is this Jewish universalism that Boyarin critiques, thus opening a dialogue with Paul's politics rather than reclaiming them. However, Boyarin does not imagine that Paul's audience similarly engaged, resisted, or revised Paul's political vision.

23. See Slavoj Žižek, *The Fragile Absolute: Or, Why Is the Christian Legacy Worth Fighting For* (London: Verso, 2000); Alain Badiou, *Saint Paul: The Foundation of Universalism*, trans. Ray Brassier, Cultural Memory in the Present (Stanford: Stanford University Press, 2003); Giorgio Agamben, *The Time that Remains: A Commentary on the Letter to the Romans*, Meridian, Crossing Aesthetics (Stanford: Stanford University Press, 2005).

24. For example, for Žižek, Christianity becomes a religion of love that insists on conversion; Judaism becomes the sign of constant particularity, while Christianity stands for a passage into universality "that achieves Redemption by coming to terms with its traumatic Origins, by ritualistically

enacting the founding Crime and the Sacrifice that erases its traces, by bringing about reconciliation in the medium of the Word" (*Fragile Absolute*, 99).

25. Ibid., 120. See also Badiou, *Saint Paul*, 9, 14.

26. These philosophers have done their work with little or no regard for Pauline scholarship. For a reading of Paul's political philosophy that presupposes the work of the New Perspective on Paul, see Theodore W. Jennings, Jr., *Reading Derrida/Thinking Paul: On Justice*, Cultural Memory in the Present (Stanford: Stanford University Press, 2006). There is much to recommend in this reading, but Jennings, too, focuses almost exclusively on Paul's thought, thus rendering Paul's political discourse timeless and without rhetorical context or dialogical contestation.

27. Allen Dwight Callahan suggests that 1 Corinthians represents Paul's directions "in emancipatory theory and practice," a "project inherently political because manumission, morality, and mutualism are by definition communal practices, collective concerned action" ("Paul, *Ekklēsia*, and Emancipation in Corinth: A Coda on Liberation Theology," in Horsley, *Paul and Politics*, 223). Like Yung Suk Kim (*Christ's Body in Corinth*), Callahan roots Paul's politics in his identification with those who suffer at the bottom of Roman imperial structures. For both, Paul leads the way in theorizing beyond liberation theology toward a truly emancipatory politics. See also the work of Davina Lopez discussed below.

28. Abraham Smith counters popular North American apocalypticism with an anti-imperial reading of 1 and 2 Thessalonians. He disrupts dichotomous and monolithic constructions of Paul by noting that Brazilian apocalypticism differs from North American versions and by discussing the way in which Paul's sexual othering in 1 Thess 4:3 reinscribes imperial ideologies ("The First and Second Letters to the Thessalonians," in *A Postcolonial Commentary on the New Testament Writings*, ed. Fernando F. Segovia and R. S. Sugirtharajah, Bible and Postcolonialism 13 [London and New York: T & T Clark, 2007], 308, 315–16).

29. Boyarin, *Radical Jew*, 3.

30. See the articles by Schussler Fiorenza, Wire, Kittredge, and Briggs in Horsley, *Paul and Politics*, and the article by Jennifer Wright Knust in Horsley, *Paul and the Roman Imperial Order* ("Paul and the Politics of Virtue and Vice"). See also Marchal, *Politics of Heaven*, ch. 1. As Kittredge notes, "Those who seek to interpret Paul in an imperial context have thus far restricted themselves to emphasizing Paul's radical stance and underplaying the ways in which Paul's language replicates and reinscribes imperial power relations. In doing so, they continue to operate within the traditional paradigm in which Paul's position, now 'correctly' interpreted within his imperial context, is the only important one and other voices must be subordinated to his. The strength of this paradigm testifies to the effectiveness of Paul's rhetoric as it has been amplified throughout the history of interpretation" ("Corinthian Women Prophets," 108–9).

31. While he does not discuss sexual othering in his article in Horsley, *Paul and the Roman Imperial Order*, Abraham Smith does incorporate the work of Knust into his postcolonial commentary article on 1 and 2 Thessalonians.

32. Elliott is explicit about this interest: "No legitimate reading of Romans in our contemporary situation can remain oblivious to the effects of empire today" (*The Arrogance of Nations: Reading Romans in the Shadow of Empire*, Paul in Critical Contexts [Minneapolis: Fortress Press, 2008], 9). See also Brad R. Braxton, "Paul and Racial Reconciliation: A Postcolonial Approach to 2 Corinthians 3:12-18," in *Scripture and Traditions: Essays on Early Judaism and Christianity in Honor of Carl R. Holladay*, ed. Patrick Gray and Gail R. O'Day, Supplements to Novum Testamentum 129 (Leiden: Brill, 2008), 413.

33. Elliott, *Arrogance of Nations*, 8.

34. Ibid., 3.

35. Although Elliott notes his interest in letting "first-century Judeans, Paul above all, speak

for themselves" (*Arrogance of Nations,* 16), it is clear throughout his book that he also identifies with Paul's anti-imperial critique and gives it voice precisely to engage the contemporary U.S. context (p. 9).

36. See Peter Oakes (*Reading Romans in Pompeii: Paul's Letter at Ground Level* [Minneapolis: Fortress Press, 2009]), who brings together archaeological remains from Pompeii's *insulae* with Paul's letter to the Romans to imagine how four "Christians," all of low status but at various levels, might have interpreted the letter. Oakes largely upholds Paul's authority throughout his analysis; while the responses vary, none of the persons whom Oakes invents in his project of historical reconstruction questions Paul's letter, even the slave woman who struggles with her ongoing requirement of sexual slavery, which is in tension with Paul's injunctions regarding purity (see especially p. 143).

37. A sustained consideration of the diverse perspectives of Haitian women and Latin American theologians would also take our eyes off the problem of whether *we* are the ones prophetically challenging Paul or the status-obsessed Gentiles. In *Arrogance of Nations,* all of the Judeans in Rome are "weak" and all the Gentiles are status-conscious (p. 158). As with Marxist analysis, these kinds of dichotomies can romanticize the oppressed and leave the category of the oppressor equally undifferentiated.

38. Davina C. Lopez, *Apostle to the Conquered: Reimagining Paul's Mission,* Paul in Critical Contexts (Minneapolis: Fortress Press, 2008), xi, xiii.

39. Ibid., xii.

40. Ibid., 3. Wire notes that Paul's vision of liberation for Gentiles (including women and slaves) is more apparent in Galatians than in 1 Corinthians, suggesting that Paul's politics, like his theology, should be seen as contextual, rhetorical, and intersubjective ("Response: Paul and Those Outside Power," 226).

41. For example, Lopez argues that Paul recognized his top-down hegemonic stance as he sought to ravage or destroy the *ekklēsia* and that he was transformed after his travels to Arabia. During that time, he became vulnerable and even pursued a "life of penetrated, defeated masculinity" (*Apostle to the Conquered,* 138). Certainly in Galatians and elsewhere Paul presents his body as homologous to Christ's abused body. But is it possible, as some feminist scholars have argued, that Paul's assertion of his homology between his body and Christ's might be an *authorizing* move and thus another assertion of power, even if cast in a key different from that of the imperial masculinity depicted in statuary such as the *Prima Porta Augustus*? If we decenter Paul and assume that his subjectivity is embedded in his multiple relationships, should we not ask about the *variety of modes* of employing gender and one's own gender mutability for the purposes of persuasion? Paul's assertion of maternal status in relation to the Galatians would then need to be placed alongside his image of himself as a nurse in 1 Thessalonians and his self-depiction as a father with a punishing rod in 1 Corinthians.

42. He, too, locates his writing in the context of the American empire, but he is less explicit than Lopez about producing a view of Paul that is useful in public debates and more concerned with crafting an analysis that will further nuance politically-attuned Pauline scholarship. See Marchal, *Politics of Heaven,* vii-viii.

43. Ibid., 44.

44. Ibid., 111.

45. Ibid., 11.

46. Although Kim (*Christ's Body in Corinth*) claims to agree with Wire that the women in Corinth are claiming voice and agency in the *ekklēsia,* his reconstruction of Paul's opponents in Corinth as imperially minded elites with oppressive views renders the women's voices silent in 1 Corinthians, which is figured primarily as a dialogue between Paul (as he identifies with the oppressed) and his oppressive and triumphalist opponents.

47. Marchal applies this question to Paul alone, concluding that he positions "himself as a

provincial governor or colonial administrator for the divine *imperator*" (*Politics of Heaven*, 51). However, if we consider the social and economic status of both Paul and the communities to which he writes, might Paul's travels look more like the circumambulations of a migrant worker than the visits of a Roman imperial governor? Might they look that way to some contemporary communities, too?

48. For the notion of tracing the effective history of Paul's rhetoric, see Smith, "First and Second Letters to the Thessalonians," 307–9.

49. MacArthur is the pastor of Grace Community Church in Sun Valley, Idaho. He has a regular radio program (*Grace to You*), appeared frequently on *Larry King Live*, and in 2006 was named one of the twenty-five most influential preachers in America by *Christianity Today* (see http://www.christianitytoday.com/anniversary/features/top25preachers.html).

50. This self-conscious caveat both recognizes the history of violence in Christian missions and dismisses it as avoidable through benevolent moderation.

51. John MacArthur, "The Qualities of a Great Missionary—Part 1," http://www.biblebb.com/files/mac/sg1747.htm (accessed May 29, 2010).

52. To our knowledge, not much work has been done to trace the place of Pauline literature in the history of European missionary expansion in the eighteenth and nineteenth centuries (though see the article by Robert Seesengood in the present volume). For some brief references, see R. S. Sugirtharajah, "A Postcolonial Exploration of Collusion and Construction in Biblical Interpretation," in *The Postcolonial Bible,* ed. R. S. Sugirtharajah, Bible and Postcolonialism 1 (Sheffield: Sheffield Academic, 1998), 91–117, especially 96–98.

53. Smith begins to get beyond this problem with his treatment of the Pauline assemblies as alternative communities of resistance. These are not, however, sites of struggle and debate around the challenges of empire so much as the result of Paul's work in the Greek cities ("The First and Second Letters to the Thessalonians," 311–13).

54. For an extended example of interrogating Paul's rhetorical construct of a community, see Antoinette Clark Wire, *The Corinthian Women Prophets: A Reconstruction through Paul's Rhetoric* (Minneapolis: Fortress Press, 1990).

55. See Colin Adams and Ray Laurence, ed., *Travel and Geography in the Roman Empire* (London and New York: Routledge, 2005). For theorizing intersectional analysis in a context of highly increased population mobility, see Avtar Brah, "Diaspora, Border, and Transnational Identities," in Reina Lewis and Sara Mills, ed., *Feminist Postcolonial Theory: A Reader* (New York: Routledge, 2003), 613–34.

56. For a contemporary exploration of the importance of identifying the material (often military-driven) technologies of empire and their use as sites of resistance to empire, see Jenna Tiitsman, "Planetary Subjects after the Death of Empire," in *Planetary Loves: Spivak, Postcoloniality, and Theology*, ed. Stephen D. Moore and Mayra Rivera, Transdisciplinary Theological Colloquia (New York: Fordham University Press, 2011).

57. See John S. Kloppenborg and Stephen G. Wilson, eds., *Voluntary Associations in the Graeco-Roman World* (London and New York: Routledge, 1996); and Richard S. Ascough, *Paul's Macedonian Associations: The Social Context of Philippians and 1 Thessalonians*, Wissenschaftliche Untersuchungen zum Neuen Testament 2/161 (Tübingen: Mohr Siebeck, 2003).

58. For a discussion of the Thessalonian *ekklēsia* as a voluntary association and the economic and gendered imagery in 1 Thessalonians, see Melanie Johnson-DeBaufre, "'Gazing Upon the Invisible': Archaeology, Historiography, and the Elusive Women of 1 Thessalonians," in *From Roman to Early Christian Thessalonikē: Studies in Religion and Archaeology*, ed. Laura Nasrallah, Charalambos Bakirtzis, and Steven J. Friesen, Harvard Theological Studies 64 (Cambridge, Mass.: Harvard University Press, 2010).

59. In his sermon on 1 Thess 2:1-6 ("Leading the Charge: Fail-Proof Spiritual Leadership"),

MacArthur replicates Paul's politics of othering and thus constructs his own audience as standing in need of the preacher's (and Paul's) guidance: "Somehow and in some way not known to us, the church in Thessalonica was being told lies about Paul. Someone was attacking his integrity and someone or some group was attacking his sincerity. They were doing everything they could to be hostile toward the church and one way to tear up the church was to destroy its confidence in the one that God used to found it, namely Paul. This group may have included the Jews who were so utterly hostile to the gospel, it may also have included pagan Gentiles who would be hostile to it as well." The audience is thus identified with a community that faces hostile religious Others bent on disrupting the proper relations between the assembly and its leader and founder.

60. Marchal (*Politics of Heaven*, 119) warns that a reconstruction of a political Paul who opposes the Roman imperial cult can become an anti-pagan missionary Paul who is thus available to support the missionary ambitions of European empires against Africa and the Americas.

61. See Lopez, *Apostle to the Conquered*. Dube's first question asks about "distant and inhabited lands," while her third question asks, "How does this text construct difference: does it promote dialogue and liberating interdependence or condemnation of all that is foreign?" In the case of 1 Thessalonians, Paul, Timothy, and Silvanus travel to inhabited cities, but the cities are not figured as distant nor foreign. The construction of difference is cast not geographically or in terms of foreignness but in terms of allegiances—the Thessalonians are to be different from Gentiles who are "not of God" (4:5). In this, they are like Jews who are "in Christ." Gentiles who are "not of God" are painted with the usual sexual slanders (4:5). In the same way, the outsider Jews in faraway Judea are murderous and have killed the Lord and abused Paul (both insider Jews).

62. See Elliott, *Arrogance of Nations*. See also the roundtable discussion between Amy-Jill Levine and third-world feminists in *Journal of Feminist Studies in Religion* 20, no. 1 (Spring 2004).

63. See, among others, Stefan Weinstock, "The Geographical Catalogue in Acts II, 9–11," *Journal of Roman Studies* 38, no. 1–2 (1948): 43–46; Gary Gilbert, "The List of Nations in Acts 2: Roman Propaganda and Lukan Response," *Journal of Biblical Literature* 121, no. 3 (2002): 497–529; Allen Brent, *The Imperial Cult and the Development of Church Order: Concepts and Images of Authority in Paganism and Early Christianity before the Age of Cyprian*, Supplements to Vigiliae Christianae 45 (Leiden: Brill, 1999), 101–23.

64. Loveday Alexander, "Mapping Early Christianity: Acts and the Shape of Early Church History," *Interpretation* 57, no. 2 (2003): 163–75; and eadem, "'In Journeyings Often': Voyaging in the Acts of the Apostles and in Greek Romance," in *Luke's Literary Achievement: Collected Essays*, ed. C. M. Tuckett, Journal for the Study of the New Testament Supplement Series 116 (Sheffield: Sheffield Academic Press, 1995), 17–49; James M. Scott, "Luke's Geographical Horizon," in *The Book of Acts in Its First Century Setting*, vol. 2, *The Book of Acts in Its Graeco-Roman Setting*, ed. David W. J. Gill and Conrad Gempf (Grand Rapids: Eerdmans, 1994), 483–544; Hans Conzelmann, *The Theology of St. Luke*, trans. Geoffrey Buswell (1961; Philadelphia: Fortress Press, 1982). On the eclipsing of Jerusalem, see Richard I. Pervo, "My Happy Home: The Role of Jerusalem in Acts 1–7," *Forum* n.s. 3.1 (2000): 31–55, especially 38.

65. For a fuller analysis of Acts and the Panhellenion, see Laura S. Nasrallah, *Christian Responses to Roman Art and Architecture: The Second-Century Church Amid the Spaces of Empire* (New York: Cambridge University Press, 2010), ch. 3. On the Panhellenion, see A. S. Spawforth and Susan Walker, "The World of the Panhellenion, I. Athens and Eleusis," *Journal of Roman Studies* 75 (1985): 88–104; eidem, "The World of the Panhellenion, II. Three Dorian Cities," *Journal of Roman Studies* 76 (1986): 88–105; Ilaria Romeo, "The Panhellenion and Ethnic Identity in Hadrianic Greece," *Classical Philology* 97, no. 1 (2002): 21–40; Christopher P. Jones, *Kinship Diplomacy in the Ancient World*, Revealing Antiquity 12 (Cambridge, Mass.: Harvard University Press, 1999).

66. Shelly Matthews, "The Need for the Stoning of Stephen," in *Violence in the New Testament*,

ed. Shelly Matthews and E. Leigh Gibson (New York: T & T Clark, 2005), 124–39; see also Shelly Matthews, *Perfect Martyr: The Stoning of Stephen and the Construction of Christian Identity* (Oxford: Oxford University Press, 2010); Lawrence Wills, "The Depiction of the Jews in Acts," *Journal of Biblical Literature* 110 (1991): 631–54; Richard I. Pervo, "Meet Right—and Our Bounden Duty," *Forum* n.s. 4.1 (2001): 57–60.

67. Schüssler Fiorenza, *Rhetoric and Ethic*, 196–98.

12. To What End?

1. Elisabeth Schüssler Fiorenza, "Paul and the Politics of Interpretation," in *Paul and Politics: Ekklesia, Israel, Imperium, Interpretation. Essays in Honor of Krister Stendahl*, ed. Richard A. Horsley (Harrisburg, Pa.: Trinity Press International, 2000), 47–51.

2. It is with this demarcated territory that any scholar seeking liberative messages for females must contend, often requiring an admission, however (in)directly, of Paul's authority and power. It is striking that the most convincing or effective argument against an oppressive interpretation of Paul is still dependent on him.

3. One could certainly include any nonempowered people as being colonized by Paul's writings in certain situations—people of lower classes, various ethnicities, and non-heterosexual orientations, among others. I leave the discussion on the level of gender because of the focus of this essay.

4. See Caroline Vander Stichele and Todd Penner, "Paul and the Rhetoric of Gender," in *Her Master's Tools? Feminist and Postcolonial Engagements of Historical-Critical Discourse*, ed. Caroline Vander Stichele and Todd Penner, Global Perspectives on Biblical Scholarship 9 (Atlanta: Society of Biblical Literature, 2005), 287–310; and Preston Massey, "The Meaning of κατακαλυπτω and κατα κεφαλης εχων in 1 Corinthians 11.2-16," *New Testament Studies* 53, no. 4 (2007): 502–23, for more comprehensive lists of references addressing this passage.

5. Even among the scholars who hold to this method of reading the passage, there has been debate as to whether Paul does this once or twice in this passage. The relatively few scholars that I have found who suggest a dialogical reading are David O'Dell Scott (*A Post-Patriarchal Christology*, American Academy of Religion Academy Series 78 [Atlanta: Scholars Press, 1991]), Margaret Mitchell (*Paul and the Rhetoric of Reconciliation: An Exegetical Investigation of the Language and Composition of 1 Corinthians*, Hermeneutische Untersuchungen zur Theologie 28 [Tübingen: J. C. B. Mohr, 1991]), and Alan Padgett ("The Significance of αντι in 1 Corinthians 11:15," *Tyndale Bulletin* 45, no. 1 [1994]: 181–87). Daniel Arichea somewhat dodges the issue by noting that Paul is acknowledging the subordination ideas that are found in Scripture while arguing that they are to be renounced because of the newness in Christ ("The Covering on the Woman's Head: Translation and Theology in 1 Corinthians 11.2-16," *Bible Translator* 55, no. 4 [2004]: 460–69).

6. For instance, Francis Watson ("The Authority of the Voice: A Theological Reading of 1 Cor 11.2-16," *New Testament Studies* 46, no. 4 [2000]: 520–36), seeking a coherent reading of this passage, suggests that Paul's modification of the female head-covering practice turns it into a symbol of women's freedom from an erotic basis for the relationship of male and female derived from creation. Ann Jervis ("The Story That Shaped Paul's Way with Women," in *Loving God with Our Minds: The Pastor as Theologian. Essays in Honor of Wallace M. Alston*, ed. Michael Welker and Cynthia A. Jarvis [Grand Rapids: Eerdmans, 2004], 265–79) suggests that "correctly identifying" the myth that informed Paul's "way with women" as that of the crucified Christ "can allow us to see the way the conflicting pieces of his words and actions may, in fact, rest comfortably together" (p. 268). See also Judith M. Gundry-Volf, "Gender and Creation in 1 Corinthians 11:2-16: A Study in Paul's Theological Method," in *Evangelium, Schriftauslegung, Kirche: Festschrift für Peter Stuhlmacher zum 65.*

Geburtstag, ed. Jostein Ådna et al. (Göttingen: Vandenhoeck & Ruprecht, 1997), 151-71. Interestingly, Gundry-Volf does not actually resolve anything in her contribution; see the discussion below.

7. While there are scholars who find the veiling-versus-hairstyles question an important one to settle, I am deliberately not addressing it here. The final effect, as I understand it, is to maintain the decency or order required of the woman in terms of her hair, whether it is covered or seen, so that it must be neatly kept. See Massey, "The Meaning of κατακαλυπτω," 502-23; and Khiok-Khng Yeo, "Differentiation and Mutuality of Male-Female Relations in 1 Corinthians 11:2-16," *Biblical Research* 43 (1998): 7-21, for strong arguments in favor of veiling and hairstyles, respectively.

8. Most significant here is Jervis, "Story That Shaped Paul's Way"; see also note 6 above.

9. I am indebted to David O'Dell-Scott's work *A Post-Patriarchal Christology*, for this insight, as well as for his reading of 1 Corinthians 14:33b-36.

10. It is worth noting here that something similar happened within the Christian movement once it was adopted as "the" religion of the empire: the forces that Jesus was critiquing and most likely resisting were now the ones "taking up" his cause. This is an effective means of control that we have seen play out numerous times in historical events around the world.

11. The following description of my approach is adapted to this particular passage and its scholarship from a more thoroughly framed description in the first chapter of my book *Abuse, Power and Fearful Obedience: Reconsidering 1 Peter's Commands to Wives* (New York: T&T Clark, forthcoming).

12. See also Elisabeth Schüssler Fiorenza, *In Memory of Her: A Feminist Theological Reconstruction of Christian Origins* (New York: Crossroad, 1883), 14, 45, 50, 226-30.

13. See Antoinette Clark Wire, *The Corinthian Women Prophets: A Reconstruction through Paul's Rhetoric* (Minneapolis: Fortress Press, 1990), 10. She argues that we ought to ascribe authority to Paul only if/when he is convincing, not simply because his writings are in the canon. Only God is worthy of "intrinsic authority," according to Wire.

14. I prefer to speak about "a" or "my" feminist postcolonial method as an indication that my approach is not the only one that is possible under this rubric.

15. Joseph A. Marchal, *The Politics of Heaven: Women, Gender and Empire in the Study of Paul*, Paul in Critical Contexts (Minneapolis: Fortress Press, 2008), 11.

16. Elisabeth Schüssler Fiorenza, *Rhetoric and Ethic: The Politics of Biblical Interpretation* (Minneapolis: Fortress Press, 1999), 48-55.

17. This neologism was coined by Elisabeth Schüssler Fiorenza in order to highlight the fact that oppression due to hierarchies and various forms of inequalities happens within any situation or society on more than one level at a time. The term is derived from the combination of the Greek words for "ruler" (*archē*) and "lord" (*kyrios*); it refers to a male who is in the superior role of a master-slave relation, and most likely also in husband-wife and father-child relationships. Thus, the term "kyriarchy" is intended to draw our attention to the inequalities in gendered, economic, political, social, and familial relations, at the very least.

18. Schüssler Fiorenza explains that this play on words is not a pejorative term but a descriptive one. The discourses that are usually referred to as "mainstream" are typically defined by and therefore benefit certain males. Because the main-/malestream we are discussing is that of Western biblical scholarship, I must also point out that these males are typically white, heterosexual, and elite, and contribute scholarly interpretations of biblical passages that are notably more positivistic than critical. Thus, in this discussion, the point is that any scholar—male, female, or otherwise—can employ malestream language. It is quite common to see someone who is harmed by such language, knowledge, or power taking it up as her/his own, simply because that is what she/he has been socialized, and now theologically grounded, to use; see Schüssler Fiorenza, *Rhetoric and Ethic*, 1-14.

19. Elizabeth A. Castelli, *Imitating Paul: A Discourse of Power*, Literary Currents in Biblical Interpretation (Louisville: Westminster John Knox, 1991); Jorunn Økland, *Women in Their Place:*

Paul and the Corinthian Discourse of Gender and Sanctuary Space, Journal for the Study of the New Testament Supplement Series 269 (New York: T&T Clark, 2004); Mitchell, *Paul and the Rhetoric of Reconciliation*; Vander Stichele and Penner, "Paul and the Rhetoric of Gender," 287–310, and "*Unveiling Paul*: Gendering *ēthos* in 1 Corinthians 11:2-16," in *Rhetoric, Ethic and Moral Persuasion in Biblical Discourse: Essays from the 2002 Heidelberg Conference,* ed. Thomas H. Olbricht and Anders Eriksson, Emory Studies in Early Christianity 11 (New York: T&T Clark, 2005), 214–37. Kathy Ehrensperger's article, "Be Imitators of Me as I Am of Christ: A Hidden Discourse of Power and Domination in Paul?" *Lutheran Theological Quarterly* 38, no. 4 (2003): 241–61, could also be listed here, but that would require a full discussion of Castelli's work *Imitating Paul* as well. Ehrensperger directly challenges Castelli's work and the conclusions that she draws regarding the detrimental effect of Paul's rhetoric. Interestingly, her main argument hinges on *mimesis* terminology that does not imply "copying" or "sameness." While I agree that Paul is not saying that his audiences must be exactly like him, it seems that Ehrensperger is missing part of the powerful effect that such commands to "imitate" Paul have on the recipient(s) of his letters.

20. Schüssler Fiorenza discusses this concern in "Paul and the Politics of Interpretation," 47–51.

21. Because of space limitations, I will limit my attention to materials in which the scholar assumes that the entire content of 1 Cor 11:2-16 originated with Paul and focuses on the content of the passage, ignoring its rhetorical effects.

22. Schüssler Fiorenza, "Paul and the Politics of Interpretation," 47–51.

23. Watson, "Authority of the Voice," 524, 528, 530; Gundry-Volf, "Gender and Creation in 1 Corinthians 11:2-16"; Jervis, "Story That Shaped Paul's Way."

24. See also Castelli, *Imitating Paul*.

25. Gundry-Volf, "Gender and Creation," 151–71.

26. Ibid., 165.

27. Ibid., 171.

28. See also Cynthia Briggs Kittredge's discussion of Ephesians in *Community and Authority: The Rhetoric of Obedience in the Pauline Tradition*, Harvard Theological Studies 45 (Harrisburg, Pa.: Trinity Press International, 1998), 176. "The conventional connotations of obedience language in the social contexts of the patriarchal family and in the political context of ruling and being ruled *are not transformed* within Paul's argument, despite the reversal of that system proclaimed in Phil 2:6-11" (p. 176 [emphasis added]).

29. Mitchell, *Paul and the Rhetoric of Reconciliation*, 262–63.

30. See also the discussion below regarding Jervis's article.

31. Andrew C. Perriman, "The Head of a Woman: The Meaning of in 1 Cor 11:3," *Journal of Theological Studies* 45, no. 2 (1994): 602–22.

32. Ibid., 621–22.

33. I find it difficult to make strong claims based on proof-texting. I offer this comparison here because of its prevalence within the scholarship on 1 Cor 11:2-16.

34. Jouette M. Bassler, "1 Corinthians," in *Women's Bible Commentary, with Apocrypha*, ed. Carol A. Newsom and Sharon H. Ringe (expanded ed.; Louisville: Westminster John Knox, 1998), 417.

35. I am among those scholars who read this myth etiologically, wherein '*ādām* is generic humanity and male and female ('*îš* and '*iššâ*) are then "introduced" with the creation of the second human.

36. Bassler, "1 Corinthians," 411–19.

37. Jervis, "Story That Shaped Paul's Way," 268.

38. Ibid., 278–79.

39. Luise Schottroff, "Purity and Holiness of Women and Men in 1 Corinthians and the

Consequences for Feminist Hermeneutics," in *Distant Voices Drawing Near: Essays in Honor of Antoinette Clark Wire*, ed. Holly E. Hearon (Collegeville, Minn.: Liturgical, 2004), 90.

13. Wrestling with the "Macedonian Call"

1. Portions of this essay appear as "Paul and the Age of Colonialism," chapter 6 of *Paul: A Brief History* (Oxford: Wiley-Blackwell, 2010).
2. Robert Paul Seesengood, "Hybridity and the Rhetoric of Endurance: Reading Paul's Athletic Metaphors in the Context of Postcolonial Self-Construction," *Bible and Critical Theory* 2.1 (2005), http://publications.epress.monash.edu/doi/abs/10.2104/bc050016 (accessed May 20, 2010); later expanded and published as chapter 2 of my book *Competing Identities: The Athlete and Gladiator in Early Christian Literature*, Library of New Testament Studies 346, Playing the Texts 12 (New York: T&T Clark, 2006), 20–34. An earlier version of the essay was presented at the International Meeting of the Society of Biblical Literature in 2004.
3. Fernando F. Segovia, "Biblical Criticism and Postcolonial Studies: Towards a Postcolonial Optic," in *The Postcolonial Bible*, ed. R. S. Sugirtharajah, Bible and Postcolonialism 1 (Sheffield: Sheffield Academic, 1998), 58–63.
4. Ibid., 61.
5. Homi K. Bhabha, "The Vernacular Cosmopolitan," in *Voices of the Crossing: The Impact of Britain on Writers from Asia, the Caribbean and Africa*, ed. Ferdinand Dennis and Naseem Khan (London: Serpent's Tail, 2000), 139.
6. Sara Suleri, "The Rhetoric of English India," in *The Postcolonial Studies Reader*, ed. Bill Ashcroft, Gareth Griffiths, and Helen Tiffin (New York: Routledge, 1995), 112.
7. See, for example, Homi Bhabha, *The Location of Culture* (New York: Routledge, 1994). For a history of Christian missions, see David J. Bosch, *Transforming Mission: Paradigm Shifts in Theology of Mission*, American Society of Missiology Series 16 (Maryknoll, N.Y.: Orbis, 1991). Bosch argues that early Christian missions were closely tied to colonialism and linked to hegemonic impositions of European culture upon the "native." In time, mission movements became "more indigenous," less colonial, and more "successful" (in terms of conversion and retention). Contrasting views that in some cases end up demonstrating the thesis of Bosch can be found in earlier histories of missions such as those by John M. Reid, *Missions and Missionary Society of the Methodist Episcopal Church* (2 vols.; New York: Hurst and Eaton, 1879); Clarence P. Shedd, *Two Centuries of Student Christian Movements: Their Origin and Intercollegiate Life* (New York: Association Press, 1934); Gustav Warneck, *Outline of a History of Protestant Missions from the Reformation to the Present Time: A Contribution to Modern Church History* (3rd ed.; New York: Fleming H. Revell, 1906); Charles Henry Robinson, *History of Christian Missions*, International Theological Library (New York: Charles Scribner's Sons, 1915); and the modern work by Stephen Neill, *Christian Missions* (Grand Rapids: Eerdmans, 1964).
8. *Oxford English Dictionary*, s.v. "mission."
9. William Carey, "An Inquiry Into the Obligations of Christians to Use Means for the Conversion of the Heathens" (sermon, 1793). See also Bosch, *Transforming Mission*; Ruth A. Tucker, *From Jerusalem to Irian Jaya: A Biographical History of Christian Missions* (Grand Rapids: Zondervan, 1983); Neill, *Christian Missions*.
10. The idea remained a staple chestnut in calls for Christian missions: "If Paul could accomplish... then we can...." For example, James M. Thoburn, in *The Christian Conquest of India* (Cleveland: J. H. Lamb, 1906), 244, states: "In her most palmy days, Rome ruled over only one hundred and twenty million people, while in India today nearly three hundred million souls are subject, more or less directly, to the rule of the king-emperor.... Instead of the wretched little vessels in which Paul

Notes to Chapter 13 335

coasted around the Mediterranean ports, the Indian missionary has floating palaces to convey him at sea, while palatial cars await him when he wishes to travel by land."

11. As quoted (without reference) in ibid., 149.

12. Tucker, *From Jerusalem*, 73. My point is not that Tucker's comparison is inappropriate but that this particular superlative—"none like him since Paul"—was particularly ubiquitous.

13. On the birth of the Bible societies, see, in addition to the sources cited above, William Canton, *A History of the British and Foreign Bible Society* (5 vols.; London: John Murray, 1904–10); Lucien Febvre and Henri-Jean Martin, *The Coming of the Book: The Impact of Printing, 1450–1800* (1976; London: Verso, 1997); and the series of titles issued under the auspices of the British and Foreign Bible Society, each bearing the subtitle "An Illustrated and Popular Report."

14. W. H. Wyckoff, *The American Bible Society and the Baptists, the Question Discussed, Shall the Whole Word of God be Given to the Heathen* (New York: Bigelow, 1842).

15. On the connection between early missions and colonization, see Bosch, *Transforming Missions*, 226–29, 302–36. On the fusion of economic, political, and religious interests in the dissemination of the Bible, see R. S. Sugirtharajah "Textual Pedlars: Distributing Salvation—Colporteurs and Their Portable Bibles," chapter 5 in *The Bible and the Third World: Precolonial, Colonial and Postcolonial Encounters* (Cambridge: Cambridge University Press, 2001), 140–74.

16. Argued explicitly by Bosch (*Transforming Mission*, 4–6, 123–80; note that he refers to Paul as "the first missionary") and implicitly by Reid, Shedd, Warneck, and Robinson (see n. 7 above), all of whom begin their histories with Paul. Most go on to summarize late antiquity and the medieval period very briefly before rushing to the "modern" era where they remain for two-thirds to three-fourths of their often distressingly thick studies.

17. On Baur's views, see Baur, "Die Christuspartei in der korinthischen Gemeinde, der Gegensatz des petrinischen und paulinischen Christenthums in der ältesten Kirche der Apostel Peterus in Rom," *Tübinger Zeitschrift für Theologie* 5 (1831): 61–206, and *Paulus, der Apostel Jesu Christi, Sein Leben und Wirken, seine Briefe und seine Lehre. Ein Beitrag zu einer kritischen Geschichte des Urchristenthums* (Stuttgart: Becher and Müller, *1845*), currently available in English as *Paul the Apostle of Jesus Christ: His Life and Works, His Epistles, and His Teachings* (Peabody, Mass.: Hendrickson, 2003).

18. One might also see an earlier rebuttal to Baur in J. B. Lightfoot's 1865 commentary on Galatians (*Saint Paul's Epistle to the Galatians* [London: MacMillan, 1865]). Certainly this would be valid; Ramsay, for example, frequently cited Lightfoot as his precursor. But Ramsay's rebuttals are, I think, both inclusive of Lightfoot's best critiques and also more developed and dramatic. For a general overview of Ramsay's views on Paul, see Ramsay, *Pauline and Other Studies in Early Christian History* (New York: Hodder & Stoughton, 1906) and *St. Paul, the Traveller and Roman Citizen* (2nd ed.; London: Hodder & Stoughton, 1895).

19. William M. Ramsay, *The Bearing of Recent Discovery on the Trustworthiness of the New Testament* (2nd ed.; London: Hodder & Stoughton, 1915), vii.

20. In the preface to the fourteenth edition of *St. Paul* (n. 18), Ramsay argues that historians who are tendentious and inaccurate produce works that have no value to anyone. Yet historians of the "highest order"—and here he refers to Luke, whom he describes, along with Paul, as a "man among men"—results in a work that produces "not just truth in each detail, but truth in the general effect."

21. Ramsay, *Bearing of Recent Discovery*, viii.

22. Ibid., ix.

23. Ramsay's fingerprints remain indelibly stained onto the pages of F. F. Bruce's *Paul: Apostle of the Heart Set Free* (Grand Rapids: Eerdmans, 1977), and his influence on such evangelical Pauline scholars as Ben Witherington III is apparent. Indeed, Ramsay's *St. Paul* was edited by Mark Wilson and re-released as *Paul: The Traveler and Roman Citizen* by the evangelical press Kregel in 2001.

24. For the following, I am indebted to Markus Barth and Helmut Blanke, *The Letter to*

Philemon: A New Translation with Notes and Commentary, Eerdmans Critical Commentary (Grand Rapids: Eerdmans, 2000) and L. Joseph Kreitzer, *Philemon, Readings* (Sheffield: Sheffield Phoenix, 2009).

25. Moses Stuart, *Conscience and the Constitution: With Remarks on the Recent Speech of the Hon. Daniel Webster in the Senate of the United States on the Subject of Slavery* (Boston: Croker and Brewster, 1850). For an extraordinarily adept treatment of the scholarship surrounding Philemon in the nineteenth century, see Kreitzer, *Philemon*, 70–106.

26. Kreitzer, *Philemon*.

27. Baur, of course, had denied Pauline authorship of Philemon.

28. Bhabha, *Location of Culture*, 167–68. Bhabha follows this with an interesting presentation of the "other side" of that debate—the view of those who were given these innumerable Bibles from the West (ibid., 168–74).

14. Galatians and the "Orientalism" of Justification by Faith

1. On the Occidental construct of civilization versus barbarians and its colonial implications, see Edith Hall, *Inventing the Barbarian: Greek Self-Definition through Tragedy*, Oxford Classical Monographs (Oxford: Oxford University Press, 1989), 5–6, 51–55, 68. On Galatians/Gauls as barbarians, see Brigitte Kahl, *Galatians Re-imagined: Reading with the Eyes of the Vanquished*, Paul in Critical Contexts (Minneapolis: Fortress Press, 2010), 42–48, 95–98; on the linkage between Galatians and Orientals, see ibid., 130–34.

2. Coming from an Eastern European background, and being a citizen of East Germany until its downfall, I am keenly aware how much the West–East binary has shaped the history of the twentieth century, especially in Germany. During the twelve years of German fascism, the East was the territory ruled by the evil empire of godless/Jewish bolshevism (that is, the Soviet type of communism), a territory occupied by racially inferior Slavic/Asiatic peoples who had to make room for the German superior race "without space." After 1945 and throughout the over four decades of the Cold War, many of the old East/West stereotypes remained present in new forms. In all of this, the German mainline churches were closely aligned with the "Christian West" as opposed to the "atheist East."

3. "So it is that the Turks perform different works from the papists, and the papists perform different works from the Jews, and so forth. But . . . the content remains the same, only the quality is different. . . . For they are still works. And those who do them are not Christians, they are hirelings, whether they are called Jews, Mohammedans, papists, or sectarians" (*Luther's Works*, vol. 26, *Lectures on Galatians, 1535, Chapters 1–4*, ed. and trans. J. J. Pelikan and W. A. Hansen [Saint Louis: Concordia, 1963], 9–10).

4. Luther's anti-Muslim stance is linked to the appearance of the Turkish armies on the doorsteps of Vienna, and thus the Christian Occident, in 1529, an event that has been compared to the shock waves after the attacks on the World Trade Center in 2001; see Hans-Martin Barth, *Die Theologie Martin Luthers: Eine kritische Würdigung* (Gütersloh: Gütersloher Verlagshaus, 2009), 64; for the long-standing Western tradition of counting Islam not as a separate religion but a Christian heresy, see ibid., 70; for Muslim "works-righteousness" as well as the connections between Islam and Satan in the eyes of Luther, see ibid., 71–72.

5. Edward Said, *Orientalism* (New York: Pantheon, 1978; repr., New York: Vintage, 1994).

6. On Said's definition of postcolonialism and his impact on Western academia, especially in the United States, see R. S. Sugirtharajah, "Charting the Aftermath: A Review of Postcolonial Criticism," in *The Postcolonial Bible*, ed. R. S. Sugirtharajah, Bible and Postcolonialism 1 (Sheffield: Sheffield Academic, 1998), 9–10

7. Said, *Orientalism*, 207.

8. Colonialism is generally understood to be a specific mode of imperialism. According to Said (*Culture and Imperialism* [New York: Vintage Books, 1993], 9), imperialism means "the practice, the theory, and the attitudes of a dominating metropolitan center ruling a distant territory." Colonialism, on the other hand, implies the "implanting of settlements on distant territories."

9. R. S. Sugirtharajah, for example, criticizes the "textualism" and "inherent biblicism" of liberation hermeneutics that remains text-centered and trusts the "now suspicious historical-critical tools" to "recover the biblical message" over against its later ideological interpretations, thereby conveniently disregarding "texts which speak of dehumanizing aspects" (*Postcolonial Criticism and Biblical Interpretation* [Oxford: Oxford University Press, 2002], 114).

10. In a study on Paul's letter to the Philippians, Joseph A. Marchal tries, in an exemplary way, to demonstrate that empire-critical readings of Paul, including those of Richard Horsley, Efraín Agosto, N. T. Wright, Peter Oakes, Richard Cassidy, and Erik Heen, fall short of understanding how much Paul, though competing with the Roman Empire, employs imperial and colonizing strategies himself with regard to his colonizing missionary travel scheme, his authority claims, and his response to his opponents. See Marchal, *The Politics of Heaven: Women, Gender, and Empire in the Study of Paul*, Paul in Critical Contexts (Minneapolis: Fortress Press, 2008), 37–57.

11. For a critical reassessment of the intertextuality between Paul and Acts, see Brigitte Kahl, "Acts of the Apostles: Pro(to)-Imperial Script and Hidden Transcript," in *In the Shadow of Empire: Reclaiming the Bible as a History of Faithful Resistance*, ed. Richard A. Horsley (Louisville: Westminster John Knox, 2008), 137–56.

12. In a most insightful study, Shawn Kelley has shown how the East–West divide became racialized in nineteenth-century Germany and subsequently found its way into biblical scholarship, including the Orientalizing anti-Jewish traits of Bultmann's interpretation of Paul, which was influenced by Heidegger, the Tübingen School, and Hegel. See *Racializing Jesus: Race, Ideology and the Formation of Biblical Scholarship*, Biblical Limits (London: Routledge, 2002).

13. Said, *Orientalism*, 286.

14. Ibid., 346–47.

15. For more on Ramsay, see William H. C. Frend, *The Archaeology of Early Christianity: A History* (Minneapolis: Fortress Press, 1996), 93–104; and the essay by Robert Seesengood in the present volume.

16. William M. Ramsay, *A Historical Commentary on St. Paul's Epistle to the Galatians* (London: Hodder & Stoughton, 1899), 70.

17. Ibid., 76.

18. Ibid., 148.

19. Ibid., 26.

20. Ibid., 28.

21. Ibid., 29–30.

22. Ibid., 31.

23. Ibid., 43.

24. Ibid., 40–41.

25. Ibid., 32–33. For a more recent exploration of the Anatolian mother goddess in relation to the Galatian crisis, see Susan M. Elliott, *Cutting Too Close for Comfort: Paul's Letter to the Galatians in Its Anatolian Cultic Context*, Journal for the Study of the New Testament Supplement Series 248 (London and New York: T&T Clark, 2004).

26. Ramsay, *Historical Commentary*, 194–95.

27. Ibid., 195–96.

28. Ibid., 70.

29. Ibid., 183.

30. Ibid., 322.
31. Ibid.
32. Ibid., 320-21.
33. William M. Ramsay, *The Church in the Roman Empire before A.D. 170*, Mansfield College Lectures 1892 (London: Hodder & Stoughton, 1893), 191-92.
34. Ramsay, *Historical Commentary*, 2.
35. See, for example, Robert Jewett, *Romans: A Commentary*, Hermeneia (Minneapolis: Fortress Press, 2007); Neil Elliott, *The Arrogance of Nations: Reading Romans in the Shadow of Empire*, Paul in Critical Contexts (Minneapolis: Fortress Press, 2008). On Galatians specifically, see Davina C. Lopez, *Apostle to the Conquered: Reimagining Paul's Mission*, Paul in Critical Contexts (Minneapolis: Fortress Press, 2008); Aliou Cissé Niang, *Faith and Freedom in Galatia and Senegal: The Apostle Paul, Colonists and Sending Gods*, Biblical Interpretation Series 97 (Leiden and Boston: Brill, 2009). For an earlier liberationist rereading of Paul's justification theology in Romans in the context of Latin America, see Elsa Tamez, *The Amnesty of Grace: Justification by Faith from a Latin American Perspective*, trans. Sharon H. Ringe (Nashville: Abingdon, 1993).
36. For Paul's justification theology as messianic transformation of the combative, competitive, and consumptive Occidental Self-Other binary, see the more comprehensive treatment in Kahl, *Galatians Re-imagined*.
37. Paul Zanker, *The Power of Images in the Age of Augustus*, trans. Alan Shapiro, Jerome Lectures, 16th Series (Ann Arbor: University of Michigan Press, 1988).
38. Cf. Kahl, *Galatians Re-imagined*, 27-29, 250-53; for a similar approach, see also Lopez, *Apostle to the Conquered*.
39. For an introduction to the iconography and history of the *Dying Gaul*, see R. R. R. Smith, *Hellenistic Sculpture: A Handbook* (London: Thames & Hudson, 1991), 99-104; and the more comprehensive treatment by John R. Marszal, "Ubiquitous Barbarians: Representation of the Gauls at Pergamon and Elsewhere," in *From Pergamon to Sperlonga: Sculpture and Context*, ed. Nancy T. de Grummond and Brunilde S. Ridgway, Hellenistic Culture and Society 34 (Berkeley: University of California Press, 2000), 191-234. For the history of the Galatians in Asia Minor in particular, see Stephen Mitchell, *Anatolia: Land, Men and Gods in Asia Minor*, vol. 1, *The Celts in Anatolia and the Impact of Roman Rule* (Oxford: Clarendon, 1993).
40. For example, Livy 38.16-17; see Bernhard Kremer, *Das Bild der Kelten bis in augusteische Zeit: Studien zur Instrumentalisierung eines antiken Feindbildes bei griechischen und römischen Autoren*, Historia, Einzelschriften 88 (Stuttgart: Franz Steiner, 1994), 64-65.
41. On the Great Altar and the *Dying Gaul*, see Kahl, *Galatians Re-imagined*, 77-128.
42. Karl Strobel, *Die Galater: Geschichte und Eigenart der keltischen Staatenbildung auf dem Boden des hellenistischen Kleinasien* (Berlin: Akademie Verlag, 1996).
43. Karl Strobel, "Keltensieg und Galatersieger: Die Funktionalisierung eines historischen Phänomens als politischer Mythos der hellenistischen Welt," in *Forschungen in Galatien*, ed. Elmar Schwertheim, Asia Minor Studien 12 (Bonn: Rudolf Habelt, 1994), 97-103. On the perception of (Western) Gauls as Other in line with both Roman and Western conceptualizations of the imperial/colonial Self, see Jane Webster, "Ethnographic Barbarity: Colonial Discourse and the 'Celtic Warrior Societies,'" in *Roman Imperialism: Post-Colonial Perspectives*, ed. Jane Webster and Nicholas J. Cooper (Leicester: University of Leicester Press, 1996), 111-23. For the overall issue of ancient barbarian stereotypes in the dominant "discourse of the conqueror" and their afterlife in Occidental scholarship, see Peter S. Wells, *The Barbarians Speak: How the Conquered Peoples Shaped Roman Europe* (Princeton: Princeton University Press, 1999), 99-106.
44. Hall, *Inventing the Barbarian*, 51-54, 187, 198.
45. David L. Balch, "Paul's Portrait of Christ Crucified (Gal 3:1) in Light of Paintings of

Notes to Chapter 15

Suffering and Death in Pompeiian Houses," in *Early Christian Families in Context: An Interdisciplinary Dialogue*, ed. David L. Balch and Carolyn Osiek (Grand Rapids: Eerdmans, 2003), 84–108.

46. Martin Hengel, *Crucifixion in the Ancient World and the Folly of the Message of the Cross* (Philadelphia: Fortress Press, 1977), 86–87.

47. For the need of public visibility, see ibid., 50.

48. K. M. Coleman ("Fatal Charades: Roman Executions Staged as Mythological Enactments," *Journal of Roman Studies* 80 [1990]: 47) observes that public humiliation (like in the soldiers' mockery of Jesus as king and god) belonged in the standard repertoire of Roman capital punishment and aimed at alienating and distancing the onlookers from the perpetrator and, in the case of Jesus, from the obviously false claims of a messianic usurper.

49. This "wrong" perception of the crucified is, in a way, mirrored in Luke's passion narrative, where the centurion "sees" (*idōn*) that Jesus was righteous (*dikaios*), while the crowds viewing the "spectacle" (*theōrian/theōrēsantes*)) "beat their breasts" (Luke 23:47-48).

50. Jewett, *Romans*, 295–96.

51. For the imperial "resurrection" of the *Dying Galatians* between 189 B.C.E. and 50 C.E., see Kahl, *Galatians Re-imagined*, 169–208.

52. Paula Fredriksen, *Jesus of Nazareth, King of the Jews: A Jewish Life and the Emergence of Christianity* (New York: Knopf, 1999), 135.

53. See Bruce W. Winter, *Seek the Welfare of the City: Christians as Benefactors and Citizens*, First-century Christians in the Graeco-Roman World (Grand Rapids: Eerdmans, 1994), 141–42; Mark D. Nanos, *The Irony of Galatians: Paul's Letter in First-Century Context* (Minneapolis: Fortress Press, 2002), 257–71.

15. Paul, Nation, and Nationalism

1. I will discuss below the distinction that Aijaz Ahmad makes between "progressive" and "retrograde" nationalism (*In Theory: Classes, Nations, Literatures* [London: Verso, 1992], 38).

2. Ernest Renan regarded national amnesia with respect to violent origins as a virtue ("What Is a Nation?" (1882), in *Nation and Narration*, ed. Homi K. Bhabha [London: Routledge, 1990], 10–11).

3. Homi K. Bhabha, "Introduction: Narrating the Nation," and "DissemiNation: Time, Narrative, and the Margins of the Modern Nation," in *Nation and Narration*, 1–7, 291–322; idem, "Ethics and Aesthetics of Globalism: A Postcolonial Perspective," in *The Urgency of Theory*, ed. António Pinto Ribeiro (Manchester: Carcanet, 2007), 2.

4. Noted by Judith Butler in Judith Butler and Gayatri Chakravorty Spivak, *Who Sings the Nation-State? Language, Politics, Belonging* (London: Seagull, 2007), 4–5.

5. See Richard Rohrbaugh, "The Pre-Industrial City in Luke-Acts: Urban Social Relationships," in *The Social World of Luke-Acts: Models for Interpretation*, ed. Jerome H. Neyrey (Peabody, Mass.: Hendrickson, 1991), 129–37.

6. See Ahmad, *In Theory*, 7.

7. Note that it is Paul who asserts his identity as an "Israelite" (Rom 11:1; 2 Cor 11:22; Phil 3:5).

8. Jonathan Hall, *Ethnic Identity in Greek Antiquity* (Cambridge: Cambridge University Press, 1997), 6–16.

9. Timothy Brenna, "The National Longing for Form," in Bhabha, *Nation and Narration*, 45.

10. Davina C. Lopez, *Apostle to the Conquered: Reimagining Paul's Mission*; Paul in Critical Contexts (Minneapolis: Fortress Press, 2008), 6. So also Neil Elliott, *The Arrogance of Nations:*

Reading Romans in the Shadow of the Empire, Paul in Critical Contexts (Minneapolis: Fortress Press, 2008).

11. See Jae Won Lee, "Paul and Ethnic Difference in Romans," in *They Were All Together in One Place: Toward Minority Biblical Criticism*, ed. Randall C. Bailey, Tat-siong Benny Liew, and Fernando F. Segovia, Semeia Studies 57 (Atlanta: Scholars, 2009), 141–57.

12. On behavior as an aspect of identity, see Dominic Abrams, "Social Identity, Social Cognition, and the Self: The Flexibility and Stability of Self-Categorization," in *Social Identity and Social Cognition*, ed. Dominic Abrams and Michael A. Hogg (Oxford: Blackwell, 1999), 205–6; Ahmad, *In Theory*, 7.

13. See especially Fernando F. Segovia, *Decolonizing Biblical Studies: A View from the Margins* (Maryknoll, N.Y.: Orbis, 2000).

14. See Butler and Spivak, *Who Sings the Nation-State?* 31.

15. Mikhail M. Bakhtin, *Speech Genres and Other Late Essays*, ed. Caryl Emerson and Michael Holquist (Austin: University of Texas Press, 1986), 2.

16. See R. S. Sugirtharajah, "Introduction," in *Voices from the Margin: Interpreting the Bible in the Third World*, ed. R. S. Sugirtharajah (Maryknoll, N.Y.: Orbis, 1995), 2; Geoffrey Bennington, "Postal Politics and the Institution of the Nation," in Bhabha, *Nation and Narration*, 121.

17. Bhabha, "Introduction," 4.

18. Homi Bhabha, *The Location of Culture* (New York: Routledge, 1994), 5.

19. Judith Butler makes a similar point with regard to what she calls "bare life" in *Who Sings the Nation-State?* 10. See also R. S. Sugirtharajah's critical position toward nativist and nationalist biblical interpretation in the Indian context in *Asian Biblical Hermeneutics and Postcolonialism: Contesting the Interpretations*, Biblical Seminar 64 (Sheffield: Sheffield Academic, 1998), 3–25, 101–11.

20. Bhabha, "DissemiNation," 292–93, 312–14.

21. Bhabha, "Ethics and Aesthetics," 8.

22. Bhabha, "DissemiNation," 296, 312.

23. Ahmad, *In Theory*, 7, 12, 41; Simon During, "Literature—Nationalism's Other? The Case for Revision," in Bhabha, *Nation and Narration*, 139. See also Benita Parry, "Directions and Dead Ends in Postcolonial Studies," in *Relocating Postcolonialism*, ed. David Theo Goldberg and Ato Quayson (Oxford: Blackwell, 2002), 66–81.

24. Tat-siong Benny Liew, *What Is Asian American Biblical Hermeneutics? Reading the New Testament*, Intersections (Honolulu: University of Hawai'i Press, 2008), 24–27.

25. Ibid., 27.

26. Ahmad, *In Theory*, 36.

27. Christine DiStefano, "Dilemmas of Difference," in *Feminism/Postmodernism*, ed. Linda J. Nicholson (London: Routledge, 1990). 75.

28. Ahmad, *In Theory*, 38.

29. Ironically, Liew argues later for such a "contextually concrete and specific" interpretation (*What Is Asian American Biblical Hermeneutics?* 56).

30. Ibid., 29–30.

31. Ibid., 27.

32. Richard A. Horsley, "Rhetoric and Empire—and 1 Corinthians," in *Paul and Politics: Ecclesia, Israel, Imperium, Interpretation*, ed. Richard A. Horsley (Harrisburg, Pa.: Trinity Press International, 2000), 72–102.

33. Efraín Agosto, "Patronage and Commendation, Imperial and Anti-Imperial," in Horsley, *Paul and Politics*, 104.

34. The construction of the arch by Domitian after the death of Titus more than a decade after the defeat of Jerusalem shows how prominent the disdain for the Jews remained in Roman memory.

35. Indeed, Horsley shows how Jewish apocalyptic was an attempt to make sense out of Israel's long history of imperial domination ("Rhetoric and Empire," 94–95).

36. See Elliott, *Arrogance of Nations*, 119 and passim; idem, "Political Formation in the Letter to the Romans," in *Character Ethics and the New Testament: Moral Dimensions of Scripture*, ed. Robert L. Brawley (Louisville: Westminster John Knox, 2007), 186–87.

37. Joel Marcus, "Crucifixion as Parodic Exaltation," *Journal of Biblical Literature* 125 (2006): 73–87.

38. Brigitte Kahl, "Reading Galatians and Empire at the Great Altar of Pergamon," *Union Seminary Quarterly Review* 59 (2005): 21–43. For her provocative rereading of Paul and Galatians against the Roman imperial context, see her recent book *Galatians Re-imagined: Reading with the Eyes of the Vanquished*, Paul in Critical Contexts (Minneapolis: Fortress Press, 2010).

39. Lopez, *Apostle to the Conquered*, 6.

40. See the critique of Ahmad, *In Theory*, 41.

41. Ibid., 38.

42. Ibid., 41.

43. For instance, N. T. Wright views the pre-conversion Paul as a (politically and religiously) revolutionary nationalist and then ironically confuses Paul's activity after conversion as (theologically) anti-imperial, but non-nationalist. See Wright, *What Saint Paul Really Said: Was Paul of Tarsus the Real Founder of Christianity?* (Grand Rapids: Eerdmans, 1997), 25–37.

44. Michael Billig, *Banal Nationalism* (London: Sage, 1995), 4–8 and passim. Billig makes the point that nationalistic presumptions are so common as to go unnoticed (ibid., 12).

45. Ibid., 1.

46. Denise Kimber Buell and Caroline Johnson Hodge, "The Politics of Interpretation: The Rhetoric of Race and Ethnicity in Paul," *Journal of Biblical Literature* 123 (2004): 235–51. See also Caroline Johnson Hodge, *If Sons Then Heirs: A Study of Kinship and Ethnicity in the Letters of Paul* (Oxford: Oxford University Press, 2007).

47. I follow here my argument in "Paul and Ethnic Difference," 151–52.

48. Lopez, *Apostle to the Conquered*, 25.

49. Sze-kar Wan, "Collection for the Saints as Anticolonial Act: Implications of Paul's Ethnic Reconstructions," in Horsley, *Paul and Politics*, 191–215.

50. Ibid., 199, 203, 209–10.

51. Ibid., 200–203.

52. Calvin Roetzel, "Reponse: How Anti-Imperial Was the Collection and How Emancipatory Was Paul's Project," in Horsley, *Paul and Politics*, 228.

53. Billig, *Banal Nationalism*, 12.

54. Mark D. Nanos, "The Jerusalem Oriented Geopolitical Perspective of Paul's Autobiographical Material in Gal. 1:17–2:12" (unpublished paper, 1999).

55. See also Horsley, "Rhetoric and Empire," 72–87.

56. Ernst Käsemann, *Commentary on Romans*, trans. Geoffrey W. Bromiley (Grand Rapids: Eerdmans, 1980), 308. Nanos implies that the root is a metaphor only for the remnant (*The Mystery of Romans: The Jewish Context of Paul's Letter* [Minneapolis: Fortress Press, 1996], 252–53 n. 31, 260). But the remnant is implied only at the level of the branches that have been broken off.

57. Hodge, *If Sons Then Heirs*, 143–46.

16. Constructions of Paul in Filipino Theology of Struggle

A version of this paper was presented at the Paul and Politics Group, Society of Biblical Literature annual meeting, Atlanta, November 2003. It was previously published in *Asia Journal of Theology* 19, no. 1 (2005): 188–220, and is republished here with permission.

1. On the emergence and character of the theology of struggle, see Eleazar S. Fernandez, *Toward a Theology of Struggle* (Maryknoll, N.Y.: Orbis, 1994), 19–63; Erme R. Camba, "The Making of a Theology of Struggle: A Testimony of Theological Praxis in the Philippines" (unpublished paper presented at Emmanuel College, University of Toronto, March 21, 2002). For the most recent bibliographic survey of Filipino contextual theology, including theology of struggle, see "Contextual Theology in the Philippines 1800–2000," in *Asian Christian Theologies: A Research Guide to Sources, Movements, Authors,* ed. John C. England et al. (3 vols.; Maryknoll, N.Y.: Orbis, 2002–4), 2:331–497.

For multiauthor anthologies of the theology of struggle, see Socio-Political Institute, ed., *With Raging Hope: A Compilation of Talks on the Themes Involved in Social Transformation and Its Emerging Theology* (2 vols.; Quezon City: Claretian, 1985); Mary R. Battung et al., eds., *Religion and Society: Towards a Theology of Struggle* (Manila: FIDES, 1988); Victoria Narciso-Apuan, Mary Rosario Battung, and Liberato Bautista, eds., *Witness and Hope amid Struggle: Towards a Theology and Spirituality of Struggle* (Manila: FIDES, 1991); Nonie Aviso et al., eds., *Currents in Philippine Theology,* Kalinangan Book Series 2 (Quezon City: IRC, 1992).

For single-author anthologies, see Melanio Aoanan, *Spirituality for the Struggle: Biblico-Theological Reflections from Mindanao* (Quezon City: Ecumenical Council for Theological Education by Extension in the Philippines, 1988); Edicio de la Torre, *Touching Ground, Taking Root: Theological and Political Reflections on the Philippine Struggle* (Quezon City: Socio-Pastoral Institute, 1986); Luis Hechanova, *Church, Politics and Transformation: Essays by Fr. Luis G. Hechanova,* ed. Juan V. Sarmiento, Jr. (Quezon City: Claretian, 2002).

2. See Feliciano Cariño, "What about the Theology of Struggle," in Battung, *Religion and Society,* ix–xi; Oscar Suarez, "Theology of Struggle: Reflections on Praxis and Location," *Tugón* [Journal of the National Council of Churches in the Philippines] 6, no. 3 (1986): 47–60.

3. Embracing a sociopolitical perspective that is more radical and revolutionary than reformist or liberal, the theology of struggle also emphasizes the struggle for cultural integrity and re-rooting. In theological method, including the use of the Bible, it is diverse; in regard to political ideology and affiliation it is pluralist on the left spectrum (or divided, depending on the point of view). For an earlier account of the revolutionary movement and the role of Christians, including Christians for National Liberation, within it, see William Chapman, *Inside the Philippine Revolution* (New York: W. W. Norton, 1987); Anne Harris, "The Theology of Struggle: Recognizing Its Place in Recent Philippine History," *Kasarinlan: The Journal of Third World Studies* 21, no. 2 (2006): 83–107. The sharp divisions within the progressive movement (Philippine left) since the early 1990s have put a particular strain on discourse about Christian participation in the radical political arena. The story is yet to be fully documented.

4. Oscar Suarez, "The Phenomenon of Power: Biblical and Theological Perspectives, *Tugón* 5, no. 1 (1985): 52. For a similar explanation, that "the key to understanding this passage [Romans 13] is that Paul is also a Roman citizen" and had enjoyed some of its benefits, see Elizabeth Dominguez, "New Testament Reflections on Political Power," in *New Eyes for Reading: Biblical and Theological Reflections by Women from the Third World,* ed. John S. Pobee and Bärbel von Wartenberg-Potter (Geneva: WCC, 1986), 45–49.

5. Explanations for Paul's so-called "social conservatism" include his Roman citizenship, the imminent expectation and nonfulfillment/postponement of the *parousia,* his Greco-Roman

contextualization, the practical survival of the Christian movement, and the dynamics of personal appropriation. See below.

6. This was the general conclusion at the Silliman University Divinity School Faculty Forum, October 7, 2003, which discussed my essay "The Politics of Paul: His Supposed Social Conservatism and the Impact of Postcolonial Readings," *Conrad Grebel Review* 21, no. 1 (Winter 2003): 82–103. For a "hermeneutics of appreciation," see José de Mesa, "A Hermeneutics of Appreciation: Approach and Methodology," in *Why Theology Is Never Far from Home* (Manila: De La Salle University Press, 2003), 112–96.

7. For instance, in the recent collection of essays by Luis Hechanova, who is credited with coining the phrase "theology of struggle" to describe this emerging theology in the early 1980s, there is only one reference to Paul, where, linked with John the Baptist, he is presented as a model of those who commit themselves to decreasing in relation to Jesus (*Church, Politics and Transformation*, 117). In reflections on Christology, the focus is on the historical Jesus, with passing reference to Paul in regard to themes of vindication through resurrection; see Luna Dingayan, "Towards a Christology of Struggle: A Proposal for Understanding the Christ," in *Doing Theology with Asian Resources*, vol. 4, *Mission and Human Ecology*, ed. Yeow Choo Lak (Singapore: ATESEA, 1999), 132–57; Virginia Fabella, "Christology from an Asian Woman's Perspective," in *Asian Faces of Jesus*, ed. R. S. Sugirtharajah, Faith and Cultures (Maryknoll, N.Y.: Orbis, 1993), 211–22. Pauline texts likewise do not appear in Melanio Aoanan's collection of "Biblico-Theological Reflections" (see n. 1 above). Noriel Capulong ("Reading the Bible from a Holistic Yet Partisan Perspective," *Silliman Ministry Magazine* 72 [2002]: 10–17) provides a survey of the theme of justice, going through the Old Testament and stopping after Jesus. Perhaps more telling is the project of the Ecumenical Center for Development's People's Theology Committee, chaired by Oscar Suarez, to engage in Bible studies with the grassroots. In the published summaries of the studies, no texts from Paul were included; see *Faith in Struggle*, Book I, trans. J. A. Q. Maglipon (2nd ed.; Quezon City: Ecumenical Center for Development, 1985); *Faith in Struggle*, Book II, compiled and arranged by Sammie P. Formilleza (Quezon City: People's Theology Publication, Ecumenical Center for Development, 1990). On this project, see further Everett Mendoza, "Theology in the Philippines: The Future of Local Theologies in an Age of Globalization," *Tugón* 13, no. 1 (1999): 61–69.

8. On the struggle of women for emancipation as a part of the larger people's struggle, see Liberato Bautista and Elizabeth Rifareal, eds., *And She Said No! Human Rights, Women's Identities, and Struggles* (Quezon City: Program Unit on Human Rights, National Council of Churches in the Philippines, 1990); Fernandez, *Toward a Theology of Struggle*, 17–18. Many writings by Filipina authors are discussed in England, "Contextual Theology in the Philippines," 331–497. The Autumn 1993 issue of *In God's Image* [Journal of the Asian Women's Resource Centre for Culture and Theology] 12, no. 3, on "Reclaiming Women's Partnership with the Earth," was authored by Filipinas. Note also Mary John Mananzan, "Globalization and the Perennial Question of Justice," *In God's Image* 21, no. 2 (2002): 22–27; eadem, "Feminist Theology in Asia: A Ten Year's Overview," *In God's Image* 14, no. 3 (1995): 38–48.

9. For an exception, see Muriel Orevillo-Montenegro, "Saying Yes! To Our Mission: A Bible Study Based on 2 Cor 8:8-15," *Silliman Ministry Magazine* 62 (December 1997): 13–17. In her article "The Bible and Violence against Women," *Silliman Ministry Magazine* 63 (March 1998): 15–19, she does not specifically deal with Paul, except to observe the presence of "positive" texts such as Rom 8:38-39 over against "oppressive" texts such as Eph 5:22. Nor does Paul figure in her *The Jesus of Asian Women*, Women from the Margins (Maryknoll, N.Y.: Orbis, 2006). Helen Graham ("Empowerment of Women for Peace," in *Woman and Religion*, ed. Mary John Mananzan [3rd ed.; Manila: Institute of Women's Studies, 1998], 24–37) discusses biblical interpretation from a women's perspective but is silent on Paul.

10. Mary John Mananzan, "Women and Religion," in Battung, *Religion and Society*, 107-20.
11. Virginia Fabella, "Mission of Women in the Church in Asia: Role and Position," in Pobee and von Wartenberg-Potter, *New Eyes for Reading*, 81-89.
12. Elizabeth Dominguez, "New Testament Reflections on Political Power," in Pobee and von Wartenberg-Potter, *New Eyes for Reading*, 45-49.
13. Sharon Rose Joy Ruiz-Duremdez, "The Biblical, Theological, and Moral Foundation of Human Rights," in *Basic Human Rights Course for Church People* (Iloilo: Western Visayas Ecumenical Council, 1992), 9-14.
14. Arche Ligo, "Women in Biblical Patriarchy," in Mananzan, *Woman and Religion*, 15-23; quotations from 20-21.
15. Jurgette Honclada, "Notes on Women and Christianity in the Philippines," *In God's Image* (October 1985): 13-20.
16. Nacpil holds a Ph.D. from Drew University in systematic theology and philosophy of religion, has served as a professor of theology at Union Theological Seminary, and has been a resident bishop in the Manila area for the United Methodist Church. He has also served as president of the (international) Council of Bishops of the United Methodist Church. His most recent major contribution is *Jesus' Strategy for Social Transformation* (Manila: United Methodist Church, 1998). He retired as a bishop of the United Methodist Church in the Philippines in 2000.
17. Mariano C. Apilado (*The Dream Need Not Die: Revolutionary Spirituality 2* [Quezon City: New Day, 2000], 16-17) includes Nacpil in his sampling of contributions under the general rubric of "theology of struggle," yet makes sharp criticisms of Nacpil's perspective as "setting back the struggle of the Filipino to be and become." In the mid-1980s Nacpil was a key player in the reaction by the United Methodist College of Bishops against the forthright criticism of the government and the political perspective of the Executive Committee of the National Council of Churches in the Philippines. See Oscar S. Suarez, *Protestantism and Authoritarian Politics: The Politics of Repression and the Future of Ecumenical Witness in the Philippines* (Quezon City: New Day, 1999), 75-81.
18. Emerito Nacpil, "A Gospel for the New Filipino," in *Asian Voices in Christian Theology*, ed. Gerald H. Anderson (Maryknoll, N.Y.: Orbis, 1976), 117-45. Page references in the text in subsequent paragraphs in this subsection are to this essay.
19. For another essay in which he draws decisively on Paul, see "One in Christ, A New Creation," *Tugón* 8, no. 3 (1987): 49-53. Addressing the annual assembly of the National Council of Churches in the Philippines on the theme "Unity in Christ, A New Creation" in a speech based on Col 1:15-20, he drew attention to Gal 3:28; 6:15; 2 Cor 5:14-21; and Eph 2:1-33, explaining that the new human and the new community in Christ are visible signs of the new creation, over against racism, classism, imperialism, and nationalism.
20. Labayen was ordained a priest in Rome in 1955 and there obtained his licentiate in theology and canon law. In 1966 he organized the National Secretariat of Social Action, Justice, and Peace (NASSA) of the Catholic Bishops' Conference of the Philippines (CBCP) and served as its National Director until 1981, when he was eased out, in his words, "by certain timorous bishops" (*Revolution and the Church of the Poor* [Quezon City: Claretian Publications, 1995], 110; page references in the text in subsequent paragraphs in this subsection are to this work). Labayen was appointed by the Federation of Asian Bishops' Conferences (FABC) as the Executive Chairman of the Office for Human Development (1972-86); he initiated the Asian Cultural Forum on Development (ACFOD) for the Pontifical Commission on Justice and Peace (1975), and he has served as chair of the Ecumenical Bishops' Forum (EBF) and as executive chairman of the Socio-Pastoral Institute. In recent years, his ecumenical work has focused on ecological and interfaith concerns; see *Revolution*, 157-67; and idem, "Gospel and Culture," *Silliman Ministry Magazine* 58 (August 1996): 17-22.
21. See Julio Labayen, *To Be the Church of the Poor* (2nd ed.; Manila: Communications Foun-

dation of Asia, 1987); idem, *Spirituality: Challenge to the Church of the Poor Today* (Manila: Socio-Pastoral Institute, 1990); idem, *The Call of the Church of the Poor: Challenge to Christians Today* (Manila: Socio-Pastoral Institute, 1991).

22. *Acts and Decrees of the Second Plenary Council of the Philippines*, held January 20—February 17, 1991 (Manila: Catholic Bishops Conference of the Philippines, 1992).

23. Claiming that "in its primary concern for equitable distribution of goods, socialism carries sympathetic vibrations with Christianity" (*Revolution*, 75), Labayen nevertheless observes that socialist revolutions (as in the Philippines) have often gone wrong in suppressing pluralism in favor of centralism, in not giving attention to the human factor such as power and greed in the human heart, in underemphasizing the role of culture and counterculture, and in favoring ideology over people, the party over the masses (ibid., 61–75, 140–41).

24. See Labayen, "Faith in the Global City," in Battung, *Religion and Society*, 197. There he interweaves comments regarding spiritual redemption and faith in Jesus with reflections on the historical arena of good news to the poor and the vision of the fullness of time and of humanity (citing Gal 3:28; Rom 4:9-12; Eph 3:8).

25. For Labayen's particular interest in the "spirituality" of the struggle, see his "Introduction" in Narciso-Apuan, Battung, and Bautista, *Witness and Hope amid Struggle*, ix–xi.

26. His other accomplishments and involvements include the roles of adjunct professor at many theological institutes; co-founder of the Socio-Pastoral Institute; member of THRUST (Theologians for Renewal, Unity and Social Transformation); theological consultant for the National Secretariat for Social Action, Justice and Peace, and the Pontifical Council for Justice and Peace, East Asia Regional Council. His theological training took him to Innsbruck, Austria, where he was ordained a Jesuit priest. There he could count among his professors Karl Rahner, although he confesses that it was biblical studies that most deeply inspired him. "Although as students, my classmates and I were privileged to study under the reputedly most renowned systematic theologian in the Catholic Church, it was biblical studies that taught me several liberating insights. One of them is that Jesus eludes systems, including the one we have saddled ourselves with today" (Carlos Abesamis, *A Third Look at Jesus* [3rd ed.; Quezon City: Claretian Publications, 1999], 6).

27. Karl Gaspar ("Doing Theology [in a Situation] of Struggle," in Battung, *Religion and Society*, 47) claims that Abesamis's paper "Faith and Life Reflections from the Grassroots in the Philippines," presented at the 1979 Asian Theological Conference (published in *Asia's Struggle for Full Humanity: Towards a Relevant Theology. Papers from the Asian Theological Conference, January 7–20, 1979, Wennappuwa, Sri Lanka*, ed. Virginia Fabella [Maryknoll, N.Y.: Orbis, 1980], 123–39), was "the first serious attempt to articulate [what sort of] theology would be most relevant to Filipinos." See also his "Doing Theological Reflection in a Philippine Context," in *The Emergent Gospel: Theology from the Underside of History. Papers from the Ecumenical Dialogue of Third World Theologians, Dar es Salaam, August 5–12, 1976*, ed. Sergio Torres and Virginia Fabella (Maryknoll, N.Y.: Orbis, 1978), 112–23.

28. For example, *Salvation—Historical and Total* (Quezon City: JMC Press, 1977); *Where Are We Going: Heaven or New World?* (Manila: Foundation Books, 1983); "Good News to the Poor," in Battung, *Religion and Society*, 203–14; "The Mission of Jesus and Good News to the Poor: Exegetico-Pastoral Considerations for a Church in the Third World," *Asia Journal of Theology* 1, no. 2 (October 1987): 429–60; *Exploring the Core of Biblical Faith: A Biblico-Catechetical Primer* (Quezon City: Claretian, 1988); "Some Paradigms in Re-Reading the Bible in a Third-World Setting," *Mission Studies* 17, no. 1 (1990): 21–34; *What Is Inside the Wooden Bowl? Ano Po ang Laman ng Mangkok? Or, How (Not) to Move towards a Contextual Theology* (Manila: Socio-Pastoral Institute, 1997); and *A Third Look at Jesus* (see n. 26 above).

29. Abesamis, *Third Look*, 3–7.

30. Abesamis, *Inside the Wooden Bowl*, 5–35; idem, *Exploring the Core*, xii–xvi.
31. Abesamis, *Inside the Wooden Bowl*, 10, 31–33.
32. Abesamis, *Third Look*, 4.
33. Abesamis, *Inside the Wooden Bowl*, 43.
34. Ibid., 43–44.
35. Abesamis, *Third Look*, 212.
36. Abesamis, *Exploring the Core*, 103–6; idem, *Third Look*, 207.
37. Abesamis, *Exploring the Core*, 98–100.
38. Ibid., 103–7; idem, *Third Look*, 206–14.
39. Abesamis, *Exploring the Core*, 106–7, 111 n. 41; idem, *Where Are We Going*, 27–28.
40. Abesamis, *Third Look*, 94–95, 211–12.
41. Abesamis, *Exploring the Core*, 2.
42. Abesamis, "Mission of Jesus," 207; idem, *Third Look*, 200.
43. Abesamis, *Third Look*, 195.
44. Ibid., 197, 200; idem, "Mission of Jesus," 207; idem, *Exploring the Core*, 101–2.
45. Abesamis, *Third Look*, 10.
46. Ibid., 195.
47. Ibid., 193.
48. Ibid., 194–95.
49. Ibid., 150 n. 58.
50. Ibid., 63.
51. Abesamis, *Where Are We Going*, 43–44; idem, *Third Look*, 217.
52. Levi Oracion completed doctoral studies at the University of Chicago in 1969 and returned to the Philippines in the brewing storm of the martial law years, where the existentialist theology that he had imbibed in graduate school was transformed into an explicit theology of struggle (Camba, "Making of a Theology of Struggle"). See also "Introduction" in Levi Oracion, *God with Us: Reflections on the Theology of Struggle in the Philippines* (Dumaguete City: Silliman University Divinity School, 2001), vi–viii. Oracion has served as dean of the Divinity School at Silliman University and as president of Union Theological Seminary; later he worked in Geneva with the World Council of Churches (CCPD office). He has now upon retirement returned to the Philippines, where he is teaching and writing.

In addition to *God with Us*, his publications include *Human Realizations of Grace: A Look at the Christian Faith from the Perspective of the Theology of Struggle* (Dumaguete City: Silliman University Divinity School, 2005). Among his noteworthy articles are "The Filipino Pastor as Theologian," *Silliman Ministry Magazine* 13 (November 1977): 7–12; "A Theological Perspective on Human Rights," *Wednesday Forum Journal*, August 1979, 2–8, reprinted in *Living Theology in Asia*, ed. John England (Maryknoll, N.Y.: Orbis, 1982), 103–11; "Religious Perspectives and the Social Imperatives of Education in the Philippines," *Tugón* 3, no. 2 (November 1982); "Theology and Ideology," *Tugón* 4, no. 1 (January 1984): 60–70, reprinted in *Theology and Ideology in Asian People's Struggle* (Singapore: CCA-URM, 1985), 4–17; "Theological Reflections on a Spirituality of Struggle," *Tugón* 7, no. 1 (1987): 100–107; "God's Dialectic of Liberation," in *Doing Theology with the Spirit's Movement in Asia*, ed. John England, ATESEA Occasional Papers No. 11 (Singapore: ATESEA, 1991), 136–44.

53. Oracion is among the few who explicitly discuss the question of violence and nonviolence and Christian participation in armed revolution, favoring nonviolent resistance (*God with Us*, 235–52, 257–62; *Human Realizations*, 364). Oracion's assessment is that the Christian will "not absolutely refuse to be drawn into the vortex of violent revolution," even though any adopted political ideology will require constant interrogation against the logic of the gospel ("Theology and Ideology," 65–69).

54. Oracion, "Theology and Ideology," 68.
55. On reading and using the Bible, especially the "people's way of reading," see *God with Us*, 49–53.
56. Oracion, "Spirituality of Struggle," 104.
57. Oracion, *God with Us*, 1, 17, 21, 78, 88, 94, 97, 168; especially chapter 4, "The Nature and Predicament of the Human Reality," 88–109.
58. Ibid., 21.
59. Ibid., 228.
60. Oracion, "Theological Reflection on Church and State," and "Theses on the Relationship between Church and State," unpublished presentations at the 1978 General Assembly of the United Church of Christ in the Philippines. The presentations of Oracion were decisive for the final assembly resolution calling for the lifting of martial law. See Victor R. Aguilan, "A Critical-Historical Analysis of the Church-State Relations under Martial Law from the Perspective of the United Church of Christ in the Philippines" (M.Theol. thesis, South East Asia Graduate School of Theology, 2003), 104–5.
61. Oracion, *God with Us*, 77.
62. Ibid., 43, 97, 140–42, 170–71, 228–29, 234, 248–49; idem, "Human Rights," 109–11.
63. See Oracion, *God with Us*, 46–48, 70–71, 140–42, 150, 170, 211–14, 249; idem, "Human Rights," 109–10; idem, "Spirituality of Struggle," 105; idem, *Human Realizations*, 141.
64. Oracion, *God with Us*, 46–47, 80–81, 82, 173.
65. Oracion, "Dialectic of Liberation," 142–43; idem, *God with Us*, 44, 48, 234.
66. Oracion, "Pastor as Theologian," 11.
67. Oracion, *God with Us*, 150.
68. Ibid., 158–59.
69. Benito Dominguez, now retired, has been a professor of New Testament at Union Theological Seminary and has served as the coordinator of the United Church of Christ in the Philippines' (UCCP) Commission on Evangelism and Ecumenical Relations, as pastor of the Church of the Risen Lord on the campus of University of the Philippines at Diliman, and as a bishop for the UCCP. His publications include "New Testament: Quest for a New Spirituality," "New Testament: Call for a New Responsibility," and "New Testament: Call for a New Witness," in *Human and the Holy*, ed. Emerito Nacpil (Maryknoll, N.Y.: Orbis, 1978), 24–35, 81–88, 177–88; "Theology of Struggle: Towards a Struggle with Human Face," *Kalinangan* 6, no. 1 (1986) [reprinted in Aviso, *Currents in Philippine Theology*, 83–88]; "Heaven or New Earth," in *Witnessing Praxis in Mission: Proceedings of Training Workshop for Emerging URM Leadership, 1986* (Hong Kong: CCA-URM, 1986); *And No One Shall Go Hungry: Stewardship of All Creation* (Quezon City: NCCP, 1988); *We Believe . . . in God* (Quezon City: UCCP, 1988); *A Theology of Struggle and the Jesus Tradition* (Manila: SPI, 1990); "God's Partners in the Kingdom," in *Turn Around: Called to Witness Together amidst Asian Plurality. CCA Asia Mission Conference, Seoul 1994* (Hong Kong: CCA, 1995).
70. Dominguez, *We Believe*, 14–15; idem, "New Responsibility," 81, 87 n. 1.
71. Dominguez, "New Spirituality," 32.
72. Ibid., 25, 33, 34 n. 2; idem, "New Witness," 182.
73. Dominguez, "New Witness," 188 n. 12.
74. Dominguez, "Theology of Struggle," 86.
75. Ibid., 84, 87.
76. Everett Mendoza is an ordained minister of the United Church of Christ in the Philippines (UCCP) and has served as professor and dean at the Silliman University Divinity School and as vice president for academic affairs at Silliman University. He received his doctorate in systematic theology

from the Southeast Asia Graduate School of Theology (1900) and has served as chairperson of the General Assembly (1998-2002) and as theologian in residence for the UCCP.

In addition to the articles cited below, materials consulted for this paper include "Jesus Lives: Sermon Guide for 1 Cor 15:12-19," *Silliman Ministry Magazine* 7 (March-May 1977): 19-20; "Faith under Fire: Sermon Guide for Acts 12; 2 Cor 4:7-18," *Silliman Ministry Magazine* 18 (April-June 1978): 20-21; "Three Bible Studies on the Poor," in *Mission in the Context of Endemic Poverty*, ed. Lourdino Yuzon (Singapore: CCA, 1983); "Bible Studies on the Transformation of Church and Society," *Tugón* 6, no. 2 (1986): 10-24; "The Basis of Our Faith: 1 Cor 1:26—2:5," *Silliman Ministry Magazine* 40 (March 1989): 7-8; "Peace with Nature," *Tugón* 11, no. 3 (1991): 555-61; "'Growing in Faith': Eph 4:1-7, 11-15," *Silliman Ministry Magazine* 53 (December 1993): 13-15; "Philippine Realities and the Theology of Struggle," *Silliman Ministry Magazine* 57 (March 1995): 19-22; "The Cross of Christ: 1 Cor 1:18-25," *Silliman Ministry Magazine* 60 (March 1997): 16-18; "Stewardship of Life: A Bible Study: Texts, Gen 1; Rom 6:1-11," *Silliman Ministry Magazine* 63 (March 1998): 20-21; "Theology in the Philippines: The Future of Local Theologies in the Age of Globalization," *Tugón* 13, no. 1 (1999): 61-69; "Naming and Confronting the Idols of Our Time," *Silliman Ministry Magazine* 68 (December 2000): 25-26; "America's Adobo, the Philippines," *Silliman Ministry Magazine* 71 (March 2002): 8-11; "Power for Creative Living: Sermon Guide for Col 2:16—3:4," *Silliman Ministry Magazine* 6 (February 1977): 5-6; See also "The Church Meets Trouble: Sermon Guide for Acts 5:12-42," *Silliman Ministry Magazine* 18 (April-June 1978): 12-13.

77. Everett Mendoza, "Hope in the Midst of Despair: Sermon Guide for Rom 5:1-11," *Silliman Ministry Magazine* 11 (September 1977): 6-7; idem, "The Reformation Faith for Today's Living: Text, Rom 1:16-17," *Silliman Ministry Magazine* 62 (December 1997): 1, 3-5.

78. Everett Mendoza, "The Letter to the Romans: Paul's Theology of Salvation," *Silliman Ministry Magazine* 30 (September-October 1980): 5-7.

79. Everett Mendoza, "Archetypes of a Spiritual Person: Guidelines for Bible Study," in Battung, *Religion and Society*, 237-45.

80. Ibid., 241.

81. Ibid., 242.

82. Everett Mendoza, "Jesus Assures His Disciples: Sermon Guide for 1 Cor 15:1-11," *Silliman Ministry Magazine* 7 (March-May 1977): 20-21.

83. In his earlier writings, Mendoza puts particular emphasis on the ecclesiology of providing a counterethic in which the church plays a subversive role; see "A New Person in Christ: Sermon Guide for Rom 8:1-4; Eph 2:1-10," *Silliman Ministry Magazine* 22 (January 1979): 2-3; "Concern for the Church: Sermon Guide Guide for 1 Cor 1:1-3; 2 Cor 1:21-24; 13:10-11," *Silliman Ministry Magazine* 23 (February-March 1979): 3-4; "Church Meets Trouble," 12-13. In more recent publications, the emphasis turns to the involvement or impact of the individual Christian as he or she joins political movements for social transformation.

84. By contrast, Suarez (*Authoritarian Politics*, 98-103) decries the dualistic dichotomy of the private and public, the sacred and secular, and the notion of autonomous zones of jurisdiction. For a further debate on the meaning of Lutheranism for the theology of struggle, see the issue of *Tugón* 8, no. 1 (1988).

85. Everett Mendoza, *Radical and Evangelical: Portrait of a Filipino Christian* (Quezon City: New Day, 1999). Page references in the text of the remainder of this subsection are to this work.

86. "Thus ... the question of violence and armed struggle is settled according to the norm of God's external or civil justice, not according to the precepts of the Gospel as may be discerned in Jesus' Sermon on the Mount" (*Radical and Evanglical*, 107). Moreover, it can be settled only according to an "inward perspective," the status of the conscience (ibid., 20, 26, 177).

Notes to Chapter 16

87. Ibid., 199–209; cf. vi, 19, 31, 75, 177.

88. José de Mesa and Lode Wostyn, *Doing Christology: The Re-Appropriation of a Tradition* (Quezon City: Claretian, 1989). Page references in the text of this subsection are to this work.

89. De Mesa and Wostyn are Catholic scholars who have spent much of their active careers teaching systematic theology at the Maryhill School of Theology. De Mesa is a married lay theologian and has served as chair of the department of applied theology at De La Salle University in Manila. Wostyn has served since the 1970s as a CICM (Congregation of the Immaculate Heart of Mary) missionary to the Philippines and has also served as director of the Institute of Philosophy and Religion at Saint Louis University in Baguio City; see the interview entitled "Doing Liberation Theology: A Filipino Agenda" that is available for download at http://www.theo.kuleuven.ac.be/clt/Annual%20 Report%20Academic%20Year%202002-2003.doc (accessed May 21, 2010).

90. They hint that they prefer a pluralist approach to liberation politics (*Doing Christology*, 320–21), rejecting the clamor to make one socioeconomic political program the only Christian option, and preferring the method of nonviolence (ibid., 326).

91. They recognize that it "remains difficult to understand Paul outside the religious-cultural ambit in which he tried to re-appropriate the Jesus event" (*Doing Christology*, 240).

92. It is for this reason, not for the specific content of Paul's thought, that de Mesa can refer to Paul as "the first great Christian theologian." See de Mesa, "Hermeneutics of Appreciation," 177.

93. Richard Hays, *Echoes of Scripture in the Lettters of Paul* (New Haven: Yale University Press, 1989).

94. This idea is presented to a lesser extent also in the writings of Oracion and Mendoza. See also Noriel Capulong, "Creation and Human Responsibility: Christ and Creation (Christology and Cosmology)," in Lak, *Doing Theology with Asian Resources*, 93; Artemio Zabala, "Advent Reflections on Col. 1:15-20 in the Philippine Setting," *Asia Journal of Theology* 3, no. 1 (1989): 315–29; Catalino Arevalo, "Notes for a 'Theology of Development,'" *Philippine Studies* 19, no. 1 (1971): 66; Domingo Diel, "On the Three-fold Office (Function) of Christ," *Tugón* 4, no. 2 (1984): 9–23; Apilado, *Dream Need Not Die*, 69–72.

95. See also Mariano Apilado, "Transformation of Church and Society: A UCCP Stance," *Tugón* 6, no. 2 (1986): 43–44; Feliciano Cariño, "Theology, Politics and Struggle," *Tugón* 6, no. 3 (1986): v.

96. See also Capulong, "Creation and Human Responsibility, 89–90.

97. Apilado, *Dream Need Not Die*, 97–99.

98. As a matter of fact, forms of millennialism (both so-called irrational peasant and rational urban forms), as reactions against colonial incursion, have had a long history of motivating people's struggles in the Philippines. On the role of millennialism/eschatology in the theology of struggle, see also Fernandez, *Toward a Theology of Struggle*, 43–52. See also Francisco Nemenzo, Jr., "The Millenarian-Populist Aspects of Filipino Marxism," *Marxism in the Philippines* (Quezon City: Third World Studies Center, 1984), 9; Benigno P. Beltran, "The End is Nigh: Militant Millenarianism and Revolutionary Eschatology in the Philippines," *Diwa* 23, no. 1 (1998): 17–41. For expressions of millennialism earlier in the history of the Philippines, see esp. Reynaldo C. Ileto, *Pasyon and Revolution: Popular Movements in the Philippines, 1840–1910* (Quezon City: Ateneo de Manila Press, 1979). On the significance of Paul's millennial vision for appreciating Paul's politics, see also my "Politics of Paul," 82–103.

99. For example, J. Christiaan Beker, *Paul the Apostle: The Triumph of God in Life and Thought* (Philadelphia: Fortress Press, 1980).

100. The theme is present with lesser emphasis also in Oracion and Dominguez, who also address the classic themes of human depravity (Romans 7). On the loss of the image of God (Rom 1:21), see Oracion, *God with Us*, 16; and Capulong, "Creation and Human Responsibility."

101. On Gal 5:1, see also Apilado, "Transformation of Church and Society," 33; Suarez, *Authoritarian Politics*, 158, applying it to the body politic. For the use of Gal 5:1 as a slogan calling on church people to be vigilant in response to recent American imperial incursion, see Reuel Marigza, "Never Again Submit to the Yoke of Slavery: A Reflection on the RP-US Balikatan War Activities," *Silliman Ministry Magazine* 71 (March 2002): 31–33.

102. For the frequent citations of these texts, see also Mendoza, "Faith under Fire," 20–21; Salvador Martinez, "Using our Troubles," *Silliman Ministry Magazine* 22 (Jan 1979): 4–5; Capulong, "Creation and Human Responsibility," 92; Domingo Diel, "On the Three-fold Office," 9–23; Apilado, *Dream Need Not Die*, 31 (discussing 2 Cor 4:8-9). On the dying and rising up of the Filipino people, see Fernandez, *Toward a Theology of Struggle*, 97–126; Dingayan, "Christology of Struggle," 146–47.

103. Galatians 2:20; 4:6-7; Rom 8:10-11, 14-17; 1 Cor 2:6-16; 15:45; 2 Cor 3:18; Phil 1:19; Eph 3:17.

104. Romans 8:22-25, 31-39; Phil 3:10; 2 Cor 4:7-12. See also Apilado, *Dream Need Not Die*, 31, 51 (2 Cor 5:19), 73 (Phil 3:13-14), 75 (1 Cor 13:13), 84 (Phil 4:13).

105. Ephesians 6 also provides the framework for a manifesto of the National Movement for Civil Liberties—Church Sector; see National Movement for Civil Liberties, "People of God, Stand Your Ground," in Battung, *Religion and Society*, 249–51.

106. From the Philippines context, see now contributions from the professors at De La Salle University in Manila: Daniel Kroger, "Paul and the Civil Authorities: An Exegesis of Romans 13:1-7," *Asia Journal of Theology* 7, no. 2 (1993): 344–66; Arnold T. Monera, "Paul and the 'Powers That Be': An Exegesis of Romans 13,1-7" (Ph.D. diss., Katholieke Universiteit Leuven, 2002). In his history of interpretation, Monera shows that Romans 13 has been "grievously perverted, to support the political interests of the readers and interpreters," and illustrates how it is a "potentially dangerous exhortation," using examples from the Philippines (p. 474).

107. See also Suarez, "Phenomenon of Power," 52–54; Elizabeth Dominguez, "New Testament Reflections on Political Power," 45–49, explaining Romans 13 in connection with Paul's Roman citizenship; Jose Fuliga, "Church–State Relations and Civil Disobedience," *Asia Journal of Theology* 1, no. 2 (1987): 472–76, who states a preference for nonviolent resistance alone when the state overreaches; Cirilo A. Rigos, "God and Caesar," in *Church and State and Other Public Issues and Concerns*, ed. Liberato C. Bautista (Quezon City: NCCP, 1986), who highlights the contrast with Revelation 13 and Acts 5.

108. Klaus Wengst, *Pax Romana and the Peace of Jesus Christ*, trans J. Bowden (Philadelphia: Fortress Press, 1987), 75.

109. "Salvaging" was the term used in the turbulent Marcos era to describe the dumping of disappeared, executed political prisoners onto urban garbage heaps.

Index

Passages

HEBREW BIBLE/ OLD TESTAMENT

Genesis
1	348n76
1:26-28	239
1:27	182
2:7-25	182

Leviticus
18:5	291n30

Deuteronomy
23:15-16	201

Job
5:12-13	307n58

Psalms
8	239
69:9	229
93:11	307n58

Isaiah
29:14	307n58
40:13	307n58
44:2-8	285n78
45:1-7	285n78
54:2-3	192
64:4	307n58

Jeremiah
9:22-23	59, 279n54, 307n58
25:9	285n78
27:6	285n78
43:10	285n78

Daniel
2:37	285n78

1 Maccabees
1:41-49	137
1:60-61	137
2:42-48	137

2 Maccabees
6:7-11	137

NEW TESTAMENT

Luke
18:9-14	218
18:14	219
23:47-48	339n49
23:48	217

Acts
1:8	192
5	350n107
5:12-42	348n76
5:29	255
12	348n76
14:5-20	211
16–17	171
16:20-21	171
16:23	70
16:24	285n71
16:37-38	70
17:6-7	172
17:10-13	172
18:11	194
20:21	194
21:27—26:32	70
21:38	300n15
21:39	70
22:25-29	70
23:27	70

Romans
1:1	162
1:3-4	285n63
1:5	103
1:12	59
1:14	59, 119, 120, 220
1:16-17	348n77
1:16	120, 231
1:17	103
1:18	121, 283n45, 283n47
1:20	231
1:21	349n100
1:25	231
1:26	121
1:28	290n14
2:5-16	121, 283n47
2:9-10	120
2:9	231
2:17-29	120, 124
2:17-24	120
2:24	229
2:25-29	121
2:26-27	120
3:9	120, 292n41
3:10	102
3:18	106
3:21	99, 102
3:22	285n64
3:26	285n64
3:27-28	218

351

Romans (continued)		7:5	121	8:19-25	249, 253
3:29	120, 231	7:6	105	8:19-23	231, 242, 243, 246
3:30	120	7:7-25	102, 291n25		
4	253, 290n20	7:7-12	291n25	8:21-23	49
4:9-12	345n24	7:7-8a	106	8:22-25	239, 350n104
4:10-12	231	7:7	98, 102, 108	8:23	283n43
4:11-12	120	7:8	98	8:26	229
4:13	283n47	7:8b-13	101–5	8:29	67
4:17-18	231	7:8b-9	291n27	8:30	283n49
5	243, 290n20	7:9-25	99	8:31-39	245, 350n104
5:1-11	348n77	7:9-13	102	8:32	283n47, 283n53
5:6-8	121	7:9	291n28		
5:10	103	7:9b-11	109	8:33-34	70
5:12-14	98, 291n28	7:9b-10	108	8:37	283n47, 283n53
5:12	102, 107	7:12	100, 102, 105		
5:13	291n27	7:13—8:11	248	8:38-39	343n9
5:14	98	7:13-25	163	8:38	103
5:17	103	7:13	291n25	8:39	283n48
5:18-20	106	7:14-25	105–8, 291n25	9–11	239
5:18	103	7:14-24	108	9:3	230
5:20	98, 106	7:14	99, 102, 121, 292n41	9:24	120
5:21	102, 103, 107			9:30-33	120
6	100, 103, 292n42	7:15-24	102	9:30-32	122
		7:15-23	107	9:30-31	120
6:1-11	348n76	7:16	102	10:1-3	120
6:2	103	7:18-24	244	10:4	291n30
6:4	103, 104	7:21	102	10:5	291n30
6:5	104	7:23	102	10:12	120
6:6	104	7:24-25	102	11	234-35
6:10	103	7:24	202	11:1	225
6:11	101, 103, 291n22	7:25—8:1	108	11:7	122
		7:25	109	11:11-25	120
6:12-23	104	8	252	11:14	120
6:12	104, 291n22	8:1-4	348n83	11:25-26	283n47
6:13	68, 103, 248, 249, 291n22	8:1	107	11:26-32	231
		8:2	103	11:26	231, 283n45
6:17	103	8:4	106, 108, 109, 292n44	11:29	231
6:18	103			11:32	283n47
6:19	248, 249	8:6	103	11:36	243, 253, 283n47
6:20-21	121	8:7-8	292n44		
6:20	106	8:9-11	243	12:1-2	68
6:22	102, 103	8:9	106	12:13-14	71
6:23	103	8:10-11	241, 350n103	12:17-21	71
7	95–109, 349n100	8:10	103	12:19-20	71
		8:12-21	4	12:21	68
7:1-8a	99–100	8:12-13	106	13	48, 58, 65, 70–73, 164, 236, 237, 244–45, 247, 252, 254–55, 278n43, 350n107
7:1	99, 102, 103	8:13	283n49		
7:2	103	8:14-17	241, 350n103		
7:3	103	8:17	283n49		
7:4	99, 101	8:18-39	283n42		
7:5-7	99	8:18-25	67, 283n47		

Index of Passages

13:1-7	48, 49, 71, 224, 233, 281n12, 285n80, 350n106	1:18-29	254	3:23	61	
		1:18-25	133, 241, 348n76	4	60	
				4:1-4	136	
		1:18	219	4:3	131	
13:1-4	71	1:19	137, 307n58	4:4-5	131, 283n47	
13:9	105	1:20-21	58	4:5	283n47	
13:10	109, 292n44	1:21	133	4:6-21	131	
13:11-14	121, 283n51, 283n53	1:22-24	133	4:6-19	302n20	
		1:22	120, 133, 142	4:6	131, 132, 305n37	
14:10-12	283n47	1:23	57, 120, 219			
14:10	68	1:24	120	4:7-21	132	
14:17	67, 73, 244, 249, 253	1:25	58	4:8-13	132, 305n37	
		1:26—2:5	348n76	4:9-12	252	
14:17-19	248	1:26-31	58, 131, 132, 302n20, 307n58	4:10-13	134	
15:3	229			4:11-13	143	
15:6	296n38			4:14-21	134	
15:8-9	120	1:26-29	246	4:14-16	60	
15:12	283n42, 283n47	1:26	59, 132, 133	4:14-15	61	
		1:27-28	133	4:15	162	
15:14	59	1:28	132	4:16—5:10	283n43	
15:19	233	1:29	132	4:16	138, 289n30	
15:25-27	230	1:31	59, 137, 279n54	4:18-19	131	
15:27	120			4:20	133	
15:31	230	2:1-5	59	5:1—6:20	134	
16	285n84	2:1-2	131, 132	5:1-8	142	
16:1	201	2:2	57	5:1-2	136, 311n94	
16:17-20	59	2:3	132, 134	5:1	120, 133, 137	
16:20	283n42, 283n47	2:4-5	131	5:2	133	
		2:4a	132	5:4	136	
		2:6—3:3	142	5:5-13	136, 311n94	
1 Corinthians		2:6-16	131, 241, 350n103	5:10-11	141	
1–4	59			6:1-6	142	
1–3	279n54	2:6-8	65, 66, 73, 283n42	6:1-3	69	
1:1-3	348n83			6:2-3	283n42, 283n47	
1:4-9	131	2:8	57			
1:4-5	133	2:9	137, 307n58	6:7-8	142	
1:5c	134	2:10	142	6:9-10	141	
1:7a	133	2:15	139	6:9	311n92	
1:8	283n47	2:16—3:3	139	6:11	141	
1:9-13	136	2:16	137, 307n58	6:12-20	136, 311n94	
1:10—4:21	305n37	3	60	6:13-20	141	
1:10	57, 131	3:1-9	131	6:13-14	134	
1:11-25	131	3:1	132	6:13	244	
1:11	131, 201	3:3	131, 132	6:15a	136	
1:12	305n36, 305n37	3:4-9	305n37	6:16-17	141	
		3:5-6	61	6:19-20	136, 141	
1:13	305n37	3:10-17	131	7	72	
1:17—3:23	134	3:12-15	131	7:1-40	134	
1:17	131, 132, 133	3:18-23	131, 137	7:1-9	141	
1:18—2:16	66	3:18-20	133	7:4	141, 307n54	
1:18-31	58, 59, 60	3:19	307n58	7:5-7	307n54	

354   Index of Passages

1 Corinthians (continued)		10:6-10	121	13:5b	136
7:10	138	10:7	137	13:10-12	283n48
7:12-16	307n54, 312n108	10:11	66	13:13	350n104
		10:18-22	137	14:11	119, 133
7:12	138	10:18	133	14:18	137
7:15	307n54	10:21-22	136, 141	14:21-22	137
7:17-24	281n12, 304n26	10:22	121	14:21	133, 137
		10:23—11:1	131, 136	14:31	137
7:18-19	132, 306n44	10:23-30	143	14:33-35	238
7:18	120, 307n56	10:23-24	292n39	14:33	138, 286n84
7:19	103, 122, 137, 307n56	10:31-32	133	14:33b-36	176, 311n86
		10:32-33	137, 138	14:34-35	46, 47, 281n12
7:20-24	137	11	71–72, 164	14:37	103, 138
7:21	143	11:1	138, 289n30	14:40	138, 286n84
7:23	136, 141	11:2-16	175-85, 238, 281n12, 331n6, 333n21, 33n33	15	243, 252, 253
7:25 38	311n86			15:1-58	134
7:25	138			15:1-11	135, 348n82
7:26	66			15:3-4	136
7:29-31	163	11:3-10	311n86	15:9-10	134, 143
7:29	66, 68	11:3-9	181	15:12-19	348n76
7:31	66	11:3-4	180, 181, 185	15:19	283n43
7:32	143	11:3	72, 179, 180, 333n31	15:20-57	134
7:35	286n84			15:20-28	58, 139, 283n43, 283n47
7:40	139	11:7-9	72, 179, 180, 182		
8:1—14:40	134				
8:1—9:23	136	11:7	182	15:20	243
8:1-13	131	11:10	181, 184	15:21-28	66
8:1-4		11:11-12	179, 180	15:23-29	283n42
8:9—9:22	143	11:13-16	181	15:23	285n65
8:11-12	136	11:16	181	15:24-28	66, 73, 242, 243, 253
9:1-27	134	11:17-34	132, 302n20		
9:1-18	131, 143	11:17-30	136	15:24	239
9:1-15	278n47	11:20-22	244, 253	15:28	67, 243
9:1-2	135	11:27-32	283n47	15:29-37	134
9:3	131	11:29	184	15:30-34	136
9:5	141	12:1-2	137	15:32-54	135
9:8-9	137	12:2	133	15:35-57	283n47
9:18	131	12:3	139, 252	15:36	135, 139
9:19-27	307n54	12:12-30	143	15:39-41	135
9:19-23	131, 137	12:12-21	136	15:42-44	135, 139
9:19-22	308n70	12:13	120, 133, 137, 311n86	15:45	138, 243, 291n32, 350n103
9:20-23	120				
9:20-21	120, 133, 162	12:22-26	136		
9:21-22	308n63	12:22-25	137, 308n60	15:50	283n43
9:22	193	12:22-24		15:51-57	139
9:22c	137	12:27-28	135, 137	15:51-52	135
9:24-27	132, 136	12:27	136	15:54-57	135
10:1-22	136, 311n94	12:28	135	15:54	138
10:1-6	301n15	12:31—14:40	135	15:58	136, 143
10:1-4	138	13:1—14:1	143	16:1-4	134
10:4	241	13:5	136	16:14	143

Index of Passages

16:19	311n86	11:32-33	70	4:3	121
16:24	143	12:8-10	252	4:5	220
		12:14-17	278n47	4:6-7	241, 350n103
2 Corinthians		12:20	286n84	4:6	242, 243
1:3-7	70	13:10-11	348n83	4:7	220
1:5	252	13:10	283n54	4:8-9	221
1:8	70			4:13	220
1:21-24	348n83	Galatians		4:14	220
2:14-16	70	1:1	162	4:19	91, 213, 220
3:12-18	21	1:4	68, 218,	4:21-31	122
3:14-18	122		283n42	4:25	230
3:18	243, 350n103	1:6-9	207	4:26	278n43,
4:1-6	251	1:8-9	207, 221		283n45
4:7-18	348n764	1:15-16	251, 254	5:1-12	207
4:7-12	246, 252, 254,	1:17	233	5:1	254,
	350n104	1:18	233		350n101
4:10	103	2:1	233	5:6	122
4:16—5:5	70	2:2	233	5:11	70
4:16	254	2:3	207	5:13	221
4:17	283n49	2:6-10	232	5:14	220, 221
5:2	283n45	2:7-9	207	6:2	220, 221
5:4	103, 283n43	2:8-9	120	6:7	283n49
5:10	283n47	2:10	50	6:12-13	207
5:11	68	2:11	103	6:12	70, 207, 221
5:14-21	344n19	2:12-14	120	6:13	218
5:19	350n104	2:15-21	217	6:15	344n19
6:5	70	2:15	218	6:17	220
6:7	68	2:16	219, 285n64,		
6:8-10	252		292n38	Ephesians	
8–9	238, 278n43	2:19-20	220, 283n48	1:9-11	239
8:8-15	343n9	2:19	91	1:9-10	242, 243, 253
8:9	241, 254	2:20	218, 241, 242,	1:10	239, 241
9:2	296n38		243, 285n64,	1:20-21	239, 253
9:4	119		350n103	1:23	243
10–13	279n54,		253	2	253
	279n59	3–4	59, 119, 212,	2:1-33	344n19
10:3-4	283n51,	3:1	217, 338n45	2:1-10	348n83
	283n53	3:3	59	3:8	345n24
10:4	68	3:13	67	3:17	243, 350n103
10:5-6	283n54	3:21	103	4:1-7	348n76
10:8	283n54	3:22	285n64	4:10	243
10:10	132, 310n79	3:23-24	239, 254	4:11-15	348n76
10:17	279n54	3:26-28	73	5:21-23	238
11	288n27	3:28	120, 164, 182,	5:22	343n9
11:22	225, 301n15		202-3, 220,	6	350n105
11:23-27	289n27		237, 238, 241,	6:10-20	253, 254,
11:23-25	289n28		253, 326n21,		283n53
11:23	70, 229		344n19,	6:15	68
11:24	70		345n24		
11:25-26	70	3:29	220	Philippians	
11:26	70	4:1-5	239, 254	1:3-11	157, 320n75

Philippians (continued)		2:17-18	156	4:16	170
1:7	158	2:17	70	4:20	283n49
1:8	156	2:19-30	153	4:21-22	320n73
1:9	70	2:21	154	4:22	158
1:12-17	70	2:23-24	320n75		
1:12-14	157, 320n75	2:24	153, 154	Colossians	
1:12	153	2:25	283n51	1:5	283n43, 283n45
1:13	70, 153	2:29	320n75		
1:15-17	154	3:1-11	247	1:12-13	283n48
1:15	154	3:2-11	155, 255	1:12	283n43
1:17	154	3:2	155	1:13-14	239, 253
1:19	243, 350n103	3:3	122, 157	1:13	68
1:20-23	153	3:4-6	157	1:15-20	241, 242, 246, 253, 344n19
1:21	103	3:5	225		
1:23-26	157, 283n48	3:7-11	157, 320n75	1:15-16	245
1:24-26	157, 320n75	3:8-11	245, 254	1:16-20	58
1:24	153	3:10	246, 350n104	1:17-20	243
1:25	153	3:13-14	350n104	1:18	243
1:26	153, 156	3:14-17	154, 157, 158	1:24	70
1:27-30	283n42, 283n47	3:15	158, 321n79	1:25-28	59
		3:17-21	156, 255, 283n47	1:27	68
1:27-28	283n47			2:2-4	59
1:27	62, 153, 156	3:17	158, 289n30	2:3	241
1:28	154, 156	3:18-19	158	2:6	286n84
1:29-30	70	3:18-21	155, 255	2:8	59
1:29	156	3:19-20	156	2:14-15	58
1:30	320n75	3:20-21	19, 283n42	2:15	66, 239, 243, 253
2:1-5	158	3:20	62, 68, 69, 156, 157, 255, 278n43, 283n43, 283n45, 284n57		
2:3	154, 158			2:16—3:4	348n76
2:4-11	254			3:3	283n48, 283n49
2:5-11	69, 245, 246				
2:6-11	289n29, 333n28			3:11	119
				3:18—4:1	281n12, 282n22, 286n84
2:6-8	241	3:21	66, 157, 158, 283n43		
2:7-8	43				
2:7	157, 202, 322n96	4:1	158	3:18-25	238
		4:2-3	158		
2:8-9	243	4:2	157, 305n37, 320n75, 323n102	1 Thessalonians	
2:8	157			1:6—2:2	68
2:9-11	19, 283n42, 283n47, 323n96			1:6-7	289n30
		4:3	321n79	1:6	68, 168
		4:5	323n103	1:7	169
2:9	157	4:7	156, 323n103	1:9	168
2:10	157	4:8-9	154, 157	1:10	283n45, 283n47
2:11	157	4:9	156, 158, 323n103		
2:12	153, 155, 157			1:14-16	120
2:13	154, 157	4:10-20	155	2:1-6	329n59
2:14	155	4:11-13	320n75	2:2-13	168
2:15	155	4:13	350n104	2:2	70, 168, 285n71
2:16-18	157, 320n75	4:14-20	278n47	2:4	168
2:16	103, 283n47	4:15-16	320n73	2:5	170

Index of Passages

2:7	162, 170	2 Peter		20.8.7	296n40
2:9	168, 170, 278n47	3:13	239, 241	20.8.9	296n40
		3:15-16	53	*Jewish War*	
2:11	170			1.4.3	296n40
2:12	68	Revelation		2.13.7	296n40
2:14-16	168	13	72, 247, 255, 350n107	2.18.2	296n40
2:14-15	120–21, 124			2.306-8	70
2:14	70, 289n30	21	239	5.1.3	296n41
2:15	168	21:4-5	241	6.3.3	296n41
2:18	168			6.335-36	233
2:19	285n65			7.8.7	296n40
3:1-5	170	**GREEK AND ROMAN**			
3:1	168	**TEXTS**		Juvenal	
3:3	68			*Satires*	
3:7	168	Cassius Dio		3.10-18	132
3:13	285n65	37.16.5–17.4	302n20	3.58–125	301n19
4:3	327n2			6.542-47	132
4:5	120, 330n61	Cicero		14.96-106	302n20
4:11	169	*Pro Cluentio (Clu.)*		14.96-104	130
4:13—5:11	283n42	5.14–6,16	142		
4:13-18	283n43, 283n48	*De natura deorum (Nat. d.)*		Livy	
		2.3.8	130	38.16–17	338n40
4:15	285n65	*De provinciis consularibus*			
4:16	283n45, 283n47	*(Prov. cons.)*		Martial	
		5.10	310n79	7.30	140
5:1-11	283n47			7.35	140
5:3	68, 278n43	Dionysius		7.82	140
5:8	68	*Roman Antiquities*		11.94	140
5:14	286n84	1.4-5	143	12.57.13	132
5:23	285n65	1.89	143		
		2.17	143	Petronius	
1 Timothy		7.66.4-5	143	*Satyricon*	
2:3-6	58			102	137
		Herodotus			
2 Timothy		*Histories*		Philo	
3:14-17	195	9.122.3	225	*De Abrahamo*	
3:16-17	192, 193			136	296n41
		Isocrates		*De confusione linguarum*	
Titus		*Panegyricus*		190	296n41
2:3-9	238	50	297n54	*De ebrietate*	
				193	296n41
Philemon		Josephus		*Legum allegoriae*	
1	201	*Antiquities of the Jews*		166	296n40
2	283n51	1.3.9	296n41	200–201	296n40
11	200	4.2.1	296n41	205	296n40
15-16	202	8.11.3	296n41	*De vita Mosis*	
19	200	11.7.1	296n41	2.44	306n44
22	201	15.5.3	296n41	*De mutatione nominum*	
		16.6.8	296n41	35	296n41
1 Peter		18.1.5	296n41	*De opificio mundi*	
3:1-7	238	18.9.9	296n40	128	296n41
4:17	68	18.65-84	141		

358 — Index of Passages and Authors

Plutarch
Lycurgus
27.4   143

Plutarch
Quaestiones convivales
1.2   129

Pseudo-Hippocrates
De aere
24   225

Quintilian
Institutio oratoria
11.3.74   140
12.11.1-3   132

Strabo
Geography
8.6.23   57
12–14   296n31

Suetonius
Domitian
12.1-2   130, 137
Tiberius
36   130

Tacitus
Annals
2.85   130
Histories
5.4-5   302n20
5.5   130, 137, 229, 311n94, 312n104

Theon
Progymnasmata
9.15-24   308n62
10.13-18   308n62

Valerius Maximus
1.3.3   130

RABBINIC TEXTS

m. Parah
3:6, 11   225
m. Šeqalim
4:2   225
m. Yoma
6:4   225
b. Roš Haššanah
31a   225

Authors

Abesamis, Carlos H., 238, 241–44, 253, 254, 345n26–346n51
Abrams, Dominic, 340n12
Achebe, Chinua, 3, 11
Adams, Colin, 329n55
Adorno, Theodor W., 303n24
Agamben, Giorgio, 50, 164, 269n69, 326n23
Agosto, Efraín, 149, 256n1, 262n85, 316n30, 316n31, 319n68, 320n70, 321n83, 322n95, 326n20, 337n10, 340n33
Aguilan, Victor R., 347n60
Ahearn, L. M., 275n16
Ahmad, Aijaz, 39–40, 49, 227–28, 258n10, 268n50, 339n1
Ahn, Yong-Sung, 258n9
Alcock, Susan E., 272n107
Alcoff, Linda Martin, 273n119
Alexander, Loveday, 330n64
Alexander, M. Jacqui, 317n51
Ang, Ien, 27, 28, 29, 265nn5–8, 295n23, 295n28

Anthias, Floya, 115, 294n18, 294n19, 294n20, 294n21, 295n23, 295n24, 295n25, 298n56, 314n7
Aoanan, Melanio, 342n1, 343n7
Apilado, Mariano C., 344n17, 349n94, 349n95, 349n97, 350n101, 350n102, 350n104
Arevalo, Catalino, 349n94
Arichea, Daniel, 331n5
Ascough, Richard S., 329n57
Ashcroft, Bill, 9, 257n4, 268n54, 277n32
Aviso, Noni, 342n1, 347n69

Badiou, Alain, 45, 50, 164, 269n69, 271n89, 271n92, 273n119, 273n120, 326n23, 327n25
Bailey, Randall C., 325n7
Bakhtin, Mikhail, 226, 340n15
Balakrishnan, Gopal, 273n124
Balch, David, 217, 338n45
Balsdon, J. P. V. D., 297n52
Barclay, John, 270n77

Barrett, C. K., 291n35
Barrier, Jeremy, 288n25
Barth, Hans-Martin, 336n4
Barth, Frederik, 292n1
Barth, Karl, 38
Barth, Markus, 335n24
Barthes, Roland, 128, 299n9
Barton, Stephen C., 280n69
Barvosa-Carter, E., 277n31
Bassler, Jouette, 182–83, 279n56, 280n68, 310n86, 333n34, 333n36
Battung, Mary R., 342n1
Bauman, Zygmunt, 138, 308n66
Baur, F. C., 196–98, 199, 300n15, 335n17, 335n18, 336n27
Bautista, Liberato, 342n1, 343n8
Beard, Mary, 289n33, 304n30
Beker, J. Christiaan, 67–68, 73, 282n23, 282n28, 284n50, 284n59, 285n77, 286n86, 286n87, 349n99
Beltran, Benigno P., 349n98

Index of Authors

Betz, Hans Dieter, 280n1, 282n18
Bhabha, Homi, 4, 6, 9, 10–11, 14, 18–19, 48, 56, 76–77, 89, 97, 113–16, 122–26, 138, 142, 144, 189–90, 204, 224, 226–27, 234, 258n7, 258n9, 262n72, 262n73, 272n112, 276n27, 287n11, 287n12, 287n14, 287n16, 290n9, 290n10, 293n6–294n18, 294n20, 295n26, 297n46, 308n68, 311n96, 312nn118–119, 313n1, 320n76, 321n77, 324n114, 334n5, 334n7, 336n28, 339n2, 339n3, 339n9, 340nn16–18, 340nn20–23
Bhatia, Sunil, 295n23, 295n26
Billig, Michael, 230, 231, 233, 341nn44–45, 341n53
Bird, Jennifer, 6
Bird, Phyllis A., 314n4
Blanke, Helmut, 335n24
Blanton, Ward, 286n8
Blount, Brian K., 324n2, 324n4–5
Blumenfeld, Bruno, 272n109
Bockmuehl, Markus, 320n75
Boer, Roland, 34, 41, 258n10, 262n72, 262n85, 266n3, 267n24, 268n51, 268n59, 268n60, 269n69, 277n33, 313n1
Bordo, Susan, 298n2
Borg, Marcus J., 282n17
Boron, Atilio A., 273n124
Bosch, David J., 334n7, 334n9, 335n16
Botha, Jan, 285n81
Boyarin, Daniel, 123, 139, 143, 163–64, 165, 270n78, 287n12, 297n47, 300n15, 304n25, 305n55, 309n74, 326nn16–19, 326n22, 327n29
Brah, Avtar, 329n55
Braxton, Brad, 21–22, 264nn98–100, 304n26, 307n56, 327n32
Brenna, Timothy, 339n9

Brent, Alan, 330n63
Brett, Mark G., 263n85
Briggs, Sheila, 14, 148–49, 275n13, 315n23, 315n24, 316n33, 323n96, 327n30
Broeck, Sabine, 294n21
Bronfen, Elisabeth, 309n75
Brown, Michael Joseph, 300n15
Bruce, F. F., 335n23
Bryan, Christopher, 278n48
Buell, Denise Kimber, 231, 270n80, 296n29, 300n15, 303n22, 304n30, 306n44, 307n58, 309n70, 311n88, 311n94, 311n97, 341n46
Burrus, Virginia, 324n110
Butler, Judith P., 277n30, 277n31, 303n24, 339n4, 340n14, 340n19
Byron, Gay L., 300n15, 301n19, 306n44

Callahan, Allen Dwight, 326n20, 327n27
Camba, Erme, 342n1, 346n52
Campbell, William S., 270n77, 302n20
Canton, William, 335n13
Capulong, Noriel, 343n7, 349n94, 349n96, 349n100, 350n102
Caputo, John D., 273n119
Cariño, Feliciano, 342n2
Carter, Sean, 295n23
Carter, Warren, 20, 263n90, 263n91, 281n17
Cassidy, Richard J., 262, 320n70, 337n10
Castelli, Elizabeth A., 142. 178, 280n67, 285n82, 289n31, 306n41, 312n100, 312n105, 320n74, 321n77, 325n11, 332n19, 333n24
Cayton, Horace R., 301n15
Césaire, Aimé, 3, 11
Chakrabarty, Dipesh, 40, 268n53
Chapman, William, 342n3
Charles, Ronald, 272n112
Chan, Jeffrey, 310n85

Chan, Sucheng, 305n32
Chen, Tina, 298n8
Chin, Frank, 140, 310n85
Chow, John K., 269n72
Chow, Rey, 19, 321n76
Clines, David J. A., 309n77
Coleman, K. M., 339n48
Conzelmann, Hans, 330n64
Copher, Charles B., 300n15
Cosgrove, Charles H., 325n6
Cranfield, C. E. B., 290n19
Crossan, John Dominic, 58, 263n85, 278n42, 281n17, 288n18
Crossley, James, 38, 266n6, 267n35, 267n37
Cullmann, Oscar, 282n21, 285n70

Dahl, Nils, 305n37
D'Angelo, Mary Rose, 323n104, 324n110
Danker, Frederick W., 271n96
Davies, Penelope J. E., 288n22
Deidun, Thomas, 270n78
Deissmann, Adolf, 38–39, 75–76, 79, 267n38, 286n2, 286n4
Derrida, Jacques, 13, 32, 33, 114, 259nn24–25
deSilva, David A., 15, 260nn45–46
Desjardins, Michel R., 284n55
de Vos, Craig S., 323n101
Dickson, Kwesi, 321n7
Diel, Domingo, 349n94, 350n102
Diller, Aubrey, 297n53
Dingayan, Luna, 343n7, 350n102
DiStefano, Christine, 228, 340n27
Dirlik, Arif, 40, 63, 268n55, 280n3
Dollimore, Jonathan, 141, 311n93
Dominguez, Benito, 246–47, 253, 254, 255, 347nn69–75, 349n100
Dominguez, Elizabeth, 237–38, 342n4, 344n12, 350n107

Donaldson, Laura, 12, 13, 150, 151, 257n5, 258n9, 259n13, 259n28, 259n29, 260n30, 314n10, 316n35, 317n42, 317n48, 317n51, 318n53, 324n108
Donfried, Karl, 322n91
Douglas, Mary, 46, 56, 272n101
Douglass, Frederick, 203
Dove, Kenneth James, 308n60
Drake, St. Clair, 301n15
Dube, Musa, 17–18, 19, 41, 146, 148, 150, 151, 152–59, 167, 168, 261nn61–66, 264n103, 264n105, 268n62, 277n29, 281n6, 313n1, 313n3, 314n4, 314n6, 315n11, 315nn14–17, 315n19, 315n22, 316n35, 317n40, 317n40, 317n47, 317n50, 318nn53–55, 318n62, 319nn66–67, 321n78, 321n79, 321nn84–86, 323n106, 324n113, 325n10, 330n61
Du Bois, W. E. B., 39
Dunn, James D. G., 270n75, 272n114, 283n31, 290n19, 291n31
During, Simon, 227

Eagleton, Terry, 34, 266n1, 273n116, 273n117
Edwards, Catherine, 310n78
Ehrensperger, Kathy, 333n19
Eilberg-Schwartz, Howard, 129, 303n24
Eisenbaum, Pamela, 14, 163, 270n78, 270n81, 303n25, 325n13–326n15
Elliott, Neil, 5, 14, 15–17, 19–20, 57, 64, 72, 165–66, 259n10, 260n34, 261n50–57, 262n79, 262nn80–82, 262n84, 263n86, 267n42, 268n43, 269n69, 270n73, 270n80, 271n94, 271n95, 271n97, 272n104, 272n111, 273n115, 273n116, 273n123, 274n6, 278n40, 278n43, 279n60, 281n10, 281n13, 281n15, 281n17, 282n27, 283nn38–40, 285n68, 285n73, 285n78, 285n80, 302n20, 316n31, 318n59, 321n79, 322n91, 322n95, 325n8, 326n19, 326n20, 327nn32–35, 330n62, 338n35, 339n10, 341n36
Elliott, Susan M., 337n25
Eng, David L., 298n3, 310n84
Engels, Frederick, 37, 267n25
England, John, 342n1
Esler, Philip F., 119, 270n76, 292n2, 295n29, 296n39, 297n53

Fabella, Virginia, 237, 343n7, 344n11
Fabi, M. Giulia, 308n67
Fanon, Frantz, 3, 11, 26, 39, 96, 98, 100, 113, 114, 135, 139, 259n11, 269n49, 289n3, 290n5, 290n6, 290n16, 291n23, 293n12, 306n45, 306n47, 309n71
Febvre, Lucien, 335n13
Fee, Gordon D., 283n36
Felder, Cain Hope, 300n15
Feldman, Louis H., 297n44, 301n20
Fernandez, Eleazar S., 342n1, 343n8, 349n98, 350n102
Fitzgerald, John T., 322n93
Fitzmyer, Joseph A., 291n29
Foucault, Michel, 10, 78, 208, 298n2, 303n24
Fredriksen, Paula, 339n52
Frend, William H. C., 337n15
Freud, Sigmund, 114, 139, 141, 143, 144, 309n75
Friedman, Jonathan, 295n22
Friesen, Steven, 34–35, 38–39, 258n9, 266n7, 267n38, 267nn40–42, 268nn44–47
Frilingos, Christopher A., 258n9
Fuliga, Jose, 350n107
Furnish, Victor Paul, 321n79

Gabba, Emilio, 312n106
Galinsky, Karl, 47, 271n96, 272n106

Gallagher, Susan VanZanten, 21, 264n93
Gandhi, Leela, 26, 30, 40, 41, 96, 265n3, 265nn13–14, 268nn52–53, 268n54, 268n55, 268n61, 290n4, 290n7, 315n12
Garlington, D. B., 103, 290n19, 291n34
Garnsey, Peter, 269n69
Gaspar, Karl, 345n27
Gaston, Lloyd, 301n20, 307n58
Gaventa, Beverly Roberts, 289n30
Georgi, Dieter, 12, 14, 64, 260n34, 269n72, 274n6, 281n16, 283n34, 283n41, 284nn59–60, 285n64, 285n67, 286n84, 322n91
Gilbert, Gary, 330n63
Gilman, Sander L., 139, 143, 309n73
Gilroy, Paul, 303n24
Glad, Clarence, 308n70
Glancy, Jennifer A., 289n28, 299n14, 307n50
Gleason, Maud W., 140, 309n77
Godiwala, Dimple, 295n26
Goldhill, Simon, 301n19
Goodman, Martin, 304n31
Gordon, Richard, 271n84
Gotanda, Neil T., 298n3
Gottwald, Norman K., 266n4
Graham, Helen, 343n9
Gramsci, Antonio, 60, 128, 165, 277n34
Griffiths, Gareth, 9, 257n4, 268n54, 277n32
Gruen, Erich S., 297n44, 312n99
Gunderson, Erik, 309n77
Gundry-Volf, Judith, 179–80, 331n6, 333n23, 333nn25–27

Haarhof, T. J., 297n53, 297n54
Haddad, Beverley, 319n64
Hall, Edith, 297n53, 336n1, 338n44
Hall, Jonathan M., 225, 297n53, 311n94, 339n8

Index of Authors

Hall, Stuart, 290n11
Han, Jin Hee, 258n9, 294n20
Hannertz, Ulf, 293n6
Hardt, Michael, 273n124
Harrill, J. Albert, 300n15, 307n50, 310n79
Harris, William V., 288n24
Hawley, John C., 264n102, 277n31
Hays, Richard B., 141, 275n17, 291n30, 299n10, 302n21, 307n55, 309n77, 311nn91–92, 312n101, 349n93
Hechanova, Luis, 342n1, 343n7
Heen, Erik, 284n63, 319n68, 326n20, 337n10
Hegel, Georg W. H., 96, 98, 290n17, 337n12
Heil, John Paul, 307n58
Henderson, John, 289n33
Hengel, Martin, 338n46
Heschel, Susannah, 270n79
Hodge, Bob, 264n101
Hodge, Caroline Johnson, 231, 234, 270n80, 296n35, 296n42, 297n51, 298n55, 302n20, 303n22, 307n58, 308n61, 308n63, 308n70, 311n88, 311n94, 341n46, 341n57
Hogan, Patrick Colm, 97, 290n10, 290n13
Holladay, Carl R., 312n99
Hollingshead, J. R., 276n18
Hölscher, Tonio, 288n17
Honclada, Jurgette, 238, 344n15
Hoogvelt, Ankie, 280n4
Horrell, David G., 267n39
Horsley, Richard, 5, 12–15, 16, 20, 34, 54, 57, 64, 72, 148–49, 228–29, 259nn14–15, 259nn17–23, 260nn31–33, 260nn37–39, 261n57, 262n79, 263n85, 263n88, 264n92, 266n6, 269n72, 275n10, 276n18, 277n35, 278n38, 280n74, 281n17, 282n19, 282n27, 282n28, 283n35, 283n37, 285n67, 301n21, 301n22, 304n26, 305n34, 305n36, 306n40,
306n42, 311n92, 313n2, 315n21, 316n28, 316n30, 316n32, 316n35, 318n59, 320n68, 321n79, 321n83, 325n8, 326n20, 337n10, 340n32 341n35, 341n55
Huddart, David, 294n18
Huet, Valérie, 288n23
Hutnyk, John, 294n18, 294n20, 295n22, 295n25
Hurd, John C., 299n11

Ignatiev, Noel, 301n15
Ileto, Reynaldo, 282n26, 349n98
Isaac, Benjamin, 129, 297n52, 300n15, 301n20, 304n31, 306n44, 310n79, 312n108
Itzkovitz, Daniel, 308n64

James, C. L. R., 3, 11, 39
Jameson, Fredric, 16, 36–37, 48, 165, 266n10, 266nn20–24, 269n69, 273n116, 287n15, 293n12
JanMohamed, Abdul R., 144, 312n117
Jenkins, Richard, 292n1
Jeffreys, S., 277n31
Jennings, Jr., Theodore W., 45, 260n34, 263n85, 271n89, 327n26
Jervis, Ann, 183–84, 325n12, 331n6, 332n8, 333n23, 333nn37–38
Jewett, Robert, 218, 326n20, 338n35, 339n50
Jobling, David, 34, 41–42, 259n10, 266n2, 266n3, 268n64–260n66
Johnson-DeBaufre, Melanie, 329n58
Jones, Jr., Amos, 274n1
Jones, Christopher P., 330n65
Joseph, Clara A. B., 264n102
Joy, C. I. David, 258n9

Kabbani, Rana, 317n44
Kahl, Brigitte, 6, 45, 229, 257n8, 263n85, 266n5, 269n70, 271n86, 271n97,
288n18, 292n2, 336n1, 337n11, 338n36, 338n38, 338n41, 339n51, 341n38
Kalra, Virinder S., 294n18, 295n22, 295n25
Kantorowicz, Ernst, 306n49
Käsemann, Ernst, 234, 272n110, 291n26, 341n56
Karner, Christian, 115, 294n22
Kaur, Raminder, 294n18, 295n22, 295n25
Kautsky, Karl, 37–38, 48, 75, 94, 267nn26–32, 272n109, 286n5, 289n34
Keck, Leander E., 272n110
Kee, Alistair, 42
Keesmaat, Sylvia C., 264n103, 278n43
Keller, Catherine, 41, 268n63, 269n67
Kelley, Shawn, 149–50, 274n8, 280n77, 302n20, 303n22, 316n38, 317n40, 337n12
Kim, Duk Ki, 263n85
Kim, Seyoon, 263n85
Kim, Yung Suk, 324n6, 327n27, 328n46
Kinukawa, Hisako, 151, 317n52
Kittredge, Cynthia Briggs, 14, 140, 148–49, 153, 157, 180, 272n100, 274n9, 275n11, 279n64, 280n72, 280n75, 285n82, 305n37, 311n87, 313n2, 315n23, 315nn26–27, 316nn33–34, 318n59, 319n67, 320n69, 321n80, 322n89, 322n95, 322n96, 323n97, 323n102, 323n105, 324n6, 327n30, 333n28
Kloppenborg, John S., 329n57
Knust, Jennifer Wright, 280n69, 312n105, 316n29, 321n81, 327n30–31, 332n11
Koester, Helmut, 284n56, 320n71
Kolakowski, Leszek, 266n11
Kondo, Dorinne, 312n120
Kovaks, Judith, 282n29
Kreitzer, L. Joseph, 336nn24–26
Kremer, Bernhard, 338n39

Krentz, Edgar M., 322n92
Krishna, Sankaran, 264n102
Krishnaswamy, Revathi, 264n102
Kristeva, Julia, 150
Kroger, Daniel, 350n106
Kuortti, Joel, 295n26
Kuriyama, Shigehisa, 307n51
Kwok, Pui-lan, 19, 41, 48, 146, 148, 150, 151–52, 154, 159, 161–62, 166, 266n8, 268n62, 270n79, 272n100, 272n108, 274n4, 275n13, 275n15, 278n46, 313n3, 314n5, 314n8, 315n10, 315n11, 315nn18–20, 316n35, 316n38, 317n40, 317n42, 317n44, 317n45, 317n47, 317n50, 318n53, 318nn54–57, 318nn60–62, 318n64, 318n65, 321n78, 323n107, 324n115, 324n3

Labayen, Julio Xavier, 240–41, 253, 254, 344n20–345n25
Lacan, Jacques, 77, 114, 287n15
Lanci, John R., 301n16, 302n21, 312n102
Lapham, Lewis A., 280n2
Larson, Jennifer, 289n28, 309n77
Laurence, Ray, 329n55
Lee, Jae Won, 340n11, 341n47
Lee, James Kyung-Jin, 311n89
Levine, Amy-Jill, 13, 259n26, 270n79, 316n35, 316n39, 330n62
Lewis, Raina, 26–27, 265n4, 294n21, 318n51
Liew, Tat-siong Benny, 6, 20, 44, 154, 227, 258n9, 263n85, 263n88, 270n83, 295n26, 298, 320n76, 340n24, 340n29
Lightfoot, J. B., 335n18
Ligo, Arche, 238, 344n14
Lincoln, Andrew T., 283n46
Loomba, Ania, 264n102, 265n25, 293n13
Lopez, Davina C., 6, 45, 166–67, 225, 229, 231, 257n8,
262n79, 264n99, 266n5, 269n70, 271n86, 282n17, 286n6, 287n13, 288n18, 292n2, 324n109, 327n27, 328nn38–42, 330n61, 338n35, 338n38, 339n10, 341n39, 341n48
Lorde, Audre, 27–29
Lowe, Lisa, 298n3
Luther, Martin, 207, 250, 292n43, 336nn3–4

MacArthur, John, 329n49, 329n51, 330n59
MacMullen, Ramsey, 128–29, 130, 272n105, 301n17
Malherbe, Abraham, 39, 267n39
Malina, Bruce J., 267n43, 280n66
Mananzan, Mary John, 237, 343n8, 344n10
Marchal, Joseph, 13, 19–20, 166, 167, 168, 257n8, 259n27, 262nn77–79, 262n83, 266n8, 266n10, 271n98, 285n82, 287n10, 287n13, 294n21, 295n26, 297n55, 318n61, 319n63, 320n68, 320n69, 320n72, 320n74, 321n83, 322n92, 322n93, 322n94, 323n99, 323n102, 324n111, 324n115, 325n11, 327n30, 327nn42–45, 328n47, 330n60, 332n15, 337n10
Marcus, Joel, 229, 341n37
Marigza, Reuel, 350n101
Marotta, Vince P., 293n6
Marshall, John, 48, 272n112
Marshall, Peter, 272n104, 299n12
Marszal, John R., 338n39
Martin, Dale B., 128, 137, 138, 268n45, 278n39, 278n45, 278n47, 279n61, 279n62, 280n66, 280n71, 299nn12–13, 299n15, 299n16, 302n22, 305n36, 306n38, 306n39, 306n48, 307nn52–54, 307n57, 307n59, 307n60, 308n69,
311n86, 311n92, 312n108
Martin, Henri-Jean, 335n13
Martinez, Salvador, 350n102
Martínez-Vázquez, Hjamil A., 319n68
Martyn, J. Louis, 288n25
Marx, Karl, 35, 36, 39, 41, 42, 249, 259n10, 266n3, 266n11, 266n13, 268n51, 268n59, 268n60, 271n87, 271n90, 277n33
Massey, Preston, 331n4, 332n7
Matthews, Shelly, 172, 309n76, 310n83, 311n90, 330n66
Mazrui, Ali, 148, 311n90, 315n14
McCabe, Colin, 24, 265n1
McClintock, Anne, 19, 147–48, 151, 314n4, 314nn8–10, 317n51, 321n76, 324n109
McKinlay, Judith, 151, 318n52
McLeod, John, 315n12
Meeks, Wayne, 39, 267n39, 277n29
Meggitt, Justin, 38, 39, 43, 267n34, 268n45, 269n72
Memmi, Albert, 3, 11, 142, 311n95
Mendoza, Everett, 248–50, 253, 254, 343n7, 347n76–348n83, 348n85–349n87, 349n94, 350n102
Mesa, José de, 251–52, 253, 254, 255, 343n6, 349nn88–92
Meyer, Paul W., 281n11, 291n21, 291n25, 291n27, 292n40
Míguez, Néstor, 325n12
Milbank, John, 273n119
Mills, Sara, 26–27, 265n4, 294n21, 318n51
Minh-ha, Trinh T., 151, 317n51
Miranda, José Porfirio, 45, 271n87, 271n90
Mishra, Vijay, 264n101
Mitchell, Katharyne, 294n18, 294n19, 295n25, 295n26
Mitchell, Margaret M., 181, 305n36, 306n39, 331n5, 332n19, 333n29

Index of Authors

Mitchell, Stephen, 296n31, 338n39
Mofokeng, Takatso, 268n64
Mohanty, Chandra Talpade, 29–30, 31, 44, 147–48, 151, 265n12, 270n82, 314n6, 317n51, 318n58, 321n84
Monera, Arnold T., 350n106
Moore, Stephen D., 256n2, 257n5, 258n5, 258n6, 258n9, 259n12, 263n87, 263n89, 276n28, 313n1, 315n23
Mount, Christopher N., 279n63
Moxnes, Halvor, 286n8

Nacpil, Emerito P., 238–40, 253, 254, 344nn16–19
Nanos, Mark D., 129, 130, 221, 233, 270n78, 292n2, 302n20, 303n25, 304n26, 339n53, 341n54, 341n56
Narciso-Apuan, Victoria, 342n1
Nasrallah, Laura, 319n65, 330n65
Negri, Antonio, 273n124
Neill, Stephen, 334n7, 334n9
Nemenzo, Francisco, Jr., 349n98
Neufeld, Thomas R. Yoder, 284n52
Newman, Carey C., 284n49
Neyrey, Jerome H., 280n66
Nguyen, Viet Thanh, 301n15
Niang, Aliou Cissé, 287n10, 338n35
Nissinen, Martti, 311n92
North, John, 304n30
Nyman, Jopi, 295n26

Oakes, Peter, 39, 263 n, 85, 268n45, 323n101, 328n36, 337n10
Oakman, Douglas E., 276n21
Økland, Jorunn, 178, 310n86, 323n100, 332n19
Ong, Aihwa, 298n4, 298n6
Oracion, Levi, 244–46, 253, 254, 346n52–347n68, 349n94, 349n100

Orevillo-Montenegro, Muriel, 343n9
Osiek, Carolyn L., 320n69, 323n98

Packer, James E., 288n21
Padgett, Alan, 331n5
Palumbo-Liu, David, 127, 298n1
Park, Eung Chun, 270n77
Parry, Benita, 11, 258n10, 295n22, 340n23
Penner, Todd, 142, 286n1, 286n7, 299n10, 310n86, 312n98, 320n68, 322n87, 324n110, 331n4, 333n19
Perriman, Andrew, 181–82, 333nn31–32
Pervo, Richard I., 330n64, 331n66
Peterson, Kirsten Holst, 314n6
Phelan, Peggy, 299n8
Pilch, John J., 267n43
Pile, Steve, 139, 309n72
Pixley, George, 252
Plaskow, Judith, 270n79
Pogoloff, Stephen M., 299n12, 300n15, 301n16, 301n19, 306n38, 307n58
Polaski, Sandra Hack, 149, 275n14, 279n55, 280n70, 316n35
Pratt, Mary Louise, 317n44, 318n61
Pregeant, Russell, 273n1
Price, S. R. F., 14–15, 260nn40–41, 277n34, 304n30, 326n19
Prior, Michael, 261n54
Punt, Jeremy, 262n85, 276n22, 276n26, 279n54

Quint, David, 315n22

Radhakrishnan, Rajagopalan, 295n22
Räisänen, Heikki, 286n85
Rajan, Rajeswari Sunder, 317n51
Ram, Anjali, 295n23
Ramsaran, Rollin, 326n20

Ramsay, William, 196, 198–200, 209–13, 220, 335nn18–23, 337n15–338n34
Rancière, Jacques, 288n17
Reasoner, Mark, 45, 269n72, 271n85, 279n60
Reed, Jonathan, 58, 263n85, 278n42, 281n17, 288n18
Rehmann, Jan, 273n116
Rehmann, Luzia Sutter, 149, 316n36
Reid, John M., 334n7, 335n16
Renan, Ernst, 339n2
Richlin, Amy, 309n77
Rieger, Joerg, 263n85, 279n53, 325n12
Rifareal, Elizabeth, 343n8
Rigos, Cirilo A., 350n107
Ringe, Sharon H., 151, 317n52
Robinson, Charles Henry, 334n7, 335n16
Rodgers, Rene, 324n109
Roetzel, Calvin, 341n52
Rohrbaugh, Richard, 339n5
Romeo, Ilario, 330n65
Rowland, Christopher, 274n5
Royce, Anya Peterson, 292n1
Ruiz-Duremdez, Sharon Rose Joy, 237, 253, 344n13
Runions, Erin, 258n9
Rushdie, Salman, 293n11
Rutherford, Anna, 314n6

Said, Edward, 3, 9, 10, 11 14, 16, 208–9, 211–12, 257n1, 257n2, 258n8, 258n9, 262n72, 268n48, 276n24, 293n4, 313n1, 316 n, 38, 321n81, 336n5–337n8, 337nn13–14
Saller, Richard, 269n69
Samuel, Simon, 258n9
Sanders, E. P., 300n15
Sanneh, Lamin O., 274n3
Santiago, Osvaldo Torres, 256n4
Saunders, R. 277n36
Schäfer, Peter, 129, 297n44, 300n15, 301n20, 304nn31–32, 308n61, 310n82, 312nn103–4

Schermerhorn, Richard A., 292n1
Schlossberg, Linda, 298n7
Schottroff, Luise, 149, 184, 267n37, 270n79, 316n37, 322n96, 333n39
Schrage, Wolfgang, 299n11
Schroer, Silvia, 270n79
Schüssler Fiorenza, Elisabeth, 14, 17–18, 19, 20, 35, 47, 72, 148–49, 167, 237, 260n36, 260n37, 261n49, 261n67–262n72, 263n86, 265n105, 266n9, 272n100, 272n103, 274n1, 274n7, 275n12, 278n42, 282n25, 284n57, 285n82, 285n83, 287n13, 305n34, 310n78, 310n86, 314n5, 315n23, 315n24, 315n25, 316n33, 317n46, 317n47, 317n49, 317n50, 318 59, 318n60, 319n62, 319n64, 319n65, 319n67, 321n83, 324n6, 324n7, 324n9, 324n10, 326n21, 327n30, 331n67, 331n1, 332n12, 332nn16–18, 333n20, 333n22
Scott, David O'Dell, 331n5, 332n9
Scott, James C., 16, 56, 149, 257n6, 263n85, 269n72, 278n37, 313n2, 316n32, 316n33
Scott, James M., 330n64
Sedgwick, Eve Kosofsky, 323n108
Seesengood, Robert P., 18–19, 122, 262nn74–79, 287n10, 287n12, 297n46, 320n68, 321n76, 323n101, 325n9, 334n2
Segal, Alan, 290n19
Segovia, Fernando, xiii–xiv, 4, 21, 40, 189–91, 256n3, 257n8, 259n13, 263n85, 263n91, 264n94, 268n57, 269n68, 276n20, 276n23, 281n5, 281n6, 313n1, 315n13, 315n23, 319n64, 325n10, 334nn3–4, 340n13

Seifrid, Mark, 290n19
Seshadri-Crooks, Kalpana, 31–32, 265nn21–24
Sharpe, Jenny, 317n44
Shaw, George Bernard, 273n1
Shedd, Clarence P., 334n7, 335n16
Shimakawa, Karen, 302n22
Shohat, Ella, 30–31, 265nn16–20, 314n4
Shome, Raka, 295n26
Sibeko, Malika, 319n64
Slemon, Stephen, 277n32
Smith, Abraham, 260n38, 313n2, 316n31, 320n68, 326n20, 327n28, 327n31, 329n48, 329n53
Smith, George, 192, 193
Smith, R. R. R., 338n39
Smith, Sidonie, 298n2
Sobrino, Jon, 50, 270n73, 273n123
Song, Young In, 130, 304n27, 304n28
Spawforth, A. S., 330n65
Spivak, Gayatri Chakravorty, 3, 4, 9, 10, 11, 14, 24, 25, 28–29, 30, 31, 32–33, 40, 145, 147–48, 150, 151, 258n6, 258n9, 258n10, 262n72, 265nn1–2, 265n15, 265nn26–29, 268n56, 268n61, 294n22, 312n121, 313n1, 314n5, 316n31, 317n43, 317n51, 339n4, 340n14
Stanley, Christopher D., 295n29, 307n58
Ste. Croix, G. E. M. de, 35–36, 266nn12–13, 269n69, 271n99, 272n105
Stendahl, Krister, 66, 161, 260n37, 270n74, 282n30, 324n1
Sterling, Gregory E., 142, 312n99
Still, Todd D., 267n39
Stoler, Ann Laura, 317n51
Stowe, Harriet Beecher, 203
Strobel, Karl, 215, 338n42, 338n43

Stuart, Moses, 336n25
Stubbs, Monya, 269n72
Suarez, Oscar, 236, 342n4, 348n84, 350n101, 350n107
Sugirtharajah, R. S., xiii, 4, 16–17, 61, 63, 76, 256n3, 257n5, 257n8, 258n9, 260n44, 261n58, 261n60, 263n85, 264n97, 268n60, 269n68, 280n76, 280n4, 281nn5–9, 281n14, 287n9, 303n23, 313n1, 312n90, 329n52, 335n15, 336n6, 337n9, 340n16, 340n19
Suh, Sharon A., 298n5, 298n6, 311n97
Suleri, Sara, 190, 334n6
Sung, Jung Mo, 325n12
Swancutt, Diana A., 279n57

Tajfel, Henri, 292n1
Tamez, Elsa, 45, 271n88, 271n91, 338n35
Tannehill, Robert C., 275n13, 325n9
Taubes, Jacob, 260n34, 281n17, 284n58, 285n63
Theissen, Gerd, 38, 267n33, 267n36, 268n45, 299n12
Therborn, Göran, 49, 266n11
Thimmes, Pamela, 314n4
Tiffin, Helen, 9, 257n4, 268n54, 277n32
Thiong'o, Ngugi wa, 3, 11
Thoburn, James M., 334n10, 335n11
Tiitsman, Jenna, 329n56
Tolbert, Mary Ann, 314n4, 319n65
Torre, Edicio de la, 342n1
Tucker, Ruth A., 193, 334n9, 335n12
Tyson, Joseph B., 302n22

Ukpong, Justin S., 264n103

Vander Stichele, Caroline, 178, 286n1, 310n86, 320n68, 322n87, 324n110, 331n4, 333n19
Vout, Caroline, 288n23

Wacker, Marie-Theres, 270n79
Wald, Gayle, 308n67
Walker, Susan, 330n65
Wallace, Richard, 296n30
Walsh, Brian J., 264n103
Walters, James C., 270n76
Wan, Sze-Kar, 14, 134, 232, 260n38, 269n72, 278n43, 285n69, 287n10, 306n43, 313n2, 320n68, 326n20, 326n22, 341n49
Wansink, Craig S., 320n70
Warneck, Gustav, 334n7, 335n16
Watson, Duane F., 279n59
Watson, Francis, 331n6, 333n23
Webster, Jane, 338n43
Weinstock, Stefan, 330n63
Weiss, Herold, 325n6
Welborn, Lawrence, 269n72
Wells, Peter S., 338n43
Wengst, Klaus, 64, 70, 255, 281n16, 282n19, 285nn72-73, 285n75, 285n79, 350n108
West, Gerald, 21, 264n94, 264n96, 269n64, 319n64
Whitelam, Keith W., 258n9
Wicker, Kathleen O'Brien, 151, 318n52, 318n53

Wiegman, Robyn, 140, 310n80, 310n81
Wiley, Tatha, 263n85
Williams, Wynne, 296n30
Wills, Lawrence, 172, 331n65
Wilson, Bryan, 282n24
Wilson, Janet, 264n102
Wilson, Mark, 335n23
Wilson, Stephen G., 329n57
Wink, Walter, 283n32, 283 n 33, 283n38
Winter, Bruce W., 339n53
Wire, Antoinette Clark, 14, 46-47, 148, 149, 271n100-272n103 275n9, 285n82, 305n34, 310n86, 315n23, 315n25, 316n33, 318n59, 319n67, 323n101, 324n6, 327n30, 328n40, 328n46, 329n54, 332n13
Woolf, Greg, 271n84, 288n19
Wostyn, Lode L., 251-53, 253, 254, 255, 349nn88-92
Wright, N. T., 57-58, 69, 156, 272n113, 272n114, 275n17, 278n37, 278n41, 278n43, 278n44, 278n49-279n52, 284nn60-62, 320n68, 321n82, 321n83, 322n88, 326n20, 337n10, 341n43

Wyckoff, W. H., 194, 335n14

Yamamoto, Hisaye, 144, 312nn109-16
Yee, Gale, 151, 266n4, 266n8, 318n52
Yeğenoğlu, Meyda, 19, 321n76
Yeo, K.-K., 268n58, 319n68, 325n6, 332n7
Yoder, John Howard, 283n33
Yorke, Gosnell L., 263n85
Young, Iris Marion, 298n7
Young, Robert J. C., 256n2
Yuval-Davis, Nira, 314n7

Zabala, Artemio, 349n94
Zanker, Paul, 213, 269n70, 288n20, 338n37
Zerbe, Gordon M., 275n11, 279n65, 282n17, 282n30, 324n3, 325n9, 343n6, 349n98
Zetterholm, Magnus, 264n95
Žižek, Slavoj, 50, 164, 272n105, 273n119, 273n121, 326n23, 326n24

www.ingramcontent.com/pod-product-compliance
Lightning Source LLC
Chambersburg PA
CBHW021826090426
42811CB00032B/2032/J